GRADE 4

P9-AGN-957

MATH Trailblazers®

A BALANCED MATHEMATICS PROGRAM INTEGRATING SCIENCE AND LANGUAGE ARTS

Teacher Implementation Guide

THIRD EDITION

KENDALL/HUNT PUBLISHING COMPANY
4050 Westmark Drive   Dubuque, Iowa 52002

A TIMS® Curriculum
University of Illinois at Chicago

Teacher Implementation Guide

Math Trailblazers®

A Balanced Mathematics Program Integrating Science and Language Arts

A TIMS® Curriculum from the University of Illinois at Chicago

---

Dedication

This book is dedicated to the children and teachers who let us see the magic in their classrooms and to our families who wholeheartedly supported us while we searched for ways to make it happen.

—*The TIMS Project*—

UIC The University of Illinois at Chicago

The original edition was based on work supported by the National Science Foundation under grant No. MDR 9050226 and the University of Illinois at Chicago. Any opinions, findings, and conclusions or recommendations expressed in this publication are those of the authors and do not necessarily reflect the views of the granting agencies.

Acknowledgments

Teaching Integrated Mathematics and Science (TIMS) Project Directors

Philip Wagreich, Principal Investigator

Joan L. Bieler

Howard Goldberg (emeritus)

Catherine Randall Kelso

Director
Third Edition   Joan L. Bieler

Curriculum Developers

Third Edition	Lindy M. Chambers-Boucher	Philip Wagreich
	Janet Simpson Beissinger	

Contributors

Third Edition	Eileen Wynn Ball	Sandy Niemiera
	Jenny Bay-Williams	Christina Nugent
	Ava Chatterjee-Belisle	Janet M. Parsons
	Elizabeth Colligan	Leona Peters
	Marty Gartzman	Catherine Reed
	Carol Inzerillo	

Editorial and Production Staff

Third Edition	Kathleen R. Anderson	Christina Clemons
	Lindy M. Chambers-Boucher	Anne Roby

TIMS Professional Developers

	Barbara Crum	Cheryl Kneubuhler
	Catherine Ditto	Lisa Mackey
	Pamela Guyton	Linda Miceli

TIMS Director of Media Services

Henrique Cirne-Lima

TIMS Research Staff

	Stacy Brown	Catherine Ditto
	Reality Canty	Kathleen Pitvorec
	Alison Castro	Catherine Randall Kelso

TIMS Administrative Staff

	Eve Ali Boles	Enrique Puente
	Kathleen R. Anderson	Alice VanSlyke
	Nida Khan	

Director

Second Edition
Catherine Randall Kelso

Curriculum Developers

Second Edition

Lindy M. Chambers-Boucher
Elizabeth Colligan
Marty Gartzman
Carol Inzerillo
Catherine Randall Kelso

Jennifer Mundt Leimberer
Georganne E. Marsh
Leona Peters
Philip Wagreich

Editorial and Production Staff

Second Edition

Kathleen R. Anderson
Ai-Ai C. Cojuangco
Andrada Costoiu
Erika Larsen

Georganne E. Marsh
Cosmina Menghes
Anne Roby

Principal Investigators

First Edition
Philip Wagreich
Howard Goldberg

Senior Curriculum Developers

First Edition

Janet Simpson Beissinger
Joan L. Bieler
Astrida Cirulis
Marty Gartzman
Howard Goldberg

Carol Inzerillo
Andy Isaacs
Catherine Randall Kelso
Leona Peters
Philip Wagreich

Curriculum Developers

First Edition

Janice C. Banasiak
Lynne Beauprez
Andy Carter
Lindy M. Chambers-Boucher
Kathryn Chval
Diane Czerwinski

Jenny Knight
Sandy Niemiera
Janice Ozima
Polly Tangora
Paul Trafton

Illustrator

First Edition
Kris Dresen

Editorial and Production Staff

First Edition

Glenda L. Genio-Terrado
Mini Joseph
Lynette Morgenthaler

Sarah Nelson
Birute Petrauskas
Anne Roby

Research Consultant

First Edition
Andy Isaacs

Mathematics Education Consultant

First Edition
Paul Trafton

National Advisory Committee

First Edition

Carl Berger
Tom Berger
Hugh Burkhart
Donald Chambers
Naomi Fisher
Glenda Lappan

Mary Lindquist
Eugene Maier
Lourdes Monteagudo
Elizabeth Phillips
Thomas Post

Preface

This third edition of *Math Trailblazers* is the product of about 20 years of concerted effort by the TIMS (Teaching Integrated Mathematics and Science) Project. The TIMS Project has its roots in the pioneering work of Howard Goldberg, Professor of Physics at the University of Illinois at Chicago (UIC) and a Carnegie Foundation Professor of the Year in 1995. Over the past two decades, the TIMS Project has worked with children, teachers, and administrators to improve the quality of mathematics and science curricula and instruction in the Chicago area and nationwide. In 1990, the TIMS Project was awarded a grant by the National Science Foundation to develop a new elementary mathematics curriculum to meet the needs of children who will be entering the world of work in the 21st century. After years of research and development, including pilot- and field-testing in hundreds of classrooms, the first edition of the curriculum was published as *Math Trailblazers* in 1997 and 1998.

The primary goal of *Math Trailblazers* has been to create an educational experience that results in children who are flexible mathematical thinkers, who see the connections between the mathematics they learn in school and the thinking they do in everyday life, and who enjoy mathematics. The curriculum is based on the premise that children can succeed in mathematics and that if more is expected of them, more will be achieved. The curriculum incorporates the best of traditional mathematics, while widening the horizons of students' mathematical thinking.

Since the initial publication of *Math Trailblazers*, the TIMS Project has continued its research and development work, studying how to implement the curriculum in the most effective ways. We have learned considerably more about the importance of teacher professional development and whole-school change. The dedication and insight of our teacher collaborators constantly encouraged us. Feedback from hundreds of teachers who tested early versions of *Math Trailblazers* and thousands of others who used the program over the past ten years significantly reshaped our view of the curriculum and inspires our continuing efforts to improve it.

The first edition of *Math Trailblazers* was grounded in mathematics education research literature as well as our own research and experience as curriculum and staff developers. It was also inspired by the 1989 publication of the National Council of Teachers of Mathematics *Curriculum and Evaluation Standards for School Mathematics*. In this edition we drew from advances in research over the decade as well as NCTM's updated vision for school mathematics, as embodied in the NCTM's *Principles and Standards for School Mathematics*.

New editions of *Math Trailblazers* have made the curriculum easier for teachers to use. The math facts program was realigned in the 2nd edition and in this edition assessment and review components of the curriculum are more clearly highlighted. This edition also features an improved format for the *Unit Resource Guide* as well as new content in the *Teacher Implementation Guide* aimed at teachers and administrators. This content was suggested and shaped by our experience as professional developers working with schools and districts across the country that implement *Math Trailblazers*. It includes **Building the *Math Trailblazers* Classroom,** strategies and tips gathered from classroom teachers; **Teaching the *Math Trailblazers* Student: Meeting Individual Needs,** integral structures and features of *Math Trailblazers* that make it accessible to all children, including sections on working with English Language Learners, Special Education students and gifted and talented students; **Language in the *Math Trailblazers* Classroom,** strategies to help students learn to effectively communicate in the math classroom; and an **Administrator Handbook,** strategies to successfully guide implementation of the curriculum.

This third edition of *Math Trailblazers* is one more step in the continuing evolution of the curriculum. The Project is now housed within UIC's Learning Sciences Research Institute, providing a permanent home for interdisciplinary collaboration between mathematicians, scientists, mathematics educators, learning scientists, and teachers as we continually work at providing the best possible mathematics curriculum. We hope that teaching *Math Trailblazers* will be an enjoyable and productive experience for you and your students.

Philip Wagreich
Professor, Department of Mathematics, Statistics, and Computer Science
Director Emeritus, TIMS Project
University of Illinois at Chicago

Joan L. Bieler and Catherine R. Kelso
Co-Directors, TIMS Project
University of Illinois at Chicago

GRADE 4

Teacher Implementation Guide
Table of Contents

SECTION 9

TIMS Tutors 217

SECTION 10

Building the *Math Trailblazers* Classroom 357

SECTION 11

Teaching the *Math Trailblazers* Student: Meeting Individual Needs 365

SECTION 12

Language in the *Math Trailblazers* Classroom 407

Grade 4 *Math Trailblazers*
Table of Contents

This Table of Contents includes page numbers for the teacher material in the *Unit Resource Guide* plus corresponding page numbers in the student books (*Student Guide, Discovery Assignment Book,* and *Adventure Book*).

Introduction

Introduction

The Introduction outlines the *Teacher Implementation Guide's* various sections and explains how best to use them.

A teacher and a student explore equivalent fractions.

Introduction

What Is the *Teacher Implementation Guide?*

The *Teacher Implementation Guide* is the reference manual for *Math Trailblazers®*. It, combined with the *Grade 4 Facts Resource Guide* and the *Unit Resource Guide* (URG), provides teachers and schools with a comprehensive set of resources to assist in the implementation of the curriculum. The *Unit Resource Guide* is the teacher's working guide, providing information and instructions related to the planning and teaching of units and individual lessons—it is intended to be used on a day-to-day basis. The *Grade 4 Facts Resource Guide* is a compilation of the components of the fourth grade math facts program, including background material. The *Teacher Implementation Guide* supplements the *Unit Resource Guide* and the *Grade 4 Facts Resource Guide* by addressing larger issues related to the curriculum. Information in the *Teacher Implementation Guide* can be roughly categorized into three groups: general background about *Math Trailblazers;* specific information about the program; and deep background about important math and science concepts. The *Teacher Implementation Guide* is a valuable resource for long-range planning for math instruction, curriculum, related implementation issues, and staff development.

Brief descriptions of sections found in the *Teacher Implementation Guide* follow:

- **Foundations of *Math Trailblazers***
  The underlying philosophy of the program is described.

- **Components and Features Guide**
  Math Trailblazers is a multicomponent program. Grade 4 includes three books for students (the *Student Guide, Discovery Assignment Book,* and *Adventure Book*) and three volumes for teachers (the *Teacher Implementation Guide,* the *Grade 4 Facts Resource Guide,* and the *Unit Resource Guide*). A *Teacher Resource CD* is also available for teachers. The Components and Features Guide is a road map for understanding the purposes of the various components and where to find key information. Important features taken from actual student and teacher pages are illustrated.

- **Grade 4 Overview**
  The Overview is an extended table of contents for the Grade 4 curriculum. Pacing Suggestions in unit outlines help you in plan your instruction schedule. Unit summaries include a narrative description of each unit's content and a list of important math concepts covered. This provides a snapshot view of the curriculum for your grade.

- **Connections with the NCTM *Principles and Standards***
  Math Trailblazers was developed to reflect the goals and approaches outlined in the *Principles and Standards for School Mathematics* of the National Council of Teachers of Mathematics (NCTM).This section includes detailed information, about how the program aligns with the *Principles and Standards*.

- **Scope and Sequence**

  The Scope and Sequence is organized to correspond with the NCTM *Principles and Standards,* providing additional detailed information about *Math Trailblazers'* alignment with the *Standards.* The scope and sequence chart is divided into two sections—one for the unit lessons and one for the Daily Practice and Problems and the Home Practice.

- **Summary of Approaches to Math Facts and Whole-Number Operations**

  The *Math Trailblazers* program for presenting the math facts and whole-number operations is summarized in this section. Background information about our approach and expectations for the grades are outlined.

- **Daily Practice and Problems and Home Practice Guide**

  An essential component of *Math Trailblazers* is a carefully designed sequence of short problems in Grades 1–5, called the Daily Practice and Problems (DPP). Beginning in third grade, a component called Home Practice is introduced. This component provides additional practice with skills and concepts.

- **Assessment**

  Math Trailblazers includes a comprehensive program of student assessment. The philosophy and components of this program are described in the Assessment section. Assessment materials from the curriculum illustrate key ideas. Specific suggestions for implementing the assessment program are included.

- **TIMS Tutors: Background Information for Teachers**

  This section includes a series of documents called TIMS Tutors. Which provide extensive information on topics in pedagogy, mathematics, and science. The tutors serve as a source of deep background information. Some tutors, such as the tutor on math facts, supply specific information needed by teachers to plan particular portions of the *Math Trailblazers* program. Other tutors, such as the tutor on mass, focus on math and science content. Still others, such as the tutor on portfolios, address teaching strategies.

- **Building the *Math Trailblazers* Classroom**

  This section contains strategies and tips gathered from classroom teachers. Topics include the organization of materials and classrooms, as well as student groupings to best implement *Math Trailblazers.*

- **Teaching the *Math Trailblazers* Student: Meeting Individual Needs**

  From its earliest days, the authors developed the *Math Trailblazers* curriculum on a foundation of equity. This means that all children in all classrooms have the right to access rigorous mathematics. This section describes the integral structures and features of *Math Trailblazers* that make it accessible to all children. It also contains a section for working with English Language Learners and Special Education students, as well as suggestions for working with gifted and talented students.

- **Language in the *Math Trailblazers* Classroom**

  Language plays an important role in the *Math Trailblazers* Classroom. Language is used to convey mathematical problems. For example, vignettes of everyday situations are often used as contexts for establishing and exploring mathematical content. Both written and spoken language are essential to communicate mathematical ideas, strategies, and solutions.

This section describes strategies to help students learn to effectively communicate in the math classroom, including tips on how to help students learn mathematical vocabulary in context.

- **Manipulatives List**
  A listing of the manipulatives required for program implementation is included in this section.

- **Literature List**
  Math Trailblazers uses commercially available trade books in many lessons. A listing of these trade books is included in this section.

- **Games List**
  Games are often used in *Math Trailblazers* to engage students in practicing basic arithmetic skills and other math concepts. Once introduced, these games can be used throughout the year for ongoing practice. A complete listing and description of the games for your grade are provided.

- **Software List**
  Math Trailblazers does not require the use of computers. We do, instead, suggest some software programs that can supplement the curriculum. A listing of these programs and some suggested uses for them are provided.

- **Suggestions for Working with Parents**
  When adopting a math program that is new and different, such as *Math Trailblazers*, it is important to keep parents informed and educated about the program. Some hints for working with parents regarding *Math Trailblazers* are outlined in this section. A brochure about the curriculum and a parent letter describing the math facts program are also provided. The documents are in both English and Spanish.

- **Glossary**
  Most *Math Trailblazers* lessons include mathematical terms relevant to the lesson. The glossary defines many of these terms and can also be used to locate key vocabulary in the lessons. Most definitions cite the locations of the term in the curriculum.

- **Index**
  The index is a list of major mathematical topics and their locations in the curriculum. The *Student Guide, Discovery Assignment Book, Adventure Book, Unit Resource Guides,* and *Teacher Implementation Guide* are all referenced in this index.

How to Use the *Teacher Implementation Guide*

Use of this guide will differ depending upon your purpose. Suggestions for using it for different purposes are described here.

If you are a teacher considering whether to use *Math Trailblazers*:
The *Teacher Implementation Guide* provides useful information for adoption committees or individual teachers who are considering *Math Trailblazers*. General information about the program that will be most helpful for this group includes the Foundations, alignment with the NCTM *Principles and Standards,* Scope and Sequence, and the Overview. The Components and

Features Guide will help reviewers understand the purposes of the different student and teacher books. Other specific information, such as the Math Facts and Whole-Number Operations section and the Assessment section, may also be useful for potential users of the curriculum.

If you are a teacher who is about to use *Math Trailblazers* for the first time:

There is too much information in the *Teacher Implementation Guide* and the *Unit Resource Guide* for any teacher to digest all at once. To make effective use of the *Teacher*

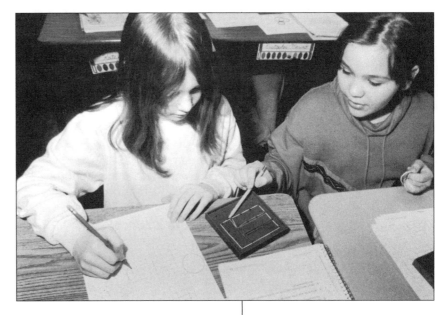

Implementation Guide, it is best to select portions to examine at different points in the curriculum implementation. Prior to using *Math Trailblazers,* glance at the Foundations section to get a sense of our overall philosophy. However, you will probably want to spend more time reviewing the sections that provide specific information about using the curriculum. This information will help you get started and plan for the year.

Carefully review the Components and Features Guide to see the big picture of the program's components and features. This information will eventually become second nature as you gain experience with the curriculum, but it will be helpful at first to see what is included in the program. We suggest you review the Overview to get a feel for what is covered over the year and can plan ahead. It will be easier to make instructional decisions if you know what

is planned for later lessons. The Assessment section and the Daily Practice and Problems Guide are essential and should be read prior to beginning the curriculum. Among the TIMS Tutors, we suggest that you first review *Math Facts.* It outlines our philosophy and plan for introducing the math facts. The manipulatives and literature lists are useful tools if you are ordering manipulatives. The section on working with parents will also be useful to read prior to using the curriculum. Use the rest of the *Teacher Implementation Guide* as the need arises.

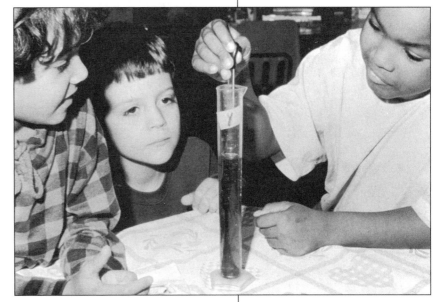

If you are a teacher who is already using *Math Trailblazers:*

During your first several years of using *Math Trailblazers,* you will likely refer to the *Teacher Implementation Guide* on an ongoing basis. You will find the TIMS Tutors particularly valuable in helping you better understand the content and approaches of key parts of the curriculum. There are numerous pointers in the *Unit Resource Guide* to individual tutors. The Scope and Sequence supplements the Overview in providing detailed information about when specific concepts are covered. Review the Games List and Software List periodically to help you in lesson planning. Any background information not found in the *Unit Resource Guide* is probably in the *Teacher Implementation Guide.*

If you are a school administrator in a school using *Math Trailblazers:*

The school administrator is the leader of the *Math Trailblazers* implementation. As the instructional leader, the school administrator works with the staff to establish, communicate, and support the goals of the mathematics program as the implementation unfolds. The *Administrator Handbook* section contains a description of the important components of a math implementation and explanations of strategies to successfully guide the implementation. It also contains blackline masters to use in presentations with staff and other audiences. Important sections from the *Teacher Implementation Guide* are also included.

If you are planning staff development sessions about *Math Trailblazers:*

Implementation of *Math Trailblazers* is most effective when accompanied by a comprehensive professional development program. An orientation to *Math Trailblazers* is made available to schools using *Math Trailblazers* through Kendall/Hunt Publishing. We recommend that schools continue their professional development throughout the lifetime of the implementation. The TIMS Project has developed presenters' guides for a variety of professional development sessions. These guides, called Teacher Enhancement Resource Modules (TERMs), contain a guide for presenters with explanatory text, discussion questions and answers, and blackline masters. Most TERMs include video that demonstrates the *Math Trailblazers* curriculum in action. Used together the 18 TERMs provide approximately 70 hours of staff development in both the content and pedagogy of *Math Trailblazers.* The TERMs are available through Kendall/Hunt Publishing.

For specific suggestions about planning local staff development related to *Math Trailblazers,* contact the Teaching Integrated Mathematics and Science (TIMS) Project at 800-454-TIMS or Kendall/Hunt Publishing Company at 800-542-6657. Information is also available on the *Math Trailblazers* Implementation Center website at *www.math.uic.edu/IMSE* and at *www.mathtrailblazers.com.*

Foundations of *Math Trailblazers*

The Foundations of *Math Trailblazers* describes the principles behind *Math Trailblazers* and discusses the curriculum's key features.

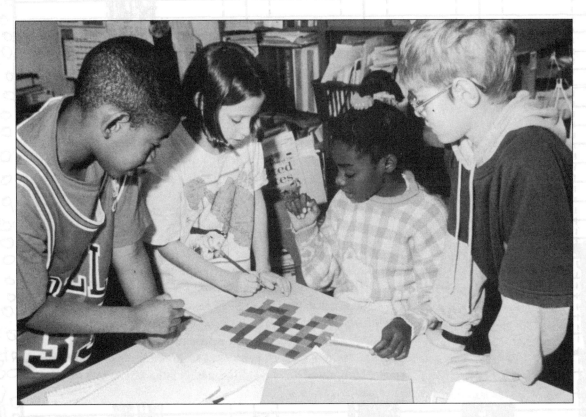

Students work together to solve problems.

Foundations of *Math Trailblazers*

Math Trailblazers is an elementary mathematics curriculum for schools that want their math programs to reflect the goals and ideas of the National Council of Teachers of Mathematics (NCTM) *Principles and Standards for School Mathematics.* With funding from the National Science Foundation (NSF) the TIMS (Teaching Integrated Mathematics and Science) Project at the University of Illinois at Chicago created a comprehensive program that embodies the *Principles and Standards.*

Math Trailblazers is based on the ideas that mathematics is best learned in real-world contexts that make sense to children; that all students deserve a richer and more challenging curriculum; and that a balanced and practical approach to learning mathematics is what students need and teachers want.

Features of *Math Trailblazers*
Alignment with Reform Recommendations

The *Principles and Standards,* which was released in 2000, is an update of three groundbreaking volumes published a decade earlier that collectively became known as the "NCTM *Standards.*" This publication was extended in 2006 with the release of the *Curriculum Focal Points for Prekindergarten through Grade 8 Mathematics: A Quest for Coherence,* which was "offered as a starting point in a dialogue on what is important at particular levels of instruction as an initial step toward a more coherent, focused curriculum in this country." (NCTM 2006, p. vii) However, in describing the relationship between the documents, the NCTM states that the *Principles and Standards* "remains the definitive reference on the development of mathematical content and processes across the grades." (NCTM 2006, p. 1)

The NCTM documents outline a vision for school mathematics that includes: a mathematically challenging curriculum that is coherent and covers a broad range of mathematical content; a strong focus on engaging students in mathematical problem solving; conceptually oriented instruction that stresses thinking, reasoning, and applying; appropriate uses of calculators and computers; and a strong commitment to promoting success in mathematics among all students—not merely those who traditionally have done well. Most states incorporated this vision for mathematics teaching and learning into their mathematics standards.

The first edition of *Math Trailblazers* took more than six years of work that included extensive pilot and field testing of the materials. After publication of the first edition, continued NSF support enabled the TIMS Project to develop implementation models and professional development materials that assisted teachers and schools as they adopted the program.

In developing the second edition of *Math Trailblazers,* we looked carefully at the NCTM *Principles and Standards* and reorganized portions of the *Math Trailblazers,* such as the math facts program, to keep *Math Trailblazers* closely aligned with the new NCTM recommendations. TIMS researchers also studied how the program impacted student achievement. The second edition of *Math Trailblazers* therefore represented more than twelve years of NSF-supported work related to the curriculum.

The third edition provides materials in an easier-to-use format, as well as new content for teachers and administrators. This content was suggested and shaped by other lessons learned from our years of professional development work with schools and districts across the country that implement *Math Trailblazers.*

The importance of a coherent, well-developed curriculum is clear in the *Principles and Standards,* which states:

A curriculum is more than a collection of activities: it must be coherent, focused on important mathematics, and well articulated across the grades. *A school mathematics curriculum is a strong determinant of what students have an opportunity to learn and what they do learn. In a coherent curriculum, mathematical ideas are linked to and build on one another so that students' understanding and knowledge deepens and their ability to apply mathematics expands. An effective mathematics curriculum focuses on important mathematics—mathematics that will prepare students for continued study and for solving problems in a variety of school, home, and work settings. A well-articulated curriculum challenges students to learn increasingly more sophisticated mathematical ideas as they continue their studies.* (NCTM, 2000, p. 14)

Math Trailblazers was developed with that goal in mind. It is a *Standards-*based curriculum in the truest sense—developed explicitly to reflect national standards for K–5 mathematics, and now revised to maintain close alignment with those standards as they have evolved.

More specific connections between *Math Trailblazers* and the NCTM *Principles and Standards* are discussed in Scope and Sequence & the NCTM *Principles and Standards* (Section 5).

High Expectations and Equity

The first principle in the *Principles and Standards* is the Equity Principle. It challenges a myth prevalent in the United States that only a few students are capable of rigorous mathematics. The Equity Principle states:

> *Excellence in mathematics education requires equity—high expectations and strong support for all students.* (NCTM, 2000, p. 12)

Accordingly, we introduce challenging content in every grade: computation, measurement, data collection, statistics, geometry, ratio, probability, graphing, algebraic concepts, estimation, mental arithmetic, and patterns and relationships.

Contexts for this demanding content begin with students' lives. Lessons are grounded in everyday situations, so abstractions build on experience. By presenting mathematics in rich contexts, the curriculum helps students make connections among real situations, words, pictures, data, graphs, and symbols. The curriculum also validates students' current understandings while new understandings develop. Students can solve problems in ways they understand while being encouraged to connect those ways to more abstract and powerful methods. Within the same lesson, some students may work directly with the manipulatives to solve the problems while other students may solve the same problems using graphs or symbols. The use of varied contexts and diverse representations of concepts allows children of varying abilities to access the mathematics.

Problem Solving

A fundamental principle of *Math Trailblazers* is that mathematics is best learned through actively solving real problems. Questions a student can answer immediately may be worthwhile exercises, but *problems,* by definition, are difficult, but not impossible.

The importance of problem solving is echoed in the NCTM *Principles and Standards,* which states:

> *Problem solving is the cornerstone of school mathematics. . . . The goal of school mathematics should be for all students to become increasingly able and willing to engage with and solve problems.*

> *Problem solving is also important because it can serve as a vehicle for learning new mathematical ideas and skills (Schroeder and Lester). A problem-centered approach to teaching mathematics uses interesting and well-selected problems to launch mathematical lessons and engage students. In this way, new ideas, techniques, and mathematical relationships emerge and become the focus of discussion.* (NCTM, 2000, p. 182)

As recommended by NCTM, problem solving in *Math Trailblazers* is not a distinct topic but permeates the entire program, providing a context for learning concepts and skills. Throughout the curriculum, students apply the mathematics they know and construct new mathematics as needed. Students' skills, procedures, and concepts emerge and develop as they solve complex problems.

Connections to Science and Language Arts

Real-world problems are naturally interdisciplinary, so any problem-solving curriculum should integrate topics that are traditionally separated. Accordingly, we have integrated mathematics with many disciplines, especially science and language arts.

Connections to Science
Math Trailblazers is a full mathematics program that incorporates many important scientific ideas. Traditionally, school science has focused on the results of science. Students learn about plate tectonics, the atomic theory of matter, the solar system, the environment, and so on. Knowing basic facts of science is seen as part of being educated, today more than ever. However, the facts of science,

important and interesting as they are, do not alone constitute a comprehensive and balanced science curriculum.

Science has two aspects: results and method. The results of scientific inquiry have enriched human life the world over. More marvelous than the results of science, however, is the method that established those results. Without the method, the results would never have been achieved. *Math Trailblazers* aims to teach students the method of science through scientific investigation of everyday phenomena. During these investigations, students learn both mathematics and science.

The method scientists use is powerful, flexible, and quantitative. The TIMS Project has organized this method in a way that is simple enough for elementary school children to use. Students use the TIMS Laboratory Method in a rich variety of mathematical investigations. In these investigations, students develop and apply important mathematical skills and concepts in meaningful situations. Their understanding of fundamental scientific concepts is also enhanced through the use of quantitative tools.

Investigations begin with discussions of experimental situations, variables, and procedures. Then students draw pictures that indicate the experimental procedures and identify key variables. Next students gather and organize data in data tables. Then they graph their data. By analyzing their data or studying their graphs, students are able to see patterns. These patterns show any relationships between the variables. Students can use the relationships to make predictions about future data. The last phase of the experiment is an in-depth analysis of the experimental results, structured as a series of exploratory questions. Some questions ask students to make predictions and then to verify them. Other questions probe students' understanding of underlying concepts and explore the role of controlled variables. As students advance through the curriculum, the questions progress from simple to complex, building eventually to problems that require proportional reasoning, multiple-step logic, and algebra.

The TIMS Laboratory Method initiates children into the authentic practice of science. Identifying variables, drawing pictures, measuring, organizing data in tables, graphing data, and looking for and using patterns are a major part of many scientists' work. This is a major goal of science: to discover and use relationships between variables—usually expressed in some mathematical form—in order to understand and make predictions about the world.

The science content in *Math Trailblazers* focuses on a small set of simple variables that are fundamental to both math and science: length, area, volume, mass, and time. Understanding these basic variables is an essential step to achieving scientific understanding of more complex concepts. Measurement is presented in meaningful, experimental situations.

Emphasizing the scientific method and fundamental science concepts helps students develop an understanding of how scientists and mathematicians think. These habits of mind will be important in all aspects of life in the 21st century. See the TIMS Tutor: *The TIMS Laboratory Method* for more discussion of these ideas.

Connections to Language Arts

Reading, writing, and talking belong in mathematics class, not only because real mathematicians and scientists read, write, and talk mathematics and science constantly, but also because these activities help students learn. The NCTM *Principles and Standards* emphasizes the importance of communication and discourse for students to achieve at higher levels.

In school mathematics, results should be accepted not merely because someone in authority says so, but rather because persuasive arguments can be made for them. A result and a reason are often easier to remember than the result alone. By discussing the mathematics they are doing, students increase their understanding. They also extend their abilities to discuss mathematics and so to participate in a community of mathematicians. Talking or writing about mathematics is part of every lesson. Journal and discussion prompts are standard features in the teacher's guide for each lesson.

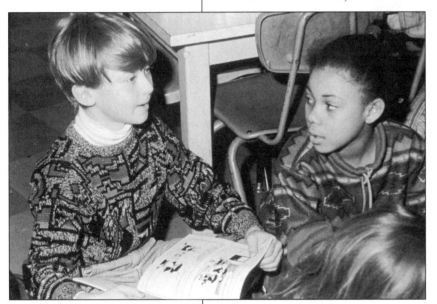

Reading is also built into this curriculum. Many lessons, especially in the primary grades, use trade books to launch or extend mathematical investigations. The curriculum also includes many original stories, called *Adventure Books,* that show applications of concepts or sketch episodes from the history of mathematics and science. Literature is used to portray mathematics as a human endeavor, so that students come to think of mathematicians and scientists as people like themselves. Mathematics embedded in a narrative structure is also easier to understand, remember, and discuss. And, of course, everyone loves a good story. In addition, students regularly write about their mathematical investigations, even in the early grades.

Collaborative Work

Scientists, mathematicians, and most others who solve complex problems in business and industry have always worked in groups. The reasons for this are simple: Most interesting problems are too difficult for one person. Explaining one's work to another person can help clarify one's thinking. Another person's perspective can suggest a new approach to a problem. Ideas that have been tested through public scrutiny are more trustworthy than private notions.

All these are reasons for collaborating in schools as well. But there are other reasons, too. Students can learn both by receiving and by giving explanations. The communication that goes with group work provides practice in verbal and symbolic communication skills. In group discussion, a basic assumption is that mathematics and science ought to make sense—something, unfortunately, that many students stop believing after only a few years of school. Social skills, especially cooperation and tolerance, increase, and the classroom community becomes more oriented towards learning and academic achievement.

Assessment

There are three major purposes for assessment. First, assessment helps teachers learn about students' thinking and knowledge: information that can then be used to guide instruction. Secondly, it communicates the goals of instruction to students and parents. Finally, it informs students and parents about progress toward these goals and suggests directions for further efforts.

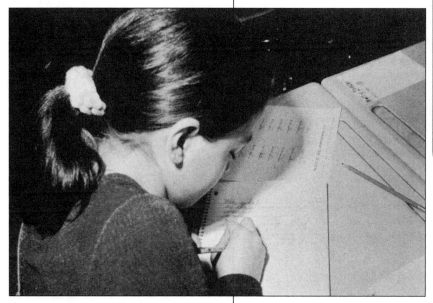

Assessment in *Math Trailblazers* reflects the breadth and balance of the curriculum. Numerous opportunities for both formal and informal assessment of student learning are integrated into the program. Many assessment activities are incorporated into the daily lessons; others are included in formal assessment units. Assessment activities include a mix of short, medium-length, and extended activities. Some are hands-on investigations, others are paper-and-pencil tasks. In all cases, assessment activities further students' learning.

For a detailed discussion of assessment in *Math Trailblazers,* refer to Assessment (Section 8) and the TIMS Tutor: *Portfolios.*

More Time Studying Mathematics

One cannot reasonably expect to cover all the concepts in a traditional program, add many new topics, and utilize an approach that emphasizes problem solving, communication, reasoning, and connections in the same amount of time used to teach a traditional math curriculum. In developing *Math Trailblazers,* we have attempted to achieve some efficiencies, such as building review into new concepts and using effective strategies to teach math facts and procedures. However, there is no magic in *Math Trailblazers.* Implementing a comprehensive, reform mathematics curriculum will require a significant amount of time. **We assume that in Grades 1–5 one hour**

every day will be devoted to teaching mathematics. In Kindergarten, the class make-up and the activity will determine the length of the class.

In some schools, finding an hour per day for math instruction may require a restructuring of the daily school schedule. Please note, however, that because *Math Trailblazers* includes extensive connections with science and language arts, *some* time spent with *Math Trailblazers* can be incorporated within science or language arts time. Thus, it may be possible to allot the one hour per day of mathematics instruction by simply scheduling math and science instruction back to back or including literature connections and journal writing in language arts.

Hard work on the part of students and more time engaged in mathematical problem solving are important ingredients to success in mathematics—no matter what program you are using. Because students using *Math Trailblazers* are actively involved in applying mathematics in meaningful contexts, our experience is that students will be highly motivated to spend extra time studying mathematics.

Staff Development and Broad School Support: Essential Ingredients

Developing the curriculum and working with schools over the last 20 years has taught us that implementing a *Standards*-based mathematics program will progress more smoothly if it is accompanied by a solid support system for teachers. Ideally, this includes a professional development program that includes workshops on content and pedagogy, leadership development, in-school support, and the means to address a variety of concerns as they arise.

Overall implementation of *Math Trailblazers* will be much easier in a school that organizes support for the new program. Necessary tools such as manipulatives, overhead projectors, and transparency masters need to be provided in adequate quantities. Institutional considerations, such as classroom schedules that allot necessary time for instruction and provide time for teachers to meet and plan together, need to be implemented. In-classroom support from resource teachers is extremely helpful. Storage and check-out systems for shared manipulatives need to be in place. Ways to engender parental support for the program, including possible ways to involve some parents in providing classroom assistance to interested teachers during math time, should be developed.

Administrators need to maintain a long-term perspective recognizing that program implementation will take some time—and they need to communicate this clearly to teachers. In short, schools need to examine their current situations and make necessary modifications to develop a school environment that supports the kind of teaching and learning that characterizes *Math Trailblazers*.

A Balanced Approach

A reform mathematics program should take a balanced and moderate approach. *Math Trailblazers* is balanced in many different ways with whole-class instruction, small-group activities, and individual work. New mathematical content is included, but traditional topics are not neglected.

Children construct their own knowledge in rich problem-solving situations, but they are not expected to reinvent 5000 years of mathematics. Concepts, procedures, and facts are important, but are introduced thoughtfully to engender the positive attitudes, beliefs, and self-image that are also important in the long run. Hands-on activities of varied length and depth, as well as paper-and-pencil tasks, all have their place. The program's rich variety of assessment activities reflects this broad balance.

Either-or rhetoric has too often short-circuited real progress in education: problem solving vs. back-to-basics, conceptual understanding vs. procedural skill, paper-and-pencil computation vs. calculators. *Math Trailblazers* is based on the view that these are false dichotomies. Students must solve problems, but of course they need basic skills to do so. Both concepts and procedures are important, and neglecting one will undermine the other. There is a place in the curriculum both for paper-and-pencil algorithms and for calculators, and for mental arithmetic and estimation. The careful balance in *Math Trailblazers* allows teachers and schools to move forward with a reform mathematics curriculum while maintaining the strengths of their current teaching practices.

Research Foundations of *Math Trailblazers*

The first edition of *Math Trailblazers* was completed in 1997. The roots of the curriculum, however, date back to the late 1970s and the work of Howard Goldberg, a particle physicist at the University of Illinois at Chicago (UIC). Building on the work of Robert Karplus and others, Goldberg developed a framework for adapting the scientific method for elementary school children and applied that framework within a series of elementary laboratory investigations (Goldberg & Boulanger, 1981). Goldberg was joined in 1985 by UIC mathematician Philip Wagreich and, together with others, formed the Teaching Integrated Mathematics and Science Project (TIMS).

Thus, the motivation behind TIMS came from two sources, one with roots in science and one with roots in mathematics. The scientific impetus stemmed from the desire to teach science to children in a manner that reflects the practice of scientists. Modern science is fundamentally quantitative; therefore, quantitative investigations should have an important role in children's science education. The mathematical impetus was to find a way to make mathematics meaningful to children. Engaging children in quantitative investigations of common phenomena harnesses their curiosity in a way that builds on their understanding of the natural world, which, in turn, helps promote study of rigorous mathematics (Isaacs, Wagreich, & Gartzman, 1997).

Initially, TIMS focused primarily on the development and implementation of a series of quantitative, hands-on activities, the *TIMS Laboratory Investigations* (Goldberg, 1997). The laboratory investigations continue the tradition of Dewey (1910) and others in focusing on the method of science and on exploring a relatively small set of fundamental scientific concepts in depth. Several studies provided clear evidence that the *TIMS Laboratory Investigations* are effective in promoting students' development of mathematics and science concepts (Goldberg & Wagreich, 1990; Goldberg, 1993).

Based largely on the success with the supplemental *TIMS Laboratory Investigations,* the National Science Foundation (NSF) supported the TIMS Project to develop a comprehensive, elementary mathematics curriculum that would align with the National Council of Teachers of Mathematics (NCTM) *Curriculum and Evaluation Standards for School Mathematics* (NCTM, 1989). The first edition of *Math Trailblazers* is the result of this work. As part of the revision process for the second edition, the authors made changes so that the new edition aligns with the current NCTM recommendations as outlined in the *Principles and Standards for School Mathematics* (NCTM, 2000).

The third edition provides materials in an easier-to-use format, as well as new content for teachers and administrators. This content embodies the lessons learned from our TIMS Project's 20 years of professional development work with schools and districts that implement *Math Trailblazers.*

In developing each edition of *Math Trailblazers,* the authors drew upon research findings from a wide variety of sources, as well as from the broad experiences of the authoring group. In this section we highlight a portion of the research that helped guide the curriculum's development and other current research that validates the approaches used.

A Problem-Solving Curriculum

A distinguishing element of any *Standards*-based mathematics curriculum is that problem solving is used as a context for students to learn new concepts and skills. Throughout *Math Trailblazers,* students apply the mathematics they know and construct new mathematics as needed. Students' skills, procedures, and concepts emerge and develop as they solve problems. Students also practice skills and procedures as they apply them in diverse and increasingly challenging contexts. Problem-solving contexts can emerge from real-life investigations or from more mathematical situations. The problems serve as the motivation for purposeful use of mathematics.

Using problem solving as a cornerstone of the mathematics curriculum has been promoted by educators dating back to Dewey and has received considerable support from current mathematics education researchers. (See Hiebert et al., 1996; Schoenfeld, 1985 and 1994; National Research Council, 2001; and NCTM 1989 and 2000 for a discussion of problem solving in the curriculum.)

A curriculum that emphasizes solving problems can use many different contexts. In developing *Math Trailblazers,* the authors first identified the key mathematical concepts and skills to be developed and then selected problem-solving contexts to support student learning in these areas. Our earlier work and that of others (e.g., Cognition and Technology Group at Vanderbilt, 1997) had confirmed the value of using quantitative laboratory investigations for this purpose. Drawing from this work, eight to ten laboratory investigations were adapted and integrated into *Math Trailblazers* in each grade, beginning with first grade. These investigations are supplemented by many other contexts for problem solving.

Challenging Mathematics in All Grades for All Students

An assumption in the development of *Math Trailblazers* was that students can learn more challenging mathematics than is covered in traditional mathematics curricula. This has been underscored in international comparison studies (Heibert, 1999; McKnight et al., 1987; Stigler & Perry, 1988; Schmidt, McKnight, & Raizen, 1996; Stigler & Hiebert, 1997; Stevenson & Stigler, 1992) and in analyses of U.S. mathematics instruction (Flanders, 1987; Lindquist, 1989). Maintaining high expectations and providing access to rigorous mathematics for all students has proven effective regardless of the socioeconomic status and ethnicity of the students (National Research Council, 2001; Newmann, Bryk, & Nagaoka, 2001; Smith, Lee, & Newmann, 2001). Therefore, mathematical expectations in *Math Trailblazers* are high and grow steadily. Review of concepts and skills is carefully built into new and increasingly challenging problems as the program builds upon itself both within and across grades.

Balancing Concept and Skill Development

The importance of developing a strong conceptual foundation is emphasized in research that guided the development of all content strands in *Math Trailblazers*. Many educators have long recognized the importance of balancing conceptual and skill development. New conceptual understandings are built upon existing skills and concepts; these new understandings in turn support the further development of skills and concepts.

A wide body of research affirms that instructional programs that emphasize conceptual development can facilitate significant mathematics learning without sacrificing skill proficiency (see Hiebert, 1999). Research affirms that well-designed and implemented instructional programs can facilitate both conceptual understanding and procedural skill.

This research had a profound effect on development of *Math Trailblazers*. For example, such research helped define the curriculum's program for developing number sense and estimation skills (Sowder, 1992) and for learning math facts and whole-number operations (Carpenter, Carey, & Kouba, 1990; Carpenter, et al., 1999; Fuson, 1987, 1992; Fuson & Briars, 1990; Fuson et al., 1997; Isaacs & Carroll, 1999; Lampert, 1986a, 1986b; Thornton, 1978, 1990a, 1990b). Work with fractions and decimals was informed by research that stressed the need to develop conceptual understandings of fractions and decimals prior to introducing procedures with the four arithmetic operations (see Behr & Post, 1992; Ball, 1993; Cramer, Post, & del Mas, 2002; Lesh, Post, & Behr, 1987; Mack, 1990; Hoffer & Hoffer, 1992). Similar research findings on student understanding of geometric concepts shaped the development of lessons in geometry (see Burger & Shaughnessy, 1986; Crowley, 1987; Fuys, Geddes, & Tishler, 1988).

In direct response to research such as that cited here, every content strand within *Math Trailblazers* interweaves the promotion of conceptual understanding with distributed practice of skills and procedures.

Field Testing and Research on the Curriculum in Classrooms

NSF funding allowed sequential development of the program to be coupled with extensive field testing in schools. As a result, curriculum development became an iterative process involving considerable interaction between the developers and field-test teachers. Comments and suggestions from teachers were incorporated into revisions that were often retested in classrooms one or more times before final revisions were made. Field-test teachers met regularly with the program's authors, and classrooms were often visited as part of the development process. Teachers using the early versions in their classrooms addressed content, language, format, practical considerations, and other issues related to each lesson.

In addition to assessing feedback from field-test teachers, independent researchers and TIMS Project staff conducted preliminary studies that helped affirm the efficacy of the content placement and approaches in the early versions of the materials (Burghardt, 1994; Perry, Whiteaker, & Waddoups, 1996; Whiteaker, Waddoups, & Perry, 1994). These preliminary studies provided an additional means for the authors to monitor the effectiveness of the developing program.

Early studies of student achievement in *Math Trailblazers* classrooms in both urban and suburban schools have shown that students using the curriculum performed as well, and often better, on mandated standardized tests than students in those schools prior to implementation of *Math Trailblazers*. (Carter, et al., 2003; Putnam, 2003) "[The results] indicate that the balanced problem-solving approach found in *Math Trailblazers* has been successful in improving student learning and achievement in mathematics." (Carter, et al., 2003)

In developing the second edition, we benefited from the suggestions and comments of teachers throughout the country who were using the published *Math Trailblazers* materials. Input from teachers, for example, resulted in the major changes to the second edition's teacher guides. Teachers' feedback also directed us to modify or eliminate some lessons.

In third edition development, changes were made to the format and content for teachers and administrators based on surveys, focus groups, and feedback from teachers and administrators. The format of the third edition materials is easier for teachers to use. New content for teachers and administrators assists with implementation issues in the classroom, school, and district. This content embodies 20 years of professional development work by the TIMS Project with schools and districts that implement *Math Trailblazers*.

Extensive field testing during the program's development, current research and evaluation in schools, and our ongoing conversations with *Math Trailblazers* teachers have helped us develop a challenging, yet grade-level-appropriate program that reflects the needs and realities of teachers and students.

References

The following references are cited in the above document. Additional references to research literature are included in many *Unit Resource Guides* following the Background and in many sections of the *Teacher Implementation Guide* including the Assessment section and the TIMS Tutors.

Ball, D. "Halves, Pieces, and Twoths: Constructing and Using Representational Contexts in Teaching Fractions." In T. P. Carpenter, E. Fennema, and T.A. Romberg (Eds.), *Rational Numbers: An Integration of Research,* pp. 157–195. Lawrence Erlbaum Associates, Hillsdale, NJ, 1993.

Behr, M.J., and T.R. Post. "Teaching Rational Number and Decimal Concepts." In *Teaching Mathematics in Grades K–8: Research Based Methods.* Allyn and Bacon, Boston, 1992.

Burger, W., and J.M. Shaughnessy. "Characterizing the Van Hiele Levels of Development in Geometry." *Journal for Research in Mathematics Education,* 17, pp. 31–48, National Council of Teachers of Mathematics, Reston, VA, 1986.

Burghardt, B. Results of Some Summative Evaluation Studies: 1993–1994 Evaluation Report. (An unpublished report to the National Science Foundation.) 1994.

Carpenter, T.P., D. Carey, and V. Kouba. "A Problem-Solving Approach to the Operations." J.N. Payne, ed., *Mathematics for the Young Child.* National Council of Teachers of Mathematics, Reston, VA, 1990.

Carpenter, T.P., E. Fennema, M.L. Franke, L. Levi, and S.E. Empson. *Children's Mathematics: Cognitively Guided Instruction.* Heinemann, Westport, CT, 1999.

Carter, M.A., J.S. Beissinger, A. Cirulis, M. Gartzman, C.R. Kelso, and P. Wagreich. "Student Learning and Achievement with *Math Trailblazers.*" S.L. Senk and D.R. Thompson, eds., *Standards-Based School Mathematics Curricula: What Does the Research Say about Student Outcomes?* Lawrence Erlbaum Associates, Inc., Hillsdale, NJ, 2003.

Cognition and Technology Group at Vanderbilt. *The Jasper Project: Lessons in Curriculum, Instruction, Assessment, and Professional Development.* Erlbaum, Mahwah, NJ, 1997.

Cramer, K., T. Post, and R. del Mas. "Initial Fraction Learning by Fourth- and Fifth-Grade Students: A Comparison of the Effects of Using Commercial Curricula with the Effects of Using the Rational Number Project Curriculum." *Journal for Research in Mathematics Education,* 33(2), pp. 111–144.

Crowley, M.L. "The Van Hiele Model of Development of Geometric Thought." *Learning and Teaching Geometry, K–12, 1987 Yearbook.* Edited by Mary Montgomery Lindquist. National Council of Teachers of Mathematics, Reston, VA, 1987.

Curriculum and Evaluation Standards for School Mathematics. National Council of Teachers of Mathematics, Reston, VA, 1989.

Dewey, J. "Science as Subject-Matter and as Method." *Science,* 31(787), pp. 121–127, 1910.

Flanders, J. "How Much of the Content in Mathematics Textbooks Is New?" *The Arithmetic Teacher,* 35(1), pp. 18–23, 1987.

Fuson, K.C. "Teaching Addition, Subtraction, and Place-Value Concepts." L. Wirszup and R. Streit (eds.), *Proceedings of the UCSMP International Conference on Mathematics Education: Developments in School Mathematics Education Around the World: Applications-Oriented Curricula and Technology-Supported Learning for All Students.* National Council of Teachers of Mathematics, Reston, VA, 1987.

Fuson, K.C. "Research on Whole Number Addition and Subtraction." *Handbook of Research on Mathematics Teaching and Learning,* pp. 243–275, D.A. Grouws, ed. Macmillan Publishing Company, New York, 1992.

Fuson, K.C., and D.J. Briars. "Using a Base-Ten Blocks Learning/Teaching Approach for First- and Second-Grade Place-Value and Multidigit Addition and Subtraction." *Journal for Research in Mathematics Education,* 21, pp. 180–206, 1990.

Fuson, K.C., D. Wearne, J. Hiebert, H. Murray, P. Human, A. Olivier, T. Carpenter, and E. Fennema. "Children's Conceptual Structures for Multidigit Numbers and Methods of Multidigit Addition and Subtraction." *Journal for Research in Mathematics Education,* 28, pp. 130–162, 1997.

Fuys, D., D. Geddes, and R. Tishler. "The Van Hiele Model of Thinking in Geometry among Adolescents." *Journal for Research in Mathematics Education, Monograph Number 3.* National Council of Teachers of Mathematics, Reston, VA, 1988.

Goldberg, H. *A Four Year Achievement Study: The TIMS Program.* University of Illinois at Chicago Institute for Mathematics and Science Education, Chicago, IL, 1993.

Goldberg, H. *The TIMS Laboratory Investigations.* Kendall/Hunt, Dubuque, IA, 1997.

Goldberg, H.S., and F.D. Boulanger. "Science for Elementary School Teachers: A Quantitative Approach." *American Journal of Physics,* 19(2), pp. 120–124, 1981.

Goldberg, H., and P. Wagreich. "A Model Integrated Mathematics Science Program for the Elementary School." *International Journal of Educational Research,* 14(2), pp. 193–214, 1990.

Goldberg, H., and P. Wagreich. "Teaching Integrated Math and Science: A Curriculum and Staff Development Project for the Elementary School." *Issues in Mathematics Education: Mathematicians and Education Reform.* N. Fisher, H. Keynes, and P. Wagreich, eds., American Mathematical Society, Providence, RI, 1990.

Hiebert, J. "Relationships between Research and the NCTM Standards." *Journal for Research in Mathematics Education,* 30(1), pp. 3–19, 1999.

Hiebert, J., T.P. Carpenter, E. Fennema, K.C. Fuson, P. Human, H. Murray, A. Olivier, D. Wearne. "Problem Solving as a Basis for Reform in Curriculum and Instruction: The Case of Mathematics." *Educational Researcher,* 25(4), pp. 12–21, 1996.

Hoffer, A.R., and S.A.K. Hoffer. "Ratios and Proportional Thinking." In *Teaching Mathematics in Grades K–8: Research Based Methods.* Allyn and Bacon, Boston, 1992.

Isaacs, A.C., and W.M. Carroll. "Strategies for Basic-Facts Instruction." *Teaching Children Mathematics,* 5(9), pp. 508–515, 1999.

Isaacs, A.C., P. Wagreich, and M. Gartzman. The Quest for Integration: School Mathematics and Science. *American Journal of Education,* 106(1), pp. 179–206, 1997.

Lampert, M. "Knowing, Doing, and Teaching Multiplication." *Cognition and Instruction,* 3 (4), pp. 305–342, 1986a.

Lampert, M. "Teaching Multiplication." *Journal of Mathematical Behavior,* 5, pp. 241–280, 1986b.

Lesh, R., T. Post, and M. Behr. "Representations and Translations Among Representations in Mathematics Learning and Problem Solving." C. Janvier, ed., *Problems of Representation in the Teaching and Learning of Mathematics.* Lawrence Erlbaum Associates, Hillsdale, NJ, 1987.

Lindquist, M.M., ed. *Results from the Fourth Mathematics Assessment of the National Assessment of Educational Progress.* National Council of Teachers of Mathematics. Reston, VA, 1989.

Mack, N.K. "Learning Fractions with Understanding: Building on Informal Knowledge." *Journal for Research in Mathematics Education,* 21(1), National Council of Teachers of Mathematics, Reston, VA, January 1990.

McKnight, C.C., F.J. Crosswhite, J.A. Dossey, E. Kifer, J.O. Swafford, K.T. Travers, and T.J. Cooney, *The Underachieving Curriculum: Assessing U.S. School Mathematics from an International Perspective.* Stipes Publishing Company, Champaign, IL, 1987.

National Research Council. *Adding It Up: Helping Children Learn Mathematics.* J. Kilpatrick, J. Swafford, and B. Findell, eds. National Academy Press, Washington, DC, 2001.

Newmann, F.M., A.S. Bryk, and J.K. Nagaoka. *Authentic Intellectual Work and Standardized Tests: Conflict or Coexistence?* Consortium on Chicago School Research, Chicago, 2001.

Perry, M., M. Whiteaker, and G.L. Waddoups. "Students' Participation in a Reform Mathematics Classroom: Learning to Become Mathematicians." In K. Fuson (Chair), *Effects of Reform Mathematics Curricula on Children's Mathematical Understanding.* Symposia conducted at the annual meeting of the American Educational Research Association, New York, 1996.

Principles and Standards for School Mathematics. National Council of Teachers of Mathematics, Reston, VA, 2000.

Putnam, R.T. "Commentary on Four Elementary Mathematics Curricula." S.L. Senk and D.R. Thompson, eds., *Standards-Based School Mathematics Curricula: What Does the Research Say about Student Outcomes?* Lawrence Erlbaum Associates, Inc., Hillsdale, NJ, 2003.

Schmidt, W.H., C.C. McKnight, and S.A. Raizen. *A Splintered Vision: An Investigation of U.S. Science and Mathematics Education.* Kluwer, Norwell, MA, 1996.

Schoenfeld, A.H. *Mathematical Problem Solving.* Academic Press, Orlando, FL, 1985.

Schoenfeld, A.H. "What Do We Know about Mathematics Curricula?" *Journal of Mathematical Behavior,* 13(1), pp. 55–80, 1994.

Schroeder, T.L., and F.K. Lester, Jr. "Developing Understanding in Mathematics via Problem Solving." In *New Directions for Elementary School Mathematics,* 1989 Yearbook. National Council of Teachers of Mathematics, Reston, VA, 1989.

Smith, J.B., V.E. Lee, and F.M. Newmann. *Instruction and Achievement in Chicago Elementary Schools.* Consortium on Chicago School Research, Chicago, 2001.

Sowder, J. "Estimation and Number Sense." *Handbook of Research on Mathematics Teaching and Learning,* pp. 243–275, D.A. Grouws, ed., Macmillan Publishing Company, New York, 1992.

Stevenson, H.W., and J.W. Stigler. *The Learning Gap.* Simon & Schuster, New York, 1992.

Stigler, J.W., and J. Hiebert. "Understanding and Improving Classroom Mathematics Instruction: An Overview of the TIMSS Study." *Phi Delta Kappan,* 79(1), pp. 14–21.

Stigler, J.W., and M. Perry. "Mathematics Learning in Japanese, Chinese, and American Classrooms." G.B. Saxe and M. Gearhart, eds., *New Directions for Child Development, No. 41: Children's Mathematics.* Jossey Bass, San Francisco, CA, 1988.

Thornton, C.A. "Emphasizing Thinking Strategies in Basic Fact Instruction." *Journal for Research in Mathematics Education,* 9 (3), pp. 214–227, 1978.

Thornton, C.A. "Solution Strategies: Subtraction Number Facts." *Educational Studies in Mathematics,* 21 (1), pp. 241–263, 1990a.

Thornton, C.A. "Strategies for the Basic Facts." *Mathematics for the Young Child,* pp. 133–151, J.N. Payne, ed. National Council of Teachers of Mathematics, Reston, VA, 1990b.

Whiteaker, M., G.L. Waddoups, and M. Perry. "Implementing a New Mathematics Curriculum: Constructing Models for Success." Paper presented at annual meeting of the American Educational Research Association, New Orleans, 1994.

Components and Features Guide

The Components and Features Guide presents reduced-size curriculum pages and descriptive boxes that cover each element of *Math Trailblazers*.

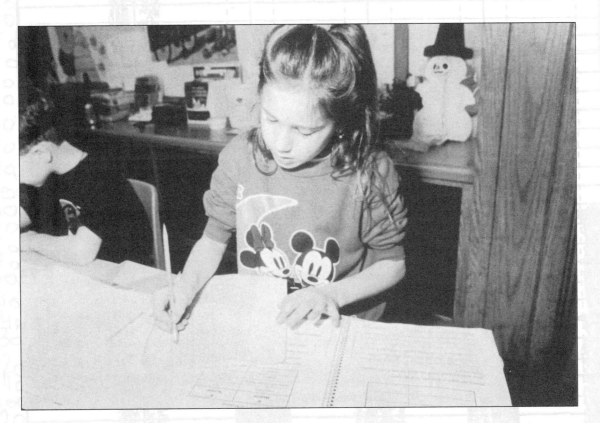

Students use Activity, Lab, and Game Pages, which are provided in the student books.

Components & Features

Components of *Math Trailblazers*

The following pages offer a walk-through of the *Teacher Implementation Guide, Unit Resource Guide, Facts Resource Guide, Teacher Resource CD, Student Guide, Discovery Assignment Book,* and *Adventure Book.*

Teacher Materials

TEACHER IMPLEMENTATION GUIDE (TIG)

- reference guide for teachers, containing program philosophy, overview, and in-depth reference documents, including a section on assessment
- black and white, nonconsumable
- glossary, including locations of key vocabulary terms in the curriculum
- curriculum index with page references to key vocabulary terms

TEACHER RESOURCE CD

Teacher resource containing:
- Daily Practice and Problems (DPP) items
- Observational Assessment Record
- Individual Assessment Record Sheet
- Letters Home (English and Spanish)
- Sections from the Facts Resource Guide
- Assessment, Transparency, and Blackline Masters
- Reproducibles
- Student and Teacher Rubrics

UNIT RESOURCE GUIDE (URG)

- comprehensive guide providing essential background information and materials for day-to-day planning, instruction, and assessment
- four-color, nonconsumable
- contains:
  Letters Home (English & Spanish)
  Unit Outlines
  Daily Practice and Problems
  Observational Assessment Record
  Lesson Guides
  Materials Lists
  Assessment Pages
  Transparency and Blackline Masters
  Answer Keys
  Glossary

FACTS RESOURCE GUIDE GRADES 2–5

- compilation of most math facts materials for each grade
- black and white, nonconsumable
- contains:
  DPP and Home Practice math facts items
  Facts Quizzes
  Games
  Lessons focusing on math facts
  Math Facts Philosophy
  Triangle Flash Cards

Student Materials

STUDENT GUIDE (SG)

- core materials for students
- four-color
- soft-cover, consumable: Grades 1, 2
- hard-cover, nonconsumable: Grades 3, 4, 5
- glossary and index: Grades 1, 2
- glossary-embedded index: Grades 3, 4, 5

DISCOVERY ASSIGNMENT BOOK (DAB) GRADES 3–5

- consumable student pages
- soft-cover, black and white
- double- and single-sided worksheets

ADVENTURE BOOK (AB)

- collections of illustrated stories focused on math and science concepts
- available in four-color Big Adventure Book and consumable black-and-white books in Grades 1, 2
- available in soft-cover, four-color, nonconsumable format in Grades 3, 4, 5

Administrator Materials

ADMINISTRATOR HANDBOOK

- Describes important components of a math implementation
- Strategies for administrators to successfully guide implementation
- Blackline Masters for presentations to staff, parents, or other audiences
- Important sections for administrators from *Teacher Implementation Guides*
- black and white, nonconsumable

Letter Home (Parent Letter)

The Letter Home is designed to be signed and sent by the teacher. It explains what students will study and how their families can help. Spanish versions of letters are also provided.

Carta al hogar
Predicciones usando datos

Fecha: _____

Estimado miembro de familia:

En esta unidad, la clase de su hijo/a hará predicciones usando gráficas y patrones observados en los datos.

También realizaremos un experimento llamado Rebote de pelotas. Los patrones en los datos del Rebote de pelotas nos ayudarán a hacer predicciones acerca de hasta qué altura rebotará una pelota cuando se la deja caer desde cierta altura. Mientras hacen estas predicciones, los estudiantes resolverán problemas y usarán las matemáticas en la manera en que se usan en la ciencia, la tecnología y el mundo de los negocios.

Saltos largos ganados
en las olimpiadas de hor...

Longitud en pulgadas

Tiempo en años

Ayude a su hijo/a en casa preguntándole acerca de sus predicciones.

- Pídale a su hijo/a que le cuente la historia de la gráfica que aparece en esta página. P... longitud del salto largo ganador en las próximas Olimpiadas de verano.
- Pídale a su hijo/a que le cuente acerca del experimento del Rebote de pelotas. ¿Qué ... recolectó su grupo? ¿Qué predicciones hizo el grupo?
- En esta unidad, seguiremos repasando las tablas de multiplicación, poniendo énfasis ... grupo, los números cuadrados ($3 \times 3 = 9$, $4 \times 4 = 16$, $5 \times 5 = 25$, etc.). Su hijo/a ... ticar usando las tarjetas triangulares.

Gracias por su interés continuo en el aprendizaje de las matemáticas de su hijo/a.

Atentamente,

_____

Letter Home
Using Data to Predict

Date: _____

Dear Family Member:

In this unit, your child's class will make predictions using graphs and patterns in data.

We will also conduct an experiment called *Bouncing Ball*. Patterns in the *Bouncing Ball* data will allow us to make predictions about how high a ball will bounce when dropped from a given height. While making these predictions, students will solve problems and use math in much the same way as it is used in science, technology, and the business world.

Men's Winning Olympic Long Jumps

Length in Inches

Time in Years

Help your child at home by asking about his or her predictions.

- Ask your child to tell you the story of the graph shown here. Predict the length of the winning long jump for the next Summer Olympic Games.
- Encourage your child to tell you about the *Bouncing Ball* lab. What data did his or her group collect? What predictions did the group make?
- In this unit, we continue reviewing the multiplication facts focusing on the third group of facts, the square numbers ($3 \times 3 = 9$, $4 \times 4 = 16$, $5 \times 5 = 25$, etc.). Your child can practice these facts using *Triangle Flash Cards*.

Thank you for your continued interest in your child's mathematical explorations.

Sincerely,

_____

Components & Features

Art — Most letters include an illustration relating to the unit's activities.

Outline

The Outline indicates the number of lessons, what they are about, supplies you will need for them, how much time they will take, and other materials you may want to introduce. The Outline also includes helpful planning information such as a summary of the unit, Pacing Suggestions, Assessment Indicators, related trade books and software as well as ideas for differentiation.

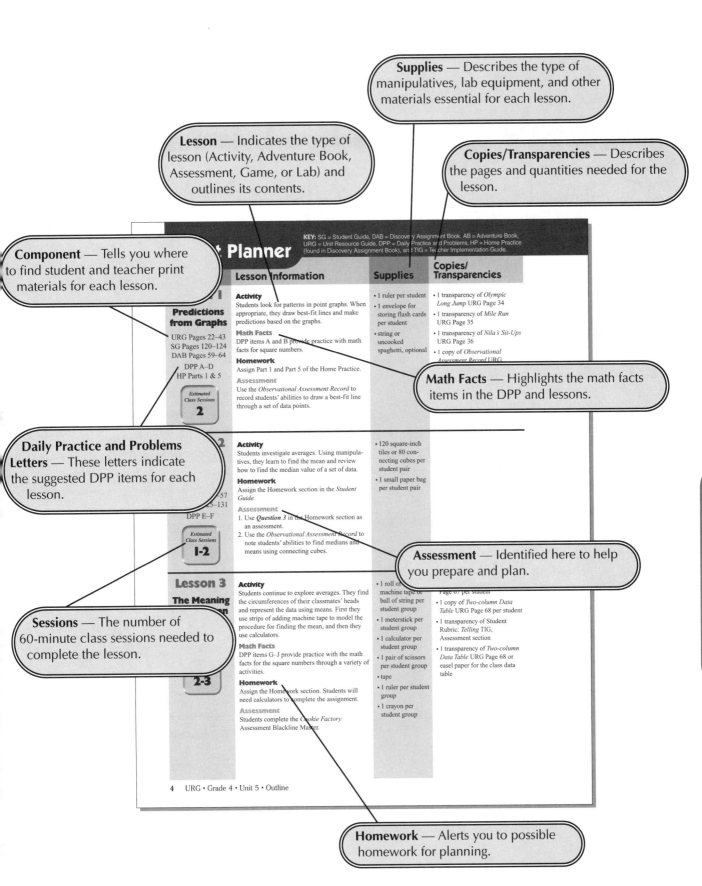

Supplies — Describes the type of manipulatives, lab equipment, and other materials essential for each lesson.

Lesson — Indicates the type of lesson (Activity, Adventure Book, Assessment, Game, or Lab) and outlines its contents.

Copies/Transparencies — Describes the pages and quantities needed for the lesson.

Component — Tells you where to find student and teacher print materials for each lesson.

Daily Practice and Problems Letters — These letters indicate the suggested DPP items for each lesson.

Sessions — The number of 60-minute class sessions needed to complete the lesson.

Math Facts — Highlights the math facts items in the DPP and lessons.

Assessment — Identified here to help you prepare and plan.

Homework — Alerts you to possible homework for planning.

KEY: SG = Student Guide, DAB = Discovery Assignment Book, AB = Adventure Book, URG = Unit Resource Guide, DPP = Daily Practice and Problems, HP = Home Practice (found in Discovery Assignment Book), and TIG = Teacher Implementation Guide.

t Planner

Lesson Information	Supplies	Copies/Transparencies

Predictions from Graphs

URG Pages 22–43
SG Pages 120–124
DAB Pages 59–64

DPP A–D
HP Parts 1 & 5

Estimated Class Sessions **2**

Activity
Students look for patterns in point graphs. When appropriate, they draw best-fit lines and make predictions based on the graphs.

Math Facts
DPP items A and B provide practice with math facts for square numbers.

Homework
Assign Part 1 and Part 5 of the Home Practice.

Assessment
Use the *Observational Assessment Record* to record students' abilities to draw a best-fit line through a set of data points.

- 1 ruler per student
- 1 envelope for storing flash cards per student
- string or uncooked spaghetti, optional

- 1 transparency of *Olympic Long Jump* URG Page 34
- 1 transparency of *Mile Run* URG Page 35
- 1 transparency of *Nila's Sit-Ups* URG Page 36
- 1 copy of *Observational Assessment Record* URG

Estimated Class Sessions **1-2**

Activity
Students investigate averages. Using manipulatives, they learn to find the mean and review how to find the median value of a set of data.

Homework
Assign the Homework section in the *Student Guide.*

Assessment
1. Use *Question 3* in the Homework section as an assessment.
2. Use the *Observational Assessment Record* to note students' abilities to find medians and means using connecting cubes.

- 120 square-inch tiles or 80 connecting cubes per student pair
- 1 small paper bag per student pair

DPP E–F

Lesson 3

The Meaning

Estimated Class Sessions **2-3**

Activity
Students continue to explore averages. They find the circumferences of their classmates' heads and represent the data using means. First they use strips of adding machine tape to model the procedure for finding the mean, and then they use calculators.

Math Facts
DPP items G–J provide practice with the math facts for the square numbers through a variety of activities.

Homework
Assign the Homework section. Students will need calculators to complete the assignment.

Assessment
Students complete the *Cookie Factory* Assessment Blackline Master.

- 1 roll of machine tape or ball of string per student group
- 1 meterstick per student group
- 1 calculator per student group
- 1 pair of scissors per student group
- tape
- 1 ruler per student group
- 1 crayon per student group

Page 67 per student
- 1 copy of *Two-column Data Table* URG Page 68 per student
- 1 transparency of Student Rubric: *Telling* TIG, Assessment section
- 1 transparency of *Two-column Data Table* URG Page 68 or easel paper for the class data table

Components & Features

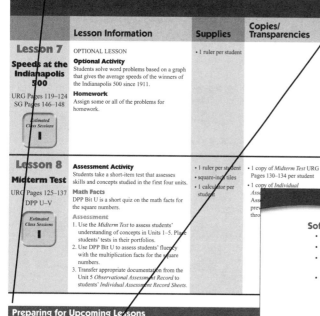

Preparing for Upcoming Lessons — Suggestions to help you plan ahead.

Connections — The material in *Math Trailblazers* lessons often can be related to books, magazine articles, and computer programs. When a Connection is recommended for use with a specific lesson, it is included in the Lesson Guide.

	Lesson Information	Supplies	Copies/ Transparencies
Lesson 7 **Speeds at the Indianapolis 500** URG Pages 119–124 SG Pages 146–148 *Estimated Class Sessions* 1	OPTIONAL LESSON **Optional Activity** Students solve word problems based on a graph that gives the average speeds of the winners of the Indianapolis 500 since 1911. **Homework** Assign some or all of the problems for homework.	• 1 ruler per student	
Lesson 8 **Midterm Test** URG Pages 125–137 DPP U–V *Estimated Class Sessions* 1	**Assessment Activity** Students take a short-item test that assesses skills and concepts studied in the first four units. **Math Facts** DPP Bit U is a short quiz on the math facts for the square numbers. **Assessment** 1. Use the *Midterm Test* to assess students' understanding of concepts in Units 1–5. Place students' tests in their portfolios. 2. Use DPP Bit U to assess students' fluency with the multiplication facts for the square numbers. 3. Transfer appropriate documentation from the Unit 5 *Observational Assessment Record* to students' *Individual Assessment Record Sheets*.	• 1 ruler per student • square-inch tiles • 1 calculator per student	• 1 copy of *Midterm Test* URG Pages 130–134 per student • 1 copy of *Individual Ass... Ass... prev... thro...*

Preparing for Upcoming Lessons

In an optional lesson in Unit 6, students will fill jars with objects and estimate the num jars. Begin asking students to collect jars from home.

In Unit 6, students will cut out articles that use big numbers from newspapers and mag ing newspapers and magazines for students.

Connections

A current list of literature and software connections is available at www.mathtrailblaze also find information on connections in the *Teacher Implementation Guide* Literature L List sections.

Literature Connections
Suggested Titles
• Peterson, Ivars and Nancy Henderson. *Math Trek: Adventures in the Math Zone.* Francisco, 2000.
• Tang, Greg. *The Grapes of Math: Mind-Stretching Math Riddles.* Scholastic Press

6   URG • Grade 4 • Unit 5 • Outline

Software Connections
• *Graph Master* provides practice with collecting data and creating graphs. (Lessons 1, 3, and 4)
• *Kid Pix* helps students create their own illustrations.
• *Math Mysteries: Measurement* provides practice with multistep problem solving involving distance, weight, and capacity.
• *TinkerPlots* allows students to record, compare, and analyze data in tables and graphs.

Teaching All Math Trailblazers Students

Math Trailblazers lessons are designed for students with a wide range of abilities. The lessons are flexible and do not require significant adaptation for diverse learning styles or academic levels. However, when needed, lessons can be tailored to allow students to engage their abilities to the greatest extent possible while building knowledge and skills.

To assist you in meeting the needs of all students in your classroom, this section contains information about some of the features in the curriculum that allow all students access to mathematics. For additional information, see the Teaching the *Math Trailblazers* Student: Meeting Individual Needs section in the *Teacher Implementation Guide.*

Differentiation Opportunities in this Unit

Laboratory Experiments

Laboratory experiments enable students to solve problems using a variety of representations including pictures, tables, graphs, and symbols. Teachers can assign or adapt parts of the analysis according to the student's ability. The following lesson is a lab:
• Lesson 4 *Bouncing Ball*

Journal Prompts

Journal prompts provide opportunities for students to explain and reflect on mathematical problems. They can help both students who need practice explaining their ide... from answering... with various... using pictur... alter journal... The followi...
• Lesso...
• Lesson 3...
• Lesson 4 *Bou...*

• Lesson 5 *Two Heads Are Better Than One*
• Lesson 6 *Professor Peabody Invents a Ball*

DPP Challenges

DPP Challenges are items from the Daily Practice and Problems that usually take more than fifteen minutes to complete. These problems are more thought-provoking and can be used to stretch students' problem-solving skills. The following lessons have a DPP Challenge in them:
• DPP Challenge F from Lesson 2 *Another Average Activity*
• DPP Challenge P from Lesson 4 *Bouncing Ball*
• DPP Challenge V from Lesson 8 *Midterm Test*

Extensions

• Lesson 2 *Another Average Activity*

URG • Grade 4 • Unit 5 • Outline   7

Teaching All Math Trailblazers Students — Helps you plan lessons that challenge all your students.

Differentiation Opportunities in this Unit — This section identifies the games, laboratory experiments, journal prompts, and extensions you can use to meet the varying needs of your students.

Background

The Background explains what students will learn in the unit and places the material in the larger context of the *Math Trailblazers* curriculum.

Unit 5

Background
Using Data to Predict

In this unit, students use data from different sources to make predictions. For example, using a graph of data from past Olympic contests and studying the patterns in the data, they make predictions about contests in future Olympics. We introduce several new ideas that help students become more sophisticated in their skills with data collection and analysis. They begin using the terms manipulated, responding, and fixed to describe variables in a controlled scientific experiment. While these terms will be new, students have used the concepts that underlie them in previous grades in laboratory experiments. We will continue to use these terms in many experiments. Students will have ample opportunities to gain confidence and facility in using this new vocabulary.

Best-fit lines. Students further explore the use of best-fit lines to make predictions from graphs. Drawing best-fit lines is done here simply by eye. The technique of fitting lines to data is frequently used by mathematicians and scientists to analyze data.

For more information on best-fit lines or manipulated, responding, and fixed variables, see the TIMS Tutor: *The TIMS Laboratory Method* in the *Teacher Implementation Guide*.

Averages. Also in this unit, we review the use of medians as averages and introduce a second kind of average, the mean. Use of the mean provides students with another tool for finding a representative value for a data set. We first introduce the concept concretely, through the use of cubes and measurement. Students then practice finding means using a calculator. See the TIMS Tutor: *Averages* in the *Teacher Implementation Guide* for a more detailed discussion.

Bouncing Ball lab. This lab is the centerpiece of the unit and integrates many of the skills and concepts students learned in previous units and

previous grades. Students use the four steps of the TIMS Laboratory Method to collect and display interesting data about how high a ball will bounce. Within the context of the lab, they draw a best-fit line on the graph to make predictions from the data. They use patterns in the data table and the graph to solve problems involving proportional reasoning. They use their problem-solving skills to solve problems in the lab.

Assessment. After completing the *Bouncing Ball* lab, students use similar data to solve an open-ended problem, *Professor Peabody Invents a Ball*. As part of this activity, students are introduced to the Student Rubric: *Solving*. Include their responses to the problems in this activity in their portfolios. For more information about the *TIMS Multidimensional Rubric*, see the Assessment section in the *Teacher Implementation Guide*.

Math Facts. The systematic review and practice of the math facts continues in this unit with the square numbers. Students use *Triangle Flash Cards* to practice these multiplication facts. They will study the division facts through the use of fact families.

Resources

- Korithoski, Theodor P., and Patricia A. "Mean or Meaningless?" in *The Arithmetic Teacher*. The National Council of Teachers of Mathematics, Reston, VA, December 1993, pp. 194–197.
- Matsumoto, A.N. "Correlation, Junior Varsity Style." In A.P. Shulte and J.R. Smart (Eds.), *Teaching Statistics and Probability: 1981 Yearbook*. The National Council of Teachers of Mathematics.
- Wallechinsky, *Summer Olympics*, York, 2000.

Resources — Listed at the end of the Background to provide additional information on the ideas covered in the unit.

Components & Features

Observational Assessment Record

The *Observational Assessment Record* is a form used to record observations of students' progress.

Assessment Indicators — These are the Assessment Indicators listed in the Unit Outline. They highlight the skills and concepts you should look for as you observe students working on activities in the unit.

Additional lines are provided to help document students' progress with other content.

Observational Assessment Record

(A1) Can students draw and interpret best-fit lines?

(A2) Can students find the median and mean of a data set?

(A3) Can students identify and use variables?

(A4) Can students measure length in centimeters?

(A5) Can students use patterns in data tables and graphs to make predictions?

(A6) Can students collect, organize, graph, and analyze data?

(A7) Can students solve open-response problems and communicate solution strategies?

(A8) Do students demonstrate fluency with the multiplication facts for the square numbers?

(A9) Can students write the two number sentences in the fact families for the square numbers?

(A10) _____

Name	A1	A2	A3	A4	A5	A6	A7	A8	A9	A10	Comments
1.											
2.											
3.											
4.											
5.											
6.											
7.											
8.											
9.											
10.											
11.											
12.											
13.											

URG • Grade 4 • Unit 5 • Observational Assessment Record   9

Daily Practice and Problems

The Daily Practice and Problems (DPP) is a series of short exercises that provide continuing review of math concepts, skills, and facts. Each DPP set includes a Teacher's Guide, which provides specific information on the study and assessment of the math facts in the current unit.

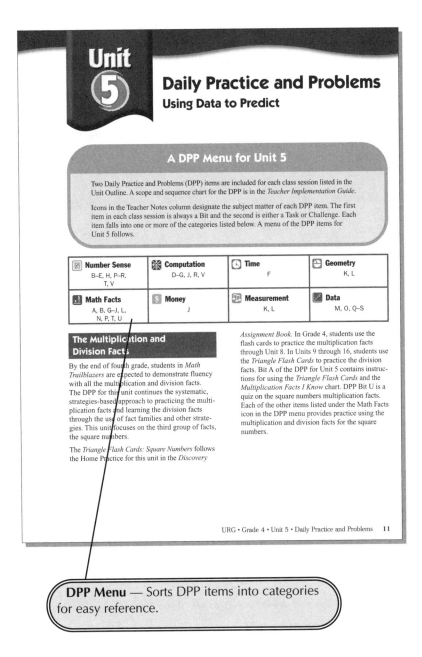

Unit 5

Daily Practice and Problems
Using Data to Predict

A DPP Menu for Unit 5

Two Daily Practice and Problems (DPP) items are included for each class session listed in the Unit Outline. A scope and sequence chart for the DPP is in the *Teacher Implementation Guide*.

Icons in the Teacher Notes column designate the subject matter of each DPP item. The first item in each class session is always a Bit and the second is either a Task or Challenge. Each item falls into one or more of the categories listed below. A menu of the DPP items for Unit 5 follows.

N Number Sense B–E, H, P–R, T, V	Computation D–G, J, R, V	Time F	Geometry K, L
Math Facts A, B, G–J, L, N, P, T, U	Money J	Measurement K, L	Data M, O, Q–S

The Multiplication and Division Facts

By the end of fourth grade, students in *Math Trailblazers* are expected to demonstrate fluency with all the multiplication and division facts. The DPP for this unit continues the systematic, strategies-based approach to practicing the multiplication facts and learning the division facts through the use of fact families and other strategies. This unit focuses on the third group of facts, the square numbers.

The *Triangle Flash Cards: Square Numbers* follows the Home Practice for this unit in the *Discovery*

Assignment Book. In Grade 4, students use the flash cards to practice the multiplication facts through Unit 8. In Units 9 through 16, students use the *Triangle Flash Cards* to practice the division facts. Bit A of the DPP for Unit 5 contains instructions for using the *Triangle Flash Cards* and the *Multiplication Facts I Know* chart. DPP Bit U is a quiz on the square numbers multiplication facts. Each of the other items listed under the Math Facts icon in the DPP menu provides practice using the multiplication and division facts for the square numbers.

URG • Grade 4 • Unit 5 • Daily Practice and Problems   11

DPP Menu — Sorts DPP items into categories for easy reference.

The Daily Practice and Problems may be used in class for practice and review, as assessment, or for homework. Notes for teachers provide the answers as well as suggestions for using the items.

Eight icons indicate the subject matter of each item:

N **Number Sense** (estimating, partitioning numbers, skip counting, etc.);

Computation (solving problems using paper-and-pencil methods, estimation, mental math, or calculators);

Time (telling time, solving problems involving elapsed time);

Geometry (work with shapes, coordinates, or other geometric topics);

$\frac{5}{x7}$ **Math Facts** (practice with addition, subtraction, multiplication, or division facts);

$ **Money** (counting change, combining various coins, or estimating total cost);

Measurement (measuring length, area, mass, volume, or time); and

Data (collecting, organizing, graphing, or analyzing data).

Components & Features

There are two Daily Practice and Problems items for each nonoptional class session noted in a Unit Outline. The first of these is always a TIMS Bit and the second is either a TIMS Task or a TIMS Challenge.

On the teacher note for an item, you will usually find one or more icons which indicate the subject matter of the item.

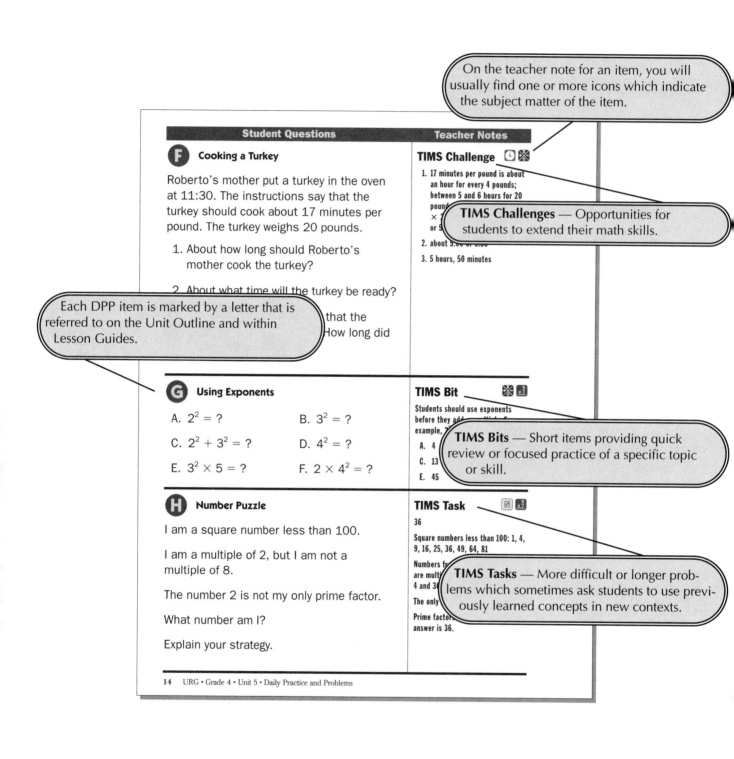

Student Questions

F **Cooking a Turkey**

Roberto's mother put a turkey in the oven at 11:30. The instructions say that the turkey should cook about 17 minutes per pound. The turkey weighs 20 pounds.

1. About how long should Roberto's mother cook the turkey?

2. About what time will the turkey be ready?

that the How long did

Teacher Notes

TIMS Challenge

1. 17 minutes per pound is about an hour for every 4 pounds; between 5 and 6 hours for 20 pound
   × or 5

2. about 5.00 or 5.50

3. 5 hours, 50 minutes

TIMS Challenges — Opportunities for students to extend their math skills.

Each DPP item is marked by a letter that is referred to on the Unit Outline and within Lesson Guides.

G **Using Exponents**

A. $2^2 = ?$ B. $3^2 = ?$

C. $2^2 + 3^2 = ?$ D. $4^2 = ?$

E. $3^2 \times 5 = ?$ F. $2 \times 4^2 = ?$

TIMS Bit

Students should use exponents before they ad   Hi h 5 example, 2
A. 4
C. 13
E. 45

TIMS Bits — Short items providing quick review or focused practice of a specific topic or skill.

H **Number Puzzle**

I am a square number less than 100.

I am a multiple of 2, but I am not a multiple of 8.

The number 2 is not my only prime factor.

What number am I?

Explain your strategy.

TIMS Task

36

Square numbers less than 100: 1, 4, 9, 16, 25, 36, 49, 64, 81

Numbers fr are mult 4 and 36 The only Prime facto answer is 36.

TIMS Tasks — More difficult or longer problems which sometimes ask students to use previously learned concepts in new contexts.

14   URG • Grade 4 • Unit 5 • Daily Practice and Problems

Lesson Guide

The Lesson guide is a how-to manual explaining what you need for the lesson and what it involves.

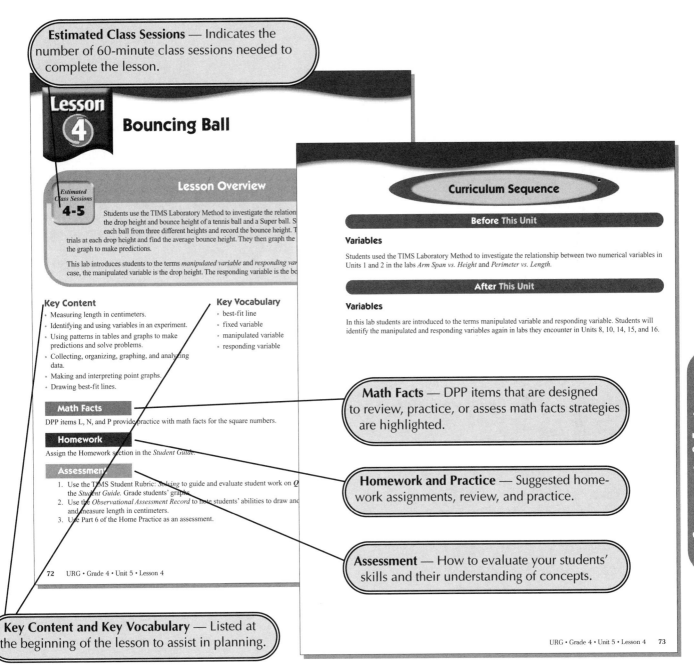

Estimated Class Sessions — Indicates the number of 60-minute class sessions needed to complete the lesson.

Lesson 4

Bouncing Ball

Estimated Class Sessions
4-5

Lesson Overview

Students use the TIMS Laboratory Method to investigate the relation[ship between] the drop height and bounce height of a tennis ball and a Super ball. S[tudents drop] each ball from three different heights and record the bounce height. T[hey do] trials at each drop height and find the average bounce height. They then graph the [data and use] the graph to make predictions.

This lab introduces students to the terms *manipulated variable* and *responding var[iable]*. [In this] case, the manipulated variable is the drop height. The responding variable is the bo[unce height.]

Key Content
- Measuring length in centimeters.
- Identifying and using variables in an experiment.
- Using patterns in tables and graphs to make predictions and solve problems.
- Collecting, organizing, graphing, and analyzing data.
- Making and interpreting point graphs.
- Drawing best-fit lines.

Key Vocabulary
- best-fit line
- fixed variable
- manipulated variable
- responding variable

Math Facts
DPP items L, N, and P provide practice with math facts for the square numbers.

Homework
Assign the Homework section in the *Student Guide*.

Assessment
1. Use the TIMS Student Rubric: *Solving* to guide and evaluate student work on *Q[uestions]* the *Student Guide.* Grade students' graphs.
2. Use the *Observational Assessment Record* to note students' abilities to draw an[d] and measure length in centimeters.
3. Use Part 6 of the Home Practice as an assessment.

72   URG • Grade 4 • Unit 5 • Lesson 4

Curriculum Sequence

Before This Unit

Variables

Students used the TIMS Laboratory Method to investigate the relationship between two numerical variables in Units 1 and 2 in the labs *Arm Span vs. Height* and *Perimeter vs. Length.*

After This Unit

Variables

In this lab students are introduced to the terms manipulated variable and responding variable. Students will identify the manipulated and responding variables again in labs they encounter in Units 8, 10, 14, 15, and 16.

Math Facts — DPP items that are designed to review, practice, or assess math facts strategies are highlighted.

Homework and Practice — Suggested homework assignments, review, and practice.

Assessment — How to evaluate your students' skills and their understanding of concepts.

URG • Grade 4 • Unit 5 • Lesson 4   73

Key Content and Key Vocabulary — Listed at the beginning of the lesson to assist in planning.

Components & Features

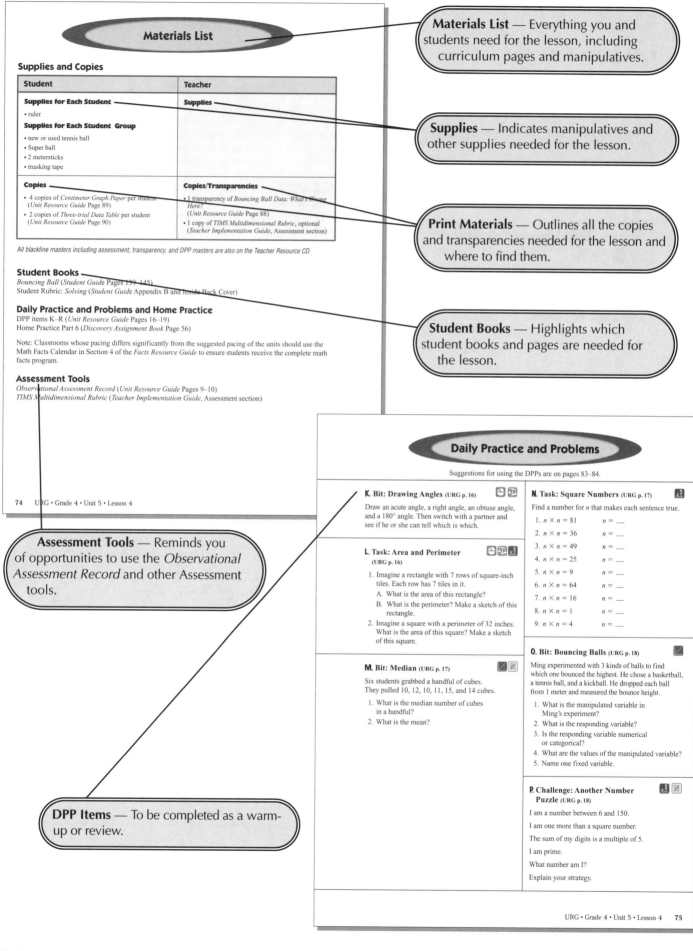

Materials List

Materials List — Everything you and students need for the lesson, including curriculum pages and manipulatives.

Supplies and Copies

Student	Teacher
Supplies for Each Student	**Supplies**
• ruler	
Supplies for Each Student Group	
• new or used tennis ball	
• Super ball	
• 2 metersticks	
• masking tape	
Copies	**Copies/Transparencies**
• 4 copies of *Centimeter Graph Paper* per student (*Unit Resource Guide* Page 89)	• 1 transparency of *Bouncing Ball Data: What's Wrong Here?* (*Unit Resource Guide* Page 88)
• 2 copies of *Three-trial Data Table* per student (*Unit Resource Guide* Page 90)	• 1 copy of *TIMS Multidimensional Rubric*, optional (*Teacher Implementation Guide*, Assessment section)

All blackline masters including assessment, transparency, and DPP masters are also on the Teacher Resource CD.

Supplies — Indicates manipulatives and other supplies needed for the lesson.

Print Materials — Outlines all the copies and transparencies needed for the lesson and where to find them.

Student Books
Bouncing Ball (*Student Guide* Pages 139–145)
Student Rubric: Solving (*Student Guide* Appendix B and Inside Back Cover)

Student Books — Highlights which student books and pages are needed for the lesson.

Daily Practice and Problems and Home Practice
DPP items K–R (*Unit Resource Guide* Pages 16–19)
Home Practice Part 6 (*Discovery Assignment Book* Page 56)

Note: Classrooms whose pacing differs significantly from the suggested pacing of the units should use the Math Facts Calendar in Section 4 of the *Facts Resource Guide* to ensure students receive the complete math facts program.

Assessment Tools
Observational Assessment Record (*Unit Resource Guide* Pages 9–10)
TIMS Multidimensional Rubric (*Teacher Implementation Guide*, Assessment section)

Assessment Tools — Reminds you of opportunities to use the *Observational Assessment Record* and other Assessment tools.

74   URG • Grade 4 • Unit 5 • Lesson 4

Daily Practice and Problems

Suggestions for using the DPPs are on pages 83–84.

K. Bit: Drawing Angles (URG p. 16)

Draw an acute angle, a right angle, an obtuse angle, and a 180° angle. Then switch with a partner and see if he or she can tell which is which.

L. Task: Area and Perimeter (URG p. 16)

1. Imagine a rectangle with 7 rows of square-inch tiles. Each row has 7 tiles in it.
   A. What is the area of this rectangle?
   B. What is the perimeter? Make a sketch of this rectangle.
2. Imagine a square with a perimeter of 32 inches. What is the area of this square? Make a sketch of this square.

M. Bit: Median (URG p. 17)

Six students grabbed a handful of cubes. They pulled 10, 12, 10, 11, 15, and 14 cubes.

1. What is the median number of cubes in a handful?
2. What is the mean?

N. Task: Square Numbers (URG p. 17)

Find a number for n that makes each sentence true.

1. $n \times n = 81$ $n = \_\_$
2. $n \times n = 36$ $n = \_\_$
3. $n \times n = 49$ $n = \_\_$
4. $n \times n = 25$ $n = \_\_$
5. $n \times n = 9$ $n = \_\_$
6. $n \times n = 64$ $n = \_\_$
7. $n \times n = 16$ $n = \_\_$
8. $n \times n = 1$ $n = \_\_$
9. $n \times n = 4$ $n = \_\_$

O. Bit: Bouncing Balls (URG p. 18)

Ming experimented with 3 kinds of balls to find which one bounced the highest. He chose a basketball, a tennis ball, and a kickball. He dropped each ball from 1 meter and measured the bounce height.

1. What is the manipulated variable in Ming's experiment?
2. What is the responding variable?
3. Is the responding variable numerical or categorical?
4. What are the values of the manipulated variable?
5. Name one fixed variable.

P. Challenge: Another Number Puzzle (URG p. 18)

I am a number between 6 and 150.

I am one more than a square number.

The sum of my digits is a multiple of 5.

I am prime.

What number am I?

Explain your strategy.

URG • Grade 4 • Unit 5 • Lesson 4   75

DPP Items — To be completed as a warm-up or review.

Samples of Student Work — Reproductions or transcriptions of work by actual students from the same grade level as your class allow you to compare your students' work to other students' work.

Before the Lab/Activity — Covers what you need to prepare ahead of time for the lesson.

Before the Lab

A drawing of the lab setup is shown in Figure 6. You will need a lab setup for each group of three students. For each group, tape two metersticks to the wall vertically, one on top of the other, with the 100 cm mark at the top of each meterstick. If you cannot find places on your classroom's walls to tape two metersticks, tape them to door jambs or on the walls in the hall.

Figure 6: *Lab setup for* Bouncing Ball

It is important that student groups use the same ball to collect the data and check their predictions. Number each ball with a permanent marker so students can find and use the same ball on succeeding days of the lab.

TIMS Tips — Practical suggestions to help you get the most out of each lesson.

TIMS Tip

Used tennis balls work as well as or better than new ones. High school or other tennis teams often have a surplus of used tennis balls. One way to obtain free tennis balls is to ask a coach to donate them.

Teaching the Lab

Part 1 Defining the Variables and Drawing the Picture

To introduce the lab, read the opening vignette on the *Bouncing Ball* Lab Pages in the *Student Guide*. One important aspect of this lab is identifying the **manipulated variable,** the **responding variable,** and the controlled, or **fixed variables.** Use the discussion in the Identifying the Variables section on the *Bouncing Ball* Lab Pages to introduce these terms to your class.

Teaching the Lab/Activity — Describes what students will do in each activity.

Student Guide - page 139

Reduced-Size Student Pages — Most student pages are reproduced in the Lesson Guide.

Components & Features

Discussion Prompts — Italicized questions designed to use in class.

...porate *Questions 1–5* in ...class discussion. If ...wering the first three ...m as suggested below:

- *The two main variables in an experiment are called the manipulated and responding variables. The **manipulated variable** is the variable with values we know at the beginning of the experiment. Which variable, the drop height or the bounce height, is the manipulated variable in this experiment?* (The drop height. ***Question 1***)

- *The **responding variable** is the variable with values we learn by doing the experiment. What is the responding variable?* (The bounce height. ***Question 2***)

- *What other variables might affect the bounce height besides the drop height? What should stay the same in the experiments so we know that the change in the bounce height is due to the drop height? What things should stay the same so the experiments are fair?* (The type of ball will be the same in each experiment. The surface of the floor. The way we drop the ball—dropping it gently, not adding any force. The same ball should be used for each trial. ***Question 3***)

Once students can identify the variables and understand the procedure, they are ready to draw a picture. A student's picture is shown in Figure 7. Note that ...tified the manipulated and ...showed the three values for

Content Notes — Specific content information relating to lesson activities.

Figure 7: Student ...

Each experiment should tell you how much the bounce height changes when you change the drop height. Usually there are other variables involved in an experiment. Look at the experimental setup. Try bouncing a ball on the floor a few times. Other than the drop height, what could change the bounce height? List some variables.

The variables in your list should remain the same during an experiment, so the only thing that affects the bounce height is the drop height. These variables are called **fixed variables**. The results of a carefully controlled experiment will help you make accurate predictions.

Discuss

1. What is the manipulated variable in both the tennis ball experiment and the Super Ball experiment?
2. What is the responding variable?
3. What are the fixed variables in each of the experiments?
4. **A.** Is the bounce height a categorical or numerical variable?
   B. Is the drop height a categorical or numerical variable?
   C. Is the type of ball a categorical or numerical variable?
5. Mrs. Dewey's class dropped the ball three times from each drop height. They measured the bounce height each time. Why is it a good idea to do three trials?

Draw

Draw a picture of the lab. Show the tools you will use. Be sure to label the two main variables. A student from another class should be able to look at your picture and know what you are going to do during the lab.

Bouncing Ball   SG · Grade 4 · Unit 5 · Lesson 4   **141**

Student Guide - page 141 *(Answers on p. 91)*

Content Note

Manipulated, Responding, and Fixed Variables.
In simple experiments, students look for the relationship between two main variables. We call these two variables the manipulated variable and the responding variable. These variables are also commonly called the independent and dependent variables. After many years of working with students on identifying variables, we found the terms manipulated and responding are less confusing than independent and dependent. However, the important idea is for students to understand that as we change the values for the manipulated variable, we look for a corresponding change (a response) in the values of the responding variable.

The idea of controlled, or fixed, variables in an investigation ... very important. In this lab, students change t... look for corresponding changes in t... keep the other variables ... release—con... vari...

Tennis Ball Graph

Question 9

Question 8

B Bounce Height in cm — 100 90 80 70 60 50 40 30 20 15 10 5 0

D Drop Height in cm — 0 10 20 30 40 50 60 70 80 90 100 110 120 130 140 150

Figure 9: Sample graph of the tennis ball experiment

Super Ball Graph

Question 11

B Bounce Height in cm — 100 90 80 70 60 50 40 30 20 15 10 5

D Drop Height in cm — 0 10 20 30 40 50 60 70 80 90 100 110 120 130 140 150

Figure 10: Sample graph of the Super ball experiment

Graphs and Tables — Shows sample graphs and data tables.

In **Question 9A,** students are asked to predict the drop height of their tennis balls when the bounce height is 75 cm. This is extrapolation (**Question 9B**) since 75 cm is beyond the original data points. The graph in Figure 9 shows the extrapolation process that begins at 75 cm on the vertical axis and ends at 139 cm on the horizontal axis. If a student checked the prediction (**Question 9C**), by dropping the same ball from 139 cm and the ball bounced to 70 cm, the actual bounce height of 70 cm would be considered close to 75 centimeters. Actual bounce heights from 68 cm to 82 cm could be considered close.

Questions 10 and 12 ask students to make predictions about heights that are probably not on the graph. They will have to devise different strategies to solve these problems. The following paragraph is a student response to **Question 12.** Many other strategies are possible. Ask students to share theirs with the class.

> "I knew that if it bounced to 1 meter the drop height would be 130, but I needed 2 meters so I doubled it and I got 260."

You can use **Questions 13–15** as part of a final whole-class discussion of the lab. These questions challenge students to think critically about what they have learned. Here is a student's answer for **Question 14:**

> "The tennis ball. I think the tennis ball because on the graph I put my finger on 50 cm at the bottom and I went up and the tennis ball was closer to 18 cm than the super ball."

Math Facts

DPP Task L provides practice with the math facts for the square numbers by finding areas of squares. Task N provides practice with the square numbers using number sentences with unknowns. Challenge P is a math riddle that uses square numbers.

Homework and Practice

- Assign the Homework section on the *Bouncing Ball* Lab Pages in the *Student Guide.* Note that students will need a piece of *Centimeter Graph Paper* and a ruler to solve the problems.
- Assign the problems *Speeds at the Indianapolis 500* (Lesson 7 in the *Student Guide*) for homework. Students may be interested in looking up recent winning speeds at the Indianapolis 500 in an almanac or on the Internet.

URG • Grade 4 • Unit

Journal Prompts — Suggested writing prompts that can be assigned to students in class or for homework.

Journal Prompt

Did your group work together cooperatively? Describe something someone in your group said that helped your group work together better.

Math Facts — DPP items designed to review, practice, or assess math facts are highlighted.

Student Guide - page 144 (Answers on pp. 92–93)

Homework and Practice — Suggested homework assignments, review, and practice.

assigned as homework.

Answers for Part 6 of the Home Practice are in the Answer Key at the end of this lesson and at the end of this unit.

Assessment

- Introduce the TIMS Student Rubric: *Solving,* found in Appendix B in the *Student Guide.* This rubric sets goals for good problem-solvers. As students complete **Questions 10** and **12,** use the rubric to help them solve the problem. Refer to this rubric as you comment on their written work. Students will use the *Solving* rubric to guide their work on the assessment problem in Lesson 6 *Professor Peabody Invents a Ball.* The teacher's version of this rubric, the Solving dimension of the *TIMS Multidimensional Rubric,* is in the Assessment section in the *Teacher Implementation Guide.*
- Use this lab to assess students' graphing skills. Grade students' graphs based on the following criteria:
  1. Does the graph have a title?
  2. Are the axes scaled correctly and labeled clearly? Labeling should be consistent with the picture and the data table and should include appropriate units of measure.
  3. Are the points plotted correctly?
  4. Did the student correctly draw a best-fit line with a ruler?
  5. Did the student show any interpolation or extrapolation on the graph?
- Use the *Observational Assessment Record* to record students' abilities to fit a best-fit line to a set of data points and measure length in centimeters.
- Place students' work from all or part of this lab in their collection folders. Their work will be used in the *Experiment Review* in Unit 8.
- Use Home Practice Part 6 *Bouncing Balls* as an individual assessment of students' abilities to find medians, identify variables, and graph data.

Answers for Part 6 of the Home Practice are in the Answer Key at the end of this lesson and at the end of this unit.

Assessment — How to evaluate your students' skills and their understanding of concepts.

Student Guide - page 145 (Answers on p. 93)

Discovery Assignment Book - page 56 (Answers on p. 94)

84   URG • Grade 4 • Unit 5 • Lesson 4

Components & Features

Software Connection

Students can use a graphing program such as *Graph Master* to enter the data from the lab and then make a graph. *Graph Master* and other programs will draw a best-fit line. Some programs will plot the points and the students can then draw the best-fit line. If you use *Graph Master*, students first create a scatter plot. The manipulated variable is the independent variable and the responding variable is the dependent variable. Students should use the data table to enter the three drop heights and the three average bounce heights, as well as (0,0).

Student Rubric: Solving

In My Best Work in Mathematics:

• I read the problem carefully, make a good plan for solving it, and then carry out that plan.

• I use tools like graphs, pictures, tables, or number sentences to help me.

• I use ideas I know from somewhere else to help me solve a problem.

• I keep working on the problem until I find a good solution.

• I look back at my solution to see if my answer makes sense.

• I look back at my work to see what more I can learn from solving the problem.

442   SG · Grade 4 · Appendix B

Student Guide - Appendix B

Connections — How to connect the lesson to children's literature, computer programs, and other content areas such as science and social studies.

---

20. Which average is easier to find?

21. Roberto rolled a toy car down a ramp and measured the distance it rolled. The first time it rolled 13 cm; the second time it rolled 14 cm; the third time it rolled 18 cm.
    A. Find the median distance the car rolled.
    B. Find the mean.
    C. Which number, the mean or the median, better describes the distance the car rolls? Explain your answer.

Homework

Dear Family Member:

In class, students used towers of cubes to learn how to find two kinds of averages, the mean and the median. You can look back at the previous pages in this section to see how this is done. In the next lesson, students will learn how to compute an average using calculators.

Use pennies or small building blocks to build towers to solve the following problems. You will need about 30 pennies or blocks.

1. Linda counted the number of plants her mom has in each room in her house. She filled in the following data table.
   A. Find the median number of plants in the house.
   B. Find the mean.

Linda's Data

Room	Number of Plants
Kitchen	5
Living Room	8
Family Room	7
Linda's Room	1
Bathroom	2
Dining Room	2
Mom's Room	3

130   SG · Grade 4 · Unit 5 · Lesson 2   *Another Average Activity*

Student Guide - page 130 (Answers on p. 56)

2. John wanted to see how many free-throws he could make in one minute. The first minute he made 6 baskets. The second minute he made only 3. The third minute he made 6 baskets again. The fourth minute he made 9.
   A. Find the median number of baskets.
   B. Find the mean.

3. The students in Mrs. Dewey's class record the number of books they read each week. Here is Jerome's data for five weeks.

Jerome's Data

Week	Number of Books
Week #1	3
Week #2	2
Week #3	5
Week #4	2
Week #5	3

the median.

towers to find the mean. Give your answer

book.

average the median or the

of books that

Extensions — Activities or suggestions for further explorations on the same topic.

---

found by finding the number in the middle of the data *(Question 19)*. The median is often the easiest to find because it is simply a matter of lining up the data values from smallest to largest and choosing the middle value *(Question 20)*.

For *Questions 21A–21B* students again use cubes to find the mean and median of three distances a car rolls: 13 cm, 14 cm, and 18 cm. *Question 21C* asks students which of the two averages better describes the distances. Reasonable arguments can be made for both the median and the mean. Since the shorter two distances are much closer together than the third distance, the median (14 cm) may be a better predictor of the distance the car will roll on a fourth try. However, the mean (15 cm) takes the 18 cm roll into account

Homework and Practice

• Assign the Homework section in the *Student Guide*. Students use towers of pennies or building blocks to find medians and mean

• DPP Bit E asks students to find the prime ization of 90. Challenge F presents a prob which students calculate how long to cook 20 pound turkey.

Assessment

• Use *Question 3* in the Homework section assessment. Ask students to write their ans and explanations.

• Use the *Observational Assessment Record* students' abilities to find medians and me manipulating connecting cubes.

Extension

Tell the class that each student will pull one han cubes from a bag or bucket and build a tower. A them to predict the average number of cubes th be pulled. Let each student grab a handful and tower. Find the median number of cubes in a to lining up all the towers and choosing the middle Find the mean b the towers. Disc resul tions?

Estimated Class Sessions **4-5**

At a Glance

Math Facts and Daily Practice and Problems

DPP items L, N, and P provide practice with math facts for the square numbers. Item K reviews angle measurement. Items M, Q, and R provide practice finding averages. Item O is a review of terminology.

Before the Lab

Number the tennis balls and Super balls. Set up the lab stations.

Part 1. Defining the Variables and Drawing the Picture

1. Discuss *Questions 1–5* on the Bouncing Ball Lab Pages in the *Student Guide*.
2. Discuss the **manipulated, responding,** and **fixed variables** in the lab.
3. Model the procedure.
4. Students draw the picture.

Part 2. Collecting and Recording the Data

1. Review the procedures, reminding students of the variables that should remain constant.
2. Discuss the transparency *Bouncing Ball Data: What's Wrong Here?*
3. Decide with the class whether they will use the median or mean to average the data for the three trials.
4. Students collect the data and complete the data tables.

Part 3. Graphing the Data

Students graph the data for each ball on a separate sheet of graph paper.

Part 4. Exploring the Data

1. In *Questions 6–7*, students add a point at (0,0) and draw a best-fit line.
2. In *Questions 8–12*, students make predictions using the data and check their predictions for *Questions 8–11*.
3. Introduce the Student Rubric: Solving to guide students as they answer *Questions 10* and *12*.
4. Discuss the lab in *Questions 13–15*.
5. Place students' work in their collection folders.

Homework

Assign the Homework section in the *Student Guide*.

n *Questions 10* and *12* of the

and interpret best-fit lines

At a Glance — Summarizes suggested steps for teaching the lesson and highlights math facts, practice, other DPP items, homework, and assessment.

86   URG · Grade 4 · Unit 5 · Lesson 4

Lesson Guide for the Adventure Book

The Lesson guide is a how-to manual explaining what you need and what is involved in each lesson.

Student Pages

Reproducibles — Frequently used blackline masters. They can be printed from the *Teacher Resource CD*.

Name _____   Date _____

Bouncing Ball Data: What's Wrong Here?

D Drop Height in cm	B Bounce Height in cm			
	Trial 1	Trial 2	Trial 3	Average
40	29	29	29	29
80	50	50	50	50
120	70	70	70	70

D Drop Height in cm	B Bounce Height in cm			
	Trial 1	Trial 2	Trial 3	Average
40	20	22	20	21
80	41	42	38	40
120	61	85	67	71

Copyright © Kendall/Hunt Publishing Company

Blackline Masters, Transparency Masters, and Assessment Blackline Masters — Pages to be photocopied as review, assessment, or transparency masters; located at the end of the Lesson Guide. They can be printed from the *Teacher Resource CD*.

URG • Grade 4 • Unit 5 • Lesson 4   89

88   URG • Grade 4 • Unit 5 • Lesson 4

UNIT RESOURCE GUIDE

Answer Key

An Answer Key at the end of each lesson provides answers to questions on *Student Guide, Unit Resource Guide,* and *Discovery Assignment Book* pages, including recommended Home Practice. The Home Practice Answer Key at the end of the unit includes the answers to all the Home Practice in the *Discovery Assignment Book* for that unit. Reduced pages showing the questions are provided beside the answers.

Book and Page References — Assist you in finding the answers to specific problems.

Asterisk — Indicates this question is discussed in the Lesson Guide. These answers are often based upon data or information in the Lesson Guide discussion of the question.

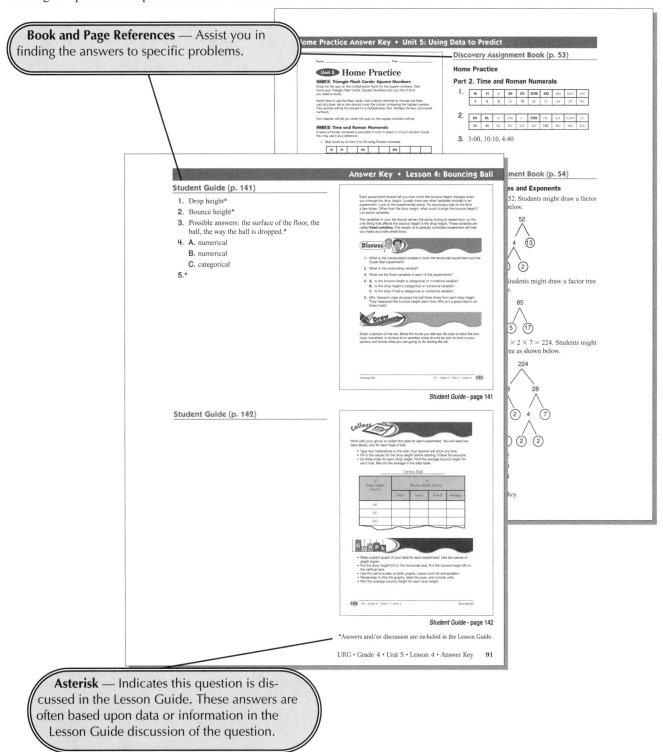

TEACHER IMPLEMENTATION GUIDE

The *Teacher Implementation Guide* is the reference manual for *Math Trailblazers*. Information in the *Teacher Implementation Guide* can be roughly categorized into three groups: general background about *Math Trailblazers*, specific information about the program, and deep background about important math and science concepts.

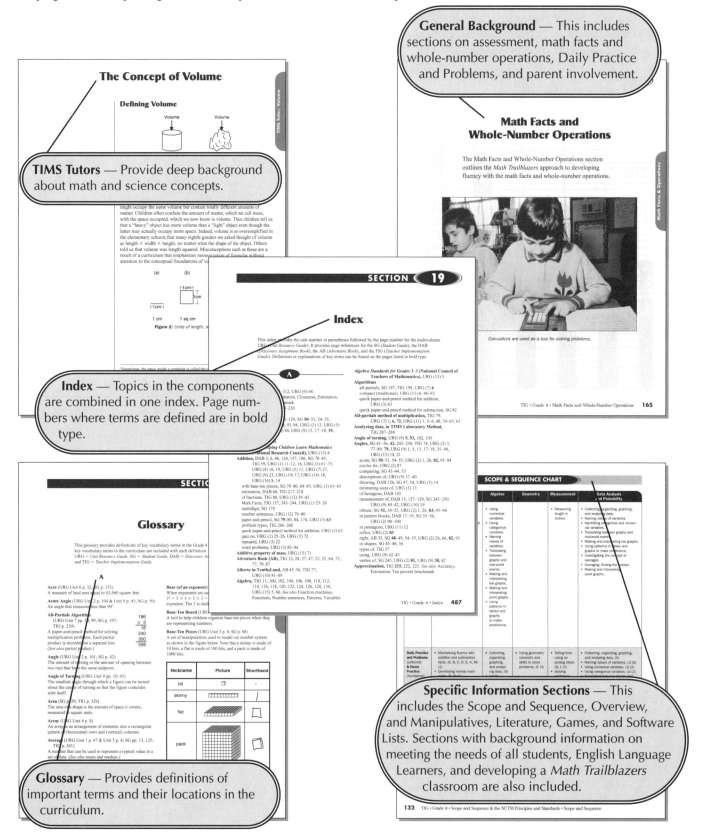

General Background — This includes sections on assessment, math facts and whole-number operations, Daily Practice and Problems, and parent involvement.

TIMS Tutors — Provide deep background about math and science concepts.

Index — Topics in the components are combined in one index. Page numbers where terms are defined are in bold type.

Glossary — Provides definitions of important terms and their locations in the curriculum.

Specific Information Sections — This includes the Scope and Sequence, Overview, and Manipulatives, Literature, Games, and Software Lists. Sections with background information on meeting the needs of all students, English Language Learners, and developing a *Math Trailblazers* classroom are also included.

FACTS RESOURCE GUIDE

The *Facts Resource Guide* provides a single location for all math facts materials for the grade and a schedule for classrooms that differ significantly from the suggested pacing of units. Almost all of the student materials in the *Facts Resource Guide* are also located in the *Student Guide, Discovery Assignment Book,* or *Unit Resource Guides.*

Games — Games help students practice math facts.

Lessons Focusing on Math Facts — Specific lessons from the *Unit Resource Guide* that focus on math facts instruction.

Calendar — An alternative calendar for covering the math facts for classrooms that depart significantly from the recommended schedule.

DPPs — DPP items that address math facts are compiled and reproduced.

Facts Assessments — Includes Facts Quizzes and Inventory Tests for the grade.

Components & Features

The *Teacher Resource CD* provides key items from other components of the curriculum. This CD includes: Letters Home (Spanish and English); Daily Practice and Problems (with and without teacher notes); *Observational Assessment Record* pages; *Individual Assessment Record Sheet;* all Blackline Masters and Transparency Masters; Teacher Rubrics and Student Rubrics; frequently used masters; and appropriate sections of the *Facts Resource Guide.*

Daily Practice and Problems — Allows you to search DPP items by topic and to print Student Questions without the Teacher Notes.

Observational Assessment Record and Individual Assessment Record Sheet — Interactive files can be copied to disk so you can enter and maintain data electronically.

Facts Resource Guide — Includes appropriate sections from the *Facts Resource Guide.*

Rubrics — All three student rubrics and the related teacher rubrics are included.

Blackline Masters — All Blackline Masters from the *Unit Resource Guide* are collated and included on the CD for convenient reproduction from your personal computer.

The *Student Guide* contains most nonconsumable student materials, including activities, labs, and games.

Unit Opener — A list of lesson numbers, names, and locations in the curriculum materials.

Illustrations — Student pages include a variety of illustrations relating to unit activities.

Unit 5

Using Data to Predict

	Student Guide	Discovery Assignment Book	Adventure Book	Unit Resource Guide*
Lesson 1				
Predictions from Graphs	●	●		
Lesson 2				
Another Average Activity				
Lesson 3				
The Meaning of the Mean				
Lesson 4				
Bouncing Ball				
Lesson 5				
Two Heads Are Better Than One				
Lesson 6				
Professor Peabody Invents a Ball				
Lesson 7				
Speeds at the Indianapolis 500				
Lesson 8				
Midterm Test				

*Unit Resource Guide pages are

Bouncing Ball

Ana and Tanya wanted to play jacks at lunch time. Tanya brought jacks from home, but forgot the ball. Mrs. Dewey told the girls that they could look for a ball in the closet where the class keeps playground equipment. They found an old tennis ball and a Super Ball.

Ana said, "I'll use the Super Ball, and you can use the tennis ball."

"No, that wouldn't be fair," said Tanya. "The balls won't bounce the same. We have to use the same ball."

"Oh, you're right. Which one should we use?" Ana began to bounce the balls to try them out. "They both bounce pretty well when I drop them from here; but when we play jacks, we are sitting down."

Mrs. Dewey said, "You girls better go outside and get your game started or lunch will be over. Experiment with both of the balls before you start to play. You've given me an idea for an experiment we can do in class."

After lunch, Mrs. Dewey asked Tanya and Ana to let her have the tennis ball and the Super Ball. She asked the class, "Can you predict how high the tennis ball will bounce if I drop it from 1 meter?"

Students answered:

"One meter."

"Yeah, one meter."

"Half as high. 50 centimeters."

"Higher than a meter."

Bouncing Ball   SG • Grade 4 • Unit 5 • Lesson 4   **139**

Components & Features

Work with your group to collect the data for each experiment. You will need two data tables, one for each type of ball.

- Tape two metersticks to the wall. Your teacher will show you how.
- Fill in the values for the drop height before starting. Follow the example.
- Do three trials for each drop height. Find the average bounce height for each trial. Record the average in the data table.

Tennis Ball

D Drop Height (in cm)	B Bounce Height (in cm)			
	Trial 1	Trial 2	Trial 3	Average
40				
80				
120				

> **Tables, Graphs, and Figures** — Student pages include examples of tables and graphs students can use to organize data.

- Make a point graph of your data for each experiment. Use graph paper.
- Put the drop height (D) on the horizontal axis. Put the bou the vertical axis.
- Use the same scales on both graphs. Leave room for extr
- Remember to title the graphs, label the axes, and include
- Plot the average bounce height for each drop height.

> **Icons** — Icons in the student pages identify steps in the TIMS Laboratory Method such as Draw, Collect, Graph, and Explore.

> **Key Vocabulary** — When appearing in student pages, key words in bold type are defined. The page number for each definition is noted in bold in the Curriculum Index and the *Student Guide* Index.

Mrs. Dewey said, "Are you guessing? Or can you give a reason for your answers? How can we make accurate predictions?"

Jessie said, "We'd have to try it out. We'd have to write down where we want to drop the ball. Then drop the ball and measure how high it bounces."

Mrs. Dewey said, "Here is the challenge: If I give you a drop height, can you predict the bounce height? Can you make a prediction that is close to the actual bounce height?"

You will use the TIMS Laboratory Method to carry out two experiments—one with a tennis ball and one with a Super Ball. Using the results of your experiments, you should be able to accurately predict the bounce height of either ball when you know the drop height.

Identifying the Variables

One of the first tasks in setting up an experiment is identifying the variables. The two main variables in these two experiments are the drop height (D) and the bounce height (B).

We have special names for the two main variables in any experiment. The variable with values we know at the beginning of the experiment is called the **manipulated variable.** We can often choose the values of the manipulated variable. The variable with values we learn by doing the experiment is called the **responding variable.**

The values for the manipulated and responding variables change during an experiment. In these experiments, good values for the drop height (D) are 40 cm, 80 cm, and 120 cm. Each time you change the drop height, you measure the bounce height (B).

Homework

You will need a sheet of *Centimeter Graph Paper* and a ruler to complete this homework.

Here are the results of an experiment using a ball Frank found on the way to school:

1. Make a point graph of this data. Put the drop height (*D*) on the horizontal axis. Put the bounce height (*B*) on the vertical axis. The scale on the horizontal axis should go to at least 150 cm. The scale on the vertical axis should go to at least 100 cm.

2. **A.** If the drop height were 0 cm, what would be the bounce height?

   B. Put this point on your graph.

3. Draw a best-fit line.

4. Frank dropped his ball from 150 cm.

   A. Use your graph to predict the bounce height of the ball. Show how you found your answer on your graph. *D* = 150 cm, predicted *B* = ?

   B. Did you use interpolation or extrapolation to find your answer?

5. Frank dropped his ball and it bounced 25 cm.

   A. From what height was it dropped? Show how you found your answer on your graph. *B* = 25 cm, predicted *D* = ?

   B. Did you use interpolation or extrapolation to find your answer?

6. Frank wants his ball to bounce to a height of 100 cm. should he drop the ball? Explain how you found you

Frank's Data

D Drop Height in cm	B Bounce Height in cm
30	11
60	18
120	44

> **Homework** — Most lessons include homework. These pages often have notes to the family on the assignment and how they can help the student complete it.

Bouncing Ball   SG • Grade

Grade 4

Index

This index provides page references for the *Student Guide.* Definitions or explanations of key terms can be found on the pages listed in bold.

(A)

Addition
  with base-ten pieces, 78–80, 84–85
  multidigit, 174
  paper-and-pencil, 79–80, 84, 174
Angle, 41–56, **42,** 243–250
  acute, **50**–51, 54–55
  comparing, 43–44, 53
  drawing, 47, 54
  measuring, 243–250
  obtuse, **51,** 54–55
  in pattern blocks, 55–56
  right, **48**–49, 54–55
  in shapes, 45–46, 56
  vertex of, 243
Area, 28–38, **29**
  counting square units, 433–436
Arm span, 20–23
Average, 12, **13,** 22, **125**

(B)

Bar graph
  interpreting, 5, 9, 11, 14. *See also* Labs
  making, 4, 10. *See also* Labs

Base (with exponents), 113
Base-ten
  division, 364–378
  multiplication, 298–303
Base-Ten Board, 68
Base-ten pieces, 68–85
  bit, **68**
  flat, **68**
  pack, **68**
  skinny, **68**
Base-Ten Recording Sheet, 68
Base-ten shorthand, 71–85, 280–282, 285–287
Best-fit line, 123–124

(C)

Categorical variable, 7, 20
Certain event, 385
Center of turning, 251–254
Centimeter, 272
Circumference, 132
Comparing
  angles, 43–44, 53
  fractions, 351–352, 354
Convenient number, 202, 203
Cubic centimeter, 216
Cubic foot, 220

> **Index** — Includes page references in bold type indicating the page where the definition can be found in the *Student Guide.*

Index   SG • Grade 4   **445**

Components & Features

DISCOVERY ASSIGNMENT BOOK

The *Discovery Assignment Book* contains consumable student materials for activities, labs, and homework.

Name and Date Lines — Since the *Discovery Assignment Book* is consumable, a name and date line has been provided.

The Home Practice is a series of problems that supplements homework assignments.

Each Home Practice is divided into several parts. Each part can be assigned separately.

Name _____ Date _____

Unit 5 Home Practice

PART 1 *Triangle Flash Cards: Square Numbers*

Study for the quiz on the multiplication facts for the square numbers. Take home your *Triangle Flash Cards: Square Numbers* and your list of facts you need to study.

Here's how to use the flash cards. Ask a family member to choose one flash card at a time. He or she should cover the corner containing the highest number. This number will be the answer to a multiplication fact. Multiply the two uncovered numbers.

Your teacher will tell you when the quiz on the square numbers will be.

PART 2 *Time and Roman Numerals*

A table of Roman numerals is provided in Unit 3 Lesson 2 of your *Student Guide*. You may use it as a reference.

1. Skip count by 3s from 3 to 30 using Roman numerals.

III	VI		XII			XXI			
3	6	9		15					

2. Skip count by 20s from 20 to 200 using Roman numerals.

XX	XL			CXX					
20	40					140			

3. What time does each clock show?

A.   B.   C.

Name _____ Da____

Using Best-Fit Li____

1. Each year, Mrs. Welch, a gym teacher at Bessie C____ the number of sit-ups each student can do. Nila u____ a graph which shows the number of sit-ups she c____

   A. Describe the graph.

   B. If you read the graph from left to right, do the points go uphill or downhill?

   C. What does the graph tell you about the number of sit-ups Nila can do?

   D. Do the points lie close to a straight line? If so, use a ruler to draw a best-fit line.

   E. If possible, predict the number of sit-ups Nila will be able to do when she is 12.

   F. Does knowing Nila's age help you predict the number of sit-ups she can do?

Number of Sit-Ups vs. Age in Years

Footer — The Home Practice footer provides you with information about the page location:

DAB: *Discovery Assignment Book*
Grade __: Grade Level
Unit __: Unit Number and Name

Activity Page — Consumable activity pages are located in the *Discovery Assignment Book.*

ADVENTURE BOOK

Illustrated stories that present mathematics and science concepts.

QUICK REFERENCE GUIDE

What I Want to Know	Where to Find It
What does this lesson cover?	*Unit Resource Guide*–Unit Outline *Unit Resource Guide*–Lesson Guide *Teacher Implementation Guide*–Overview
What are the "big ideas" in this lesson or the entire unit?	*Unit Resource Guide*–Unit Outline *Unit Resource Guide*–Lesson Guide–Key Content *Unit Resource Guide*–Unit Background *Teacher Implementation Guide*–Overview
What do I need to prepare for this lesson?	*Unit Resource Guide*–Unit Outline–Preparing for Upcoming Lessons *Unit Resource Guide*–Lesson Guide–Before the Activity *Unit Resource Guide*–Lesson Guide–Materials List
What manipulatives do I need for this lesson?	*Unit Resource Guide*–Unit Outline *Unit Resource Guide*–Lesson Guide–Materials List
What have students covered on this topic in previous grades or previous units?	*Unit Resource Guide*–Lesson Guide–Curriculum Sequence—Before This Unit *Teacher Implementation Guide*–Scope and Sequence *Teacher Implementation Guide*–Overview
What will students cover on this topic in later units?	*Unit Resource Guide*–Lesson Guide–Curriculum Sequence—After This Unit *Teacher Implementation Guide*–Scope and Sequence *Teacher Implementation Guide*–Overview
How do I teach this lesson?	*Unit Resource Guide*–Lesson Guide
Where is a quick summary of each lesson to help teach the lesson?	*Unit Resource Guide*–Lesson Guide–At a Glance
How long will it take to do this lesson (or the entire unit)?	*Unit Resource Guide*–Unit Outline–Estimated Class Sessions *Unit Resource Guide*–Lesson Guide *Teacher Implementation Guide*–Overview
How do I deal with potential trouble spots?	*Unit Resource Guide*–Lesson Guide–TIMS Tip *Unit Resource Guide*–Lesson Guide–Content Notes *Teacher Implementation Guide*–TIMS Tutors
How do I organize my class to do this lesson?	*Unit Resource Guide*–Lesson Guide
Where are the Blackline and Transparency Masters?	*Unit Resource Guide*–Letter Home *Unit Resource Guide*–Lesson Guide *Teacher Resource CD*
Where are Journal Prompts?	*Unit Resource Guide*–Lesson Guide
Where are the remediation activities?	*Unit Resource Guide*–Daily Practice and Problems *Unit Resource Guide*–Unit Outline–Optional Review Lessons *Grade 4 Facts Resource Guide*–Addition and Subtraction Math Facts Review section

What I Want to Know	Where to Find It
Where is the skill practice and review?	*Unit Resource Guide*–Daily Practice and Problems *Student Guide*–Homework sections *Discovery Assignment Book*–Home Practice *Grade 4 Facts Resource Guide*–Daily Practice and Problems, Home Practice, and the Addition and Subtraction Math Facts Review section *Teacher Resource CD*
Where are the enrichment activities?	*Unit Resource Guide*–Lesson Guide–Extensions *Unit Resource Guide*–Daily Practice and Problems–Challenges *Unit Resource Guide*–Optional Lessons

What information is available for parents?	*Unit Resource Guide*–Letter Home
	Unit Resource Guide–Unit 3–Information for Parents:
	    Math Facts Philosophy
	Teacher Implementation Guide–Parents and Math Trailblazers–
	    Parent Brochure; Information for Parents: Math Facts Philosophy
	    (English and Spanish)

What should I assign as homework?	*Unit Resource Guide*–Lesson Guide–Homework and Practice, At a Glance *Discovery Assignment Book*–Home Practice
How do I assess students' progress?	*Unit Resource Guide*–Unit Background–Assessment Indicators *Unit Resource Guide*–Daily Practice and Problems–Facts Quizzes *Unit Resource Guide*–Observational Assessment Record *Unit Resource Guide*–Assessment Units *Unit Resource Guide*–Assessment Lessons *Unit Resource Guide*–Lesson Guide–Assessment Pages *Unit Resource Guide*–Lesson Guide–Assessment *Unit Resource Guide*–Lesson Guide–Journal Prompts *Teacher Implementation Guide*–Assessment section *Teacher Implementation Guide*–Assessment section– *Individual Assessment Record Sheet* *Teacher Resource CD*
Where do I find connections to literature, computer software, and other content areas such as social studies and science?	*Unit Resource Guide*–Unit Outline *Unit Resource Guide*–Lesson Guide–Connections *Teacher Implementation Guide*–Literature List *Teacher Implementation Guide*–Software List
How do I find background information about concepts underlying each activity?	*Unit Resource Guide*–Unit Background *Unit Resource Guide*–Lesson Guide–Content Notes *Teacher Implementation Guide*–TIMS Tutors
How does this activity or unit fit into the "big picture" for my grade?	*Teacher Implementation Guide*–Overview *Teacher Implementation Guide*–Scope and Sequence *Unit Resource Guide*–Unit Background *Unit Resource Guide*–Lesson Guide–Curriculum Sequence

Components & Features

What I Want to Know	Where to Find It
What will my students do this year?	*Teacher Implementation Guide*–Overview *Teacher Implementation Guide*–Scope and Sequence
What manipulatives do I need for the entire year?	*Teacher Implementation Guide*–Manipulatives List
Where is the scope and sequence?	*Teacher Implementation Guide*–Scope and Sequence *Teacher Implementation Guide*–Scope and Sequence & the NCTM *Principles and Standards*
Does this curriculum match my district's objectives?	*Teacher Implementation Guide*–Overview *Teacher Implementation Guide*–Assessment section– *Individual Assessment Record Sheet* *Unit Resource Guide*–Unit Background–Assessment Indicators
Where is the *Student Guide* Index?	*Student Guide*—Index
Where is the index for the curriculum?	*Teacher Implementation Guide*—Index

Overview

The Overview presents brief descriptions and lists of featured concepts for each unit. It provides a quick reference to locate concepts and activities.

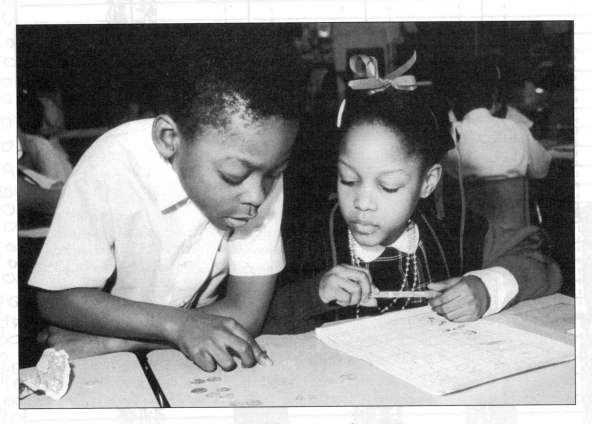

Students solve a problem using money.

Overview

The overview reflects the scope, sequence, and tone of the fourth-grade curriculum. The fundamental assumption of all the units is that math concepts and skills are best acquired through active involvement in problem solving. Thus, problem-solving activities are pervasive. Mathematics content—measurement, graphing, computation, logical reasoning, fractions, data analysis, geometry, and estimation—is included within problems in each unit. The TIMS Laboratory Method, used in laboratory experiments throughout the curriculum, incorporates experiences with important tools for investigation and experimentation: drawing a picture, measuring, collecting and organizing data, constructing a graph, and posing and answering questions about the data.

Units also include:

- Suggestions for journal writing;
- Recommended homework assignments for most lessons;
- Parent letters that discuss the important ideas within the unit and provide suggestions for home activities that support lessons in school;
- Assessment, both through formal instruments and through the informal observations that a discourse-rich curriculum makes possible.

Adventure Books. Many units include *Adventure Book* stories and recommendations for using related trade books and children's literature. A recommended software list accompanies most units. Some of the units in the first semester include activities that review materials from third grade so students new to the curriculum will have the necessary skills and concepts for fourth grade.

Home Practice. The Home Practice in the *Discovery Assignment Book* consists of short problems that can be assigned as homework or assessment throughout the unit. The Home Practice includes skill practice and problems that are related to the current unit or previous units. Problems can be solved in many ways with a variety of tools including calculators, data tables and charts, graphs, manipulatives, and paper-and-pencil strategies.

Daily Practice and Problems. The Daily Practice and Problems (DPP) is a vital component of the curriculum and can be found in the *Unit Resource Guide* and on the *Teacher Resource CD*. These short exercises provide ongoing practice and review. Two DPP items are provided for each class session. TIMS Bits are short items that provide quick review of a topic or focused practice on a specific skill. TIMS Tasks and TIMS Challenges are problems that ask students to use previously learned concepts in a new context or to extend those concepts in a challenging new situation. The content includes:

- estimation
- computation
- number sense
- using data
- addition and subtraction facts review
- multiplication and division facts review and practice
- counting and numeration
- money
- geometry
- problem solving
- time
- logic
- measurement
- using graphs

Summaries, pacing suggestions, and outlines of the fourth-grade units in the *Math Trailblazers* curriculum follow.

Unit 1: Data About Us

Unit Summary

This unit introduces students to fourth-grade mathematical content and establishes a positive classroom atmosphere for the beginning of the school year. The activities are adaptable to individual, pair, or group work. They establish a basis for learning mathematics by solving problems and communicating mathematical thinking and solution strategies.

In the first two lessons, students study categorical and numerical variables and their values. Students organize data in tables and analyze it using graphs. They learn to represent sets of data using medians as an average. The four steps of the TIMS Laboratory Method are reviewed through an Adventure Book, *The Four Servants.* Then in a lab *Arm Span vs. Height,* students use the four steps of the TIMS Laboratory Method to investigate the relationship between fourth-graders' arm spans and heights. This investigation sets a tone of inquiry and exploration in mathematics. The DPP for this unit reviews the addition facts.

Major Concept Focus

- TIMS Laboratory Method
- variables and values
- average (median)
- addition facts review
- estimation
- point graphs
- bar graphs
- *Adventure Book:* TIMS Laboratory Method
- numerical and categorical variables
- word problems
- predictions from data
- length in inches

Pacing Suggestions

- The pacing schedule for the year assumes that mathematics instruction begins on the first day of school and that students receive 60 minutes of mathematics instruction each day. The first lesson is a data collection activity specifically designed to engage students on the first day of school.
- If students have had *Math Trailblazers* in previous grades, use the minimum number of recommended class sessions as a guide for lesson planning. If students have not had *Math Trailblazers,* use the maximum number of days as a guide.
- Take advantage of connections to science and language arts. Lesson 4 in the Adventure Book *The Four Servants* reviews the TIMS Laboratory Method in a fairy tale format. Lesson 5 *Arm Span vs. Height* is a laboratory investigation. Students can read the story as part of language arts or collect data for the lab during science time.
- It is not necessary to stop and make sure students have mastered each skill before moving on to Unit 2, since later units review and extend the skills and concepts developed in Unit 1. Students will also review skills in the Daily Practice and Problems (in each *Unit Resource Guide*) and Home Practice (in the *Discovery Assignment Book*).

The table below shows resources that provide information on the development of concepts and skills throughout the year.

Resources for Pacing	Location
Curriculum Sequence	In Most Lesson Guides
Unit Scope and Sequence	*Teacher Implementation Guide*
Daily Practice and Problems and Home Practice Scope and Sequence	*Teacher Implementation Guide*
Individual Assessment Record Sheet	*Teacher Implementation Guide*

Preparing for Upcoming Lessons

Place pattern blocks, square-inch tiles, and base-ten pieces in a learning center for students to explore.

Unit Planner

	Lesson Information	Supplies	Copies/Transparencies
Lesson 1 **Getting to Know Room 204** URG Pages 31–47 SG Pages 2–6 DPP A–B HP Part 1 *Estimated Class Sessions* **1-2**	**Activity** Students are introduced to a classroom of fourth graders through a class picture and a data table displaying characteristics of the class. Students investigate categorical variables, organize data in a data table, and make bar graphs. **Math Facts** DPP items A and B provide practice with addition. **Homework** 1. Assign *Questions 1–9* in the Homework section. Students need one sheet of *Centimeter Graph Paper.* 2. Assign Part 1 of the Home Practice. **Assessment** Use the *Observational Assessment Record* to document students' abilities to make and interpret bar graphs.	• 3 pieces of easel paper or poster-size graph paper or several transparencies of *Three-column Data Table* URG Page 44 • 1 piece of poster-size graph paper or a transparency of *Centimeter Graph Paper* URG Page 43	• 2 copies of *Centimeter Graph Paper* URG Page 43 per student • 1 copy of *Three-column Data Table* URG Page 44 per student group, optional • 1 copy of *Observational Assessment Record* URG Pages 11–12 to be used throughout this unit • 1 transparency of *Bar Graph I: What's Wrong Here?* URG Page 42
Lesson 2 **Getting to Know Room 204 a Little Better** URG Pages 48–61 SG Pages 7–11 DPP C–F HP Part 2 *Estimated Class Sessions* **2**	**Activity** Students differentiate between numerical and categorical variables. They investigate a numerical variable that describes themselves. They then collect, organize, and graph data about that variable. **Math Facts** DPP items C, D, and E provide practice with addition facts. **Homework** 1. Assign the Homework section on the *Getting to Know Room 204 a Little Better* Activity Pages. Students need a piece of *Centimeter Graph Paper.* 2. Assign Part 2 of the Home Practice. **Assessment** 1. Use the *Observational Assessment Record* to document students' progress in identifying categorical and numerical variables. 2. Use *Question 1* of the Homework section to assess students' abilities to create a bar graph.	• easel paper or poster-size graph paper • class-generated data table, *Variables and Possible Values,* from Lesson 1 • 2 pieces of easel paper or poster-size graph paper or several transparencies of *Three-column Data Table* URG Page 44 • 1 piece of poster-size graph paper or a transparency of *Centimeter Graph Paper* URG Page 43	• 2 copies of *Centimeter Graph Paper* URG Page 43 per student • 1 copy of *Three-column Data Table* URG Page 44 per student group, optional • 1 transparency of *Bar Graph II: What's Wrong Here?* URG Page 57 • 1 transparency of *Bar Graph III: What's Wrong Here?* URG Page 58

(Continued)

Overview

	Lesson Information	Supplies	Copies/Transparencies
Lesson 3 **An Average Activity** URG Pages 62–75 SG Pages 12–16 DPP G–J HP Part 3 *Estimated Class Sessions* **2**	**Activity** Students explore the concept of averages. They learn to find the median value of a set of data. **Homework** Assign *Questions 1–3* in the Homework section. **Assessment** 1. Use *Questions 7–8* from the Explore section as an assessment. 2. Use *Questions 1–2* from the Homework section in the *Student Guide* as an assessment. 3. Use DPP Task J to assess students' understanding of variables and values. 4. Use Home Practice Part 3 as an assessment. 5. Use the *Observational Assessment Record* to document students' abilities to find a median.	• class data table, *Variables and Possible Values,* from Lesson 2 • class graph from Lesson 2	
Lesson 4 **The Four Servants** URG Pages 76–88 AB Pages 1–14 DPP K–L HP Parts 4–5 *Estimated Class Sessions* **1**	**Adventure Book** In this fairy tale, four servants solve a puzzle. After collecting pertinent data, they predict the height of a giant from the length of a handprint. The TIMS Laboratory Method is introduced through the story. **Math Facts** DPP Bit K is a written assessment of addition facts: Doubles, 2s, and 3s. **Homework** 1. Ask students to read and discuss the story with an adult at home. 2. Assign Parts 4 and 5 of the Home Practice.		• 1 copy of *Doubles, 2s, 3s* URG Page 29 per student
Lesson 5 **Arm Span vs. Height** URG Pages 89–112 SG Pages 17–23 DAB Pages 7–8 DPP M–T *Estimated Class Sessions* **4-5**	**Lab** Students collect, organize, graph, and analyze data using the TIMS Laboratory Method as they explore the relationship between height and arm span. **Math Facts** DPP Bit M assesses addition facts. **Homework** Assign the Homework section on the *Arm Span vs. Height* Lab Pages for homework or assessment.	• 4 metersticks or yardsticks at each station • 1 ruler per student group • 1 calculator per student group • masking tape • 1 class data table on poster-size graph paper or transparencies of *Three-column Data Table* URG Page 44	• 1 copy of *More Addition Facts* URG Page 30 per student • 1 copy of *More Arm Span vs. Height Data* URG Page 104 per student • 2 copies of *Centimeter Grid Paper* URG Page 107 per student, optional • 2 copies of *Centimeter Graph Paper* URG Page 43 per student • 1 copy of *Three-column Data Table* URG Page 44 per student group • 1 transparency of *Jerome's Family: Hand Lengths and Heights* URG Page 105

Lesson Information	Supplies	Copies/Transparencies
Assessment 1. Use the *More Arm Span vs. Height Data* Assessment Blackline Master to assess students' abilities to estimate medians in data and to plot points accurately. 2. Use DPP Task T to assess students' abilities to make and interpret bar graphs. 3. Use the *Observational Assessment Record* to note students' abilities to measure length in inches. 4. Transfer appropriate documentation from the Unit 1 *Observational Assessment Record* to students' *Individual Assessment Record Sheets.*	• 1 sheet of poster-size graph paper or 1 transparency of *Centimeter Graph Paper* URG page 43	• 1 transparency of *Point Graph: What's Wrong Here?* URG Page 106 • 1 copy of *Individual Assessment Record Sheet* TIG Assessment section per student, to be used throughout the year

Lesson 6

Solving Problems About Room 204

URG Pages 113–121
SG Pages 24–25

DPP U–V
HP Part 6

Estimated Class Sessions

1

Activity
Students solve a variety of word problems. The problems require various tools, strategies, skills, and operations.

Homework
Assign Part 6 of the Home Practice that continues work with solving word problems.

• 1 calculator per student

Unit 2: Geometric Investigations:
A Baseline Assessment Unit ....15–16 Sessions

Unit Summary

This unit has two major goals: to develop basic geometry concepts and to provide opportunities to gather information about students' mathematical abilities and attitudes at the beginning of the school year. In the first lesson, students review perimeter and area. In the second lesson, *Perimeter vs. Length,* students use the TIMS Laboratory Method to investigate the relationship between the length and width of rectangles and their perimeters. Using the Student Rubric: *Telling* as a guide, students then communicate their conclusions.

To solve a problem, *Helipads for Antopolis,* they must apply area and perimeter concepts and then communicate their problem-solving strategies. Each student starts a collection folder and places work in a portfolio to establish a baseline for documenting growth throughout the year. Students also explore angles in this unit. They identify acute, right, and obtuse angles by exploring the amount of turning in an angle. The DPP for this unit reviews the subtraction facts.

Major Concept Focus

- perimeter
- length
- width
- Student Rubric: *Telling*
- subtraction facts review
- estimating angle size

- area
- portfolios and collection folders
- TIMS Laboratory Method
- acute, obtuse, and right angles
- point graphs
- communicating problem-solving strategies

Pacing Suggestions

- Lesson 2 *Perimeter vs. Length* is a laboratory investigation in which students must collect, organize, graph, and analyze data using data tables and line graphs. If these skills are new to your students, use the maximum number of class sessions to complete the lab.
- Lesson 6 *Angles* and Lesson 7 *Angles in Pattern Blocks* introduce angles. Students estimate angle measures and identify acute, obtuse, and right angles. Students practice these skills in the Daily Practice and Problems and Home Practice in succeeding units before they measure angles using protractors in Unit 9. Use the recommended number of class sessions for Lessons 6 and 7.

Preparing for Upcoming Lessons

Place pattern blocks, base-ten pieces, connecting cubes, and square-inch tiles in a learning center for students to explore.

Unit Planner

	Lesson Information	Supplies	Copies/ Transparencies

Lesson 1

Investigating Perimeter and Area

URG Pages 35–49
SG Pages 28–30
DAB Pages 15–16
DPP A–D
HP Part 3

Estimated Class Sessions
2

Activity
Students use string to explore the perimeter of shapes. They also investigate the area and perimeter of shapes in the imaginary town of Antopolis using square-inch tiles.

Homework
1. Assign the Homework section of *Investigating Perimeter and Area* Activity Pages.
2. Assign Part 3 of the Home Practice for additional practice finding area and perimeter.

Assessment
1. Use the Student Rubric: *Telling* to guide students as they communicate the problem-solving process.
2. Use the *Observational Assessment Record* to document students' abilities to find perimeter and area.

Supplies:
- 1 piece of string about 39 inches long per student pair
- 10 square-inch tiles per student
- 1 ruler per student, optional
- overhead square-inch tiles, optional

Copies/Transparencies:
- 1 copy of *Two-column Data Table* URG Page 45 per student, optional
- 1 copy of *Square-Inch Grid Paper* URG Page 46 per student
- 1 transparency of *Square-Inch Grid Paper* URG Page 46, optional
- 1 transparency or poster of Student Rubric: *Telling* TIG, Assessment section
- 1 copy of *Observational Assessment Record* URG Pages 11–12 to be used throughout this unit

Lesson 2

Perimeter vs. Length

URG Pages 50–68
SG Pages 31–36
DPP E–J
HP Parts 1–2

Estimated Class Sessions
3-4

Assessment Lab
Students help Myrna the ant plan rectangular runways made of square-inch tiles for the Antopolis airport. They apply the TIMS Laboratory Method to find the relationship between length and perimeter for rectangles of fixed width.

Math Facts
DPP items G, H, and I provide practice with addition and subtraction.

Homework
1. Assign the two parts of the Homework section of the *Perimeter vs. Length* Lab Pages on different nights.
2. You may assign Parts 1 and 2 of the Home Practice at any time.

Assessment
1. Evaluate students' work on the lab following the suggestions in the Assessment section of the *Teacher Implementation Guide*.
2. Students should save their work from *Perimeter vs. Length* Lab Pages to put in their portfolios. (See Lesson 5.)
3. Use DPP Task J to assess area and perimeter.

Supplies:
- 60 square-inch tiles per student group
- rulers

Copies/Transparencies:
- 1 copy of *Centimeter Graph Paper* URG Page 64 per student
- 1 copy of *Three-column Data Table* URG Page 65 per student
- 1 transparency of *Three-column Data Table* URG Page 65
- 1 transparency of *Centimeter Graph Paper* URG Page 64

Lesson 3

Letter to Myrna

URG Pages 69–80
DPP K–N

Estimated Class Sessions
2

Assessment Activity
Students write a letter to an ant named Myrna explaining the results of their investigation in Lesson 2.

Math Facts
DPP Bit M is a diagnostic test for the subtraction facts.

Homework
Have students revise their letters for homework.

Copies/Transparencies:
- 1 copy of *Subtraction Facts: Count-Ups* URG Page 31 per student
- 1 copy of *A Letter to Myrna* URG Page 80 per student
- 1 transparency or poster of Student Rubric: *Telling* TIG, Assessment section
- 1 copy of *TIMS Multidimensional Rubric* TIG, Assessment section

(Continued)

Overview

	Lesson Information	Supplies	Copies/ Transparencies
	Assessment 1. Use the students' work *A Letter to Myrna* to assess their current abilities to communicate their solution strategies in writing. 2. DPP Bit M is a diagnostic test for the subtraction facts.		
Lesson 4 **Helipads for Antopolis** URG Pages 81–90 SG Pages 37–38 DPP O–R HP Part 6 *Estimated Class Sessions* **2**	**Activity** Students design helipads for the Antopolis airport. Each helipad must be a rectangle with a perimeter of 24 inches. Students find the design with the biggest area. **Math Facts** DPP Bits O and Q are diagnostic tests for the subtraction facts. **Homework** 1. Ask students to explore helipads with different perimeters. (optional) 2. Assign Part 6 of the Home Practice. **Assessment** 1. You can use *Questions 4–7* to assess problem-solving and communication skills. 2. Use the *Observational Assessment Record* to document students' progress in communicating problem-solving strategies.	• 50 square-inch tiles per student group • 24-inch piece of wire or string per student group	• 1 copy of *Subtraction Facts: Count-Backs* URG Page 32 per student • 1 copy of *Subtraction Facts: Using a Ten* URG Page 33 per student • 1 copy of *Square-Inch Grid Paper* URG Page 46 per student, optional • transparencies of *Square-Inch Grid Paper* URG Page 46
Lesson 5 **Portfolios** URG Pages 91–96 SG Pages 39–40 DPP S–T *Estimated Class Sessions* **1**	**Assessment Activity** Students organize collection folders and portfolios, choose one or two pieces for the portfolio, and begin a table of contents. **Math Facts** DPP Bit S is the fourth diagnostic test for the subtraction facts. **Homework** Assign *Questions 1–2* as homework. **Assessment** 1. Evaluate portfolios using criteria established in class. 2. DPP Bit S is the fourth diagnostic test for the subtraction facts.	• 2 file folders per student • rack for hanging files or a file box	• 1 copy of *Subtraction Facts: Doubles and Others* URG Page 34 per student
Lesson 6 **Angles** URG Pages 97–115 SG Pages 41–54 DPP U–Z HP Parts 4–5 *Estimated Class Sessions* **3**	**Activity** Angles are introduced. Students identify acute, obtuse, and right angles. **Homework** 1. Assign the Homework section on the *Angles* Activity Pages in the *Student Guide*. 2. Assign Parts 4 and 5 of the Home Practice. **Assessment** Use the *Observational Assessment Record* to document students' abilities to identify right, acute, and obtuse angles with their angle circles.	• 1 pair of scissors per student and 2 pairs with blades of different lengths for the teacher • 2 rulers • 1 calculator per student • 2 metersticks	• 2 copies of *Angle Circles* URG Page 108 per student group of 4, copied on heavy stock paper in contrasting colors

	Lesson Information	Supplies	Copies/Transparencies

Lesson 7

Angles in Pattern Blocks

URG Pages 116–126
SG Pages 55–56
DAB Pages 17–19

DPP AA–DD

Estimated Class Sessions

2

Activity
Students investigate angles in pattern blocks.

Math Facts
DPP Bit AA provides practice with subtraction.

Homework
Students complete the Homework section on the *Angles in Pattern Blocks* Activity Pages in the *Student Guide.*

Assessment
1. Use the *Observational Assessment Record* to document students' abilities to identify acute, obtuse, and right angles and estimate angle measures.
2. Transfer appropriate documentation from the Unit 2 *Observational Assessment Record* to students' *Individual Assessment Record Sheets.*

Supplies
- 1 set of pattern blocks (6 green triangles, 3 each of the orange squares, red trapezoids, yellow hexagons, and blue and tan rhombuses) per student
- 1 calculator per student

Copies/Transparencies
- 1 transparency of *Pattern Block Outlines* DAB Page 17
- 1 transparency of *Angle Measures in Pattern Blocks* DAB Page 19
- 1 transparency of *Angle Measures in Pattern Blocks Answers* URG Page 124
- 1 copy of *Individual Assessment Record Sheet* TIG Assessment section per student, previously copied for use throughout the year

Overview

Unit 3: Numbers and Number Operations ....7–12 Sessions

Unit Summary

This unit develops several topics involving numbers and operations. Students are introduced to Roman numerals. The study of a different number system helps them further understand the Hindu-Arabic number system and place value. They gain an appreciation of the evolution of numbers and mathematics. Place value with ones, tens, hundreds, and thousands then becomes the focus. Addition and subtraction algorithms are reviewed using connecting cubes and base-ten pieces through grouping, trading, and regrouping. Negative numbers are introduced in the context of temperature. The DPP for this unit begins the strategies-based yearlong process of reviewing the multiplication facts and developing fluency with the division facts. This unit reviews the multiplication facts and practices the division facts for the fives and tens.

Major Concept Focus

- number systems
- base-ten system
- addition algorithm review
- patterns
- Roman numerals
- multiplication and division facts for fives and tens
- negative numbers
- place value from ones to thousands
- subtraction algorithm review
- grouping, trading, and regrouping
- estimating sums and differences

Pacing Suggestions

Students' fluency with multiplication facts, their knowledge of place value, and their skills with addition and subtraction of whole numbers will determine how quickly the class proceeds through this unit. The following recommendations will help you adapt the unit to your students' needs.

- In Lesson 1 *Multiplying and Dividing with 5s and 10s* students assess their fluency with the multiplication facts and begin a systematic review of those facts they need to study. They also begin work on the division facts. In this unit they review the multiplication facts and develop strategies for the division facts for the fives and tens. Work with the remaining groups of facts is distributed throughout the Daily Practice and Problems (DPP) and Home Practice in subsequent units. All students should continue learning new concepts and skills while working on the facts.

  Because the math facts program is closely linked to the recommended schedule for teaching lessons, classrooms that differ significantly from the suggested pacing will need to make accommodations in order to ensure that students receive a consistent program of math facts practice and assessment throughout the year. The *Grade 4 Facts Resource Guide* outlines a schedule for studying the math facts in classrooms that move much more slowly through lessons than is recommended in the Lesson Guides. For more information, see the TIMS Tutor: *Math Facts* in the *Teacher Implementation Guide*.

The unit includes three optional lessons:

- Lesson 2 *Roman Numerals*. Use this lesson if your state or local standards suggest work with Roman numerals or other number systems. This lesson can also serve as an extension for students who show an interest in ancient number systems.
- Lesson 3 *Place Value*. This lesson includes an assessment you can use to determine students' understanding of place value concepts. The lesson reviews place value and the use of base-ten pieces to represent numbers. All the concepts and skills in the lesson are included in the third-grade materials. Use this lesson if your students have not used base-ten pieces to study place value or if the results of the assessment show that they need a review.
- Lesson 6 *What's Below Zero?* Use this lesson if your standards recommend that students study negative numbers. The lesson can also be used as an extension for students who do not need extensive work with math facts, place value, addition, or subtraction.

Preparing for Upcoming Lessons

Place connecting cubes and base-ten pieces in a learning center for students to explore prior to beginning Lesson 3.

Unit Planner

	Lesson Information	Supplies	Copies/Transparencies
Lesson 1 **Multiplying and Dividing with 5s and 10s** URG Pages 24–39 SG Pages 58–63 DAB Pages 29–33 DPP A–D HP Parts 1 & 4 *Estimated Class Sessions* **2**	**Activity** Students review the multiplication facts for fives and tens. This activity, along with the DPP for this unit, launches the yearlong math facts program that reviews the multiplication facts and develops fluency with the division facts. **Math Facts** DPP items B and C provide practice with the multiplication and division facts for the fives and tens. **Homework** 1. Assign Parts 1 and 4 of the Home Practice. 2. Assign *Questions 1–10* in the Homework section of the *Student Guide*. **Assessment** Students begin a record of their progress with the facts by using the *Multiplication Facts I Know* chart in the *Discovery Assignment Book*.	• 1 or 2 envelopes for storing flash cards per student	• 1 copy of *Triangle Flash Cards: 5s* URG Page 35 per student, optional • 1 copy of *Triangle Flash Cards: 10s* URG Page 36 per student, optional • 1 copy of Information for Parents: *Grade 4 Math Facts Philosophy* URG Pages 11–12 per student • 1 transparency of *Triangle Flash Cards: 5s* DAB Page 29 • 1 transparency of *Triangle Flash Cards: 10s* DAB Page 31
Lesson 2 **Roman Numerals** URG Pages 40–47 SG Pages 64–67 *Estimated Class Sessions* **1**	OPTIONAL LESSON **Optional Activity** Students learn about this ancient number system and compare it to their own. **Homework** Assign the Homework section on the *Roman Numerals* Activity Pages. **Assessment** Use the Journal Prompt to assess students' understanding of how the Roman and the Hindu-Arabic systems compare.		• 1 transparency of Roman Numerals and Symbols chart SG Page 65, optional
Lesson 3 **Place Value** URG Pages 48–59 *Estimated Class Sessions* **1**	OPTIONAL LESSON **Optional Activity** Students use connecting cubes to review place value concepts. **Assessment** 1. Use the *Working with Base-Ten Pieces* Assessment Blackline Master to provide baseline information. 2. Use the *Observational Assessment Record* to document students' abilities to use base-ten pieces to represent two-digit numbers.	• 70 connecting cubes per student pair and some for the teacher • 1 set of base-ten pieces (14 flats, 30 skinnies, and 50 bits) per student pair if using the assessment	• 1 copy of *Working with Base-Ten Pieces* URG Page 56 per student, optional • 1 copy of *Base-Ten Board Part 1* URG Page 57 per student • 1 copy of *Recording Sheet* URG Page 58 per student plus extras • 1 transparency of *Base-Ten Board Part 1* URG Page 57 • 1 transparency of *Recording Sheet* URG Page 58 • 1 copy of *Observational Assessment Record* URG Pages 13–14 to be used throughout this unit

(Continued)

	Lesson Information	Supplies	Copies/ Transparencies
Lesson 4 **The TIMS Candy Company** URG Pages 60–78 SG Pages 68–77 DPP E–F HP Part 5 *Estimated Class Sessions* **1-2**	**Activity** Students work with base-ten pieces to review and expand their understanding of place value. **Math Facts** DPP items E and F provide practice with the math facts for the fives and tens. **Homework** 1. Assign students *The TIMS Candy Company* Homework Page in the *Student Guide*. 2. Assign Part 5 of the Home Practice. **Assessment** Use the *Observational Assessment Record* to document students' abilities to represent numbers using base-ten pieces.	• 1 set of base-ten pieces (2 packs, 14 flats, 30 skinnies, 50 bits) per student pair • overhead base-ten pieces, optional	• 2 copies of *Base-Ten Pieces* (bits, skinnies) URG Page 69 per student pair, optional • 3 copies of *Base-Ten Pieces* (flats, packs) URG Page 70 per student pair, optional • 1 copy of *Base-Ten Board Parts 1* and *2* URG Pages 57 & 71 per student pair • 1 copy of *Recording Sheet* URG Page 58 per student plus extras • 1 transparency of *Recording Sheet* URG Page 58, optional
Lesson 5 **Addition and Subtraction** URG Pages 79–98 SG Pages 78–85 DPP G–L HP Parts 2–3 *Estimated Class Sessions* **3**	**Activity** Students review and expand their understanding of addition and subtraction algorithms. **Math Facts** DPP items H, K, and L provide math facts practice. **Homework** 1. Students complete *Questions 1–19* in the Homework section of the *Addition and Subtraction* Activity Pages in the *Student Guide*. 2. Have students complete Parts 2 and 3 of the Home Practice. **Assessment** 1. You may use the *Place Value Addition and Subtraction Quiz* as an assessment. 2 Use the *Observational Assessment Record* to note students' abilities to add and subtract multidigit numbers and check the reasonableness of their answers.	• 1 set of base-ten pieces (2 packs, 14 flats, 30 skinnies, 50 bits) per student pair • overhead base-ten pieces, optional	• 1 copy of *Place Value Addition and Subtraction Quiz* URG Page 92 per student • 2 copies of *Base-Ten Pieces* (bits, skinnies) URG Page 69 per student pair, optional • 3 copies of *Base-Ten Pieces* (flats, packs) URG Page 70 per student pair, optional • 1 copy of *Base-Ten Board Parts 1* and *2* URG Pages 57 & 71 per student pair • 1 copy of *Recording Sheet* URG Page 58 per student plus extras • 1 transparency of *Recording Sheet* URG Page 58 • 1 transparency of *Base-Ten Board Part 1* URG Page 57
Lesson 6 **What's Below Zero?** URG Pages 99–108 SG Pages 86–91 DAB Page 35 *Estimated Class Sessions* **1**	OPTIONAL LESSON **Optional Activity** Students explore negative numbers in contexts such as temperature, altitudes, and bank balances. **Homework** Assign the Homework section on the *What's Below Zero?* Activity Pages. **Assessment** Have students complete the *Professor Peabody Made a Mess!* Assessment Blackline Master.	• 1 calculator per student • 1 pair of scissors per student • tape or glue • large classroom number line, optional • classroom weather thermometer, optional	• 1 copy of *Professor Peabody Made a Mess!* URG Page 106 per student

Lesson 7

At the Hardware Store

URG Pages 109–118
SG Pages 92–93
DPP M–N
HP Parts 6–7

Estimated Class Sessions

1-2

Activity

Students solve word problems based on concepts in this and previous units.

Math Facts

DPP Bit M is a quiz on the fives and tens multiplication facts.

Homework

Assign Home Practice Part 6.

Assessment

1. DPP Bit M assesses the fives and tens multiplication facts.
2. Use Home Practice Part 7 as an assessment.
3. Use the *Observational Assessment Record* to record students' abilities to compute multidigit addition and subtraction problems.
4. Transfer appropriate documentation from the Unit 3 *Observational Assessment Record* to students' *Individual Assessment Record Sheets.*

• 1 copy of *Individual Assessment Record Sheet* TIG Assessment section per student, previously copied for use throughout the year

Unit 4: Products and Factors . . . . .10–12 Sessions

Unit Summary

This unit is the first of four multiplication and division units in fourth grade. The array model for multiplication is used to illustrate factors and multiples. The study of factors and multiples then leads to a study of prime numbers and square numbers. Work with factors gives students an opportunity to explore the relationship between multiplication and division, as well as to practice the multiplication facts. The DPP for this unit reviews the multiplication facts and provides practice with the division facts for the twos and threes. This unit includes two games, *Floor Tiler* and *Product Bingo,* which provide practice with the multiplication facts.

Major Concept Focus

- prime numbers
- square numbers
- prime factors
- exponents
- factor trees
- number puzzles
- factors
- array model for multiplication
- multiples
- multiplication and division facts for twos and threes

Pacing Suggestions

Lesson 6 *Multiplying to Solve Problems* is an optional lesson. You may assign these problems as homework throughout the unit or solve them in class. Since the lesson requires little teacher preparation, it is appropriate to leave for a substitute teacher.

Unit Planner

KEY: SG = Student Guide, DAB = Discovery Assignment Book, AB = Adventure Book, URG = Unit Resource Guide, DPP = Daily Practice and Problems, HP = Home Practice (found in Discovery Assignment Book), and TIG = Teacher Implementation Guide.

	Lesson Information	Supplies	Copies/ Transparencies
Lesson 1 **Multiplication and Rectangles** URG Pages 26–44 SG Pages 96–101 DAB Page 45 DPP A–F HP Part 1 *Estimated Class Sessions* **3**	**Activity** Students investigate the dimensions of rectangles they can make with a specified number of square-inch tiles. They use their rectangles to investigate multiples, prime numbers, and square numbers. Using exponents to write square numbers is introduced. **Math Facts** DPP items A–C and E–F provide practice with math facts for 2s and 3s. **Homework** 1. Assign *Questions 1–10* in the Homework section on the *Multiplication and Rectangles* Activity Pages. 2. Assign Part 1 of the Home Practice. **Assessment** Use the *Observational Assessment Record* to document students' abilities to represent multiplication and division using arrays.	• 50 square-inch tiles per student group • 1 resealable plastic bag for storing tiles per student group, optional • easel paper or construction paper • tape • 1 pair of scissors per student group • envelopes for storing flash cards • sheets of easel paper or construction paper for mounting rectangles on the class chart, one for each number 1–25	• 1 table from *Small Multiplication Tables* URG Page 39 per student to tape on desk • 4–5 copies of *Square-Inch Grid Paper* URG Page 40 per student group • 1 copy of *Observational Assessment Record* URG Pages 11–12 to be used throughout this unit
Lesson 2 **Factors** URG Pages 45–59 SG Pages 102–106 DPP G–J *Estimated Class Sessions* **2**	**Activity** Using rectangular arrays of square-inch tiles, students discuss factors and prime numbers. **Math Facts** DPP items G and J provide practice with math facts for the twos and threes. **Homework** 1. Assign the More Tiles Problems section of the Homework section in the *Student Guide* after Part 1. 2. Assign the More Finding Factors Problems section of the Homework section after Part 2. **Assessment** Use the *Observational Assessment Record* to record students' abilities to use rectangular arrays to represent multiplication and division problems and to find the factors of a number, using either an array or a calculator.	• 50 square-inch tiles per student group • 1 calculator per student group • completed rectangles from class chart from Lesson 1	• 1 table from *Small Multiplication Tables* URG Page 39 per student to tape on desk • 3–4 copies of *Square-Inch Grid Paper* URG Page 40 per student • 2 copies of *Three-column Data Table* URG Page 55 per student, optional

(Continued)

	Lesson Information	Supplies	Copies/ Transparencies
Lesson 3 **Floor Tiler** URG Pages 60–66 SG Pages 107–108 DAB Page 47 DPP K–L *Estimated Class Sessions* **1** 	**Game** Students play a game that provides practice with the multiplication facts. After using spinners to find two numbers, a player uses the product of the two numbers to color in rectangles on grid paper. Players take turns spinning and filling in rectangles until someone completely fills in his or her grid. **Math Facts** DPP items K and L provide practice with math facts. **Homework** Students take home the *Floor Tiler* Game Pages in the *Student Guide,* the *Spinners 1–4 and 1–10* Game Page, *Centimeter Grid Paper,* and a small multiplication table. They play the game at home using pencil-and-paper-clip spinners. **Assessment** Use DPP Bit K as an assessment.	• 1 paper clip and pencil or clear plastic spinner per student pair • crayons or markers • 1 calculator per student • 1 pair of scissors per student	• 2 tables from *Small Multiplication Tables* URG Page 39 per student to tape on desk and to take home • 2–3 copies of *Centimeter Grid Paper* URG Page 66 per student pair • 1 transparency of *Centimeter Grid Paper* URG Page 66, optional • 1 transparency of *Spinners 1–4 and 1–10* DAB Page 47 for the Extension, optional
Lesson 4 **Prime Factors** URG Pages 67–82 SG Pages 109–115 DPP M–R HP Part 2 *Estimated Class Sessions* **3-4** 	**Activity** Students use factor trees to find the prime factorization of numbers. They use exponents as a shortcut for writing repeated factors. **Math Facts** DPP Bit M provides further practice in finding factors. DPP Task R provides practice with math facts. **Homework** 1. Assign *Questions 1–7* in the Homework section after Parts 1 and 2. 2. Assign homework *Questions 8–10* after Part 3. 3. Assign Part 2 of the Home Practice. **Assessment** Use the *Unit 4 Test* Assessment Pages in the *Unit Resource Guide* as an assessment.	• 1 calculator per student • square-inch tiles	• 1 table from *Small Multiplication Tables* URG Page 39 per student to tape on desk • 1 copy of *Unit 4 Test* URG Pages 75–76 per student
Lesson 5 **Product Bingo** URG Pages 83–90 SG Pages 116–117 DAB Page 49 DPP S–T HP Part 3 *Estimated Class Sessions* **1** 	**Game** Students use two spinners to generate multiplication problems. They find the products and place markers on them on a bingo card. Players find that one card is most likely to win because more of its numbers can be obtained as products in several ways. **Math Facts** DPP item S is a quiz on the multiplication facts for the twos and threes. **Homework** 1. Have students play the game at home. 2. Assign word problems in Lesson 6 for homework. 3. Assign Part 3 of the Home Practice.	• 1 paper clip and pencil or clear plastic spinner per student • small objects such as beans to use as game markers	• 1 table from *Small Multiplication Tables* URG Page 39 per student to tape on desk • 1 copy of *Individual Assessment Record Sheet* TIG Assessment section per student, previously copied for use throughout the year

	Lesson Information	Supplies	Copies/ Transparencies
	Assessment 1. DPP Bit S is a multiplication facts quiz. 2. Use the *Observational Assessment Record* to record students' proficiency finding products playing the game. Also document students' abilities to explain their reasoning as they tell the class why one Product Bingo card is better. 3. Transfer appropriate documentation from the Unit 4 *Observational Assessment Record* to students' *Individual Assessment Record Sheets*.		
Lesson 6 **Multiplying to Solve Problems** URG Pages 91–95 SG Page 118 *Estimated Class Sessions* **1**	OPTIONAL **Optional Activity** Students solve a variety of word problems on content from this and previous units. **Homework** Assign some or all of the problems for homework.	• 1 calculator per student group • 50 square-inch tiles per student group	• 1 table from *Small Multiplication Tables* URG Page 39 per student to tape on desk

Unit 5: Using Data to Predict . . . . 11–17 Sessions

Unit Summary

In this unit, students use data from different sources to make predictions. They interpret point graphs, draw best-fit lines, and make predictions where appropriate. The *Bouncing Ball* lab reinforces the four steps of the TIMS Laboratory Method while introducing the terms manipulated, responding, and fixed variables. Students collect data, organize it in a data table, and plot points on a graph.

They fit a line to the points, then make predictions using their lines. Students solve a problem, *Professor Peabody Invents a Ball,* using data similar to *Bouncing Ball* and communicate their problem-solving strategies in words, tables, and graphs. An Adventure Book, *Two Heads Are Better Than One,* illustrates the lab and a problem students might encounter while completing it.

Students are also introduced to a new kind of average, the mean. Students learn to calculate the mean and compare the median and the mean of the same set of data. The DPP for this unit reviews the multiplication facts and practices the division facts for the square numbers.

Major Concept Focus

- best-fit lines
- point graphs
- Student Rubric: *Solving*
- TIMS Laboratory Method
- manipulated, responding, and fixed variables
- predictions from data
- averages (mean and median)
- *Adventure Book:* collaborative learning
- measuring length in centimeters
- communicating problem-solving strategies
- interpolation and extrapolation
- multiplication and division facts for the square numbers

Pacing Suggestions

Students' knowledge of averages and familiarity with best-fit lines will determine how quickly the class can proceed through this unit. Use the smaller of the recommended number of sessions if students worked with these concepts and skills in third grade. Students will have numerous opportunities to use averages and draw and interpret best-fit lines in laboratory investigations, Daily Practice and Problems items, and Home Practice assignments in this and subsequent units.

The unit includes two optional lessons:

- Lesson 5 *Two Heads Are Better Than One* is an *Adventure Book* story about two students who work together to correct a mistake in their graphs. Students can be challenged to find the mistake as they read the story. You can also use this lesson as an extension.
- The second optional lesson, Lesson 7 *Speeds at the Indianapolis 500,* is a set of word problems that reviews concepts and skills developed in this and preceding units. You can distribute the problems as homework throughout the unit or use them as an in-class review.

Math Trailblazers includes many connections to other subjects, especially science and language arts. Linking appropriate lessons with your instruction in other subjects can help maximize time available to complete lessons. For example, consider using some science time to collect data for the *Bouncing Ball* lab in Lesson 4. The *Adventure Book* story can be linked with language arts.

Preparing for Upcoming Lessons

In an optional lesson in Unit 6, students will fill jars with objects and estimate the number of objects in the jars. Begin asking students to collect jars from home.

In Unit 6, students will cut out articles that use big numbers from newspapers and magazines. Begin collecting newspapers and magazines for students.

Unit Planner

	Lesson Information	Supplies	Copies/ Transparencies
Lesson 1 **Predictions from Graphs** URG Pages 22–43 SG Pages 120–124 DAB Pages 59–64 DPP A–D HP Parts 1 & 5 *Estimated Class Sessions* **2**	**Activity** Students look for patterns in point graphs. When appropriate, they draw best-fit lines and make predictions based on the graphs. **Math Facts** DPP items A and B provide practice with math facts for square numbers. **Homework** Assign Part 1 and Part 5 of the Home Practice. **Assessment** Use the *Observational Assessment Record* to record students' abilities to draw a best-fit line through a set of data points.	• 1 ruler per student • 1 envelope for storing flash cards per student • string or uncooked spaghetti, optional	• 1 transparency of *Olympic Long Jump* URG Page 34 • 1 transparency of *Mile Run* URG Page 35 • 1 transparency of *Nila's Sit-Ups* URG Page 36 • 1 copy of *Observational Assessment Record* URG Pages 9–10 to be used throughout this unit
Lesson 2 **Another Average Activity** URG Pages 44–57 SG Pages 125–131 DPP E–F *Estimated Class Sessions* **1-2**	**Activity** Students investigate averages. Using manipulatives, they learn to find the mean and review how to find the median value of a set of data. **Homework** Assign the Homework section in the *Student Guide.* **Assessment** 1. Use *Question 3* in the Homework section as an assessment. 2. Use the *Observational Assessment Record* to note students' abilities to find medians and means using connecting cubes.	• 120 square-inch tiles or 80 connecting cubes per student pair • 1 small paper bag per student pair	
Lesson 3 **The Meaning of the Mean** URG Pages 58–71 SG Pages 132–138 DPP G–J *Estimated Class Sessions* **2-3**	**Activity** Students continue to explore averages. They find the circumferences of their classmates' heads and represent the data using means. First they use strips of adding machine tape to model the procedure for finding the mean, and then they use calculators. **Math Facts** DPP items G–J provide practice with the math facts for the square numbers through a variety of activities. **Homework** Assign the Homework section. Students will need calculators to complete the assignment. **Assessment** Students complete the *Cookie Factory* Assessment Blackline Master.	• 1 roll of adding machine tape or ball of string per student group • 1 meterstick per student group • 1 calculator per student group • 1 pair of scissors per student group • tape • 1 ruler per student group • 1 crayon per student group	• 1 copy of *Cookie Factory* URG Page 67 per student • 1 copy of *Two-column Data Table* URG Page 68 per student • 1 transparency of Student Rubric: *Telling* TIG, Assessment section • 1 transparency of *Two-column Data Table* URG Page 68 or easel paper for the class data table

	Lesson Information	**Supplies**	**Copies/ Transparencies**
Lesson 4 **Bouncing Ball** URG Pages 72–94 SG Pages 139–145 DPP K–R HP Part 6 *Estimated Class Sessions* **4-5**	**Lab** Students look for the relationship between the drop height and the bounce height of a tennis ball and a Super ball. They collect, record, and graph the data, using the data to make predictions. **Math Facts** DPP items L, N, and P provide practice with math facts for the square numbers. **Homework** Assign the Homework section in the *Student Guide.* **Assessment** 1. Use the TIMS Student Rubric: *Solving* to guide and evaluate student work on **Questions 10** and **12** of the *Student Guide.* Grade students' graphs. 2. Use the *Observational Assessment Record* to note students' abilities to draw and interpret best-fit lines and measure length in centimeters. 3. Use Part 6 of the Home Practice as an assessment.	• 1 new or used tennis ball per student group • 1 Super ball per student group • 2 metersticks per student group • masking tape • 1 ruler per student	• 4 copies of *Centimeter Graph Paper* URG Page 89 per student • 2 copies of *Three-trial Data Table* URG Page 90 per student • 1 transparency of *Bouncing Ball Data: What's Wrong Here?* URG Page 88 • 1 copy of *TIMS Multidimensional Rubric* TIG, Assessment section, optional
Lesson 5 **Two Heads Are Better Than One** URG Pages 95–102 AB Pages 15–28 HP Part 2 *Estimated Class Sessions* **1**	OPTIONAL LESSON **Optional Adventure Book** In this story, two students work together to complete the *Bouncing Ball* experiment. They arrive at different answers to a question from the lab, then they work cooperatively to solve the problem. **Homework** Assign Part 2 of the Home Practice if students completed Unit 3 Lesson 2 *Roman Numerals.*		
Lesson 6 **Professor Peabody Invents a Ball** URG Pages 103–118 DPP S–T HP Parts 3–4 *Estimated Class Sessions* **1-2**	**Assessment Activity** Students solve problems similar to those posed in the *Bouncing Ball* lab. They use the Student Rubrics: *Solving* and *Telling* to guide their work. **Math Facts** Task T provides practice with math facts. **Homework** Assign Parts 3 and 4 of the Home Practice. **Assessment** Use the *Professor Peabody Invents a Ball* Assessment Blackline Master to assess problem solving and communication.	• 1 ruler per student • 1 calculator per student	• 1 copy of *Professor Peabody Invents a Ball* URG Page 116 per student • 1 copy of *Centimeter Graph Paper* URG Page 89 • 1 copy of *TIMS Multidimensional Rubric* TIG, Assessment section • 1 transparency or poster of Student Rubric: *Solving* TIG, Assessment section • 1 transparency or poster of Student Rubric: *Telling* TIG, Assessment section

(Continued)

Overview

	Lesson Information	Supplies	Copies/Transparencies
Lesson 7 **Speeds at the Indianapolis 500** URG Pages 119–124 SG Pages 146–148 *Estimated Class Sessions* **1**	OPTIONAL LESSON **Optional Activity** Students solve word problems based on a graph that gives the average speeds of the winners of the Indianapolis 500 since 1911. **Homework** Assign some or all of the problems for homework.	• 1 ruler per student	
Lesson 8 **Midterm Test** URG Pages 125–137 DPP U–V *Estimated Class Sessions* **1**	**Assessment Activity** Students take a short-item test that assesses skills and concepts studied in the first four units. **Math Facts** DPP Bit U is a short quiz on the math facts for the square numbers. **Assessment** 1. Use the *Midterm Test* to assess students' understanding of concepts in Units 1–5. Place students' tests in their portfolios. 2. Use DPP Bit U to assess students' fluency with the multiplication facts for the square numbers. 3. Transfer appropriate documentation from the Unit 5 *Observational Assessment Record* to students' *Individual Assessment Record Sheets.*	• 1 ruler per student • square-inch tiles • 1 calculator per student	• 1 copy of *Midterm Test* URG Pages 130–134 per student • 1 copy of *Individual Assessment Record Sheet* TIG Assessment section per student, previously copied for use throughout the year

Unit 6: Place Value Patterns

Unit Summary
This unit focuses on number sense and numeration. Students explore numbers in the thousands, ten thousands, hundred thousands, and millions. They collect articles that have large numbers from newspapers and place them in order on a newswire. They also work together as a class to build models that extend the base-ten pieces to the millions. Collecting data from the real world extends students' opportunities to develop an intuition about numbers. Students learn to read and write big numbers, which leads to computing with larger numbers. They practice two types of estimation: estimating sums and differences and estimating the number of objects in a collection.

Computational estimation is guided by using convenient numbers, benchmarks, and rounding techniques. When students estimate "how many," they determine if an estimate is close to the actual number by using 10 percent as a guide. In the succeeding units, 10% continues as a standard for estimation. In the context of an ancient story about the inventor of the game of chess, students explore the patterns of the powers of two using diagrams, data tables, and graphs. The DPP for this unit reviews the multiplication facts and provides practice with the division facts for the nines.

Major Concept Focus
- Student Rubric: *Knowing*
- exponents
- convenient numbers
- powers of two and ten
- computational estimation
- ordering large numbers
- place value to the millions
- reading and writing large numbers
- 10% as a standard for error analysis
- using diagrams to solve problems
- estimating the number of objects in a collection
- multiplication and division facts for the nines

Pacing Suggestions
The unit includes two optional lessons:
- Lesson 5 *Close Enough* discusses accuracy in estimation and measurement. Students learn to use 10 percent as a benchmark to judge the accuracy of their estimates. This concept is then applied in the *Volume vs. Number* laboratory investigation in Unit 8, as well as in laboratory investigations in future units. If you elect to omit this lesson, you will need to skip related questions in subsequent lessons.
- Lesson 7 *9 to 5 War* provides multiplication math facts practice in a game setting.

Preparing for Upcoming Lessons
In an optional lesson, Lesson 5, students will estimate the number of objects in jars. If students are to complete this lesson, assign them the task of preparing a mystery jar by filling (or partially filling) a clear jar with the same kind of object. See the Homework section in Lesson 4 and Before the Activity in Lesson 5 for details.

Overview

Unit Planner

	Lesson Information	Supplies	Copies/Transparencies
Lesson 1 **Newswire** URG Pages 25–36 SG Pages 150–153 DAB Page 73 DPP A–B HP Parts 1 & 5 *Estimated Class Sessions* **1** 	**Activity** Students collect large numbers from newspapers. They arrange the numbers in numerical order on a wire (clothesline) in the classroom. **Math Facts** DPP Bit A begins review and practice of the nines multiplication facts. **Homework** 1. Assign the Homework section in the *Student Guide.* Students look for numbers in newspapers at home. They bring in the numbers and add them to the newswire. 2. Assign Parts 1 and 5 of the Home Practice. **Assessment** Use the *Observational Assessment Record* to note students' abilities to read and order large numbers.	• newspapers • highlighter markers, optional • string, twine, or cord for the newswire • 4 paper clips or clothespins per student pair • 1 pair of scissors per student pair • paper hole punch • 2 3-by-5-inch index cards cut in half lengthwise per student pair • envelopes for storing flash cards	• 1 transparency of *Place Value Chart* DAB Page 73 • 1 copy of *Observational Assessment Record* URG Pages 11–12 to be used throughout this unit
Lesson 2 **Doubles** URG Pages 37–51 SG Pages 154–156 DPP C–F HP Part 2 *Estimated Class Sessions* **2-3**	**Activity** Students read a story about the inventor of the game of chess who asks for a specific reward. Within this context, students investigate doubling patterns and develop number sense for large numbers. **Math Facts** DPP Bit C provides practice with the multiplication facts for the nines. **Homework** 1. Assign the Homework section of the *Doubles* Activity Pages. 2. Assign Home Practice Part 2. **Assessment** 1. Use DPP item D as an assessment. 2. Score homework *Question 1* using the Telling dimension of the *TIMS Multidimensional Rubric.*	• several colored pencils • 2 large sheets of paper, optional	• 1 copy of *Three-column Data Table* URG Page 47 per student, optional • 1 copy of *Centimeter Graph Paper* URG Page 48 per student • 1 transparency of *Three-column Data Table* URG Page 47, optional • 1 copy of *TIMS Multidimensional Rubric* TIG, Assessment section • 50 copies of *10,000 Sq Mm Grid* URG Page 49, optional
Lesson 3 **Big Base-Ten Pieces** URG Pages 52–65 SG Pages 157–159 DAB Page 75 DPP G–J HP Part 3 *Estimated Class Sessions* **2-3** 	**Activity** Students are introduced to the powers of 10 using a place value chart. They also build large base-ten pieces to represent ten thousand, one hundred thousand, and one million. **Math Facts** DPP items G, H, and J provide practice with math facts. **Homework** 1. Students play the game *Draw, Place, and Read* at home. 2. Assign Home Practice Part 3. **Assessment** Use the Journal Prompt as an assessment.	• 1 meterstick per student group and 24 for the teacher • masking tape • 6–16 base-ten packs • 4–8 rulers • paper for covering the big base-ten pieces, optional	• 1 copy of *Digit Cards 0–9* URG Pages 61–62 per student group copied back to back • 1 transparency of *Place Value Chart II* URG Page 63

	Lesson Information	Supplies	Copies/Transparencies
Lesson 4 **News Number Line** URG Pages 66–76 SG Pages 160–163 DPP K–L HP Part 6 *Estimated Class Sessions* **1**	**Activity** The class newswire is converted into a number line. Large numbers collected from newspapers are placed in order on this number line. **Math Facts** DPP items K and L provide practice with multiplication and division facts. **Homework** 1. Assign the homework in the *Student Guide*. Omit *Questions 8–10* if Lesson 5 will be omitted. 2. Assign Part 6 of the Home Practice. **Assessment** 1. Use homework *Questions 5–7* as a quiz. 2. Use the *Observational Assessment Record* to note students' abilities to order large numbers.	• number newswire created in Lesson 1 • 1 or 10 metersticks • red and green markers • 10-meter strip of adding machine tape, string, twine, or cord • 1 calculator per student group • paper clips	
Lesson 5 **Close Enough** URG Pages 77–90 SG Pages 164–168 DAB Page 77 *Estimated Class Sessions* **2-3**	OPTIONAL LESSON **Optional Activity** Students use 10 percent as a benchmark to establish whether or not an estimate is close to an actual amount. **Homework** Assign the Homework section in the *Student Guide*. **Assessment** Use *Questions 1–2* in the Homework section as an assessment.	• 1 calculator per student • meterstick • clear centimeter ruler • mystery jar from Lesson 4 homework • clear jar filled with 123 objects, optional • large and small clear jars, optional • objects for estimation such as connecting cubes, marbles, or beans, optional	• 1 copy of *Three-column Data Table* URG Page 47 per student group, optional • 1 transparency of *10% Chart* DAB Page 77 or large paper for class data table • 1 transparency of *Three-column Data Table* URG Page 47, optional
Lesson 6 **Using Estimation** URG Pages 91–109 SG Pages 169–174 DPP M–P HP Parts 4 & 7 *Estimated Class Sessions* **2-3**	**Activity** Students use a number line to find convenient numbers expressed to the nearest 1000, 10,000, 100,000, and 1,000,000. They practice paper-and-pencil procedures for addition and subtraction. **Math Facts** DPP item M provides practice with math facts for the nines. Bit O is a short quiz on the multiplication facts for the nines. **Homework** 1. Assign *Questions 1–4* in the Homework section after Part 1. 2. Assign *Questions 5–12* in the Homework section after Part 2. 3. Assign Parts 4 and 7 of the Home Practice.		• 1 copy of *Check-Up Time* URG Pages 102–103 per student • 1 copy of *Individual Assessment Record Sheet* TIG Assessment section per student, previously copied for use throughout the year • 1 copy of *TIMS Multidimensional Rubric* TIG, Assessment section • 1 transparency or poster of Student Rubric: *Knowing* TIG, Assessment section • 1 transparency of a blank number line, optional

(Continued)

	Lesson Information	Supplies	Copies/Transparencies

Assessment

1. Students complete the skill assessment *Check-Up Time.*
2. Use DPP item O *Multiplication Quiz: 9s* as an assessment.
3. Use the Knowing dimension of the *TIMS Multidimensional Rubric* to assess students' abilities to use computational estimation.
4. Use the *Observational Assessment Record* to document students' abilities to represent larger numbers on number lines and estimate sums and differences.
5. Transfer appropriate documentation from the Unit 6 *Observational Assessment Record* to students' *Individual Assessment Record Sheets.*

Lesson 7

9 to 5 War

URG Pages 110–115
SG Pages 175–177
DAB Pages 79–82

Estimated Class Sessions

1

OPTIONAL LESSON

Optional Game
Students draw cards from decks to find products of multiplication facts for the fives and nines.

Math Facts
The *9 to 5 War* Game provides practice with multiplication facts for the fives and nines.

Homework
Ask students to play the game at home.

• 1 pair of scissors per student pair
• 1 calculator per student pair
• 1 deck of playing cards with face cards removed per student pair, optional

• 2 copies of *Digit Cards 0–9* URG Pages 61–62 per student copied back to back
• 1 table from *Small Multiplication Tables* URG Page 115 per student

Unit 7: Patterns in Multiplication . . . . .15–18 Sessions

Unit Summary

This unit focuses on multiplication, order of operations, divisibility rules, and estimation strategies. Students explore multiplication patterns when multiplying a one-digit number by numbers with ending zeros. They also use paper-and-pencil methods to multiply one-digit by two-digit numbers.

They further explore multiplication strategies as they pretend that certain keys on calculators are broken. They must list keystrokes to obtain products in different ways in the assessment lesson, *Oh, No! My Calculator Is Broken*. Students learn the conventional rules for the order of operations in number sentences. They identify patterns in multiples that lead to rules they can use to determine if a number is divisible by 2, 3, 5, 6, 9, or 10.

Finally, students practice estimation and identify when it is appropriate to estimate and when it is appropriate to find an exact answer. The DPP for this unit reviews the last six multiplication facts (4×6, 4×7, 4×8, 6×7, 6×8, 7×8) and practices the related division facts.

Major Concept Focus

- order of operations
- factors
- estimation
- divisibility rules
- multiples
- inverse relationship between multiplication and division
- Student Rubrics: *Solving* and *Knowing*
- multiplication of numbers with ending zeros
- paper-and-pencil methods for multiplication
- multiplication and division facts for the last six facts

Pacing Suggestions

- This unit develops mental math, estimation, and paper-and-pencil skills for multiplication. Use the recommended session numbers for each lesson as a guide. It is not necessary to wait until students master each skill, especially paper-and-pencil procedures. Students will revisit them in later units, particularly in Unit 11.

- The Daily Practice and Problems includes review of the last group of multiplication facts. This group is called the Last Six Facts (4×6, 4×7, 4×8, 6×7, 6×8, 7×8). These facts are often the most difficult for students to learn. Allow time for students to practice, share, and use strategies to solve problems. Systematic review of the facts is also found in the *Grade 4 Facts Resource Guide*. Use this guide if your pacing is significantly different from the recommended schedule.

Preparing for Upcoming Lessons

In Unit 9, students will cut up boxes to explore three-dimensional geometry. Have students bring in small boxes for a class collection.

Overview

Unit Planner

KEY: SG = Student Guide, DAB = Discovery Assignment Book, AB = Adventure Book, URG = Unit Resource Guide, DPP = Daily Practice and Problems, HP = Home Practice (found in Discovery Assignment Book), and TIG = Teacher Implementation Guide.

	Lesson Information	Supplies	Copies/Transparencies
Lesson 1 **Order of Operations** URG Pages 30–44 SG Pages 180–183 DPP A–B HP Parts 1–2 *Estimated Class Sessions* **1-2**	**Activity** Students learn the conventional order for carrying out basic arithmetic operations. A game *Operation Target* provides practice with this order and basic math facts. **Math Facts** DPP items A and B provide practice with the last six facts using flash cards and fact families. **Homework** 1. Assign *Operation Target* for homework. 2. Assign Parts 1 and 2 in the Home Practice.	• 1 calculator per student and 2 for the teacher, 1 that follows the order of operations and 1 that does not • 1 pair of scissors per student • 1 envelope for storing flash cards per student	• 1–2 copies of *Digit Cards 0–9* URG Pages 39–40 per student group copied back to back • 1 copy of *Operation Cards* URG Pages 41–42 per student group copied back to back
Lesson 2 **Divisibility Rules** URG Pages 45–60 SG Pages 184–189 DPP C–F HP Part 3 *Estimated Class Sessions* **2**	**Activity** Students find ways to determine whether a multidigit number is evenly divisible by 2, 3, 5, 6, 9, or 10. **Math Facts** DPP items E and F develop math facts strategies, using doubles and breaking apart numbers. **Homework** 1. Assign *Questions 12–15* in the *Student Guide* as homework after Part 1. 2. Assign *Questions 1–2* in the Homework section in the *Student Guide* after Part 1. 3. Assign *Questions 3–19* after Part 2. Students need one or two clean copies of the *100 Chart* and a calculator. **Assessment** 1. Use *Question 6* in the Homework section as an assessment. 2. Use Part 3 of the Home Practice as a quiz.	• 1 calculator per student • blue and red crayons or colored pencils • blue and red overhead markers	• 2–3 copies of *100 Chart* URG Page 56 per student • 1 transparency of *100 Chart* URG Page 56
Lesson 3 **Oh, No! My Calculator Is Broken** URG Pages 61–78 SG Pages 190–192 DPP G–L HP Part 4 *Estimated Class Sessions* **3**	**Assessment Activity** Students use the order of operations and a "broken" calculator to generate the numbers from 1 to 50. **Math Facts** DPP Bit G reviews order of operations and Challenge H uses a game to develop number sense using order of operations. Task J asks for a math story. **Homework** Assign Home Practice Part 4. **Assessment** 1. Score student work using the Solving and Knowing dimensions of the *TIMS Multidimensional Rubric*. 2. Students place scored work in their portfolios.	• 1 calculator per student	• 1 copy of *The Broken Calculator* URG Page 76 per student • 1 transparency or poster of Student Rubric: *Knowing* TIG, Assessment section • 1 transparency or poster of Student Rubric: *Solving* TIG, Assessment section • 1 copy of *TIMS Multidimensional Rubric* TIG, Assessment section

	Lesson Information	Supplies	Copies/ Transparencies
Lesson 4 **Multiplying by 10s** URG Pages 79–93 SG Pages 193–196 DPP M–P HP Part 5 *Estimated Class Sessions* **2**	**Activity** Students explore patterns when multiplying 1-digit numbers by multidigit numbers ending in zeros. Finding unknowns in number sentences is introduced. **Math Facts** DPP items M, N, and O provide math facts strategies for the last six facts. **Homework** Assign the Homework section in the *Student Guide*. **Assessment** Use Home Practice Part 5 as a quiz.	• 1 set of base-ten pieces per student pair • 1 calculator per student pair • overhead base-ten pieces, optional	• 1 copy of *Base-Ten Board Parts 1* and *2* URG Pages 87–88 per student pair • 1 table from *Small Multiplication Tables* URG Page 90 per student or completed *Multiplication Facts I Know* charts • 1 transparency of *Base-Ten Board Part 1* URG Page 87 • 1 transparency of *Recording Sheet* URG Page 89
Lesson 5 **Multiplication** URG Pages 94–105 SG Pages 197–201 DPP Q–V *Estimated Class Sessions* **3-4**	**Activity** Students are introduced to the all-partials method of multiplication. **Homework** Assign the Homework section on the *Multiplication* Activity Pages. **Assessment** Use the *Observational Assessment Record* to document students' progress with multiplication.	• 1 set of base-ten pieces per student pair • overhead base-ten pieces, optional	• 1 copy of *Base-Ten Board Parts 1* and *2* URG Pages 87–88 per student pair • 1 copy of *Recording Sheet* URG Page 89 per student plus extras • 1 table from *Small Multiplication Tables* URG Page 90 per student or completed *Multiplication Facts I Know* charts • 1 transparency of *Base-Ten Board Part 1* URG Page 87 • 1 transparency of *Recording Sheet* URG Page 89 • 1 copy of *Observational Assessment Record* URG Pages 11–12 to be used throughout this unit
Lesson 6 **Estimation** URG Pages 106–115 SG Pages 202–206 DPP W–Z *Estimated Class Sessions* **2**	**Activity** Students explore computational estimation. Students develop techniques for finding convenient numbers for estimation. **Math Facts** DPP Bit Y provides practice multiplying numbers with ending zeros. **Homework** Students complete *Questions 1–7* in the Homework section of the *Estimation* Activity Pages after Part 1 of this lesson and *Questions 8–13* after Part 2. **Assessment** 1. Use DPP item Y as an assessment. 2. You may use *Questions 1–7* in the Homework section for assessment. Review the TIMS Student Rubric: *Solving* with the class. 3. Use the *Observational Assessment Record* to record students' abilities to make reasonable estimates.		

(Continued)

Overview

	Lesson Information	Supplies	Copies/Transparencies
Lesson 7 **Multiplying Round Numbers** URG Pages 116–127 SG Pages 207–210 DPP AA–BB HP Part 6 *Estimated Class Sessions* **1**	**Activity** Students use patterns to multiply multidigit numbers ending in zeros. They practice estimation. **Math Facts** DPP item AA is a quiz on the last six multiplication facts. **Homework** 1. Assign the Homework section in the *Student Guide*. 2. Assign Part 6 of the Home Practice to review multiplication. **Assessment** 1. DPP item AA is a multiplication facts quiz. 2. Students complete the *Multiplication* Assessment Page.	• 1 calculator per student	• 1 copy of *Multiplication* URG Page 123 per student
Lesson 8 **A Camping Trip** URG Pages 128–135 SG Pages 211–213 DPP CC–DD HP Part 7 *Estimated Class Sessions* **1-2**	**Activity** Students solve word problems centered around a camping trip. **Homework** Assign some or all of the problems for homework. **Assessment** 1. Use Home Practice Part 7 as a quiz. 2. Document students' progress solving problems involving multiplication on the *Observational Assessment Record*. Transfer information from the *Observational Assessment Record* to students' *Individual Assessment Record Sheets*.		• 1 copy of *Individual Assessment Record Sheet* TIG Assessment section per student, previously copied for use throughout the year

Unit 8: Measuring Up: An Assessment Unit . . . . .11–15 Sessions

Unit Summary

This unit reviews the concepts developed in the first seven units while revisiting volume, a concept explored in earlier grades. The unit's activities assess students' learning in a variety of ways. Assessments are individual as well as group oriented and include short, medium, and longer activities. This unit includes an assessment lab *Volume vs. Number,* which asks students to demonstrate their progress in carrying out a laboratory investigation. Students complete a shorter task, *Hour Walk,* which allows you to evaluate their problem-solving abilities as well as their abilities to communicate solution strategies. The *Midyear Test* is also included in this unit and the DPP includes a test on all the multiplication facts.

Major Concept Focus

- review of previously studied concepts
- midyear test
- point graphs
- divisibility rules
- portfolio review
- estimation
- best-fit lines
- experiment review
- Student Rubrics: *Solving, Knowing*, and *Telling*
- volume by displacement
- TIMS Laboratory Method
- order of operations
- communicating problem-solving strategies
- interpolation and extrapolation
- multiplication test on all the facts

Pacing Suggestions

This unit includes a variety of review and assessment activities that provide opportunities for teachers to assess individual growth in mathematics. Students continue learning as they apply concepts and skills in new contexts.

- Lesson 4 *Review Problems* is an optional lesson. This set of problems reviews skills and concepts from the first seven units and helps students prepare for the *Midyear Test* in Lesson 6. You can assign the problems for homework. Lesson 4 is also appropriate for use by a substitute teacher.

- Lessons 1–3 provide connections to science. Students can review volume measurement in Lesson 1 *Volume* or collect data for the lab in Lesson *3 Volume vs. Number* during science time. Part 3 of Lesson 1 is an optional activity that uses material from Grade 3 to review measuring volume by displacement. If your students measured volume in Grades 2 and 3, omit this activity.

- Lesson 8 *Facts I Know: Multiplication and Division Facts* completes students' review of the multiplication facts with an inventory test of all the multiplication facts. (See DPP Bit U.) This lesson also begins the study and assessment of the division facts that will continue in the Daily Practice and Problems and Home Practice in Units 9–16. All students should continue working on new concepts and skills while they are learning the division facts. Because the math facts program is closely linked to the recommended schedule for teaching lessons, classrooms that differ significantly from the suggested pacing will need to make accommodations to ensure that students receive a consistent program of math facts practice and assessment throughout the year. The *Grade 4 Facts Resource Guide* outlines a schedule for the study of math facts in classrooms that move much more slowly through lessons than is recommended in the Lesson Guides. For more information, see the TIMS Tutor: *Math Facts* in the *Teacher Implementation Guide.*

Preparing for Upcoming Lessons

In Unit 9, students will cut up boxes to explore three-dimensional shapes. Have students bring in boxes such as cereal boxes, gelatin boxes, and cracker boxes that are relatively easy to cut with scissors. Students will also need juice boxes (which are not easy to cut up) for use in Unit 9.

Place three-dimensional solids in a learning center for students to explore prior to beginning Unit 9.

Unit Planner

	Lesson Information	**Supplies**	**Copies/ Transparencies**

Lesson 1

Volume

URG Pages 30–52
SG Pages 216–220
DAB Pages 101–106

DPP A–B
HP Part 1

Estimated Class Sessions
1-2

Activity
Students discuss volume and review methods for measuring volume. This lesson includes an optional review section for students who have not taken part in volume activities in previous grades. Students review the multiplication facts for homework.

Math Facts
DPP Bit A provides practice with multiplication facts.

Homework
1. Assign Part 1 of the Home Practice and the *Mixed-Up Tables* Homework Pages in the *Discovery Assignment Book*.
2. Assign the *Estimating and Measuring Volume* Homework Pages in the *Discovery Assignment Book* after Part 3 (optional).

Assessment
Use the *Estimating and Measuring Volume* Homework Pages in the *Discovery Assignment Book* to determine how well students are able to read a graduated cylinder.

Supplies:
- 1 eyedropper per student pair, optional and 1 for the teacher
- 1 container of water per student pair, optional and 1 for the teacher
- 1 ruler per student pair
- 1 centimeter cube or base-ten bit per student pair
- 1 decimeter cube or base-ten pack per student pair
- 1 250-cc graduated cylinder per student pair, optional and 1 for the teacher
- small objects to measure in a graduated cylinder such as overhead pens, markers, small rocks, erasers, glue sticks, and lumps of clay, optional
- paper towels, optional
- 2-liter soda bottle, optional

Copies/Transparencies:
- 1 copy of *Three-column Data Table* URG Page 46 per student, optional
- 1 transparency of *100-cc Graduated Cylinder Scale* URG Page 42
- 1 transparency of *250-cc Graduated Cylinder Scale* URG Page 43
- 1 transparency of *Reading a Graduated Cylinder* URG Page 44
- 1 transparency of *Meniscus* URG Page 45

Lesson 2

Fill It First

URG Pages 53–59
SG Pages 221–224
DAB Page 107

DPP C–D

Estimated Class Sessions
1

Game
Students find volume by displacement using graduated cylinders. They play a game in which teams of students compete to predict the rise in water level as they add marbles to graduated cylinders. Homework in the *Student Guide* reviews the order of operations.

Homework
Assign the Order of Operations Review in the Homework section in the *Student Guide*.

Assessment
As students play the *Fill It First* game, assess their skills in measuring volume by displacement. Record your observations on the *Observational Assessment Record*.

Supplies:
- 1 clear plastic spinner, paper clip and pencil, or a number cube per student group
- 1 100-cc graduated cylinder per student pair
- 12 marbles in a container per student pair
- 1 eyedropper per student pair
- paper towels
- 1 container of water per student pair

Copies/Transparencies:
- 1 copy of *Three-column Data Table* URG Page 46 per student, optional
- 1 copy of *Observational Assessment Record* URG Pages 11–12 to be used throughout this unit

(Continued)

Overview

	Lesson Information	**Supplies**	**Copies/Transparencies**

Lesson 3

Volume vs. Number

URG Pages 60–78
SG Pages 225–229
DAB Pages 109–111

DPP E–J
HP Parts 2–3

Estimated Class Sessions
3-4

Assessment Lab
Students collect, organize, and graph data to solve problems involving volume. For homework they review drawing best-fit lines and using graphs to make predictions.

Math Facts
DPP items E–G and I provide practice with math facts.

Homework
1. Assign the *Predicting Prices* Activity Pages in the *Discovery Assignment Book*.
2. Assign Parts 2 and 3 of the Home Practice.
3. Assign the *Review Problems* Activity Pages in Lesson 4 of the *Student Guide*.

Assessment
1. Use the *Observational Assessment Record* to note students' skills in measuring volume by displacement.
2. Use the Assessment section of the *Teacher Implementation Guide* to provide a framework for scoring the *Volume vs. Number* lab.
3. Use **Question 12** to assess students' problem-solving abilities. Score their work using the Solving dimension of the *TIMS Multidimensional Rubric*.
4. Students add their labs to their collection folders.

Supplies:
- 1 eyedropper per student pair
- 1 container of water per student pair
- 1 ruler per student pair
- 25 standard-size marbles per student pair
- 1 250-cc graduated cylinder per student pair
- 10–12 three-quarter-inch plastic spheres or marbles larger than the standard size per student pair
- paper towels
- 1 container for marbles per student pair

Copies/Transparencies:
- 2 copies of *Two-column Data Table* URG Page 72 per student, optional
- 1 copy of *Centimeter Graph Paper* URG Page 73 per student
- 1 transparency or poster of Student Rubric: *Solving* TIG Assessment section, optional

---

Lesson 4

Review Problems

URG Pages 79–84
SG Pages 230–231

Estimated Class Sessions
1

OPTIONAL LESSON

Optional Activity
Students solve problems that review skills and concepts from previous units.

Homework
Assign the *Review Problems* for homework.

Supplies:
- 1 calculator per student
- 1 ruler per student

Lesson 5

Hour Walk

URG Pages 85–101

DPP K–L
HP Parts 4–5

Estimated Class Sessions
1-2

Assessment Activity
Using the student rubrics as guides, students solve a problem and communicate the solution. They estimate the number of steps they will take if they walk for one hour.

Homework
1. Students can complete their explanations for homework.
2. Students study for the *Multiplication Facts Inventory Test* in Lesson 8.
3. Assign Parts 4 and 5 of the Home Practice for homework.

Supplies:
- 1 calculator per student group
- classroom clock or 1 stopwatch per student group

Copies/Transparencies:
- 1 copy of *Hour Walk* URG Page 99 per student
- 1 copy of *TIMS Multidimensional Rubric* TIG, Assessment section
- 1 transparency or poster of Student Rubrics: *Solving, Telling,* and *Knowing* TIG Assessment section, optional

---

	Lesson Information	Supplies	Copies/ Transparencies
Lesson 6 **Midyear Test** URG Pages 102–115 DPP M–P *Estimated Class Sessions* **2**	**Assessment Activity** Students take a short-item test that assesses skills and concepts studied since the beginning of the year. **Math Facts** DPP Bit M provides practice with the multiplication and division facts. **Homework** For homework, students study for the *Multiplication Facts Inventory Test.* **Assessment** Place students' tests in their collection folders.	• 1 ruler per student • 1 calculator per student • square-inch tiles	• 1 copy of *Midyear Test* URG Pages 107–112 per student
Lesson 7 **Midyear Experiment and Portfolio Review** URG Pages 116–125 SG Pages 232–233 DAB Pages 113–114 DPP Q–T *Estimated Class Sessions* **2**	**Assessment Activity** Students review the experiments completed during the first half of the school year. They then organize and review their portfolios. **Math Facts** Bit S provides multiplication facts practice. **Homework** Students review for the *Math Facts Inventory Test* using their *Triangle Flash Cards.*	• 1 portfolio folder per student • 1 collection folder per student	• 1 transparency of *Experiment Review Chart* DAB Pages 113–114
Lesson 8 **Facts I Know: Multiplication and Division Facts** URG Pages 126–138 SG Pages 234–236 DAB Pages 115–119 DPP U–V *Estimated Class Sessions* **1**	**Assessment Activity** Students take the *Multiplication Facts Inventory Test* and learn to use the *Triangle Flash Cards* to practice the division facts. **Math Facts** DPP Bit U is the *Multiplication Facts Inventory Test.* Task V provides practice with multiplication and division facts. **Assessment** 1. Use the *Multiplication Facts Inventory Test* in DPP Bit U and the *Observational Assessment Record* to document students' fluency with the multiplication facts. 2. Transfer appropriate documentation from the Unit 8 *Observational Assessment Record* to students' *Individual Assessment Record Sheets.*	• 1 envelope for storing flash cards per student • 1 pair of scissors per student, optional • 1 ruler per student, optional	• 1 copy of *Multiplication Facts Inventory Test* URG Page 29 per student • 1 copy of *Dot Paper* URG Page 135 per student, optional • 1 copy of *Triangle Flash Cards: 5s* URG Page 136 per student, optional • 1 copy of *Triangle Flash Cards: 10s* URG Page 137 per student, optional • 1 transparency of *Triangle Flash Cards: 5s* DAB Page 115 • 1 transparency of *Triangle Flash Cards: 10s* DAB Page 117 • 1 transparency of *Division Facts I Know* DAB Page 119 • 1 copy of *Individual Assessment Record Sheet* TIG Assessment section per student, previously copied for use throughout the year

Overview

TIG • Grade 4 • Overview • Unit 8   **89**

Unit 9: Shapes and Solids . . . . .11–16 Sessions

Unit Summary

The theme of this unit is representing and describing shapes in two and three dimensions. Students begin by reviewing basic concepts of two-dimensional geometry. They learn to name and describe lines and angles. They also explore line and turn symmetry. Exploring three-dimensional geometry, they draw prisms and investigate nets. An Adventure Book, *Journey to Flatopia,* tells the tale of a three-dimensional person traveling to a two-dimensional world. An assessment activity is included to observe students' understanding of prisms, symmetry, angles, and volume. The DPP for this unit provides practice with and assesses the division facts for the fives and tens.

Major Concept Focus

- parallel lines
- symmetry
- prisms
- volume
- division facts for the fives and tens
- nets
- polygons
- perpendicular lines
- *Adventure Book:* dimensions
- lines and segments
- angles and rays
- dimensions
- measuring angles

Pacing Suggestions

- The Daily Practice and Problems continues the practice and assessment of the division facts begun in Unit 8 Lesson 8. In Unit 9 students practice the first group of facts, the fives and tens. Allow time for students to practice, share strategies, and use them to solve problems. Students continue to practice small groups of facts throughout Units 10–16. They take an inventory test of all the division facts in Unit 16. This work with the division facts is also in the *Grade 4 Facts Resource Guide.* Use this guide if your pacing schedule is significantly different from the recommended schedule.

- Lessons 4 and 7 are optional lessons. Both lessons extend concepts and make connections to other subject areas. Lesson 4 *Journey to Flatopia* connects math and language arts in an *Adventure Book* story. Lesson 7 *Building an Octahedron* makes connections to art. Students can make use of language arts and art time to complete these lessons.

Preparing for Upcoming Lessons

Collect boxes and prisms with different bases. See Before the Activity in Lessons 5 and 6. Arrange for students to bring juice boxes, one per student group, for Lesson 6. Students will measure the volume of the box in Lesson 6.

In Unit 10, students will participate in an experiment called *Downhill Racer.* Ask students to bring in toy cars, skates, or other vehicles that roll well for this lab.

Unit Planner

	Lesson Information	Supplies	Copies/ Transparencies
Lesson 1 **Lines** URG Pages 30–40 SG Pages 238–242 DPP A–B HP Part 1 *Estimated Class Sessions* **1-2**	**Activity** Students learn about points, lines, line segments, and rays. They investigate parallel lines. **Math Facts** DPP Task B uses fact families to practice multiplication and division facts. **Homework** 1. Students complete the homework questions in the *Student Guide.* 2. Assign Home Practice Part 1 that reminds students to use the *Triangle Flash Cards* to study the math facts for the fives and tens.	• 1 ruler per student	
Lesson 2 **What's Your Angle?** URG Pages 41–58 SG Pages 243–250 DAB Pages 127–129 DPP C–F HP Part 2 *Estimated Class Sessions* **2**	**Activity** Students learn to measure angles with a protractor and draw angles. Lines, line segments, rays, and points are discussed. **Math Facts** DPP Bits C and E provide division facts practice. **Homework** 1. Students complete the Homework section. 2. Remind students to use *Triangle Flash Cards* to study the division facts for the fives and tens with a family member. 3. Assign Part 2 of the Home Practice to develop mental math skills. **Assessment** 1. Use the *Measuring Angles II* Activity Page in the *Discovery Assignment Book* to assess students' abilities to measure and identify types of angles. 2. Use the *Observational Assessment Record* to record your observations of students as they measure and identify types of angles.	• 1 protractor per student and 1 for the teacher • 1 cardboard corner or plastic right triangle per student, optional and 1 for the teacher	• 1 transparency of *Measuring Angles I* DAB Page 127, optional • 1 transparency of *Measuring Angles II* DAB Page 129, optional • 1 copy of *Observational Assessment Record* URG Pages 13–14 to be used throughout this unit
Lesson 3 **Symmetry** URG Pages 59–75 SG Pages 251–255 DAB Pages 131–139 DPP G–J HP Part 3 *Estimated Class Sessions* **2**	**Activity** Students investigate turning (rotational) and line (reflective) symmetry. **Homework** 1. Assign the *More Symmetry* Homework Page in the *Discovery Assignment Book.* 2. Assign Home Practice Part 3 that provides computation problems. **Assessment** 1. Use DPP item I as a quiz on identifying types of angles and shapes. 2. Observe students' abilities to identify line and turn symmetry. Record your observations on the *Observational Assessment Record.*	• 1 protractor per student and 1 for the teacher • 1 ruler per student • a few of each shape of pattern blocks per student • 1 pair of scissors per student • 1 calculator per student • 4 blank sheets of paper and extras per student • 1 envelope per student, optional	• 2 transparencies of *Pattern Block Shapes* (one with shapes cut out) DAB Page 131 • 1 transparency of *Line Symmetry Examples* DAB Page 133, optional • 1 transparency of *Turn Symmetry Examples* DAB Page 135, optional • 1 transparency of *Blank Spinners* DAB Page 137, optional

Overview

(Continued)

	Lesson Information	Supplies	Copies/Transparencies
		• large square or construction paper cutout for class demonstration	
Lesson 4 **Journey to Flatopia** URG Pages 76–83 AB Pages 29–44 *Estimated Class Sessions* **1**	OPTIONAL LESSON **Optional Adventure Book** Students explore two- and three-dimensional worlds in a story about travel through the fourth dimension.		
Lesson 5 **Prisms** URG Pages 84–104 SG Pages 256–262 DAB Pages 141–149 DPP K–N HP Part 4 *Estimated Class Sessions* **2-3**	**Activity** Students learn about rectangular prisms by cutting them to form nets. Students explore nets of various prisms and build their own prisms. **Math Facts** DPP items K and M provide math facts practice. **Homework** 1. Students complete the homework questions in the *Student Guide: Question 1* after Part 1, *Questions 2–5* after Part 3, and *Questions 6–12* after Part 4. 2. Assign Part 4 of the Home Practice. **Assessment** Use the *Observational Assessment Record* to document students' abilities to identify the net of a prism.	• 1 ruler per student • 1–2 medium-sized boxes such as cereal boxes • transparent tape • 1 pair of scissors per student • 1 protractor per student • several rectangular solids or boxes, other than cubes • other examples of prisms (wooden solids), optional • 1 small cardboard box per student	• 1 transparency of *Nets 1* URG Page 98 • 1 transparency of *Nets 2* URG Page 99 • extra copies of *Nets 1* and *2* URG Pages 98–99 • extra copies of *A Hexagonal Prism* DAB Pages 145–147 • 1 copy of *Right Triangular Prism* DAB Page 149
Lesson 6 **Finding the Volume of a Prism** URG Pages 105–119 SG Pages 263–267 DPP O–R HP Part 5 *Estimated Class Sessions* **2-3**	**Activity** Students find the volumes of various prisms. **Math Facts** DPP items O and R provide practice with multiplication and division facts. **Homework** Assign the Homework section in the *Student Guide*. **Assessment** 1. Use *Questions 1–3* of Home Practice Part 5 as an assessment. 2. Use the *Observational Assessment Record* to document students' abilities to measure the volume of a prism.	• 75 centimeter connecting cubes per student group and 75 for the teacher • 1 right triangular prism from the net in Lesson 5 per student group and 1 for the teacher • 1 250-cc graduated cylinder per student group, optional and 1 for the teacher, optional	• 2–3 copies of *Centimeter Grid Paper* URG Page 116 per student • 1 transparency of *Centimeter Grid Paper* URG Page 116 • 1 copy of *Individual Assessment Record Sheet* TIG Assessment section per student, previously copied for use throughout the year

	Lesson Information	Supplies	Copies/Transparencies
	3. Transfer appropriate documentation from the Unit 9 *Observational Assessment Record* to students' *Individual Assessment Record Sheets*.	• paper towels, optional • 1 set of geometric solids or prisms with different shapes as bases per student group • various prisms small enough to fit into the graduated cylinder per student group, optional and some for the teacher, optional • 1 calculator per student group • 1 base-ten pack • 10 base-ten flats • 1 250-ml juice pack or half-pint milk carton per student group • 1 eyedropper per student group, optional and 1 for the teacher, optional • 1 small container for water per student group, optional and 1 for the teacher, optional	
Lesson 7 **Building an Octahedron** URG Pages 120–122 DAB Page 151 *Estimated Class Sessions* **1**	OPTIONAL LESSON **Optional Activity** Students construct an octahedron and discuss the mathematics they see.	• 1 pair of scissors per student and 1 for the teacher • tape • string, optional	• 1 copy of *Net of an Octahedron* DAB Page 151

(Continued)

Overview

Lesson 8
Constructing a Prism

URG Pages 123–130

DPP S–V

Estimated Class Sessions

2

Assessment Activity

Students design a net for a triangular prism and answer questions about symmetry, angles, and volume.

Math Facts

DPP Bit U is a quiz on the division facts for the fives and tens. Challenge V contains riddles that develop number sense.

Assessment

1. Use DPP item U *Quiz: 5s and 10s* to assess students' fluency with the division facts in these groups.
2. Score students' work on Part 2 using the Solving dimension of the *TIMS Multidimensional Rubric*.

- 1 protractor per student group
- 1 ruler per student group
- 1 pair of scissors per student group
- tape
- 1 calculator per student group

- 1 copy of *Constructing a Prism* URG Page 129 per student
- 1 copy of *Centimeter Grid Paper* URG Page 116 per student
- 1 copy of *TIMS Multidimensional Rubric* TIG, Assessment section

Unit 10: Using Decimals

Unit Summary
The goal of this unit is for students to develop connections between decimals and physical models, pictures, real situations, symbols, and words. Students explore decimals as they measure lengths in meters, decimeters, centimeters, and millimeters. They learn to read, write, and order decimals to the hundredths. They make connections between common fractions and decimals.

Students use the TIMS Laboratory Method to complete the *Downhill Racer* lab. This unit also includes a game that practices comparing decimals. The Adventure Book, *Alberto in TenthsLand,* tells the story of a child who falls asleep in a library and dreams of a world where everything involves tenths. The DPP for this unit provides practice with and assesses the division facts for the twos and threes.

Major Concept Focus
- TIMS Laboratory Method
- best-fit lines
- tenths and hundredths
- common fractions
- point graphs
- Student Rubric: *Knowing*
- division facts for the twos and threes
- *Adventure Book:* decimals
- fractional units of measure
- length in mm, dm, cm, and m
- reading, comparing, and writing decimals
- number sense for decimals
- interpolation and extrapolation

Pacing Suggestions
This unit will take 12 to 14 days to complete depending on your students' familiarity with decimals. Students began their formal study of decimals in Grade 3 Unit 15.

- Lesson 4 *Downhill Racer* provides connections to science. Students can collect the data for the lab during science time.
- Lesson 5 *Decimal Hex* is an optional lesson. It is a challenging game that provides practice comparing decimals.
- Lesson 6 *Alberto in TenthsLand* is an *Adventure Book* story that provides a connection to language arts. It is based on *The Adventures of Alice in Wonderland.* Alberto grows ten times larger than normal and shrinks to one-tenth his normal size. Students can read the story as part of language arts time.

Preparing for Upcoming Lessons
Ask students to bring in toy cars, roller skates, or other things with wheels for the experiment in Lesson 4.

Overview

Unit Planner

	Lesson Information	Supplies	Copies/Transparencies
Lesson 1 **m, dm, cm, mm** URG Pages 30–45 SG Pages 270–275 DAB Pages 163–166 DPP A–D HP Parts 1–2 *Estimated Class Sessions* **2**	**Activity** Students measure objects in the classroom first to the nearest whole meter, and then to the nearest tenth, hundredth, and thousandth of a meter. They discuss appropriate units of measure for various situations. **Math Facts** DPP items B and C provide practice with division facts. Task D provides practice with base-ten shorthand and multiplying with multiples of 10. **Homework** 1. Assign *Questions 1–2* in the Homework section of the *m, dm, cm, mm* Activity Pages after Part 1. 2. Assign *Question 3* in the Homework section of the *m, dm, cm, mm* Activity Pages after Part 3. 3. Assign Parts 1 and 2 of the Home Practice. **Assessment** 1. Use the *Observational Assessment Record* to document students' abilities to measure length to the nearest mm, cm, dm, and m. 2. Set up a performance assessment task in which students measure specified objects.	• 1 or 2 metersticks per student group • about 10 skinnies and 10 bits per student group • 1 meter of string per student • 1 centimeter ruler per student • masking tape • 1 envelope for storing flash cards per student	• 1 transparency of *Class Measurement Tables* DAB Page 163 • 1 copy of *Observational Assessment Record* URG Pages 13–14 to be used throughout this unit
Lesson 2 **Tenths** URG Pages 46–61 SG Pages 276–282 DAB Pages 167–171 DPP E–H HP Parts 4–5 *Estimated Class Sessions* **2-3**	**Activity** Students work with decimal notation for tenths. The emphasis is on connections between base-ten pieces, shorthand, and written notation for common and decimal fractions. **Math Facts** DPP item G provides practice with division facts. **Homework** 1. Complete the *Exploring Tenths* Activity Pages in the *Discovery Assignment Book* as homework. 2. Assign Parts 4 and 5 of the Home Practice. **Assessment** Use the *Observational Assessment Record* to document students' abilities to translate between concrete, pictorial, and symbolic representations of decimals.	• 2 packs, 14 flats, and 30 skinnies per student pair • 1 meterstick per student pair • overhead base-ten pieces	• 1 transparency of *Tenths Helper* DAB Page 167

	Lesson Information	**Supplies**	**Copies/ Transparencies**

Lesson 3

Hundredths

URG Pages 62–79
SG Pages 283–287
DAB Pages 173–177

DPP I–N
HP Part 3

Estimated Class Sessions
3

Activity
Students work with decimal notation for hundredths. The emphasis is on connections between base-ten pieces, shorthand, and written notation for common and decimal fractions.

Math Facts
DPP Bits K and M provide math facts practice.

Homework
1. Assign the *More Hundredths* Activity Pages in the *Discovery Assignment Book* after Part 1.
2. Assign the Homework section, *Playing Hundredths, Hundredths, Hundredths,* in the *Student Guide* after Part 2.
3. Assign Home Practice Part 3.

Assessment
1. Score the *Linda's Base-Ten Pieces* Assessment Blackline Master using the Knowing dimension of the *TIMS Multidimensional Rubric*.
2. Use the *Observational Assessment Record* to document students' abilities to translate between different representations of decimals.

• 2 packs, 14 flats, 30 skinnies, and 50 bits per student pair
• overhead base-ten pieces, optional

• 1 copy of *Linda's Base-Ten Pieces* URG Page 73 per student
• 1 transparency of *Shorthand and Fractions Table* DAB Page 177
• 1 copy of *TIMS Multidimensional Rubric* TIG, Assessment section, optional
• 1 transparency or poster of Student Rubric: *Knowing* TIG, Assessment section

---

Lesson 4

Downhill Racer

URG Pages 80–103
SG Pages 288–295

DPP O–V

Estimated Class Sessions
4

Lab
Students collect, organize, graph, and analyze data as they study the relationship between the height of a ramp and the distance a car rolls. They use decimals to measure the distance the car rolls.

Math Facts
DPP Bit Q provides practice with division facts.

Homework
1. Assign some or all of the questions in the Explore section.
2. Assign the Homework section on the *Downhill Racer* Lab Pages after students complete the *Roberto's Data* Assessment Blackline Master.

Assessment
1. Use *Roberto's Data* Assessment Blackline Master to assess students' understanding of the *Downhill Racer* lab.
2. Use the *Observational Assessment Record* to document students' abilities to collect, organize, graph, and analyze data.
3. Transfer information from the Unit 10 *Observational Assessment Record* to students' *Individual Assessment Record Sheets*.

• 1 wood or metal ramp at least 50 cm long per student group
• 1 toy car or roller skate per student group
• 2–3 metersticks per student group
• 4–5 blocks or books of equal size per student group
• masking tape
• 1 calculator per student group

• 1 copy of *Roberto's Data* URG Pages 95–96 per student
• at least 3 copies of *Centimeter Graph Paper* URG Page 97 per student
• 1 copy of *Three-trial Data Table* URG Page 98 per student
• 1 transparency of *Centimeter Graph Paper* URG Page 97
• 1 copy of *Individual Assessment Record Sheet* TIG Assessment section per student, previously copied for use throughout the year

Overview

(Continued)

	Lesson Information	Supplies	Copies/ Transparencies
Lesson 5 **Decimal Hex** URG Pages 104–107 DAB Pages 179–181 *Estimated Class Sessions* **1**	OPTIONAL LESSON **Optional Game** As part of a game, students compare decimals. **Homework** Students take home the *Decimal Hex* Game Pages to play with family members. **Assessment** Use the *Observational Assessment Record* to note students' abilities to compare and order decimals.	• 2 same-color centimeter cubes as game markers per student • 1 clear plastic spinner or paper clip and pencil per student • base-ten pieces	
Lesson 6 **Alberto in TenthsLand** URG Pages 108–116 AB Pages 45–56 DPP W–X HP Part 6 *Estimated Class Sessions* **1**	**Adventure Book** The hero of this story falls asleep in the library and has a dream about a place called TenthsLand. He has a series of adventures in which he meets several fantastic creatures. Decimals and 10 percent are emphasized. **Math Facts** DPP item W is a quiz on the division facts for the twos and threes. Task X asks students to solve a division problem, write a story about it, and draw a picture. **Homework** 1. Have students read and discuss the *Adventure Book* with family members. 2. Assign Part 6 of the Home Practice. **Assessment** Use DPP Bit W to assess students on the division facts for the twos and threes.	• 1 calculator per student	

Unit 11: Multiplication ....11–14 Sessions

Unit Summary

Students learn to multiply two-digit by two-digit numbers using paper-and-pencil methods. Students learn that there are many ways to complete multiplication problems. Egyptian multiplication, called duplation, is shown in the Adventure Book, *Phil and Howard's Excellent Egyptian Adventure.* Students also identify patterns in multiplying numbers with ending zeros. The DPP for this unit provides practice with and assesses the division facts for the square numbers.

Major Concept Focus

- multiplication of numbers with ending zeros
- estimating products
- *Adventure Book:* other number systems
- paper-and-pencil methods for multiplication

Pacing Suggestions

- Use the recommended number of sessions for each lesson as a guide. Students extend their multiplication skills in this unit, but it is not necessary to stop until all students master each concept and skill. Distributed practice of small sets of multiplication problems and sets of word problems are included in each of the succeeding units in the lessons, Daily Practice and Problems, and Home Practice.
- Lesson 5 *More Compact Multiplication* is an optional lesson that challenges students to extend the compact method of multiplication to larger numbers.
- Lesson 7 *Visiting Egypt* is an optional lesson in which students solve multistep word problems and practice multiplication skills. You can assign these problems for homework. They are also appropriate for use by a substitute teacher since preparation is minimal.

Unit Planner

KEY: SG = Student Guide, DAB = Discovery Assignment Book, AB = Adventure Book, URG = Unit Resource Guide, DPP = Daily Practice and Problems, HP = Home Practice (found in Discovery Assignment Book), and TIG = Teacher Implementation Guide.

	Lesson Information	Supplies	Copies/ Transparencies
Lesson 1 **Modeling Multiplication** URG Pages 26–48 SG Pages 298–303 DPP A–F HP Parts 1–2 *Estimated Class Sessions* **3**	**Activity** Students review the concept of multiplication using base-ten pieces and square-inch tiles. They review and expand their understanding of multiplying by multiples of ten and the all-partials method. **Math Facts** DPP Bits A, C, and E provide practice with math facts. **Homework** 1. Assign Parts 1 and 2 of the Home Practice. 2. Assign homework *Questions 1–20* in the *Student Guide* after Part 1. 3. Assign homework *Questions 21–38* after Part 2. **Assessment** Use the *Observational Assessment Record* to document students' progress representing multiplication using base-ten pieces.	• 2 packs, 14 flats, 30 skinnies, and 50 bits per student group • square-inch tiles, optional • 1 envelope for storing flash cards per student • overhead base-ten pieces • overhead square-inch tiles	• 1 table from *Small Multiplication Tables* URG Page 39 per student • 1 copy of *Base-Ten Board Part 1* and *Part 2* URG Pages 40–41 per student • 1 copy of *Recording Sheet* URG Page 42 per student, optional • 2 copies of *Centimeter Grid Paper* URG Page 43 per student • 1 copy of *Observational Assessment Record* URG Pages 11–12 to be used throughout this unit
Lesson 2 **More Multiplication** URG Pages 49–60 SG Pages 304–307 DPP G–J HP Parts 3–5 *Estimated Class Sessions* **2**	**Activity** Students review multiplying one-digit numbers by multidigit numbers. They explore exercises that lead to developing traditional, compact methods of multiplication. **Math Facts** DPP Bits G and I provide division facts practice. **Homework** 1. Assign the homework problems in the *Student Guide*. 2. Assign Home Practice Parts 4 and 5. **Assessment** 1. Use Home Practice Part 3 to assess students' abilities to multiply with multiples of 10. 2. Use the *Observational Assessment Record* to note students' abilities to multiply a multidigit number by a one-digit number.	• 2 packs, 14 flats, 30 skinnies, and 50 bits per student group • overhead base-ten pieces, optional	• 1 copy of *Base-Ten Board Part 1* and *Part 2* URG Pages 40–41 per student • 2 copies of *Centimeter Grid Paper* URG Page 43 per student
Lesson 3 **Compact Multiplication** URG Pages 61–70 SG Pages 308–312 DPP K–N HP Parts 6 & 8 *Estimated Class Sessions* **2**	**Activity** Students are introduced to a traditional multiplication algorithm that is referred to as the compact method. **Homework** 1. Assign homework *Questions 1–21* as needed. 2. Home Practice Part 6 is more multiplication practice with multiples of 10. Part 8 builds skills with metric measurement. **Assessment** Use the *Observational Assessment Record* to note students' abilities to estimate products.	• 1 set of base-ten pieces per student, optional	

	Lesson Information	Supplies	Copies/ Transparencies
Lesson 4 **All-Partials Revisited** URG Pages 71–84 SG Pages 313–316 DPP O–T HP Parts 7 & 9–11 *Estimated Class Sessions* **3**	**Activity** Students expand the use of the all-partials method to solve two-digit by two-digit multiplication problems. A quiz is provided. **Math Facts** DPP items Q and T provide practice with math facts. **Homework** 1. Assign the homework in the *Student Guide*. 2. Part 7 of the Home Practice provides two-digit by two-digit multiplication practice. Part 9 is a logic problem using money. Parts 10 and 11 review divisibility rules. **Assessment** 1. Use the *Quiz* Assessment Blackline Master to assess multiplication skills. 2. Use the *Observational Assessment Record* to note students' progress with multiplication. Transfer appropriate documentation from the Unit 11 *Observational Assessment Record* to students' *Individual Assessment Record Sheets*.	• 1 set of base-ten pieces per student, optional • overhead base-ten pieces	• 1 copy of *Quiz* URG Page 79 per student • 1 copy of *Individual Assessment Record Sheet* TIG Assessment section per student, previously copied for use throughout the year
Lesson 5 **More Compact Multiplication** URG Pages 85–93 SG Pages 317–321 *Estimated Class Sessions* **2**	OPTIONAL LESSON **Optional Activity** The compact method is expanded to two-digit by two-digit multiplication problems. The method is tied to the all-partials method. **Homework** Assign homework *Questions 1–16* at the end of the lesson. **Assessment** Use homework questions to assess students' skills.		
Lesson 6 **Phil and Howard's Excellent Egyptian Adventure** URG Pages 94–103 AB Pages 57–70 DPP U–V *Estimated Class Sessions* **1**	**Adventure Book** Phil and Howard travel through time with Professor Peabody to learn how the ancient Egyptians multiplied. **Math Facts** DPP item U is a quiz on the division facts for the square numbers. **Homework** Assign some or all of the problems in Lesson 7 for homework. **Assessment** Use DPP Bit U as a quiz on the division facts for the square numbers.		• 1 transparency of *Egyptian Numbers and Symbols* URG Page 103, optional

Overview

(Continued)

	Lesson Information	Supplies	Copies/Transparencies
Lesson 7 **Visiting Egypt** URG Pages 104–108 SG Pages 322–323 *Estimated Class Sessions* **1**	OPTIONAL LESSON **Optional Activity** Students solve a variety of word problems involving multiplication. **Homework** Assign any or all of the problems for homework. **Assessment** Use the problems to assess problem-solving and multiplication skills.		• 1 table from *Small Multiplication Tables* URG Page 39 per student, optional

Unit 12: Exploring Fractions . . . . .12–16 Sessions

Unit Summary

Through the use of manipulatives, students continue to build a strong conceptual understanding of fractions. Students explore part-whole fractions with fraction strips and pattern blocks. They use manipulatives to compare and order fractions as well as add and subtract fractions with like denominators. An open-response problem involving fraction pattern block puzzles, *Puzzle Problem,* is included as an assessment lesson. This unit also includes a midterm test that covers concepts from this and past units. The DPP reviews and assesses the division facts for the nines.

Major Concept Focus

- writing fractions
- equivalent fractions
- ordering fractions
- part-whole fractions
- midterm test
- adding and subtracting fractions with like denominators
- division facts for the nines

- modeling fractions with manipulatives
- communicating problem-solving strategies
- fractions in measurement
- Student Rubrics: *Solving* and *Telling*
- adding and subtracting fractions with manipulatives

Pacing Suggestions

- Lesson 4 *Frabble Game and Bubble Sort* is an optional lesson. These activities provide opportunities to practice and extend fraction concepts in game situations.
- Lesson 6 *Pattern Block Fractions* contains an optional activity from third grade that introduces students to using pattern blocks to represent fractions. Use it with students who have not had these experiences.

Unit Planner

KEY: SG = Student Guide, DAB = Discovery Assignment Book, AB = Adventure Book, URG = Unit Resource Guide, DPP = Daily Practice and Problems, HP = Home Practice (found in Discovery Assignment Book), and TIG = Teacher Implementation Guide.

	Lesson Information	Supplies	Copies/Transparencies
Lesson 1 **Fraction Strips** URG Pages 28–47 SG Pages 326–332 DAB Pages 199–201 DPP A–F HP Parts 1–2 *Estimated Class Sessions* **3**	**Activity** Students fold uniform strips of paper to show equal parts, labeling each part according to the fractional part it represents. Students will fold halves, thirds, fourths, fifths, sixths, eighths, ninths, tenths, and twelfths. Students will then use the strips to find equivalent fractions. **Math Facts** DPP items B and C and Home Practice Part 1 review and provide practice with the division facts for the nines. **Homework** 1. Assign homework *Questions 1–7* in the *Student Guide* any time after Part 1, homework *Questions 8–13* after Part 2, and homework *Questions 14–21* after Part 3. 2. Students take their flash cards home to study the division facts for the nines. 3. Assign Home Practice Part 2 in the *Discovery Assignment Book.* **Assessment** Use the *Observational Assessment Record* to record students' abilities to represent fractions with paper folding.	• 1 pair of scissors per student • 2 envelopes per student (1 for flash cards and 1 for fraction strips) • crayons, markers, or colored pencils • 1 ruler per student	• 1 copy of *Fraction Strips for the Teacher* URG Pages 42–43 • 1 copy of *Observational Assessment Record* URG Pages 13–14 to be used throughout this unit
Lesson 2 **Adding and Subtracting with Fraction Strips** URG Pages 48–53 SG Pages 333–335 DPP G–H *Estimated Class Sessions* **1**	**Activity** Students use fraction strips to add and subtract fractions with like denominators. **Math Facts** DPP Bit G provides practice with division facts and Task H provides practice with prime factorization. **Homework** Assign homework *Questions 1–7* in the *Student Guide.* Students will need their fraction strips. **Assessment** Use the *Observational Assessment Record* to note students' progress adding and subtracting fractions with like denominators using manipulatives.	• 1 set of fraction strips from Lesson 1 per student	• 1 set of cut strips, folded, colored, and labeled copied from *Fraction Strips for the Teacher* URG Pages 42–43
Lesson 3 **Comparing Fractions** URG Pages 54–63 SG Pages 336–338 DPP I–J *Estimated Class Sessions* **1**	**Activity** Students organize their fraction strips in a chart and then use the chart to compare and order fractions according to size. **Homework** Assign homework *Questions 1–8* in the *Student Guide.* **Assessment** Use the *Observational Assessment Record* to note students' abilities to order fractions.	• glue • 1 sheet of blank paper per student • 1 set of fraction strips from Lesson 1 per student	• 1 copy of *Fraction Strips for the Teacher* URG Pages 42–43 • 1 transparency of *Fraction Chart* URG Page 61

104 TIG • Grade 4 • Overview • Unit 12

	Lesson Information	Supplies	Copies/ Transparencies
Lesson 4 **Frabble Game and Bubble Sort** URG Pages 64–70 SG Pages 339–342 DAB Pages 203–209 *Estimated Class Sessions* **1-2**	OPTIONAL LESSON **Optional Game** Students use a deck of fraction cards to complete two activities. First, students play a game in small groups in which they order fractions according to size by strategically placing cards on the table. Then in an activity called Bubble Sort, each student holds a fraction card as he or she stands in line. Following simple rules, they rearrange themselves so the cards are in order. **Homework** Students play *Frabble* at home. They should take home a deck of *Frabble* cards, six wild cards, and their *Student Guides*. **Assessment** Use the *Observational Assessment Record* to note students' abilities to compare and order fractions.	• 1 pair of scissors per student • envelopes, optional • 1 fraction chart from Lesson 3 per student	• 1 transparency of *Standard Frabble Cards* DAB Pages 203–205, optional • 1 transparency of *Fraction Chart* URG Page 61 or fraction chart from Lesson 3
Lesson 5 **Equivalent Fractions** URG Pages 71–79 SG Pages 343–345 DPP K–L HP Part 3 *Estimated Class Sessions* **1**	**Activity** Students find equivalent fractions using their fraction charts from Lesson 3, write number sentences to represent the fractions, and look for patterns in the number sentences. They use the patterns to write an equivalent fraction for a given fraction. **Math Facts** Use DPP items K and L to practice multiplication and division facts as students build number sense. **Homework** Assign the Homework section on the *Equivalent Fractions* Activity Pages in the *Student Guide*. Students will need their fraction charts to complete this assignment. **Assessment** 1. Use the *Observational Assessment Record* to note students' abilities to find equivalent fractions. 2. Use Home Practice Part 3 as an assessment.	• 1 fraction chart from Lesson 3 per student	

Overview

	Lesson Information	Supplies	Copies/ Transparencies
Lesson 6 **Pattern Block Fractions** URG Pages 80–95 SG Pages 346–349 DPP M–P HP Parts 4–5 *Estimated Class Sessions* **2-3**	**Activity** Students explore the use of pattern blocks to model fractions. They name fractions when a given pattern block is defined as one whole, and they identify the whole when a fraction is given. They also model easy addition problems using pattern blocks. **Math Facts** DPP Bit M provides practice with math facts. Item P focuses on different aspects of division. **Homework** 1. Assign *Questions 1–7* in the Homework section of the *Student Guide.* These questions review skills and concepts addressed in Lessons 1–5. 2. Assign Home Practice Parts 4 and 5. 3. Students continue practicing division facts using the *Triangle Flash Cards: 9s.* **Assessment** Use the *Observational Assessment Record* to note students' abilities to identify the whole when given a fractional part of the whole.	• 1 set of pattern blocks (2–3 yellow hexagons, 6 red trapezoids, 10 blue rhombuses, 10 green triangles, 6 brown trapezoids) per student pair • overhead pattern blocks, optional	• 1 copy of *What's 1?* URG Pages 88–89 per student, optional
Lesson 7 **Solving Problems with Pattern Blocks** URG Pages 96–103 SG Pages 350–352 DPP Q–R *Estimated Class Sessions* **1**	**Activity** Students use pattern blocks to order fractions by looking at patterns. They develop a strategy for ordering fractions. They also solve word problems involving addition of fractions using pattern blocks. **Homework** Assign *Questions 1–5* in the Homework section in the *Student Guide.* **Assessment** Use DPP items Q and R as assessments.	• 1 set of pattern blocks (2–3 yellow hexagons, 6 red trapezoids, 10 blue rhombuses, 10 green triangles, 6 brown trapezoids) per student pair • 1 fraction chart from Lesson 3 per student pair • overhead pattern blocks, optional	
Lesson 8 **Fraction Puzzles** URG Pages 104–117 SG Pages 353–355 DPP S–V HP Part 6 *Estimated Class Sessions* **2**	**Assessment Activity** Students work cooperatively in groups of four to solve fraction puzzles. Four clues are given to help the groups solve each puzzle. After finding a solution, students write a paragraph explaining their solutions and the problem-solving strategies used by their groups. **Homework** 1. Assign homework *Questions 1–7* in the *Student Guide.* 2. Assign Home Practice Part 6.	• 1 set of pattern blocks per student group • envelopes, optional • paper clips, optional	• 1 copy of *Fraction Puzzle Clues* URG Pages 112–113 per student group • 1 copy of *Puzzle Problem* URG Page 114 per student • 1 transparency or poster of Student Rubric: *Solving* TIG, Assessment section • 1 transparency or poster of Student Rubric: *Telling* TIG, Assessment section

	Lesson Information	Supplies	Copies/ Transparencies
	Assessment 1. Puzzle D and the *Puzzle Problem* Assessment Blackline Master provide an assessment of students' problem-solving and communication skills. 2. Use the *Observational Assessment Record* to note students' abilities to solve open-response problems and communicate solution strategies. 3. Transfer appropriate documentation from the Unit 12 *Observational Assessment Record* to students' *Individual Assessment Record Sheets*.		• 1 copy of *TIMS Multidimensional Rubric* TIG, Assessment section • 1 copy of *Individual Assessment Record Sheet* TIG Assessment section per student, previously copied for use throughout the year
Lesson 9 **Midterm Test** URG Pages 118–129 DPP W–X *Estimated Class Sessions* **1-2**	**Assessment Activity** Students take a test on concepts in this and past units. **Math Facts** DPP Bit W is a short quiz on division facts.	• 1 calculator per student • 1 ruler per student • 1 protractor per student • base-ten pieces • pattern blocks • 1 fraction chart from Lesson 3 per student	• 1 copy of *Midterm Test* URG Pages 122–126 per student

Unit 13: Division . . . . .13–14 Sessions

Unit Summary
This unit develops students' conceptual understanding of division and introduces a paper-and-pencil method for division. Division is reviewed through word problems before computation is introduced. Using the context of *TV Survey,* students solve multiplication and division problems involving time. They model division with base-ten pieces and then make connections to paper-and-pencil methods. The *Plant Growth* lab also begins in this unit. Students plant seeds and begin collecting data that they will analyze in Unit 15. The DPP provides practice with and assesses the division facts for the last six facts.

Major Concept Focus
- division symbols
- modeling division with base-ten pieces
- TIMS Laboratory Method
- paper-and-pencil methods for division
- length in centimeters
- choosing appropriate methods of computation
- interpreting remainders
- estimating products and quotients
- bar graphs
- division facts for the last six facts

Pacing Suggestions
- Use the recommended number of sessions for each lesson as a guide. Students develop their division skills in this unit, but it is not necessary to stop until all students master each concept and skill. Distributed practice of small sets of division problems and sets of word problems are included in each of the succeeding units in the lessons, Daily Practice and Problems, and Home Practice.
- Lesson 5 *Plant Growth* begins a laboratory investigation that shows the growth patterns in plants. In this lesson students identify the variables in the experiment, draw pictures, set up data tables, and plant seeds. Students collect data on the height of their plants for approximately 21 days. Unit 15 Lesson 1 *Plant Growth Conclusion* begins the study of patterns in that unit. Students analyze their plant growth data by identifying patterns in their data tables and graphs. Note that there are less than 21 days between these two lessons according to the suggested number of sessions in the unit outlines for Units 14 and 15. You may need to teach this lesson later in Unit 15. Setting up the laboratory investigation and planting seeds are appropriate activities for science as well as math.

Unit Planner

	Lesson Information	Supplies	Copies/ Transparencies

Lesson 1
TV Survey

URG Pages 30–53
SG Pages 358–363
DAB Pages 219–221

DPP A–F
HP Part 1–2

Estimated Class Sessions
3

Activity
In an introductory session, students plan the *TV Survey.* Then students collect data about the amount of TV they watch in a four-day period while continuing with this unit's other lessons. After the four-day period, students organize, graph, and analyze the data.

Math Facts
DPP items B, C, and D provide multiplication and division practice with the last six facts.

Homework
1. Students complete homework *Questions 1–10* in the *Student Guide.*
2. Assign Parts 1 and 2 of the Home Practice in the *Discovery Assignment Book.*

Assessment
Document students' abilities to collect, organize, graph, and analyze data on the *Observational Assessment Record.*

Supplies:
- 1 calculator per student
- 1 envelope for storing flash cards per student

Copies/Transparencies:
- 1 copy of *TV Survey: Letter Home* URG Page 46 per student
- 2 copies of *Centimeter Graph Paper* URG Page 47 per student
- 2 copies of *Three-column Data Table* URG Page 48 per student
- several transparencies of *Four-column Data Table* URG Page 49 or a laminated data table wall chart or large chart paper
- 1 transparency of *Centimeter Graph Paper* URG Page 47
- 1 copy of *Observational Assessment Record* URG Pages 11–12 to be used throughout this unit

Lesson 2
Division

URG Pages 54–69
SG Pages 364–370

DPP G–L
HP Parts 5–6

Estimated Class Sessions
3

Activity
Introduce students to long division by modeling with the base-ten pieces. Discuss the symbols for division, and introduce the "forgiving method" for long division.

Math Facts
DPP items H and K provide practice with multiplication and division facts.

Homework
1. Assign homework *Questions 1–6* after Part 1 and discuss them with the class.
2. Assign homework *Questions 7–16* after Part 2.
3. Assign Home Practice Parts 5 and 6.
4. Students continue to practice division facts using the *Triangle Flash Cards: Last Six Facts.*

Assessment
Ask students to model 49 divided by 3 using base-ten pieces and then compute the quotient using paper and pencil. Record students' abilities on the *Observational Assessment Record.*

Supplies:
- 1 set of base-ten pieces (2 packs, 14 flats, 30 skinnies, 50 bits) per student pair
- overhead base-ten pieces, optional

(Continued)

Overview

	Lesson Information	Supplies	Copies/Transparencies
Lesson 3 **More Division** URG Pages 70–83 SG Pages 371–373 DAB Page 223 DPP M–R HP Parts 3–4 *Estimated Class Sessions* **3-4**	**Activity** Students represent division problems with base-ten pieces and use the forgiving method. This lesson emphasizes three- and four-digit dividends. Using estimation to make good predictions is stressed. **Math Facts** DPP Bit Q provides division facts practice. **Homework** 1. Assign the homework questions in the *Student Guide* over several nights. 2. Assign the *Division Dot-to-Dot* Activity Page in the *Discovery Assignment Book.* 3. Assign Home Practice Part 3. **Assessment** 1. Record students' abilities to model division using base-ten pieces on the *Observational Assessment Record.* 2. Use Home Practice Part 4 as an assessment.	• 1 set of base-ten pieces (2 packs, 14 flats, 30 skinnies, 50 bits) per student group • overhead base-ten pieces, optional	
Lesson 4 **Solving Problems Using Multiplication and Division** URG Pages 84–96 SG Pages 374–378 DPP S–V HP Part 7 *Estimated Class Sessions* **2**	**Activity** Students solve a variety of word problems involving multiplication and division. A quiz is included in this lesson. **Math Facts** DPP item S is a quiz on the 12 division facts related to the last six multiplication facts. Bit U reviews division and zero. **Homework** 1. Assign the Homework section in the *Student Guide.* 2. Assign Part 7 of the Home Practice. **Assessment** 1. Use the *Unit 13 Quiz* Assessment Blackline Master to assess students' multiplication and division skills. 2. Use DPP Bit S to assess students' fluency with the division facts in the Last Six Facts group. 3. Document students' abilities to solve multiplication and division problems on the *Observational Assessment Record.* Transfer appropriate documentation to students' *Individual Assessment Record Sheets.*	• 1 calculator per student	• 1 copy of *Unit 13 Quiz* URG Page 91 per student • 1 table from *Small Multiplication Tables* URG Page 92 per student • 1 copy of *Individual Assessment Record Sheet* TIG, Assessment section per student, previously copied for use throughout the year

	Lesson Information	Supplies	Copies/Transparencies
Lesson 5 **Plant Growth** URG Pages 97–108 SG Pages 379–381 DPP W–Z *Estimated Class Sessions* **2**	**Lab** Students begin a lab that investigates the growth pattern of plants. They identify the manipulated, responding, and fixed variables for this experiment. Students plant seeds, choose one plant to follow, and take measurements of the plant's growth over time. Students will graph and analyze their data in Lesson 1 of Unit 15. **Homework** Students can draw their pictures for homework. **Assessment** Use students' drawings of the lab setup as an assessment.	• 1 container for planting seeds per student pair • 4 seeds (lima beans or sunflower) per student pair • 1 graduated cylinder per student pair • rulers • 1 cup of potting soil per student pair • paper towels • 1 centimeter ruler per student pair • craft sticks marked at $\frac{1}{2}$-inch, optional	• 1 copy of *Three-column Data Table* URG Page 48 per student • 1 transparency of *Three-column Data Table* URG Page 48, optional

Overview

Unit 14: Chancy Predictions:
An Introduction to Probability . . . . .8–9 Sessions

Unit Summary

This unit investigates probabilities using a probability line, number cubes, and spinners. Students learn to describe probabilities qualitatively in words such as "likely," "unlikely," and "impossible" as well as with probability lines. Students also describe probabilities quantitatively using fractions. This unit includes a laboratory investigation, *Rolling a Number Cube,* in which students explore the outcome of a random process. It also includes an Adventure Book, *Prob_e Quest,* that reviews probability concepts. The DPP reviews and assesses the division facts for the twos, fives, tens, and square numbers.

Major Concept Focus

- random process
- probability lines
- creating spinners
- the meaning of "or"
- bar graphs
- Law of Large Numbers
- probabilities as fractions

- TIMS Laboratory Method
- *Adventure Book:* probability review
- probabilities of rolling number cubes
- equivalent probabilities
- probabilities of spinning spinners
- expressing fractions as decimals and percents
- division fact review for the 2s, 5s, 10s, and square numbers

Pacing Suggestions

- Lesson 6 *Make Your Own Spinners* is an optional lesson. It extends students' work with probability by asking students to apply concepts to new situations.
- Lesson 7 *Prob_e Quest* is an *Adventure Book* story that makes connections to language arts. Students can read the story during language arts time.

Unit Planner

KEY: SG = Student Guide, DAB = Discovery Assignment Book, AB = Adventure Book, URG = Unit Resource Guide, DPP = Daily Practice and Problems, HP = Home Practice (found in Discovery Assignment Book), and TIG = Teacher Implementation Guide.

	Lesson Information	Supplies	Copies/ Transparencies
Lesson 1 **Chance Discussions** URG Pages 26–38 SG Pages 384–386 DPP A–B HP Part 1 *Estimated Class Sessions* **1**	**Activity** Students discuss probability in qualitative and quantitative terms while constructing a probability line. **Math Facts** DPP Bit A uses math facts to solve a puzzle. Task B reminds students to use the *Triangle Flash Cards* to study division facts. **Homework** 1. Assign the Homework section on the *Chance Discussions* Activity Pages. 2. Assign Part 1 of the Home Practice.	• 4 self-adhesive notes per student group	• 1 copy of *Triangle Flash Cards: 2s, 5s, 10s,* and *Square Numbers* URG Pages 34–37 per student, optional
Lesson 2 **Bean Counter's Game** URG Pages 39–45 SG Page 387 DPP C–D HP Parts 4–5 *Estimated Class Sessions* **1**	**Game** Students play a game that focuses on the rolls of a number cube. This game helps students develop concepts needed for Lesson 3. **Math Facts** DPP Bit C reviews division facts for the 2s, 5s, 10s, and square numbers. **Homework** 1. Students can play the game at home with family members. 2. Assign Home Practice Parts 4 and 5.	• 12 beans, small tokens, or centimeter connecting cubes per student • 1 number cube per student group • scratch paper	
Lesson 3 **Rolling a Number Cube** URG Pages 46–62 SG Pages 388–391 DPP E–H HP Part 3 *Estimated Class Sessions* **2**	**Lab** Students investigate the outcome of a random process by rolling a number cube and analyzing the results. A discussion of the results is tied to both the *Bean Counter's Game* from Lesson 2 and to probability. **Math Facts** DPP Bit G provides practice with division facts using fact families. **Homework** 1. Use **Questions 12–16** in the *Student Guide* as homework. 2. Assign Home Practice Part 3 from the *Discovery Assignment Book.* 3. Students practice division facts using the *Triangle Flash Cards.* **Assessment** 1. Students complete the *Check-up* Assessment Page that follows the lesson guide in the *Unit Resource Guide.* 2. Use the *Observational Assessment Record* to note students' abilities to express probabilities as fractions and to make and interpret bar graphs.	• 1 number cube per student pair • 1 calculator per student pair • 1 small paper cup for rolling number cubes per student pair, optional	• 1 copy of *Check-up* URG Page 57 per student • 2 copies of *Centimeter Graph Paper* URG Page 58 per student • 1 copy of *Three-column Data Table* URG Page 59 per student pair • 1 copy of *Observational Assessment Record* URG Pages 13–14 to be used throughout this unit

Overview

(Continued)

	Lesson Information	Supplies	Copies/Transparencies
Lesson 4 **From Number Cubes to Spinners** URG Pages 63–71 SG Page 392 DAB Page 231 DPP I–J HP Part 2 *Estimated Class Sessions* **1**	**Activity** Students construct spinners that reflect the number cube investigation. **Homework** 1. Students can test their spinners at home for homework *(Question 6)*. 2. Assign Home Practice Part 2 in the *Discovery Assignment Book*. **Assessment** Use the Journal Prompt to assess students' understanding of this concept.	• 1 clear plastic spinner or paper clip per student pair • 1 protractor per student pair and 1 for the teacher	• 1 copy of *Centimeter Graph Paper* URG Page 58 per student • 1 copy of *Three-column Data Table* URG Page 59 per student • 1 transparency of *From Number Cubes to Spinners: Class Data Table* URG Page 70 • 1 transparency of *Number Cube Rolls: Class Data Table* URG Page 56 prepared in Lesson 3 • 1 transparency of class data table from Lesson 3 or large poster paper, optional
Lesson 5 **Exploring Spinners** URG Pages 72–87 SG Pages 393–396 DAB Page 233 DPP K–N *Estimated Class Sessions* **2**	**Activity** Students use models of two different spinners to explore probability. **Math Facts** DPP Bit K provides division facts practice. Bit M is a division facts quiz. **Homework** Assign *Questions 19A–G* in the *Student Guide*. **Assessment** 1. Use the *Observational Assessment Record* to note students' abilities to use probabilities to make predictions. 2. Use the *Spinners Quiz* to evaluate students' understanding of probability. 3. DPP Bit M is a quiz on the division facts for the 2s, 5s, 10s, and the square numbers. 4. Transfer appropriate documentation from the Unit 14 *Observational Assessment Record* to students' *Individual Assessment Record Sheets*.	• 1 clear plastic spinner or paper clip per student pair or group	• 1 copy of *Spinners Quiz* URG Page 83 per student • 2 copies of *Centimeter Graph Paper* URG Page 58 per student • 2 transparencies of *Spinners Class Data Table* URG Page 84 or large poster paper, optional • 1 copy of *Individual Assessment Record Sheet* TIG Assessment section per student, previously copied for use throughout the year
Lesson 6 **Make Your Own Spinners** URG Pages 88–95 SG Pages 397–399 DAB Pages 235–236 *Estimated Class Sessions* **1**	OPTIONAL LESSON **Optional Activity** Students create spinners that reflect scientific probabilities. **Homework** Students can continue to collect more data at home to test spinners. Have them spin a given number of spins, record the data in a table, and add it to a class data table on the following day. **Assessment** Use the *Spinners Quiz* Assessment Blackline Master to assess students' concepts of probability.	• 1 clear plastic spinner or paper clip per student pair • 1 ruler per student pair	

	Lesson Information	Supplies	Copies/Transparencies

Lesson 7

Prob_e Quest

URG Pages 96–102
AB Pages 71–90

DPP O–P
HP Part 6

Estimated Class Sessions

1

Adventure Book
Students read a story and solve problems about probability.

Math Facts
DPP Bit O is an assessment of the division facts for the 2s, 5s, 10s, and square numbers.

Homework
1. Students can share the story with family members.
2. Assign Part 6 of the Home Practice.

Assessment
Use DPP Bit O to assess division facts.

Unit 15: Using Patterns . . . .8–13 Sessions

Unit Summary

This unit engages students in identifying and using patterns. Students explore, analyze, and extend patterns in many contexts. They complete the *Plant Growth* lab, which began in Unit 13, and explore the patterns that result in their data tables and graphs. An Adventure Book, *In the Shade of the Old Meranpi Tree,* relates the lab to a scientific investigation of the rain forest. The investigation of patterns continues as students record patterns in data tables as functions. The unit also reviews mass in the *Taste of TIMS* laboratory investigation. In this lab, students study the pattern from a decreasing function where the mass of the sandwich decreases as bites are eaten. The DPP reviews and assesses the division facts for the threes, nines, and the last six facts.

Major Concept Focus

- patterns in data
- functions
- number patterns
- function machines
- length
- best-fit lines
- geometric patterns

- *Adventure Book:* growth patterns
- TIMS Laboratory Method
- interpolation and extrapolation
- mass
- point graphs
- "story of the graph"
- division fact review for the 3s, 9s, and the last six facts

Pacing Suggestions

The laboratory investigations and the *Adventure Book* story in this unit make strong connections to science. Use science time to collect data for these labs.

- Lesson 1 concludes the *Plant Growth* lab begun in Unit 13. Students should begin this lesson after the growth of their plants has leveled off. This is usually about 20 days after the seeds sprout.
- Lesson 2 *In the Shade of the Old Meranpi Tree* is an optional lesson. It is appropriate to read this story as part of science or language arts after completing Lesson 1.
- Lesson 3 *Planet Gzorp* introduces students to a context for investigating numerical patterns. This context is used again in the open-response assessment problem in Unit 16 Lesson 4. Students can complete this assessment in Unit 16 anytime after completing Lesson 3 of this unit.
- Lesson 5 *Taste of TIMS* includes an optional activity *Mass Review* in the *Unit Resource Guide* for those students who have not had previous experiences measuring mass.
- Lesson 6 *Patterns and Problems* is optional. It is a set of word problems that students can complete in class or for homework.

Preparing for Upcoming Lessons

In Lesson 5 *Taste of TIMS,* students will find the mass of sandwiches. Ask students to bring in a sandwich for this lab. Refer to Lesson 5, Before the Lab, for a description of appropriate sandwiches.

Unit Planner

	Lesson Information	Supplies	Copies/Transparencies
Lesson 1 **Plant Growth Conclusion** URG Pages 24–43 SG Pages 402–405 DAB Page 243 DPP A–D HP Parts 1–2 *Estimated Class Sessions* **2**	**Lab** Students use the data they began collecting in Unit 13 Lesson 5 to generate a graph, explore its characteristics, and answer discussion questions. **Math Facts** DPP Task B reminds students to use the *Triangle Flash Cards* to review division facts. **Homework** 1. Assign homework *Questions 1–5* in the *Student Guide*. 2. Assign Parts 1 and 2 of the Home Practice. **Assessment** 1. Use students' completed graphs and the *Observational Assessment Record* to note their abilities to make and interpret point graphs. 2. Score students' responses to *Questions 11, 14,* and *15* using the Telling dimension of the *TIMS Multidimensional Rubric*.	• 1 calculator per student	• 2 copies of *Centimeter Graph Paper* URG Page 35 per student • 1 copy of *Two-Column Data Table* URG Page 36 per student • 1 copy of *Triangle Flash Cards: 3s, 9s,* and *Last Six Facts* URG Pages 37–39 per student, optional • 1 transparency of *Two-column Data Table* URG Page 36 • 1 copy of *TIMS Multidimensional Rubric* TIG, Assessment section • 1 copy of *Observational Assessment Record* URG Pages 11–12 to be used throughout this unit
Lesson 2 **In the Shade of the Old Meranpi Tree** URG Pages 44–52 AB Pages 91–106 *Estimated Class Sessions* **1**	OPTIONAL LESSON **Optional Adventure Book** Dr. Clark and her son travel to Borneo to study the effects of gap cutting on the rain forest. They find a relationship between the area of the gap and its ability to regenerate meranpi trees. **Homework** Have students share the story with their families.	• map or globe, optional	• 1 transparency of *Two-column Data Table* URG Page 36, optional
Lesson 3 **Planet Gzorp** URG Pages 53–72 SG Pages 406–410 DPP E–H HP Parts 3–4 *Estimated Class Sessions* **2**	**Activity** Students describe number patterns in the context of an imaginary planet, Gzorp, where creatures are made of squares. **Math Facts** DPP Bits E and G provide math facts practice. **Homework** 1. Assign the Homework section in the *Student Guide*. 2. Assign Parts 3 and 4 of the Home Practice. **Assessment** 1. Use the *Make Your Own* Assessment Blackline Masters to assess students' abilities to make and extend patterns. Record observations on the *Observational Assessment Record*. 2. Ask students to complete the open-response problem in Unit 16 Lesson 4 to assess students' growth in solving problems and communicating solutions.	• 1 calculator per student pair • 30–35 square-inch tiles per student pair • overhead square-inch tiles, optional	• 1 copy of *Make Your Own* URG Pages 65–66 per student • 2 copies of *Two-column Data Table* URG Page 36 per student • 1 transparency of *Gzorp Rules* URG Page 64 • 1 transparency of *Two-column Data Table* URG Page 36

(Continued)

Overview

	Lesson Information	Supplies	Copies/ Transparencies
Lesson 4 **Function Machines** URG Pages 73–86 SG Pages 411–416 DPP I–L HP Part 6 *Estimated Class Sessions* **2-3**	**Activity** Students are introduced to function machines and play the game *Guess My Rule*. **Math Facts** DPP item J provides practice with patterns. Task L provides practice with math facts and division with multiples of 10. **Homework** 1. Assign the Homework section in the *Function Machines* Activity Pages in the *Student Guide*. 2. Students practice division facts using the *Triangle Flash Cards*. **Assessment** Use Home Practice Part 6 as an assessment.	• 1 calculator per student	• 1 copy of *Centimeter Grid Paper* URG Page 81 per student • 8 copies of *Two-column Data Table* URG Page 36 per student • 1 transparency of *Two-column Data Table* URG Page 36 per student
Lesson 5 **Taste of TIMS** URG Pages 87–105 SG Pages 417–423 DPP M–P HP Part 5 *Estimated Class Sessions* **2-3**	**Lab** Students find the mass of a sandwich. Then they take a bite and find the mass again. Students find the relationship between the mass of the sandwich and the number of bites they take. They plot this decreasing relationship on a graph. **Math Facts** DPP Bits M and O are quizzes on division facts. **Homework** 1. Assign the Homework section on the *Taste of TIMS* Lab Pages. 2. Assign the problems in the *Student Guide* for Lesson 6. 3. Assign Part 5 of the Home Practice. **Assessment** 1. Use the *Observational Assessment Record* to rate students' skills measuring mass. 2. Transfer appropriate documentation from the Unit 15 *Observational Assessment Record* to students' *Individual Assessment Record Sheets*. 3. Score students' responses to **Questions 13, 14,** or **15** in the *Student Guide* using the Telling dimension of the *TIMS Multidimensional Rubric*. 4. DPP Bits M and O quiz students on division facts.	• 1 two-pan balance per student group and 1 for the teacher • 1 set of standard masses per student group and 1 for the teacher • 1 napkin, piece of plastic wrap, or wax paper per student and 1 for the teacher • 1 sandwich per student and 1 for demonstration • 1 calculator per student	• 1 copy of *Mass Review* URG Pages 99–101 per student, optional • 1 copy of *Two-column Data Table* URG Page 36 per student • 2 copies of *Centimeter Graph Paper* URG Page 35 per student • 1 transparency of *Graphing Mistakes: What's Wrong Here?* URG Page 98 • 1 transparency of *Two-column Data Table* URG Page 36, optional • 1 transparency of *Centimeter Graph Paper* URG Page 35, optional • 1 copy of *TIMS Multidimensional Rubric* TIG, Assessment section • 1 copy of *Individual Assessment Record Sheet* TIG Assessment section per student, previously copied for use throughout the year
Lesson 6 **Patterns and Problems** URG Pages 106–111 SG Pages 424–427 *Estimated Class Sessions* **1-2**	OPTIONAL LESSON **Optional Activity** Students solve problems based on concepts learned in the unit. **Homework** Students complete some or all of the problems for homework.	• 1 calculator per student	• 1 copy of *Centimeter Graph Paper* URG Page 35 per student

Unit 16: Assessing Our Learning . . . . .9–11 Sessions

Unit Summary

This unit reviews, extends, and assesses concepts students learned throughout the school year. The activities are similar to those in other assessment units. Students begin by reviewing past laboratory investigations. This prepares them for completing the experiment, *Area vs. Length,* which assesses their abilities to use and apply the TIMS Laboratory Method. An open-response problem, *The Many-Eyed Dragonfly,* is included to see if students can combine many of the skills they have acquired to solve a problem. Students then complete a short item test of concepts and skills taught in previous units. Finally, students review past work in their portfolios and compare it to recently completed work to see growth over time. The DPP includes a test on all the division facts.

Major Concept Focus

- TIMS Laboratory Method
- number patterns
- area
- length
- geometric patterns
- end-of-year test
- Student Rubrics: *Solving, Knowing,* and *Telling*

- patterns in data
- point graphs
- problem solving
- portfolio review
- communicating problem-solving strategies
- division fact test

Pacing Suggestions

This unit includes a variety of review and assessment activities that provide opportunities for teachers to assess individual growth in mathematics. Students continue learning as they apply concepts and skills in new contexts.

Lesson 2 *Problems and Practice* is an optional lesson. It is a set of problems that reviews skills and concepts and helps students prepare for the *End-of-Year Test* in Lesson 5. The problems can be assigned for homework.

Unit Planner

	Lesson Information	Supplies	Copies/Transparencies
Lesson 1 **Experiment Review** URG Pages 23–39 SG Page 430 DAB Pages 251–252 DPP A–B HP Parts 1–2 *Estimated Class Sessions* **1**	**Activity** Students review the labs they worked on during the past year. They recount the various elements of each lab. **Math Facts** DPP Task B provides practice with division facts using the *Triangle Flash Cards.* **Homework** 1. The Journal Prompt may be assigned for homework. 2. Assign Part 2 of the Home Practice. 3. Lesson 2 of this unit, *Problems and Practice,* may be assigned as homework. **Assessment** Use the *Observational Assessment Record* to document students' understanding of the use of variables in experiments.	• 1 student portfolio per student	• 1 copy of *Triangle Flash Cards* URG Pages 32–38 per student, optional • 1 transparency of *Downhill Racer Graph* URG Page 31 • 1 copy of *Observational Assessment Record* URG Pages 9–10 to be used throughout this unit • 1 transparency of *Experiment Review Chart* DAB Pages 251–252 or large sheet of chart paper for class chart
Lesson 2 **Problems and Practice** URG Pages 40–45 SG Pages 431–434 *Estimated Class Sessions* **1**	OPTIONAL LESSON **Optional Activity** Students complete a series of applied problems. You can use these problems to review major concepts before the end-of-year test. **Homework** Assign the *Problems and Practice* Activity Pages.	• 1 calculator per student • pattern blocks • square-inch tiles • base-ten pieces, optional	
Lesson 3 **Area vs. Length** URG Pages 46–63 SG Pages 435–438 DPP C–H HP Parts 7–8 *Estimated Class Sessions* **3**	**Assessment Lab** Students use the TIMS Laboratory Method to investigate the relationship between area and length for rectangles of fixed width. **Math Facts** DPP Bit C provides practice with division facts. **Homework** Students complete Parts 7 and 8 of the Home Practice. **Assessment** 1. Use the *TIMS Multidimensional Rubric* or a point scale to assess students' abilities to implement the steps of the TIMS Laboratory Method. 2. Assess students' letters to Myrna using the Telling dimension of the *TIMS Multidimensional Rubric.* 3. Use the *Observational Assessment Record* to document students' abilities to collect, organize, graph, and analyze data.	• 50 square-inch tiles per student group • 1 ruler per student	• 1 copy of *Three-column Data Table* URG Page 59 per student • 1 copy of *Centimeter Graph Paper* URG Page 60 per student • 1 copy of *TIMS Multidimensional Rubric* TIG, Assessment section • 1 transparency or poster of Student Rubric: *Telling* TIG, Assessment section

	Lesson Information	Supplies	Copies/ Transparencies
Lesson 4 **The Many-Eyed Dragonfly** URG Pages 64–84 DPP I–L HP Parts 3–4 *Estimated Class Sessions* **2**	**Assessment Activity** Students identify and extend patterns to solve an open-response problem and write about their solutions. **Math Facts** DPP Bit I provides practice with math facts. **Homework** Assign Parts 3 and 4 of the Home Practice. **Assessment** Use the Solving, Knowing, and Telling dimensions of the *TIMS Multidimensional Rubric* to assess student work on *The Many-Eyed Dragonfly* Assessment Blackline Masters.	• square-inch tiles • 1 calculator per student	• 1 copy of *The Many-Eyed Dragonfly* URG Pages 77–80 per student • 1 copy of *Two-column Data Table* URG Page 81 per student • 1 transparency or poster of Student Rubrics: *Knowing, Solving,* and *Telling* TIG, Assessment section • 1 copy of *TIMS Multidimensional Rubric* TIG, Assessment section
Lesson 5 **End-of-Year Test** URG Pages 85–94 DPP M–P HP Parts 5–6 *Estimated Class Sessions* **2**	**Assessment Activity** Students complete a short item test on the concepts and skills taught in previous units. **Math Facts** DPP Bit O provides practice computing with multiples of 10 and Task P reviews multiplication and division with zeros and ones. **Homework** 1. Assign Parts 5 and 6 of the Home Practice either in this lesson or in Lesson 6. 2. Students study for the *Division Facts Inventory Test* using *Triangle Flash Cards.*	• 1 calculator per student • 1 ruler per student • pattern blocks • base-ten pieces	• 1 copy of *End-of-Year-Test* URG Pages 90–92 per student
Lesson 6 **Portfolios** URG Pages 95–99 SG Page 439 DPP Q–R *Estimated Class Sessions* **1-2**	**Assessment Activity** Students review the contents of their collection folders and their portfolio folders. Students select pieces to include in their final portfolios. **Math Facts** DPP Task R is an assessment of all the division facts. **Homework** Students share their portfolios with their parents for homework. **Assessment** 1. DPP Task R is the *Division Facts Inventory Test* and assesses fluency with the division facts. Record students' fluency with the division facts on the *Observational Assessment Record.* 2. Transfer appropriate Unit 16 observations to students' *Individual Assessment Record Sheets.*	• 1 portfolio folder from Unit 2 per student • 1 collection folder from Unit 2 per student • two different-colored pencils or a pen and pencil per student	• 1 copy of *Division Facts Inventory Test* URG Page 22 per student • 1 copy of *Individual Assessment Record Sheet* TIG Assessment section per student, previously copied for use throughout the year

Overview

Scope and Sequence
& the NCTM *Principles and Standards*

This section provides descriptions and tables that show how *Math Trailblazers* relates to the National Council of Teachers of Mathematics *Principles and Standards for School Mathematics*. A comprehensive scope and sequence for Grade 4 units and Daily Practice and Problems is included.

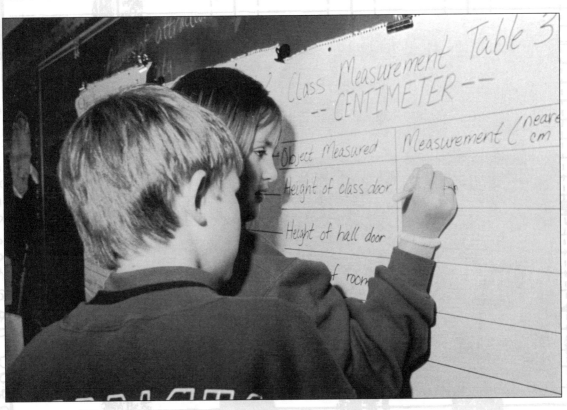

Students share their data by recording it on a class data table.

Math Trailblazers and the Principles and Standards

The National Council of Teachers of Mathematics (NCTM) *Principles and Standards for School Mathematics* and *Math Trailblazers* complement each other: The *Principles and Standards* is a vision of what school mathematics should be. *Math Trailblazers* is the curricular structure so teachers can turn that vision into reality. This section starts with an outline of how *Math Trailblazers* complements the five content and five process standards in the *Principles and Standards.* It concludes with a scope and sequence that specifies how the Grade 4 curriculum develops through the year. For information on the scope and sequence across the grades, see the *Math Trailblazers Scope and Sequence Chart* available from Kendall/Hunt Publishing Company.

Content Standards

Principles and Standards for School Mathematics outlines an articulated vision of how learning and teaching in each of five content areas should develop across the grades. These content areas are number and operations, algebra, geometry, measurement, and data analysis and probability. In *Math Trailblazers* the standards for all five content areas are addressed appropriately at every grade level, from Kindergarten through Grade 5. Five process standards prescribe a curriculum where problem solving, communication, reasoning, connections, and representation are integral, not ancillary, issues. By looking at the Scope and Sequence Chart in this section, one can see how mathematical ideas develop throughout the grade.

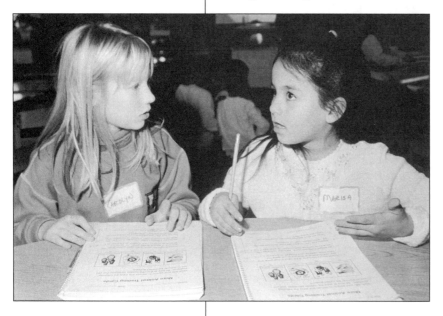

Many activities in *Math Trailblazers* address more than one of the content standards. Consider, for example, *Bouncing Ball,* a fourth-grade laboratory experiment in which students investigate the relationship between the drop height and the bounce height of a tennis ball. The investigation begins with a question: "What is the relationship between how far a tennis ball drops and how high it bounces?" Through class discussion, the variables are identified and named (D, the drop height and B, the bounce height) and experimental procedures are devised. A picture records this information. Next, the students drop the tennis balls repeatedly, measure drop height and bounce height each time, and record the data in a table. As students gather the data, they monitor the measurements for consistency and sense. Then when the data is complete, they examine the data table to see if they can discern a pattern. Next, students graph their data. As they work, they are asked how the data table and the graph relate to the physical system, what the relationship between drop height and bounce height is, and how that relationship is evident in the table and graph. Then students make and verify predictions. Finally, students generalize: "What would the graph look like for a Super ball?" "What would happen if the experiment were repeated on a carpeted floor?"

This single experiment involves measurement, data analysis, number sense, estimation, graphing, multiplication, patterns and functions (algebra), and mathematical reasoning. All these topics, moreover, relate to a single context that unites them. By weaving so many themes into one complex whole, that whole becomes more meaningful and the mathematics more powerful.

Lessons such as *Bouncing Ball* are embedded in a careful sequence of lessons and units that address all the standards. Other lessons develop single skills or concepts that students can then practice in the Daily Practice and Problems. These skills and concepts are extended and applied in more complex lessons and investigations. *Math Trailblazers* is therefore a comprehensive and balanced curriculum that includes geometry, statistics and probability, measurement, algebra, estimation, fractions, numeration, and computation—just what the *Principles and Standards* requires.

For more information on the *Math Trailblazers* approach to selected content areas, see the TIMS Tutors in Section 9 of this *Teacher Implementation Guide.*

Process Standards

The process standards highlight ways to acquire and use content knowledge. Each process standard is connected to the others. Moreover, the learning of mathematical processes is deeply embedded in the learning of content.

Problem Solving. A strong emphasis on problem solving is evident in the NCTM recommendations. Throughout *Math Trailblazers,* students are immersed in complex problem situations in which they both apply the mathematics they know and learn new mathematics. Students develop skills, procedures, and concepts as they work on the problems. For example, in the third-grade laboratory experiment, *The Better "Picker Upper,"* students explore the absorbency of various brands of paper towels by dropping water on each type of towel and comparing the areas of the spots. As students work through this complex problem, they learn about area (by tracing the spots on grid paper and counting square centimeters to find the areas), fractions (as they piece parts of square centimeters together to make whole square centimeters), averaging (as they aggregate the results of several trials), graphing (as they display and interpret their data in graphs), and computation (as they calculate the number of drops of water a whole paper towel absorbs). All this mathematics grows out of one problem: "Which is the more absorbent towel?"

Putting problems first is a different and difficult way to organize a mathematics curriculum. Having the focus on problems requires careful design, meticulous planning, and continual assessment to ensure the timely development of skills and concepts. Despite the difficulties, the benefits are clear: students not only master skills and concepts, they can apply them flexibly to solve problems.

Reasoning and Proof. This standard requires that reasoning permeate the curriculum. Students constantly explain their thinking and justify their solutions, first in small groups and then to the class as a whole. Sometimes they explain their thoughts orally and other times in writing or by using pictures and other tools. Students are always encouraged to find solutions in more than one way and to compare and contrast various solution methods. Thus, meaning and understanding are emphasized, and students find that mathematics makes sense.

"Mathematical reasoning develops in classrooms where students are encouraged to put forth their own ideas for examination. Teachers and students should be open to questions, reactions, and elaborations from others in the classroom. Students need to explain and justify their thinking and learn how to detect fallacies and critique others' thinking. They need to have ample opportunity to apply their reasoning skills and justify their thinking in mathematical discussion." (NCTM 2000, p. 188)

One example of an important area of mathematical reasoning that receives particular attention in *Math Trailblazers,* especially in Grades 3 through 5, is pre-proportional and proportional reasoning. This kind of reasoning is carefully developed over time through a sequence of real-life problems that students can solve with manipulatives, patterns, graphs, or symbols. Students choose the strategies and tools that make sense to them. Using these tools helps students create visual images of this important mathematical concept, which historically has largely been taught symbolically or procedurally and has been difficult for many students to grasp.

Communication. Students need frequent opportunities to communicate their mathematics. "Communication is an essential part of mathematics and mathematics education… Students gain insight into their thinking when they present their methods for solving problems, when they justify their reasoning to a classmate or teacher, or when they formulate a question about something that is puzzling to them." (NCTM 2000, p. 60) Communication is integral to *Math Trailblazers.* In many activities, students handle manipulatives, draw pictures, make graphs, and grapple with mathematical ideas. Many activities are collaborative exercises involving groups of students who work together to obtain, analyze, and generalize their results.

Just as people explain how they solve problems on the job, students who use the labs and activities talk about their mathematics. Students discuss, compare, contrast, and write about their problem-solving methods in both small-group and whole-class settings. This "publication" of students' mathematical thinking gives students access to a broader range of solution strategies and helps them become more reflective about mathematics.

Connections. This standard calls for connections within mathematics, between mathematics and other parts of the school curriculum, and between mathematics and their own interests. Integration of subject matter is a major focus of *Math Trailblazers.* Mathematics arises naturally in science, language, history, and daily life. *Math Trailblazers* does not artificially merge disparate ideas from distinct disciplines, but rather builds up the underlying unity between disciplines that we see in the real world. For example, the basic measurement variables that the curriculum covers extensively —length, area, volume, mass, and time—are fundamental not only to mathematics but also to science and daily life. The TIMS Laboratory Method effectively incorporates the method of science into the mathematics curriculum as a problem-solving tool.

The *Adventure Books* and Literature Connections integrate language arts and social studies with the mathematics curriculum. Some *Adventure Books* recount the history of science and mathematics; others show how the concepts and procedures students are learning apply to the work of real scientists or to everyday life. Students are continually required to communicate their mathematical thinking orally and in writing. *Math Trailblazers* is committed to the ideal of "writing across the curriculum."

Connections within mathematics are equally important. Like most real-world problems, activities in *Math Trailblazers* generally involve a combination of mathematical topics. A single laboratory experiment, for example, might involve arithmetic, data collection, estimation, geometry, probability, and algebraic concepts—each covered at an appropriate level for students.

Representation. "Representing ideas and connecting their representations to mathematics lies at the heart of understanding mathematics." (NCTM 2000, p. 136) *Math Trailblazers* is rich in the many opportunities it gives students to represent mathematical ideas. For example, whole numbers are represented as collections of objects (using manipulatives or drawings), as measurements, as points on a number line, or as items on a *100 Chart.* When children collect data they may organize it in a data table or represent it graphically. If there are patterns in the data, they can describe them numerically or graphically. Ultimately, they describe some relations symbolically.

Throughout *Math Trailblazers* students are encouraged to draw pictures and diagrams to illustrate their ideas and support their thinking. This communicates their reasoning, and as students create these representations, they clarify and build their thinking.

Developing a *Standards*-Based Classroom

The *Professional Standards for Teaching Mathematics* (NCTM, 1991) and the Teaching Principle in the *Principles and Standards* specify what classroom teachers, supervisors, teacher educators, and policy makers should do to improve mathematics instruction. Much of this discussion concerns four key areas: tasks, discourse, environment, and analysis. Teachers decide what tasks to set for students, foster discourse about mathematics, establish a classroom environment conducive to high achievement and positive attitudes, and engage in analysis of students' thinking and their own teaching. While accomplishing these things depends more on teachers' expertise than on curricula, materials that embody the *Principles and Standards* can make the work easier.

Tasks. *Math Trailblazers* provides a logical sequence of well-conceived tasks. Professional mathematicians and scientists helped develop the curriculum so lessons focus on significant concepts and skills. Teachers and mathematics educators also helped write the curriculum, so tasks are engaging, practical, and developmentally appropriate. Lessons develop both skills and concepts, so they make connections within mathematics and between mathematics and other subjects, portray mathematics as a human endeavor, and promote communication and problem solving.

Discourse. Many features of *Math Trailblazers* support discourse. Tasks in the curriculum have enough depth for significant discussion to be possible. An emphasis on multiple solutions to problems encourages students to talk about their own thinking. The *Student Guide* often displays and discusses multiple solutions to problems. Journal and discussion prompts in the teacher materials stimulate and focus classroom discussions. *Adventure Books* and children's literature help students understand that people really do talk about mathematics and science. The wide range of tools and technology in *Math Trailblazers*—manipulatives, calculators, pictures, tables, graphs, and symbols—enhance discourse by broadening the means of communication beyond what is traditional.

Environment. Creating a classroom environment conducive to the development of each student's mathematical power is necessary for the *Principles and Standards* to come alive. This involves arranging space, time, and materials in ways that maximize student learning. *Math Trailblazers'* diverse range of lessons—activities of varied length, activities for groups and individuals, hands-on and paper-and-pencil investigations, and activities that encourage multiple solution paths—all help teachers develop a classroom that builds mathematical understandings and skills for a wide range of students.

Analysis. The curriculum's activities and assessment program provide teachers with many opportunities to analyze students' learning. Teachers using the curriculum will know more about their students' mathematical abilities than they ever have before. The extensive background information in the unit guides and in the *Teacher Implementation Guide* provides accessible ways for teachers to gain additional insight into how students learn mathematics. This enhanced knowledge motivates the teaching of subsequent lessons. *Math Trailblazers* will help you become more attuned both to your students and to your teaching.

For additional discussion on these and related topics, see the following sections in the *Teacher Implemention Guide:*

- Building the *Math Trailblazers* Classroom
- Teaching the *Math Trailblazers* Student: Meeting Individual Needs
- Language in the *Math Trailblazers* Classroom
- Working with *Math Trailblazers* Parents and Families

Math Trailblazers:
A Standards-Based Curriculum

In summary, NCTM calls for curricula to be coherent within and across the grades, to be conceptually oriented, to involve students actively, to emphasize development of students' mathematical thinking and reasoning abilities, to emphasize applications, to include a broad range of content, and to make appropriate use of calculators and computers.

These are admirable goals and high expectations. No curriculum can finally and fully attain such goals and fulfill such expectations—not only will there always be improvements to be made, but in the end much depends upon individual teachers and students. Yet a curriculum that has been developed specifically to be aligned with the *Principles and Standards* will provide the foundation. The goals and characteristics described above are all hallmarks of *Math Trailblazers*.

The best test of alignment with the *Principles and Standards,* however, is to observe students using the curriculum. Are they actively involved? Do they grapple with significant concepts while learning and applying basic skills? Are they thinking and reasoning? Do they use a broad range of tools to solve realistic problems? We think you will find that *Math Trailblazers* more than meets this test.

References

An Agenda for Action: Recommendations for School Mathematics of the 1980s. National Council of Teachers of Mathematics, Reston, VA, 1980.

Assessment Standards for School Mathematics. National Council of Teachers of Mathematics, Reston, VA, 1995.

Curriculum and Evaluation Standards for School Mathematics. National Council of Teachers of Mathematics, Reston, VA, 1989.

Essential Mathematics for the 21st Century: The Position of the National Council of Supervisors of Mathematics. National Council of Supervisors of Mathematics, Minneapolis, MN, 1988.

National Research Council. "Conclusions and Recommendations." In *Adding It Up: Helping Children Learn Mathematics.* J. Kilpatrick, J. Swafford, and B. Findell (Eds.). National Academy Press, Washington, DC, 2001.

Principles and Standards for School Mathematics. National Council of Teachers of Mathematics, Reston, VA, 2000.

Professional Standards for Teaching Mathematics. National Council of Teachers of Mathematics, Reston, VA, 1991.

Scope and Sequence

Scope and Sequence for Units

Math Trailblazers was developed to meet the NCTM *Principles and Standards for School Mathematics*. The scope and sequence on white on the following pages indicates how each unit aligns with the *Principles and Standards*. By reading the chart horizontally, you will see the integration of the various standards within a given unit. By reading the chart vertically, you can track the development of a specific standard throughout the fourth-grade curriculum.

Scope and Sequence for the Daily Practice and Problems

Every unit includes a series of Daily Practice and Problems (DPP). The scope and sequence chart on gray on the following pages indicates how the DPP aligns with the *Principles and Standards*. By reading the chart vertically, you can track the development of a specific standard throughout the fourth-grade DPP. Each DPP item, which is denoted by a letter, has been correlated with one or more of the standards. The appropriate letters are indicated in parentheses following each entry. Thus the scope and sequence can also serve as a content map for the DPP.

For more information about the Daily Practice and Problems, see the Daily Practice and Problems Guide (Section 7).

	Number and Operations	Algebra	Geometry	Measurement	Data Analysis and Probability
Unit 1: **Data** **About Us** **Lessons**	• Choosing appropriate methods and tools to calculate (calculators, pencil and paper, or mental math). • Choosing to find an estimate or an exact answer. • Estimating quantities.	• Using numerical variables. • Using categorical variables. • Naming values of variables. • Translating between graphs and real-world events. • Making and interpreting bar graphs. • Making and interpreting point graphs. • Using patterns in tables and graphs to make predictions.		• Measuring length in inches.	• Collecting, organizing, graphing, and analyzing data. • Naming values of variables. • Identifying categorical and numerical variables. • Translating between graphs and real-world events. • Making and interpreting bar graphs. • Using patterns in tables and graphs to make predictions. • Investigating the concept of averages. • Averaging: finding the median. • Making and interpreting point graphs.
Daily Practice and Problems (Lettered) **& Home Practice** (Numbered)	• Maintaining fluency with addition and subtraction facts. (A, B, C, D, E, K, M) (1) • Developing mental math skills. (B, D) (1) • Telling time using an analog clock. (G, I, O) • Solving problems involving time. (I, O) (6) • Solving problems involving addition and subtraction. (L, N, P) (6) • Solving problems involving money. (N) • Solving problems using manipulatives. (P) • Choosing appropriate methods and tools to calculate (calculators, pencil and paper, or mental math). (P)	• Collecting, organizing, graphing, and analyzing data. (4) • Using numerical variables. (J) (2) • Using categorical variables. (J) (2) • Naming values of variables. (J) (2) • Translating between graphs and real-world events. (Q, T) • Making and interpreting bar graphs. (Q, T)	• Using geometric concepts and skills to solve problems. (F, H)	• Telling time using an analog clock. (G, I, O) • Solving problems involving time. (I, O) (6) • Measuring length in inches. (R, V) (4, 5) • Measuring length in centimeters. (R, V) (5) • Translating between metric and English measurements. (R) (5) • Estimating length. (S, V) (4) • Choosing appropriate units of measure. (V)	• Collecting, organizing, graphing, and analyzing data. (4) • Naming values of variables. (J) (2) • Using numerical variables. (J) (2) • Using categorical variables. (J) (2) • Translating between graphs and real-world events. (Q, T) • Making and interpreting bar graphs. (Q, T) • Averaging: finding the median. (U) (3)

Problem Solving	Reasoning and Proof	Communication	Connections	Representation
• Promoting these beliefs: Problems can be solved by more than one method and different methods should yield solutions that agree. • Solving multistep word problems. • Choosing appropriate methods and tools (calculators, pencil and paper, or mental math) to calculate. • Choosing to find an estimate or an exact answer.	• Using patterns in tables and graphs to make predictions.	• Communicating solutions verbally and in writing.	• Connecting mathematics and science to real-world situations: surveying classmates and investigating the relationship between arm span and height. • Translating between graphs and real-world events. • Connecting mathematics and language arts: reading a story that uses mathematics.	• Collecting, organizing, graphing, and analyzing data. • Translating between graphs and real-world events. • Making and interpreting bar graphs. • Using numerical variables. • Using categorical variables. • Making and interpreting point graphs.
• Using geometric concepts and skills to solve problems. (F, H) • Solving multistep word problems. (L, N, P) (6) • Solving problems involving addition and subtraction. (L, N, P) (6) • Using data to solve problems. (Q, T) • Choosing appropriate methods and tools (calculators, pencil and paper, or mental math) to calculate. (P) • Using logical reasoning to solve puzzles. (A, C, E) • Solving problems involving time. (I, O) (6)	• Evaluating the reasonableness of a conjecture. (S) • Using logical reasoning to solve puzzles. (A, C, E)	• Communicating solutions verbally and in writing. (L, P, Q, S) (1, 3, 5, 6) • Developing, writing, and explaining word problems. (6)	• Connecting mathematics and science to real-world situations. (L, Q) (6) • Making connections between English and metric measurements. (R) (5)	• Representing length in both metric and English units. (R) (5) • Collecting, organizing, graphing, and analyzing data. (4) • Translating between graphs and real-world events. (Q, T) • Making and interpreting bar graphs. (Q, T) • Translating between different representations of numbers (concrete, pictorial, and symbolic). (P) • Using numerical variables. (J) (2) • Using categorical variables. (J) (2) • Naming values of variables. (J) (2)

Scope and Sequence

	Number and Operations	Algebra	Geometry	Measurement	Data Analysis and Probability
Unit 2: Geometric Investigations: A Baseline Assessment Unit **Lessons**		• Using numerical variables. • Investigating how a change in one variable leads to a change in another variable. • Using patterns in data tables and graphs to make and test conjectures. • Making and interpreting point graphs.	• Investigating the relationship between length and perimeter. • Finding the area of a polygon. • Finding the perimeter of a polygon. • Estimating angle measures using benchmarks. • Identifying acute, obtuse, and right angles. • Making and testing conjectures about geometric properties. • Using geometric concepts and skills to solve problems.	• Estimating angle measures using benchmarks. • Measuring length in inches. • Finding the perimeter of a polygon. • Finding the area of a polygon. • Identifying acute, obtuse, and right angles.	• Collecting, organizing, graphing, and analyzing data. • Using patterns in data tables and graphs to make and test conjectures. • Making and interpreting point graphs.
Daily Practice and Problems (Lettered) **& Home Practice** (Numbered)	• Maintaining fluency with addition and subtraction facts. (H, I, M, O, S, AA) (1, 4) • Adding and subtracting whole numbers with paper and pencil. (F, G, N, P) (6) • Using effective strategies to add and subtract whole numbers. (G, K, U, AA) (4) • Using effective strategies to multiply and divide whole numbers. (R) • Solving problems involving time. (A, B, E, W, Y, Z) (5, 6) • Solving problems involving addition, subtraction, multiplication, and division. (CC) (6) • Developing number sense. (C, D, H, I, K, N, P, R, T, V, X, AA, CC) • Developing mental math skills. (G, I, K, AA, CC) (1, 4) • Solving problems involving money. (R, U) (6) • Choosing when to estimate and when to find exact answer. (V)	• Translating between graphs and real-world events. (2) • Making and interpreting a bar graph. (2) • Using numerical and categorical variables. (2)	• Using geometric concepts and skills to solve problems. (J, L, Y, Z, BB, DD) (3, 5) • Investigating the relationship between area and perimeter. (J, L, BB) (3) • Finding the area of a polygon. (J) (3) • Finding the perimeter of a polygon. (J) (3) • Using manipulatives to solve geometric problems. (J, BB) • Drawing shapes with determined measure. (J, L, BB) (3) • Estimating angle measures using benchmarks. (Z) (5) • Identifying acute, obtuse, and right angles. (Y, DD) (5)	• Translating between English and metric units. (C) • Measuring in both English and metric units. (C) • Estimating measure in both English and metric units. (D) • Estimating angle measure using benchmarks. (Z) • Identifying acute, obtuse, and right angles. (Y, DD) (5) • Solving problems involving time. (A, B, E, W, Y, Z) (5, 6)	• Using data to estimate. (T) • Making and interpreting bar graphs. (2) • Using numerical and categorical variables. (2)

Problem Solving	Reasoning and Proof	Communication	Connections	Representation
• Using geometric concepts and skills to solve problems. • Using area and perimeter to solve problems.	• Making and testing conjectures about geometric properties. • Developing mathematical arguments to support a statement. • Using patterns in tables and graphs to make and test conjectures. • Communicating solution strategies.	• Using portfolios. • Communicating solution strategies verbally and in writing. • Using the student Rubric: *Telling* as a guide for writing solutions.		• Collecting, organizing, graphing, and analyzing data. • Using numerical variables. • Drawing angles and shapes with determined measures. • Representing angles using angle wheels. • Making and interpreting point graphs.
• Using geometric concepts and skills to solve problems. (J, L, Y, Z, BB, DD) (3, 5) • Solving problems involving time. (A, B, E, W, Y, Z) (5, 6) • Solving problems involving money. (R, U) (6) • Using pictures, tables, graphs, or other representations to solve a problem. (X) (2) • Solving multistep word problems. (X, CC) (6)	• Evaluating the reasonableness of a conjecture. (D) • Using geometric reasoning to draw shapes with determined measures. (J, L)	• Identifying and describing 2-dimensional shapes. (DD) • Communicating estimation strategies. (V) • Communicating solution strategies. (I, R, U, AA) • Communicating solutions with drawings. (BB)		• Translating between English and metric units. (C) • Translating between graphs and real-world events. (2) • Using pictures, tables, graphs, or other representations to solve problems. (X) (2) • Using numerical and categorical variables. (2)

	Number and Operations	Algebra	Geometry	Measurement	Data Analysis and Probability
Unit 3: Numbers and Number Operations **Lessons**	• Maintaining fluency with the multiplication facts for the 5s and 10s. • Developing strategies for the division facts for the 5s and 10s. • Writing the four number sentences in the fact families for the 5s and 10s. • Naming the value of a digit based upon its place in a number. • Developing number sense for larger numbers. • Representing 2-, 3-, and 4-digit numbers using base-ten pieces. • Understanding place value: ones, tens, hundreds, and thousands. • Representing addition and subtraction with base-ten pieces. • Adding and subtracting multidigit numbers using paper and pencil. • Estimating sums and differences. • Multiplying by 0 and 1. • Choosing to find an estimate or an exact answer. • Exploring negative and positive numbers. • Solving problems involving addition and subtraction. • Choosing appropriate methods and tools to calculate (calculator, paper and pencil, or mental math).	• Using patterns to solve problems.			
Daily Practice and Problems (Lettered) **& Home Practice** (Numbered)	• Maintaining fluency with the addition and subtraction facts. (D) • Maintaining fluency with the multiplication facts for the 5s and 10s. (B, C, F, H, K, L, M) (1, 4, 5) • Skip counting by 5s and 10s. (B, E, H, K) • Developing strategies for the division facts: fact families. (C, F, L) (4, 5) • Solving problems involving addition, subtraction, multiplication, and division. (D, G, I) (3) • Solving problems involving time. (E, K) • Solving problems involving money. (B, D) (3) • Adding and subtracting whole numbers using paper and pencil. (D, G, I) (2, 7) • Developing number sense. (F, G, H, I, J, K) • Developing mental math skills. (D, J) (7) • Choosing to find an estimate or an exact answer. (H) • Representing addition and subtraction with base-ten pieces. (7)	• Identifying acute, obtuse, and right angles. (A) (6) • Drawing shapes with determined measure. (6) • Estimating angles using benchmarks. (6) • Finding the area of polygons by counting square units. (N) • Finding the perimeter of polygons by counting square units. (N)	• Developing a sense of the passage of time. (K)	• Solving problems involving time. (E, K)	

Problem Solving	Reasoning and Proof	Communication	Connections	Representation
• Solving multistep word problems. • Solving problems involving addition and subtraction. • Choosing appropriate methods and tools to calculate (calculator, paper and pencil, or mental math). • Determining the reasonableness of a solution. • Choosing to find an estimate or an exact answer.		• Communicating solutions verbally and in writing.	• Connecting mathematics and history: Roman Numerals.	• Representing 2-, 3-, and 4-digit numbers using base-ten pieces. • Representing addition and subtraction with base-ten pieces. • Translating between different representations of numbers (concrete, pictorial, and symbolic). • Representing positive and negative numbers on a number line.
• Solving problems involving time. (E, K) • Solving problems involving money. (B, D) (3) • Solving multistep word problems. (3) • Solving problems involving addition, subtraction, multiplication, and division. (D, G, I) (3) • Choosing to find an estimate or an exact answer. (H)		• Communicating solutions verbally and in writing. (H) (3, 7) • Communicating strategies. (J) • Creating a story and a drawing for a number sentence. (F)		• Translating between different representations of numbers (concrete, pictorial, and symbolic). (7) • Creating a story and a drawing for a number sentence. (F)

Scope and Sequence

	Number and Operations	Algebra	Geometry	Measurement	Data Analysis and Probability
Unit 4: Products and Factors **Lessons**	• Choosing appropriate methods and tools to calculate (calculators, pencil and paper, or mental math). • Solving problems involving multiplication and division. • Representing multiplication and division problems using arrays. • Determining whether one number is a multiple of another. • Using exponents. • Identifying prime, composite, and square numbers. • Solving problems involving multiples, factors, primes, and squares. • Finding all the factors of numbers. • Using factor trees to find the prime factorization of a number. • Identifying and describing number patterns. • Using patterns to build number sense. • Practicing multiplication facts.	• Using turn-around facts (commutativity) to multiply. • Using exponents.	• Using arrays to identify prime numbers and square numbers.		
Daily Practice and Problems (Lettered) **& Home Practice** (Numbered)	• Maintaining fluency with the multiplication facts for the 2s and 3s. (A, C, E, F, G, S) (1) • Developing strategies for the division facts for the 2s and 3s. (E, G) • Multiplying with multiples of 10. (C) • Solving problems involving unknowns. (D) • Developing number sense. (B, J, K, N, O, R, T) • Understanding place value. (O) • Finding factors and multiples of a number. (K, M) (2) • Identifying prime and composite numbers. (2) • Using exponents. (2) • Identifying, describing, and extending number patterns. (B) • Maintaining fluency with math facts. (B) • Developing mental math skills. (C) • Adding, subtracting, multiplying, and dividing using paper and pencil. (P) (3) • Estimating sums, differences, products, and quotients. (P) • Solving problems involving addition, subtraction, multiplication, and division. (F, I, J, L, N) (3) • Solving problems involving time. (I, Q, T) • Solving problems involving money. (J, N) (3) • Averaging: finding the median. (T)	• Solving problems with unknowns. (D) • Finding factors and multiples of a number. (K, M) (2) • Identifying variables. (T) • Using exponents. (2)	• Finding area by counting square units. (H, L)	• Converting between units of measurement. (H) • Finding area by counting square units. (H, L) • Measuring the passage of time. (T)	• Averaging: finding the median. (T) • Identifying variables. (T)

Problem Solving	Reasoning and Proof	Communication	Connections	Representation
• Solving problems involving multiplication and division. • Solving multistep word problems. • Choosing appropriate methods and tools to solve problems (calculators, paper and pencil, mental math). • Solving problems involving multiples, factors, primes, and squares.	• Using mathematical definitions. • Analyzing fair and unfair games. • Explaining mathematical reasoning using definitions of multiples, factors, and primes.	• Using the *Telling* Rubric to self-assess communication skills. • Using mathematical definitions. • Communicating solutions verbally and in writing.		• Representing multiplication and division using arrays. • Representing prime and square numbers using arrays. • Using exponents.
• Solving problems involving addition, subtraction, multiplication, and division. (F, I, J, L, N) (3) • Solving multistep word problems. (F, J, N, R) (3) • Solving problems involving time. (I, Q, T) • Solving problems involving money. (J, N) (3)	• Identifying, describing, and extending number patterns. (B) • Using factors and multiples to solve problems. (K, M)	• Identifying, describing, and extending number patterns. (B) • Communicating solutions and solution strategies verbally and in writing. (P)		• Using exponents. (2)

Scope and Sequence

	Number and Operations	Algebra	Geometry	Measurement	Data Analysis and Probability
Unit 5: Using Data to Predict **Lessons**	• Choosing appropriate methods and tools to calculate (calculator, pencil and paper, or mental math).	• Using numerical variables. • Identifying the manipulated, responding, and fixed variables in an experiment. • Making and interpreting point graphs. • Using interpolation and extrapolation to estimate and predict from a data set. • Using patterns in data to make predictions and solve problems. • Drawing and interpreting best-fit lines. • Translating between graphs and real-world events. • Investigating how a change in one variable relates to a change in a second variable.		• Measuring length in centimeters.	• Collecting, organizing, graphing, and analyzing data. • Identifying the manipulated, responding, and fixed variables in an experiment. • Making and interpreting point graphs. • Using interpolation and extrapolation to estimate and predict from a data set. • Using patterns in data to make predictions and solve problems. • Drawing and interpreting best-fit lines. • Translating between graphs and real-world events. • Investigating the concept of averages. • Averaging: finding the median and the mean. • Comparing the median and the mean.
Daily Practice and Problems (Lettered) **& Home Practice** (Numbered)	• Maintaining fluency with the multiplication facts for the square numbers. (A, G, H, I, L, N, P, T, U) (1) • Developing strategies for the division facts for the square numbers. (I, L, N, T) • Developing number sense. (B, C, D, E, H, M, P, Q, R, T, V) (3) • Developing fluency for the multiplication and division facts. (A, B, G, H, I, J, L, N, P, T) • Modeling numbers using base-ten shorthand. (C) • Understanding place value. (C, V) • Adding and subtracting whole numbers using calculators, paper and pencil, and mental math. (D, V) (4) • Developing mental math skills. (4) • Understanding other number systems: Roman Numerals. (2) • Skip counting by 2s and 3s. (2) • Solving problems involving multiplication and division. (F, J, R) • Finding the prime factorization of a number. (E) (3) • Solving problems involving time. (F) • Solving problems with unknowns. (D, N, T) (4) • Using exponents. (G) • Averaging: finding the median and the mean. (M, Q, R) (6) • Choosing appropriate methods and tools to calculate (calculator, pencil and paper, mental math). (R) (4)	• Solving problems with unknowns. (D, N, T) (4) • Identifying the manipulated, responding, and fixed variables. (O, S) (6) • Naming the value of a variable. (O, S) (6) • Using exponents. (G) • Identifying numerical and categorical variables. (O, S) (5, 6) • Using patterns in data to make predictions and solve problems. (5) • Drawing and interpreting best-fit lines. (5) • Deciding whether to draw a point graph or a bar graph. (6)	• Identifying and drawing right, acute, and obtuse angles. (K) • Calculating area of a rectangle. (L) • Calculating perimeter of a rectangle. (L)	• Identifying and drawing right, acute, and obtuse angles. (K) • Telling time. (2)	• Identifying the manipulated, responding, and fixed variables. (O, S) (6) • Identifying numerical and categorical variables. (O, S) (5, 6) • Averaging: finding the median and the mean. (M, Q, R) (6) • Naming the value of a variable. (O, S) (6) • Using patterns in data to make predictions and solve problems. (5) • Drawing and interpreting best-fit lines. (5) • Deciding whether to draw a point graph or a bar graph. (6)

Problem Solving	Reasoning and Proof	Communication	Connections	Representation
• Solving multistep word problems. • Choosing appropriate methods and tools (calculators, pencil and paper, or mental math) to calculate. • Using the Student Rubrics: *Solving* and *Telling* to self-assess problem-solving skills. • Solving open-response problems. • Using patterns in data to make predictions and solve problems. • Comparing the mean and the median.	• Choosing whether to use the median or the mean. • Using patterns in data to make predictions and solve problems. • Using interpolation and extrapolation to estimate and predict from a data set. • Investigating how a change in one variable relates to a change in a second variable. • Communicating solution strategies.	• Communicating solutions verbally and in writing. • Using the Student Rubrics: *Solving* and *Telling* to self-assess communication skills.	• Connecting mathematics to real-world situations: interpreting graphs of sports records over time. • Connecting mathematics and science to real-world situations: exploring the bounce height of balls. • Translating between graphs and real-world events.	• Collecting, organizing, graphing, and analyzing data. • Translating between graphs and real-world events. • Using numerical variables. • Making and interpreting point graphs. • Choosing an appropriate graph to display data. • Drawing and interpreting best-fit lines.
• Solving problems involving multiplication. (F, J, R) • Solving problems involving time. (F) • Solving problems with unknowns. (D, N, T) (4) • Using geometric concepts to solve problems. (L) • Solving problems involving money. (J) • Solving multistep problems. (O, S) • Choosing appropriate methods and tools to calculate (calculator, pencil and paper, or mental math). (R) (4)	• Using place value to solve problems. (V)	• Communicating solution strategies verbally and in writing. (B, H, P, V)	• Making connections between mathematics and real-world situations: prices. (J)	• Translating between different representations of a number (concrete, pictorial, and symbolic). (C) • Using exponents. (G)

Scope and Sequence

	Number and Operations	Algebra	Geometry	Measurement	Data Analysis and Probability
Unit 6: Place Value Patterns **Lessons**	• Exploring large numbers: doubles and powers of ten. • Using exponents. • Reading and writing large numbers (millions). • Comparing and ordering large numbers (millions). • Representing large numbers (to the millions) using place value charts, number lines, and base-ten pieces. • Developing number sense for large numbers (to the millions). • Rounding large numbers. • Choosing convenient numbers. • Translating between different representations of large numbers (concrete, pictorial, and symbolic). • Understanding place value (to the millions). • Estimating sums and differences of large numbers. • Using 10% as a standard for error analysis.	• Using exponents. • Identifying, extending, and making generalizations about number patterns. • Using patterns in data tables and graphs to make predictions and solve problems. • Making and interpreting point graphs (curves).			• Making and interpreting point graphs (curves). • Using patterns in data tables and graphs to make predictions and solve problems.
Daily Practice and Problems (Lettered) **& Home Practice** (Numbered)	• Maintaining fluency with the multiplication facts for the nines. (A, C, G, J, K, M, O) (1) • Developing strategies for the division facts for the nines. (G, K, M) • Practicing multiplication facts. (2) • Reading and writing large numbers. (D) (5) • Comparing and ordering large numbers. (B, P) (5) • Adding, subtracting, multiplying, and dividing whole numbers using pencil and paper. (B) (3, 4) • Estimating sums and differences. (3, 4) • Rounding large numbers. (7) • Developing number sense. (B, D, E, F, H, I, L, N, P) (5, 7) • Understanding place value. (7) • Representing large numbers on the number line. (7) • Developing mental math skills. (G, M) (6) • Averaging: finding the median and the mean. (E) • Skip counting by 3s and 9s using the calculator. (H) • Solving problems involving money. (I) • Solving problems involving addition, subtraction, multiplication, and division. (I) • Exploring large numbers: doubles and powers of ten. (F) • Using exponents. (F, N) • Solving problems involving time. (H)	• Using exponents. (F, N) • Solving problems with unknowns. (2)		• Estimating distance in feet. (P) • Solving problems involving time. (H)	• Averaging: finding the median and the mean. (E) • Interpreting a data table. (4)

Problem Solving	Reasoning and Proof	Communication	Connections	Representation
• Using the *Knowing* rubric to self-assess problem-solving skills. • Choosing to find an estimate or an exact answer. • Using patterns in data tables and graphs to make predictions and solve problems.	• Identifying, extending, and making generalizations about number patterns. • Using patterns in data tables and graphs to make predictions and solve problems.	• Communicating solutions verbally and in writing. • Identifying and describing number patterns.	• Connecting mathematics to real-world situations: comparing large numbers used in news stories. • Connecting mathematics and social studies: interpreting data about national parks.	• Translating between different representations of large numbers (concrete, pictorial, and symbolic). • Representing large numbers (to the millions) using place value charts, number lines, and base-ten pieces. • Using exponents. • Reading and writing large numbers (to the millions). • Making and interpreting point graphs (curves).
• Solving problems involving money. (I) • Solving problems involving time. (H) • Solving multistep word problems. (I, L, N) • Using logical reasoning to solve word problems. (L, N, P) • Solving problems with unknowns. (2)	• Communicating in writing an explanation of multiplication strategies. (J, N) • Using logical reasoning to solve word problems. (L, N, P) • Using mathematical definitions. (L)	• Communicating solutions and strategies verbally and in writing. (J, N)	• Connecting mathematics to social science: analyzing census data. (4)	• Representing large numbers on a number line. (7) • Using exponents. (F, N)

SCOPE & SEQUENCE CHART

	Number and Operations	Algebra	Geometry	Measurement	Data Analysis and Probability
Unit 7: Patterns in Multiplication **Lessons**	• Using order of operations. • Identifying and describing number patterns. • Exploring the inverse relationship of multiplication and division. • Choosing appropriate methods and tools to calculate (calculator, mental math, and pencil and paper). • Using factors and multiples to solve problems. • Understanding place value. • Using divisibility rules. • Multiplying numbers with ending zeros. • Developing mental math skills. • Developing number sense. • Representing multiplication with base-ten pieces. • Understanding multiplication as repeated addition. • Multiplying numbers (1-digit x 2-digit) using paper and pencil. • Estimating sums, differences, and products. • Using convenient numbers to round and estimate. • Solving problems involving multiplication.	• Using order of operations. • Using unknowns in number sentences. • Identifying and describing number patterns.			
Daily Practice and Problems (Lettered) **& Home Practice** (Numbered)	• Developing strategies for the division facts: the last six facts. (B) • Maintaining fluency with the multiplication facts: the last six facts. (A, B, E, F, G, J, M, N, O, Y, AA) (1) • Skip counting. (C) • Using order of operations. (G, H, R) (2) • Solving problems involving time. (C) • Using number patterns to solve problems. (E, M, O, Q) • Understanding place value. (D, O, Q) • Estimating to check the reasonableness of an answer. (V, Z, CC) • Developing number sense. (D, F, H, I, K, L, N, O, P, Q, S, T, U, V, W, X, CC, DD) (2, 5) • Multiplying and dividing numbers with ending zeros. (O, Q, Y) (5, 7) • Using divisibility rules. (I, P) (3) • Rounding large numbers. (T, W) • Using benchmarks on a number line. (T) • Comparing and ordering large numbers. (T) • Representing large numbers on a number line. (T) • Using convenient numbers to estimate. (W) (6) • Choosing appropriate tools and methods to calculate (paper and pencil, mental math, or calculators). (G, S, V, W, Y, Z, CC) (2, 3, 6, 7) • Developing mental math skills. (G, O, S, V, W, Y, Z, CC) (3, 6, 7) • Adding, subtracting, multiplying, and dividing using pencil and paper. (G, S, V, Z, CC) (2, 3, 6, 7) • Using 10% as a standard of error analysis. (L, DD) • Solving problems involving money. (R, X) • Averaging: finding the median and the mean. (K, U) • Solving problems using negative numbers. (X) • Solving problems with unknowns. (5)	• Averaging: finding the median and the mean. (K, U) • Solving problems using negative numbers. (X) • Solving problems with unknowns. (5)	• Using geometric figures to model multiplication and division. (F, N) • Using geometric definitions and concepts to solve problems. (BB, DD) • Finding area and perimeter. (BB)	• Estimating length in centimeters. (L) • Measuring length in centimeters. (L) • Finding area and perimeter. (BB) • Solving problems involving time. (C)	• Averaging: finding the median and the mean. (K, U)

Problem Solving	Reasoning and Proof	Communication	Connections	Representation
• Solving multistep word problems. • Choosing appropriate methods and tools to calculate (calculator, mental math, and pencil and paper). • Choosing to find an estimate or an exact answer. • Using the calculator efficiently in problem solving. • Using factors and multiples to solve problems. • Solving problems involving money. • Solving problems involving time. • Solving problems involving multiplication. • Solving open-response problems.	• Exploring the inverse relationship of multiplication and division. • Communicating solution strategies.	• Identifying and describing number patterns. • Writing number sentences. • Communicating solutions verbally and in writing.		• Writing number sentences. • Translating between different representations of numbers (concrete, pictorial, and symbolic). • Representing multiplication using base-ten pieces. • Using unknowns in number sentences.
• Solving problems involving time. (C) • Using mathematical reasoning to solve problems. (D, H, P) (2) • Using geometric definitions and concepts to solve problems. (BB, DD) • Solving multistep word problems. (P, R, W) (7) • Solving problems involving money. (R, X) • Solving problems with unknowns. (5)	• Using mathematical reasoning to solve problems. (D, H, P) (2) • Using number patterns to solve problems. (E, M, O, Q)	• Using geometric definitions and concepts to solve problems. (BB, DD) • Communicating solutions verbally and in writing. (E, L, M, Q, R, S, Z, CC, DD) (3) • Creating a story and a drawing for a number sentence. (J)		• Translating between different representations of numbers (concrete, pictorial, and symbolic). (F, N) • Using geometric figures to model multiplication and division. (F, N) • Representing large numbers on a number line. (T) • Creating a story and a drawing for a number sentence. (J)

	Number and Operations	Algebra	Geometry	Measurement	Data Analysis and Probability
Unit 8: Measuring Up: An Assessment Unit **Lessons**	• Practicing the multiplication facts. • Choosing appropriate methods and tools to calculate (calculators, pencil and paper, or mental math). • Solving problems involving addition, subtraction, multiplication, or division. • Using order of operations. • Developing strategies for the division facts for the 5s and 10s. • Writing the four related number sentences in a fact family.	• Using numerical variables. • Making and interpreting point graphs. • Using patterns in data to make predictions and solve problems. • Drawing and interpreting best-fit lines. • Using extrapolation and interpolation to estimate and predict. • Using order of operations. • Translating between graphs and real-world events. • Comparing and contrasting elements of different laboratory investigations: problems solved, types of graphs, and variables.	• Estimating volume by building centimeter cube models.	• Measuring volume by displacement. • Estimating volume by building centimeter cube models. • Dealing with precision and accuracy. • Reporting a volume measure using a number and a unit.	• Collecting, organizing, graphing, and analyzing data. • Using numerical variables. • Making and interpreting point graphs. • Using patterns in data to make predictions and solve problems. • Drawing and interpreting best-fit lines. • Translating between graphs and real-world events. • Comparing and contrasting elements of different laboratory investigations: problems solved, types of graphs, and variables. • Identifying the manipulated, responding, and fixed variables in an experiment.
Daily Practice and Problems (Lettered) **& Home Practice** (Numbered)	• Maintaining fluency with the multiplication facts. (A, E, I, M, S, U, V) (1) • Developing strategies for the division facts. (E, G, M, Q, S, V) • Developing number sense. (A, B, C, D, F, G, I, J, O, S, T, V) (2) • Identifying prime numbers, factors, and prime factors. (2) • Maintaining fluency with the addition and subtraction facts. (P, T) • Comparing and ordering large numbers. (O) (5) • Estimating to check the reasonableness of an answer. (B, N) (4) • Using convenient numbers to estimate. (I, O) (3, 4, 5) • Developing mental math skills. (I, O) (3) • Representing large numbers using base-ten shorthand. (5) • Solving problems involving addition, subtraction, multiplication, and division. (B, F, H, I, K, O, Q, T) • Adding, subtracting, multiplying, and dividing using paper and pencil. (B, N) (3, 4) • Choosing appropriate tools and methods to calculate (paper and pencil, mental math, or calculators). (O, R) (3, 5) • Using order of operations. (F) • Averaging: finding the median and the mean. (C, D) • Solving problems with unknowns. (E, V) • Solving problems involving time. (P, R) • Solving problems involving money. (Q, R) (3, 4) • Solving problems using negative numbers. (T)	• Solving problems with unknowns. (E, V) • Solving problems using negative numbers. (T)	• Finding area and perimeter of a rectangle. (H) • Using geometric concepts to solve problems. (H) • Using geometric figures to model multiplication and division facts. (S) • Estimating volume. (J, L)	• Estimating volume. (J, L) • Measuring volume in cubic centimeters. (J, K, L) • Translating between metric units: milliliters and cubic centimeters. (K) • Solving problems involving passage of time. (P, R) • Measuring change in temperature using negative numbers. (T)	• Averaging: finding the median and the mean. (C, D) • Interpreting census data. (O)

Problem Solving	Reasoning and Proof	Communication	Connections	Representation
• Solving multistep word problems. • Solving open-response problems. • Choosing appropriate methods and tools (calculators, pencil and paper, or mental math) to calculate. • Using the *Knowing, Solving,* and *Telling* Rubrics to self-assess problem-solving skills. • Using patterns in data to make predictions and to solve problems. • Solving problems involving multiplication and division.	• Using extrapolation and interpolation to estimate and predict. • Communicating solution strategies. • Using patterns in data to make predictions and solve problems.	• Communicating solutions verbally and in writing. • Using the *Telling* Rubric to self-assess problem-solving skills. • Using portfolios.	• Connecting mathematics and real-world situations: interpreting statistical data. • Comparing and contrasting elements of different laboratory investigations: problems solved, types of graphs, and variables. • Connecting mathematics and science: measuring volume by displacement.	• Translating between words, pictures, tables, and graphs to express mathematical concepts. • Translating between graphs and real-world events. • Using numerical variables. • Drawing and interpreting best-fit lines. • Collecting, organizing, graphing, and analyzing data. • Making and interpreting point graphs.
• Using mathematical definitions and concepts to solve problems. (D) • Using patterns in data to make predictions and solve problems. (D) • Using logical reasoning to solve problems. (F, P) • Using geometric concepts to solve problems. (H) • Solving problems involving time. (P, R) • Solving problems involving money. (Q, R) (3, 4) • Solving multistep word problems. (C, D, H, K, P, R) (3, 4)	• Using mathematical definitions and concepts to solve problems. (D) • Using logical reasoning to solve problems. (F, P) • Using geometric concepts to solve problems. (H)	• Communicating solutions verbally and in writing. (D, G, J, L, Q)	• Connecting mathematics, science, and social studies: estimating annual rainfall in Borneo. (D) • Connecting mathematics, science, and social studies: interpreting census data. (O) • Connecting mathematics and science: measuring temperature change. (T)	• Representing large numbers using base-ten shorthand. (5) • Translating between different representations of large numbers (concrete, pictorial, and symbolic). (5)

	Number and Operations	Algebra	Geometry	Measurement	Data Analysis and Probability
Unit 9: Shapes and Solids **Lessons**			• Identifying acute, obtuse, and right angles. • Identifying and describing parallel, perpendicular, and intersecting lines. • Identifying and using symbolic notation for lines, line segments, rays, points, angles, and polygons. • Identifying and describing line and rotational symmetry. • Measuring angles with a protractor. • Finding the volumes of prisms. • Drawing rectangular solids. • Identifying and describing 3-dimensional shapes using their properties. • Translating between a rectangular prism and its net. • Using geometric definitions and concepts to solve problems.	• Measuring angles with a protractor. • Measuring area in square centimeters. • Measuring the volumes of prisms. • Measuring length (height) in centimeters.	
Daily Practice and Problems (Lettered) **& Home Practice** (Numbered)	• Developing fluency with the division facts for the 5s and 10s. (B, C, K, M, R, U) (1) • Maintaining fluency with the multiplication facts for the 5s and 10s. (B, K, M, O, R) • Estimating sums, differences, products, and quotients. (D, S) (3) • Using convenient numbers to estimate. (3) • Adding, subtracting, multiplying, and dividing whole numbers using paper and pencil. (D, S) (3) • Multiplying numbers with ending zeros. (O) (2) • Solving problems involving addition, subtraction, multiplication, and division. (E, M) • Solving problems involving money. (F) (2) • Solving problems involving time. (T) (4) • Developing number sense. (D, F, G, O, V) (2, 3) • Developing mental math skills. (G, S, V) (2, 3) • Solving problems with unknowns. (K)	• Solving problems with unknowns. (K) • Using symbolic notation to denote lines, line segments, and angles. (N) (5)	• Identifying acute, obtuse, and right angles. (A, I, J) • Estimating angle size using benchmarks. (J) • Identifying and naming polygons. (I) • Identifying parallel, perpendicular, and intersecting lines. (N) • Using symbolic notation to denote lines, line segments, and angles. (N) (5) • Measuring angles using a protractor. (5) • Identifying line and rotational symmetry. (P) • Identifying geometric shapes. (P) • Measuring volume by displacement. (Q) • Finding volume by counting cubic centimeters. (5) • Estimating volume. (5)	• Identifying acute, obtuse, and right angles. (A, I, J) • Estimating angle size using benchmarks. (J) • Measuring volume by displacement. (Q) • Measuring the volume using cubic centimeters. (Q) • Interpreting a time schedule. (T) • Measuring the passage of time. (4) • Converting between units of time. (4)	

Problem Solving	Reasoning and Proof	Communication	Connections	Representation
• Using geometric definitions and concepts to solve problems.	• Using geometric definitions and concepts to solve problems. • Translating between a rectangular prism and its net.	• Communicating solutions verbally and in writing.		• Translating between a rectangular prism and its net. • Using symbolic notation to denote lines, line segments, rays, points, angles, and polygons. • Drawing rectangular solids.
• Solving multistep word problems. (E, Q, V) (4) • Solving problems involving addition, subtraction, multiplication, and division. (E, M) • Solving problems involving money. (F) (2) • Solving problems involving time. (T) (4) • Using logical reasoning to solve problems. (H, L) • Solving problems with unknowns. (K)	• Using logical reasoning to solve problems. (H, L)	• Communicating solutions verbally and in writing. (D, N)		• Writing number sentences. (3)

	Number and Operations	Algebra	Geometry	Measurement	Data Analysis and Probability
Unit 10: Using Decimals **Lessons**	• Representing decimals using base-ten pieces, number charts, and number lines. • Developing number sense for decimals to the hundredths. • Reading and writing decimals to the hundredths. • Understanding place value: decimals. • Translating between different representations of decimals (concrete, pictorial, verbal, and symbolic). • Comparing and ordering decimals. • Using fractions and decimals to represent the same quantity. • Averaging: finding the mean. • Counting by tenths and hundredths.	• Using numerical variables. • Identifying manipulated, responding, and fixed variables. • Using interpolation and extrapolation to estimate and predict. • Translating between graphs and real-world events. • Using patterns in data to make predictions and solve problems. • Making and interpreting point graphs. • Drawing and interpreting best-fit lines. • Investigating how a change in one variable relates to a change in a second variable.		• Measuring length in meters, decimeters, centimeters, and millimeters. • Choosing an appropriate unit of measure. • Converting between millimeters, centimeters, decimeters, and meters. • Dealing with precision and accuracy.	• Collecting, organizing, graphing, and analyzing data. • Identifying the manipulated, responding, and fixed variables in an experiment. • Using interpolation and extrapolation to estimate and predict. • Translating between graphs and real-world events. • Using patterns in data to make predictions and solve problems. • Making and interpreting point graphs. • Drawing and interpreting best-fit lines. • Averaging: finding the median.
Daily Practice and Problems (Lettered) **& Home Practice** (Numbered)	• Developing fluency with the division facts for the 2s and 3s. (B, C, G, K, Q, W, X) (1) • Developing number sense for metric measure. (I, T, V) (3) • Dividing numbers when there is a remainder. (K, X) • Understanding place value. (I) • Developing mental math skills. (M) (5) • Skip-counting by tenths, quarters, and hundredths. (O, P) • Developing number sense for decimals. (O, P, R, S) (3) • Comparing and ordering decimals. (R, S, U) (3) • Comparing and ordering large numbers. (2) • Maintaining fluency with the multiplication facts. (C, D, G, M, Q) (2) • Adding, subtracting, multiplying, and dividing whole numbers using paper and pencil. (H) (5) • Estimating to check the reasonableness of an answer. (H) • Using convenient numbers to estimate. (2, 4) • Rounding large numbers. (2) • Representing large numbers using base-ten shorthand. (D) • Representing decimals using base-ten shorthand. (R, U) (3) • Choosing to find an estimate or an exact number. (E) • Solving problems involving money. (4, 6) • Solving problems involving addition, subtraction, multiplication, and division. (6)	• Solving problems with an unknown. (2)	• Using geometric concepts to solve problems. (J, L) • Using lines of symmetry to complete a diagram. (J) • Drawing polygons according to specifications. (L) • Measuring angles. (L)	• Choosing appropriate units of measure. (A, E) • Developing number sense for metric measure. (A, F, I, T, V) (3) • Converting between units of measure: millimeters, centimeters, and meters. (F, T, V) (3) • Measuring length in centimeters to the nearest tenth. (I) • Measuring angles. (L) • Converting between units of time. (N)	

Problem Solving	Reasoning and Proof	Communication	Connections	Representation
• Solving problems involving decimals. • Using the *Knowing* rubric to self-assess problem-solving skills. • Using patterns in data to make predictions and solve problems.	• Analyzing a graph, identifying errors, and writing a critique. • Using interpolation and extrapolation to estimate and predict. • Using patterns in data to make predictions and solve problems.	• Communicating solutions verbally and in writing. • Analyzing a graph, identifying errors, and writing a critique.	• Connecting mathematics and science: investigating the height of a ramp and the distance a car rolls.	• Translating between different representations of decimals: concrete, pictorial, verbal, and symbolic. • Translating between graphs and real-world events. • Using numerical variables. • Making and interpreting point graphs. • Drawing and interpreting best-fit lines. • Representing decimals using base-ten pieces, number charts, and number lines. • Using fractions and decimals to represent the same quantity. • Collecting, organizing, graphing, and analyzing data.
• Using geometric concepts and definitions to solve problems. (J, L) • Solving multistep word problems. (4, 6) • Solving problems involving money. (4, 6)	• Using geometric concepts and definitions to solve problems. (J, L)	• Communicating solution strategies verbally and in writing. (S, T) (4) • Describing a math fact with a written story and a picture. (X)		• Representing large numbers using base-ten shorthand. (D) • Representing decimals using base-ten shorthand. (R, U) (3) • Translating between units of metric measure: millimeters, centimeters, and meters. (F, T, V) (3) • Translating between units of time. (N)

	Number and Operations	Algebra	Geometry	Measurement	Data Analysis and Probability
Unit 11: **Multiplication** **Lessons**	• Estimating products. • Representing multiplication with base-ten pieces. • Multiplying multidigit (1-digit x 4-digit and 2-digit x 2-digit) numbers using paper and pencil. • Solving problems involving multiplication. • Developing mental math skills. • Multiplying and dividing numbers with ending zeros. • Translating between different representations of multiplication (concrete, pictorial, and symbolic).	• Using unknowns in multiplication sentences.			
Daily Practice and Problems (Lettered) **& Home Practice** (Numbered)	• Developing fluency with the division facts for the square numbers. (A, E, G, I, T, U) (1) • Maintaining fluency with the multiplication facts. (C, E, G, I, Q, T) (3) • Developing number sense for decimals. (D, M) • Developing number sense for fractions. (H, N) • Developing number sense for large numbers. (K) (2, 4) • Comparing and ordering decimals. (D) • Comparing and ordering large numbers. (K) • Translating between different representations of numbers (concrete, pictorial, and symbolic). (D, H, L, N, O) • Representing fractions with geometric shapes. (H) • Modeling multiplication of whole numbers using base-ten shorthand. (L, O) • Estimating products, sums, and differences. (B, P, V) (5, 6, 7) • Estimating volume. (J) • Understanding place value. (K, M, O) • Developing mental math skills. (B, C, D, P) (3, 5, 6) • Adding, subtracting, and multiplying whole numbers using pencil and paper. (B, P, V) (5, 6, 7, 11) • Multiplying and dividing numbers with ending zeros. (C, E, O, Q) (3, 6, 7) • Using rules of divisibility to solve problems. (T) (10, 11) • Solving problems with unknowns. (E) • Solving problems involving multiplication. (S) • Solving problems involving money. (9)	• Solving problems with unknowns. (E)	• Using geometric definitions. (F) • Drawing a shape with specified properties. (F) • Representing fractions with geometric shapes. (H) • Finding the volume of a cylinder. (J, S)	• Measuring length in centimeters. (J, M) • Translating between different units of metric measurement. (M, S) • Choosing appropriate units of metric measurement. (8)	

Problem Solving	Reasoning and Proof	Communication	Connections	Representation
• Solving multistep word problems. • Solving problems involving multiplication.	• Communicating estimation strategies verbally and in writing.	• Communicating estimation strategies verbally and in writing.	• Connecting mathematics and social studies: counting and multiplication in ancient Egypt.	• Translating between different representations of multiplication (concrete, pictorial, and symbolic). • Representing multiplication with base-ten pieces. • Using unknowns in multiplication sentences.
• Using mathematical definitions to solve problems. (F) • Solving problems involving multiplication. (S) • Solving problems in more than one way. (L, V) • Using logical reasoning to solve problems. (R) (9) • Using divisibility rules to solve problems. (T) (10, 11)	• Drawing a shape with specified properties. (F) • Using place value to solve problems. (K) • Using logical reasoning to solve problems. (R) (9) • Using rules of divisibility to solve problems. (T) (10, 11)	• Describing patterns in numbers. (C) • Representing fractions of a set using pictures. (N) • Communicating estimation strategies verbally and in writing. (P) (5, 6) • Communicating solutions verbally and in writing. (9, 10)	• Connecting mathematics and social studies: counting and multiplication in ancient Egypt. (V)	• Translating between different representations of numbers (concrete, pictorial, and symbolic). (D, H, L, N, O) • Representing fractions with geometric shapes. (H) • Modeling multiplication of whole numbers using base-ten shorthand. (L, O)

Scope and Sequence

	Number and Operations	Algebra	Geometry	Measurement	Data Analysis and Probability
Unit 12: Exploring Fractions **Lessons**	• Defining numerator and denominator. • Identifying the unit whole when a fractional part is given. • Finding a fraction for a given quantity when a unit whole is given. • Representing fractions with paper folding and pattern blocks. • Adding and subtracting fractions with like denominators using manipulatives, pictures, or symbols. • Developing number sense for fractions. • Comparing and ordering fractions using fraction charts and benchmarks 0, $\frac{1}{2}$, and 1. • Finding equivalent fractions. • Writing number sentences using fractions. • Solving problems involving fractions using manipulatives.	• Identifying and describing number patterns.			
Daily Practice and Problems (Lettered) **& Home Practice** (Numbered)	• Developing fluency with the division facts for the nines. (B, C, G, K, L, M, P, W) (1) • Maintaining fluency with the multiplication facts. (L, M) (2) • Developing number sense. (E, H, I, J, O, Q, R, S, T, U, V) (2) • Identifying prime and composite numbers. (H) • Finding the prime factorization of a number. (H) • Developing number sense for decimals and fractions. (E, I, Q, R, T) (3, 4, 5) • Identifying and extending a decimal pattern. (E) • Comparing and ordering fractions. (Q) (3) • Finding equivalent fractions. (3) • Solving problems involving time. (A, F) • Solving problems involving money. (F, V) (6) • Adding, subtracting, multiplying, and dividing using paper and pencil. (D, J, L) (6) • Solving problems using addition, subtraction, multiplication, and division. (F, V) • Developing mental math skills. (D, L) (2, 6) • Using order of operations. (2) • Performing operations using 0 and 1. (2) • Estimating products and quotients. (D) (6) • Rounding numbers in more than one way. (J) • Solving problems with unknowns. (G, K) • Translating between different representations of decimals and fractions (concrete, pictorial, and symbolic). (I, Q, R, S, T) (4) • Using divisibility rules to solve problems. (O, U)	• Identifying and extending a decimal pattern. (E) • Solving problems with unknowns. (G, K)	• Drawing shapes with specific areas. (N) • Measuring perimeter. (N) • Using geometric concepts and definitions to solve problems. (X)	• Measuring the passage of time. (A, F) • Measuring perimeter in centimeters. (N) • Measuring length in centimeters. (X) • Comparing metric measures. (5)	

Problem Solving	Reasoning and Proof	Communication	Connections	Representation
• Solving problems involving fractions using manipulatives. • Solving multistep word problems. • Solving open-response problems. • Using the *Solving* and *Telling* Rubrics to self-assess problem-solving skills.	• Communicating solutions with manipulatives.	• Identifying and describing number patterns. • Communicating solutions verbally and in writing. • Communicating solutions with manipulatives. • Using the *Solving* and *Telling* Rubrics to self-assess communication skills.		• Translating between different representations of fractions: concrete, pictorial, and symbolic. • Writing number sentences using fractions. • Representing fractions with paper folding and pattern blocks.
• Solving problems involving time. (A, F) • Solving problems involving money. (F, V) (6) • Solving problems using addition, subtraction, multiplication, and division. (F, V) • Solving multistep word problems. (F, O, Q, R, V) (6) • Solving problems with unknowns. (G, K) • Using divisibility rules to solve problems. (O, U) • Solving problems in more than one way. (V)	• Using divisibility rules to solve problems. (O, U) • Explaining mathematical reasoning. (Q, R, T, U)	• Communicating solutions verbally and in writing. (D, F, O) (6) • Creating a story and a drawing for a number sentence. (P) • Translating between different representations of decimals and fractions (concrete, pictorial, and symbolic). (I, Q, R, S, T) (4) • Explaining mathematical reasoning. (Q, R, T, U)	• Connecting mathematics and language arts: creating a story to illustrate a number sentence. (P)	• Translating between different representations of decimals and fractions (concrete, pictorial, and symbolic). (I, Q, R, S, T) (4) • Creating a story and a drawing for a number sentence. (P) • Using a diagram to explain a mathematical concept. (Q, R, T)

	Number and Operations	Algebra	Geometry	Measurement	Data Analysis and Probability
Unit 13: Division **Lessons**	• Representing division with base-ten pieces. • Dividing with 1-digit divisors using paper and pencil. • Interpreting remainders. • Solving problems using addition, subtraction, multiplication, and division. • Developing mental math skills. • Estimating products and quotients. • Averaging: finding the mean. • Choosing appropriate methods and tools (calculators, pencil and paper, or mental math) to calculate. • Understanding place value. • Multiplying and dividing with 0. • Choosing to find an estimate or an exact answer. • Solving problems involving money. • Solving problems involving time. • Using division symbols ($\div$ and $\overline{)}\ $).	• Identifying manipulated, responding, and fixed variables. • Using numerical variables. • Making and interpreting bar graphs. • Translating between graphs and real-world events.		• Converting between different measures of time. • Measuring length in centimeters.	• Averaging: finding the mean. • Collecting, organizing, graphing, and analyzing data. • Binning data. • Identifying manipulated, responding, and fixed variables. • Using numerical variables. • Planning and conducting a survey. • Making and interpreting bar graphs. • Translating between graphs and real-world events.
Daily Practice and Problems (Lettered) **& Home Practice** (Numbered)	• Developing fluency with the division facts for the last six facts. (B, D, H, K, Q, S) (1) • Maintaining fluency with the multiplication facts. (C, D, H) • Adding, subtracting, multiplying, and dividing using paper and pencil. (A, M, P, Q, R) (3, 4) • Solving problems involving addition, subtraction, multiplication, and division. (J, M, N, P) (2, 7) • Using divisibility rules to solve problems. (R, V) (2) • Estimating products and quotients. (A) (3, 4) • Developing number sense for fractions and decimals. (E, F, W, Y) (5) • Comparing and ordering fractions. (Y) (5) • Adding and subtracting fractions. (W) • Developing mental math skills. (A, M) (3, 4) • Modeling division using connecting cubes and base-ten pieces. (J, N) • Interpreting remainders. (J, P, R, T) (2) • Skip counting. (G) • Multiplying and dividing with zero. (U) • Multiplying and dividing numbers with ending zeros. (H) • Solving problems involving time. (E, F, M) (7) • Solving problems involving money. (T, X) (6) • Averaging: finding the median and the mean. (I)		• Finding a fraction when the unit whole is given. (L)	• Converting between different measures of time. (E, F) (7)	• Averaging: finding the median and the mean. (I) • Using data to solve problems. (O)

Problem Solving	Reasoning and Proof	Communication	Connections	Representation
• Choosing to find an estimate or an exact answer. • Choosing appropriate methods and tools (calculators, pencil and paper, or mental math) to calculate. • Solving multistep word problems. • Solving problems involving money. • Solving problems involving time. • Solving problems using addition, subtraction, multiplication, and division.	• Interpreting remainders. • Using fact families to justify responses to division problems involving zero.	• Communicating solutions verbally and in writing. • Writing a story to illustrate a division sentence.	• Connecting mathematics and science to real-world situations: measuring plant growth. • Connecting mathematics and social studies: using statistics about time spent watching TV.	• Representing division with base-ten pieces. • Translating between graphs and real-world events. • Making and interpreting bar graphs. • Using numerical variables. • Collecting, organizing, graphing, and analyzing data. • Using division symbols ($\div$ and $\overline{)\ }$).
• Using divisibility rules to solve problems. (R, V) (2) • Solving problems involving addition, subtraction, multiplication, and division. (J, M, N, P) (2, 7) • Solving problems involving time. (E, F, M) (7) • Solving problems involving money. (T, X) (6) • Solving multistep word problems. (E, F, M, V, Z) (2, 6, 7) • Solving problems in more than one way. (J, P)	• Using mathematical reasoning to develop solutions to new problems. (E, Z) (6) • Using fact families to justify responses to division problems involving zero. (U) • Using divisibility rules to solve problems. (R, V) (2)	• Communicating solutions verbally and in writing. (A) (3) • Writing a story to illustrate a division problem. (P)		• Translating between different representations of numbers (concrete, pictorial, and symbolic). (L)

	Number and Operations	Algebra	Geometry	Measurement	Data Analysis and Probability
Unit 14: Chancy Predictions: An Introduction to Probability **Lessons**	• Representing probabilities on a number line. • Expressing probabilities as fractions. • Finding the probability of an event.	• Making and interpreting bar graphs. • Translating between graphs and real-world events. • Identifying the manipulated and responding variables in an experiment.	• Dividing circles into equal parts by measuring angles with a protractor. • Using geometric concepts and skills to solve problems.	• Dividing circles into equal parts by measuring angles with a protractor.	• Defining probability. • Finding the probability of an event. • Expressing probabilities as fractions. • Collecting, organizing, graphing, and analyzing data from a random process. • Making and interpreting bar graphs. • Representing probabilities on a number line. • Describing events as certain, likely, not likely, equally likely, or impossible. • Exploring probabilities involved in number cubes and spinners. • Using probabilities to make predictions. • Translating between graphs and real-world events. • Identifying patterns that emerge as the number of random events increases.
Daily Practice and Problems (Lettered) **& Home Practice** (Numbered)	• Developing fluency with the division facts for the 2s, 5s, 10s, and square numbers. (B, C, G, K, M, O) (1) • Developing number sense. (A, C, F, H) (5) • Comparing and ordering decimals and large numbers. (H) (5) • Maintaining fluency with the multiplication facts. (A, G) • Using divisibility rules to solve problems. (A) • Developing mental math skills. (D, E, F, G, J, L) (2, 3) • Multiplying and dividing numbers with ending zeros. (G) (5) • Adding, subtracting, multiplying, and dividing using paper and pencil. (D, L) (2, 3, 5, 6) • Expressing probabilities as fractions. (N, P) • Estimating sums and differences, products and quotients. (D, F, L) (3) • Solving word problems involving multiplication and division. (E) (2, 6) • Choosing appropriate methods and tools to calculate: calculators, mental math, or pencil and paper. (E) (2, 6) • Solving problems involving money. (E, F) (2) • Solving problems involving time. (H) (6) • Averaging: finding the median and the mean. (H) • Representing probabilities on a number line. (P) (4)	• Using patterns in data to solve problems. (H) • Identifying and describing number patterns. (K) (5)	• Using geometric concepts and definitions to solve problems. (I) • Identifying parallel and perpendicular lines. (I)	• Solving problems involving time. (H) (6)	• Using patterns in data to solve problems. (H) • Finding the probability of an event. (N, P) • Expressing probabilities as fractions. (N, P) • Representing probabilities on a number line. (P) (4)

Problem Solving	Reasoning and Proof	Communication	Connections	Representation
• Solving multistep word problems. • Choosing appropriate methods and tools to calculate (calculator, pencil and paper, or mental math). • Using geometric concepts and skills to solve problems.	• Using probabilities to make predictions. • Making and testing conjectures about probable outcomes. • Analyzing fair and unfair chance situations. • Using the word "or" to combine probabilities.	• Communicating solutions verbally and in writing. • Choosing an appropriate graph to display data. • Expressing probabilities as fractions. • Describing events as likely, not likely, equally likely, or impossible.	• Connecting mathematics to real-world situations: games of chance. • Comparing probabilities to real-world data: rolling one number cube and spinning spinners.	• Collecting, organizing, graphing, and analyzing data. • Translating between different representations of probability (concrete, pictorial, and symbolic). • Making and interpreting bar graphs. • Translating between graphs and real-world events. • Expressing probabilities as fractions. • Representing probabilities on a number line.
• Finding the probability of an event. (N, P) • Solving multistep word problems. (E, H) (2, 6) • Solving problems involving money. (E, F) (2) • Solving problems involving time. (H) (6) • Using divisibility rules to solve problems. (A)	• Using the word "or" to combine probabilities. (P) • Using divisibility rules to solve problems. (A)	• Communicating solutions verbally and in writing. (D, F, J, L) (2, 3) • Identifying and describing number patterns. (K) (5) • Expressing probabilities as fractions. (N, P)	• Connecting mathematics and real-world events: games of chance. (N, P)	• Representing probabilities on a number line. (P) (4) • Expressing probabilities as fractions. (N, P)

	Number and Operations	Algebra	Geometry	Measurement	Data Analysis and Probability
Unit 15: Using Patterns **Lessons**	• Identifying, extending, and making generalizations about number patterns. • Using number and geometric patterns to make predictions and solve problems. • Relating number patterns and geometric patterns. • Averaging: finding the mean. • Investigating and using square roots.	• Identifying manipulated, responding, and fixed variables. • Investigating and using square roots. • Making and interpreting point graphs. • Translating between tables, graphs, and real-world events. • Identifying, extending, and making generalizations about number and geometric patterns. • Representing patterns and functions as input-output tables, words, symbols, and graphs. • Expressing mathematical relationships using variables. • Drawing and interpreting best-fit lines. • Using patterns in data to make predictions and solve problems. • Using numerical variables. • Investigating how a change in one variable relates to a change in a second variable. • Identifying and describing situations with varying rates of change.	• Identifying, extending, and making generalizations about geometric patterns. • Relating number patterns and geometric patterns.	• Measuring mass in grams. • Measuring length in centimeters. • Dealing with precision and accuracy. • Solving problems involving mass.	• Identifying manipulated, responding, and fixed variables. • Collecting, organizing, graphing, and analyzing data. • Making and interpreting point graphs. • Translating between tables, graphs, and real-world events. • Drawing and interpreting best-fit lines. • Using patterns in data to make predictions and solve problems. • Averaging: finding the mean.
Daily Practice and Problems (Lettered) **& Home Practice** (Numbered)	• Developing fluency with the division facts for the 3s, 9s, and the last six facts. (B, E, G, L, M, O) (1, 2) • Maintaining fluency with the multiplication facts. (E, G, L) (2) • Expressing probabilities as fractions. (A) • Finding a fraction for a given quantity when the unit whole is given. (A) • Solving problems involving time. (C) (4) • Estimating products and quotients. (D, H) • Adding, subtracting, multiplying, and dividing using pencil and paper. (D, H) (3) • Solving problems involving addition, subtraction, multiplication, and division. (5) • Choosing appropriate methods and tools to solve problems (pencil and paper, mental math, and calculators). (5) • Multiplying and dividing numbers with ending zeros. (E, L) • Developing number sense. (A, F, H, I, J, L, N) • Developing mental math skills. (D, E, H, L) (3) • Identifying common factors. (E) • Averaging: finding the median and the mean. (K) • Solving problems with unknowns. (L) • Solving problems involving money. (5)	• Identifying and extending a geometric pattern. (I) • Representing functions as input-output tables. (J, N) (6) • Using order of operations. (J) • Solving problems with unknowns. (L) • Using numerical variables. (J) (6) • Identifying, extending, and making generalizations about number patterns. (J, N) (6)	• Identifying angle measures on a clock face. (C) • Identifying and extending a geometric pattern. (I) • Drawing angles of determined measure. (P)	• Drawing angles of determined measure. (P) • Solving problems involving time. (C) (4)	• Finding the probability of an event. (A) • Expressing probabilities as fractions. (A) • Averaging: finding the median and the mean. (K)

Problem Solving	Reasoning and Proof	Communication	Connections	Representation
• Solving multistep word problems. • Using patterns to make predictions and solve problems. • Solving problems involving mass.	• Identifying, extending, and making generalizations about number and geometric patterns. • Using patterns to make predictions and solve problems.	• Communicating data analysis verbally and in writing. • Communicating solutions verbally and in writing. • Describing situations with varying rates of change.	• Connecting mathematics and science: measuring mass in grams. • Connecting mathematics and science: measuring plant growth. • Connecting geometric and number patterns.	• Translating between tables, graphs, and real-world events. • Representing patterns and functions using input-output tables, words, symbols, and graphs. • Expressing mathematical relationships using variables. • Using numerical variables. • Making and interpreting point graphs. • Drawing and interpreting best-fit lines. • Collecting, organizing, graphing, and analyzing data.
• Solving problems involving time. (C) (4) • Solving multistep word problems. (5) • Choosing appropriate methods and tools to solve problems (pencil and paper, mental math, and calculators). (5) • Choosing to find an estimate or an exact answer. (5) • Solving problems involving addition, subtraction, multiplication, and division. (5) • Solving problems involving money. (5)	• Using mathematical reasoning to solve problems. (F) • Identifying, extending, and making generalizations about number patterns. (J, N) (6)	• Expressing probabilities as fractions. (A) • Communicating solutions verbally and in writing. (D) (3)		• Using numerical variables. (J) (6) • Representing functions as input-output tables. (J, N) (6)

	Number and Operations	Algebra	Geometry	Measurement	Data Analysis and Probability
Unit 16: Assessing Our Learning **Lessons**	• Solving problems involving addition, subtraction, multiplication, and division. • Estimating sums, differences, products, and quotients. • Choosing appropriate methods and tools to calculate (calculators, pencil and paper, or mental math). • Choosing to find an estimate or an exact answer. • Identifying, extending, and making generalizations about number patterns.	• Identifying, extending, and making generalizations about geometric and number patterns. • Using patterns in tables and graphs to make predictions and solve problems. • Using numerical variables. • Identifying manipulated, responding, and fixed variables. • Making and interpreting point graphs. • Generalizing the area of a rectangle as length times width. • Comparing elements of different laboratory investigations: problems solved, types of graphs, and variables.	• Identifying, extending, and making generalizations about geometric patterns. • Generalizing the area of a rectangle as length times width.	• Measuring length in inches. • Measuring areas of rectangles in square inches.	• Comparing elements of different laboratory investigations: problems solved, types of graphs, and variables. • Collecting, organizing, graphing, and analyzing data. • Using numerical variables. • Identifying manipulated, responding, and fixed variables. • Making and interpreting point graphs. • Using patterns in tables and graphs to make predictions and solve problems.
Daily Practice and Problems (Lettered) **& Home Practice** (Numbered)	• Developing fluency with the division facts. (B, C, I, O, P) (1) • Maintaining fluency with the multiplication facts. (I) (2) • Using order of operations. (2, 7) • Solving problems with unknowns. (O) (7) • Developing number sense for fractions, decimals, and whole numbers. (G, N, P) (4) • Finding a fraction for a given quantity when the unit whole is given. (N) • Translating between different representations of numbers (concrete, pictorial, and symbolic.) (4) • Using fractions and decimals to represent the same quantity. (4) • Multiplying and dividing with 0 and 1. (P) • Solving problems using positive and negative numbers. (R) • Comparing and ordering fractions and decimals. (G) • Comparing and ordering large numbers. (D) • Developing number sense for large numbers. (Q) • Rounding large numbers. (D, Q) • Adding, subtracting, multiplying, and dividing using paper and pencil. (K, L) (2, 6) • Estimating sums, differences, products, and quotients. (K, L) (5, 6) • Solving problems involving addition, subtraction, multiplication, and division. (H) • Developing mental math skills. (A, K, L) (2, 6) • Solving problems involving time. (M) • Multiplying numbers with ending zeros. (O)	• Solving problems using positive and negative numbers. (R) • Using order of operations. (2, 7) • Making and interpreting point graphs. (8) • Drawing best-fit lines. (8) • Using patterns in data to make predictions and solve problems. (8) • Translating between graphs and real-world events. (8) • Solving problems with unknowns. (O) (7) • Representing functions as input-output tables. (7) • Identifying, extending, and making generalizations about number patterns. (7)	• Finding the area and perimeter of a rectangle. (E, F) • Measuring length in inches. (E) • Using geometric definitions to solve problems. (F) • Identifying fractional parts of a geometric shape. (N) • Identifying and describing rotational and line symmetry. (3)	• Finding the area and perimeter of a rectangle. (E, F) • Measuring length in inches. (E) • Converting between units of metric measurement. (J) • Measuring the passage of time. (M)	• Using data to solve problems. (Q, R) (5, 8) • Making and interpreting point graphs. (8) • Drawing best-fit lines. (8) • Using patterns in data to make predictions and solve problems. (8) • Translating between graphs and real-world events. (8)

Problem Solving	Reasoning and Proof	Communication	Connections	Representation
• Solving multistep word problems. • Solving open-response problems. • Choosing appropriate methods and tools to calculate (calculators, mental math, and pencil and paper). • Using the Student Rubrics: *Solving, Knowing,* and *Telling* to self-assess problem-solving skills. • Solving problems involving addition, subtraction, multiplication, and division. • Using patterns in tables and graphs to make predictions and to solve problems. • Choosing to find an estimate or an exact answer.	• Identifying, extending, and making generalizations about geometric and number patterns. • Generalizing the area of a rectangle as length times width. • Communicating solution strategies.	• Communicating solution strategies verbally and in writing. • Using the Student Rubrics: *Solving, Knowing* and *Telling* to self-assess communication skills. • Identifying and describing geometric and number patterns. • Using portfolios.	• Comparing and contrasting elements of different laboratory investigations: problems solved, types of graphs, and variables. • Connecting geometric patterns and number patterns.	• Using numerical variables. • Making and interpreting point graphs. • Collecting, organizing, graphing, and analyzing data.
• Using geometric definitions to solve problems. (F) • Solving multistep word problems. (H) • Solving problems involving addition, subtraction, multiplication, and division. (H) • Solving problems involving time. (M) • Using data to solve problems. (Q, R) (5, 8)	• Using geometric definitions to solve problems. (F) • Explaining mathematical reasoning when multiplying and dividing with 0 and 1. (P) • Identifying, extending, and making generalizations about number patterns. (7)	• Communicating solutions verbally and in writing. (A, G, K, L) • Explaining mathematical reasoning when multiplying and dividing with 0 and 1. (P)		• Translating between different representations of numbers (concrete, pictorial, and symbolic). (4) • Translating between graphs and real-world events. (8) • Making and interpreting point graphs. (8) • Representing functions as input-output tables. (7)

Math Facts and Whole-Number Operations

The Math Facts and Whole-Number Operations section outlines the *Math Trailblazers* approach to developing fluency with the math facts and whole-number operations.

Calculators are used as a tool for solving problems.

Math Facts & Operations

Math Facts and Whole-Number Operations

Work with whole numbers pervades the elementary mathematics curriculum. A major goal of *Math Trailblazers* is to prepare students to compute accurately, flexibly, and appropriately in all situations. Standard topics in arithmetic—acquisition of basic math facts and fluency with whole-number operations—are covered extensively.

In this section, we briefly describe our approach to developing fluency with the math facts and whole-number operations. Table 1 outlines the development of these two topics in Grades K–5. We also summarize below the fundamental characteristics of our work with whole numbers. You can obtain more detailed information from the following sources:

- Two TIMS Tutors *Arithmetic* and *Math Facts;* and
- Background sections and lesson guides from individual *Math Trailblazers* units.

Introduction to the Math Facts in *Math Trailblazers*

In developing our program for the math facts, we sought a careful balance between strategies and drill. This approach is based on a large body of research and is advocated by the NCTM *Principles and Standards for School Mathematics.* The research indicates that the methods used in the *Math Trailblazers* math facts program lead to more effective learning and better retention of the math facts and also helps develop essential math skills.

The *Math Trailblazers* program for teaching the math facts is characterized by these elements:

- *Early emphasis on problem solving.* Students first approach the basic facts as problems to solve rather than as facts to memorize. Students invent their own strategies to solve these problems or learn appropriate strategies from others through class discussion. Students' natural strategies, especially for counting, are explicitly encouraged. In this way, students learn that math is more than memorizing facts and rules that "you either get or you don't."
- *De-emphasis of rote work.* Fluency with the math facts is an important component of any student's mathematical learning. Research shows, however, that overemphasizing memorization and frequent timed tests are counterproductive. We encourage the use of strategies to find facts, so students become confident they can find answers to fact problems that they do not immediately recall.
- *Gradual and systematic introduction of facts.* Students study the facts in small groups of problems that can be solved using similar strategies. Students first work on simple strategies for easy facts and then progress to more sophisticated strategies and harder facts. By the end of the process, they gain fluency with all the required facts.

- *Ongoing practice.* Work on the math facts is distributed throughout the curriculum, especially in the Daily Practice and Problems (Grades 1–5), Home Practice (Grades 3–5), and games. This practice for fluency, however, takes place only after students have a conceptual understanding of the operations and have achieved proficiency with strategies for solving basic fact problems. Delaying practice in this way means that less practice is required to achieve fluency.

- *Appropriate assessment.* Teachers assess students' knowledge of the facts through observations as they work on activities, labs, and games as well as through the appropriate use of written tests and quizzes. Beginning in first grade, periodic, short quizzes in the Daily Practice and Problems naturally follow the study of small groups of facts organized around specific strategies. As self-assessment in Grades 3–5, each student records his or her progress on *Facts I Know* charts and determines which facts he or she needs to study. Inventory tests of all facts for each operation are used sparingly in Grades 2–5 (no more than twice per year) to assess students' progress with fact fluency. The goal of the math facts assessment program is to determine whether students can find answers to fact problems quickly and accurately and retain this skill over time.

- *Multiyear approach.* In Grades 1 and 2, *Math Trailblazers* emphasizes strategies that lead to fluency with the addition and subtraction facts. In Grade 3, students gain fluency with the multiplication facts while reviewing the addition and subtraction facts. In Grade 4, students achieve fluency with the division facts and verify fluency with the multiplication facts. In Grade 5, the multiplication and division facts are systematically reviewed and assessed. This is outlined in Table 1.

- *Facts are not gatekeepers.* Students are not prevented from learning more complex mathematics because they do not perform well on fact tests. Use of strategies, calculators, and other math tools (e.g., manipulatives, hundreds charts, printed multiplication tables) allows students to continue to work on interesting problems and important mathematical concepts while still learning the facts.

Whole-Number Operations in *Math Trailblazers*

Math Trailblazers helps students develop efficient and accurate methods for computation with the four basic operations. The treatment of whole-number computation proceeds in several stages. The grade levels for the stages vary with the operation—full development of division, for example, comes long after addition—but the general pattern is similar for all the operations. Roughly speaking, the stages are:

- developing meaning for the operation,
- inventing procedures for solving problems, and
- becoming more efficient at carrying out procedures, all leading to
- developing mathematical power.

Developing mathematical power with an operation means that students understand *when* to apply the operation and *how* to use varied computational methods to solve problems, even complex or nonroutine problems.

With each operation, we seek a balance between conceptual understanding and procedural skill. Standard methods for solving problems are not introduced until students develop good conceptual and procedural understandings. Research has shown that introducing such procedures too early may short-circuit students' common sense, encouraging mechanical and uncritical behavior. As a result, formal instruction in some standard procedures is delayed slightly beyond the traditional time, but problems that would normally be solved by standard procedures are often introduced sooner than is customary. This forces students to use their prior knowledge to devise their own methods to solve the problems.

Students practice using the operations in activities, games, and laboratory investigations. More practice is provided in the Daily Practice and Problems in Grades 1–5 and in the Home Practice in Grades 3–5. Even after analyzing and practicing standard methods, students are still encouraged to solve problems in more than one way. Flexible thinking and mathematical power are our goals, not rote fluency with a handful of standard algorithms.

The *Math Trailblazers* approach to all mathematics topics promotes the coordinated development of both procedural skill and conceptual understanding. This is particularly apparent in our approach to computation.

The following table describes the development of math facts and whole-number operations in *Math Trailblazers*. The shaded portions of the table highlight development of the math facts program in each grade. Expectations for fluency with math facts are indicated in bold. The white portions of the table highlight development of the whole-number operations.

Grade	Addition	Subtraction	Multiplication	Division
K	Introduce concepts through problem solving and use of manipulatives.			
1	Develop strategies for addition facts. Solve addition problems in context.	Develop strategies for subtraction facts. Solve subtraction problems in context.	Develop concepts through problem solving and use of manipulatives.	
2	Continue use of addition facts in problems. Continue use of strategies for addition facts. **Assess for fluency with addition facts.** Continue solving addition problems in context. Introduce procedures for multidigit addition using manipulatives and paper and pencil.	Continue use of subtraction facts in problems. Continue use of strategies for subtraction facts. **Assess for fluency with subtraction facts.** Continue solving subtraction problems in context. Introduce procedures for multidigit subtraction using manipulatives and paper and pencil.	Continue concept development through problem solving and use of manipulatives.	
3	Diagnose and remediate with addition facts as needed. Develop procedures for multidigit addition using manipulatives and paper and pencil. Practice and apply multidigit addition in varied contexts.	Maintain fluency with subtraction facts through review and assessment. Develop procedures for multidigit subtraction using manipulatives and paper and pencil. Practice and apply multidigit subtraction in varied contexts.	Continue use of multiplication facts in problems. Develop strategies for multiplication facts. **Assess for fluency with multiplication facts.** Solve multiplication problems in context. Introduce paper-and-pencil multiplication (1-digit × 2-digits).	Continue use of division facts in problems. Develop strategies for division facts. Continue concept development. Solve division problems in context.
4	Diagnose and remediate with addition facts as needed. Practice and apply multidigit addition in varied contexts. Review paper-and-pencil procedures for multidigit addition.	Diagnose and remediate with subtraction facts as needed. Practice and apply multidigit subtraction in varied contexts. Review paper-and-pencil procedures for multidigit subtraction.	Maintain fluency with multiplication facts through review and assessment. Develop procedures for multiplication using manipulatives and paper and pencil (1-digit and 2-digit multipliers). Practice and apply multiplication in varied contexts.	Continue use of division facts in problems. Continue development of strategies for division facts. **Assess for fluency with division facts.** Solve division problems in context. Develop procedures for division using manipulatives and paper and pencil (1-digit divisors).
5	Diagnose and remediate with addition facts as needed. Practice and apply multidigit addition in varied contexts.	Diagnose and remediate with subtraction facts as needed. Practice and apply multidigit subtraction in varied contexts.	Maintain fluency with multiplication facts through review and assessment. Review paper-and-pencil procedures. Practice and apply multiplication in varied contexts.	Maintain fluency with division facts through review and assessment. Develop paper-and-pencil procedures (1-digit and 2-digit divisors). Practice and apply division in varied contexts.

Table 1: *Math Facts and Whole-Number Operations Overview*

Daily Practice and Problems and Home Practice Guide

The Daily Practice and Problems (DPP) and Home Practice (HP) Guide explains the purpose and use of the DPP and HP within the curriculum.

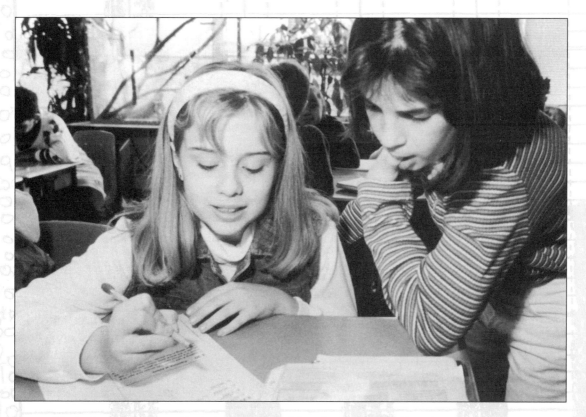

Students work cooperatively to solve a problem from the Daily Practice and Problems.

Daily Practice and Problems
and Home Practice Guide

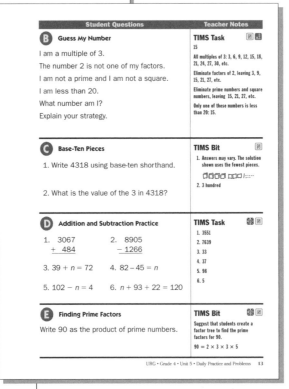

Figure 1: *Two pages from the DPP for Grade 4 Unit 5.*

Daily Practice and Problems

The Daily Practice and Problems (DPP) is a set of short exercises that provides ongoing review, practice, and study of math concepts and skills. These exercises are in each *Unit Resource Guide* immediately preceding the lesson guides and on the *Teacher Resource CD*. The DPP should become a routine part of daily instruction since the problems serve several important functions in the curriculum:

- They provide distributed practice in computation and a structure for systematic study of the basic math facts.
- They develop concepts and skills such as number sense, telling time, and working with money throughout the year; and
- They review topics from earlier units, presenting concepts in new contexts and linking ideas from unit to unit.

There are three types of items: Bits, Tasks, and Challenges. Bits are short and should take no more than 5 or 10 minutes to complete. They often provide practice with a skill or the basic math facts. Tasks take 10 or 15 minutes to complete. Challenges usually take longer than 15 minutes to complete and the problems are more thought-provoking. Use them to stretch students' problem-solving skills.

Two DPP items are included for each class session listed on the Unit Outline. The first item is always a Bit and the second is either a Task or a Challenge. Each item is composed of Student Questions and Teacher Notes as shown in Figure 1.

The Teacher Notes give the answers and often discuss possible problem-solving strategies. Eight icons designate the subject matter of the problems. See Figure 2.

The Scope and Sequence chart in Section 5 of the *Teacher Implementation Guide* lists the topics covered in the DPP in each unit. This chart correlates the items in the DPP to the standards from the National Council of Teachers of Mathematics *Principles and Standards for School Mathematics*. Teachers can use this chart to track the development of a particular standard

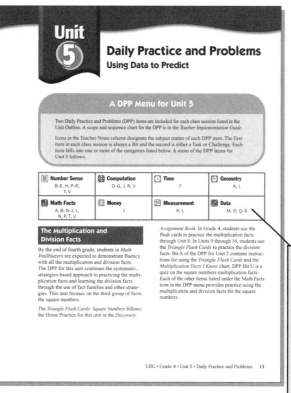

Figure 2: *DPP icons and DPP menu on a DPP page*

Eight icons indicate the subject matter of each problem:

N **Number Sense** (estimating, partitioning numbers, skip counting, etc.);

Math Facts (practice with addition, subtraction, multiplication, and division facts);

Computation (solving problems using paper-and-pencil methods, estimation, mental math, or calculators);

$ **Money** (counting change, combining various coins, or estimating total cost);

Time (telling time, solving problems involving elapsed time);

Measurement (measuring length, area, mass, volume, and time);

Geometry (work with shapes, coordinates, or other geometric topics); and

Data (collecting, organizing, graphing, or analyzing data).

throughout third grade and locate items on particular topics to use for review, extra practice, or enrichment. For example, by looking at the Number and Operations column, teachers can follow the sequence of items providing computation and facts practice. By looking at the Measurement column in the same way, teachers can find all the items that deal with measuring length and area. For a specific description of the study and assessment of the math facts as organized in the DPP, see the TIMS Tutor: *Math Facts*.

How to Use the Daily Practice and Problems

The Suggestions for Teaching the Lesson section and the At a Glance in most lessons provide suggestions on how and when to use each DPP item. These are only suggestions. The following provides further description on how to incorporate the DPP into your math instruction.

Assign a Bit each day to provide students with the review and fact practice they need. Bits are short, quick questions that need little instruction from the teacher. Students should be able to complete them independently. For many problems, it will be appropriate for students to work in pairs or groups. For other items such as facts quizzes, students should answer the questions individually. If students take more than 5 or 10 minutes to complete the problems, they are probably unfamiliar with a topic. For example, items intended to review second-grade topics may be new to students who are using *Math Trailblazers* for the first time in third grade. If students need more instruction on the material presented in the DPP, defer the problems and the instruction until a later date, possibly during an upcoming unit that covers similar subject matter.

Choose from the Tasks and Challenges as time permits according to the interests and needs of your students. Tasks can extend a topic or provide extra practice. Challenges can provide enrichment for those students who need less skill practice and are ready for more complex problems. Not all students will be able to complete all the Tasks and Challenges, but all should have the opportunity to try.

Teachers use the Daily Practice and Problems in many ways. Many problems can easily be written on the board or displayed using an overhead projector. Items can also be photocopied or printed (without the teacher portion) from the *Teacher Resource CD* and distributed to students daily, or several items can be stapled together in a packet and distributed weekly. For many items (such as facts practice or mental arithmetic), it is appropriate for students to just write answers on scrap paper. For others (such as skip counting), students can respond orally. One way to establish routines is to have students use their math journals for any written responses. This will also preserve a record of their work. Teacher notes sometimes recommend conducting a discussion of students' problem-solving strategies. These discussions are an important part of the problem-solving process, but they need not be extensive since topics are revisited many times.

When to Use the Daily Practice and Problems

At the Beginning of Math Class. Use Bits and other DPP items to begin class and focus students' attention on mathematics. Students immediately answer the questions and then the class can discuss the answers before they begin work on the current lesson. Alternatively, the teacher can assign the items at the beginning of a lesson and students can solve the problems as they have time during class. This is especially effective if students are collecting data for an experiment and have to take turns using equipment.

During Daily Routines. Bits can be used as part of morning (or afternoon) routines that also include taking the roll, calendar work, language arts practice, or geography questions. A "Problem of the Day" can also be part of the daily routine in which the teacher presents students with a Task or a Challenge that they can work on throughout the day or take home to complete for homework or as extra credit. For some Tasks and Challenges, it may be appropriate to ask students to describe their problem-solving process.

During Transition Times. You can use many items, especially practice with the math facts, during transition times throughout the day. Possible times include when students have completed an assignment, when money or permission slips are being collected, when an activity is delayed, or when an activity ends earlier than expected.

As Homework or Assessment. You can also assign problems for homework or use them for short assessments. See the TIMS Tutor: *Math Facts* for information on facts assessment in the DPP and the Assessment Overview in Part VI of the Assessment Section for specific locations of Facts Quizzes.

Home Practice

The Home Practice (HP) is a series of problems that supplement the homework included in the lessons. The HP, like the DPP, distributes skill practice throughout the units and reviews concepts studied in previous units. For each unit, the *Discovery Assignment Book* begins with problems divided into different parts as shown in Figure 3.

How to Use the Home Practice

The At a Glance in many lessons provides guidance for how and when to use the Home Practice. Here are further suggestions.

One way to assign the HP is to send all parts home with students at some point during the unit. Students are responsible for completing the pages and returning them on a given day. This schedule allows flexibility for the teacher, students, and students' families. If some evenings are filled with athletic practices, meetings, family commitments, or the completion of other homework, students can choose their own times to work on the HP.

The HP is designed to be used in addition to (not as a replacement for) the unit homework. Since some parts may include content directly related to the current unit, often it is not appropriate to assign these parts during the first week of the unit. Rather, use such HP items after students solve similar problems in class.

Another way to occasionally use the HP is for the teacher (or parents) to complete one or more parts of the assignment. The adult makes some intentional mistakes and shows how he or she solved the problems. Then, students grade the adult's work, justifying the number of points awarded to each problem.

From time to time, teachers may ask students to reflect on how they completed the HP either in a short paragraph attached to the homework or in math journals. Did they need help? Who helped them? Did the helper give them new strategies for solving problems? How did they organize their time?

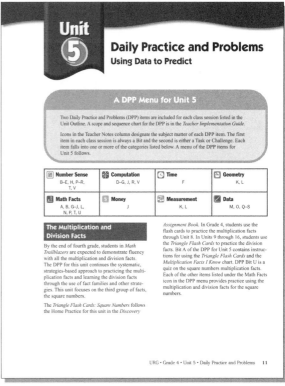

Figure 3: *Home Practice pages from Grade 4 Unit 5.*

Calculations: Paper-and-Pencil, Calculators, Mental Math, or Estimation?

The HP provides many opportunities for practice of computational skills. Practice of paper-and-pencil calculations is emphasized throughout the HP. However, besides developing skill with paper-and-pencil computations, students also need to be able to choose when it is appropriate to use paper-and-pencil procedures, calculators, mental math, or estimation.

The following problem serves as an example:

> *The Student Council is selling 1000 pencils to make money for a school project. They have already sold 450 pencils. How many more do they have to sell?*

Students may use paper-and-pencil procedures, but subtracting across zeros is difficult and not particularly efficient. They may estimate that the student council needs to sell about 500 more, but a more exact answer is probably needed in this situation. Using a calculator is possible, but probably not necessary. Using a mental math strategy of counting up is effective and efficient. (Count up 50 from 450 to 500, then count up 500 more to 1000 to arrive at the answer of 550 pencils.) Before sending home the HP, you may discuss the possible strategies for particular problems and whether or not it is appropriate to use a calculator or another method of calculating. For more information on helping students choose appropriate strategies for computation, see the TIMS Tutor: *Arithmetic*.

Assessment

The Assessment section details the philosophy, goals, and components of assessment in the curriculum.

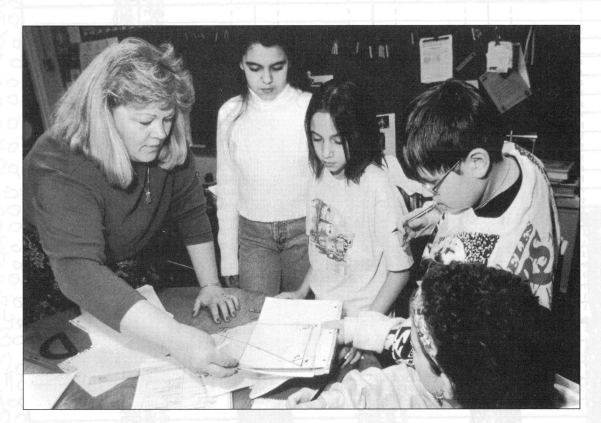

A teacher and her students assess their work on a problem.

Assessment

 PART I | # Philosophy of the Assessment Program in *Math Trailblazers*

Assessment in *Math Trailblazers* is ongoing and reflects the program's content and goals. Throughout the program, assessment serves several purposes:

- It helps teachers learn about students' thinking and knowledge. This information is then used to guide instruction.
- It communicates the instruction goals to students, parents, and others.
- It informs students, parents, and others about progress toward these goals.

The assessment program is built around two main principles: assessment should reflect the breadth and balance of the curriculum; and assessment activities should be valuable educational experiences.

Alignment with Goals

The National Council of Teachers of Mathematics (NCTM) *Principles and Standards for School Mathematics* describes the understanding, concepts, and skills students need to acquire. These principles and standards call for a mathematically rich curriculum for all students. The curriculum must teach a broad range of content and develop mathematical processes including problem solving, reasoning, and communication.

Math Trailblazers is designed to meet recommendations in the *Principles and Standards.* As such, the program requires significant shifts in emphases relative to a traditional program—changes in content, learning, teaching, evaluation, and expectations. The implications with regard to student assessment are also significant. We can no longer focus narrowly on the assessment of only isolated skills and procedures, using single sources of information at the end of a learning cycle. Instead, assessment needs to shift toward collecting information over the course of the year from a variety of sources, covering a wide range of mathematical content, and incorporating the rich problem-solving situations that are characteristic of the curriculum. The NCTM *Principles and Standards for School Mathematics* describes this as follows:

> *Many assessment techniques can be used by mathematics teachers, including open-ended questions, constructed-response tasks, selected-response items, performance tasks, observations, conversations, journals, and portfolios.* (NCTM, 2000, p. 23)

Integral with Instruction

Assessment is an integral part of instruction. All assessment activities are valuable educational experiences that have their own merit. By making assessment both integral to instruction and reflective of the overall mathematical content of the curriculum, we communicate what we value in mathematics. Again, the NCTM *Principles and Standards* addresses this idea:

> *To ensure deep, high-quality learning for all students, assessment and instruction must be integrated so that assessment becomes a routine part of ongoing classroom activity rather than an interruption.* (NCTM, 2000, p. 23)

Our assessment program gives teachers frequent opportunities to assess student progress. It assesses concepts and skills in many different ways but especially within the context of solving problems. Assessments are designed to elicit more than just an answer. In solving problems, students show their thinking and give a picture of their understanding of mathematical concepts, strategies, tools, and procedures.

Integrating assessment with instruction has significant implications for the structure of the assessment program. There is no separate assessment book; assessment activities and other components of the assessment program are fully integrated into units. Furthermore, because much of the curriculum's content is revisited many times in varying contexts, students are assessed many times on many concepts. This flavors both instruction and assessment. Teachers can focus on student progress since they know there will be other opportunities to review and assess and thus do not expect mastery at every juncture. At the same time, students' mathematical progress is not put on hold until they pass any particular assessment.

Balanced Assessment

The assessment program reflects the curriculum's instruction in another important way: it is varied and balanced. The *Math Trailblazers* curriculum is balanced across several dimensions:

- **Math Content.** The program incorporates a broad range of mathematical content and procedures, and connections between different topics abound.
- **Communication.** Students are expected to communicate their mathematical work and represent mathematical ideas in many different ways, such as written and oral explanations, number sentences, tables, graphs, pictures, and models.

- **Student Groupings.** Students work individually, in pairs, and in small groups.
- **Length of Activities.** There are short activities (5–15 minutes), tasks that take a full class period, and longer investigations that take several days.
- **Amount of Teacher Direction.** Some activities involve considerable teacher direction; others are more student-directed.
- **Varied Contexts.** Mathematics is presented in a variety of contexts, such as laboratory experiments, real-life settings, word problems, and numerical problems.

Our assessment program is balanced in similar ways. A balanced assessment program gives each student an opportunity to demonstrate what he or she knows by allowing multiple approaches. It covers a wide range of content, allows access to tools when appropriate, varies the difficulty and pedagogy, and assesses within different kinds of contexts.

Using multiple sources of evidence improves the validity of judgments made about students' learning. With more than one source of information about students' progress, strengths in one source can compensate for weaknesses in others. It also helps teachers judge the consistency of students' mathematical work. (NCTM, 2000, p. 24)

Promoting Student Reflection

Assessment activities in *Math Trailblazers* do more than provide momentary snapshots of a student's progress. Students are often asked to revise work based on commonly understood criteria for excellence. In Grades K–2, these criteria are communicated largely by the teachers. Beginning in Grade 3, the Student Rubrics provide an additional source of information to students about what is expected of them. As students become more involved in the assessment process, they become more reflective and can make constructive, critical judgments about their work and the work of others.

Components in Grades 1-5

Watching students grow intellectually throughout the school year is one of the great satisfactions of teaching. The components of the assessment program provide teachers with the tools necessary to document students' progress over time as they acquire skills and concepts, develop their abilities to solve problems, and learn to communicate their thinking. While most components are included at all grade levels, the assessment program does vary from grade to grade based on the students' needs.

All materials provided to assess student learning are located in the units, either in the student materials or the *Unit Resource Guide.* Each unit contains assessment ideas and activities appropriate for the unit's content and goals. Many components are also available in electronic form on the *Teacher Resource CD.* This section describes the following components:

Observational Assessment
Assessment Indicators
Observational Assessment Record
Individual Assessment Record Sheet

Written Assessments
Assessment Pages
Math Journals
Assessment Section in
 the Lesson Guide
Assessment Lessons
 Assessment Labs
 Open-Response Problems
 Tests
Assessment Units
Portfolios
Facts Assessment

Observational Assessment

Teachers have always assessed student learning through informal classroom observations, thus integrating instruction and assessment. The NCTM *Principles and Standards* confirms the importance of these observations.

Observations and conversations in the classroom can provide insights into students' thinking, and teachers can monitor changes in students' thinking and reasoning over time with reflective journals and portfolios. (NCTM, 2000, p. 24)

Teachers use the information gathered from classroom observations to guide instruction. While watching, questioning, and listening to students, they make moment-to-moment instructional decisions that change the direction and emphasis of the lesson. Teacher evaluation of student responses during a lesson will also affect the content of succeeding lessons.

Teachers can also use classroom observations to evaluate student achievement and monitor student progress. Skills such as using a graduated cylinder to measure volume, habits such as estimating regularly to check results, and behaviors such as working effectively within a group are best assessed through observing students at work. Assessing students through observation is

Assessment

especially important in the primary grades, because students at this age can often communicate their thinking very well in a discussion, but not always in writing. Also, what we assess becomes what we value. If we only assess written work, we may neglect other important behaviors such as verbal communication. Finding a manageable way to organize and record these observations is critical to an effective assessment program.

Each unit includes two tools to help teachers organize and document informal assessments: Assessment Indicators and the *Observational Assessment Record.*

Assessment Indicators

The Background for each unit in Grades 1–5 lists several Assessment Indicators that orient teachers to important skills, behavior, and knowledge they should assess in the unit. See Figure 1.

Assessment Indicators

- Can students group and count objects by twos, fives, and tens?
- Can students divide a collection of objects into groups of a given size and count the leftovers?
- Can students collect, organize, graph, and analyze data?
- Can students identify the relationships among pennies, nickels, and dimes?

Figure 1: *Assessment Indicators from Grade 1 Unit 5*

Observational Assessment Record

An *Observational Assessment Record* similar to the one shown for Grade 1 Unit 5 in Figure 2 follows the Background in each unit. The Assessment Indicators for that unit are listed at the top of each sheet. Each indicator is identified with an icon. An additional line is provided for teachers to include their own ideas. Each sheet has 32 rows for student names with columns for recording observations and extra space for comments. It is not necessary to record an observation about each child in each column. The grid provides a snapshot of the class's understanding of the unit's main concepts, procedures, and skills.

Observational Assessment Record

- **A1** Can students group and count objects by twos, fives, and tens?
- **A2** Can students divide a collection of objects into groups of a given size and count the leftovers?
- **A3** Can students collect and organize data in a table?
- **A4** Can students identify the relationships among pennies, nickels, and dimes?
- **A5**

Name	A1	A2	A3	A4	A5	Comments
1.						
2.						
3.						
4.						
5.						
6.						
7.						
8.						
9.						
10.						
11.						
12.						
13.						

URG • Grade 1 • Unit 5 • Observational Assessment Record   9

Figure 2: *Sample* Observational Assessment Record *from Grade 1 Unit 5*

In first and second grade, the icons are also placed in the At a Glance sections of the Lesson Guides. These indicate which skills and concepts described in the Assessment Indicators teachers might assess during that particular lesson. Figure 3 is a sample At a Glance section from Grade 1 Unit 5 Lesson 2. The use of the icon (A1) shows that during this lesson teachers can assess students on their abilities to count objects by twos, fives, and tens.

Individual Assessment Record Sheets

Information from the *Observational Assessment Record* can be transferred to *Individual Assessment Record Sheets*. The *Individual Assessment Record Sheet* is located at the end of Part VI of this section and provides an organizational tool for compiling a year-long, anecdotal record for each child. Assessment Indicators for the entire year are listed by unit along with a line for comments as shown in Figure 4.

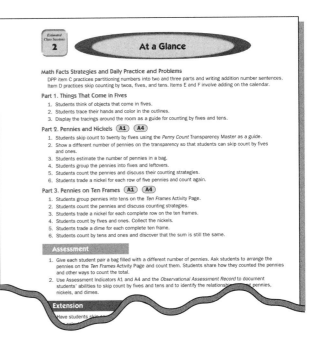

Figure 3: *Sample At a Glance from Grade 1 Unit 5 Lesson 2*

Figure 4: Observational Assessment Record *from Grade 5 Unit 1 and* Individual Assessment Record Sheet *from Grade 5*

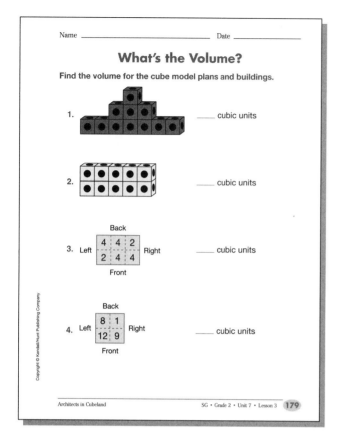

Name _____ Date _____

What's the Volume?

Find the volume for the cube model plans and buildings.

1. _____ cubic units

2. _____ cubic units

3. Left | Back | Right _____ cubic units

   | 4 | 4 | 2 |
   | 2 | 4 | 4 |

   Front

4. Left | Back | Right _____ cubic units

   | 8 | 1 |
   | 12 | 9 |

   Front

Architects in Cubeland   SG • Grade 2 • Unit 7 • Lesson 3   179

Figure 5: *Assessment Page from Grade 2 Unit 7*

Written Assessments

Assessment Pages

Many lessons in *Math Trailblazers* include short paper-and-pencil assessments that teachers can use to check skills or concepts developed in a unit. While teachers can use some assessment pages to assess students as they work in groups, they can often use these pages as quizzes to assess students individually. Checking student work gives both the teacher and the students feedback on their current abilities. The *What's the Volume?* Assessment Page from Grade 2 Unit 7 is shown in Figure 5. Students must combine their arithmetic skills with their measurement skills to complete the page correctly.

Math Journals

Students' entries in their math journals are a rich source of assessment information. Journal Prompts, a regular feature in the lesson guides, elicit information about students' understanding of specific concepts. Figure 6 shows an example of a Journal Prompt in Grade 5 Unit 1 Lesson 3.

Journal Prompt

A stream has an average depth of 1 meter. Can you wade across?

Figure 6: *A Journal Prompt from Grade 5 Unit 1 Lesson 3*

2/18/92   Double Challenge

Today My class did Some Math and We did

Some Writ Some Math too! I Like it!

Figure 7: *A second-grade journal entry*

Regular journal writing provides teachers and parents with a means of documenting a student's growth in mathematical thinking, attitudes, and communication skills. (For information on math journals, see the TIMS Tutor: *Journals.*) Young children often begin by drawing pictures in their journals or combining pictures with a few words. The journal entry in Figure 7 is an early effort by Jayne, a second grader, at communicating her thoughts about a math lesson on doubling. Jayne used six circles and six squares to show two examples of doubling three. She also wrote a short paragraph about the class:

> *Today my class did some math. and we did some writ (write) some math too! I like it!*

Assessment Section

The Assessment section at the end of most lesson guides lists ideas for assessing the lesson's content. The following components are often recommended as assessment: Assessment Pages, Journal Prompts, classroom observations corresponding to the Assessment Indicators, and appropriate questions from the student pages and Homework sections. The teacher can also record the level of a student's response to these questions on the *Observational Assessment Record* or in a grade book. Figure 8 shows assessment for Grade 1 Unit 6 Lesson 2.

Assessment Lessons

Some units include specially designed assessment lessons. These lessons are generally one of three types: assessment labs, open-response problems, or written tests composed of short items. Each type provides different kinds of information to teachers so that they can develop and document a complete picture of their students' progress toward the curriculum's goals.

Assessment Labs

Two or three laboratory experiments in each grade are designated as assessment labs. Teachers can use them to assess students' abilities to work with a group on an investigation that takes several days. Teachers can also observe students to see if they are confident enough to tackle new ideas and to use previously learned mathematics in new contexts. Working on projects such as these—problems requiring integration and application of many concepts and skills over a period of time—more closely resembles the work of mathematicians and scientists (as well as working adults in many occupations) than any other kind of work students do in school. Suggestions for evaluating labs are included in Part III.

Open-Response Problems

In these lessons, students are given a task that requires them to demonstrate their problem-solving skills individually or while working in a group. Students are also assessed on their understanding of the mathematical content and their abilities to communicate their strategies. They must produce a product that allows teachers to examine their processes as well as their final answers. More than a few minutes are required to solve such a problem and students will often need a whole class period to find solutions and describe their strategies. To encourage students to give full explanations and improve their writing skills, teachers can comment on students' initial responses and ask them to make revisions. Part III includes rubrics for scoring student responses to these problems.

Math Facts Strategies

DPP item D provides practice with addition math facts.

Homework and Practice

- The *Two Car Roll-off* Homework Page shows a diagram of two cars that rolled down different ramps. Students count the links and compare the distances.
- DPP item C practices addition in a measurement context. For DPP item E, students estimate lengths of objects. Item F reviews even and odd numbers. Item G practices partitioning numbers. Students divide groups of cookies among 4 people and count leftovers. Item H asks students to solve problems using skip counting.

Assessment

- The *Brian's Class* Assessment Page asks students to examine the data for a fictional class. *Questions 1–4* are similar to questions found in the class discussion while *Question 5 is* a challenge.
- Use children's journal entries to assess whether students understand the connection between "fairness" and controlled variables.
- Use the *Observational Assessment Record* to record students' abilities to make and interpret bar graphs and also to solve problems using data involving length.

Extension

Provide additional measurement practice by leaving the ramp in an activity center for student use.

Figure 8: *Grade 1 Unit 6 Lesson 2—Math Facts Strategies, Homework and Practice, Assessment, and Extension*

Name _____ Date _____

Class Party

Suppose there are 25 students in your class and you have $10 for a class party. Use the prices in the table to plan a party.

Tell how you would spend the money, and explain why you would spend it that way. Use as much of the $10 as you can, but do not plan to spend more than $10. (There is no tax.) Be sure your plan works for a class of 25.

Write your plan on another piece of paper. Be sure to explain how you solved the problem and how you made your decisions.

Item	Cost
pitcher of lemonade (10 servings)	$2.50
paper cups (package of 24)	69¢
ice cream bars	30¢
oatmeal cookies (package of 16)	99¢
bag of popcorn (30 servings)	$1.09
napkins (package of 50)	49¢

Assessment Blackline Master   URG • Grade 3 • Unit 10 • Lesson 3   73

Figure 9 shows Jayne's response to an open-response problem written at midyear of third grade. Jayne is the same student who wrote the journal entry shown in Figure 7. Compare her writing here with her paragraph from second grade and also with her work at the end of third grade on the Earning Money problem shown in Figure 19 in Part III. Comparing these three responses shows how she has developed her communication skills.

Tests

Tests that assess students' conceptual understanding and procedural skills are short items that teachers can easily grade. There is a test in the final unit of both first and second grade. In third grade, there is a midyear and an end-of-year test. In fourth and fifth grades, there is a midterm test in both the fall and spring semesters in addition to a midyear and end-of-year test.

Jayne

Steps
1. Lemonade $7.50
   $2.50 \times 3 = \$7.50$

2. Paper Cups $1.38
   $69 \times 2 = \$1.38$

3. Popcorn
   1.09
   $1.09 \times 1 = 1.09$

4.
   $\begin{array}{r} \overset{1}{7.50} \ \text{Lemonade} \\ 1.38 \ \text{Paper Cups} \\ + 1.09 \ \text{Popcorn} \\ \hline \$9.97 \end{array}$

4. 3¢ left over

I solved the problems the way I did because number sentences help you get the awnser

My way works because it helped me get the awnser.

The math is the same as other math because they both have driffrent ways of solving their problems and awnsering them.

Figure 9: *Jayne's work for an open-response problem*

Assessment Units

In each grade, specific units are designated as assessment units. They include lessons that emphasize assessment at the same time that content is reviewed and new material is introduced. Teachers can assess students' abilities to apply previously studied concepts in new contexts and their willingness to approach new mathematics.

Assessment units at the beginning of each grade provide opportunities to observe students and collect baseline data on students' mathematical knowledge. Teachers can use this information to plan instruction that meets students' needs and to begin documenting students' mathematical growth over the course of the year. See the Assessment Overview in Part VI for specific information on the assessment units.

Portfolios

Portfolios are important tools for documenting students' growth throughout the year. They are collections of students' written work and teachers' anecdotal records. To provide a complete picture of a student's learning, a portfolio should include assessments that demonstrate the range of the child's abilities. Samples of student work on labs, open-response problems, assessment activity pages, and tests can be included along with samples of students' daily work. Work from the year's beginning to end will show students' growth over time. Certain lessons in the assessment units are especially appropriate for inclusion in portfolios. Refer to the TIMS Tutor: *Portfolios* for more information.

Facts Assessment

In *Math Trailblazers,* teachers assess students' knowledge of the facts by observing them as they work on activities, labs, and games and through the appropriate use of quizzes and tests. Periodic, short quizzes in the Daily Practice and Problems naturally follow the study of small groups of facts organized around specific strategies. As self-assessment in third, fourth, and fifth grades, each student can record his or her progress on *Facts I Know* charts and determine which facts he or she needs to study. The goal of the math facts assessment program is to determine the degree to which students can find answers to fact problems quickly and accurately and whether they can retain this skill over time. For more information on teaching and assessing the math facts, see the TIMS Tutor: *Math Facts.*

PART III | Implementing the Assessment Program

Evaluating and reporting on a broad range of student achievement throughout the school year is a complex task. It is only practical if the assessment process is built into day-to-day instruction. Components of the assessment program are designed so teachers can gather information about students as they are learning. This section outlines a plan for gradually introducing the various components of the assessment program during the first weeks of instruction and provides information on evaluating and scoring written work.

Getting Started

An assessment program that emphasizes the documentation of students' growth over time establishes a climate in which each child is valued for the knowledge and skills he or she brings to the classroom and in which each student is expected to make significant gains in mathematics. These are high expectations that also reflect reality. Students begin and end the school year with varying abilities, backgrounds, and accomplishments. Therefore, it is important to record what each student can do initially, as well as during the learning process, so that the teacher, student, and parents can fully appreciate progress throughout the year.

Begin Observational Assessments

Activities in the first two or three units of each grade provide many opportunities to observe students as they use mathematics. These observations provide a rich source of baseline information about students. For example, in Units 1–3 of first grade, students count objects in many contexts. By routinely observing four or five students during appropriate lessons, the teacher can note those students who can count and those who may need additional help. At the same time, all students are working on their counting skills as well as on related concepts such as comparing numbers and organizing data.

Unit 2 of third grade is also designated as an assessment unit. In this unit, students review strategies to maintain fluency with the subtraction facts. Students discuss strategies, play games, work with flash cards, assess themselves using *Facts I Know* charts, and use subtraction facts as part of a data collection activity. Observing students participating in these activities gives teachers information about students' knowledge of the facts and, more importantly, about students' abilities to use the facts to solve problems. Since students will continually use the facts in many activities as well as in the Daily Practice and Problems, the teacher need only record observations for a small number of students at a time. (For more information on assessment of the math facts, see the TIMS Tutor: *Math Facts.*)

Using the *Observational Assessment Record.* Before beginning assessment observations, teachers need a system for recording short, anecdotal records. Such a system should allow recording of a broad range of evidence of students' behavior, attitudes, and understanding of mathematics and should make recording and retrieving information easy and convenient. The *Observational Assessment Record* and the Assessment Indicators help organize data from observations. Teachers can develop their own shorthand to denote satisfactory progress toward a goal or proficiency with a skill or concept.

In Grades 1–5, information from the *Observational Assessment Record* can be transferred to *Individual Assessment Record Sheets* to create a year-long anecdotal record of growth for each child. The *Individual Assessment Record Sheet* is located at the end of Part VI of this section. Teachers can copy and place it in each student's portfolio. It is also available on the *Teacher Resource CD*. Teachers can use it to maintain records of each student's progress electronically.

As part of lesson planning, the teacher can choose one or two behaviors, concepts, or skills to check during class. The Assessment Indicators for each unit and the Assessment section in the lesson guides can facilitate this process. The teacher should choose no more than four or five students to observe in a day. Additional students can be observed in succeeding lessons or units to provide further information about individual students' progress and the improvement of the class as a whole.

Figure 10 is an example of an *Observational Assessment Record* for Grade 1 Unit 1 that shows one possible scheme for recording classroom observations. Note that the teacher chose to observe students' abilities to work together as well as counting skills.

Other suggestions from teachers for organizing anecdotal records follow:

Student Grid. A teacher can make a grid that allows note-taking about all students on one piece of paper as shown in Figure 11. The grids include as many cells as there are students in the class, labeling each cell with a student's name. Observations are written in the cells. Like the *Observational Assessment Record,* this provides a view of the entire class's progress.

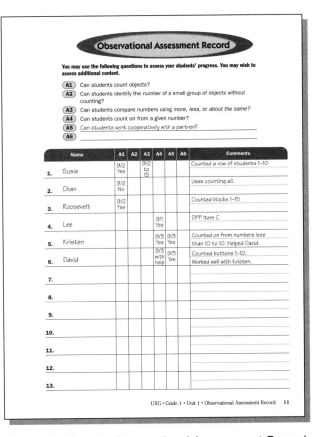

Figure 10: *Sample* Observational Assessment Record *for Grade 1 Unit 1*

Sally Adamji	Feliz Arnez	John Boyd	Barb Crown
Willie Darno	Sarah Frank	Lee Guzman	etc.

Figure 11: *Student grid*

Flip Chart. A flip chart can be made by lining up index cards and taping them to a clipboard or a piece of heavy cardboard so they overlap by all but a strip of about $\frac{1}{2}$ inch as shown in Figure 12. Students' names are written on the uncovered area of each card, so the teacher can easily flip to a student's card and write a quick, dated note about the observation. As a card is filled, it can be removed to a card file or a student's portfolio and replaced with a new card.

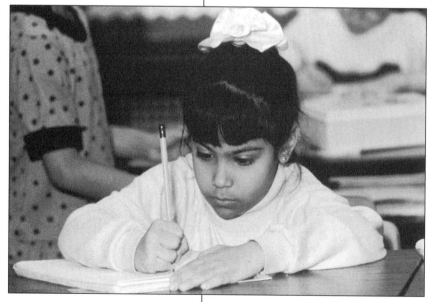

Figure 12: *Flip chart*

Flip Cards. A variation of the flip chart can be made by fastening together a set of index cards—one card labeled for each student in the class. A binder ring is placed through a hole in a corner of each card.

Self-Adhesive Notes. Some teachers prefer to write their observations about individual students on self-adhesive notes, which are then attached to a sheet of paper in the student's portfolio. These notes have the advantage of being easily transferable, so they can be grouped and regrouped by student, subject, day, etc.

Begin Math Journals

At the beginning of the year, math journals provide a safe place for students to start communicating their insights. By writing regularly in their journals, they gain the experience necessary to write more and learn to express themselves clearly. Students can write in response to journal prompts or record answers to questions from the *Student Guide* or Daily Practice and Problems. See the TIMS Tutor: *Journals* for more information on using journals to assess students.

Begin Portfolios

The TIMS Tutor: *Portfolios* recommends establishing portfolios by starting small with modest goals. This implies using portfolios to document progress in one or two specific areas such as communicating mathematically or collecting and analyzing data. One way to begin is to assign each student a collection folder in which early examples of student work are saved. Later in the process, teachers can designate or students can select a smaller number of pieces that show growth in these areas.

It is important to choose examples of work from the beginning of the year so a student's first efforts can be compared to later work. The earliest entries in the portfolio will most likely show much less sophisticated results than those that are added toward the end of the year. For example, to compare students' use of the TIMS Laboratory Method at the beginning of the year to their abilities to conduct an experiment at the end of the year, include a data table and a graph from an early lab in each student's portfolio. Good choices of initial labs to collect in portfolios include the following: In Grade 1, save students' weather graphs from Unit 2; in Grade 2, use the Button Sizer Graph from Unit 3; and in Grade 3, choose student work from the lab *Kind of Bean* in Unit 1 or the graph and write-up from *Spinning Differences* in Unit 2. At the beginning of Grade 4, include *Arm Span vs. Height* from Unit 1 and *Perimeter vs. Length* from Unit 2. In Grade 5, begin portfolios with the labs *Searching the Forest* from Unit 1 and *Distance vs. Time* from Unit 3.

Scoring Open-Response Problems

In *Math Trailblazers,* most lessons involve multiple mathematical topics, skills, and processes. Assessing student progress requires tools that allow students to respond using multiple approaches and that let teachers evaluate student communication and problem-solving strategies as well as mathematical knowledge.

TIMS Multidimensional Rubric

To assist teachers in evaluating student performance and in communicating progress to students and parents, we have developed a rubric—a scoring guide—for evaluating student work on open-response problems. The *TIMS Multidimensional Rubric* addresses three dimensions of mathematical learning: (i) knowing, (ii) solving, and (iii) telling. Using these three dimensions broadens the assessment focus from the traditional emphasis on rote procedures to a more complete view of mathematics learning. The rubric outlines our criteria for excellence and provides an explicit indication of what we value in mathematics. Examples of using the rubric to score student work are included in lesson guides beginning in Grade 3. The ideas embodied in the rubric are generally applicable to younger children and can be modified for use in earlier grades. The rubric is displayed in Part V.

The three dimensions of mathematical understanding emphasized in the *TIMS Multidimensional Rubric* are described here briefly.

- *Solving.* This section focuses on students' understanding of a problem and their abilities to devise a plan for solving it, organize information, analyze results, and reflect on its mathematical implications.
- *Knowing.* This portion of the rubric examines students' comprehension of mathematical concepts and their abilities to apply procedures, rules, and facts to a given mathematical situation. This includes effective use of representations, such as written numbers, words, graphs, tables, or pictures, and the ability to make connections among different mathematical ideas.
- *Telling.* This part stresses students' abilities to explain their problem-solving strategies, justify their solutions, use symbols and terminology correctly, and discuss connections among mathematical topics.

The *TIMS Multidimensional Rubric* specifies criteria for assigning scores on each dimension to one piece of student work. Level 4 is the highest and is intended to represent excellence in that particular dimension. A paper might earn, for example, a 3 in *Solving*, a 4 in *Knowing*, and a 3 in *Telling*. It is not necessary to assign a score for all three dimensions for every task. For many tasks, it may be more appropriate to give scores for only one or two dimensions.

Student Rubrics

Corresponding Student Rubrics for each dimension make the expectations of student performance clear. These rubrics provide students with goals as they solve problems, communicate their solutions, and revise their work. Students also use these rubrics as guides when assessing their own work. The student rubrics are introduced gradually in the *Student Guide* throughout the first semester of third, fourth, and fifth grades. They are included in lessons with open-response problems.

The Student Rubrics are shown in Figure 13.

The Student Rubrics are located in Appendices A, B, and C and on the inside backcover of the *Student Guides* for Grades 3–5. Blackline Masters of the Student Rubrics are included in Part V so teachers can make transparencies or use a copier to enlarge the rubrics to make classroom posters.

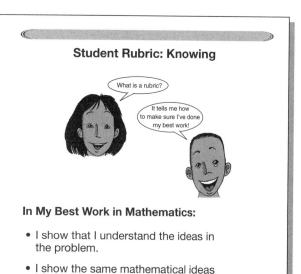

Student Rubric: Knowing

What is a rubric?

It tells me how to make sure I've done my best work!

In My Best Work in Mathematics:

- I show that I understand the ideas in the problem.

- I show the same mathematical ideas in different ways. I use pictures, tables, graphs, and sentences when they fit the problem.

- I show that I can use tools and rules correctly.

- I show that I can use the mathematical facts that apply to the problem.

TIG • Grade 4 • Assessment • Master Copies of Rubrics **201**

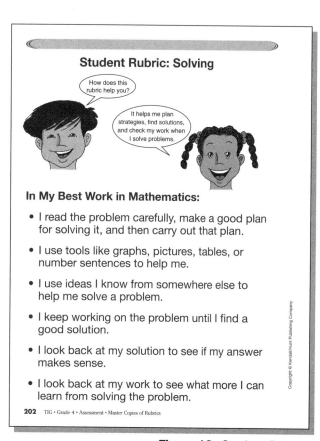

Student Rubric: Solving

How does this rubric help you?

It helps me plan strategies, find solutions, and check my work when I solve problems.

In My Best Work in Mathematics:

- I read the problem carefully, make a good plan for solving it, and then carry out that plan.

- I use tools like graphs, pictures, tables, or number sentences to help me.

- I use ideas I know from somewhere else to help me solve a problem.

- I keep working on the problem until I find a good solution.

- I look back at my solution to see if my answer makes sense.

- I look back at my work to see what more I can learn from solving the problem.

202 TIG • Grade 4 • Assessment • Master Copies of Rubrics

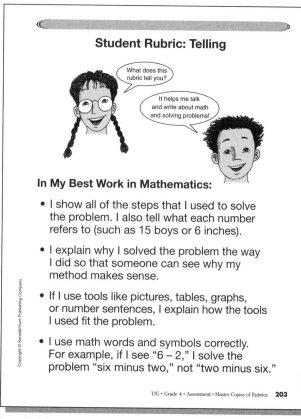

Student Rubric: Telling

What does this rubric tell you?

It helps me talk and write about math and solving problems!

In My Best Work in Mathematics:

- I show all of the steps that I used to solve the problem. I also tell what each number refers to (such as 15 boys or 6 inches).

- I explain why I solved the problem the way I did so that someone can see why my method makes sense.

- If I use tools like pictures, tables, graphs, or number sentences, I explain how the tools I used fit the problem.

- I use math words and symbols correctly. For example, if I see "6 − 2," I solve the problem "six minus two," not "two minus six."

TIG • Grade 4 • Assessment • Master Copies of Rubrics **203**

Figure 13: *Student Rubrics: Knowing, Solving, and Telling*

Using the Rubrics: An Early Example

Using the student rubrics to inform students of your expectations as well as using the *TIMS Multidimensional Rubric* to score student work is a process that evolves throughout the year. For example, Grade 3 Unit 2 includes the first assessment lesson with an open-response problem. This is the students' first exposure to the student rubrics. The problem is shown in Figure 14.

To begin the lesson the class reads and discusses the problem. It is similar to the problem in an earlier lesson (Unit 2 Lesson 2 *Spinning Sums*), so students should be familiar with the procedures. They also read and discuss the Student Rubric: *Knowing.* The teacher may ask students what tools, rules, and mathematical facts apply to the problem. She explains that she will grade their work based on the rubric.

After students understand the problem, they work in groups to plan a strategy for solving the problem and to carry out their plans. Then students write paragraphs describing their problem-solving processes and their results. The teacher directs students either to write the paragraph with their groups or to write the paragraph individually. When students have completed their paragraphs, the teacher reviews their work and makes suggestions for improvement.

It is a good idea to make transparencies of exemplary work from previous years or the lesson guide. The teacher discusses the exemplary work with the class, comparing the work to the rubric's standards. Finally, students revise their work based on the teacher's comments. A student response with teacher comments is shown in Figure 15.

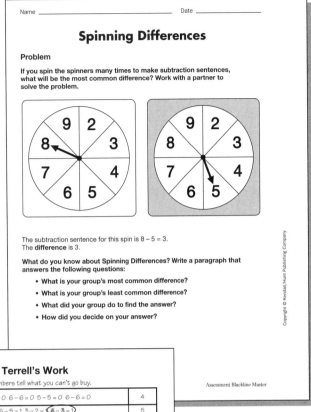

Figure 14: *Assessment lesson from Grade 3 Unit 2*

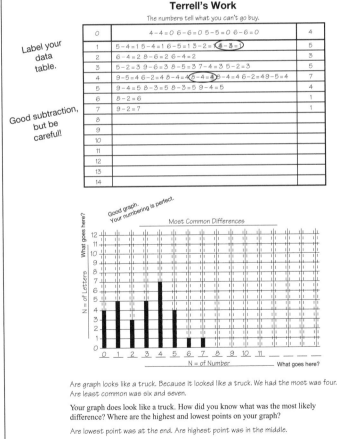

Figure 15: *A student response to a teacher's comments*

The teacher used the Knowing dimension of the *TIMS Multidimensional Rubric* to score students' work. The Lesson Guide provides questions specific to this problem to guide the teacher's scoring. The questions provided for this problem are given below:

- Were the data table and graph appropriately labeled?
- Was the graph scaled properly?
- Were the bars correctly drawn?
- Were the subtraction sentences correct?
- Were the most common differences identified?

Many of the criteria in the rubric overlap. In addition, the student's data table, graph, and written paragraphs tell us about more than one component of the problem. Consequently, the score for a dimension will result from the compilation of all the evidence, not necessarily from an arithmetic average of scores in each cell of the rubric. Figure 16 shows the Knowing dimension of the *TIMS Multidimensional Rubric* with the teacher's notations after she scored Terrell's paper.

How would you score Terrell's work? Terrell's teacher decided that he earned a 3. He worked with his group using tools to spin the spinners 30 times, record the results in a table, and display the data in a graph. The bars are drawn correctly on the graph and the axes are scaled correctly. However, the incorrect labels on both the data table ("The numbers that tell what you can't go buy") and graph ("Most Common Differences" and "N = of Letters") indicate that he was not clear on his goal for collecting data and therefore did not completely understand the problem's concepts and applications. The incorrect labels also show major errors translating between tables, graphs, and real situations, although he did correctly identify the most common and least common differences. The correct number sentences are evidence that he knows the subtraction facts. (See the Lesson Guide for *Spinning Differences* in Grade 3 Unit 2 for other examples of student work scored using the rubric.)

Knowing	Level 4	Level 3	Level 2	Level 1
Understands the task's mathematical concepts, their properties and applications…	Completely	Nearly completely	Partially	Not at all
Translates between words, pictures, symbols, tables, graphs, and real situations…	Readily and without errors	With minor errors	With major errors	Not at all
Uses tools (measuring devices, graphs, tables, calculators, etc.) and procedures…	Correctly and efficiently	Correctly or with minor errors	Incorrectly	Not at all
Uses knowledge of the facts of mathematics (geometry definitions, math facts, etc.)…	Correctly	With minor errors	With major errors	Not at all

Figure 16: *Scoring an open-response problem using one dimension of the* TIMS Multidimensional Rubric

Using the Rubrics: A Second Example

During the school year, students become familiar with all three student rubrics and use them as they solve problems. Depending on the problem, they may use one or more of the rubrics. The results of these assessments are often saved in portfolios to show students and parents progress over time. The problem in Figure 17 is posed to students in the final assessment unit of third grade.

Before students begin solving the problem, the class reads and discusses the problem. Students should understand that play money will be available to help solve the problem and that they will be asked how they can use calculators to solve the problem. The teacher also reviews all three student rubrics and advises students that their work for this problem will be scored using all three dimensions.

Students use the tools available to them to find solutions and write about their strategies. The teacher may use samples of students' work to provide good examples for students to emulate. The teacher also comments on students' first drafts and students revise their work accordingly.

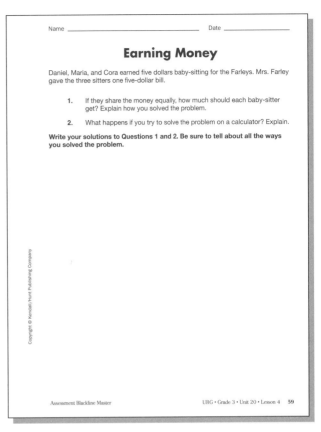

Figure 17: *An open-response problem from Grade 3 Unit 20*

Figure 18: *Marco's work*

Samples of two students' work are shown in Figures 18 and 19. Scores for both students for all three dimensions of the *TIMS Multidimensional Rubric* are discussed below. The teacher was guided by additional questions in the Lesson Guide that are specific to this problem and that point out elements to consider while scoring.

The teacher gave Marco a 2 on Solving. Marco chose a legitimate problem-solving strategy—guess and check—but did not use it systematically or efficiently, nor did he organize his work. His work does show evidence that he persisted in the problem-solving process, but does not show that he identified all the elements of the problem since he does not indicate that he knows that there will be money left over. He makes no connections to previously studied mathematics or previously solved problems.

On the Knowing dimension, the teacher gave Marco a 3 since he correctly used his knowledge of mathematics and he used appropriate tools (a calculator) and procedures (repeated addition and multiplication) to solve the problem. He did not demonstrate that he completely understood the nature of the task or show that he can translate between symbols and real situations since he did not calculate the amount of money that would be left over.

Marco received a 1 on the Telling dimension. His explanation was very short and totally unclear, with no supporting arguments. Since he did not identify which trial was successful, we are not even sure of his final answer. He used symbols to show his trials, but made no attempt to organize them. Appropriate terminology is not present.

A second sample of student work on the Earning Money problem is shown below:

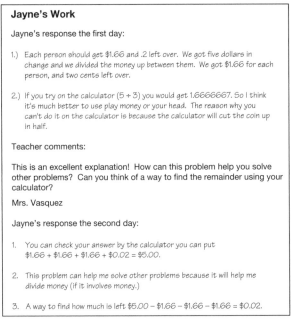

Jayne's Work

Jayne's response the first day:

1.) Each person should get $1.66 and .2 left over. We got five dollars in change and we divided the money up between them. We got $1.66 for each person, and two cents left over.

2.) If you try on the calculator (5 ÷ 3) you would get 1.6666667. So I think it's much better to use play money or your head. The reason why you can't do it on the calculator is because the calculator will cut the coin up in half.

Teacher comments:

This is an excellent explanation! How can this problem help you solve other problems? Can you think of a way to find the remainder using your calculator?

Mrs. Vasquez

Jayne's response the second day:

1. You can check your answer by the calculator you can put $1.66 + $1.66 + $1.66 + $0.02 = $5.00.

2. This problem can help me solve other problems because it will help me divide money (if it involves money.)

3. A way to find how much is left $5.00 − $1.66 − $1.66 − $1.66 = $0.02.

Figure 19: *Jayne's work*

Jayne's teacher gave her a score of 4 for Solving. She fully met the criteria in the rubric. She clearly identified the elements of the problem when she described the problem first as dividing the play money "up between them." She then found the amount left over and used a calculator to divide (5 ÷ 3) resulting in a repeating decimal. With prompting from the teacher, she looked for other strategies and found she could use repeated addition and subtraction to find the remainder. All her strategies are effective and they are presented in an organized fashion. Jayne's first conclusion that "you can't do it (find the remainder) on the calculator is because the calculator will cut the coin up in half" is insightful, although not quite correct mathematically. Using both repeated addition and subtraction on the calculator to find the remainder shows that she made meaningful connections between the operations and that she was willing to persist in the problem-solving process.

Jayne also received a 4 in Knowing since she clearly understood the problem's mathematical concepts. She readily translated the real situation into words when she described the process of dividing up the money and then translated words into symbols using correct addition, subtraction, and division sentences. The use of play money and a calculator is evidence that she can use tools correctly and efficiently and her calculations show that she can use the facts of mathematics correctly as well.

The teacher gave Jayne a score of 3 for the Telling dimension. Her explanations and responses were fairly complete and clear. However, we are not entirely sure how the group shared the money. Did they trade the dollars for quarters and then the quarters for dimes, etc., or were they able to make the process more efficient in some way? Her supporting arguments are sound, but they contain a few minor gaps. Did she use repeated subtraction or repeated addition first to find the remainder? Why did she choose these operations? She used many symbols and terms correctly. However, she reported that two cents were left over and wrote it first as ".2."

Like any new tool, using the rubric efficiently will require practice. As you begin to work with the rubric, we suggest that you work closely with other teachers. For example, you might score a half-dozen papers and ask one or more colleagues to score the same set; then compare and discuss the results, negotiating any differences. Repeating this process over the course of the year will help establish school-wide norms for applying the rubrics.

Using Assessment Observations, Math Journals, and Portfolios

The rubrics can be combined with other components of the assessment program to provide a more complete picture of students' skills at solving open-response problems. For example, to assess students' willingness to tackle new problems or work cooperatively in a group, teachers can observe students as they work on the problem or ask them to write in their journals about the process. For example, the Journal Prompt for the Earning Money problem concerns students' feelings about working in groups in math class. (See Figure 20.)

Journal Prompt

How did your group share the work on this problem? How do you feel about working with a group in math class?

Figure 20: *Journal prompt for Earning Money (Grade 3 Unit 20)*

Considerable growth in mathematical power is often evident when several write-ups of open-response problems from different times of the year are included in a student's portfolio. We can see growth in Jayne's problem-solving and communication skills when we look at her work on both the Class Party and Earning Money problems. (See Figure 9 in Part II and Figure 19.)

Evaluating Labs

Teachers have used the following ideas to evaluate student performance on labs:

Group Work

Students work in their groups to polish a lab write-up and turn in one completed lab or to prepare an oral report to be presented to the class. Their reports may include how the work was distributed among the group members. Students can also write a paragraph in their journals describing how each member functioned in the group and how to improve the process.

Using the Multidimensional Rubric

Choose one or two important questions to score using one or more dimensions of the *TIMS Multidimensional Rubric*. Often suitable questions are suggested in the Assessment section of the Suggestions for Teaching the Lesson in the Lesson Guide. These are usually open-response questions that ask students to make predictions or solve a problem using the data collected during the experiment.

Self-Assessment

Students can grade their own labs in class. This provides a forum for discussing the most important aspects of the lab.

Using a Point System

To grade a lab, teachers can assign a given number of points to each part of the lab and grade each part based on the criteria below. Teachers can also choose to grade only a portion of the lab such as the picture or the graph.

1. Drawing the Picture
   - Are the procedures and the materials clearly illustrated?
   - Are the variables labeled?
2. Collecting and Recording the Data
   - Are the data organized in a table?
   - Are the columns in the data table labeled correctly?
   - Are the data reasonable?
   - Are the correct units of measure included in the data table?
   - If applicable, did students average the data (find the median or mean) correctly?
3. Graphing the Data
   - Does the graph have a title?
   - Are the axes scaled correctly and labeled clearly? Labeling should be consistent with the picture and the data table and should include appropriate units of measure.
   - If it is a bar graph, are the bars drawn correctly?
   - If it is a point graph, are the points plotted correctly?
   - If the points suggest a straight line or a curve, did the student draw a best-fit line or fit a curve to the points?
   - Did the students show any interpolation or extrapolation on the graph?

4. Solving the Problems
   - Are the answers correct based on the data?
   - Did students use appropriate tools (calculators, rulers, graphs, etc.) correctly?
   - Are the answers, including the explanations, clear and complete?

References

Elementary Grades Assessment. *Balanced Assessment for the Mathematics Curriculum.* University of California. Dale Seymour Publications, White Plains, NY, 1999.

Lane, Suzanne. "The Conceptual Framework for the Development of a Mathematics Performance Assessment Instrument" in *Educational Measurement: Issues and Practice.* Vol. 12, Number 2. National Council on Measurement in Education, Washington, DC, 1993.

Mathematics Resource Guide for Fourth- and Eighth-Grade Teachers. Vermont Department of Education, Montpelier, VT, 1996.

Middle Grades Assessment. *Balanced Assessment for the Mathematics Curriculum.* University of California. Dale Seymour Publications, White Plains, NY, 2000.

Pellegrino, J.W., N. Chadowsky, and R. Glaser (Eds.) *Knowing What Students Know: The Science and Design of Educational Assessment.* National Research Council. National Academy Press, Washington, DC, 2001.

Performance Assessment in Mathematics: Approaches to Open-Ended Problems. Illinois State Board of Education, Springfield, IL, 1994.

Principles and Standards for School Mathematics. National Council of Teachers of Mathematics, Reston, VA, 2000.

Stenmark, J.K. (Ed.) *Mathematics Assessment: Myths, Models, Good Questions, and Practical Suggestions.* National Council of Teachers of Mathematics, Reston, VA, 1991.

Master Copies of Rubrics

This section contains the blackline masters of the *TIMS Multidimensional Rubric* and the three Student Rubrics: *Knowing, Solving,* and *Telling.* The Scoring Open-Response Problems section in Part III describes the rubrics and provides examples of their use in the curriculum. The *TIMS Multidimensional Rubric* is provided here so that teachers can use it to score student work. The copies of the three student rubrics in this section can be used to make transparencies for the overhead projector or enlarged to make posters for the classroom.

TIMS Multidimensional Rubric

Solving	Level 4	Level 3	Level 2	Level 1
Identifies the elements of the problem and their relationships to one another.	All major elements identified	Most elements identified	Some, but shows little understanding of relationships	Few or none
Uses problem-solving strategies which are . . .	Systematic, complete, efficient, and possibly elegant	Systematic and nearly complete, but not efficient	Incomplete or unsystematic	Not evident or inappropriate
Organizes relevant information . . .	Systematically and efficiently	Systematically, with minor errors	Unsystematically	Not at all
Relates the problem and solution to previously encountered mathematics and makes connections that are . . .	At length, elegant, and meaningful	Evident	Brief or logically unsound	Not evident
Persists in the problem solving process . . .	At length	Until a solution is reached	Briefly	Not at all
Looks back to examine the reasonableness of the solution and draws conclusions that are . . .	Insightful and comprehensive	Correct	Incorrect or logically unsound	Not present

Knowing	Level 4	Level 3	Level 2	Level 1
Understands the task's mathematical concepts, their properties and applications . . .	Completely	Nearly completely	Partially	Not at all
Translates between words, pictures, symbols, tables, graphs, and real situations . . .	Readily and without errors	With minor errors	With major errors	Not at all
Uses tools (measuring devices, graphs, tables, calculators, etc.) and procedures . . .	Correctly and efficiently	Correctly or with minor errors	Incorrectly	Not at all
Uses knowledge of the facts of mathematics (geometry definitions, math facts, etc.) . . .	Correctly	With minor errors	With major errors	Not at all

Telling	Level 4	Level 3	Level 2	Level 1
Includes response with an explanation and/or description which is . . .	Complete and clear	Fairly complete and clear	Perhaps ambiguous or unclear	Totally unclear or irrelevant
Presents supporting arguments which are . . .	Strong and sound	Logically sound, but may contain minor gaps	Incomplete or logically unsound	Not present
Uses pictures, symbols, tables, and graphs which are . . .	Correct and clearly relevant	Present with minor errors or somewhat irrelevant	Present with errors and/or irrelevant	Not present or completely inappropriate
Uses terminology . . .	Clearly and precisely	With minor errors	With major errors	Not at all

Student Rubric: Knowing

What is a rubric?

It tells me how to make sure I've done my best work!

In My Best Work in Mathematics:

- I show that I understand the ideas in the problem.

- I show the same mathematical ideas in different ways. I use pictures, tables, graphs, and sentences when they fit the problem.

- I show that I can use tools and rules correctly.

- I show that I can use the mathematical facts that apply to the problem.

Assessment

Student Rubric: Solving

How does this rubric help you?

It helps me plan strategies, find solutions, and check my work when I solve problems.

In My Best Work in Mathematics:

- I read the problem carefully, make a good plan for solving it, and then carry out that plan.

- I use tools like graphs, pictures, tables, or number sentences to help me.

- I use ideas I know from somewhere else to help me solve a problem.

- I keep working on the problem until I find a good solution.

- I look back at my solution to see if my answer makes sense.

- I look back at my work to see what more I can learn from solving the problem.

Student Rubric: Telling

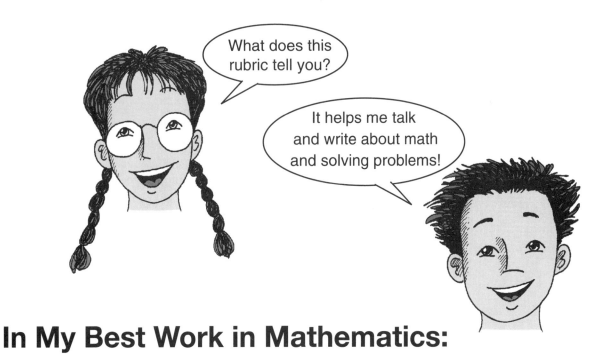

What does this rubric tell you?

It helps me talk and write about math and solving problems!

In My Best Work in Mathematics:

- I show all of the steps that I used to solve the problem. I also tell what each number refers to (such as 15 boys or 6 inches).

- I explain why I solved the problem the way I did so that someone can see why my method makes sense.

- If I use tools like pictures, tables, graphs, or number sentences, I explain how the tools I used fit the problem.

- I use math words and symbols correctly. For example, if I see "6 – 2," I solve the problem "six minus two," not "two minus six."

Assessment Overview for Fourth Grade

The assessment overview includes short descriptions of the components in the assessment program followed by a table that lists each assessment in fourth grade. The table names the assessments in each unit and gives the lesson name and number, the type of assessment, and the location of the assessment within the unit.

Component Summary

Assessment Indicators: A list of important topics covered in a given unit. The *Assessment Indicators* help the teacher focus on important skills and behaviors that should be assessed.

Observational Assessment Record: A tool that helps teachers organize student progress on the Assessment Indicators. Information about all students in the class can be recorded on the *Observational Assessment Record*. This provides a quick view of how both individual students and the class as a whole are progressing during the course of a unit. Student information can later be transferred to *Individual Assessment Record Sheets*.

Individual Assessment Record Sheet: A tool for tracking individual students' progress with the Assessment Indicators from all sixteen units.

Assessment: Suggested ways to assess student progress during a lesson are included as Assessment in the Suggestions for Teaching the Lesson section of the lesson guides. Assessment might highlight particular parts of an activity as appropriate for observations, direct teachers to an assessment page or activity, or suggest a Daily Practice and Problems (DPP) item or homework questions for assessment.

Math Journals: As a part of the assessment for a lesson, students are sometimes asked to respond in their Math Journals to a specific question or prompt.

Assessment Pages: Short paper-and-pencil assessments that can be used to check skills or concepts developed in a unit. Some are designed for use in groups; others are for individual work.

Assessment Lessons: Specially designed lessons to gauge student progress. There are three basic types of assessment lessons: assessment labs, open-response problems, and written tests composed of short items.

Assessment Labs: 2–3 laboratory experiments each year are designated as Assessment Labs. They are used to assess students' abilities to work in a group on an investigation that takes several days.

Assessment Units: Specific units in each grade that are designed to help teachers monitor student progress as part of the learning process. Units 2, 8, and 16 are the Assessment Units in Grade 4.

Facts Self-Assessment: As part of the Daily Practice and Problems (DPP), students regularly assess their knowledge of specific groups of math facts. Students categorize facts into three groups (facts I know quickly; facts I know using a strategy; facts I need to learn). They record this information on a special chart, which is updated regularly.

Facts Quizzes: Periodic quizzes of small groups of math facts are given as part of the DPP. Facts are grouped to encourage the use of strategies in learning them. Tests of the entire set of facts are given at midyear and at the end of the year.

Portfolios: Collections of students' written work and teachers' anecdotal records. Portfolios are used to document students' growth over time.

Assessment Component	Component Description	Location
Unit 1—Data About Us		
Observational Assessment Record	**Assessment Record**	**URG**
Individual Assessment Record Sheet	**Assessment Record**	**TIG**
Lesson 3—An Average Activity	**Lesson**	**URG**
DPP Item J—Variables and Values	Assessment Item	URG
Home Practice Part 3—Finding the Median	Assessment Page	DAB
Lesson 4—The Four Servants	**Adventure Book**	**URG**
DPP Item K—Addition Test: Doubles, 2s, 3s	Assessment Item	URG
Lesson 5—Arm Span vs. Height	**Lab**	**URG**
DPP Item M—Addition Test: More Addition Facts	Assessment Item	URG
DPP Item T—Favorite Sandwiches	Assessment Item	URG
More Arm Span vs. Height Data	Assessment Page	URG
Unit 2—Geometric Investigations: A Baseline Assessment Unit		
Observational Assessment Record	**Assessment Record**	**URG**
Individual Assessment Record Sheet	**Assessment Record**	**TIG**
Lesson 1—Investigating Perimeter and Area	**Lesson**	**URG**
Student Rubric: *Telling*	Student Rubric	SG/TIG
Lesson 2—Perimeter vs. Length	**Assessment Lab**	**URG, SG, DAB**
DPP Item J—Area and Perimeter	Assessment Item	URG
Lesson 3—Letter to Myrna	**Assessment Lesson**	**URG, SG**
DPP Item M—Subtraction Facts Test: Count Ups	Subtraction Facts Assessment Item	URG
A Letter to Myrna	Assessment Page	URG
Student Rubric: *Telling*	Student Rubric	SG/TIG
TIMS Multidimensional Rubric	Scoring Guide	TIG
Lesson 4—Helipads for Antopolis	**Lesson**	**URG**
DPP Item O—Subtraction Facts Test: Count-Backs	Subtraction Facts Assessment Item	URG
DPP Item Q—Subtraction Facts Test: Using a Ten	Subtraction Facts Assessment Item	URG
Lesson 5—Portfolios	**Assessment Lesson**	**URG, SG**
DPP Item S—Subtraction Facts Test: Doubles and Others	Subtraction Facts Assessment Item	URG

Assessment Component	Component Description	Location
Unit 3—Numbers and Number Operations		
Observational Assessment Record **Individual Assessment Record Sheet**	**Assessment Record** **Assessment Record**	**URG** **TIG**
Lesson 3—Place Value Working with Base-Ten Pieces	**Optional Lesson** Assessment Page	**URG** URG
Lesson 5—Addition and Subtraction Place Value Addition and Subtraction Quiz	**Lesson** Assessment Page	**URG** URG
Lesson 6—What's Below Zero? Professor Peabody Made a Mess!	**Optional Lesson** Assessment Page	**URG** URG
Lesson 7—At the Hardware Store DPP Item M—Quiz on 5s and 10s Home Practice Part 7—Arithmetic Review	**Lesson** Facts Quiz Assessment Page	**URG** URG DAB
Unit 4—Products and Factors		
Observational Assessment Record **Individual Assessment Record Sheet**	**Assessment Record** **Assessment Record**	**URG** **TIG**
Lesson 3—Floor Tiler DPP Item K—Multiples of a Number	**Game** Assessment Item	**URG** URG
Lesson 4—Prime Factors Student Rubric: *Telling* Unit 4 Test	**Lesson** Student Rubric Assessment Pages	**URG** SG/TIG URG
Lesson 5—Product Bingo DPP Item S—Quiz on 2s and 3s	**Game** Facts Quiz	**URG** URG
Unit 5—Using Data to Predict		
Observational Assessment Record **Individual Assessment Record Sheet**	**Assessment Record** **Assessment Record**	**URG** **TIG**
Lesson 3—The Meaning of the Mean Cookie Factory Student Rubric: *Telling*	**Lesson** Assessment Page Student Rubric	**URG** URG SG/TIG
Lesson 4—Bouncing Ball Home Practice Part 6—Bouncing Balls Student Rubric: *Solving* TIMS Multidimensional Rubric	**Lab** Assessment Page Student Rubric Scoring Guide	**URG** DAB SG/TIG TIG
Lesson 6—Professor Peabody Invents a Ball Professor Peabody Invents a Ball Student Rubric: *Solving* Student Rubric: *Telling* TIMS Multidimensional Rubric	**Assessment Lesson** Assessment Page Student Rubric Student Rubric Scoring Guide	**URG, SG,** **DAB** URG SG/TIG SG/TIG TIG
Lesson 8—Midterm Test DPP Item U—Quiz on the Square Numbers Midterm Test	**Assessment Lesson** Facts Quiz Assessment Pages	**URG** URG URG

Assessment Component	Component Description	Location
Unit 6—Place Value Patterns		
Observational Assessment Record **Individual Assessment Record Sheet**	**Assessment Record** **Assessment Record**	**URG** **TIG**
Lesson 2—Doubles DPP Item D—The Long and the Short Student Rubric: *Telling* Student Rubric: *Solving* TIMS Multidimensional Rubric	**Lesson** Assessment Item Student Rubric Student Rubric Scoring Guide	**URG** URG SG/TIG SG/TIG TIG
Lesson 6—Using Estimation DPP Item O—Multiplication Quiz: 9s Check-Up Time Student Rubric: *Knowing* TIMS Multidimensional Rubric	**Lesson** Facts Quiz Assessment Pages Student Rubric Scoring Guide	**URG** URG URG SG/TIG TIG
Unit 7—Patterns in Multiplication		
Observational Assessment Record **Individual Assessment Record Sheet**	**Assessment Record** **Assessment Record**	**URG** **TIG**
Lesson 2—Divisibility Rules Home Practice Part 3—Division	**Lesson** Assessment Page	**URG** DAB
Lesson 3—Oh, No! My Calculator Is Broken The Broken Calculator Student Rubric: *Knowing* Student Rubric: *Solving* TIMS Multidimensional Rubric	**Assessment Lesson** Assessment Page Student Rubric Student Rubric Scoring Guide	**URG, SG,** **DAB** URG SG/TIG SG/TIG TIG
Lesson 4—Multiplying by 10s Home Practice Part 5—Multiplying by 10	**Lesson** Assessment Page	**URG** DAB
Lesson 6—Estimation DPP Item Y—Multiplying by Multiples of 10	**Lesson** Assessment Item	**URG** URG
Lesson 7—Multiplying Round Numbers DPP Item AA—Multiplication Quiz: Last Six Facts Multiplication	**Lesson** Facts Quiz Assessment Page	**URG** URG URG
Lesson 8—A Camping Trip Home Practice Part 7—Groups and More Groups	**Lesson** Assessment Page	**URG** DAB

Assessment

Assessment Component	Component Description	Location
Unit 8—Measuring Up: An Assessment Unit		
Observational Assessment Record **Individual Assessment Record Sheet**	**Assessment Record** **Assessment Record**	**URG** **TIG**
Lesson 3—Volume vs. Number Student Rubric: *Solving*	**Assessment Lab** Student Rubric	**URG, SG, DAB** SG/TIG
Lesson 5—Hour Walk Hour Walk Student Rubric: *Knowing* Student Rubric: *Solving* Student Rubric: *Telling* TIMS Multidimensional Rubric	**Assessment Lesson** Assessment Page Student Rubric Student Rubric Student Rubric Scoring Guide	**URG, SG, DAB** URG SG/TIG SG/TIG SG/TIG TIG
Lesson 6—Midyear Test Midyear Test	**Assessment Lesson** Assessment Pages	**URG** URG
Lesson 7—Midyear Experiment and Portfolio Review	**Assessment Lesson**	**URG, SG, DAB**
Lesson 8—Facts I Know: Multiplication and Division Facts DPP Item U—Multiplication Facts Inventory Test	**Assessment Lesson** Facts Quiz	**URG, SG, DAB** URG
Unit 9—Shapes and Solids		
Observational Assessment Record **Individual Assessment Record Sheet**	**Assessment Record** **Assessment Record**	**URG** **TIG**
Lesson 2—What's Your Angle? Measuring Angles II	**Lesson** Assessment Page	**URG** DAB
Lesson 3—Symmetry DPP Item I—Geometric Gems	**Lesson** Assessment Item	**URG** URG
Lesson 6—Finding the Volume of a Prism Home Practice Part 5—Geometry	**Lesson** Assessment Page	**URG** DAB
Lesson 8—Constructing a Prism DPP Item U—Quiz: 5s and 10s Constructing a Prism	**Assessment Lesson** Facts Quiz Assessment Page	**URG** URG URG
Unit 10—Using Decimals		
Observational Assessment Record **Individual Assessment Record Sheet**	**Assessment Record** **Assessment Record**	**URG** **TIG**
Lesson 3—Hundredths Linda's Base-Ten Pieces Student Rubric: *Knowing* TIMS Multidimensional Rubric	**Lesson** Assessment Page Student Rubric Scoring Guide	**URG** URG SG/TIG TIG
Lesson 4—Downhill Racer Roberto's Data	**Lab** Assessment Pages	**URG** URG
Lesson 6—Alberto in Tenthsland DPP Item W—Quiz on 2s and 3s Division Facts	**Adventure Book** Facts Quiz	**URG** URG

Assessment Component	Component Description	Location
Unit 11—Multiplication		
Observational Assessment Record **Individual Assessment Record Sheet**	**Assessment Record** **Assessment Record**	**URG** **TIG**
Lesson 2—More Multiplication Home Practice Part 3—Multiples of 10 and 100	**Lesson** Assessment Page	**URG** DAB
Lesson 4—All-Partials Revisited Quiz	**Lesson** Assessment Page	**URG** URG
Lesson 6—Phil and Howard's Excellent Egyptian Adventure DPP Item U—Division Quiz: Square Numbers	**Adventure Book** Facts Quiz	**URG** URG
Unit 12—Exploring Fractions		
Observational Assessment Record **Individual Assessment Record Sheet**	**Assessment Record** **Assessment Record**	**URG** **TIG**
Lesson 5—Equivalent Fractions Home Practice Part 3—Fraction Chart	**Lesson** Assessment Page	**URG** DAB
Lesson 7—Solving Problems with Pattern Blocks DPP Item Q—Confused! DPP Item R—Further Confusion	**Lesson** Assessment Item Assessment Item	**URG** URG URG
Lesson 8—Fraction Puzzles Puzzle Problem Student Rubric: *Solving* Student Rubric: *Telling* TIMS Multidimensional Rubric	**Assessment Lesson** Assessment Page Student Rubric Student Rubric Scoring Guide	**URG, SG,** **DAB** URG SG/TIG SG/TIG TIG
Lesson 9—Midterm Test DPP Item W—Division Quiz: 9s Midterm Test	**Assessment Lesson** Facts Quiz Assessment Pages	**URG, SG** URG URG
Unit 13—Division		
Observational Assessment Record **Individual Assessment Record Sheet**	**Assessment Record** **Assessment Record**	**URG** **TIG**
Lesson 3—More Division Home Practice Part 4—More Division Practice	**Lesson** Assessment Page	**URG** DAB
Lesson 4—Solving Problems Using Multiplication and Division DPP Item S—Facts Quiz: Last Six Facts Unit 13 Quiz	**Lesson** Facts Quiz Assessment Page	**URG** URG URG

Assessment

Assessment Component	Component Description	Location
Unit 14—Chancy Predictions: An Introduction to Probability		
Observational Assessment Record **Individual Assessment Record Sheet**	**Assessment Record** **Assessment Record**	**URG** **TIG**
Lesson 3—Rolling a Number Cube Check-up	**Lab** Assessment Page	**URG** URG
Lesson 5—Exploring Spinners DPP Item M—Division Facts Quiz 1 Spinners Quiz	**Lesson** Facts Quiz Assessment Page	**URG** URG URG
Lesson 7—Probe Quest DPP Item O—Division Facts Quiz 2	**Adventure Book** Facts Quiz	**URG** URG
Unit 15—Using Patterns		
Observational Assessment Record **Individual Assessment Record Sheet**	**Assessment Record** **Assessment Record**	**URG** **TIG**
Lesson 3—Planet Gzorp Make Your Own	**Lesson** Assessment Pages	**URG** URG
Lesson 4—Function Machines Home Practice Part 6—Function Machines	**Lesson** Assessment Page	**URG** DAB
Lesson 5—Taste of TIMS DPP Item M—Division Facts Quiz 1 DPP Item O—Division Facts Quiz 2 Student Rubric: *Telling* TIMS Multidimensional Rubric	**Lab** Facts Quiz Facts Quiz Student Rubric Scoring Guide	**URG** URG URG SG/TIG TIG
Unit 16—Assessing Our Learning		
Observational Assessment Record **Individual Assessment Record Sheet**	**Assessment Record** **Assessment Record**	**URG** **TIG**
Lesson 3—Area vs. Length Student Rubric: *Telling* TIMS Multidimensional Rubric	**Assessment Lab** Student Rubric Scoring Guide	**URG, SG,** **DAB** SG/TIG TIG
Lesson 4—The Many-Eyed Dragonfly The Many-Eyed Dragonfly Student Rubric: *Knowing* Student Rubric: *Solving* Student Rubric: *Telling* TIMS Multidimensional Rubric	**Assessment Lesson** Assessment Pages Student Rubric Student Rubric Student Rubric Scoring Guide	**URG, SG,** **DAB** URG SG/TIG SG/TIG SG/TIG TIG
Lesson 5—End-of-Year Test End-of-Year Test	**Assessment Lesson** Assessment Pages	**URG, DAB** URG
Lesson 6—Portfolios DPP Item R—Division Facts Inventory Test	**Assessment Lesson** Facts Quiz	**URG, SG** URG

Individual Assessment Record Sheet

Name _____

Unit 1: Data About Us	✔	**Date and Comments:**

A1. Can students identify categorical and numerical variables?   _____   _____

A2. Can students find the median of a data set?   _____   _____

A3. Can students make and interpret bar graphs?   _____   _____

A4. Can students make and interpret point graphs?   _____   _____

A5. Can students use patterns in data tables and graphs to make predictions?   _____   _____

A6. Can students measure length in inches?   _____   _____

A7. Do students demonstrate fluency with the addition facts?   _____   _____

A8. _____   _____   _____

Unit 2: Geometric Investigations: **A Baseline Assessment Unit**	✔	**Date and Comments:**

A1. Can students use patterns in data tables and graphs to make and test conjectures?   _____   _____

A2. Can students collect, organize, graph, and analyze data?   _____   _____

A3. Can students make and interpret point graphs?   _____   _____

A4. Can students find the perimeter of polygons?   _____   _____

A5. Can students find the area of polygons?   _____   _____

A6. Can students estimate the size of an angle?   _____   _____

A7. Can students identify acute, obtuse, and right angles?   _____   _____

A8. Can students communicate solution strategies?   _____   _____

A9. Do students demonstrate fluency with the subtraction facts?   _____   _____

A10. _____   _____   _____

Unit 3: Numbers and Number Operations	✔	**Date and Comments:**

A1. Can students name the value of a digit based on its place in a number?   _____   _____

A2. Can students represent two-, three-, and four-digit numbers using base-ten pieces?   _____   _____

A3. Can students represent addition and subtraction using base-ten pieces?   _____   _____

A4. Can students add multidigit numbers using paper and pencil?   _____   _____

A5. Can students subtract multidigit numbers using paper and pencil?   _____   _____

A6. Can students determine the reasonableness of a solution?   _____   _____

A7. Do students demonstrate fluency with the multiplication facts for the 5s and 10s?   _____   _____

A8. Can students write the four number sentences in the fact families for the 5s and 10s?   _____   _____

A9. _____   _____   _____

Name _____

Unit 4: Products and Factors   ✔   **Date and Comments:**

A1.   Can students represent multiplication and division problems using arrays?   _____   _____

A2.   Can students determine whether one number is a multiple of another number?   _____   _____

A3.   Can students determine whether one number is a factor of another number?   _____   _____

A4.   Can students identify prime, composite, and square numbers?   _____   _____

A5.   Can students find the prime factorization of a number?   _____   _____

A6.   Can students explain their mathematical reasoning?   _____   _____

A7.   Do students demonstrate fluency with the multiplication facts for the 2s and 3s?   _____   _____

A8.   Can students write the four number sentences in the fact families for the 2s and 3s?   _____   _____

A9.   _____   _____   _____

Unit 5: Using Data to Predict   ✔   **Date and Comments:**

A1.   Can students draw and interpret best-fit lines?   _____   _____

A2.   Can students find the median and mean of a data set?   _____   _____

A3.   Can students identify and use variables?   _____   _____

A4.   Can students measure length in centimeters?   _____   _____

A5.   Can students use patterns in data tables and graphs to make predictions?   _____   _____

A6.   Can students collect, organize, graph, and analyze data?   _____   _____

A7.   Can students solve open-response problems and communicate solution strategies?   _____   _____

A8.   Do students demonstrate fluency with the multiplication facts for the square numbers?   _____   _____

A9.   Can students write the two number sentences in the fact families for the square numbers?   _____   _____

A10.   _____   _____   _____

Name _____

Unit 6: Place Value Patterns   ✔   **Date and Comments:**

A1.   Can students read and write large numbers (to the millions)?   ———   ————————————

A2.   Can students compare and order large numbers (to the millions)?   ———   ————————————

A3.   Can students represent large numbers (to the millions) using place value charts and number lines?   ———   ————————————

A4.   Can students use patterns to make predictions?   ———   ————————————

A5.   Can students estimate sums and differences for large numbers?   ———   ————————————

A6.   Do students demonstrate fluency with the multiplication facts for the 9s?   ———   ————————————

A7.   Can students write the four number sentences in the fact families for the 9s?   ———   ————————————

A8.   —————————————————   ———   ————————————

Unit 7: Patterns in Multiplication   ✔   **Date and Comments:**

A1.   Can students follow the order of operations?   ———   ————————————

A2.   Can students mentally multiply numbers with ending zeros?   ———   ————————————

A3.   Can students multiply 2-digit by 1-digit numbers using paper and pencil?   ———   ————————————

A4.   Can students estimate sums, differences, and products?   ———   ————————————

A5.   Can students solve problems involving multiplication?   ———   ————————————

A6.   Can students solve open-response problems and communicate solution strategies?   ———   ————————————

A7.   Do students demonstrate fluency with the last six multiplication facts (4×6, 4×7, 4×8, 6×7, 6×8, 7×8)?   ———   ————————————

A8.   Can students write the four number sentences for each of the fact families for the last six facts?   ———   ————————————

A9.   —————————————————   ———   ————————————

Unit 8: Measuring Up: An Assessment Unit   ✔   **Date and Comments:**

A1.   Can students collect, organize, graph, and analyze data?   ———   ————————————

A2.   Can students make and interpret point graphs?   ———   ————————————

A3.   Can students draw and interpret best-fit lines?   ———   ————————————

A4.   Can students use patterns in data tables and graphs to make predictions?   ———   ————————————

A5.   Can students measure volume by displacement?   ———   ————————————

A6.   Can students solve open-response problems and communicate solution strategies?   ———   ————————————

A7.   Do students demonstrate fluency with the multiplication facts?   ———   ————————————

A8.   Can students write the four number sentences for each of the fact families?   ———   ————————————

A9.   —————————————————   ———   ————————————

Assessment

Name _____

Unit 9: Shapes and Solids ✔ **Date and Comments:**

A1. Can students measure angles? _____ _____

A2. Can students identify acute, obtuse, and right angles? _____ _____

A3. Can students identify line and turn symmetry? _____ _____

A4. Can students describe 2- and 3-dimensional shapes
     using their properties? _____ _____

A5. Can students identify a net of a prism? _____ _____

A6. Can students find the volume of a rectangular prism? _____ _____

A7. Do students demonstrate fluency with the division facts
     for the 5s and 10s? _____ _____

A8. _____ _____ _____

Unit 10: Using Decimals ✔ **Date and Comments:**

A1. Can students represent decimals using number lines
     (metersticks) and base-ten pieces? _____ _____

A2. Can students read and write decimals to hundredths? _____ _____

A3. Can students skip count by tenths and hundredths? _____ _____

A4. Can students measure length to the nearest mm,
     cm, dm, and m? _____ _____

A5. Can students collect, organize, graph, and analyze data? _____ _____

A6. Do students demonstrate fluency with the division facts
     for the 2s and 3s? _____ _____

A7. _____ _____ _____

Unit 11: Multiplication ✔ **Date and Comments:**

A1. Can students represent multiplication using
     base-ten pieces? _____ _____

A2. Can students multiply two-digit by two-digit numbers
     using paper and pencil? _____ _____

A3. Can students multiply numbers with ending zeros mentally? _____ _____

A4. Can students estimate products? _____ _____

A5. Can students solve multistep word problems using
     multiplication? _____ _____

A6. Do students demonstrate fluency with the division
     facts for the square numbers? _____ _____

A7. _____ _____ _____

Name _____

Unit 12: Exploring Fractions   ✔   **Date and Comments:**

A1. Can students represent fractions using pattern blocks and paper folding? _____ _____

A2. Can students identify the whole when given a fractional part of the whole? _____ _____

A3. Can students find equivalent fractions using manipulatives? _____ _____

A4. Can students compare and order fractions using manipulatives? _____ _____

A5. Can students add and subtract fractions with like denominators using manipulatives? _____ _____

A6. Can students solve open-response problems and communicate solution strategies? _____ _____

A7. Do students demonstrate fluency with the division facts for the 9s? _____ _____

A8. _____ _____ _____

Unit 13: Division   ✔   **Date and Comments:**

A1. Can students collect, organize, graph, and analyze data? _____ _____

A2. Can students represent division using base-ten pieces? _____ _____

A3. Can students divide with 1-digit divisors using paper and pencil? _____ _____

A4. Can students interpret remainders? _____ _____

A5. Can students estimate quotients? _____ _____

A6. Can students solve problems involving multiplication and division? _____ _____

A7. Do students demonstrate fluency with the 12 division facts related to the last six facts ($24 \div 4$, $24 \div 6$, $28 \div 4$, $28 \div 7$, $32 \div 4$, $32 \div 8$, $42 \div 6$, $42 \div 7$, $48 \div 6$, $48 \div 8$, $56 \div 7$, $56 \div 8$)? _____ _____

A8. _____ _____ _____

Unit 14: Chancy Predictions: An Introduction to Probability   ✔   **Date and Comments:**

A1. Can students collect, organize, graph, and analyze data? _____ _____

A2. Can students make and interpret bar graphs? _____ _____

A3. Can students use fractions to give the probabilities of events? _____ _____

A4. Can students use probabilities to make predictions? _____ _____

A5. Do students demonstrate fluency with the division facts for the 2s, 5s, 10s, and square numbers? _____ _____

A6. _____ _____ _____

A7. _____ _____ _____

Assessment

Name _____

Unit 15: Using Patterns   ✔   **Date and Comments:**

A1. Can students collect, organize, graph, and analyze data?   _____   _____

A2. Can students make and interpret point graphs?   _____   _____

A3. Can students draw and interpret best-fit lines?   _____   _____

A4. Can students identify and extend patterns?   _____   _____

A5. Can students use patterns to make predictions?   _____   _____

A6. Can students represent patterns and functions using words, symbols, tables, and graphs?   _____   _____

A7. Can students identify and use variables?   _____   _____

A8. Can students measure mass?   _____   _____

A9. Do students show fluency with the division facts for the 3s, 9s, and the 12 division facts related to the last six facts ($24 \div 4$, $24 \div 6$, $28 \div 4$, $28 \div 7$, $32 \div 4$, $32 \div 8$, $42 \div 6$, $42 \div 7$, $48 \div 6$, $48 \div 8$, $56 \div 7$, $56 \div 8$)?   _____   _____

A10. _____   _____   _____

Unit 16: Assessing Our Learning   ✔   **Date and Comments:**

A1. Can students identify and use variables?   _____   _____

A2. Can students collect, organize, graph, and analyze data?   _____   _____

A3. Can students use patterns in data to make predictions and solve problems?   _____   _____

A4. Can students solve open-response problems and communicate solution strategies?   _____   _____

A5. Do students demonstrate fluency with the division facts?   _____   _____

A6. _____   _____   _____

Additional Comments:

TIMS Tutors

The TIMS Tutors section provides an in-depth exploration of the mathematical concepts and ideas behind *Math Trailblazers*.

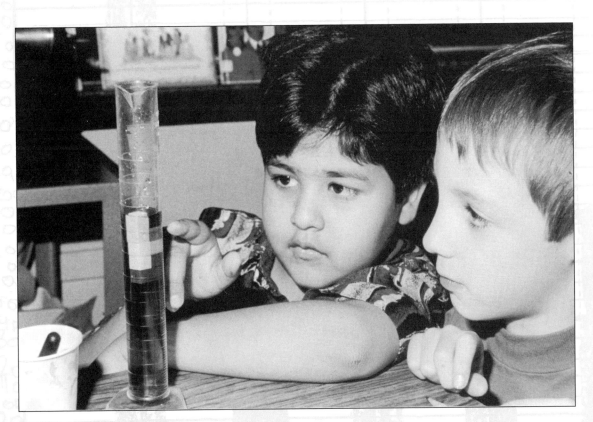

Students use a graduated cylinder to find the volume of small objects.

Introduction

TIMS Tutors

Arithmetic

Introduction

The last half-century has seen many changes in elementary school mathematics. For many people, "mathematics" is synonymous with "arithmetic." But today, while reasonable people can still debate the proper content of an elementary mathematics curriculum, nearly all agree that a curriculum focused largely on rote arithmetic will not meet the needs of students in the twenty-first century.

Much more than just arithmetic is now expected—geometry, probability, statistics, measurement, graphing, even algebra. Technology is dramatically changing the world, making it hard to imagine what our children will need to know in 20 or 40 more years, but also ensuring that many skills critical 50 years ago are less essential. Despite recent advances in psychology, educational research, and curriculum design, we are far from resolving all the uncertainties of the elementary school mathematics curriculum. A few things, however, do seem clear:

- The school mathematics curriculum can and must be more rigorous.
- Arithmetic is only one piece, albeit an important one, of a broad mathematics curriculum.
- We need to do better at helping children connect marks on paper to the real world. Too many children and adults fail to use common sense when dealing with mathematical symbolism. Discussing mathematics and integrating subject matter may help students make these connections.
- As we correct for the overemphasis on skills in the traditional mathematics curriculum, we should avoid over-correcting. Problem solving requires both procedural skill and conceptual understanding. As William Brownell (1956) noted during a previous period of reform, "In objecting to the emphasis on drill prevalent not so long ago, we may have failed to point out that practice for proficiency in skills has its place too." In *Math Trailblazers,* we consistently seek a balance between conceptual understanding and procedural skill.

The National Council of Teachers of Mathematics' (NCTM) *Principles and Standards for School Mathematics* advocates learning mathematics with understanding. "In recent decades, psychological and educational research on the learning of complex subjects such as mathematics has solidly established the important role of conceptual understanding in the knowledge and activity of persons who are proficient. Being proficient in a complex domain such as mathematics entails the ability to use knowledge flexibly, applying what is learned in one setting appropriately in another. One of the most robust findings of research is that conceptual understanding is an important component of proficiency, along with factual knowledge and procedural facility" (Bransford, Brown, and Cocking, 1999). The alliance of factual knowledge, procedural proficiency, and conceptual understanding makes all three components usable in powerful ways. Students who memorize facts or procedures without understanding often are not sure when or how to use what they know, and such learning is often quite fragile (Bransford, Brown, and Cocking, 1999; NCTM, 2000).

Several arguments support the NCTM position. One is that the computational proficiency of American students comes at too high a cost. The hundreds of hours devoted to arithmetic computation in elementary school leave too little time for other important topics. The traditional rote approach to computation undermines higher-level thinking: children learn that mathematics is blindly following rules, not thinking.

Another argument for shifting away from the traditional arithmetic curriculum is that technology has altered the role of paper-and-pencil calculation. As noted in the NCTM *Principles and Standards,* ". . . most of the arithmetic and algebraic procedures long viewed as the heart of the school mathematics curriculum can now be performed with handheld calculators. Thus more attention can now be given to understanding the number concepts and the modeling procedures used in solving problems." (NCTM, 2000) More practical topics—probability and statistics, geometry, measurement, mental computation and estimation—deserve more attention.

A final and most important argument in favor of the changes NCTM recommends is that new approaches to arithmetic instruction are more effective in helping students learn both appropriate calculation skills and how to apply those skills in solving problems. These new approaches build on students' own knowledge and intuitive methods and engage their common sense. This more meaningful approach helps students to be efficient and flexible in their computation and can reduce, though not eliminate, the amount of practice required. Thus a greater emphasis on conceptual understanding can lead to better procedural skills and problem-solving abilities (Brown & Burton, 1978; Skemp, 1978; Hiebert, 1984; Van Lehn, 1986; Carpenter, 1986; Baroody and Ginsburg, 1986; Good, Mulryan, and McCaslin, 1992; Hiebert, 1999; National Research Council, 2001).

A final and most important argument in favor of the changes NCTM recommends is that new approaches to arithmetic instruction are more effective in helping students learn both appropriate calculation skills and how to apply those skills in solving problems.

Numeration and Place Value

Numeration in kindergarten emphasizes developing oral counting skills, making one-to-one correspondence between objects and numbers, developing the concept of cardinality, discovering patterns in our number system, and writing numbers. Students in Grade 1 continue to develop these skills and concepts. They take part in activities that help them become familiar with the structure of the number system.

In kindergarten and Grade 1, students practice their counting skills. They learn to count past 100 by ones, twos, fives, and tens. They count forward and backward from any given number. They group objects for counting.

Students use counting to solve addition and subtraction problems. They learn to write numbers up to and beyond 100. Beginning in kindergarten, a ten frame is frequently used as a visual organizer. See Figure 1. The *100 Chart* is introduced and used for a variety of purposes, including solving problems and studying patterns. Students partition, or break apart, numbers in several ways (25 = 20 + 5, 25 = 10 + 10 + 5, and so on). These activities help children develop number sense that allows them to use numbers flexibly.

Figure 1: *Sample ten frame*

While formal study of place value is not a focus in kindergarten or Grade 1, the multiple grouping and counting experiences described above provide children with a foundation for building an intuitive sense for the meaning of place value.

Work with counting continues in Grade 2, especially skip counting and counting backwards. Place value is explored in the context of counting and grouping by tens. Children continue to count and group everyday objects such as buttons or beans. They use connecting cubes to represent these objects and often group the cubes by tens. Later, base-ten pieces represent these same objects, thus linking the base-ten representations with quantities of actual objects.

Students explore numbers well into the hundreds. Counting is still used for problem solving, but more elaborate procedures may be employed. For example, a student may solve 885 − 255 by counting up, first by hundreds (355, 455, 555, 655, 755, 855) and then by tens (865, 875, 885), yielding 630 as the answer.

More elaborate partitions of numbers are investigated in Grade 2. Particularly important are partitions in which every part is a single digit times 1, 10, 100, or 1000: 359 = 300 + 50 + 9 and so on. Attention is also given to partitioning numbers in more than one way:

$$
\begin{aligned}
359 &= 300 + 50 + 9 \\
&= 200 + 150 + 9 \\
&= 100 + 250 + 9
\end{aligned}
$$

This work with multiple partitioning is closely related to multidigit addition and subtraction. One way to think about addition and subtraction—indeed, one way to think about much of elementary mathematics—is as procedures for renaming numbers in more convenient forms. For example, 563 + 13 is a number we usually rename as 576. Another number, 875 ÷ 25, is renamable as 35 when it suits our purposes.

In Grade 3, more formal study of place value takes place. Students work in varied contexts involving numbers through the thousands. For example, students draw an outline of a coat and determine how many square centimeters of material are required to make the coat. Using contexts such as this encourages students to associate quantities of actual objects with representations of the quantities using base-ten pieces and with the numerals that represent them. Most of this work is closely connected with addition and subtraction of multidigit numbers. Indeed, a good reason for studying computational algorithms is that they provide a context for learning about place value.

In Grade 4, large numbers up to the millions are studied and used in various contexts. Continued efforts are made to connect the numbers with actual quantities. For example, the class creates its own base-ten pieces for large numbers—pieces we call super skinnies (10,000), super flats (100,000), and megabits (1,000,000). See Figure 2.

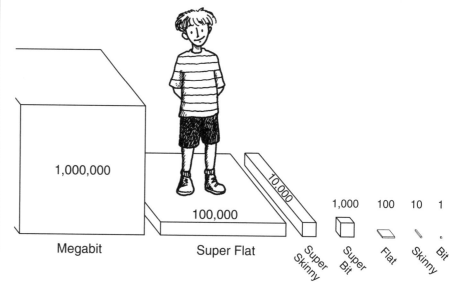

Figure 2: *Base-ten pieces for small and large numbers*

After reviewing and establishing the basics of the base-ten place value system for whole numbers, the system is extended to include decimals beginning in third grade. In Grade 4, the ten-for-one trading rules and other aspects of our number system are extended to the right of the decimal point for the first time.

In Grade 5, we extend the number system to even larger numbers. The story of Archimedes' attempt to calculate the number of grains of sand that would fill the observed universe introduces students to numbers far beyond what we encounter in everyday life. With the use of scientific calculators in Grade 5, scientific notation for large numbers is needed and introduced.

Basic Number Facts

In developing the math facts program, we sought a careful balance between strategies and drill. This approach is based on a large body of research and advocated by the NCTM *Principles and Standards for School Mathematics*. The research indicates that the methods used in the *Math Trailblazers* math facts program lead to more effective learning and better retention of the math facts and also helps develop essential math skills.

The *Math Trailblazers* program for teaching the math facts is characterized by these elements:

- *Early emphasis on problem solving.* Students first approach the basic facts as problems to solve rather than facts to memorize. Students invent their own strategies to solve these problems or learn appropriate strategies from others through class discussion. Students' natural strategies, especially counting strategies, are explicitly encouraged. In this way, students learn that math is more than memorizing facts and rules that "you either get or you don't."

- *De-emphasis of rote work.* Fluency with the math facts is an important component of any student's mathematical learning. Research has shown that an overemphasis on memorization and the frequent administration of timed tests are counterproductive. (National Research Council, 2001) We encourage the use of strategies to find facts, so students become confident they can find answers to fact problems they do not immediately recall.

- *Gradual and systematic introduction of facts.* Students study the facts in small groups that can be solved using similar strategies. Students first work on simple strategies for easy facts and then progress to more sophisticated strategies and harder facts. By the end of the process, they gain fluency with all the required facts.

- *Ongoing practice.* Work on the math facts is distributed throughout the curriculum, especially in the Daily Practice and Problems, Home Practice, and games. This practice for fluency, however, takes place only after students conceptually understand the operations and are proficient with strategies for solving basic fact problems. Delaying practice in this way means students need less practice to achieve fluency.

- *Appropriate assessment.* Teachers assess students' knowledge of the facts through observations as they work on activities, labs, and games as well as through the appropriate use of written tests and quizzes. Beginning in first grade, periodic, short quizzes in the Daily Practice and Problems naturally follow the study of small groups of facts organized around specific strategies. As self-assessment in Grades 2–5, students record their progress on *Facts I Know* charts and determine which facts they need to study. Inventory tests of all facts for each operation are used sparingly in Grades 2–5 (no more than twice per year) to assess students' progress with fact fluency. The goal of the math facts assessment program is to determine the degree to which students can find answers to fact problems quickly and accurately and whether they can retain this skill over time.

- *Multiyear approach.* In Grades 1 and 2, *Math Trailblazers* emphasizes strategies that lead to fluency with the addition and subtraction facts. In Grade 3, students gain fluency with the multiplication facts while reviewing the addition and subtraction facts. In Grade 4, students achieve fluency with the division facts and verify fluency with the multiplication facts. In Grade 5, the multiplication and division facts are systematically reviewed and assessed. This is outlined in Table 1.
- *Facts are not gatekeepers.* Students are not prevented from learning more complex mathematics because they do not perform well on fact tests. Use of strategies, calculators, and other math tools (e.g., manipulatives, hundreds charts, printed multiplication tables) allows students to continue to work on interesting problems and important mathematical concepts while they are still learning the facts.

The *Math Trailblazers* approach to the math facts is discussed more fully in the TIMS Tutor: *Math Facts.*

Concepts of Whole-Number Operations
Concepts and Skills

Throughout the past 150 years, there were numerous attempts to teach mathematics meaningfully rather than by rote. Unfortunately, as Lauren Resnick points out in *Syntax and Semantics in Learning to Subtract,* ". . . the conceptual teaching methods of the past were inadequate to the extent that they taught concepts instead of procedures and left it entirely to students to discover how computational procedures could be derived from the basic structure of the number and numeration system." (1987, p. 136)

Many educators have long recognized, however, that there is no real conflict between skills and concepts. (Whitehead, 1929; Dewey, 1938; Brownell, 1956; May, 1995; National Research Council, 2001) New conceptual understandings are built on existing skills and concepts; these new understandings in turn support the further development of skills and concepts. Thomas Carpenter describes the relationship in this way: ". . . It is an iterative process. Procedures are taught that can be supported by existing conceptual knowledge, and the conceptual knowledge base is extended to provide a basis for developing more advanced concepts. At every point during instruction, procedures are taught that can be connected to existing conceptual knowledge." (1986, p. 130) This integration of concepts and skills underlies our work with arithmetic in *Math Trailblazers.*

Subtraction in Grades K to 5
To illustrate how concepts and skills are balanced in *Math Trailblazers,* we outline in this section how one operation—subtraction—is developed with whole numbers in Grades K–4. Though the details may differ for the other operations, the same general approach described here with subtraction applies to all four arithmetic operations.

In kindergarten and Grade 1 of *Math Trailblazers,* students solve a variety of problems involving subtraction of numbers up to and even beyond 100. These problems are based on hands-on classroom activities and realistic situations from children's experiences. Different subtraction problem types are represented, including take-away, comparison, part-whole, and missing addend problems. (See the TIMS Tutor: *Word Problems* for a discussion of these and other problem types.)

Students in even the earliest grades are thus faced with problems for which they have no ready solution methods, problems that in the traditional view are beyond their ability. They do, however, have much prior knowledge that is relevant. They have their common sense—their conceptual knowledge of the problem situations. They know, for example, that if Grace begins with 50 marbles and loses 17, then she must end with fewer than 50 marbles. Young students also have considerable procedural knowledge, including various kinds of counting skills: ordinary counting, counting on, counting back, and skip counting by twos, fives, and tens. Students have tools to solve the problems. These include connecting cubes, links, *100 Charts,* ten frames, other manipulatives, paper and pencil, calculators, and number lines. Researchers note that initial work with any operation should involve classroom activities that use real-world or imaginary contexts, manipulatives, or drawings that highlight the attributes of the numbers and operations. (Carpenter et al., 1998; Fuson and Briars, 1990, Hiebert et al., 1997) This research further emphasizes the importance of long-term use of the manipulatives and of linking the manipulatives with written notation.

On one side, then, are hard problems involving many types of subtraction. On the other side are the kindergartners and first-graders, with their common sense, their counting skills, and tools. Traditionally, word problems and other applications involving subtraction (and other operations) were introduced only after students had extensive practice with a subtraction algorithm. Research on students' learning of addition and subtraction (Carpenter et al., 1998) strongly suggests that it is more effective to have students solve and pose word problems and other context-based problems (such as problems in the laboratory investigations in *Math Trailblazers*) before they learn formal, paper-and-pencil procedures for subtraction. As students apply their resources to solve the problems, they build their conceptual and procedural understanding of subtraction. They devise methods to solve the problems, make records of their work, and discuss their methods with their teacher and classmates. Their new knowledge about subtraction is closely linked to their prior knowledge, especially their out-of-school knowledge and their counting skills. (Baroody and Ginsburg, 1986)

You comment on students' methods and may show students how to use conventional symbols to describe their work, but you make no attempt to standardize students' methods. Any method that yields a correct result is acceptable—as long as it makes sense. The goal is to encourage students to apply their prior knowledge to problems they encounter and to let students know that their intuitive methods are valid.

> *As students apply their resources to solve the problems, they build their conceptual and procedural understanding of subtraction. They devise methods to solve the problems, make records of their work, and discuss their methods with their teacher and classmates.*

First grade focuses on various strategies students can use to solve single-digit subtraction problems. For example, they can solve a problem like $9 - 3$ by counting back 3 from 9: 8, 7, 6. This work aims not at achieving fluency with the subtraction facts, but rather at building conceptual understanding of subtraction and procedural skill with various strategies. (See the TIMS Tutor: *Math Facts*.)

At the beginning of Grade 2, the problem-solving approach to subtraction continues. Problems with numbers up to 1000 are introduced, but again no standard solution method is taught at this point. Students devise their own ways to solve the problems, drawing on their prior knowledge of the problem situations and the number system, and share their thinking with the class.

The strategies approach to the subtraction facts continues in Grade 2. As students' fluency with the addition facts and simple subtraction facts increases, more sophisticated strategies become feasible. For example, a child may solve $14 - 6$ by reasoning that "to take away 6 from 14, I first can take away 4, which leaves 10. Then I take away 2 more, which equals 8." These new strategies, sometimes called derived fact strategies or reasoning from known facts, illustrate how new knowledge builds on prior skills.

Later in Grade 2, systematic work begins on paper-and-pencil methods for subtracting two-digit numbers. Students solve two-digit subtraction problems using their own methods and record their solutions on paper. The class examines and discusses the various procedures that students devise. At this time, if no student introduces a standard subtraction algorithm, then the teacher does so, explaining that it is a subtraction method that many people use. The standard method is examined and discussed, just as the invented methods were. Students who do not have an effective method of their own are urged to adopt the standard method.

> *Giving children only multidigit problems that do not involve borrowing encourages the development of a rote and faulty algorithm that may not carry over into problems that require borrowing.*

Problems that require borrowing are included from the beginning. Though this differs markedly from traditional approaches, we view it as important in developing a sound conception of subtraction algorithms. Giving children only multidigit problems that do not involve borrowing encourages the development of a rote and faulty algorithm that may not carry over into problems that require borrowing.

By the beginning of Grade 3, students have a strong conceptual understanding of subtraction and significant experience devising procedures to solve subtraction problems with numbers up to 1000. They also have some experience with standard and invented paper-and-pencil algorithms for solving two-digit subtraction problems. In Grade 3, this prior knowledge is extended in a systematic examination of paper-and-pencil methods for multidigit subtraction.

This work begins with a series of multidigit subtraction problems that students solve in various ways. Many of these problems are set in a whimsical context, the TIMS Candy Company, a business that uses base-ten pieces to keep track of its production and sales. Other problems are based on student-collected data, such as a reading survey.

As in Grade 2, the class discusses and compares the several methods students use to solve these problems. Again, any method that yields correct results is acceptable, but now a greater emphasis is given to methods that are efficient and compact. This work leads to a close examination of one particular subtraction algorithm. See Figure 3. Students solve several problems with base-ten pieces and with this standard algorithm, making connections between actions with the manipulatives and steps in the algorithm. After a thorough analysis of the algorithm, including a comparison of the standard algorithm and other methods, students are given opportunities to practice the algorithm or other methods of their choice.

$$\begin{array}{r} {}^{3}{}^{16} \\ 7\ \cancel{4}\ \cancel{0} \\ -\ 4\ 3\ 9 \\ \hline 3\ 0\ 7 \end{array}$$

Figure 3: *A standard subtraction algorithm*

Practice in paper-and-pencil methods for multidigit subtraction is distributed throughout Grades 3 and 4. Students encounter sets of problems that encourage them to look at each problem and choose an efficient method to solve it. For many of these problems, a standard algorithm will be the most efficient choice. For others, students can use mental math or counting strategies. For example, students should identify the problem $4001 - 3998$ as a problem they can easily solve by counting up three from 3998 to 4001.

By the beginning of Grade 4, basic work with whole number subtraction is complete. Students have a firm conceptual understanding of subtraction and a diverse repertoire of methods they can use to solve subtraction problems. Work in Grade 4 is designed to maintain and extend these skills and understandings. Fluency with the subtraction facts is verified and remediation is provided for students who need it. In the laboratory experiments and other work, students solve a wide variety of subtraction problems using methods of their own choosing. The Daily Practice and Problems and Home Practice include distributed practice in paper-and-pencil subtraction so that those skills do not deteriorate.

In Grade 5 students continue to use subtraction in activities and labs. As in earlier grades, they are encouraged to decide when it is appropriate to use paper and pencil, calculators, or estimation. A review of subtraction modeled with base-ten pieces is included for students who have not used *Math Trailblazers* in previous grades. Distributed practice is provided in the Daily Practice and Problems and the Home Practice. Fluency with the subtraction facts is assessed in the first unit, and remediation is provided in the Addition and Subtraction Math Facts Review section in the *Facts Resource Guide.*

Whole-Number Computation in *Math Trailblazers*

Many other topics in *Math Trailblazers*—addition, multiplication, division, fractions, and decimals—are treated in ways similar to that sketched for subtraction above. In all these areas, we seek a balance between conceptual understanding and procedural skill. For all operations, standard methods for solving problems are not introduced until students have developed good conceptual and procedural understandings—the too-early introduction of such procedures may short-circuit students' common sense, encouraging mechanical and uncritical behavior. (Brownell & Chazall, 1935; Resnick & Omanson, 1987; Rathmell & Huinker, 1989; Perry, 1991; Hiebert, 1999)

Grade	Addition	Subtraction	Multiplication	Division
K	• concepts of the operation	• concepts of the operation	• concepts of the operation	• concepts of the operation
1	• concepts of the operation • informal methods	• concepts of the operation • informal methods	• concepts of the operation	• concepts of the operation
2	• concepts of the operation • invented algorithms • standard methods for small numbers	• concepts of the operation • invented algorithms • standard methods for small numbers	• concepts of the operation • informal methods	• concepts of the operation • informal methods
3	• invented algorithms • standard methods for larger numbers	• invented algorithms • standard methods for larger numbers	• concepts of the operation • invented algorithms • standard methods for small numbers	• concepts of the operation
4	• review, practice, apply, and extend	• review, practice, apply, and extend	• invented algorithms • standard methods for larger numbers	• invented algorithms • standard methods for larger numbers
5	• review, practice, apply, and extend	• review, practice, apply, and extend	• review, practice, apply, and extend	• standard methods for larger numbers

Table 1: *Whole-number operations scope and sequence*

Even after analyzing and practicing standard methods students are still encouraged to solve problems in more than one way. Flexible thinking and mathematical power are our goals, not rote fluency with a handful of standard algorithms.

Varieties of Computation

There is much more to computation than the standard paper-and-pencil algorithms for adding, subtracting, multiplying, and dividing. These algorithms are good for obtaining exact answers with simple technology, but, depending on the resources available and the result desired, there are many other kinds of computation. For example, if you are in a supermarket check-out line with several items and you find only $10 in your wallet, then a quick judgment whether you have sufficient funds is desirable. In this case, a rough mental estimate of the total cost of your purchases is what you want. If you are planning an addition to your house, however, different computational demands must be met. The situation is more complex than the supermarket checkout, and the penalty for making a mistake is more severe, so greater care must be taken. You will want more resources—paper and pencil, a calculator, time to work, perhaps a computer spreadsheet—and you will probably want rather precise estimates for the cost of various alternative designs for the addition.

A well-rounded mathematics program should prepare students to compute accurately, flexibly, and appropriately in all situations. Figure 4 shows a classification of computational situations using two criteria, the result desired and the resources available. Although you may want to move some of the questions to other cells or insert your own examples, these six categories of computation indicate the scope required of a complete mathematics curriculum (Coburn, 1989).

Resources Available

	Paper & Pencil	Machine	Mental
Exact	How many students are in the three third grades at my school?	How much will my monthly payment be on my car loan?	How much baking soda do I need if I am tripling a recipe that calls for 2 teaspoons?
Approximate	What is my share of the national debt?	House remodeling: Which design(s) can I afford?	Supermarket checkout: Do I have enough money for these items?

(Result Desired)

Figure 4: *Six varieties of computation*

The TIMS Philosophy: Meaning, Invention, Efficiency, Power

The treatment of computation in *Math Trailblazers* proceeds in several stages. The grade levels for the stages vary with the operation—ideas of division, for example, develop long after addition—but the general pattern is similar for all the operations. Roughly speaking, the stages are

- developing meaning for the operation,
- inventing procedures for solving problems, and
- becoming more efficient at carrying out procedures, all leading to
- developing mathematical power.

Developing mathematical power with an operation means that students understand *when* to apply the operation and *how* to use varied computational methods to solve problems, even complex or nonroutine problems.

The goal of the first stage is to help students understand the meaning of the operation. Most of the work involves solving problems, writing or telling "stories" that involve operations, and sharing solution strategies. These methods typically involve a great deal of mental arithmetic and creative thinking. The use of manipulatives, pictures, and counting is encouraged at this stage. Discussing these informal methods helps develop students' understanding of the operation.

In the next stage, the focus shifts from developing the concept of the operation to devising and analyzing procedures to carry out the operation. At this stage, students "invent" methods for carrying out the operation, explaining, discussing, and comparing their procedures. Multiple solution strategies—mental, paper and pencil, manipulative, calculator—are encouraged, and parallels between various methods are explored. There is evidence that this "invented algorithms" approach enhances students' number and operation sense and problem-solving abilities (Madell, 1985; Sawada, 1985; Kamii, Lewis & Jones, 1991; Burns, 1992; Kamii, Lewis & Livingston, 1993; Porter & Carroll, 1995; Carroll & Porter, 1997). Inventing their own methods helps make mathematics meaningful for children by connecting school mathematics to their own ways of thinking. The expectation that mathematics should make sense is reinforced.

In the third stage, a standard algorithm for the operation is introduced. This algorithm is not presented as the one, true, and official way to solve problems, but rather as yet another procedure to examine. The algorithms used in *Math Trailblazers* are not all identical to the traditional ones taught in school. The addition and subtraction algorithms are only a little different, but the procedures for multiplication and division are considerably different. (See Figures 5 and 6.)

$$
\begin{array}{r}
5\ 8 \\
\times\ 3\ 6 \\
\hline
4\ 8 \\
3\ 0\ 0 \\
2\ 4\ 0 \\
1\ 5\ 0\ 0 \\
\hline
2\ 0\ 8\ 8
\end{array}
$$

Figure 5: *All-partials multiplication*

```
                1 9 R 31
        3 2 ) 6 3 9
            - 3 2 0    10
            ─────────
              3 1 9
            - 1 6 0    5
            ─────────
              1 5 9
            -   9 6    3
            ─────────
                6 3
            -   3 2    1
            ─────────
                3 1 | 19
```

Figure 6: *A division algorithm*

We chose these alternative algorithms for multiplication and division for several reasons. First, they are easier to learn than the traditional methods. Second, they are more transparent, revealing what is actually happening. Third, they provide practice in multiplying by numbers ending in zero, an important skill for estimation. Finally, even though they are less efficient than the traditional algorithms, they are good enough for most purposes—any problem that is awkward to solve by these methods should probably be done by machine anyway.

Students who have no reliable method of their own are urged to adopt the standard algorithm. However, even after introducing and analyzing a standard algorithm for an operation, alternative methods are still accepted, even encouraged, for students who are comfortable with them. In particular, the standard algorithm is very inefficient with some problems. For example, students using *Math Trailblazers* should be able to compute 40×30 mentally to get 1200. Using the standard algorithm here would be inefficient. Or consider $16,000 - 5$. Using a standard algorithm to solve this problem is tedious and often results in errors.

In the last stage, students achieve mathematical power through the mastery of procedures that solve entire classes of problems: efficient and reliable computational algorithms. This procedural fluency, moreover, is based on solid conceptual understandings so that it can be applied flexibly to solve problems. These procedures become part of the students' base of prior knowledge—on which they can build more advanced conceptual and procedural understandings.

Fractions and Decimals

The approach to fractions and decimals in *Math Trailblazers* parallels that for whole numbers. At first, the focus is on developing concepts and meanings for fractions and decimals. Next comes a period in which students invent procedures for solving problems, connecting school mathematics to their own informal methods and common sense. Finally, formal procedures are investigated, not as substitutes for common sense, but as more efficient methods for achieving desired results.

Fraction Meanings

One of the problems with fractions is that they are so useful. Consider some of the meanings for $\frac{1}{2}$:

- half of a cookie (a part-whole fraction)
- $1 \div 2$ (division)
- one cup water to two cups flour (a ratio, sometimes written 1:2)
- $\frac{1}{2}$ mile (a measurement)
- the point midway between 0 and 1 (the name of a point on a number line)
- the square root of $\frac{1}{4}$ (a pure number)
- the chance a fair coin will land heads up (a probability)

Because the same notation can mean so many different things, children and even adults sometimes become confused and may manipulate fraction symbols haphazardly, often with unfortunate results. A better approach develops sound meanings for the symbols before focusing on how to manipulate them (Mack, 1990).

Part-Whole Fractions

Early fraction work focuses on part-whole fractions. Many fractions in daily life are part-whole fractions, so even young children are familiar with terms like one-half and three-fourths in part-whole contexts. Also, many key ideas about fractions are well illustrated in part-whole situations.

There are two concepts that are fundamental in understanding part-whole fractions: knowing what the whole is and understanding what a part is in relation to the whole. For example, to understand the statement, "Last night I ate three-fourths of a carton of ice cream," requires knowing what the whole is. Just how big a carton of ice cream was it? One must also understand that the parts into which the whole is divided must be equal—they should have the same area or mass or number, etc. A way to make this clear to children is to talk about "fair shares."

The whole in a part-whole fraction can be either a single thing (e.g., a pizza) or a collection (e.g., a class of students). When the whole is a collection, then counting is generally used to make fair shares; when the unit is a single thing, the fairness of the shares depends on some measurable quantity. Half of one pizza is different from half of three pizzas. Often, area is the variable that must be equally allocated among the parts; such a situation may be called an area model for fractions.

Symbols and Referents

A key idea in the *Math Trailblazers* approach to fractions is that fractions should be represented in several ways and that students should be able to make connections between those representations. The fraction two-thirds, for example, can be expressed in words, symbols, pictures, or real objects (Figure 7).

> *Because the same notation can mean so many different things, children and even adults sometimes become confused and may manipulate fraction symbols haphazardly, often with unfortunate results. A better approach develops sound meanings for the symbols before focusing on how to manipulate them.*

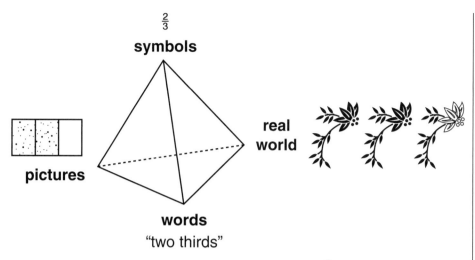

$\frac{2}{3}$

symbols

pictures

real world

words

"two thirds"

Figure 7: *Representations of $\frac{2}{3}$*

The ability to move freely between these several representations is an essential component of the mathematical understanding of fractions (Lesh, Post & Behr, 1987). Especially important are connections between fraction symbols and the real-world situations to which those fractions refer. Given symbols for a fraction, can students draw an illustrative picture or tell a story? Can students explain the relationship between a group of five girls and two boys and the fraction $\frac{5}{7}$?

Math Trailblazers makes extensive use of manipulatives in teaching fractions in all grades. Pictures, pattern blocks, geoboards, paper folding, and number lines are among many tools used to promote students' conceptual understanding of fractions. When paper-and-pencil procedures for adding, subtracting, multiplying, and dividing fractions are introduced in Grades 4 and 5, they are always linked closely with other representations of fractions, such as manipulatives or pictures.

Decimals

Decimals are treated in two ways in *Math Trailblazers:* first, as another way to write certain common fractions—those with denominators that are powers of ten—and second, as an extension of the whole number place value system. Similar to the coverage of other topics in *Math Trailblazers,* considerable attention is placed upon developing a solid conceptual foundation about decimals before formal, paper-and-pencil operations are introduced. Students with strong conceptual understandings of decimals learn procedures more easily and can apply those procedures to problem situations more effectively

The ability to move freely between these several representations is an essential component of the mathematical understanding of fractions. Especially important are connections between fraction symbols and the real-world situations to which these fractions refer.

(Ball, 1993; Behr & Post, 1992; Hiebert, Wearne & Taber, 1991; Lesh, Post & Behr, 1987). Connections between fractions (common fractions) and decimals (decimal fractions) are stressed throughout.

As with work with whole numbers and fractions, work with decimal fractions includes extensive work with manipulatives. Often these models are used to make strong connections between fractions, decimals, and percents. Figures 8 and 9 show two examples of tools used in Grade 5 lessons on decimals. These representations create visual images of the decimal fractions and link those images with students' previous work with fractions and percent.

Figure 8: *Interlocking centiwheel disks model $\frac{1}{4}$, 0.25, and 25%.*

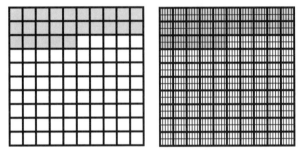

Figure 9: $\frac{25}{100} = 0.25$ and $\frac{250}{1000} = 0.250$

A Developmental Approach

Kindergarten fraction work emphasizes the idea that the fractional parts of a whole must be the same size. Work with symbols is not emphasized.

Fraction work in Grades 1–3 of *Math Trailblazers* focuses primarily on establishing links between symbols and referents for part-whole fractions. Children learn to make connections between marks on paper and the real world. Concepts of the unit—identifying the unit, knowing how the size of the unit affects the value of the fraction, appreciating the importance of fair shares—are also explored (Figure 10). Decimals are treated primarily as an alternative notation for certain fractions, and some attention is given to the interpretation of decimals that appear on calculators. Real-world situations, especially fair sharing, and area models predominate.

If [⬚] is $\frac{1}{3}$,

then what is one whole?

Figure 10: *A concept-of-unit exercise*

In Grade 3, students continue to develop concepts of the unit, but they begin to use more varied models. Children explore the relative size of fractions, especially with respect to the benchmark numbers 0, $\frac{1}{2}$, and 1. They also study equivalent fractions in Grade 3. Fractions are represented with a variety of manipulatives—paper folding, pattern blocks, geoboards. Collections of objects are divided to represent fractions.

Decimals are investigated more extensively in Grade 3, again being treated as a kind of fraction. Decimals in metric length measurement and on number lines are investigated. Base-ten pieces are used to create concrete and visual representations of decimal fractions. Translating between common fractions and decimals is again stressed.

In Grade 4, work on operations with fractions and decimals begins, but standard procedures are not taught. As discussed above, modeling concepts and procedures with manipulatives is intended to establish a basis for more algorithmic work in Grade 5. In fourth grade, students solve problems involving addition and subtraction, largely with the aid of manipulatives and other fraction models.

Operations with fractions and decimals include more than simply the four arithmetic operations. Putting fractions and decimals in order by size, renaming the same number in several equivalent forms, and estimating sums, differences, and so on, are all operations that can be carried out with fractions and decimals. Again, manipulatives, such as pattern blocks and base-ten pieces, are used to develop conceptual understanding and provide a concrete representation of the symbols.

In Grade 5, paper-and-pencil procedures for addition, subtraction, and multiplication of fractions and decimals are explored, including use of common denominators and reducing. Repeating decimals are introduced. Students also use calculators to rename fractions as decimals for comparing and ordering common fractions.

Many contexts are used to reinforce students' understanding of fraction and decimal concepts. For example, in a Grade 5 laboratory investigation, *Comparing Lives of Animals and Soap Bubbles,* students collect data about the "life spans" of soap bubbles. As they analyze the data, they convert the data first to a fractional quantity, then to the equivalent decimal fraction. Making these connections between mathematical concepts and real-world situations helps students make sense of the mathematics they are learning.

Conclusion

Our goal in developing *Math Trailblazers* is to create a balanced program that promotes the coordinated development of both procedural skill and conceptual understanding. Students will connect school mathematics with intuitive knowledge and informal procedures. They will use a variety of techniques and manipulatives for modeling the mathematical ideas. In doing so, students will not only develop skills and concepts, but will be able to use those skills and concepts to solve problems.

References

Ball, D. "Halves, Pieces, and Twoths: Constructing and Using Representational Contexts in Teaching Fractions." In T.P. Carpenter, E. Fennema, and T.A. Romberg (Eds.), *Rational Numbers: An Integration of Research.* pp. 157–195. Lawrence Erlbaum Associates, Hillsdale, NJ, 1993.

Baroody, A.J., and H.P. Ginsburg. "The Relationship between Initial Meaning and Mechanical Knowledge of Arithmetic." In J. Hiebert (ed.), *Conceptual and Procedural Knowledge: The Case of Mathematics.* Lawrence Erlbaum Associates, Hillsdale, NJ, 1986.

Behr, M.J., and T.R. Post. "Teaching Rational Number and Decimal Concepts." In *Teaching Mathematics in Grades K–8: Research Based Methods.* Allyn and Bacon, Boston, MA, 1992.

Bransford, J.D., A.L. Brown, and R.R. Cocking, eds. *How People Learn: Brain, Mind, Experience, and School.* National Academy Press, Washington, DC, 1999.

Brown, J.S., and R.R. Burton. "Diagnostic Models for Procedural Bugs in Basic Mathematical Skills." *Cognitive Science,* 2, pp. 155–192, 1978.

Brownell, W.A., and C.B. Chazal. "The Effects of Premature Drill in Third-Grade Arithmetic." *Journal of Educational Research,* 29 (1), 1935.

Brownell, W.A. "Meaning and Skill—Maintaining the Balance." *Arithmetic Teacher,* 34 (8), pp. 18–25 (Original work published in 1956), 1987.

Carpenter, T.P. "Conceptual Knowledge as a Foundation for Procedural Knowledge." In J. Hiebert (ed.), *Conceptual and Procedural Knowledge: The Case of Mathematics.* Lawrence Erlbaum Associates, Hillsdale, NJ, 1986.

Carpenter, T.P., E. Fennema, and M.L. Franke. *Cognitively Guided Instruction: Building the Primary Mathematics Curriculum on Children's Informal Mathematical Knowledge.* A paper presented at the annual meeting of the American Educational Research Association, San Francisco, CA, April 1992.

Carpenter, T.P., M.L. Franke, V.R. Jacobs, E. Fennema, and S.B. Empson. "A Longitudinal Study of Invention and Understanding in Children's Multidigit Addition and Subtraction." *Journal for Research in Mathematics Education,* 29, pp. 3–20, 1998.

Carroll, W., and D. Porter. "Invented Algorithms: Helping Students to Develop and Use Meaningful Mathematical Procedures." *Teaching Children Mathematics,* pp. 370–374, March 1997.

Coburn, T.G. "The Role of Computation in the Changing Mathematics Curriculum." In P.R. Trafton (ed.), *New Directions for Elementary School Mathematics.* National Council of Teachers of Mathematics, Reston, VA, 1989.

Dewey, J. *Experience and Education.* Macmillan, New York, 1938.

Finn, C.E., Jr. "What If Those Math Standards Are Wrong?" *Education Week,* 20 January 1993.

Fuson, K.C., and D.J. Briars. "Using a Base-Ten Blocks Learning/Teaching Approach for First- and Second-Grade Place-Value and Multidigit Addition and Subtraction." *Journal for Research in Mathematics Education,* 21, pp. 180–206, 1990.

Good, T.L., C. Mulryan, and M. McCaslin. "Grouping for Instruction in Mathematics: A Call for Programmatic Research on Small-Group Processes." In D.A. Grouws (ed.), *Handbook of Research on Mathematics Teaching and Learning: A Project of the National Council of Teachers of Mathematics* (Chapter 9). Macmillan, New York, 1992.

Greenes, C., M. Cavanagh, L. Dacey, C. Findell, and M. Small. *Navigating through Algebra in Pre-kindergarten–Grade 2.* National Council of Teachers of Mathematics, Reston, VA, 2001.

Hiebert, J. "Children's Mathematical Learning: The Struggle to Link Form and Understanding." *Elementary School Journal,* 84 (5), pp. 497–513, 1984.

Hiebert, J. "A Theory of Developing Competence with Written Mathematical Symbols." *Educational Studies in Mathematics,* 19, pp. 333–355, 1988.

Hiebert, J. "Relationships between Research and the NCTM Standards." *Journal for Research in Mathematics Education,* 30 (1), pp. 3–19, 1999.

Hiebert, J. and D. Wearne. "Procedures over Concepts: The Acquisition of Decimal Number Knowledge." In J. Hiebert (Ed.), *Conceptual and Procedural Knowledge: The Case of Mathematics.* Lawrence Erlbaum Associates, Hillsdale, NJ, 1986.

Hiebert, J., D. Wearne, and S. Taber. "Fourth Graders' Gradual Construction of Decimal Fractions during Instruction Using Different Physical Representations." *Elementary School Journal,* 91 (4), pp. 321–341, 1991.

Hiebert, J., T. Carpenter, E. Fennema, K.C. Fuson, D. Wearne, H. Murray, A. Oliver, and H. Piet. *Making Sense: Teaching and Learning Mathematics with Understanding.* Heinemann, Portsmouth, NH, 1997.

Kamii, C., B.A. Lewis, and S. Jones. "Reform in Primary Mathematics Education: A Constructivist View." *Educational Horizons,* 70 (1), pp. 19–26, 1991.

Kamii, C., B.A. Lewis, and S.J. Livingston, "Primary Arithmetic: Children Inventing Their Own Procedures." *Arithmetic Teacher,* 41 (4), pp. 200–203, 1993.

Lesh, R., T. Post, and M. Behr. "Representations and Translations among Representations in Mathematics Learning and Problem Solving." C. Janvier, ed., *Problems of Representation in the Teaching and Learning of Mathematics.* Lawrence Erlbaum Associates, Hillsdale, NJ, 1987.

McKnight, C.C., F.J. Crosswhite, J.A. Dossey, E. Kifer, J.O. Swafford, K.J. Travers, and T.J. Cooney. *The Underachieving Curriculum: Assessing U.S. School Mathematics from an International Perspective.* Stipes, Champaign, IL, 1987.

Mack, N.K. "Learning Fractions with Understanding: Building on Informal Knowledge." *Journal for Research in Mathematics Education,* 21 (1), pp. 16–32, 1990.

Madell, R. "Children's Natural Processes." *Arithmetic Teacher,* 32 (7), pp. 20–22, 1985.

Mathews, J. "Psst, Kid, Wanna Buy a Used Math Book? They're Old-Fashioned and a Bit Tedious, but John Saxon's Books are Hot Stuff in the Education Underground." *Newsweek,* 121, pp. 62–63, 1993.

May, L. "Reflections on Teaching Mathematics Today." *Illinois Mathematics Teacher,* 46 (3), pp. 5–8, 1995.

National Council of Teachers of Mathematics. *Curriculum Focal Points for Pre-kindergarten through Grade 8 Mathematics: A Quest for Coherence.* Reston, VA, 2006.

National Research Council. *Adding It Up: Helping Children Learn Mathematics.* National Academy Press, Washington, DC, 2001.

National Research Council. "The Strands of Mathematical Proficiency." *Adding It Up: Helping Children Learn Mathematics.* pp. 115–156, J. Kilpatrick, J. Swafford, and B. Findell, eds. National Academy Press, Washington, DC, 2001.

Perry, M. "Learning and Transfer: Instructional Conditions and Conceptual Change." *Cognitive Development,* 6, pp. 449–468, 1991.

Porter, D., and W. Carroll. "Invented Algorithms: Some Examples from Primary Classrooms." *Illinois Mathematics Teacher,* pp. 6–12, April 1995.

Press, M. "Drill and Practice Add Up." *San Jose Mercury News,* 27 February 1995.

Principles and Standards for School Mathematics. National Council of Teachers of Mathematics, Reston, VA, 2000.

Rathmell, E.C., and D.M. Huinker. "Using 'Part-Whole' Language to Help Children Represent and Solve Word Problems." In P.R. Trafton (ed.), *New Directions for Elementary School Mathematics,* pp. 99–110. National Council of Teachers of Mathematics, Reston, VA, 1989.

Resnick, L.B. "Syntax and Semantics in Learning to Subtract." In R. Glaser (ed.), *Advances in Instructional Psychology* (Vol. 3). Lawrence Erlbaum Associates, Hillsdale, NJ, 1987.

Resnick, L.B., and S.F. Omanson. "Learning to Understand Arithmetic." In *Advances in Instructional Psychology* (Vol. 3). Lawrence Erlbaum Associates, Hillsdale, NJ, 1987.

Resnick, L.B., S. Lesgold, and V. Bill. *From Protoquantities to Number Sense.* A paper prepared for the Psychology of Mathematics Education Conference, Oaxtapec, Mexico, 1990.

Sawada, D. "Mathematical Symbols: Insight through Invention." *Arithmetic Teacher,* 32 (6), pp. 20–22, 1985.

Shuard, H. "CAN: Calculator Use in the Primary Grades in England and Wales." In J. T. Fey (ed.), *Calculators in Mathematics Education,* Reston, VA, 1992.

Skemp, R.R. "Relational Understanding and Instrumental Understanding." *Arithmetic Teacher,* 26 (3), pp. 9–15, 1978.

Swart, W.L. "Some Findings on Conceptual Development of Computational Skills." *Arithmetic Teacher* 32 (5), pp. 36–38, 1985.

Usiskin, Z. "Paper-and-Pencil Skills in a Calculator/Computer Age." *UCSMP Newsletter,* 16, pp. 7–14, 1994.

Van Lehn, K. "Arithmetic Procedures Are Induced from Examples." In J. Hiebert (ed.), *Conceptual and Procedural Knowledge: The Case of Mathematics.* Lawrence Erlbaum Associates, Hillsdale, NJ, 1986.

Whitehead, A.N. "The Rhythmic Claims of Freedom and Discipline." In *The Aims of Education and Other Essays.* Macmillan, New York, 1929.

Averages

Introduction

"Average" is one of those words that mean different things to different people. Baseball players talk about their batting averages. A teacher might confide to a colleague that "Jim is just an average student." At the university, students always want to know what the class average is on an exam. Sometimes you hear the statement that the temperature will be about average for this time of year. When someone asks you how you feel, you may reply, "Just average." In everyday usage, "average" is a word that can be anything from a synonym for "typical," "normal," or "usual," to a number derived according to some formula or rule. This TIMS Tutor lays out some of the different numerical meanings of "average" and explains some of the importance of averages in mathematics and science.

The Mean—A Wage Dispute

In his wonderful little book, *How to Lie with Statistics,* Darrell Huff gives the example of a factory owner and his workers who are arguing over wages. There are 25 workers including the owner. The owner pays himself $45,000. The others make $15,000, $10,000, $10,000, $5700, $5000, $5000, $5000, $3700, $3700, $3700, $3700, $3000, $2000, $2000, $2000, $2000, $2000, $2000, $2000, $2000, $2000, $2000, and $2000. The owner says the average wage is $5700 but the workers claim the average wage is only $3000. Even though prices have gone way up since Huff wrote his book 50 years ago, the discrepancy is clear: there is a big disagreement over what people are being paid, let alone what they should be paid.

So, what's going on here? Who's right, the owner or the workers? Both! The factory owner's average is the (arithmetic) mean; the workers' average is the median. There are other averages too, such as the **mode** (the number or value that occurs most often in a data set). However, in *Math Trailblazers,* we primarily use the mean and/or the median when finding average values. These two averages will be the focus of our discussion in this tutor.

Usually when people use the term "average," they are referring to the **mean.** This is the familiar add-up-all-the-numbers-and-divide average you learned in school. The mean has many useful properties that make it beloved by schoolteachers, statisticians, and scientists alike. Consider finding the average height of all the children in a class. Data for 23 children from a third-grade class is shown in Figure 1.

The mean height of these 23 children is

$$<H> = \frac{\text{sum of heights}}{\text{number of children}}$$

$$= \frac{(133 + 136 + \ldots + 129 + 134) \text{ cm}}{23}$$

$$= \frac{3064 \text{ cm}}{23}$$

$$= 133.2 \text{ cm}$$

Name	H Height (in cm)
Karina	133
Federico	136
Ramon	135
Kiela	127
Aesha	126
Bravlia	128
Zuzia	133
Anthony	139
Iorta	146
Cordeli	135
Mary	137
Gennice	124

Name	H Height (in cm)
Curtis	139
Brian C	125
David	135
Anna	141
Brian M	131
Adriana	137
Boberto	134
Lucas	131
Gennifer	129
Amber	129
Nathan	134

Figure 1: *Data from a third-grade class*

Although no child may have this mean height, it gives everyone a point for making comparisons. For scientists, the mean is often the first number they calculate when looking at a data sample.

There is another way to interpret the mean height of this class. This may seem strange, but consider the following situation. Suppose you walk into another class and find 23 students all exactly the same height. The mean is clearly that height. If the mean height of this new class and the mean in our class are the same, then the sum of the heights of the children is the same. That is, imagine making two stacks of the children, one for our class and one

For scientists, the mean is often the first number they calculate when looking at a data sample.

for the new class. Stack the children one on top of another. Then the two stacks would be the same height. So, if two class means are the same and the number of children in each class is the same, then the sums of the heights in the classes are the same, even if the individual heights that make the sums are vastly different.

Statisticians like the mean because it is often the "best" estimate of an unknown quantity like a length, an area, or a mass. For example, suppose you are trying to measure the mass of a large steel sphere. You have an unbiased balance, and you know you need to take repeated readings to get an accurate measurement. So, suppose you make eleven measurements and find the sphere's mass to be 129 gm, 133 gm, 132 gm, 130 gm, 128 gm, 129 gm, 130 gm, 131 gm, 130 gm, 129 gm, and 131 gm. Then

$$\frac{(129 + 133 + \ldots + 130 + 129 + 131) \text{ gm}}{11}$$

$$= \frac{1432 \text{ gm}}{11}$$

$$= 130 \text{ gm}$$

This is the best estimate of the "true" mass of the sphere, given these measurements. (Notice that the quotient above is actually equal to 130.18181818 . . . gm. However, since our original measurements are to the nearest gram, it makes sense to give the average only to the nearest gram.)

Similar situations arise all the time in everyday life. Our factory owner is using the mean. He computes the average wage by adding up everyone's salary (including his big fat one) and dividing by the total number of workers:

$$\frac{\$142,500}{25} = \$5,700$$

As one final example, suppose Marty scores 85, 84, 86, 87, 84, 87, 85, 85, 83, and 85 on 10 rounds of golf and Ellen scores 83, 83, 95, 97, 81, 83, 82, 84, 96, and 84. Then Marty's mean score is

$$= \frac{85 + 84 + 86 + 87 + 84 + 87 + 85 + 85 + 83 + 85}{10}$$

$$= 85.1$$

and Ellen's mean score is

$$= \frac{83 + 83 + 95 + 97 + 81 + 83 + 82 + 84 + 96 + 84}{10}$$

$$= 86.8$$

So, it would appear that Marty is a better golfer than Ellen. (In golf, a lower score is a better score.)

But anyone who plays golf and bets will notice that if Marty and Ellen played 10 rounds against each other and scored as above, then Marty would win three times and Ellen would win seven times. And the factory workers still feel underpaid, despite that nice mean salary. So to get some perspective on what is happening here, let's look at another average, the median.

The Median

The **median** is the number in the middle. That is, roughly speaking, the median splits a set of numbers into two halves: one half is less than the median; the other half is more than the median.

The **median** is the number in the middle. That is, roughly speaking, the median splits a set of numbers into two halves: one half is less than the median; the other half is more than the median. So to find the median, rank the numbers from smallest to largest and take the one in the middle.

Suppose you want to find the median selling price of homes in your town. At the town office you find that 15 homes sold in the last six months. The selling prices, in rank order, were $134,000, $156,000, $164,000, $170,000, $184,000, $194,000, $224,000, $236,000, $250,000, $264,000, $266,000, $278,000, $334,000, $350,000, and $372,000. The median price was $236,000: seven houses sold for less than $236,000 and seven houses sold for more than $236,000.

When there is an even number of values, then the median can be a little harder to find. Say only 14 of the homes above have sold. Suppose that the highest-priced house, the one costing $372,000, went unsold. What is the new median? Counting up seven from the $134,000 house, we end up at the $224,000. Counting down seven from the $350,000 house, we end up at $236,000. The seventh house from the bottom is not the seventh house from the top! What to do? Easy. Go halfway between the two numbers closest to the middle. Halfway between $224,000 and $236,000. That comes out to be $230,000. So the median price of the 14 homes that sold would be $230,000.

Going back to our factory workers' example, there were 25 employees including the owner. The thirteenth salary (from the top or from the bottom) is $3000: there are 12 employees who make less than $3000, and 12 who make more than $3000. So, the median salary is $3000.

One common situation where the median may be preferred is when there are extreme values. In such cases, the mean can give a distorted picture of the "average" because the extreme values tend to "pull" the mean away from the typical values.

Sometimes the median is a better average to use than the mean. One common situation where the median may be preferred is when there are extreme values. In such cases, the mean can give a distorted picture of the "average" because the extreme values tend to "pull" the mean away from the typical values. Statisticians say the median is more "robust" than the mean; that is, the median is less affected by extreme values than the mean. This is why the factory workers prefer the median: it gives a truer picture of what a typical worker earns than the mean, which is pulled up by the owner's big salary.

The median offers some insight into our golfing example, too. Marty's (ranked) golf scores were 83, 84, 84, 85, 85, 85, 85, 86, 87, and 87. The two numbers in the middle are 85 and 85, so Marty's median score is 85. Ellen's scores were 81, 82, 83, 83, 83, 84, 84, 95, 96, and 97. The two numbers in the middle are 83 and 84, so Ellen's median score is 83.5. Thus, using medians, Ellen is a slightly better golfer, on average. Every few rounds she has a high score, but her typical score is better than Marty's typical score, so she usually wins.

Obviously, the median has several advantages with respect to the mean: it is less affected by extreme values; it requires little computation; it can be a better indicator of what is typical. You will want to be flexible, sometimes using the mean, sometimes using the median.

The Mode

The **mode** of a data set is the number that appears most often. For example, in Ellen's golf scores, the number that appears most often is 83. In our first example from *How to Lie with Statistics,* we considered the factory owner and his 25 workers who are arguing over wages. The owner pays himself $45,000. The others make $15,000, $10,000, $10,000, $5700, $5000, $5000, $5000, $3700, $3700, $3700, $3700, $3000, $2000, $2000, $2000, $2000, $2000, $2000, $2000, $2000, $2000, and $2000. To present their best argument, the workers could have argued that the modal salary was $2,000, since 12 workers had that salary.

Making Sense of Measures of Central Tendency

The median, mean, and mode are all "measures of central tendency." They each tell us something about the way the information in the data set clusters. Of course, when we replace a whole data set with one number, we lose a lot of information. Depending on the nature of the data set, the mean, median, or mode may or may not provide us with useful information. These measures of central tendency are most useful when the data clusters around some value.

Averaging in the *Math Trailblazers* Classroom

So how are averages used in *Math Trailblazers?* Suppose your second-grade students collected the data shown in Figure 2 for the TIMS Laboratory Investigation, *Rolling Along in Centimeters.* There are three experimental values for each car, and students need some measure of the middle that fairly represents their data for each car. In this case, the median is a perfectly respectable average.

T Type of Car	*D* Distance (in $\frac{cm}{unit}$)			
	Trial 1	Trial 2	Trial 3	Median
Red	83	93	86	
Blue	44	44	43	
Orange	39	53	46	
Black	194	199	189	

Figure 2: *Data from* Rolling Along in Centimeters

One way to get a median from data like this is illustrated in Figure 3. The students cross out the largest and smallest numbers in each row and use the one that is left as their average value. Finding the median value of the three trials does not require young children to do any arithmetic and conceptually illustrates quite nicely the idea of an average representing a middle value.

T Type of Car	D Distance (in $\frac{cm}{unit}$)			
	Trial 1	Trial 2	Trial 3	Median
Red	~~88~~	~~95~~	(86)	86
Blue	~~44~~	(44)	~~45~~	44
Orange	~~39~~	~~55~~	(46)	46
Black	(194)	~~189~~	~~186~~	194

Figure 3: *Finding the median*

red truck

42
45
47

You can illustrate finding the median more concretely by using links (or string, adding machine tape, etc.) to create "lengths" that match the actual distance the cars roll each time. At the end of three rolls, students will have three lengths of links each representing the distance a car rolled in a trial.

This is illustrated in Figure 4. The median value can then be found by comparing the lengths and discarding the shortest and longest; the remaining length represents the median. A similar process is used in the first-grade experiment *Rolling Along with Links.*

In fourth grade, students begin finding the mean as well as the median. Again the concepts are introduced concretely. For example, students find the median value for several towers of cubes by lining them up from shortest to tallest and

Figure 4: *Finding the median in* Rolling Along with Links selecting the tower in the middle. This is illustrated in Figures 5a and 5b. Figure 6 illustrates an even number of trials. To find the median here, students have to find the halfway point between the two middle towers.

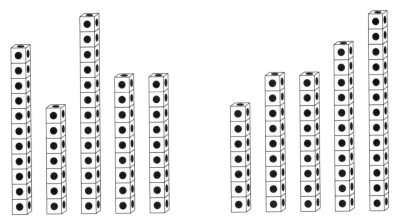

Figures 5a and 5b: *Finding the median with cubes*

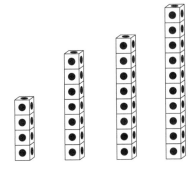

Figure 6: *The median number of cubes is $7\frac{1}{2}$.*

You can also use cubes to introduce the mean. For example, suppose students begin with the same five towers illustrated in Figure 5a. They first estimate the mean by figuring out a way to "even out the towers," as illustrated in Figure 7. The mean, to the nearest whole cube, is ten cubes. In this manner, the concept of the mean as a representative measure is stressed rather than focusing purely on the arithmetic procedure. Students then learn to calculate the mean using numerical values.

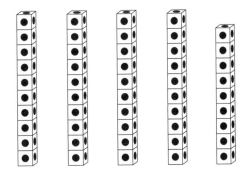

Figure 7: *Estimating the mean by "evening out" towers of cubes*

Students will often use calculators to calculate the mean of a data set. For example, the mean distance for the red car in Figure 2, when found by calculator, is:

$$\frac{(83 + 93 + 86)\text{ cm}}{3} = 87.333333\text{ cm}$$

This is an example of too much of a good thing. In this case, the calculator gives many more digits than are meaningful. Students have to determine an appropriate level of significance. Keep in mind that our goal is to get a reasonable number to use as an average. Here, the original measurements were made to the nearest cm, so it makes sense to also report the mean value also to the nearest cm.

Why Average?

Finding the average is critical in a *Math Trailblazers* experiment. It is an important step from raw data to understanding. Errors are inevitable when making measurements, and averaging is one way to detect and control them. If a group of students makes the same measurement three times and gets 67 cm, 64 cm, and 84 cm, they should notice that the 84 cm is way off. They can detect their error and redo that measurement.

When we take a measurement, many factors prevent us from getting an exact answer. First is the precision of our measuring tools. A meterstick can measure only to the nearest tenth of a centimeter. When we measure the area of an irregular figure by counting square centimeters, we have to estimate the area of the fraction pieces of square centimeters, and so on. In addition, when we perform an experiment, we might get somewhat different measurements each time. If we drop a ball from a height of 100 centimeters and try to measure how high it bounces, we will get different answers each time. This is due to the difficulty in controlling variables (can we be sure we dropped the ball exactly the same way each time?) and the difficulty in measuring how high a moving object bounces. Nevertheless, if students are careful and practice measuring, they should get answers that are reasonably close. Even when all the measurements are close, the average minimizes error. If the measurements are 67 cm, 64 cm, and 67 cm, then the mean, 66 cm, is a more accurate prediction of future measurements than any of the actual measurements.

Another function of averaging is to aggregate raw data. Unlike computers, people cannot handle too many numbers at once. If I tell you the height of every child in a school, then you will be overwhelmed by numbers. If I tell you the median height of children in the school, you know less but probably understand more. The situation in a typical *Math Trailblazers* experiment is similar. From 12 actual measurements in *Rolling Along in Centimeters,* we cut down to four medians that are then used to display the data in a graph.

References

Huff, Darrell. *How to Lie with Statistics.* W.W. Norton & Co., New York, 1954.

Johnson, Robert. *Elementary Statistics,* 3rd ed., Wadsworth, Inc., Belmont, CA, 1980.

Estimation, Accuracy, and Error

For many people, one of the most attractive aspects of mathematics is that it is exact. The story problems that we worked on in our youth were reassuring (or terrifying) in the certainty of their answers. If one potato weighs 2 pounds, then 100 potatoes weigh 200 pounds. The only problem is that the real world is not so exact. One potato does not weigh exactly 2 pounds and 100 potatoes probably do not weigh 200 pounds. In this tutor, we discuss ways we deal mathematically with situations where exactness is not called for (when we estimate) or impossible (when we measure within a certain degree of accuracy).

Virtually all mathematics educators agree that estimation should be an important part of any elementary curriculum. Unlike content areas such as number and operation and geometry, there is very little traditional curriculum on estimation as well as some disagreement about exactly what is meant by estimation. Some mathematicians and educators make a distinction between estimation and approximation, but there is no generally agreed definition of these terms. This tutor provides a general overview of the concept of estimation and discusses some of the more common strategies and applications. For a more exhaustive treatment of estimation, we recommend the NCTM yearbook (1986).

What Is Estimation?

According to *Webster's Eleventh New Collegiate Dictionary,* **to estimate** means to judge tentatively or approximately the value, worth, or significance of something. Alternatively, it means to calculate approximately. **An estimate** is a general calculation of size, value, and so on, especially an *approximate* computation of the probable cost of a piece of work. This leads one to ask for the definition of **approximate.** The dictionary states that approximate means located close together, or nearly correct or exact. Moreover, **an approximation** is an *estimate,* guess, or mathematical result that is close in value but not the same as a desired quantity.

Although these definitions appear to be circular (an estimate is an approximation and an approximation is an estimate), the dictionary does give us a general idea of what these words mean. As with most words, these words have several meanings and their exact meaning is determined by the particular context in which they are used. In particular, these words are used in a variety of ways in mathematics. You should first note that unlike most mathematical concepts, estimate and approximate do not have precise definitions. What does it mean for two numbers to be "near in position, close together?" Is 5 close to 10? Is 1250 close to 1300? Is 1000 close to 3000? It's hard to say. In spite of our inability to precisely define closeness, we shall see that the varied uses of estimation are an important ingredient in mathematical problem solving.

Pedagogical Aspects of Estimation

In her survey article, "Estimation and Number Sense," Judith Threadgill-Sowder (1992) points out that

> *Good estimators are flexible in their thinking, and they use a variety of strategies. They demonstrate a deep understanding of number and operations, and they continually draw upon that understanding. Poor estimators seem to be bound, with only slight variations, to one strategy—that of applying algorithms more suitable for finding an exact answer. Poor estimators have only a vague notion of the nature and purpose of estimation; they believe it to be inferior to exact calculation (Morgan, 1988) and equate it with guessing.*

It follows from this view that teaching estimation is a complex task. Rather than being a simple skill that follows a few basic rules, estimation requires a variety of strategies. Rather than being a separate subject, estimation is a habit of mind that is carried out in many mathematical activities. Thus, there are few lessons in the *Math Trailblazers* curriculum devoted solely to estimation, while many lessons offer opportunities for estimation. While estimation is not a simple skill, a number of simple skills, such as rounding and mental multiplication, are extremely useful when doing estimation.

Students often have difficulty with estimation because they are uncomfortable about having more than one correct answer. They want to know "the right answer" and dislike being told "that's a good estimate." So it is your task to keep reminding students of the purpose of estimation and that different strategies can result in different correct answers. The laboratory experiments in *Math Trailblazers* help students develop an appreciation of the approximate nature of measurement and the fact that some problems can have more than one solution.

To help organize our thoughts about estimation, we will break the uses of estimation in the elementary mathematics curriculum into four major categories:

1. Estimating the result of a calculation (in particular, addition, subtraction, multiplication, and division) to see if the answer is reasonable.
2. Measurement error, experimental error, and predictions.
3. Estimating the magnitude of a measurement; for example, the height of a building, the area of a wall, the volume of a jar, or the weight of a person.
4. Estimating how many; for example, the number of peanuts in a jar, the number of students in a school, the number of people at a concert.

Good estimators are flexible in their thinking, and they use a variety of strategies. They demonstrate a deep understanding of number and operations, and they continually draw upon that understanding.

It is your task to keep reminding students of the purpose of estimation and that different strategies can result in different correct answers.

Estimating the Results of a Calculation

Two primary reasons for estimating calculation results are:

1. To check that the exact answer is (possibly) correct. The estimation can be done either before or after the calculation. Getting an answer that is far from your estimate indicates that the calculation is incorrect. On the other hand, an estimate close to the calculation does not guarantee that it is correct.
2. As a substitute for the exact answer. In many situations an exact answer is not needed and may not even make sense.

We will discuss a few of the more common strategies used to estimate the results of a calculation. Undoubtedly, you and your students will find other good strategies.

Addition and Subtraction

For estimation purposes, the most important digits in a number are the ones to the left, i.e., the leading digits. When estimating a sum or difference, one strategy you can usually carry out mentally is to look at the first one or two *place-value columns*. For example, here are some statistics on the New England states from a 1987 almanac:

	Population (1984)	Area (sq mi)
Maine	1,164,000	33,215
New Hampshire	998,000	9304
Vermont	535,000	9609
Massachusetts	5,822,000	8257
Rhode Island	968,000	1214
Connecticut	3,174,000	5009

> When estimating a sum or difference, one strategy you can usually carry out mentally is to look at the first one or two place-value columns.

If we wanted to estimate the total population of New Hampshire and Vermont in 1984 using "front end estimation," we could look at the first column on the left. In this case, it is the hundred thousands column. Adding the 9 and the 5 we get 14, which tells us that the sum is approximately 14 hundred thousands; in other words, one million, four hundred thousand. In fact, the first two digits of the sum must be either 14 or 15 (depending on whether or not there is any carrying when we do the addition algorithm). Your estimate can be 1,400,000 or you can look at the next digits to see if there is likely to be any carrying. In this case, the digits in the ten thousands column are 9 and 3, so there will be carrying. Thus, 1,500,000 is an even better estimate. Of course, the whole point of estimation is to get a quick, approximate answer. If you start looking at too many digits, you might as well find the exact answer.

A second quick method for this estimate is to think that the population of New Hampshire was approximately 1 million and that of Vermont was about $\frac{1}{2}$ million, so the total is about 1.5 million. Since the "exact" answer is 1,533,000, an estimate of 1.5 million is only off by about 2 percent. A more rule-bound approach that says, "round off the nearest million" would give us 1 million plus 1 million which is 2 million. This is not a very close estimate (it's about 30 percent off). In fact, there is no simple rule that gives a good estimate in all situations. A rule that often gives good results is "round each number to one significant digit and then add." (A whole number has one significant digit if all digits after the first one equal zero.) That's what we did in this case, rounding 1,164,000 to 1,000,000 and 535,000 to 500,000.

You can apply the same strategies to estimate the results of subtraction calculations. For example, if we wanted to know how much larger the population of New Hampshire was than the population of Vermont, we could round each population to one significant digit, and subtract 500,000 from 1 million to get 500,000. Rounding to the nearest million definitely doesn't work in this problem, since both populations round to 1 million, and we would get the nonsensical estimate that there were no more people in New Hampshire than there were in Vermont! It should be noted that looking at the difference between two numbers is not always the best way of comparing them. If we wanted to compare the populations of New Hampshire and Vermont, it might be better to look at the ratio of their populations and say that New Hampshire had twice the population of Vermont.

The fact that the population figures are rounded off to the nearest thousand in the table is an acknowledgment that census figures themselves are estimates. In this case, there are two reasons that the data is not exact. Population data for the United States is based on census data. Since the U.S. population is so large and not everyone cooperates with the census takers, it is impossible to count everyone in the country. The population is also a moving target. Every day, tens of thousands of people are born or die. Finally, the figures for 1984 population are obtained by starting with the 1980 figures and extrapolating based on assumptions about the rate of population growth. Since many factors affecting population growth change, it is highly unlikely that predictions for population would be very accurate.

Rounding is also one effective strategy for mentally estimating the sum of a series of numbers. For example, to find the total population of New England from the individual state populations above, you might round the numbers in the population column to the nearest half million, namely 1, 1, $\frac{1}{2}$, 6, 1, and 3 million. Adding these mentally gives $12\frac{1}{2}$ million, which is pretty close to the actual total of 14,238,888 people. Try to estimate the total area of New England, mentally. The exact answer is 62,810 square miles.

Note that these are not the only strategies for estimating the sum or difference of several numbers. For example, if you want to purchase items that cost $3.79, $4.19, $2.23, and $6.49, you might add the dollars mentally (3 + 4 + 2 + 6 = 15) and then round the cents to the nearest quarter, i.e., 79 cents is about 75 cents, etc. This way, you see you need about $1.75 more (or 7 quarters). So, the total is pretty close to $16.75.

Multiplication: Rounding and Mental Math

The most basic technique for estimating the result of a multiplication problem is to replace (if necessary) the original numbers in the problem with other numbers that permit us to do the calculation mentally, or rapidly with paper and pencil. For example, if you want to know the number of minutes in a day, you would multiply 24 hours by 60 minutes per hour. Finding 24 × 60 is too hard for most people to do mentally, but 25 × 60 can be done by many fourth- and fifth-graders. Now, 25 × 60 is the same as 25 × 6 × 10, and 25 × 6 is 150. (Think of 6 quarters as a dollar-fifty. Most of us are pretty good at calculating

The most basic technique for estimating the result of a multiplication problem is to replace (if necessary) the original numbers in the problem with other numbers that permit us to do the calculation mentally . . .

with multiples of 5, 10, and 25, since we have had a lot of practice doing mental arithmetic with money.) Finally, if 6×25 is 150, then $6 \times 25 \times 10$ is 1500. This is a pretty good estimate for 24×60. Note that we repeatedly used the commutative property of multiplication—i.e., the order in which we multiply several numbers does not affect the result. An alternative estimate for 24×60 can be obtained by rounding off 24 to 20 and multiplying 20 by 60 to get approximately 1200 minutes in a day. This estimate is not as close, but it may suffice for many purposes.

A basic skill fundamental to being able to estimate in multiplication and division situations is the ability to multiply and divide by ten and powers of ten (100, 1000, etc.). Thus, as early as third grade in *Math Trailblazers,* we observe the pattern that multiplying a whole number by 10 amounts to adding the digit 0 to the right of the number, i.e., $10 \times 57 = 570$, $10 \times 365 = 3650$, and so on. Similarly, multiplying by 100 amounts to adding two 0 digits to the right, and so on. When we start to work with decimals, we observe that multiplying a decimal by 10 amounts to moving the decimal point to the right one place. For example, $10 \times 45.76 = 457.6$. This is really the same pattern we see with whole numbers, since $10 \times 57.0 = 570$, etc.

Another fundamental process in the examples above was finding convenient numbers that were close to the numbers we started with. Here, convenient means numbers with which we can calculate mentally. For example, we rounded 24 to 25, since multiples of 25 are easy to figure out. Often, the convenient numbers are what we call round numbers. For example, when we used our second strategy to estimate 24×60, we rounded 24 to the nearest 10, which gave us 20. All this means is that 20 is the multiple of 10 that is nearest to 24 (since 24 is between 20 and 30 but is closer to 20).

Rounding

Traditionally, students were taught a lot of rules about rounding, but they often are not able to apply them successfully since they did not understand the purpose of rounding, nor did they have a good understanding of place value. When we are doing mental estimation, we frequently want to round a number in the hundreds to the nearest hundred, a number in the thousands to the nearest thousand, and so on. For example, 457 rounded to the nearest hundred is 500, while 447 rounded to the nearest hundred is 400. That's because both numbers are between 400 and 500, and 457 is closer to 500 and 447 is closer to 400. Now 450 is exactly halfway between 400 and 500, so it is not obvious how to round 450 to the nearest hundred. Strictly speaking, it does not make sense to talk about **the** nearest hundred in this situation, since 450 is 50 away from 400 and 50 away from 500. In the context of estimation, this means that you can use either 400 or 500 as an estimate for 450. For example, if we wanted to estimate 450×321, we could say $400 \times 300 = 120,000$ is an estimate for the answer. This estimate is certainly smaller than the actual answer, since 400 is less than 450 and 300 is less than 321. On the other hand, $500 \times 300 = 150,000$, which is probably bigger than the actual answer. So the answer is probably between 120,000 and 150,000 (it's actually 144,450).

It used to be taught that numbers halfway between should always be rounded up, but there is really no reason for doing so. In general, the choice is determined by the context in which the rounding takes place and the reason you are rounding. For example, if you want to make sure you have enough money to purchase the items in your grocery cart, it is probably best to make a conservative estimate and round items that cost $12.50 up to $13.

Division

It may be surprising to realize that the operation we need to estimate most frequently in daily life is division. This is because many decisions we have to make are based on proportional reasoning.

It may be surprising to realize that the operation we need to estimate most frequently in daily life is division. This is because many decisions we have to make are based on proportional reasoning. How many miles per gallon is your car getting? Which brand of cereal is the least expensive? (One costs $2.65 for 14 oz and the other costs $3.55 for 24 oz.) A calculator can answer all these easily, but we often do not have a calculator handy. More significantly, students often perform the wrong calculations on the calculator. Letting students first solve their problem using convenient numbers allows them to focus on the essential parts of the problem, without being distracted by a lot of digits and a lot of mechanical manipulations. Once they have found a reasonable solution strategy, they can return to solve the original messy problem.

The easiest problems are ones that we can turn into a problem that requires dividing by a power of 10. Dividing by 10 is the inverse of multiplying by 10. Thus we can divide by 10 mentally by moving the decimal point one place to the left. For example, $\frac{279}{10} = 27.9$, $\frac{456.2}{10} = 45.62$, and so on. Similarly, we can divide by 100 by moving the decimal point two places to the left. When dividing a whole number by 10, we get a fairly good estimate for the result by just dropping the ones digit. For example, $\frac{279}{10}$ is approximately 27. Note that the estimate we get this way is always smaller than the exact answer.

One method for estimating the results of a division problem is to replace each number by a suitable nearby convenient number and then carry out the first step in the division algorithm. The rounding is chosen to make the division easy. For example, suppose we wanted to estimate the population density of Maine in 1984. The data in Table 1 tells us that the density is 1,164,000 people ÷ 33,215 square miles. We can round off the divisor to 30,000 square miles and round off the dividend to 1,000,000 people. To estimate 1,000,000 ÷ 30,000, we can ask what times 30,000 gives 1,000,000. Multiplying 30,000 by 10 gives 300,000 and multiplying this by 3.3 gets us near 1,000,000. So, our estimate is about 33. Another method is to replace the divisor and dividend with nearby convenient numbers. For example, 33,215 is near 30,000 and 1,164,000 is close to 1,200,000. We chose this pair of numbers because 12 is divisible by 3. So, our estimate now amounts to 1,200,000 people ÷ 30,000 square miles. Again, we see we need to multiply 30,000 by 40 to get 1,200,000. So 40 people per square mile is a reasonable estimate for the population density of Maine. Putting the numbers back into the context of the problem is important for checking any result.

A powerful technique for estimating the result of a division problem is to consider the division as a ratio. For example, suppose you traveled 637 miles and used 22 gallons of gas. To find miles per gallon, divide 22 into 637. Write the ratio 637 miles/22 gallons. Rounding 637 to 600 and 22 to 20 we get

A powerful technique for estimating the result of a division problem is to consider the division as a ratio.

$$\frac{637 \text{ mi}}{22 \text{ gal}} \approx \frac{600 \text{ mi}}{20 \text{ gal}}$$

Note that we used the symbol $\approx$ instead of the equal sign. This symbol means "approximately equal." Now, we can simplify the ratio $\frac{600}{20}$ by dividing both numerator and denominator by 10. So

$$\frac{600 \text{ mi}}{20 \text{ gal}} = \frac{60 \text{ mi}}{2 \text{ gal}}$$

and dividing numerator and denominator by 2 gives us

$$\frac{60 \text{ mi}}{2 \text{ gal}} = \frac{30 \text{ mi}}{1 \text{ gal}}$$

Putting this all together, we get 637 mi/22 gal $\approx$ 30 mi/1 gal; in other words, our estimate is 30 miles per gallon.

A note on canceling. Many people learned to simplify ratios by "canceling" the same thing in the numerator and the denominator. You might be tempted to say that when we wrote 600 mi/20 gal $\approx$ 60 mi/2 gal, we "canceled a 0" in the numerator and the denominator. Unfortunately, this can lead to some bad habits. For example, can you cancel the fives in $\frac{875}{25}$ to get $\frac{87}{2}$, or cancel the fives in $(X + 5)/(Y + 5)$ to get X/Y? You better not, since this amounts to subtracting the 5 from the numerator and denominator and results in a fraction that is not equal to the one we started with.

$$\frac{875}{25} \neq \frac{87}{2}$$

$$\frac{X + 5}{Y + 5} \neq \frac{X}{Y}$$

So canceling does not always result in an equal ratio. For this reason, we always say exactly what we are doing, dividing numerator and denominator by the same number, rather than using the word "cancel."

Here are some examples of estimation in a division context:

Example 1: Estimate the quotient $\frac{80,000}{30}$. This is approximately $\frac{8000}{3}$, which is between $\frac{7500}{3}$ and $\frac{9000}{3}$, i.e., between 2500 and 3000. Note that if we estimated $\frac{80,000}{30}$ by replacing 30 with 40 (since 40 goes into 80,000 evenly) we get $\frac{80,000}{40} = \frac{8000}{4} = 2000$, which is not as good as our previous estimate. This might be a little surprising, since we only made a change of 10 in replacing 30 by 40. But what is important here is not the size of the change (10), but the relative size of the change (10 out of 30 is 33%).

Here are some additional examples of estimation in a division context. See if you can follow the reasoning in these estimates. Can you make an estimate in a different way?

$$\frac{6206}{8271} \approx \frac{6000}{8000} = \frac{6}{8} = \frac{3}{4} = 0.75$$

$$\frac{78{,}221}{987} \approx \frac{80{,}000}{1000} = 80$$

$$\frac{77{,}921}{289} \approx \frac{75{,}000}{250} = \frac{7500}{25} = 300$$

$$\frac{828}{38{,}765} \approx \frac{800}{40{,}000} = \frac{8}{400} = \frac{2}{100} = .02$$

Measurement Error, Experimental Error, and Predictions

The theme of this tutor is the way to deal with "inexactness" in real-world mathematics. One class of situations that involve inexactness is measurement error or experimental error.

Measurement error is the unavoidable error that occurs due to the limitations inherent to any measurement instrument. Any measurement in the real world is an approximation. It is not really possible to guarantee that an object is exactly 1 meter long since any measuring instrument has a limit to its accuracy. For example, our centimeter ruler can only measure to the nearest tenth of a centimeter and the two-pan balance usually used in *Math Trailblazers* can only measure mass to the nearest gram.

Experimental error is the variation in measurement that results from the inability to control extraneous variables in an experiment.

These two types of error are closely related. Let's consider three examples of measurement in real-world contexts to get some idea of the meaning of measurement and experimental error:

Example 1: A volunteer is selected from the class and every student measures the circumference of her head to the nearest tenth of a centimeter. Most students get between 47 and 49 centimeters. One student gets 37.4 centimeters.

Example 2: Students drop a ball from a height of 80 centimeters three times to see how high it bounces. They get 41 centimeters, 45 centimeters, and 44 centimeters.

Example 3: Students measure the volume of a marble using a graduated cylinder. Most students get either 7 or 8 cubic centimeters. Two students get 67 cubic centimeters.

Example 4: A student finds that the mass of one blue pattern block is 11 grams. She predicts that 2 blue pattern blocks will have a mass of 22 grams and 4 blue pattern blocks will have a mass of 44 grams. When she checks her results, she finds that 2 pattern blocks do have a mass of 22 grams, but 4 pattern blocks have a mass of 42 grams.

> *Measurement error is the unavoidable error that occurs due to the limitations inherent to any measurement instrument. . . .*
> *Experimental error is the variation in measurement that results from the inability to control extraneous variables in an experiment.*

Errors vs. Mistakes

In Examples 1, 2, and 3, there were repeated measurements of the same thing that produced seemingly different answers. The fact that most students obtained slightly different answers in Example 1 is due to slight variations in how they performed the measurement—where they placed the tape measure, how tight they held it, etc. All these measurements are "close" to each other (see below for a discussion of "what's close?").

However, the student whose measurement was 37.4 centimeters probably made a *mistake* such as reading the tape measure incorrectly or placing the tape measure in the wrong position. In mathematics, we try to distinguish between the words "error" and "mistake." Of course, "mistake" is one of the common meanings of "error." *Webster's New World Dictionary of the American Language* gives as its first definition of the word "error," "the state of believing what is untrue, incorrect, or wrong."

In the current context, however, "error" has a different meaning. This is the fifth definition given for "error" in that dictionary, namely "the difference between a computed or estimated result and the actual value as in mathematics." The dictionary goes on to explain that "error implies deviation from truth, accuracy, correctness, right, [while] mistake suggests an error resulting from carelessness, inattention, misunderstanding, etc."

Most of the measurements in Example 1 involved some measurement error, but those measurements were correct. However, the student who measured 37.4 centimeters must have made a mistake. In this case, the teacher would help the student find the reason for the mistake and then repeat the measurement correctly.

In Example 2, it is not surprising that repeating the activity, that is, dropping the ball from 80 centimeters, results in a different measurement. It's pretty hard to measure how high the ball bounces, since the ball does not stop at the height of its bounce and wait for you to measure its distance from the floor. Also, there can be slight variations because different parts of the ball or different spots on the floor are "bouncier." This is a typical example of the experimental error that results from the inability to control all the fixed variables in an experiment. (See the TIMS Tutor: *The TIMS Laboratory Method*, Fixed Variables in Controlled Experiments.)

In Example 3, students used a graduated cylinder to measure the volume by displacement. Two students forgot to subtract the volume of the water in the cylinder, so they obtained measurements that were very different from the others. This is a clear example of a mistake. The actual volume of the marble was between 7 and 8 cubic centimeters.

Reducing Experimental Error

In Examples 1 through 3, we saw that repeating a measurement does not always give the same answer. To get more reliable and accurate results, scientists often repeat a measurement several times and then take the average of all the measurements. The "average" that we use in this situation can be

> *In mathematics, we try to distinguish between the words "error" and "mistake."*

> *To get more reliable and accurate results, scientists often repeat a measurement several times and then take the average of all the measurements.*

either the mean or the median. (See the TIMS Tutor: *Averages.*) In Example 2, we can take the median of the three measurements and say that dropping the ball from 80 centimeters results in a bounce height of 44 centimeters. We could also use the mean, in which case the bounce height would be nearly the same—approximately 43 centimeters.

In many experiments, we have another way of minimizing experimental error. If the data points plotted on a graph appear close to a straight line, we find a best-fit line that is close to all the data points. (See the TIMS Tutor: *The TIMS Laboratory Method.*) Using the best-fit line is a way of averaging out the experimental error. In *Math Trailblazers,* we draw a best-fit line "by eye," using a transparent ruler. In addition to averaging out the error, these lines help scientists and mathematicians make predictions based upon the patterns in the data. Scientists, mathematicians, and statisticians use a variety of sophisticated methods to find best-fit lines for data, but the "eyeball" method is pretty good for making approximate predictions.

One example of an activity that uses both averaging and best-fit lines to minimize experimental error is the *Math Trailblazers* fourth-grade lab, *The Bouncing Ball.* In this lab, students drop a ball from heights of 40, 80, and 120 cm and record their data in a data table. See Figure 1. Note that the ball was dropped three times from each height. When the data is graphed, we can see that the data points lie close to a straight line. In Figure 2, we see an estimated best-fit line drawn by a student. For further information, see the TIMS Tutor: *The TIMS Laboratory Method,* Point Graphs: Fitting Lines and Curves.

> Scientists, mathematicians, and statisticians use a variety of sophisticated methods to find best-fit lines for data, but the "eyeball" method is pretty good for making approximate predictions.

Tennis Ball

D Drop Height in cm	B Bounce Height in cm			
	Trial 1	Trial 2	Trial 3	Average
40	27	22	21	22
80	50	40	43	43
120	72	62	68	68

Figure 1: The Bouncing Ball *data table*

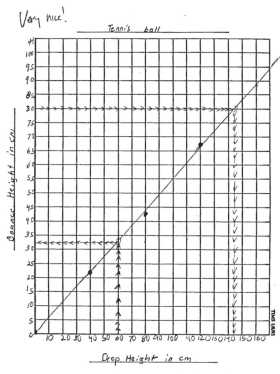

Figure 2: The Bouncing Ball *graph*

What's Close?

Recall that the notions of approximation and estimation involve the notion of finding a number that is close to a desired number. But how do we decide what is close? The most fundamental idea about closeness is that it is a **relative** idea. For example, suppose two merchants are selling the same item and the prices differ by $1. Are the prices close? If the merchants were selling cars that cost around $30,000, you would not make your decision based on a $1 difference in price. On the other hand, if you could buy a cup of coffee in one restaurant for $1 and it cost $2 at another restaurant, you might go out of your way for the $1 coffee (provided the quality was not vastly different). Why are these two choices for coffee significantly different? Because one brand costs twice as much as the other! This leads us to the fundamental idea for discussing closeness: when comparing closeness of numbers or measurements, we should look at the **ratio** of the two numbers, rather than the difference. The only problem with this approach is that the concept of ratio is difficult to understand fully. Developing this concept requires time and exposure to many experiences. We deal with this problem in two ways. First, instead of using ratios, we use a related concept—percent. Second, instead of calculating specific percentages (another difficult concept), we make comparisons to certain benchmark percentages, such as 10%. Using 10% as a benchmark for closeness, we see that $1 is not close to $2 since $2 is more than 10% bigger than $1 (in fact, it's 100% bigger). On the other hand, if we compare $30,000 and $30,001 we see that the difference, $1, is a lot less than 10% of $30,000.

> The most fundamental idea about closeness is that it is a **relative** idea.

In Example 1, the one in which many students measured the head circumference of one person, most measurements fell between 47 and 49 centimeters. A rough estimate for 10% of these numbers is 4 cm. Now the difference between 47 cm and 49 cm is 2 cm, so there is clearly less than 10% variation between the largest and smallest measurement. We can safely say these measurements are "close." On the other hand, the student who got 37.5 cm was almost 10 cm less than 47 cm. This is nowhere close to being within 10% of the other measurements, so we should suspect a mistake in that measurement. In Example 2, students took three measurements of the bounce height of a ball—41 cm, 45 cm, and 44 cm. Again, the variation is less than 10%. Finally, in Example 3, when students measured the volume of a marble, most obtained a value between 7 cc and 8 cc, while a few measured 67 cc. Now, 10% of 7 or 8 cc is less than 1 cc, so the students who measured 67 cc are nowhere close to the others. It should be pointed out that in situations such as Example 3, we do not decide who had the correct measurements by taking a majority vote. While the majority is usually right, it is not always right. The different results are a warning flag telling us to seek out the reasons for the discrepancies. Someone is making a mistake, but we can only find out who by looking more closely. Once we find the mistake, then we discard the incorrect information.

The 10 Percent Solution

It's natural to ask why we use 10% as a standard of closeness. We have a variety of reasons:

1. It's easy to find 10% of a number, or at least to estimate it. Just divide by 10. For whole numbers bigger than 10, the simplest estimate for 10% is obtained by dropping the last digit. Thus 10% of 187 is about 18 (it's between 18 and 19) and 10% of 5623 is about 562.
2. In many of the *Math Trailblazers* hands-on experiments, 10% is about the accuracy we can expect from students using the equipment they have, while 10% accuracy is still good enough for seeing the patterns in the data on graphs.
3. Psychologically, 10% is near the limit of our visual estimating ability. For example, if a person sees two drawings in sequence, one an enlargement of the other, in most cases that person will have difficulty distinguishing pictures that are less than 10% different in size, but will be able to distinguish figures that are much more than 10% different in size. Of course, this 10% borderline is not exact, and the point at which different people will be able to make distinctions is different.

Estimating the Magnitude of a Measurement

The basic measurement variables in the *Math Trailblazers* curriculum are length, area, volume, mass, and time. While much of the discussion that follows will apply to any type of measurement, it is a good idea to keep these few variables in mind. The examples given in this section will use these five variables.

There are two important types of knowledge used in many measurement estimation exercises. First, you need to know the measurements of some objects to use as a reference point. Second, you must know how to estimate unknown measurements by comparison with things you know. Very often this will involve some kind of proportional reasoning. The first type of knowledge is gained from experience. Therefore, students should have a wide variety of hands-on experiences as well as knowledge gained from external sources. For example, students should know the height of an average adult in English and metric systems ($5\frac{1}{2}$–6 feet, 160–185 cm), the length of their feet, and the width of their hands. We would hope that students have a general idea of the width of the continental United States from east to west (3000 miles) and from north to south (1000 miles). These facts can be used to make other estimates. For example, what is the area of the United States? The continental United States looks as though it would fit in a rectangle that is 3000 miles long and 1000 miles wide. This gives us an estimate of 3 million square miles. The actual area is close to 3.6 million square miles. To estimate the height of a three-story building (Figure 3), we could first estimate the height of one floor. Looking at an adult standing in the room, we might estimate that the distance from floor to ceiling is twice the height of the person. If the person is about 6 feet tall, then we get an estimate of 12 feet from floor to ceiling. If there are three floors, then the total height of the building is approximately $3 \times 12 = 36$ feet high.

Figure 3: *Estimating the height of a three-story building*

Accuracy and Precision

The accuracy required in a measurement depends on how we are going to use the measurement. By its very nature, any measurement we make in the real world is an estimation. What does it mean to say that a sheet of paper is 21.6 cm wide? How does one find this out? One way is to put the 0 cm mark on the ruler even with the left-hand edge of the paper and see that the right-hand edge of the paper is even with the 22.6 cm mark. If the paper is really 22.61 cm wide, we could not tell this with our ruler, which is only divided into tenths of a centimeter. So the measurements we make are really estimates that are accurate to the nearest tenth of a centimeter. Measuring the width of a piece of paper to an accuracy of more than a tenth of a centimeter would probably not make sense, since the sides cannot be perfectly even and measuring the width in different places would give different answers (like 22.613 cm and 22.615 cm). In any case, a measurement of 22.6 cm is probably more than sufficient for our purpose.

> *By its very nature, any measurement we make in the real world is an estimation.*

Dealing with Decimal Digits

One important fact to note is that in the course of solving a problem we can end up with a number that has many digits, most of which do not make sense in the real world (although they make mathematical sense). For example, suppose we wanted to share 16 ounces of orange juice among three students. When I divide 16 by 3 on my calculator, I get 5.3333333333. It makes no sense at all to say that we should give each student 5.3333333333 ounces of juice, since, with the tools we have, we cannot measure more accurately than to the nearest tenth of an ounce. In fact, when we say that we want to share 16 ounces of orange juice, we do not mean that we have exactly 16 ounces of juice. Unless we were using unusually sensitive measuring instruments, it would only make sense to say that we would give each student 5.3 ounces or $5\frac{1}{3}$ ounces of juice. Although 5.3 and $5\frac{1}{3}$ are not equal, they are approximately equal in this context.

Estimating "How Many"

In this type of estimation, we estimate the number of objects in some collection. It could be the number of trees in the United States, the number of students in a school district next year, or the number of beans in a jar. This class of problems has a lot in common with the estimation problems we have already discussed. Many problems that require estimating "how many" are similar to estimating a measurement in that they involve knowing how many objects there are in some known set and then comparing the unknown with the known. Here are some examples:

Example 1: Students are asked to estimate the number of peanuts in a jar. If students have no previous experience with peanuts or jars, this is not really an estimate, but rather a guess. Answers will vary widely because students do not have any idea of what the answer might be and no strategies to use to get a sensible answer. A more reasonable exercise is to give them a small jar and have them count how many peanuts can fit in the jar. If they are now given a larger jar, they should be able to make a sensible estimate by comparing the large jar to the small one. How many small jars would they think fit in the large jar? If the small jar holds 10 peanuts and it appears that 12 small jars fit in the large one, what is a reasonable estimate for the number of peanuts that fit in the large jar?

Example 2: How many students are in your school? The reference set here can be the number of students in a class. Students should know how many students are in their class. They should also be able to estimate the number of classes in the school. This gives an estimate for the number of students in the school (using multiplication).

Example 3: How many total hours of television were watched by all the children in the school? We can find the *exact* answer by asking every student how much they watched and then adding the number of hours. The answer can be *estimated* using a very important technique called sampling. Take a survey of some of the children in the school (say one class or two students in each class) and then scale up.

Example 4: We have a picture of the crowd at a basketball game. How can we determine the number of people at the game? It would be tedious to count the number of people in the picture. We could draw a square on the picture and count the number of people in that square. Then multiply that result by the number of such squares needed to cover the crowd. Figure 4 from the *Math Trailblazers* fourth-grade curriculum shows a picture used to pose a similar problem.

Figure 4: *Picture of a basketball game crowd*

Example 5: Will more people vote for Fred or Amy in the next election? This is another example of a kind of problem that frequently occurs in the real world. The common technique for estimating the answer is to take a sample of the voters and use the sample to predict the results for the whole population. For example, if 40% of the sample says they will vote for Fred and 60% says they will vote for Amy, we might predict that Amy will win. We might even predict that Fred will get 40% of the vote and Amy 60%. We know from real life that predictions like this are not always accurate. Some things that affect the accuracy of such estimates are the size of the sample (compared to the whole population) and the randomness of the sample (how well the sample represents the whole population).

Example 6: How many households are there in the United States? We can only make this estimate if we know enough facts about the population of the United States. We know that the population of the United States is about 250 million people and that the average family has 2.3 children. If we think that some households have only one person, while others have several generations living together, we might say that the average household size is about 4 or 5 people. Using a household size of 5 for our estimate (since 5 goes evenly into 25) we get a figure of 50 million households.

> *The best way to become a good estimator is to estimate.*

Conclusion

We hope that this tutor gives you an overview of the way estimation is treated in the *Math Trailblazers* curriculum. Naturally, it could not deal with all the types of estimation situations and all kinds of estimation strategies. The best way to become a good estimator is to estimate. The best way for children to learn to be good estimators is to be given meaningful situations that require estimation and to be given the opportunity to discuss their strategies with others. As with all mathematics instruction, the teacher plays a valuable role by moderating discourse and by adding new strategies when appropriate.

References

Schoen, Harold L., and Marilyn J. Zweng (eds.). *Estimation and Mental Computation—1986 Yearbook.* National Council of Teachers of Mathematics, Reston, VA, 1986.

Sowder, J., "Estimation and Number Sense," in *Handbook of Research on Mathematics Teaching and Learning.* Douglas A. Grouws (ed.). Macmillan Publishing Co., New York, 1992.

Threadgill-Sowder, J. "Computational Estimation Procedures of School Children." *Journal of Educational Research,* 77 (6), 1984.

Webster's Eleventh New Collegiate Dictionary. Merriam-Webster, Inc., Springfield, MA.

Functions

Introduction

Function is one of those words with a mathematical meaning that is not the same as its everyday meaning. In everyday life, a function can be an important celebration, a role someone or something has, or the purpose for something. In mathematics and science, a function is a special and very important kind of relationship between variables. Discovering functional relationships between variables is what science is all about.

In mathematics and science, a function is a special and very important kind of relationship between variables. Discovering functional relationships between variables is what science is all about.

Three Blind Men and an Elephant. There is a story about three blind men who encounter an elephant. The first comes up against one of the elephant's legs and says, "An elephant is like a tree." The second touches the side of the elephant and says, "No, no. An elephant is like a wall." The third blind man finds the elephant's trunk and claims, "You're both wrong. An elephant is like a big snake."

Each blind man has some notion of what an elephant is. The story doesn't tell whether they eventually resolve their differences and come to a proper understanding of elephants; we can only hope so. Our approach to functions will be similar: We will begin with three different views of functions. This, we hope, will lead to a fuller and more proper understanding of functions.

Tables

Many functions are displayed as tables. For example, consider this data table from the experiment *Mass vs. Number,* shown in Figure 1.

N Number of Erasers	M Mass (in gm)
1	39 gm
2	79 gm
4	158 gm

Figure 1: Mass vs. Number *data table*

This table displays a functional relationship between the variables N and M. For each value of N we have a value of M; we say that the mass is a function of the number of erasers. That is, if we know what N is, then we can find M. This is the essence of a function: knowing one variable's value enables us to find the corresponding value of the other variable. In this example, the data has a distinctive pattern: within experimental error, doubling one variable causes the other to double. N and M are said to be (directly) proportional.

Many functions we encounter in everyday life come to us as tables. You can think of stock tables, for example, as functions: one variable is the company, the other is the closing price. If you know the company, you can look up the price. Almanacs are filled with tables of information, most of which you can think of as functions: one variable is the name of the country, the other is the population, and so on. The sports pages are filled with tabular functions of team standings and individual statistics.

Many functions come to us first as tables, and some, like batting averages or almanac information, are normally given only as tables. Tables of numbers, however, can be very difficult to understand. Patterns in the data can go undetected—patterns that might help us better understand the function. One of the best ways to get a handle on patterns is to make a visual image of the data in the form of a graph.

Graphs

If a picture is worth a thousand words, a graph is worth a billion numbers. The graph of the *Mass vs. Number* data, seen in Figure 2, is a good example.

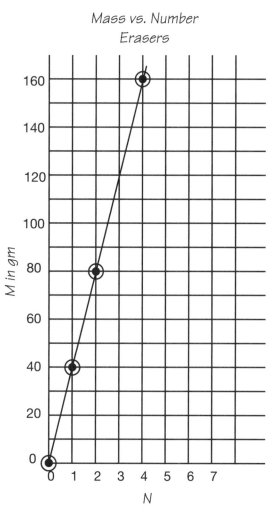

Figure 2: *Graph of* Mass vs. Number *data*

The key thing about this graph is that the data points lie on a straight line through (0,0). This confirms that N and M are proportional: we can fit a straight line through (0,0) if and only if the variables are proportional. Many other types of functions besides direct proportion are characterized by their graphs.

Often, experimental error obscures the nature of the relationship between the variables until the data is plotted. Like taking multiple measurements and averaging, graphing the data and fitting a curve can help control error. With error minimized, the true nature of the relationship between the variables may become clearer. Stock analysts graph their data to spot trends in order to make predictions (and money); such trends are unlikely to be noticed in the stock tables. Scientists graph their data almost as soon as they get it because the graph is so much more likely to be revealing than the raw data.

The graph is a crucial step on the road from the concrete apparatus to formal understanding. Sometimes, this formal understanding can be distilled in a few symbols, as in a formula.

The graph is a crucial step on the road from the concrete apparatus to formal understanding.

Formulas

A more abstract way to consider a function is as a formula. In our *Mass vs. Number* example, we can exploit the fact that when variables are proportional, their ratio is constant. The value of this constant ratio is the slope of the best-fit line. So,

$$\frac{M}{N} = \frac{39.5 \text{ gm}}{1 \text{ eraser}}.$$

This can be rewritten to give a formula for M as a function of N:

$$M = \frac{39.5 \text{ gm}}{1 \text{ eraser}} \times N$$

Such formulas are very useful when they can be found. When we do manage to obtain a formula, it allows us to solve problems quickly and accurately. We can also use formulas to ascend to higher levels of abstraction. This movement to ever greater abstraction and generality is the driving force behind much of science and mathematics.

G Number of Generations	A Number of Ancestors
1	2
2	4
3	8
4	16

Figure 3: *Ancestors data table*

Often students are not able to understand formulas, but they are, nevertheless, able to continue a pattern in a data table or devise a rule that works. For example, the pattern in the table shown in Figure 3 is easy to extend. Five generations back, you have 32 ancestors: each further generation doubles the number of ancestors (ignoring the inevitable overlap). Extending patterns like this is a first step towards formulas. Later, the students may be able to give a rule for a data table. For example, consider the table in Figure 4, the number of fence posts needed for a given length of fence.

L Length of Fence in _feet_	N Number of Fence Posts
10	2
20	3
30	4
40	5

Figure 4: *Fence posts data table*

The rule may be stated: the number of fence posts is just one more than $\frac{1}{10}$ the number of feet in the fence.

$$N = \frac{L}{10} + 1$$

It is not much harder for us to express this sentence as a formula, but this type of expression may be confusing to a third-grader. Often, a rule stated in ordinary language is more accessible.

Formulas are the most powerful way to look at functions but are often not appropriate for elementary school students. The great temptation is to move to formulas as quickly as possible. This sometimes leads to quick gains, but over the long run it is often problematic. Pushing formulas at children is like building a house of cards: students need to build a conceptual foundation by handling apparatus, gathering data, and graphing and analyzing it. Only after students develop an understanding of the relationship of the variables is it proper to distill that understanding into a formula. Extending patterns and figuring out rules are excellent alternatives for younger students moving towards higher levels of abstraction.

What Is a Function?

A **function** is a special kind of relationship between variables that can often be expressed as a data table, graph, or formula. One variable is the manipulated (or independent) variable; the other is the responding (or dependent) variable.

But not every relationship is a function. The main requirement for a relationship to be a function is that for each value of the manipulated variable, there is only one value of the responding variable. For example, suppose the manipulated variable is the edge length of a cube and the responding variable is the surface area. Then, for each given edge length there is exactly one surface area: if the edge is 3 cm, then the surface area is 54 sq cm, and so on. Or consider the manipulated variable to be the company and the responding variable to be the closing price: each stock has exactly one closing price each day. Notice that many stocks may have the same closing price; that's okay. The requirement says only that each value of the manipulated variable must have exactly one value of the responding variable. Values of the responding variable may repeat, and often do. One way to visualize this requirement is to think about functions as mappings. Figure 5 shows a map of a squaring function.

... not every relationship is a function. The main requirement for a relationship to be a function is that for each value of the manipulated variable, there is only one value of the responding variable.

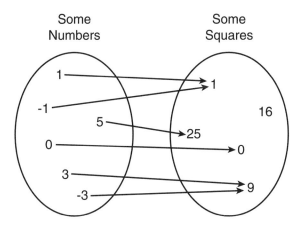

Figure 5: *Map of a squaring function*

Every number has exactly one square; this corresponds to the single arrow leaving each number on the left above. Notice that more than one arrow can end at a single number; the requirement is only that exactly one arrow leave each of the starting numbers. The mapping in Figure 6 is not a function because two arrows leave each number.

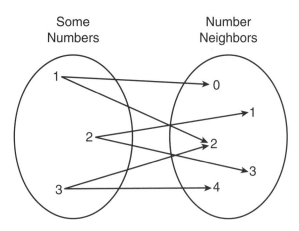

Some Numbers   Number Neighbors

Figure 6: *Map of a relationship that is not a function*

But you may object, saying that when we do experiments we often have several different values of the responding variable for each value of the manipulated variable. Isn't there a functional relationship between variables like the drop height and the bounce height in *The Bouncing Ball?* In a word, yes. But with real data, things get more complicated. Experimental error creeps in; there are other uncontrolled variables; there is uncertainty inherent in all our measurements.

One useful way to think about the situation is to suppose there is some "true" value of the responding variable that we cannot measure exactly. So, instead we measure the responding variable several times and then take the average as our best estimate of the true value.[1] Then we have a function: for each value of the manipulated variable there is exactly one *true* value of the responding variable. The only trouble is, in most real-world situations, we usually don't know what that true value is.

Mathematicians have precise and abstract definitions of function. We could go on and on describing more precisely the requirements a relationship must have to be a function. We could spell out the meanings of technical terms having to do with functions—terms like *domain, range, one-to-one, many-to-one,* and so on. For most purposes, however, thinking about functions in the terms outlined above is enough.

Functions in the Classroom

The concept of a function is a powerful one for organizing and extending mathematical ideas. From time to time, we have activities that deal with functions, for example, *Function Machines* in second grade. The best approach to functions, however, is just doing the *Math Trailblazers* lessons. As your students do TIMS Laboratory Investigations and other activities, they will move naturally from the apparatus to the data table, graph, and questions. Much of the data analysis is designed to help children see how changes in one of these correspond to changes in the others. Thus, in each experiment the students will deal with specific functions in several guises and will gain facility in moving between different representations of functions. This is the best possible preparation for the explicit study of functions later in high school and beyond.

As your students do TIMS Laboratory Investigations and other activities, they will move naturally from the apparatus to the data table, graph, and questions. Much of the data analysis is designed to help the children see how changes in one of these correspond to changes in the others. . . . This is the best possible preparation for the explicit study of functions later in high school and beyond.

[1]See the TIMS Tutor: *Averages.*

Journals

> *Writing about mathematics and science helps students consolidate ideas, see connections between school and life, and think more abstractly.*

We at TIMS embrace the idea of writing across the curriculum. We see helping students to write better as part of every teacher's job.

By writing in mathematics and science class, students improve their communication skills and develop their subject-matter understanding. Writing about mathematics and science helps students consolidate ideas, see connections between school and life, and think more abstractly.

Another reason to have students write about mathematics and science lessons is so you can gain insight into how those lessons are being received and what the students are learning. Collecting and saving students' writing is also an excellent way to document long-term student progress.

We incorporate writing into *Math Trailblazers* in several ways. We often ask for students to write a short or extended answer to a question and we may also ask students to explain how they obtained their solutions. Students may be asked to write about problems they solved in cooperative groups.

Journals are another effective way to use writing in mathematics and science. Typically, a journal is a small, bound book in which students write regularly. The writing can be in response to various prompts, or it can be rather undirected. Because each student responds at his or her own level and rate, journal writing is accessible to all students.

The teacher reads students' journals regularly, possibly responding in writing to what students wrote. Usually journal writing is not corrected for grammar, spelling, and punctuation—the focus is on the content of the writing, not the form.

The physical form of the journal is not important. A cloth-covered bound book, a spiral notebook, or even several sheets of paper stapled together all work just fine.

Journal Prompts

We urge you to have your students write regularly, every day or at least every week. Start with short periods and gradually extend the amount of time. When a student fills up one journal, give him or her another. Students will also enjoy reading their writing aloud and discussing it.

Your students' journal writing should take a variety of forms. Here are some suggestions for assignments ranging from highly structured to rather open-ended.

Sentence Completion

Give part of a sentence and ask students to complete it (Azzolino, 1990). For example, you might ask students to complete sentences like these:

"A shape is symmetric when . . ."
"Today we learned . . ."
"Before you use an equal-arm balance it's important to . . ."

A variation of this activity is to give one or more complete sentences and then to ask students to continue.

Explanations of Procedures

Ask students to explain how to measure the area of a leaf, how to use an equal-arm balance, how to add two three-digit numbers, or how to make a graph of some data. This may require an explanation of an entire procedure or only of certain steps.

Answers to Specific Questions

Sometimes you may pose a specific question about a lesson. For example, ask students to describe the shape of the graph for a certain experiment and to explain why the graph has that shape. Many *Math Trailblazers* lessons include questions that require some writing; these questions can be answered in the journals.

A question to ask sometimes is, "How did working in your group turn out?" You may get valuable information that can help you improve the dynamics of your small groups.

Descriptions of Solutions

There are usually many ways to solve a mathematics problem; it is often worth exploring multiple solutions. To correct the common misconception that there is usually only one way to solve a problem, students need to learn that the process of problem solving is often as important as the answer. In *Math Trailblazers,* they see connections by comparing different solutions. They learn that mathematics makes sense because their own ideas are validated. They are exposed to advanced ideas through other students' solutions, but without undue stress if they fail to understand those advanced ideas.

One way to encourage multiple solutions is to ask students to write about how they solved a problem. Ask them to describe all the ways they solved a problem or to describe a single way in depth. Ask them to write about failed solutions or what they did when they got stuck. Such assignments will encourage students to see such efforts not as failures but as periodic by-products of the problem-solving process.

One way to encourage multiple solutions is to ask students to write about how they solved a problem. Ask them to describe all the ways they solved a problem or to describe a single way in depth. Ask them to write about failed solutions or what they did when they got stuck.

Definitions

Ask students to define a key concept like area or volume. You may be surprised at some of their answers.

Advice to Adventure Book Characters

Often the characters in the *Adventure Books* and other activities encounter problems that yield to the techniques the students have been learning in the labs and activities. You might stop part way through an *Adventure Book* story and ask your students to write some advice, perhaps in the form of a letter, to the hero. When you finish the book, compare what the hero actually did to the students' advice.

Reactions

Ask students what they liked or didn't like about a certain lab, activity, or adventure book. Or, ask what they learned or what confused them.

Word Banks

Supply a list of words or phrases and ask students to use those words in a piece of writing (Azzolino, 1990). For example, you might supply the following words, "ten, hundred, thousand, less than, seven, more than, nine."

Problems

Students enjoy writing their own problems. Ask them to write another problem like a given problem; to write an addition, subtraction, or sharing problem; to write a number riddle; or to make up any problem that classmates would find interesting to solve.

Free Writing

Other times, simply tell students to write whatever they want about a certain lesson.

Some Tips for Getting Started

- Start with brief periods of writing and gradually extend the amount of time.
- Encourage pictures, data tables, graphs, number sentences, and other mathematical and scientific forms of communication.
- Vary the prompt. Sometimes be very specific; other times make the assignment more open-ended.
- Do not worry about grammar, spelling, and punctuation. Focus on content.

Conclusion

The name of our project—TIMS (Teaching Integrated Mathematics and Science)—expresses our conviction that the teaching of mathematics and science should be integrated. But we also believe strongly that integration should not stop there; language arts and social studies can and should be integrated with mathematics and science. Journals are one way to use writing in mathematics and science. Reading and writing are too important to be confined to language arts lessons.

References

Azzolino, A. "Writing as a Tool for Teaching Mathematics: The Silent Revolution." In *Teaching and Learning Mathematics in the 1990s: 1990 Yearbook.* T.J. Cooney and C.R. Hirsch, Eds. National Council of Teachers of Mathematics, Reston, VA, 1990.

Burns, Marilyn, and Robyn Sibley. "Incorporating Writing into Math Class." *So You Have to Teach Math? Sound Advice for K–6 Teachers.* Math Solutions Publications, Sausalito, CA, 2000.

Countryman, Joan. *Writing to Learn Mathematics.* Heinemann, Portsmouth, NH, 1992.

Math Facts

Students need to learn the math facts. Estimation, mental arithmetic, checking the reasonableness of results, and paper-and-pencil calculations require the ability to give quick, accurate responses when using basic facts. The question is not if students should learn the math facts, but how. Which teaching methods are most efficient and effective? To answer this question, we as authors of *Math Trailblazers* drew upon educational research and our own classroom experiences to develop a comprehensive plan for teaching the math facts.

Philosophy

The goal of the *Math Trailblazers* math facts strand is for students to learn the basic facts efficiently, gain fluency with their use, and retain that fluency over time. A large body of research supports an approach that is built on a foundation of work with strategies and concepts. This not only leads to more effective learning and better retention, but also to development of mental math skills. Therefore, the teaching and assessment of the basic facts in *Math Trailblazers* is characterized by the following elements:

- *Early emphasis on problem solving.* Students first approach the basic facts as problems to solve rather than as facts to memorize. Students invent their own strategies to solve these problems or learn appropriate strategies from others through class discussion. Students' natural strategies, especially counting strategies, are explicitly encouraged. In this way, students learn that math is more than memorizing facts and rules that "you either get or you don't."

- *De-emphasis of rote work.* Fluency with the math facts is an important component of any student's mathematical learning. Research shows that overemphasizing memorization and frequent administration of timed tests are counterproductive. Both can produce undesirable results (Isaacs and Carroll, 1999; Van de Walle, 2001; National Research Council, 2001). We encourage the use of strategies to find facts, so students become confident they can find answers to fact problems they do not immediately recall.

- *Gradual and systematic introduction of facts.* Students study the facts in small groups they solve using similar strategies. Students first work on simple strategies for easy facts and then progress to more sophisticated strategies and harder facts. By the end of the process, they gain fluency with all required facts.

- *Ongoing practice.* Work on the math facts is distributed throughout the curriculum, especially in the Daily Practice and Problems (DPP), Home Practice, and games. This practice for fluency, however, takes place only after students have a conceptual understanding of the operations and have achieved proficiency with strategies for solving basic fact problems. Delaying practice in this way means that less practice is required to achieve fluency.

- *Appropriate assessment.* Teachers assess students' knowledge of the facts through observations as they work on activities, labs, and games as well as through the appropriate use of written tests and quizzes. Beginning in first grade, periodic, short quizzes in the DPP naturally follow the study of small groups of facts organized around specific strategies. As self-assessment in Grades 3–5, students record their progress on *Facts I Know* charts and determine which facts they need to study. Inventory tests of all facts for each operation are used sparingly in Grades 2–5 (no more than twice per year) to assess students' progress with fact fluency. The goal of the math facts assessment program is to determine the degree to which students can find answers to fact problems quickly and accurately and whether they can retain this skill over time.

- *Multiyear approach.* In Grades 1 and 2, *Math Trailblazers* emphasizes strategies that lead to fluency with the addition and subtraction facts. In Grade 3, students gain fluency with the multiplication facts while reviewing the addition and subtraction facts. In Grade 4, students achieve fluency with the division facts and verify fluency with the multiplication facts. In Grade 5, the multiplication and division facts are systematically reviewed and assessed.

- *Facts are not gatekeepers.* Students are not prevented from learning more complex mathematics because they do not perform well on fact tests. Use of strategies, calculators, and other math tools (e.g., manipulatives, hundred charts, printed multiplication tables) allows students to continue to work on interesting problems while still learning the facts.

Expectations by Grade Level

The following goals for the math facts are consistent with the recommendations in the National Council of Teachers of Mathematics *Principles and Standards for School Mathematics:*

- In kindergarten, students use manipulatives and invent their own strategies to solve addition and subtraction problems.

- By the end of first grade, all students can solve all basic addition and subtraction problems using some strategy. Fluency is not emphasized; strategies are. Some work with beginning concepts of multiplication takes place.

- In second grade, learning efficient strategies for addition and especially subtraction continues to be emphasized. Work with multiplication concepts continues. By the end of the year, students are expected to demonstrate fluency with all the addition and subtraction facts.

- In third grade, students review the subtraction facts. They develop efficient strategies for learning the multiplication facts and demonstrate fluency with the multiplication facts.

- In fourth grade, students review the multiplication facts and develop strategies for the division facts. By the end of year, we expect fluency with all the division facts.

- In fifth grade, students review the multiplication and division facts and are expected to maintain fluency with all the facts.

This is summarized in the following chart:

Grade	Addition	Subtraction	Multiplication	Division
K	• invented strategies	• invented strategies		
1	• strategies	• strategies		
2	• strategies • practice leading to fluency	• strategies • practice leading to fluency		
3	• review and practice	• review and practice	• strategies • practice leading to fluency	
4	• assessment and remediation as required	• assessment and remediation as required	• review and practice	• strategies • practice leading to fluency
5	• assessment and remediation as required	• assessment and remediation as required	• review and practice	• review and practice

Table 1: *Math Facts Scope and Sequence*

Strategies for Learning the Facts

Students are encouraged to learn the math facts by first employing a variety of strategies. Concepts and skills are learned more easily and are retained longer if they are meaningful. By first concentrating on concepts and strategies, we increase retention and reduce the amount of time necessary for rote memorization. Researchers note that over time, students develop techniques that are increasingly sophisticated and efficient. Experience with the strategies provides a basis for understanding the operation involved and for gaining fluency with the facts. In this section, we describe possible strategies for learning the addition, subtraction, multiplication, and division facts. The strategies for each operation are listed roughly in order of increasing sophistication.

Strategies for Addition Facts

Common strategies include counting all, counting on, doubles, making or using 10, and reasoning from known facts.

Counting All

This is a particularly straightforward strategy. For example, to solve 7 + 8, the student gets 7 of something and 8 of something and counts how many there are altogether. The "something" could be beans or chips or marks on paper. In any case, the student counts all the objects to find the sum. This is perhaps not a very efficient method, but it is effective, especially for small numbers, and is usually well understood by the student.

Counting On

This is a natural strategy, particularly for adding 1, 2, or 3. Counters such as beans or chips may or may not be used. As an example, consider 8 + 3. The student gets 8 beans, and then 3 more, but instead of counting the first 8 again, she simply counts the 3 added beans: "9, 10, 11."

Even if counters are not used, finger gestures can help keep track of how many more have been counted on. For example, to solve 8 + 3, the student counts "9, 10, 11," holding up a finger each time a number word is said; when three fingers are up, the last word said is the answer.

Doubles

Facts such as 4 + 4 = 8 are easier to remember than facts with two different addends. Some visual imagery can help, too: two hands for 5 + 5, a carton of eggs for 6 + 6, a calendar for 7 + 7, and so on.

Making a 10

Facts with a sum of 10, such as 7 + 3 and 6 + 4, are also easier to remember than other facts. Ten frames can create visual images of making a 10. For example, 8 is shown in a ten frame like the one in Figure 1:

Figure 1: *A ten frame*

This visual imagery helps students remember, for example, that 8 + 2 = 10.

Using a 10

Students who are comfortable partitioning and combining small numbers can use that knowledge to find the sums of larger numbers. In particular, there are many strategies that involve using the number 10. For example, to find 9 + 7, we can decompose 7 into 1 + 6 and then 9 + 7 = 9 + 1 + 6 = 10 + 6 = 16. Similarly, 8 + 7 = 8 + 2 + 5 = 10 + 5 = 15.

Reasoning from Known Facts

If you know what 7 + 7 is, then 7 + 8 is not much harder: it's just 1 more. So, the "near doubles" can be derived from knowing the doubles.

Strategies for Subtraction Facts

Common strategies for subtraction include using counters, counting up, counting back, using 10, and reasoning from related addition and subtraction facts.

Using Counters

This method models the problem with counters like beans or chips. For example, to solve 8 − 3, the student gets 8 beans, removes 3 beans, and counts the remaining beans to find the difference. As with using the addition strategy "counting all," this relatively straightforward strategy may not be efficient but it has the great advantage that students usually understand it well.

Counting Up
The student starts at the lower number and counts on to the higher number, perhaps using fingers to keep track of how many numbers are counted. For example, to solve $8 - 5$, the student wants to know how to get from 5 to 8 and counts up 3 numbers: 6, 7, 8. So, $8 - 5 = 3$.

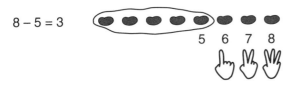

Figure 2: *Counting up*

Counting Back
Counting back works best for subtracting 1, 2, or 3. For larger numbers, it is probably best to count up. For example, to solve $9 - 2$, the student counts back 2 numbers: 8, 7. So, $9 - 2 = 7$.

$$9 - 2 = 7 \quad 9 \quad 8 \quad 7$$

Figure 3: *Counting back*

Using a 10
Students follow the pattern they find when subtracting 10, e.g., $17 - 10 = 7$ and $13 - 10 = 3$, to learn close facts, e.g., $17 - 9 = 8$ and $13 - 9 = 4$. Since $17 - 9$ will be 1 more than $17 - 10$, they can reason that the answer will be 8, or $7 + 1$.

Making a 10
Knowing the addition facts that have a sum of 10, e.g., $6 + 4 = 10$, can be helpful in finding differences from 10, e.g., $10 - 6 = 4$ and $10 - 4 = 6$. Students can use ten frames to visualize these problems as in Figure 4. These facts can then also be used to find close facts, such as $11 - 4 = 7$.

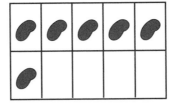

$$10 - 4 = 6$$

Figure 4: *Using a ten frame*

Using Doubles
Students can use the addition doubles, e.g., $8 + 8 = 16$ and $6 + 6 = 12$, to learn the subtraction "half-doubles" as well: $16 - 8 = 8$ and $12 - 6 = 6$. They can then use these facts to figure out close facts, such as $13 - 6 = 7$ and $15 - 8 = 7$.

Reasoning from Related Addition and Subtraction Facts
Knowing that $8 + 7 = 15$ would seem to be of some help in solving $15 - 7$. Unfortunately, however, knowing related addition facts may not be so helpful to younger or less mathematically mature students. Nevertheless, reasoning from known facts is a powerful strategy for those who can apply it and should be encouraged.

Strategies for Multiplication Facts

Common strategies for multiplication include skip counting, counting up or down from a known fact, doubling, breaking a product into the sum of known products, and using patterns.

Skip Counting

Students begin skip counting and solving problems informally that involve multiplicative situations in first grade. By the time they begin formal work with the multiplication facts in third grade, they should be fairly proficient with skip counting. This strategy is particularly useful for facts such as the 2s, 3s, 5s, and 10s, for which skip counting is easy.

Counting Up or Down from a Known Fact

This strategy involves skip counting forwards once or twice from a known fact. For example, if children know that 5×5 is 25, then they can use this to solve 6×5 (5 more) or 4×5 (5 less). Some children use this for harder facts. For 7×6, they can use the fact that $5 \times 6 = 30$ as a starting point and then count on by sixes to 42.

Doubling

Some children use doubling relationships to help them with multiplication facts involving 4, 6, and 8. For example, 4×7 is twice as much as 2×7. Since $2 \times 7 = 14$, it follows that 4×7 is 28. Since 3×8 is 24, it follows that 6×8 is 48.

Breaking a Product into the Sum of Known Products

A fact like 7×8 can be broken into the sum $5 \times 8 + 2 \times 8$ since $7 = 5 + 2$. See Figure 5. The previous two strategies are special cases of this more general strategy.

$7 \times 8 =$
$5 \times 8 + 2 \times 8 =$
$40 + 16 = 56$

Figure 5: *Breaking up 7×8*

Patterns

A. Perhaps the best-known examples of patterns are the nines patterns:

1. When the nines products are listed in a column, as shown below, it is easy to see that the digits in the tens place count up by one (0, 1, 2, 3, . . .) and that the digits in the ones place count down by one (9, 8, 7, . . .).

    9
    18
    27
    36
    45
    54
    63
    72
    81

2. The sums of the two digits in each of the nines products above are all equal to nine. For example, the sum of the digits in 36 is $3 + 6 = 9$; the sum of the digits in 72 is $7 + 2 = 9$. Adding the digits of a number to see whether they add up to nine can be a strategy in remembering a nines fact. For example, a student might think, "Let me see, does 9×6 equal 54 or 56? It must be 54 since $5 + 4$ is 9, but $5 + 6$ is not 9."

3. The digit in the tens place in a nines fact is one less than the number being multiplied. For example, $4 \times 9 = 36$, and 3 is one less than 4. This can be combined with the previous pattern to derive nines facts. For example, 3×9 is in the twenties. Since $2 + 7$ is 9, 3×9 must be 27.

4. Nines can easily be computed using the counting down strategy. Nine times a digit is the same as 10 times the digit, minus the digit. For example, 9×6 is $10 \times 6 - 6 = 54$.

B. Other patterns.

Other patterns that are useful in remembering other special facts:

1. 0 times a number equals 0.
2. 1 times a number equals the number.
3. 2 times a number is double the number.
4. 5 times a number ends in 0 or 5; even numbers times 5 end in 0 and odd numbers times five end in 5.
5. 10 times a number is the same number with a 0 on the end.

Sequencing the Study of Multiplication Facts

In kindergarten, children solve word problems involving multiplication situations. Beginning in first grade, the curriculum develops a conceptual foundation for multiplication through a variety of multiplication models, including repeated addition, the array model, and the number-line model. Fluency with the multiplication facts is expected by the end of third grade. Strategies are often introduced in specific, third-grade lessons. Practice is continued in subsequent lessons and especially in the Daily Practice and Problems and Home Practice. We do not introduce the multiplication facts in the order in which they are traditionally taught (first learning the 2s, then the

3s, then the 4s, etc.). Rather, we emphasize thinking strategies for the facts, introducing fact-groups in the following order:

2s, 3s, 5s, and 10s. The 2s, 3s, 5s, and 10s are easily solved using skip counting.

Square numbers such as $3 \times 3 = 9$, $4 \times 4 = 16$, and $5 \times 5 = 25$. These are introduced by arranging tiles into square arrays.

Nines. Students explore patterns for nines.

Last six facts. After students have learned the facts listed above and their turn-around facts ($9 \times 6 = 6 \times 9$), there are only six more facts to learn: 4×6, 4×7, 4×8, 6×7, 6×8, and 7×8.

Strategies for the Division Facts

The main strategy for learning the division facts is to think of the related multiplication fact. Therefore, students review the multiplication facts and develop fluency with the division facts by working with fact families. (Fact families are groups of related facts. An example of a fact family is $3 \times 4 = 12$, $4 \times 3 = 12$, $12 \div 3 = 4$, and $12 \div 4 = 3$.)

Using the Right Strategy

Different strategies appeal to different students. Students should not feel overburdened with the need to determine which is the "correct" strategy for a given fact. We do not intend to give them a new layer of things to learn. For example, when asked to explain a strategy for a fact, a student may say, "I've used it so much that now I just remember it." "Just remembering" is obviously an efficient strategy. The purpose of suggesting and discussing various strategies is to give students other, perhaps helpful, ways of learning the facts and to give them the confidence to think problems through when necessary. Students should have the opportunity to choose the strategies that work best for them or to invent their own.

Math Facts Lessons

The *Math Trailblazers* math facts program pervades most of the curriculum's components. Work with math facts are in different kinds of lessons. These are described in this section.

Figure 6: *Discussing fact strategies*

Everyday Work

As students work on problems in the labs and activities, encourage them to use and discuss various strategies for solving math facts problems. A number of important goals can best be reached through such discussions.

One goal is to legitimize all valid strategies, even those that may be less efficient. When students see their intuitive methods recognized and validated, they tend to perceive mathematical knowledge as continuous with everyday knowledge and common sense. We thus hope to avoid the unfortunate tendency of many students to separate their knowledge of mathematics from their knowledge of the real world.

By discussing strategies as they arise in context, students and teachers can explore how the strategies work and can verify that they are being used properly. Students should come to realize that a fact strategy that gives wrong answers is not very useful.

A second goal of our approach is to encourage students to communicate mathematical ideas. There are several reasons to stress communication: Students can learn from one another; communicating a method requires higher orders of thinking than simply applying that method; and skill at communicating is important in itself. We are social creatures. Mathematics and science are social endeavors in which communication is crucial.

A third goal of encouraging discussions of various methods is to give the teacher opportunities to learn about how students think. Knowing more about students' thinking helps the teacher ask better questions and plan more effective lessons.

Strategy Lessons

We feel that occasionally it is appropriate for lessons to focus on certain strategies that are developmentally appropriate for most students. Our plan is to begin with simple strategies that should be accessible to all students and to progress gradually to more complex forms of reasoning. For example, in the fall of first grade, we have several lessons that stress counting on to solve certain addition problems. Later, we explicitly introduce making a 10 and other, more sophisticated, strategies.

In general, you should expect your students to come up with effective strategies on their own. Our strategy lessons are intended to explore how and why various strategies work and also to codify and organize the strategies the students invent. They are not meant to dictate the only appropriate strategy for a given problem or to discourage students from using strategies they understand and like. They should be seen as opportunities to discuss strategies that may be appropriate for many students and to encourage their wider use.

Practice

Our ultimate goal is to produce students who can think mathematically, who can solve problems and deal easily with quantified information, and who enjoy mathematics and are not afraid of it. It is easier to do all of the above if one has fluency with the basic math facts. Practice strengthens students' abilities to use strategies and moves students towards fluency with the facts. Practice that follows instruction that stresses the use of strategies has been shown to improve

As students work on problems in the labs and activities, they should be encouraged to use and to discuss various strategies for solving math facts problems.

Our ultimate goal is to produce students who can think mathematically, who can solve problems and deal easily with quantified information, and who enjoy mathematics and are not afraid of it. It is easier to do all of the above if one has fluency with the basic math facts.

students' fluency with the math facts. We recommend, and have incorporated into the curriculum, the following practice to gain this fluency.

Practice in Context

The primary practice of math facts will arise naturally for the students as they participate in the labs and other activities in the curriculum. These labs and activities offer many opportunities to practice addition, subtraction, multiplication, and division in a meaningful way. The lessons involve the student visually with drawings and patterns, auditorily through discussion, and tactilely through the use of many tools such as manipulatives and calculators.

Pages of problems on the basic facts are not only unnecessary, they can be counterproductive. Students may come to regard mathematics as mostly memorization and may perceive it as meaningless and unconnected to their everyday lives.

Structured Practice

Student-friendly, structured practice is built into the curriculum, especially in the DPP, Home Practice, and games. One small group of related math facts is presented to the students at a time. The practice of groups of facts is carefully distributed throughout the year. A small set of facts grouped in a meaningful way leads students to develop strategies such as adding doubles, counting back, or using a 10 for dealing with a particular situation. Furthermore, a small set of facts is a manageable amount to learn and remember.

Beginning in the second half of first grade and continuing through fifth grade, a small group of facts to be studied in a unit is introduced in the DPP. Through DPP items, students practice the facts and take a short assessment. Beginning in second grade, students use flash cards for additional practice with specific groups of facts. Facts are also practiced in many word problems in the DPP, Home Practice, and individual lessons. These problems allow students to focus on other interesting mathematical ideas as they also gain more fact practice.

Games

A variety of games are included in the curriculum, both in the lessons and in the DPP items of many units. A summary of the games used in a particular grade can be found in the Games section. Once students learn the rules of the games, they should play them periodically in class and at home for homework. Games provide an opportunity to encourage family involvement in the math program. When a game is assigned for homework, a note can be sent home with a place for the family members to sign, affirming that they played the game with their student.

Figure 7: *Playing a game*

Use of Calculators

The relationship between knowing the math facts and the use of calculators is an interesting one. Using a multiplication table or a calculator when necessary to find a fact helps promote familiarity and reinforces the math facts. Students soon figure out that it is quicker and more efficient to know the basic facts than to have to use these tools. The use of calculators also requires excellent estimation skills so that one can easily check for errors in calculator computations. Rather than eliminating the need for fluency with the facts, successful calculator use for solving complex problems depends on fact knowledge.

When to Practice

Practicing small groups of facts often for short periods of time is more effective than practicing many facts less often for long periods of time. For example, practicing 8 to 10 subtraction facts for 5 minutes several times a week is better than practicing all the subtraction facts for half an hour once a week. Good times for practicing the facts for 5 or 10 minutes during the school day include the beginning of the day, the beginning of math class, when students have completed an assignment, when an impending activity is delayed, or when an activity ends earlier than expected. Practicing small groups of facts at home involves parents in the process and frees class time for more interesting mathematics.

> *Practicing small groups of facts often for short periods of time is more effective than practicing many facts less often for long periods of time.*

Assessment

Throughout the curriculum, teachers assess students' knowledge of the facts through observations as they work on activities, labs, and games. In Grades 3–5, students can use their *Facts I Know* charts to record their own progress in learning the facts. This type of self-assessment is very important in helping each student to become responsible for his or her own learning. Students are able to personalize their study of facts and not waste valuable time studying facts they already know.

In the second half of first grade, a sequence of facts assessments is provided in the Daily Practice and Problems. A more comprehensive facts assessment program begins in second grade. This program assesses students' progress in learning the facts, as outlined in the Expectations by Grade Level section of this tutor. As students develop strategies for a given group of facts, short quizzes accompany the practice. Students know which facts will be tested, focus practice in class and at home on those facts, then take the quiz. As they take the quiz, they use one color pencil to write answers before a given time limit, then use another color to complete the problems they need more time to answer. Students then use their *Facts I Know* charts to make a record of those facts they answered quickly, those facts they answered correctly but with less efficient strategies, and those facts they did not know at all. Using this information, students can concentrate their efforts on gaining fluency with those facts they answered correctly, but not quickly. They also know to develop strategies for those facts they could not answer at all. In this way, the number of facts studied at any one time becomes more manageable, practice becomes more meaningful, and the process less intimidating.

Tests of all the facts for any operation have a very limited role. They are used no more than two times a year to show growth over time and should not be given daily or weekly. Since we rarely, if ever, need to recall 100 facts at one time in everyday life, overemphasizing tests of all the facts reinforces the notion that math is nothing more than rote memorization and has no connection to the real world. Quizzes of small numbers of facts are as effective and not as threatening. They give students, parents, and teachers the information needed to continue learning and practicing efficiently. With an assessment approach based on strategies and the use of small groups of facts, students can see mathematics as connected to their own thinking and gain confidence in their mathematical abilities.

Conclusion

Research provides clear indications for curriculum developers and teachers about the design of effective math facts instruction. These recommendations formed the foundation of the *Math Trailblazers* math facts program. Developing strategies for learning the facts (rather than relying on rote memorization), distributing practice of small groups of facts, applying math facts in interesting problems, and using an appropriate assessment program— all are consistent with recommendations from current research. It is an instructional approach that encourages students to make sense of the mathematics they are learning. The resulting program will add efficiency and effectiveness to your students' learning of the math facts.

References

Ashlock, R.B., and C.A. Washbon. "Games: Practice Activities for the Basic Facts." In M.N. Suydam and R.E. Reys (eds.), *Developing Computational Skills: 1978 Yearbook.* National Council of Teachers of Mathematics, Reston, VA, 1978.

Beattie, L.D. "Children's Strategies for Solving Subtraction-Fact Combinations." *Arithmetic Teacher,* 27 (1), pp. 14–15, 1979.

Brownell, W.A., and C.B. Chazal. "The Effects of Premature Drill in Third-Grade Arithmetic." *Journal of Educational Research,* 29 (1), 1935.

Carpenter, T.P., and J.M. Moser. "The Acquisition of Addition and Subtraction Concepts in Grades One through Three." *Journal for Research in Mathematics Education,* 15 (3), pp. 179–202, 1984.

Cook, C.J., and J.A. Dossey. "Basic Fact Thinking Strategies for Multiplication—Revisited." *Journal for Research in Mathematics Education,* 13 (3), pp. 163–171, 1982.

Davis, E.J. "Suggestions for Teaching the Basic Facts of Arithmetic." In M.N. Suydam and R.E. Reys (eds.), *Developing Computational Skills: 1978 Yearbook.* National Council of Teachers of Mathematics, Reston, VA, 1978.

Fuson, K.C. "Teaching Addition, Subtraction, and Place-Value Concepts." In L. Wirszup and R. Streit (eds.), *Proceedings of the UCSMP International Conference on Mathematics Education: Developments in School Mathematics Education Around the World: Applications-Oriented Curricula and Technology-Supported Learning for All Students.* National Council of Teachers of Mathematics, Reston, VA, 1987.

Fuson, K.C., and G.B. Willis. "Subtracting by Counting Up: More Evidence." *Journal for Research in Mathematics Education,* 19 (5), pp. 402–420, 1988.

Fuson, K.C., J.W. Stigler, and K. Bartsch. "Grade Placement of Addition and Subtraction Topics in Japan, Mainland China, the Soviet Union, Taiwan, and the United States." *Journal for Research in Mathematics Education,* 19 (5), pp. 449–456, 1988.

Greer, B. "Multiplication and Division as Models of Situations." In D.A. Grouws (ed.), *Handbook of Research on Mathematics Teaching and Learning: A Project of the National Council of Teachers of Mathematics* (Chapter 13). Macmillan, New York, 1992.

Hiebert, James. "Relationships between Research and the NCTM Standards." *Journal for Research in Mathematics Education,* 30 January, pp. 3–19, 1999.

Isaacs, A.C., and W.M. Carroll. "Strategies for Basic Facts Instruction." *Teaching Children Mathematics,* 5 May, pp. 508–515, 1999.

Kouba, V.L., C.A. Brown, T.P. Carpenter, M.M. Lindquist, E.A. Silver, and J.O. Swafford. "Results of the Fourth NAEP Assessment of Mathematics: Number, Operations, and Word Problems." *Arithmetic Teacher,* 35 (8), pp. 14–19, 1988.

Myers, A.C., and C.A. Thornton. "The Learning-Disabled Child—Learning the Basic Facts." *Arithmetic Teacher,* 25 (3), pp. 46–50, 1977.

National Research Council. *Adding It Up: Helping Children Learn Mathematics.* National Academy Press, Washington, DC, 2001.

Principles and Standards for School Mathematics. National Council of Teachers of Mathematics, Reston, VA, 2000.

Rathmell, E.C. "Using Thinking Strategies to Teach the Basic Facts." In M.N. Suydam and R.E. Reys (eds.), *Developing Computational Skills: 1978 Yearbook.* National Council of Teachers of Mathematics, Reston, VA, 1978.

Rathmell, E.C., and P.R. Trafton. "Whole Number Computation." In J.N. Payne (ed.), *Mathematics for the Young Child.* National Council of Teachers of Mathematics, Reston, VA, 1990.

Swart, W.L. "Some Findings on Conceptual Development of Computational Skills." *Arithmetic Teacher,* 32 (5), pp. 36–38, 1985.

Thornton, C.A. "Doubles Up—Easy!" *Arithmetic Teacher,* 29 (8), p. 20, 1982.

Thornton, C.A. "Emphasizing Thinking Strategies in Basic Fact Instruction." *Journal for Research in Mathematics Education,* 9 (3), pp. 214–227, 1978.

Thornton, C.A. "Solution Strategies: Subtraction Number Facts." *Educational Studies in Mathematics,* 21 (1), pp. 241–263, 1990.

Thornton, C.A. "Strategies for the Basic Facts." In J.N. Payne (ed.), *Mathematics for the Young Child.* National Council of Teachers of Mathematics, Reston, VA, 1990.

Thornton, C.A., and P.J. Smith. "Action Research: Strategies for Learning Subtraction Facts." *Arithmetic Teacher,* 35 (8), pp. 8–12, 1988.

Van de Walle, J. *Elementary and Middle School Mathematics: Teaching Developmentally.* Addison Wesley, New York, 2001.

Portfolios

A portfolio is a purposeful collection of a student's work that provides evidence of the student's skills, understandings, or attitudes. If the portfolio includes work collected over time, then it may also reflect the student's growth.

This tutor outlines reasons portfolios may be useful and provides some guidance for getting started and going further. A bibliography includes suggestions for additional reading.

Why Portfolios?

Portfolios can help teachers:

- better assess student learning;
- foster student autonomy;
- communicate the goals of instruction to students and parents; and
- improve their own teaching.

Student Assessment

Since a portfolio contains direct samples of student work, it may, for certain purposes, be superior to indirect indicators like grades. For example, an actual graph shows a student's skill at graphing better than a grade; and the juxtaposition of two graphs, one from September and the other from January, documents learning over time much more accurately than two grades could ever do.

Portfolios can assess many outcomes that are hard to assess by more conventional methods—communication, reasoning, problem solving, confidence, perseverance, flexibility, and so on. They also can help you learn more about how students think and track the development of that thinking.

Student Autonomy

Portfolios can assess many outcomes that are hard to assess by more conventional methods . . . They also can help you learn about how students think and track the development of that thinking.

Portfolios can encourage students to assess their own learning. Students become more self-directed and motivated by examining and reflecting on their own work and the work of their peers.

Communication

Concrete examples of student work reveal much that is not easily conveyed in grades or comments. Parents and others can see progress and achievement for themselves.

The examples of student work in a portfolio also convey the content and goals of the curriculum in a specific way that complements the generalities of curriculum philosophies and scope and sequence charts. Portfolios focus on the work students actually do, not on ideology or wishful thinking. You can enhance communication between students and their parents, teachers, and peers by having particular examples to discuss.

Portfolios can help establish public norms for mathematics achievement. Focusing assessment on tests and grades communicates a narrow concept of what is valuable in mathematics. When assessment is more broadly based, it promotes a broader vision of mathematics.

Improvement of Instruction

Student portfolios are useful both for making instructional decisions and for evaluating and improving instruction.

Certainly, better understanding of how students think and feel can help you make better decisions about directions for future instruction. But portfolios can also help teachers improve their teaching more generally. Portfolios can facilitate discussions with professional colleagues about different approaches to the same topic; they can reflect the range of instructional opportunities offered; and they can indicate the use of manipulatives, group work, and technology in an implemented curriculum.

Student portfolios might be included in a Teaching Portfolio that a teacher can use for self-evaluation. You can refine your own teaching by collecting and examining several years of student portfolios. Some benefits that portfolios promise for students—collegiality, establishment of public norms, improvement of higher-level skills—may thus become available to teachers.

Getting Started

> The beginnings of all things are small.
>
> —Cicero

There is no single right way to do portfolios. The suggestions offered below have worked for others and may work for you, but you should expect to learn by trial and error and to rely on your own judgment. If you have used portfolios for writing or some other subject, then your experience will be invaluable. If you possibly can, work with a colleague as you implement portfolios for the first time.

Starting small, with modest goals, is a good idea. For example, you may organize your portfolio program around one well-defined area that is hard to assess by more traditional methods. For instance, choose one of the following areas as a theme for the portfolios:

- measurement,
- graphing,

There is no single right way to do portfolios.

- drawing pictures and diagrams, or
- communicating solution methods.

Besides starting small, start early so you have a baseline of student attitudes and achievement. Before and after comparisons are useful, but impossible without early samples. All materials in a portfolio must be dated.

A box with a file folder for each child's work is a simple way to start. If the box is easily accessible, then the portfolios are more likely to fit into classroom routines. Anticipate the need for more room as items are added to the portfolios.

What goes in the portfolios is a key decision. Figure 1 shows some kinds of materials you might include in a portfolio, although clearly no real portfolio will have such a wild collection. Figure 2 is a table of contents for a possible third-grade portfolio.

You might aim for balance in the selection of materials: group vs. individual assignments; short problems vs. longer projects; real life vs. purely mathematical problems; on-demand vs. no-deadline tasks; attitude vs. skill vs. concept-oriented work; and so on. The number of pieces should not be so few that there is not enough evidence about important outcomes, nor so many that there is no judgment about what is important or worthwhile. About eight to ten pieces might be enough for a semester.

You must also decide how to pick what to put in the portfolios. We suggest that students select items subject to constraints imposed by the teacher. Constraints might range from requiring particular items, to selecting items that meet certain criteria, to allowing complete freedom of choice by students. The amount of latitude you allow will depend on your class and goals. Younger children, for example, usually need more direction. Putting fewer constraints on what goes in the portfolios may foster student autonomy, but may result in portfolios with few overlapping items so comparisons between students are difficult, or may even yield useless collections of random scraps.

> *The number of pieces should not be so few that there is not enough evidence about important outcomes, nor so many that there is no judgment about what is important or worthwhile. About eight to ten pieces might be enough for a semester.*

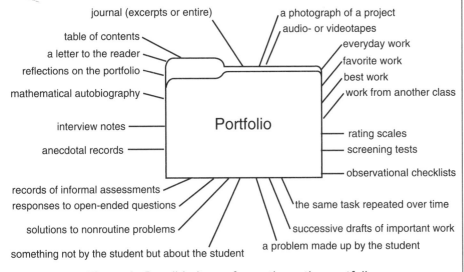

Figure 1: *Possible items for mathematics portfolios*

One way to organize the selection process is to have two folders for each child—a collection folder and the portfolio proper. Then, from time to time (once every several weeks or so), students can harvest the collection folder and add a few select items to the portfolio. At the same time, they can weed the portfolio so the total number of items does not become too large. Students can do this selection in small groups or pairs subject to teacher constraints as described above. Keep remaining items in the collection folder or send them home.

Eight to ten well-chosen and chronologically arranged pieces of work are most useful. You will have specific examples that communicate at parent conference time what your curriculum is and how your students are progressing; you will have a sampling of the products of your instruction so you can critically examine your teaching; and your students will see a cross section of their own work so they can attain greater self-awareness and autonomy. You have accomplished much even if your portfolios are no more than this.

Going Further

There are, however, other things you might want to try as you gain experience with portfolios, especially if you are working with older students. Periodic reviews of the portfolios, writing about the portfolios, and assessing the portfolios are worth considering.

Jarrett's Portfolio • Table of Contents		
Item	**Description**	**Date**
Letter to Reader	My letter tells what my portfolio shows about my math work this semester.	9/22
Journal	A few times a week we write about math in our journals. Mine has 35 pages so far!	
Spinning Differences	I used a spinner to make subtraction problems and then graphed how many times I got each difference.	9/27
The Better "Picker Upper"	I used water to make spots on different kinds of paper towels. Then I counted square cm to find the areas of the spots.	10/25
Joe the Goldfish	Joe needed a raincoat and I figured out how much cloth he would need to make it.	11/1
Palindromes	A palindrome is a number that is the same frontwards and backwards. I used addition to make numbers into palindromes.	11/10
Lemonade Stand	This was the first line graph I ever made.	11/15
Mass vs. Number	I measured the mass of different numbers of marbles. Then I made a line graph and used it to make some predictions.	12/5
Stencilrama	This was my favorite. We made stencils out of index cards and then used the stencils to make designs. We had to figure out how many times we would have to move the stencil to make a border around the bulletin board.	1/15

Figure 2: *Sample third-grade portfolio with an emphasis on graphing*

Portfolio Review

Most teachers will be hard-pressed to find time to meet with individual students to review portfolios. Whole-class discussion and peer consultations, however, can accomplish many of the same goals.

For example, ask students to look through their collection folders for their best graphs to add to their portfolios. First, through whole-class discussion, help students identify characteristics of a good graph. Then in small groups or pairs, students can examine their collections to pick out the best graphs. This opportunity for students to examine one another's work can help establish public norms for excellence.

Portfolio Writing

Asking students to write about the contents of their portfolios encourages reflection and self-assessment. This writing can take a variety of forms.

The most basic writing is a table of contents with the name of each piece, a brief description, and the date it was completed. Students can also include who chose the piece and why, who worked on the piece, and what was learned or liked or hard about the piece.

You might ask students to write a letter to the reader of the portfolio. The letter can identify favorite pieces and explain why they are favorites, or best work, or work that shows the most progress. The letter might show you what the portfolio reveals about the student as a learner of mathematics.

Assessing the Portfolios

You do not have to assess the portfolios. Most likely you already graded the work included in them, and the collection is itself a direct indicator of achievement and attitude. This indicator may be sufficient for your purposes.

Assessing the portfolios, however, can have advantages, especially if you are working with older students. For one, it shows that you care about the portfolios and so communicates to students that they should take them seriously. It can also model processes you want students to apply in peer- and self-assessment of the portfolios.

If you do intend to grade the portfolios, you should make your expectations known to the students in advance. The establishment of such public criteria for excellence, like the TIMS Student Rubrics, will help students know what they should aim for so their work can be better focused. You might concentrate on how well the portfolios are organized—table of contents, correct chronological order, completeness, etc.—or on the quality of the reflective writing about the portfolio. You may encourage a balanced selection of items, documentation of improvement over time, clarity of communication, accuracy of self-assessment, neatness, or something else. As long as your students know the criteria and you have the time to do it, such grading can be useful.

Conclusion

Portfolios will not solve all the problems of mathematics education. And there are some costs for using them. Using portfolios as part of an assessment program will certainly take extra time and can be difficult, especially at first. Getting students to reflect on their own learning is particularly hard. But despite such pitfalls, portfolios offer great promise for improving your teaching and your students' learning. The basic idea is simple: collect, select, reflect.

References

Crowley, Mary L. "Student Mathematics Portfolio: More Than a Display Case." *Mathematics Teacher,* 86 (7), pp. 544–547, 1993.

Kuhs, Therese. "Portfolio Assessment: Making It Work for the First Time." *Mathematics Teacher,* 87 (5), pp. 332–335, 1994.

Lambdin, Diana V., and Vicki L. Walker. "Planning for Classroom Portfolio Assessment." *Arithmetic Teacher,* 41 (6), pp. 318–324, 1994.

Mumme, Judith. *Portfolio Assessment in Mathematics.* (A publication of the California Mathematics Project.) University of California, Santa Barbara, CA, 1990.

Stenmark, Jean Kerr, ed. *Mathematics Assessment: Myths, Models, Good Questions, and Practical Suggestions.* National Council of Teachers of Mathematics, Reston, VA, 1991.

Word Problems

> In fact, word problems should not just be integrated into the mathematics curriculum; they should form the basis of the curriculum.
>
> —CARPENTER, FENNEMA, AND PETERSON, 1987

Although word problems are not the basis of the *Math Trailblazers* curriculum, we do agree that students should confront a wide variety of challenging word problems and exercises. Word problems can highlight applications of the mathematics students are learning. They can introduce, motivate, and develop new mathematics in meaningful contexts.

This tutor provides teachers with a summary of research and background information about word problems. It outlines the theoretical and practical frameworks that underlie the extensive use of word problems in *Math Trailblazers*.

Problem Representations

Problems are presented to us in different ways. Sometimes a problem arises from a real situation; other times we give problems in words, pictures, or symbols. These different ways are sometimes called modes of representation.

Real Situations

Consider this problem: "Jessica and Meri Joy baked 36 cookies. Then, Meri Joy dropped 12 cookies on the floor. How many were left?" Now this problem has a basis in reality: Jessica and Meri Joy are the daughters of two members of the *Math Trailblazers* development team; they really did bake cookies; some cookies really were dropped and spoiled. Note that Meri Joy and Jessica could answer the question simply by counting the cookies that were not dropped.

Such real-life situations are the most concrete level of problem representation. People rarely go wrong when they solve such problems. (Resnick, 1987)

Concrete Model

If, however, some time has passed and the cookies are no longer at hand, we can still ask and answer the question. One way is to get some beans and to pretend they are cookies. To solve the problem, we can count out 36 beans, separate 12, and count how many remain.

This use of beans to represent cookies is one step up the ladder of abstraction: a concrete model represents a real situation. Good evidence exists that even kindergarten students can handle complex problems that are represented by concrete models. (Carpenter, Ansell, Franke, Fennema, and Weisbeck, 1993)

Figure 1: *Twelve of 36 cookies dropped*

Pictures

Another way to approach the problem is via pictures. Each cookie can be represented by a circle. We can solve the problem by drawing 36 circles, crossing out 12, and counting those left.

This sort of pictorial representation is often useful in mathematics and science. Even when the picture does not lead immediately to a solution, it often helps us understand the problem situation and starts us on the road to a solution.

> *Even when the picture does not lead immediately to a solution, it often helps us understand the problem situation and starts us on the road to a solution.*

Verbal Representations

Most school problems are stated in words. This is often necessary (How else could we present our cookie problem in this essay?) and builds on a well-developed set of skills your students have—their language skills.

Language is the first and most powerful symbol system we learn. The recent emphasis on discourse and communication in learning is based at least in part on a recognition of the importance of language in human thought.

Symbols

We can also represent Jessica and Meri Joy's cookies in symbols:

$$36 - 12 = \Box$$

Such symbolic representations are abstract and powerful. Much of the explosive growth of mathematics in the last 400 years is due to the invention of more efficient symbol systems.

Unfortunately, for too many students, mathematical symbolism is a code they never crack. Such students do not see the marks on paper as meaningful or related to the real world in any way. Instead, they see the marks as part of an arcane game.

When writing number sentences, it is important to use units. Of course, constantly writing the units can be tedious. One compromise is to omit the units in the middle of a sequence of symbolic representations, but be sure to include them at the beginning and again at the end.

We want students to learn to write, read, and understand mathematical symbolism, especially number sentences. Here, word problems can be particularly useful. The situations in many word problems are straightforward enough that the corresponding number sentences are simple.

Usually, several number sentences are appropriate for each problem. Consider, for example, the following problem: "Janice had 9 stickers. Then her mother gave her some more. Now Janice has 16 stickers. How many stickers did Janice's mother give her?"

An adult might see this as a subtraction problem and write

$$16 - 9 = 7 \qquad\qquad\qquad\qquad\qquad\qquad (a)$$
or
$$16 - 9 = \square \qquad\qquad\qquad\qquad\qquad\qquad (b)$$

These number sentences are in the normal or "canonical" form. That is, the known quantities are on the left-hand side of the equals sign and the unknown or the answer is on the right-hand side.

Many students, however, write something like

$$9 + \square = 16 \qquad\qquad\qquad\qquad\qquad\qquad (c)$$
or
$$9 + 7 = 16 \qquad\qquad\qquad\qquad\qquad\qquad (d)$$

These "non-canonical" forms reflect the students' way of thinking about the problem: Janice had 9 stickers, then she got some more, and now she has 16 stickers. Often a student who writes (c) or (d) will solve the problem by counting on from 9 to 16 rather than by subtracting 9 from 16. We consider these non-canonical number sentences to be as correct as the canonical forms. They can also be more understandable for the students.

Translations between Representations

So we have a hierarchy of levels of representation: real objects, physical models, pictures, words, symbols.

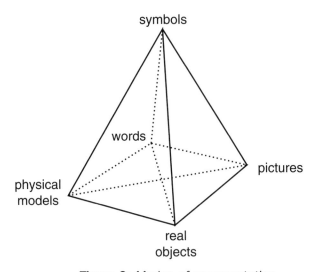

Figure 2: *Modes of representation*

But perhaps "hierarchy of levels" is not quite the right phrase; it may be better to consider that there are a number of different modes of representation, each of which has certain strengths and weaknesses. Recent cognitive theory indicates that the ability to translate from one representation to another is a crucial part of conceptual understanding and problem-solving skill. Connecting symbols with real referents, for example, permits one to understand symbolic manipulations and results in terms of real situations. Earlier, we saw how translating a problem from a real or verbal presentation to a concrete model could yield a solution by an elementary method.

Unfortunately, too much instruction in mathematics focuses exclusively on symbols. While symbolic representations are compact and powerful, they cannot stand alone. Our goal is to have students create mental "two-way streets" between symbols, words, concrete models, pictures, and real situations. Word problems are an excellent vehicle for reaching this goal.

Solving Problems

One view of problem solving is that the most critical step is developing the right representation: when we see the problem in the correct light, then the solution is obvious. Of course, the right representation for me might not be right for you. Accordingly, just as multiple representations should be part of the mathematics curriculum, so should multiple solutions. Estimation and attention to the reasonableness of results must also be part of instruction in problem solving.

Multiple Solutions

Many students think the main thing in mathematics is to get the right answer. Incorrect or partial answers are seen as failures, and re-solving a problem in a different way is considered futile.

On the contrary, students can learn much by solving problems in several ways. When different methods yield the same answer, students gain confidence both in the answer and in the various methods. This can be particularly useful for students learning more abstract and powerful methods: if a more powerful method gives the same answer as a more familiar method, then students are more likely to understand and trust the powerful method.

Students can also see connections within mathematics by comparing the points of view that generate different solutions to a problem. Making such connections is a key goal of the National Council of Teachers of Mathematics *Principles and Standards for School Mathematics* (NCTM, 2000). If students share their solution methods, then not only do they learn new methods from one another, but they also learn to communicate mathematically, another *Principles and Standards* goal.

Even incorrect or partial answers can be useful. Wrong answers are almost always the result of a student's honest attempt to get the problem right. Examining and discussing wrong answers and the procedures that generated them can make students' thinking explicit so that misconceptions can be identified and cleared up.

Sometimes a partial answer is the best we can reasonably hope for. In fact, many practical problems are impossible or prohibitively expensive to solve exactly. In some real situations, a partial answer may be all that is required.

A partial solution may be based on an idea that can be modified or extended to yield a complete solution. If a problem is hard, then making progress towards an answer is perfectly respectable, and certainly far better than giving up.

One way to get the most out of partial solutions is to encourage students to talk and write about the problem even if they cannot solve it. This will also help students stay with difficult problems longer.

Estimation

A common reason for estimating is that an exact answer is not necessary. If we have $5 and want to buy milk, bread, and eggs, a quick estimate will tell us if we have enough money. Sometimes an estimate must serve because an exact answer is impossible or impractical to obtain. The exact number of piano tuners who live in Chicago, for example, can only be estimated.

Another reason to estimate an answer is to verify the accuracy of a result obtained in some other way. This is especially important in our age of computing machines—if we do not have some idea what the answer should be, then we may be at a loss to know whether the answer the machine gives us is reasonable.

A less commonly recognized reason to make an estimate is as a step on the way to an exact answer. As one of our favorite teachers used to say, "Never solve a problem until you know the answer." We think he meant that finding an approximate answer can help in the search for the exact answer. By estimating an answer, we come to understand the problem better.

Learning to estimate builds number sense and encourages students to rely on their common sense rather than on rote procedures. Making a good estimate requires a flexible combination of common sense, experience, rules of thumb, and specific knowledge. Estimation is a high-level skill that takes a long time to develop. Estimation is, accordingly, built into *Math Trailblazers* from the beginning.

Reasonableness of Results

How often have you seen a student's paper with patently absurd answers? Such answers indicate that the student is not working at a meaningful level. Rather some procedures—half-understood, half-remembered—were carried out and something was produced, but the relationship of that product to the problem at hand is far from clear. No connection exists in the student's mind between the real situation and the symbolic manipulations.

Looking back when an answer is obtained, mapping the result of symbolic or other manipulations back onto the original problem statement, is a crucial part of the problem-solving process. George Polya, in his famous book *How to Solve It* (1957), included looking back as one of four basic steps in solving a problem. (Polya's other steps are to understand the problem; to make a plan to solve the problem; and to carry out the plan.)

When students look back at a solution, they should assess whether it is reasonable and correct. They can also look for ways to improve the solution, simplify it, or generalize it. By comparing their solution to other solutions, they can obtain further evidence of correctness and they have an opportunity to make connections between different approaches.

Addition and Subtraction Problem Types

Children typically use many varied methods to solve word problems. This, in part, relates to the fact that there is an underlying variety of problem types. Educational researchers in the last 20 years or so have explored the different problem types extensively. Several different examples are discussed here. Additional discussion about the methods children use to solve problems are in the TIMS Tutor: *Math Facts*.

Students should experience solving many different types of word problems. It is important to note, however, that in discussing the different problem types, we are not suggesting a new level of material for children to learn, i.e., we do not expect nor want children to have to learn about the different types of problems as a study in and of itself. Rather, we discuss the diversity in problem types so teachers recognize that this variety exists and subsequently are better prepared to present their students with a rich and varied collection of word problems.

Thomas Carpenter and his colleagues (Carpenter, Fennema, and Peterson, 1987; Carpenter, Carey, and Kouba, 1990; Carpenter, et al., 1999) have devised a classification scheme for problems that most adults would solve by simple addition or subtraction. They identify four general types of situations that give rise to 11 different kinds of addition or subtraction problems. (Other researchers have devised similar schemes. See, for example, Riley, Greeno, and Heller, 1983, and Rathmell and Huinker, 1989.)

Join Situations

Carpenter begins with "join" situations. Here, something is joined to a beginning quantity so a new quantity results. We think of these situations like this:

$$\text{start} + \text{change} = \text{result}$$

If the result is unknown, then we have an addition situation. Otherwise, we have a subtraction situation. Children often have more difficulty with problems in which the start is unknown than those in which the change is unknown.

Join/Result Unknown
Erick had 8 action figures. Then his father gave him 3 new ones. How many does he have now?

Join/Change Unknown
Janice had 9 stickers. Then her mother gave her some more. Now Janice has 16 stickers. How many stickers did Janice's mother give her?

Join/Start Unknown
Maria had some pennies. Then she found 3 more. Now she has 12 pennies. How many pennies did Maria have at first?

Separate Situations

Adults most often think of these situations as take-away problems:

$$\text{start} - \text{change} = \text{result}$$

If the result or change is unknown, then we have a subtraction (or take-away) situation. Otherwise, we have an addition situation.

Separate/Result Unknown
Thomas had 8 cookies. Then he ate 6. How many cookies does he have left?

Separate/Change Unknown
Leah had 12 dolls. She gave some of her dolls away. Then she had 7 dolls left. How many dolls did Leah give away?

Separate/Start Unknown
Michael had some marbles. He lost 5 of his marbles. Then he had 7 marbles. How many marbles did Michael have at first?

Part-Whole Situations

Carpenter's third category is part-whole. Here, a single whole is broken into two parts:

$$\text{part} + \text{part} = \text{whole}$$

This is similar to the join situation. The difference is that part-whole situations are static, the two parts coexisting from the beginning, whereas in join situations, two things are put together to form a new whole.

If the whole is unknown in a part-whole situation, then we have an addition situation. Otherwise, we have a subtraction situation.

Part-Whole/Whole Unknown
Ian has some action figures. He has 8 good guys and 3 bad guys. How many action figures does Ian have altogether?

Part-Whole/Part Unknown
There are 14 children who live in Clayton's building. Five of the children are boys. How many girls live in Clayton's building?

Compare Situations

Carpenter's last category is "compare." Here, two independent quantities are being compared:

$$q_1 - q_2 = \text{difference}$$

If the difference or q_2 is unknown, then we subtract. If q_1 is unknown, we add.

Compare/Difference Unknown
Samantha has $14. Kristin has $5. How much more money does Samantha have?

Compare/Q₂ Unknown
Jason has 13 crayons. Angela has 6 fewer than Jason. How many crayons does Angela have?

Compare/Q_1 Unknown

Lamar has some markers. Robin has 15 markers. Robin has 7 fewer markers than Lamar. How many markers does Lamar have?

Compare problems seem to be the hardest for children to solve. The other three types—join, separate, and part-whole—all involve a whole with parts in situations that are either static or dynamic. In compare problems, on the other hand, there is no whole. Rather, there are two independent quantities and a difference between them.

Need for Diversity in Problem Types

Traditionally, just two of these 11 kinds of problems have dominated American elementary mathematics textbooks, a dominance that contrasts sharply with customary practice abroad (Stigler, Fuson, Ham, & Kim, 1986; Fuson, Stigler, & Bartsch, 1988). These favored problem types, moreover, are the easiest to solve. Most of the subtraction problems are take-away situations (separate/result unknown). Most of the addition problems are join/result unknown. By presenting such a limited variety of problems, these texts give students a wrong impression about what addition and subtraction are. Carpenter's four situations—join, separate, part-whole, and compare—and the various types of problems reflect a much wider conception of addition and subtraction. In *Math Trailblazers,* we present this full range of addition and subtraction problems beginning in the earliest grades.

Diversity in Strategies

The description of the various problem types identified addition and subtraction situations. However, students may approach the problems in different ways. For example, while adults may immediately subtract when they encounter a take-away situation (8 cookies − 6 cookies = 2 cookies) some children may choose to use an addition strategy and count up. (Thomas ate 6 cookies and he has 2 left. Two more than 6 is 8 cookies.) Both are valid strategies.

Types of Multiplication and Division Problems

Researchers who have studied multiplication and division have identified different types of multiplication and division problems. While students do not need to be able to identify these different types of problems by name, it is important that they encounter and solve them. The different types of multiplication and division problems are outlined below.

Problems Involving a Number of Equivalent Sets

These sets can be groups of objects, arrays, or jumps on the number line. An example: Ask a class of 20 students to stand in a group. Instruct them to break into teams of four.

Using this situation, three different questions emerge. One question is interpreted as a multiplication problem, the other two as division problems.

> *Traditionally, just two of these 11 kinds of problems have dominated American elementary mathematics textbooks, a dominance that contrasts sharply with customary practice abroad. . . . These favored problem types, moreover, are the easiest to solve.*

The Unknown Is the Total Number in All the Groups

If there are 5 teams with 4 members on each team, how many players are there in all? There are two known factors and a missing product. Using established knowledge, students often interpret this correctly as a repeated addition problem (4 + 4 + 4 + 4 + 4 = 20). Through classroom experiences with many such problems, they can connect the repeated addition sentence to a multiplication sentence (5 × 4 = 20).

The Unknown Is the Number of Groups

Twenty members of a class are divided into teams of four members each. How many teams are there? The problem gives the total number in all the groups and the measure or size of each group. This aspect of division is called *measurement division*.

The Unknown Is the Number in Each Group

Twenty members of a class are divided equally into five teams. How many students are on each team? The problem gives the total number of students and the number of partitions or groups. This aspect of division is known as *partitive division*.

Jumps on a number line and arrays provide additional experience with the multiplication and division of equivalent sets. Successive jumps of equal size on a number line provide a model for multiplication as repeated addition and division as repeated subtraction. In *Math Trailblazers,* we model this situation using mythical creatures called "mathhoppers." For example, a +2 mathhopper starts at 0 and hops 4 times. On what number will it land? (8)

An array is a group of objects arranged in rows and columns. For example, a candy box that contains 5 rows with 6 pieces in each row is a 5 × 6 array. One virtue of the array model is that it makes it very clear that 5 × 6 = 6 × 5. You can rotate the box 90 degrees to form a 6 × 5 array. Another advantage is that it creates a visual image for both multiplication and division problems.

Problems Involving Scale Factors

This type of problem is often found in TIMS Laboratory Investigations. For example, after students have rolled different cars down a ramp, they might be asked if one car rolled three times as far as another. Similarly, when finding the mass of objects, they may be asked if the mass of one object is one-half the mass of another object.

A Cartesian Product

This problem involves two sets of objects (such as shirts and pants) that must be joined into pairs (shirt-and-pant sets). The answer for this type of problem then becomes the number of unique pairs that students can form from these two sets. While this type of problem is difficult for young children, they are able to solve it using manipulatives and diagrams.

Experiences with many types of problems should provide a strong conceptual foundation not only for multiplication and division, but for fractions, ratios, and proportional reasoning as well.

Problem Contexts

Most word problems in *Math Trailblazers* are embedded in a larger context; this is often an advantage since situational problems are more meaningful to students than abstract problems. Sometimes, however, providing a context is constraining or distracting. Also, problems may come to us without context; often, we have to provide extra information to make sense of a problem. Accordingly, in an attempt to provide a balance between problems embedded in situations and problems that are self-contained, we often provide free-standing word problems.

Teaching Word Problems

A variety of approaches to teaching word problems can be useful and stimulating. Here are several:

Whole Class, Then Small Groups

First, present a sample problem to your whole class. Discuss the problem and ask students to estimate the answer. Also ask students to explain how they made their estimates. Neither the estimates nor the explanations are likely to be very good, but this is only the beginning.

Next, ask students to solve the problem in groups of two or three students. Tell them you want (1) an answer for the problem, (2) an explanation of how they obtained the answer, and (3) a number sentence for the problem.

Require students who need help to seek it first from other students in their groups. Clearly, this is beneficial for the students who need the help, but those who give the help also benefit since they must make explicit what they may understand only implicitly. You will also be freed up since your students will be helping one another instead of depending so much on you.

As students work, move among the groups, listening to the various strategies. Use your judgment about what questions to ask and how much help to give, but try to restrain yourself. It is often better if students struggle on their own and find a solution themselves.

When the groups have answers, reconvene the whole class and ask students to explain their solutions and number sentences for the problem. Be sure they assess the reasonableness and correctness of their results. During these discussions, emphasize that every student is responsible for understanding his or her group's solution. One way to accomplish this is to call on random students to explain each group's work.

Encourage students to solve problems in more than one way by accepting only novel solutions during class discussions. This will motivate students to search for multiple solutions so they can contribute to the class discussion.

Small Groups, Then Whole Class

As your students gain experience, you can abbreviate or eliminate the whole-class introduction to the problem. Again, a whole-class discussion of solutions is appropriate.

Individual Work, Then Small Groups

Another approach is for students to work individually first and then to come together in pairs or small groups to compare solutions. Then, the small-group solutions can be shared with other groups during a class discussion.

Other Suggestions

Find some word problems appropriate for homework or for individual seatwork. Other problems may be so hard that no student is able to solve them; use such problems for whole-class investigations. You may use certain problems to introduce new mathematics like multiplication and division. Use an interesting problem as an "opener" when students arrive or when math class begins.

TIMS Tips

- If students cannot solve a problem, ask them to describe the problem and to restate it in their own words or ask them to draw a picture. This may lead to a better understanding of the problem and then to a solution.
- Do only a few problems at a time. Distributed practice will be more effective than bunched practice.
- Vary the format: individual, small group, whole class, homework.
- Be sure to discuss multiple solution strategies. Compare and contrast strategies, and point out advantages of each, but accept all correct strategies.
- Discuss several number sentences for each problem. Ask students to explain how a given number sentence fits the problem situation.
- Ask students to explain why their answers are reasonable.
- Provide manipulatives and calculators to each group. Just having them available in the room may not be enough—these resources should be immediately at hand.

Conclusion

As your students work word problems and share solutions, they will be applying mathematics they already know and learning new mathematics. Word problems deserve a prominent place in your mathematics lessons.

References

Carpenter, T.P., E. Fennema, M.L. Franke, L. Levi, and S.E. Empson. *Children's Mathematics: Cognitively Guided Instruction.* Heinemann, Westport, CT, 1999.

Carpenter, T.P., E. Fennema, and P. Peterson. "Cognitively Guided Instruction: The Application of Cognitive and Instructional Science to Mathematics Curriculum Development." In *Developments in School Mathematics Education Around the World,* I. Wirszup and R. Streit, eds. National Council of Teachers of Mathematics, Reston, VA, 1987.

Carpenter, T.P., D. Carey, and V. Kouba. "A Problem-Solving Approach to the Operations." In *Mathematics for the Young Child,* J.N. Payne, ed. National Council of Teachers of Mathematics, Reston, VA, 1990.

Carpenter, T.P., E. Ansell, M.L. Franke, E. Fennema, and L. Weisbeck. "Models of Problem Solving: A Study of Fourth Grade Children's Problem-Solving Processes." *Journal for Research in Mathematics Education,* 24 (5), pp. 428–441, 1993.

Fuson, K.C., J.W. Stigler, and K. Bartsch. "Grade Placement of Addition and Subtraction Topics in Japan, Mainland China, the Soviet Union, Taiwan, and the United States." *Journal for Research in Mathematics Education,* 19 (5), pp. 449–456, 1988.

National Council of Teachers of Mathematics. *Principles and Standards for School Mathematics.* National Council of Teachers of Mathematics, Reston, VA, 2000.

Polya, G. *How to Solve It.* Princeton University Press, Princeton, NJ, 1957.

Rathmell, E.C., and D.M. Huinker. "Using Part-Whole Language to Help Children Represent and Solve Word Problems." In *New Directions for Elementary School Mathematics,* P.R. Trafton, ed. National Council of Teachers of Mathematics, Reston, VA, 1989.

Resnick, L.B. "Presidential Address: Learning In School and Out." *Educational Researcher,* 16 (9), pp. 13–20, 1987.

Riley, M.S., J.G. Greeno, and J.I. Heller. "Development of Children's Problem-Solving Ability in Arithmetic." In *The Development of Mathematical Thinking,* H.P. Ginsburg, ed. Academic Press, New York, 1983.

Stigler, J.W., K.C. Fuson, M. Ham, and M.S. Kim. "An Analysis of Addition and Subtraction Word Problems in American and Soviet Elementary Mathematics Textbooks." *Cognition and Instruction,* 3 (3), pp. 153–171, 1986.

The TIMS Laboratory Method

Math Trailblazers is a comprehensive mathematics program that incorporates many important scientific ideas. Scientific concepts often provide contexts for developing and practicing math concepts and skills. The tools and processes of science are integral to mathematical problem solving throughout the curriculum.

This tutor expands upon the *Math Trailblazers* connection with science. It outlines the Teaching Integrated Math and Science (TIMS) Project's view of science and describes the TIMS Laboratory Method, a version of the scientific method. This method forms a framework throughout the curriculum for students to explore science in much the way scientists work.

The TIMS View of Science

Traditionally, school science has focused on the results of science. Students learn about parts of the body, types of rocks, the solar system, evolution, and so on. Knowing basic facts of science is seen as part of being educated, today more than ever. However, the facts of science, important and interesting as they are, do not alone comprise a comprehensive and balanced science curriculum.

The great educator and philosopher John Dewey expressed this idea some 100 years ago. In 1910, he wrote:

> *At times, it seems as if the educational availability of science were breaking down because of its sheer mass. There is at once so much of science and so many sciences that educators oscillate, helpless, between arbitrary selection and teaching a little of everything.*
>
> *Visit schools where they have taken nature study conscientiously. This school moves with zealous bustle from leaves to flowers, from flowers to minerals, from minerals to stars, from stars to the raw materials of industry, thence back to leaves and stones.*
>
> *Thus, . . . science teaching has suffered because science has been so frequently presented just as so much ready-made knowledge, so much subject-matter of fact and law, rather than as the effective method of inquiry into any subject-matter.*

Surely if there is any knowledge which is of most worth it is knowledge of the ways by which anything is entitled to be called knowledge instead of being mere opinion or guess-work or dogma.

Such knowledge ... is not information, but a mode of intelligent practise, an habitual disposition of mind.

In 1996, the National Research Council (NRC) published the *National Science Education Standards* for K–12 science education. Among the many recommendations of the NRC document is a direction for decreased emphasis on teaching scientific facts and information, and increased emphasis on teaching for understanding of scientific concepts and developing abilities of inquiry. The NRC *Standards* state:

Emphasizing active science learning means shifting away from teachers presenting information and covering science topics. The perceived need to include all the topics, vocabulary, and information in textbooks is in direct conflict with the central goal of having students learn scientific knowledge with understanding.

> *If we were to describe the TIMS approach in the most concise way possible, we would choose two words,* variable *and* experiment.

These points of view underlie the TIMS approach to science. If we were to describe the TIMS approach in the most concise way possible, we would choose two words, *variable* and *experiment*. The essence of modern science, as it is practiced by scientists, is to understand the relationships among variables. Out of the great sea of variables we have selected those that we feel are fundamental to the understanding of all areas of science, namely: length, area, volume, mass, and time. These variables might be considered the fundamental vocabulary of science. They are integral to the everyday work of biologists, chemists, physicists, astronomers, and earth scientists. The more a child explores these variables, the greater will be his or her command of scientific language and the more complete will be his or her ability to take up the adventure of science.

We have therefore made these variables the focus of experiments and activities in Grades K through 5 of *Math Trailblazers*. Explorations in kindergarten are conceptual in nature. As the curriculum progresses through the grades, students revisit the variables many times in increasingly more sophisticated ways. In Grade 5, students are able to move on to compound variables such as density and velocity, which involve two of the basic variables. For example, density involves both mass and volume while velocity involves both length and time. To understand these compound variables, it is important that students are first familiar with the more basic variables. Through repeated investigation of the variables in different contexts, fundamental science concepts and skills become generalized.

Variables in Scientific Experiments

A **variable** is a quantity that may assume any one of a set of values. The variable is the heart and soul of science because the variable is to scientific investigation what the word is to language—its foundation and the basis of its structure. All experiments center around at least two variables, and the ability to measure these variables satisfactorily will determine the success or failure of the experiment.

Variables and Values

Variables fall into two broad categories: categorical and numerical. Would you say that a person's hair color is a categorical or a numerical variable? Would you say that a person's height is a categorical or numerical variable? A **numerical variable** is one that may assume a numerical set of values. In contrast, a **categorical variable** is one that does not assume numerical values.

Color, then, which can take on values such as red, blue, or yellow, is a categorical variable. Other categorical variables are shape, kind of object, and type of material the object is made of. In each case, you have the broad classification, the variable, and then the values the variable can assume.

The simplest kind of numerical variable is the number of objects in a set. For example, if we were studying the number of students who came to class each day, the variable would be "Number of Students," and the possible values of the variable would be 0 students, 1 student, 2 students, etc. A second category of numerical variable involves measurement. The basic measurement variables stressed in *Math Trailblazers* are length, area, volume, mass, and time. The values for these variables are what we measure during the course of an experiment. For example, if we are investigating the variable length, the values might be the number of meters, centimeters, millimeters, or other appropriate unit of length. When the variable is area, the values might be the number of square centimeters. Or if volume is the variable, the value might be the number of cubic centimeters, and so on. The variable is the broad classification; the **values** for the variable describe what we are counting or measuring for that variable.

One point in studying variables that will take repeated practice for your students to master is the regular use of units of measure. In science, we never deal with numbers without understanding what their units are. For example, say that we tell you that Mary dropped a ball from a height of 30. A question your students will learn to ask is, "Thirty what?" Was it 30 centimeters, 30 feet, or 30 miles? The name after the number 30 is what we call the unit of measure, and every variable has a set of them. $5 + 4 = 9$ can be meaningless unless we know 5 of what. 5 apples + 4 apples = 9 apples, but 5 apples + 4 pears does not equal either 9 apples or 9 pears. The sum is equal to 9 pieces of fruit. Invariably, children will give you the numerical value of the variable and leave off its unit. Learning to use units is merely a matter of discipline; that is, using them correctly so often that you feel uncomfortable when you either forget them or use them incorrectly. Developing this discipline in your students will help them later in their schooling as they examine more complicated scientific concepts.

Manipulated and Responding Variables in Controlled Experiments

In an experiment, a scientist tries to find a relationship between two variables. Where possible, the experimenter chooses ahead of time the values of one of the variables. This variable is called the **manipulated variable.** The values of the second variable are determined by the results of the experiment—something that the experimenter does not know ahead of time. We shall call the variable whose values result from the experiment, the **responding variable.**

For example, consider the following situation from a fourth-grade experiment, *The Bouncing Ball*. In this experiment, children study how high a ball bounces. They drop a ball from various heights and measure how high it bounces. As the experimenters, they decide what drop heights they want to use in the experiment, say 40 cm, 80 cm, and 120 cm. The drop height is the manipulated variable. But the height to which the ball bounces can only be determined after you drop the ball. It is not known ahead of time. So, the bounce height is the responding variable.

Or, say you fill a plastic jar with different-colored blocks and choose red, yellow, and blue as the colors of your blocks. You then ask a child to reach in and pull out as many pieces as he or she can in one grab, sort the blocks by color, and count them. Color is the manipulated variable in this experiment. The number of each color that he or she pulls out is the responding variable. You choose the values of the colors that go in but you have no choice over the number of each color that comes out.

Beginning in the first grade of *Math Trailblazers*, the experimental variables are identified in all laboratory experiments. This is an essential part of conducting any scientific experiment. It is not until fourth grade, however, that we introduce the formal terms "manipulated" and "responding."

Note that in *Math Trailblazers*, we have elected to use the terms "manipulated" and "responding" to describe experimental variables. We have found manipulated and responding to be less abstract for children (and adults) and easier to understand than the more commonly used terms for variables, "independent" and "dependent."

Fixed Variables in Controlled Experiments

Experiments often have more than two variables. In an ideal experiment, more easily realized in the laboratory than in the real world, a scientist focuses on only two variables—the ones we have called manipulated and responding—and strives to hold all others constant. If too many variables change simultaneously in an experiment, obtaining meaningful results can be difficult or impossible.

Consider a laboratory experiment done in second grade, *Rolling Along in Centimeters*. Students roll different kinds of cars down a ramp and use metersticks to measure the distance each car rolls. Here, the "type of car" is the manipulated variable and the distance each car rolls is the responding variable. The height of the ramp, the starting line, the floor onto which the cars roll, and the method for releasing the car are all held constant each time a car is rolled down the ramp. We refer to these as the **fixed variables** (or controlled variables) in the experiment. Children intuitively understand this as "keeping things fair" while the data are collected during the course of the experiment.

In many situations, some variables in an experiment are hidden; that is, they are not immediately obvious, although changing them will greatly alter the results of your experiment. Consider an experiment in which you collect data on the kinds of pets owned by each child in the classroom. The kind of pet is the manipulated variable and the number of each kind of pet is the

> *In an ideal experiment, more easily realized in the laboratory than in the real world, a scientist focuses on only two variables—the ones we have called manipulated and responding—and strives to hold all others constant. If too many variables change simultaneously in an experiment, obtaining meaningful results can be difficult or impossible.*

responding variable. If you think about it, you can see that your results depend on where the pet owners live—in a high rise or a single-family house, in the city or a farm community, and even in which country. Thus the variable, "location," can drastically change the results.

One of the reasons cancer research is so difficult is because there are so many variables which are either difficult or impossible to control (such as environmental factors, personality traits, multitudinous viruses) that it is hard to pinpoint the variables that might be the cause of cancer. It is the complexity of biological and sociological systems that makes doing repeatable experiments in these areas very difficult.

Nonetheless, children can learn how to deal with simple physical systems where three or four variables are present. They should learn how to recognize the different variables involved and understand the importance of controlling all but two—the manipulated and the responding variable.

The TIMS Laboratory Method

Throughout *Math Trailblazers,* children carry out quantitative investigations in which they explore the relationships between variables. Each investigation is carried out with the same general format, which we call the TIMS Laboratory Method. One may call this our version of the scientific method. There are four phases: beginning the investigation and drawing the picture, collecting and organizing the data, graphing the data, and analyzing the experimental results. We discuss these four phases below, illustrating our discussion with references to *The Bouncing Ball* experiment described above and to *Marshmallows and Containers,* a second-grade experiment in which children study the number of marshmallows that fit into different-sized jars.

Phase 1: Beginning the Investigation and Drawing the Picture

Most investigations begin with a question. The question does not have to be momentous, but it must be meaningful to children. If the question connects in some authentic way with their experience, children will need no flashy inducements to want to find the answer. This is illustrated in the following classroom anecdote involving *Marshmallows and Containers.*

> As class begins, students sit together in groups of three. Each group has three different containers: a margarine tub, a 100 cc graduated cylinder, and a small paper cup. The teacher shows the class a bag of miniature marshmallows and asks, "Which container will hold the most marshmallows? Why do you think so?"
>
> The teacher encourages the groups to discuss their predictions and explanations and to record their ideas in their journals. When the groups report to the class, many groups think that the graduated cylinder will hold the most because it is the tallest. One boy explains that he thinks the cylinder holds the most because even if he could stretch the plastic in the bowl so it was tall like the cylinder, it still would not be as tall and would not hold as much. Other groups choose the tub because it is fatter than the other containers.

The teacher then asks, "How could you find out which container holds the most marshmallows?" This question leads naturally to an experiment: The students will fill each of the containers with marshmallows, count them, and record the numbers in a data table.

Once a suitable question has been posed—and posing such questions is far from trivial—then you must identify variables related to the question. *Marshmallows and Containers* examines the kind of container and the number of marshmallows. The size of the marshmallows and the method for packing the marshmallows into the jars is held fixed. In *The Bouncing Ball*, students measure the drop heights and bounce heights of a ball, while holding fixed the type of ball, the floor on which the ball is dropped, and the method for dropping the ball.

Through class discussion, the original question has been refined into a precise query about the relationship between two variables. These variables become defined well enough so children know how to gather information about them. Drawing a picture is an excellent way to summarize and communicate this beginning phase, and also to plan what is to come.

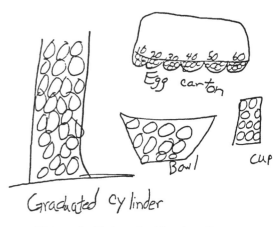

Figure 1: *Picture for* Marshmallows and Containers

Scientists often make sketches in experimental situations. In the TIMS Laboratory Method, drawing pictures helps children understand and organize what they are to do. A sketch gives the child time to think, to see relationships between variables, to place diverse relationships in a compact form, and to "explain" the experiment or problem to someone at a glance. Pictures also help teachers assess whether students are ready to proceed. Figure 1 shows one student's picture for

Figure 2: *Picture for* The Bouncing Ball

Marshmallows and Containers. The picture indicates the student's understanding of the experimental variables and the procedure. Note that the student is using an egg carton to make groups of 10 when counting marshmallows. Figure 2 shows a picture from *Bouncing Ball*, indicating the manipulated and responding variables (the drop height and the bounce height) and the procedure for the experiment. The students who drew these pictures are ready to go on to the next step, gathering data.

> *Scientists often make sketches in experimental situations. In the TIMS Laboratory Method, drawing pictures helps children understand and organize what they are to do. A sketch gives the child time to think, to see relationships between variables, to place diverse relationships in a compact form, and to "explain" the experiment or problem to someone at a glance.*

Phase 2: Collecting and Organizing the Data

In Phase 2 of the TIMS Laboratory Method, children gather the data and organize it in a table. To illustrate, we return to our classroom anecdote involving *Marshmallows and Containers*:

> On the next day, the children use their pictures to review the experiment before beginning the data collection. Each group receives a two-column data table, fills in the column headings, and writes the names (or draws pictures) of the containers in the first column. The teacher emphasizes the need for accuracy in counting, and the children discuss various methods for grouping and counting the marshmallows. As students begin to collect the data, the teacher circulates among the groups, coaching and assessing.

> After the children complete their data tables (Figure 3), the teacher leads a discussion in which the groups compare their results. This discussion centers on whether the groups' results are reasonable or not. Most groups report about 130 marshmallows in the graduated cylinder. Students agree that numbers close to 130, but not exactly 130, are acceptable. Based on this discussion, a group that had recorded only 110 marshmallows for the cylinder decides to refill the cylinder and count again.

Container	N Number of Marshmellow units
Graduated cylinder	133
Cup	121
bowl	181

Figure 3: *Data table from* Marshmallows and Containers

Tennis Ball

D Drop Height in cm	B Bounce Height in cm			
	Trial 1	Trial 2	Trial 3	Average
40	27	22	21	22
80	50	40	43	43
120	72	62	68	68

Figure 4: *Data table from* The Bouncing Ball

Figure 3 shows a student's data table for *Marshmallows and Containers.* Figure 4 is a student's data table from *The Bouncing Ball*. The name of a variable, including units if appropriate, heads each column.

When creating data tables, scientists and mathematicians generally place the manipulated variable in the left column and the responding variable in the right column. Since the experimenter chooses values for the manipulated variable before the experiment begins, the first column of the data table can be filled out prior to the experiment. Values of the responding variable can only be filled in as the experiment is conducted.

When creating data tables, scientists and mathematicians generally place the manipulated variable in the left column and the responding variable in the right column. Since the experimenter chooses values for the manipulated variable before the experiment begins, the first column of the data table can be filled out prior to the experiment. Values of the responding variable can only be filled in as the experiment is conducted.

Data tables are tools for organizing data. In a real laboratory experiment, scientists have to record the data clearly and correctly the first time, during the experiment. It has to be recorded in such a way that not only you can read it, but also your colleagues and even a stranger. A story is told about the Nobel Prize-winner James Watson, who helped discover DNA. His teacher at Indiana University was asked if he suspected that Watson might go on to great things when he graduated. Yes, he answered. Watson would go far. Why? The teacher replied that although Watson did not take great care of his personal appearance, and his desk was a mess, he kept a neat notebook. That is a lesson that even young children can understand.

The data table is also useful in controlling error and identifying patterns. Children can detect blunders when a measurement deviates too much from established patterns (as in the *Marshmallows and Containers* anecdote above), and they can control inevitable measurement error by averaging several trials.

Note that in *The Bouncing Ball* lab, the students performed three trials for each measurement. In other words, to answer the question of how high does the ball bounce when dropped from 40 centimeters, they dropped the ball three times from 40 centimeters and recorded the bounce height, in this case (Figure 4), 27, 22, and 21 centimeters. The students then take the average (they used the median for the average) bounce height for their value of the bounce height. This is done to minimize the effect of measurement and experimental error on the experiment. (See the TIMS Tutors: *Averages* and *Estimation, Accuracy, and Error.*)

Phase 3: Graphing the Data

Graphing is the heart of scientific analysis. Graphs are powerful communication tools that create a picture of the data and "tell its story." They allow you to compare, predict, and infer. If there is a pattern in the relationship between the variables, you are more likely to see it clearly in a graph. Being able to read a graph and produce a graph from data should be a major goal of school science. Graphing cuts across many disciplines: biology, chemistry, sociology, and economics. Students using *Math Trailblazers* work extensively with graphs from kindergarten on.

Bar Graphs vs. Point Graphs

In *Math Trailblazers,* data are mostly graphed as either a bar graph or a point graph; these two types of graphs will thus be the focus of our discussion in this section. Since a graph is a visual representation of the relationship between variables, the type of graph used depends upon the types of variables studied in the experiment.

When both variables are numerical, a point graph is often (though not always) appropriate. In *The Bouncing Ball,* for example, both variables—the drop height and the bounce height—are numerical. Since the values for these variables are numbers and are not discrete—that is, there are values between the data points that make sense, such as 52.5 cm—it is possible to use points and lines on the graph instead of bars to represent the data. Drawing a line or a curve makes sense only when the variables are numerical and there is a pattern in the data. Figure 5 shows a student's graph from *The Bouncing Ball.*

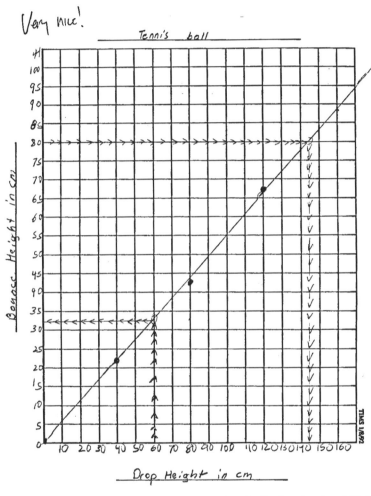

Figure 5: *Point graph from* The Bouncing Ball *showing best-fit lines, interpolation, and extrapolation*

Point graphs are introduced in *Math Trailblazers* in third grade and are used to represent a variety of different mathematical situations as well as to display data from laboratory experiments.

A bar graph is usually best when one of the variables is categorical (qualitative). In *Marshmallows and Containers,* for example, the type of container is a categorical variable and the number of marshmallows is numerical. Figure 6 shows the graph for *Marshmallows and Containers.* There are no values that make sense between the types of containers. Thus it does not make sense to connect them on the graph with a line. A bar graph, therefore, is appropriate for these kinds of situations.

A bar graph is usually best when one of the variables is categorical (qualitative).

Although point graphs are most often used when both experimental variables are numerical, that is not always the case. For example, in the experiment *First Names* from third grade, students collect data about the number of letters in the first names of classmates. The two primary variables in this experiment are the number of letters (the manipulated variable) and the number of names (the responding variable). A graph for the experiment is shown in Figure 7. While both variables in this experiment are numerical, they are also discrete—that is, it is not meaningful to speak of $6\frac{1}{2}$ letters in a name or $3\frac{1}{4}$ people who have that number of letters in their names. Thus, we can see why a point graph, in which values between the data points are represented, would not be appropriate in this case. Instead, the data is best represented on a bar graph.

Figure 6: *Bar graph from* Marshmallows and Containers

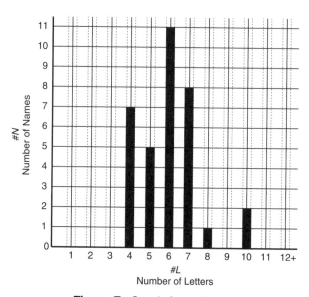

Figure 7: *Graph from* First Names

Labeling the Axes

With most types of data, it is conventional in science to place the manipulated variable along the horizontal axis and the responding variable along the vertical axis. The horizontal axis is labeled with a word or letter describing the manipulated variable and the vertical axis with a word or letter describing the responding variable. In Figure 7, for example, the horizontal axis—the manipulated variable—is labeled "#L, Number of Letters" and the vertical axis—the responding variable—is labeled "#N, Number of Names."

Once the axes are in place, the children can label the axes with the values for each variable. In the case of the *Marshmallows and Containers* in Figure 6, the student wrote in labels to represent the different kinds of containers.

> With most types of data, it is conventional in science to place the manipulated variable along the horizontal axis and the responding variable along the vertical axis.

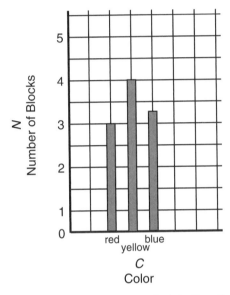

Figure 8: *Common errors in labeling the axes*

A common error in labeling axes is illustrated in Figure 8. This graph shows irregular spacing on both axes. The vertical axis in Figure 8 is incorrect with one space between 0 and 1 and two spaces between the other numbers. Technically, the categorical variables displayed on the horizontal axis do not have to be equally spaced, but it is a good idea to get your students into the habit of spacing their bars across the axis in regularly spaced intervals. This is because when dealing with numerical data, the values *must* be equally spaced.

Scaling the axes for numerical data requires an analysis of the range of the data and comparing it with the number of available intervals on your particular graph paper. Scaling by ones, two, fives, tens, or other numbers might be appropriate depending on the data for a particular experiment. What is essential, however, is that the intervals are all equal along a given axis. Students will learn that it is best to determine the appropriate interval ahead of time. Otherwise they will end up plotting their initial data points and later discovering that other points will not fit on the graph.

In most cases, the scale on the horizontal axis is independent of the scale on the vertical axis. Students should number the axes in ways that make sense for the data. For example, the horizontal axis in *The Bouncing Ball* graph

(Figure 5) is scaled by tens but the vertical axis is scaled by fives. One exception to this is when making scale maps. Here, using different scales for the different axes would create a distorted image and make it difficult to find distances on the map.

As scientists do, students using the TIMS Laboratory Investigations often use their graphs to make predictions about physical phenomena. When making point graphs, therefore, we often encourage students to scale their axes to allow room for extrapolation. (See the section below entitled *Predictions from Point Graphs: Interpolation and Extrapolation* for information about extrapolation.)

Bar Graphs in *Math Trailblazers*

As early as kindergarten, students using *Math Trailblazers* work on graphing concepts, including making and interpreting simple graphs. A quick way to make bar graphs of classroom data is to place self-adhesive notes on a labeled graph. An example of this with *First Names* is illustrated in Figure 9. In this graph, each student placed a self-adhesive note with the data for his or her name on the graph. The data are clearly represented. The one-to-one correspondence between data points and the number of students in the class is particularly apparent in this type of graph, which we use primarily in kindergarten, first, and second grades.

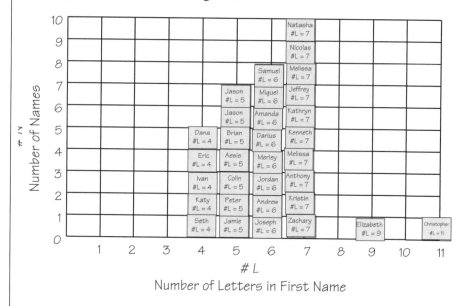

Figure 9: First Names *graph using self-adhesive notes*

In first grade, we introduce a graphing protocol that is different in *Math Trailblazers* than in some other programs. When making bar graphs, we encourage students to create their bars along the vertical lines in the graph rather than in the spaces between the lines. (See Figures 6, 7, and 9.) This does not affect the data or the reading of the graph. Rather it prepares students for making point graphs, where data points are plotted at the intersection of lines extending from the horizontal and vertical axes.

To assist students with this, we have created a special graph paper for making bar graphs. A version of this graph paper is shown in Figure 10. The dark vertical grid lines across the page are where the data for the manipulated variable is plotted. These lines are surrounded on both sides by a pair of dashed guide lines. Students make bars by coloring in the space on either side of the dark vertical lines. The result is a straight bar that is centered along a vertical line. The values for the manipulated variable are indicated on the horizontal axis directly below each bar.

Figure 10: *TIMS bar graph paper*

The benefit of making bar graphs in this manner is most apparent in third grade as students make the transition to creating point graphs. To simplify students' initial attempt at creating a point graph, they first graph a data set as a bar graph and then convert the bar graph to a point graph. This is shown in Figure 11.

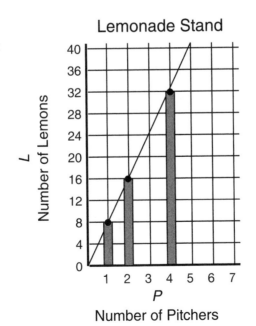

Figure 11: *Transition from bar graphs to point graphs in third grade*

Point Graphs: Fitting Lines and Curves

With point graphs, the data are plotted at the junction of the values of each variable. Once the data are plotted, we look for patterns. If the data points form a line or close to a line, we try to fit a line through the points. If the data form a curve, we try to fit a smooth curve through the points.

Figure 11 shows a graph in which the data points lie exactly on a straight line. Fitting a line to these data points is simply a matter of laying down a ruler and connecting the points.

For most experiments, we cannot expect the data to be so precise. In these experiments, the data may lie close to, but not exactly on a straight line. The "zigzags" in the data are due to experimental error. (See the TIMS Tutor: *Estimation, Accuracy, and Error.*) To average the error, one fits a line that comes as close to the data points as possible even though the line may not pass through any of these points. To assure a good fit, you would like as many points above the curve as below. You do not want to force the line through two points while missing the third by a mile. It is better to miss them all but come close to all than be too far from any one point.

As shown on *The Bouncing Ball* graph in Figure 5, you can fit a line to the data points, not by using some complicated statistical procedure, but simply "by eye." The student uses a clear ruler or a thread and moves it around until it fits the data points as closely as possible. This best-fit line is useful for minimizing error and making predictions.

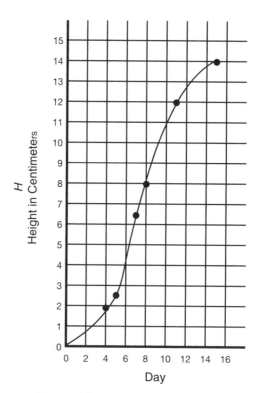

Figure 12: *Graph from* Plant Growth

Of course, not all experimental relationships result in data that yields straight lines on graphs. In *Math Trailblazers,* we also explore data that exhibits other kinds of patterns. Figure 12 shows the graph from a fourth-grade experiment, *Plant Growth,* where the data shows a pattern, but not a straight line.

When you can fit a smooth curve through the data points, you have uncovered one of nature's secrets—that the variables are related, that there is a predictable pattern to the data. We are then not restricted only to our specific data points, but can now use the pattern to predict what the value of the responding variable will be for any value of the manipulated variable.

Predictions from Point Graphs: Interpolation and Extrapolation
A major goal of mathematics and science is to find patterns in data and to use the patterns to make predictions. Interpolating and extrapolating on a point graph are two ways to do this.

Using the graph to find data points that lie between those in your data table is called **interpolation.** *Inter* means between or among. The simplest situation is when the pattern of data points produces a straight line. In the graph in Figure 5, the student interpolated to predict that a ball dropped from 60 cm would bounce about 32 cm. Note that in Figure 5 the student showed how she made her interpolation by starting at 60 cm on the horizontal axis, drawing a line (with arrows) up to the best-fit line, and then drawing a horizontal line to find the corresponding value of the bounce height—about 32 cm.

Extrapolation is an attempt to predict information beyond the last data point. *Extra* means outside or beyond. To extrapolate, we must extend the line into a region where there is no data. You can do this easily by laying a ruler on the straight line, extending the line, and reading off your prediction. In Figure 5, the student extrapolated to predict that a ball that bounced 80 cm was dropped from a height of about 144 cm. Here, the student began with values on the vertical axis (the bounce height) and predicted a value on the horizontal axis (the drop height). It is possible to interpolate and extrapolate in either of two directions: from values on the horizontal axis to values on the vertical axis or vice versa.

Having used these techniques to make predictions, it is important to have the children check their predictions experimentally and see how close their new data comes to the curve. This is one of the joys of science—to see that nature is often regular and predictable and that you can make predictions that come true! Checking predictions, though time-consuming, is worthwhile because it reinforces connections between mathematical abstractions and the real world.

Phase 4: Analyzing the Data

After making the graph, students explored the relationship between the variables in four ways: with the physical materials, in the picture, in the data table, and in the graph. The last phase of the TIMS Laboratory Method is the analysis of the entire situation, where students explore the relationship quantitatively and represent it symbolically (i.e., with numbers).

> *A major goal of mathematics and science is to find patterns in data and to use the patterns to make predictions. Interpolating and extrapolating on a point graph are two ways to do this.*

One way to structure this analysis is to ask a series of questions. The questions usually begin on the literal level: *Did the tallest container hold the most marshmallows? How high did the tennis ball bounce when dropped from 60 cm?* More demanding questions require prediction: *How many marshmallows would two bowls hold? If a ball bounced to 45 cm, what height was it dropped from?* Asking what would happen if one of the fixed variables is changed can build a broader understanding of the situation: *What would happen if we used large instead of miniature marshmallows? What would happen if we used a Super ball instead of a tennis ball?* This quantitative analysis of the data is one place in *Math Trailblazers* where students regularly practice and reinforce arithmetic and other math skills.

The end of the investigation may be a completely satisfying answer to the original question, but, more often than not, the end is another question that can lead to further investigations. *Marshmallows and Containers,* for example, might lead to an investigation of the liquid capacities of other short and tall containers. After an initial experiment with tennis balls in *The Bouncing Ball,* children carry out an investigation using another type of ball and compare the results from the two experiments.

Picture, Table, Graph, and Questions: Putting It Together

Each of the four phases previously described may require one or more class periods. In addition, you may spend time becoming familiar with the equipment at the beginning and on further experiments at the end. Thus, a lab is an extended activity that may last a week or even longer. This is much longer than a typical mathematics or science lesson, but there are significant benefits.

First, the four phases simplify the scientific method enough for children to use, but not so much that it fails to resemble what scientists do. Identifying variables, drawing pictures, measuring, organizing data in tables, graphing data, and looking for patterns are part of many scientists' work. Students are thus inducted via this method into the authentic practice of science.

The method fosters children's sense-making. Children handle numbers they have generated themselves by counting or measuring, numbers that are thus meaningful to them. As they deal with experimental error, they develop number sense and estimation skills. As they look for patterns in their tables and graphs, they make sense of the numbers before them. Arithmetic in context is more understandable.

The approach is multimodal, which has benefits for both individual students and heterogeneous groups of students. The multiple representations of relationships between the variables permit problems to be solved in more than one way, allowing different students to approach the same content in ways they understand. The container that holds the most marshmallows, for example, can be found from the graph, from the data table, or from the marshmallows themselves. A prediction about a bounce height might be obtained by extrapolating on the graph or by extending patterns in the data table, and can then be verified using the apparatus. Students can compare these various approaches, thus helping them make connections within mathematics as well as between the informal mathematics of their everyday experience and more formal mathematics.

Identifying variables, drawing pictures, measuring, organizing data in tables, graphing data, and looking for patterns are part of many scientists' work. Students are thus inducted via this method into the authentic practice of science.

Mathematics in Context

Two principles underlie the TIMS Laboratory Method. First, an investigation should begin within the children's own experiences. Children use objects from their everyday lives to investigate a familiar situation. Children's everyday knowledge, like a scientist's theory, provides a framework for interpreting the results of the investigation. Without that framework, the investigation would remain hollow and meaningless.

The second principle is that an investigation should also transcend children's everyday experiences. The exploration must go somewhere; it must lead the children both to a better understanding of the immediate situation and to improved skills, understandings, habits, and attitudes. The concepts can then be extended and transferred to new contexts.

Balancing these principles requires teacher judgment. The key is to enable students to follow their own ideas, but with the intention that those ideas will lead somewhere. How much scaffolding to provide, how much to guide students in directions that are fruitful rather than sterile, must be decided by the teacher in context. The goal is that students should advance not only in skill and understanding, but also in autonomy and perseverance. Just how much structure to provide along the way is perhaps a teacher's most important and difficult job.

The TIMS Laboratory Method helps children connect their everyday experiences with formal mathematics. As they investigate everyday situations quantitatively, children handle variables, explore relationships between variables, master a few powerful techniques for representing these relationships, and use these multiple representations to generate a wide variety of problem solutions. By beginning and ending in familiar situations, the abstractions of mathematics are linked to children's everyday knowledge. As students master this method, they become increasingly autonomous and flexible in its application. Then we can truly say they understand the fundamentals of *doing* science.

References

Archambault, Reginald D. (ed.), *John Dewey on Education: Selected Writings*. Modern Library, 1964.

Bruner, Jerome S. "The Course of Cognitive Growth." *American Psychologist* 19 (1), pp. 1–15, 1964.

Dewey, John. "Science as Subject-Matter and as Method." *Science* 31 (787), pp. 121–7, January 28, 1910.

Goldberg, Howard, and F. David Boulanger. "Science for Elementary School Teachers: A Quantitative Approach." *American Journal of Physics* 49 (2), pp. 120–124, 1981.

Goldberg, Howard, and Philip Wagreich. "Focus on Integrating Science and Math." *Science and Children* 2 (5), pp. 22–24, 1989.

Goldberg, Howard, and Philip Wagreich. "A Model Integrated Mathematics and Science Program for the Elementary School." *International Journal of Educational Research* 14 (2), pp. 193–214, 1990.

Hiebert, James. "A Theory of Developing Competence with Written Mathematical Symbols." *Educational Studies in Mathematics* 19, pp. 333–355, 1988.

Isaacs, Andrew C., and Catherine Randall Kelso. "Pictures, Tables, Graphs, and Questions: Statistical Processes." *Teaching Children Mathematics* 2 (6), pp. 340–345, 1996.

Isaacs, Andrew C., Philip Wagreich, and Martin Gartzman. "The Quest for Integration: School Mathematics and Science." *American Journal of Education* 106 (1), pp. 179–206, 1997.

Lesh, Richard, Thomas Post, and Merlyn Behr. "Representations and Translations among Representation in Mathematics Learning and Problem Solving." In C. Janvier (ed.), *Problems of Representation in the Teaching and Learning of Mathematics.* Lawrence Erlbaum Associates, Hillsdale, NJ, 1987.

National Research Council. *National Science Education Standards.* National Academy Press, Washington, DC, 1996.

Silver, Edward. "Using Conceptual and Procedural Knowledge: A Focus on Relationships." In J. Hiebert (ed.), *Conceptual and Procedural Knowledge: The Case of Mathematics.* Lawrence Erlbaum Associates, Hillsdale, NJ, 1986.

The Concept of Length

Units

In dealing with scientific problems, we must often know such things as the location of an object, the distance between objects, how tall or wide an object is, or how fast it is moving. Central to all these ideas is the concept of length. In this tutor, we shall examine the various disguises in which length can appear.

First, however, we must note the messy problem of units. The kinds of units chosen for length were for a long time quite arbitrary. The cubit, used by several ancient civilizations, was the length of a forearm between the tip of the middle finger and the elbow. The fathom was the width of a Viking sailor's embrace. (Fathom that!)

The foot was a convenient length defined as the length of a person's foot. Of course, everyone has a different-sized foot, so if we want to use, say, the king's foot as a standard, we will have to mark it permanently; we cannot very well lug the king around! Since the king is the ruler of the land, it was both rational and proper to call this marker a ruler as well. To show students the chaos caused by not having a standard length, have them measure the length of their desks in cubits or the width of the room in feet with each child using his or her own body measurements. You will have as many different values as measurers.

Nonstandard Units

At first, we have the children measure length using nonstandard units, often links. A link is shown in Figure 1 along with a chain of links. The measurement of the object shown is $4\frac{1}{2}$ links. The reasons we go to links are: (1) to make counting the unit length easy and (2) to keep the numbers manageable. Rather than dealing with hundreds of cm, we can count 50 links. And to count a link is easy since they are so large.

By alternating link colors (2 reds, 2 whites, 2 reds, etc.), one can make the counting even easier by skip counting by 2s. If you want to have the children skip count by 5s, then have a chain with 5 blues, 5 yellows, 5 blues, etc.

With links, it is also easy to round off to $\frac{1}{2}$ link as shown in Figure 1. If the edge we are measuring is near the middle, then the length is $4\frac{1}{2}$ links. If shorter, then the length is 4 links; if longer, the length is 5 links.

Figure 1: *Links*

The Metric System

Of course, links are not a commonly used standard of measure. In the United States, it is feet. Unfortunately, many objects are smaller than a foot. This means one must subdivide the standard unit. For some miserable reason, the smaller unit, the inch, is $\frac{1}{12}$ of a foot. Who likes to divide by 12? So, the French scientific community at the time of the French Revolution (c. 1790) chose as the standard unit of length a distance that they called a meter. It was chosen so that 10^7 (10 million) metersticks laid end to end would just fit between the North Pole and the equator, as shown in Figure 2. A platinum-iridium rod was constructed with two marks a meter apart and stored in a vault near Paris. Every meterstick, albeit indirectly, comes from this standard. Having defined the meter, the French were smart enough to define all subsequent subdivisions of the meter as integral powers of ten. The foot is divided into $\frac{1}{12}$s and $\frac{1}{48}$s, and other equally horrible numbers; for the meter, the divisions are $\frac{1}{10}$s, $\frac{1}{100}$s, and $\frac{1}{1000}$s. We shall now explore this point further.

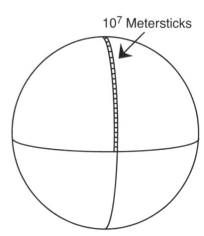

10^7 Metersticks

Figure 2: *Metersticks from the North Pole to the equator*

For measuring ordinary objects in the classroom, the meter is divided into three other units; the millimeter, the centimeter, and the decimeter (although the latter is rarely used). Without being specific as to the size of each unit, we can order them using the greater than (>) or less than (<) sign. Starting with the smallest, we have:

1 millimeter < 1 centimeter < 1 decimeter < 1 meter.

Reversing the order and starting with the largest, we have:

1 meter > 1 decimeter > 1 centimeter > 1 millimeter.

It is important that students know at least this much before going on to more exact relations.

The key to the subdivision of the meter is the prefix *milli*. Milli is related to the word mile. Mile was the distance it took a Roman soldier to step off 1000 paces, a pace being two steps. Since an average pace is approximately 5 feet (try it and see), a mile would be approximately 5000 feet. The crucial point is the number 1000 as related to the word mile. Milli is the prefix for "$\frac{1}{1000}$ of." Thus, a millimeter is one-thousandth of a meter. There are 1000 millimeters in a meter just as there are 1000 paces in a mile. In each case, we have a subunit that is one-thousandth of the main unit. The word mile is to remind us that there are 1000 paces in a mile. The word millimeter is to remind us that there are 1000 millimeters in a meter. One should try to picture this in one's mind. Millimeters are tiny; it takes a lot of them to make up any macroscopic length. (By macroscopic, we are referring to something one can see unaided versus microscopic where one would need a magnifying glass or microscope to see it.) On the other hand, because a meter is large, a millimeter is usually a fraction of most lengths one would measure in the lab. Thus, it is reasonable that a third-grader knows how to measure the length of his thumb as 3 cm or 30 mm, but not as 0.03 m.

How are mm, cm, dm, and m related? Let's start with the smallest and see how many mm are in a cm, a dm, and a meter.

> 1 centimeter contains 10 mm;
> 1 decimeter contains 100 mm;
> 1 meter contains 1000 mm.

Based on these relationships, we should be able to figure out how many centimeters are in a decimeter or in a meter. Here, however, the French have made it easy for us; the prefix for each word gives the answer away. *Centi* stands for 100th and *deci* stands for one-tenth. Thus one centimeter is one-hundredth of a meter; there are 100 cm in a meter. A decimeter is one-tenth of a meter; there are 10 dm in a meter. What this boils down to then is the following:

> 1 decimeter contains 10 cm;
> 1 meter contains 100 cm;
> 1 meter contains 10 dm.

Everything depends upon the size of the meter. Once that is fixed (by our rod in Paris), the sizes of all other metric units are determined.

Measuring Length

The simplest way to get started in the metric system is to count, using a meterstick, the number of mm or cm (and if they do not equal fractions, dm or meters) in a given length. Say we measure the width of the sheet of paper in cm. Then depending upon the accuracy of the meterstick (a cheap one could be off a bit) and the judgment of the student, one can see that there are between 21 and 22 cm across the page. If you stick to cm, then for students who are not yet comfortable with fractions or decimals, this is all you can say. As they begin to learn decimals, the children can determine the width as 21.6 cm. However, you can get still better accuracy even without decimals by going to mm instead of cm. Here, all one has to be able to do is count beyond 100. Thus, the width is 216 mm. In fact, one of the neat things about the metric system is that you can always choose a set of units to obtain almost any accuracy you want without going to fractions or decimals. On the other hand, you can purposely choose units that will give decimal or fractional answers. As we just saw, in cm units, the width of the page is a decimal, 21.6 cm. We could have asked for the width in meters. Since the width is less than a meter, we are dealing with fractions. In this case, the width is 0.216 meters or roughly $\frac{1}{5}$ of a meter. Clearly, there is great potential in the metric system for teaching math and linking this to scientific measurement.

With regard to addition, when adding numbers they must always have the same units. For example:

(a) 5 cm + 6 m = ? This is a "no-no"; the units are mixed.

(b) 5 cm + 600 cm = 605 cm. This is okay—we are adding the same units.

(c) 8 mm + 50 cm = ? We should convert the cm to mm and get:

> 8 mm + 500 mm = 508 mm.

Thus, if we ask a student to measure the length of his arm by separately measuring his hand (say in mm), his lower arm (say in cm), his upper arm (say in decimeters), and then adding them, he will first have to convert to a set of consistent units that he or she can handle. If you do not choose to have the students work with fractions, the students can change the units to millimeters as shown above. If you want to give the students a chance to work on decimal fractions, they can change the units to centimeters.

$$.8 + 50 \text{ cm} = 50.8 \text{ cm}$$

This brings us to another point—how to use a ruler. At first it seems quite apparent: just place the end of the ruler at the end of the object and read the length directly (Figure 3). However, a better test of whether students really understand how to use a ruler as well as a test of their ability to subtract is to place the object in the center of the ruler. Clearly, the length of the object should not depend upon its position vis-a-vis the ruler, but we have found that many young people (and even a few at our university) have trouble understanding how to find the length in the latter case.

Figure 3: *How to use a ruler*

Since we do not always have a ruler handy, a few "natural" rulers might be fun to discuss and use. For example, say the length of a person's upper thumb from knuckle to tip is generally about 3 cm while his spread-out fingers span about 20 cm, as shown in Figure 4. Either can now be used to measure the length of an object. Of course, as shown in Figure 3, there is the foot, a convenient measure for stepping off distances. This person's foot, without his shoes, is 23 cm or about 9 inches. Anyway, you should have the children measure a few objects using natural rulers and have them compare their results with that of a meterstick.

Figure 4: *Natural rulers*

The Concept of Area

Defining Area

The area of a shape or object can be defined in everyday words as the "amount of stuff" needed to cover the shape. Common uses of the concept of area are finding the amount of tile needed to cover a floor, the amount of wallpaper needed to cover a wall, and the amount of paint needed to cover a ceiling. You can often directly compare areas of different objects without measurement. For example, if one piece of carpet completely covers another, we know the top piece has more area.

Just as with length, to measure area we need a unit of measure. Many different units have been used throughout history. The acre is still used as a measure of land area, along with square miles. The square inch, square foot, and square yard are area units in the English system. For example, square yards is the unit of area measure for carpeting in the United States. Most of the world and all scientists use the metric system. For the classroom, the most frequent metric unit of area is the square centimeter. It is defined as the amount of flat surface within a square that is 1 cm on a side. This is illustrated in Figure 1.

Figure 1: *Units of length and area*

A note on terminology: Scientists often use the term "centimeters squared" in place of "square centimeters." This may be due to the fact that one way of writing the symbol for square centimeters is cm^2. We prefer to use sq cm for square centimeters. On occasion, the use of cm^2 can confuse students. Since 7 squared is 49, they may reason that 7 centimeters squared is 49 square centimeters. Unfortunately, the symbols 7 cm^2 and $(7 \text{ cm})^2$ sound the same when spoken, if you say cm^2 as "centimeters squared." For that reason, we stick to "square centimeters" and sq cm.

Measuring Area by Counting Square Centimeters–Part I

One way to find an area is to count the number of sq cm needed to cover a surface. To count the number of sq cm, you can construct unit squares within the desired area. For example, the rectangle in Figure 2 is 3 cm wide and 4 cm high. You can find its area by completing the following steps.

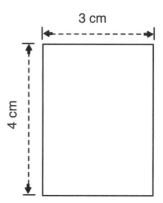

Figure 2: *A rectangle*

1. Draw a grid of lines so that each square in the grid is 1 cm on a side. (Figure 3.)

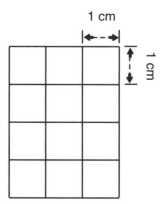

Figure 3: *A rectangle tiled with centimeter squares*

2. Count the number of sq cm enclosed in the rectangle. (Figure 4.)

1	2	3
4	5	6
7	8	9
10	11	12

Figure 4: *Counting square centimeters*

There are 12 sq cm in a rectangle that is 3 cm wide and 4 cm high. So the area of the rectangle is 12 sq cm.

Why Not Use Length × Width?

You may be wondering why we did not use the formula *length × width* to find the area of the rectangle. After all, $4 \times 3 = 12$. The formula works. Indeed, the reason the formula works is precisely because the rectangle can be represented by an ordered array of squares, 3 squares in each row and 4 rows of 3 squares each.

In any ordered array, you can count the total number of elements by multiplying the number of rows by the number of columns. Figure 5 shows 24 apples arrayed in 6 rows. Instead of counting each apple, we take advantage of the array and multiply 4×6 to obtain 24 apples. Using the length times width formula does give the area of a rectangle, but we delay teaching the formula for two reasons. First, we want students to build a mental image of the concept of area. Premature use of the formula for area of rectangles leads to rote use of the formula without understanding. In particular, many students are led to believe that the definition of area is length times width and that this formula works for any shape. While there are formulas for the areas of rectangles, circles, and other geometric shapes, there is no formula for the area of a leaf!

Figure 5: *An array of apples*

Premature use of the formula for area of rectangles leads to rote use of the formula without understanding. In particular, many students are led to believe that the definition of area is length times width and that this formula works for any shape.

Furthermore, using the formula can be harder than counting square centimeters when the sides of the rectangle are not whole numbers.

For example, what is the area of the rectangle, $3\frac{1}{2}$ cm wide and $2\frac{1}{2}$ cm high, shown in Figure 6? We asked a group of sixth-graders to find the area of this rectangle. Even though the students knew the length × width formula, 80 percent could not find the area. They were not able to multiply fractions. It is likely that these students would have been able to find the area by counting sq cm, as we shall see in the next section.

Figure 6: *Another rectangle*

Counting Square Centimeters–Part II

In Figure 7, we set up the square cm grid. To keep track of the sq cm, we first number the whole square centimeters. There are six whole sq cm in the rectangle. Next, we turn to the fractions of sq cm. Students can manipulate sq cm pieces of paper to complete the task. The two half sq cm on the right make up the seventh sq cm and so both are numbered 7. The two half sq cm along the bottom make up the eighth sq cm and are numbered 8. One half sq cm and one fourth square cm make up the remaining areas. The area is $8\frac{3}{4}$ sq cm.

Figure 7: *Whole and part centimeter squares*

Most students can count squares to find area—no multiplication is necessary. But what if there is no "order" to the figure? The shape in Figure 8 has no unique length or width; the formula *length* × *width* does not apply. The only way to find the area is to count the number of sq cm contained within the boundary of the figure.

Figure 8: *A blob*

First, construct a sq cm grid to fit over the shape of Figure 8. It's often easier if the horizontal and vertical boundary of the grid each touch the figure at one point. The grid should extend beyond the figure. The completed grid would look similar to the grid in Figure 9.

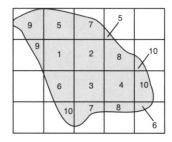

Figure 9: *Finding area by counting centimeter squares*

Next, count and number the whole sq cm. There are four. Now estimate which fractions of grid squares add together to form one square centimeter. For example, square centimeter number 5 is a big piece upper left and a little piece farther to the right. Number 6 is two pieces, a big piece on the left and a smaller piece in the lower right corner. Square centimeter number 7 is two pieces, each around a half square cm. Square centimeter 8 is made up of a $\frac{3}{4}$ and $\frac{1}{4}$ square cm piece. So is square centimeter 9. Three pieces make up square centimeter 10, two half square cm pieces and a smaller piece to the right.

Now all the shape is covered and counted in square centimeters. The shape has an area of about 10 square cm. While the method does not give an exact area, the result is usually close. And the primary benefit of this method is that students will have the opportunity to "see" area, aiding their understanding of this important mathematical concept.

Surface Area

Often, students who understand area quite well seem to have difficulty with the notion of surface area. One problem may be that they were led to believe that area and surface area are two different things. This is not surprising, since we use two different words. However, area and surface area are identical; a measure of the number of sq cm (or square units) needed to cover an object. Customarily, the term "surface area" is usually used for three-dimensional shapes and "area" for two-dimensional shapes.

To measure the surface area of a three-dimensional object, we count the number of square centimeters needed to cover it, just as with flat shapes. In some cases, this is easy as in the case of a rectangular box (since it is made up of flat pieces). Another easy example can be made by taking a sheet of flat paper and rolling it to make a cylinder (Figure 10). As long as the edges do not overlap, the surface area of the outside of the cylinder will be the same as the flat piece of paper. Another way to find the area of a cylinder is to cover it with one square centimeter "stamps." As with flat shapes, you may need some fractional pieces. With more complex shapes, like a sphere, it is hard to get an exact measurement of the surface area, but we can approximate the surface area by covering the object with square centimeters or smaller squares.

Figure 10: *Paper flat and rolled*

The Concept of Volume

Defining Volume

Figure 1: *Two meanings of volume*

Figure 1 shows a container and a rock. The space that the container surrounds (and is occupied by air) and the space that the rock takes up (and is occupied by elements such as oxygen, silicon, and aluminum) are both called **volume.**[1] The concept of volume is tricky. Two objects (like our container and rock) might occupy the same volume but contain totally different amounts of matter. Children often confuse the amount of matter, which we call mass, with the space occupied, which we now know is volume. Thus children tell us that a "heavy" object has more volume than a "light" object even though the latter may actually occupy more space. Indeed, volume is so oversimplified in the elementary schools that many eighth-graders we asked thought of volume as length × width × height, no matter what the shape of the object. Others told us that volume was length squared. Misconceptions such as these are a result of a curriculum that emphasizes memorization of formulas without attention to the conceptual foundations of volume.

Figure 2: *Units of length, area, and volume*

---

[1] Sometimes, the space inside a container is called the capacity of the container. For simplicity, we prefer to use one term, volume, to denote both "space inside" and "space occupied."

Units

As with length and area, if we wish to measure volume, we need to decide on a unit of measure. In the metric system, the metric unit of length is the centimeter (Figure 2a), and the unit of area is the square centimeter (the extent of the plane surface that is bounded by a square 1 cm on a side) (Figure 2b), so it is not unreasonable that we take as our unit of volume the space occupied within a cube that is 1 cm on a side (Figure 2c). The volume occupied by such a cube is defined as 1 cubic centimeter whether that volume is occupied by a solid object (Figure 3a) or by empty space (Figure 3b).

(a)   (b)

Figure 3: *Full and empty cubic centimeter*

Unlike area, it is very hard to divide an object up and count cubic cm. We can't trace the volume the way we trace areas on square cm paper. In theory we could slice it up into 1 cubic cm pieces, but this process will destroy the object. Therefore, learning to understand and measure volume can be more difficult than understanding and measuring area.

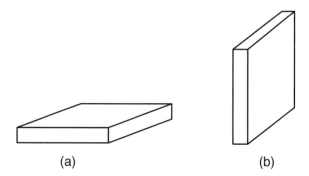

(a)   (b)

Figure 4: *Flat vs. tall shapes*

In everyday life, we are accustomed to a variety of other units of volume measure. Gallons, quarts, pints, and fluid ounces are one set of units, usually used to measure the capacity of a container. Cubic feet and cubic inches are also frequently used. For example, in the United States, air conditioners are often rated on the volume of space they can cool, measured in cubic feet. The remainder of this tutor uses metric units of measure, but many of the same underlying ideas apply to any system of measure.

Problem of Dimensionality

Another great difficulty in understanding volume is that the concept deals with three dimensions. As Piaget pointed out, it is much easier, and therefore usual, for a child to focus on one dimension. They will decide that a tall object has lots of volume because they only focus on the height and fail to take into account the other two dimensions to make a proper estimate. In Figure 4, the two objects have the same volume, but because (a) is flat and (b) is upright, young children will tell you that (b) has the greater volume.

Volume is an extremely important scientific variable. The way it is related to area and to mass and the manner in which it may change with time are all intrinsic to every area of scientific investigation. It is well worth our time to do a good job on volume.

Measuring Volume–Early Activities

Kindergarten students explore volume by filling containers with rice, water, pasta, sand, or beans. Another way to deal with volume in the primary grades is to have the children make figures out of a set of cubes. In first and second grade, we usually use connecting cubes that are about $\frac{3}{4}$-inch on a side. At the end of second grade, we start using standard centimeter linking cubes. For example, you can give each child 10 cubes and ask him or her to make a figure whose volume is 10 cubic units. You will get a variety of shapes, all of which have the same volume. This will begin to impress upon the children the idea that many different shapes can have the same volume.

Another centimeter cube activity to build the children's understanding at this level involves building shapes with different volumes. Give each child a few (3–10) centimeter cubes. Have each child make a shape with his or her centimeter cubes. Then have the children sort themselves into groups according to the volume of their shapes.

You can bring in some simple solid shapes, like a piece of chalk, a match box, a pile of washers, etc., and have the children make figures out of cubic units that approximate the volume (size and shape) of these objects. In this way, they can estimate the volume of the original object by keeping track of the number of cubic cm they used. An example is given in Figure 5 of a marking pen and cubic cms linked together to make a shape of approximately the same volume.

Figure 5: *A marker and a cm cube model*

Another great difficulty in understanding volume is that the concept deals with three dimensions. As Piaget pointed out, it is much easier, and therefore usual, for a child to focus on one dimension. They will decide that a tall object has lots of volume because they only focus on the height and fail to take into account the other two dimensions to make a proper estimate.

The next step would be for you to make several cube models and have children count the number of unit cubes in each. Pictures of three typical models, each a bit more complex than the previous, are given in Figures 6a, b, and c. There are two potential problems here. The children may confuse surface area and volume and count the faces of the cubes calling each face a cubic cm. A subtle problem, exemplified by Figure 6c, is when there are one or more "hidden" cubic centimeters buried inside the figure.

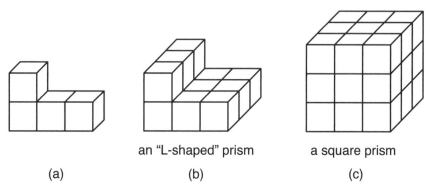

an "L-shaped" prism   a square prism

(a)   (b)   (c)

Figure 6: *Shapes made from centimeter cubes*

We want the children to learn to be systematic, look for patterns, and use simple addition and multiplication to count the cubic cm.

A very basic problem is learning to count the cubic centimeters properly. It is relatively easy to pick up 12 cubic centimeters, make a figure, and say the volume is 12 cc. It is quite another to hold a centimeter cube figure like that in Figure 6b, turn it over, and keep track of all the centimeters. We want the children to learn to be systematic, look for patterns, and use simple addition and multiplication to count the cubes. For example, Figure 6a is easy since it is only 4 cc. Figure 6b is made up of three layers, each of which is exactly like Figure 6a. Your students can then use addition to see that the volume is 4 cc + 4 cc + 4 cc, or use multiplication, 3 × 4 cc. Likewise in Figure 6c, it would be difficult to find and keep track of each cubic cm. A systematic approach allows the children to solve the problem easily. There are 9 cc in the top layer, and there are three layers; therefore the volume is

$$9 \text{ cc} + 9 \text{ cc} + 9 \text{ cc} = 27 \text{ cc.}$$

Note that Figures 6b and 6c are labeled as prisms. This means they are made of a number of identical layers. Figure 6b has three "L-shaped" layers and 6c has three "square-shaped" layers. It is important to know that these are prisms. Otherwise, there might be some hidden cubes behind the object that we cannot see, or there might be missing cubes "inside" the object.

A more difficult skill is finding the volume of an object directly from a perspective drawing, without actually building the object. You can develop this kind of spatial visualization skill by first having students build cube models from pictures. Students as early as first grade can build simple models from pictures. As the models get more complex, this task can become quite difficult. One important subtlety is that pictures such as 6b and 6c do not give enough information to reconstruct the model. For example, there might be some unexpected cubes hidden behind the model in Figure 6c (see Figure 7).

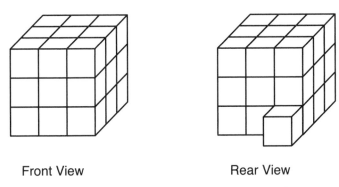

Front View   Rear View

Figure 7: *Front and rear views of Figure 6c*

For example, in Figure 7 we see what appears to be a 3 × 3 × 3 cm cube from the front, but when we view the model from the rear, we see there is an "extra" cube stuck on.

Finally, and hardest of all, you can ask the children to try to draw a figure with a given number of cubic centimeters. It is very hard for anyone to draw a cube, and a figure with several cubic centimeters is harder still. Nevertheless, it is worth a try since doing so will help them improve their spatial perception and will force them to think in three dimensions.

Let's review the four steps we just described:

1. Make figures out of a given number of centimeter cubes.
2. Count cubic centimeters in a cube model.
3. Count cubic centimeters in the drawing of a cube model—usually prisms.
4. Draw a figure with a given number of cubic centimeters.

This discussion covers volumes of objects made from cubes. The most important tool, however, for determining volume will be the graduated cylinder which we will discuss in the section after next. But first we want to talk about how to calculate the volume of prisms.

Calculating Volume—An Upper Grade Exercise

The volume of a rectangular prism made of cubic centimeters can be found using multiplication. The number of cubic centimeters in the top layer is just the product of 3 × 6 since there are 3 rows of 6 cubic cm (see Figure 8). Thus, in each layer there are 18 cc. Because there are 5 layers, the total number of cubic centimeters is 5 × 18 cc = 90 cc. As often written in math books, this type of counting is expressed as

$$V = l \times w \times h.$$

You should interpret this as the number of cubic cm in the top layer (given by the value of $l \times w$) times the number of layers (given by the value of h).

Figure 8: *A rectangular prism*

If the top layer is not rectangular but the figure is a right solid (sides perpendicular to top and bottom), then we can still find the volume by the above technique. The formula *length* $\times$ *width* $\times$ *height* will no longer work since the layers are not rectangular. However, since each horizontal slice has the same shape (see Figure 9), all we have to do is find the number of cubic cm in the top layer and multiply this by the number of layers. To find the number of cubic centimeters in the top layer, we have to find the number of square centimeters in the top surface, since each square centimeter of the surface is attached to a cubic centimeter in the top layer. Thus, if in Figure 9 by counting square cm we find that there are 22 sq cm on the top surface, then there must be 22 cubic cm in the top layer and in each subsequent layer. The total volume, then, is:

$$\frac{22 \text{ cubic cm}}{1 \text{ layer}} \times 5 \text{ layers} = 110 \text{ cubic cm}$$

for the object shown in Figure 9. As a general formula we have:

$$V = A \times h,$$

where the area A of the top tells us the number of cc in the top layer, and the value of h tells us the number of layers. Children should not just memorize each formula; they should understand what is behind the formulas.

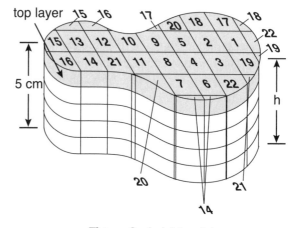

Figure 9: *A right solid*

When using a formula like $l \times w \times h$, the old bugaboo of units reappears. Since l, w, and h are all measured in centimeters, it is tempting to say that the units of volume are centimeters cubed written as $(cm)^3$. And indeed this is what is often done in scientific texts. Yes, it's technically correct to write $(cm)^3$ or cm^3, but again it can be misleading for children just as "centimeter squared" can be misleading for area. If we say a volume is 7 centimeters cubed, is that $(7 \text{ cm})^3 = 343$ cc? We can avoid this confusion by writing what we mean; that the volume is 7 cubic centimeters or 7 cc.

Figure 10: *Graduated cylinders*

Clearly, the ability to calculate volume is rather limited to certain special shapes. An irregularly shaped container or object will require a different approach.

A Volume Measurer: The Graduated Cylinder

We have seen that a ruler which is calibrated in cm can be used to measure length. There is no comparably simple device for measuring area, but there is one for measuring volume. It is the graduated cylinder calibrated in cubic centimeters. Two graduated cylinders are shown in Figure 10. They can be made of glass or Pyrex, both of which are breakable, or plastic, which is not. The cylinder most suitable for classroom use would be calibrated in 1 cc, 5 cc, or 10 cc divisions and have a capacity of 100 to 150 cc. When filled with a liquid (usually water) or a fluid substance like sand or salt, one can read the volume of the material off the side of the graduated cylinder. One cannot use this device to directly measure the volume of a number of marbles since the marbles piled in the cylinder will leave an unknown volume of air spaces between them. This is illustrated in Figure 11b. As we shall see in the next section, we can find the volume of solid objects like marbles by the method of displacement. The rest of this section will discuss using the graduated cylinder for finding the volume of liquid, particularly water.

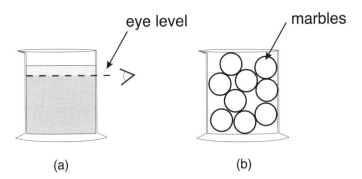

Figure 11: *Liquid and marbles in graduated cylinder*

To read the volume of water in a graduated cylinder, your eyes must be level with the liquid, as shown in Figure 11a. Since water is pulled up at the sides of the cylinder into a curved surface called a meniscus, one must measure the water level at the center of the cylinder. This is done by using the lower of the two lines that one sees (Figure 12) when looking at the water from the side. The top line is due to the pulled up water and should be ignored. (This phenomenon tends to be more pronounced when using glass rather than plastic graduated cylinders.)

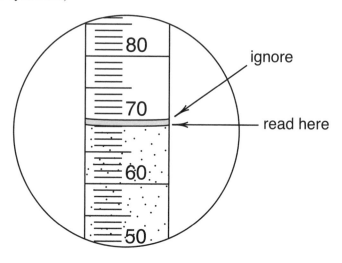

Figure 12: *The meniscus*

One must be careful about what one puts into a graduated cylinder. A tall, narrow one will generally have 1 cc divisions and thus can be used for accurate measurements. The trouble is, that because it is narrow, you can use only small objects. Many a time a student has misjudged the size of an object and found it stuck in the narrow cylinder never to come out again.

Chalk off one cylinder. A good general size that we like is one about 4 cm in diameter with a 150 cc capacity and made of plastic. The divisions are usually 5 or 10 cc. We shall discuss in the next section how to use a "big" graduated cylinder to measure the volume of small objects.

Many graduated cylinders that you purchase will have several different scales along the sides. This is due to the diversity of units for liquid measurements. Many cylinders will have a scale for fluid ounces and another for milliliters. The metric unit of volume is the milliliter, which is defined to be 1 cubic cm:

$$1 \text{ ml} = 1 \text{ cc.}$$

The liter is often encountered in daily life (for example, soda bottles are often 1 or 2 liters). It is exactly 1000 ml.

One of the first exercises the children can do with a graduated cylinder is simply to fill the cylinder to a specified level—10 cc, for example. An eyedropper is handy for getting the volume exactly right, since by pouring one usually overshoots or undershoots the mark. Whatever the divisions of the cylinder are, choose some volumes that fall right on a major division and some that fall between divisions, where the children will have to interpolate. An example is shown in Figure 13 for a cylinder with 10 cc divisions.

fill with

30 cc
46 cc
75 cc
101 cc

Figure 13: *A graduated cylinder exercise*

Once the second- or third-graders are good at reading the scale, they can use the graduated cylinder to find the capacity or volume of a set of three jars (Figure 14). You should build up a collection of jars of all shapes and volumes, from small baby food jars, through peanut butter containers, to large coffee jars. Exotic shapes are nice. To find the volume of a jar, one can either fill the jar to the brim and then keep pouring the water into the graduated cylinder, or one can keep filling the graduated cylinder and pour the water into the jar until it is filled. Either way, the children have to keep track of the number of times the graduated cylinder is filled and the total volume of water accumulated this way. This activity appears as a lesson called *Fill 'er Up* in third grade.

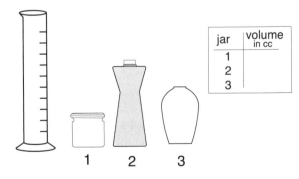

jar	volume in cc
1	
2	
3	

Figure 14: *A capacity exercise*

Volume Measurement by Displacement

How would you measure the volume of a small rock? This problem is dealt with in lessons on volume beginning in Grade 2. The technique is illustrated in Figure 15. First, you fill the graduated cylinder with a convenient amount of water, for example, 40 cc rather than 43 cc. Then you place the rock in the graduated cylinder without losing any water (there must be enough water in the cylinder initially to cover the object). You then read the new volume V. Since the volume of water V_{water} stays constant, the volume V is due to the water plus the rock. The rock displaces, or pushes aside, its volume in water and the water level rises. Thus, we have:

$$V_{rock} = V - V_{water}.$$

For example, in Figure 15 the volume of the rock is 22 cc. Note that subtraction is easier if you start with a multiple of ten for the volume of water. The technique works for any solid object no matter what its shape. To start with, then, ask children to find the volume of a wide variety of objects, some spheres, cubes, rocks, coins, washers, etc.

$$V_w \qquad\qquad V = V_{rock} + V_{water}$$

Figure 15: *Volume by displacement*

But what if the object is too big to fit into the graduated cylinder? If a bigger graduated cylinder isn't handy, then use your graduated cylinder to calibrate a large jar, and then away you go. One word of warning: When you place a large object in a graduated cylinder or jar, a considerable amount of water may splash out, even though you are very careful. You can get around this by placing the object in the graduated cylinder first and then pouring in a known amount of water V_w, and then read $V = V_{rock} + V_{water}$ off the scale. An alternative method is to find a large container and fill it with water to the brim. When the object is carefully placed in the container, it overflows, and the volume of the overflow liquid is equal to the volume of the object. If you catch all the overflow liquid in a second container, you can then use a graduated cylinder to find the volume of that liquid.

Finding the volume of small objects is also a problem, since the object may be so small you can't see the water level rise. Of course, you can always use a smaller graduated cylinder, one with 1 cc divisions instead of 5 or 10 cc divisions. The trouble is that sometimes even 1 cc per division is too large. The only way out is to measure the volume of several of the small objects at once (Figure 16b). (The volume of the several objects are identical.) For example, suppose you have 10 identical objects. To find the volume of one object, subtract the volume of the water and divide by 10. In this fashion, children can find the volume of small washers, paper clips, pins, and so on. Using 10 objects is a good idea since it is easy to divide by 10.

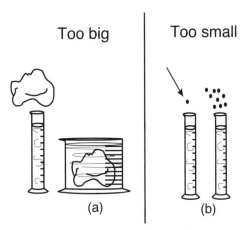

Too big | Too small

(a) (b)

Figure 16: *Finding volumes of large or small objects*

Obtaining Accurate Results

A few words about accuracy are appropriate here. Most of the time you have to interpolate between divisions in order to read the volume. This usually leads to a reading error of about 20% of the value between the scale marks. Thus, if your graduated cylinder has 10 cc divisions, you might expect an error (i.e., children will get readings that differ) by up to 2 cc. This is illustrated in Figure 17a. If the object has raised the water level several divisions, then this 20% per division uncertainty is not a serious problem. For example, our rock changed the water level from 40 cc to 62 cc. If a reading error is up to 2 cc, then three children who read the same graduated cylinder might read 62 cc, but possibly 61 cc or 63 cc (if they are careful; maybe even more if they are not). But the volume of the rock is 62 cc − 40 cc = 22 cc for one child, but 23 cc for another, and 21 cc for the third. Thus we have a spread in reading of about 2 parts in 22 or 10%. A bigger rock, with a volume of, say, 46 cc would still have the same reading error of 2 cc, but its volume error would only be 2 parts in 46 or about 5%.

$V = 62 - 40$ cc $= 22$ cc
or
$V = 63 - 40$ cc $= 23$ cc
or
$V = 61 - 40$ cc $= 21$ cc

$V = 105$ cc or 106 cc or 107 cc

$$V = \frac{105 - 40 \text{ cc}}{3} = \frac{65}{3} = 21.67 \text{ cc}$$

$$V = \frac{106 - 40 \text{ cc}}{3} = \frac{66}{3} = 22.0 \text{ cc}$$

$$V = \frac{107 - 40 \text{ cc}}{3} = \frac{67}{3} = 22.33 \text{ cc}$$

(a) (b)

Figure 17: *Measurement error*

A good rule of thumb is that your reading will not be accurate unless the object raises the water level by more than one division. There are two ways to achieve this. One, use a narrow graduated cylinder, or two, use several identical objects if they are available. In the case of the latter, you find the volume of one object by dividing by the number of identical objects, as we did above for very small objects. For example, three objects would still produce a reading error of 2 cc but a volume error of only 2 cc/3 = 0.67 cc. This is illustrated in Figure 17b where three marbles give a volume spread of only 0.67 cc in 22 cc or 3%, compared to 10% for one marble. Of course, this would not work for finding the volume of a rock, since it would be difficult to find three identical rocks.

If the object floats, you have to push it under in order to measure its volume. In this situation, what is important is how you push it under. If you use your finger, then what you measure is the volume of the object plus the volume of your submerged finger. Since the volume of your finger may be comparable to the volume of the object, this is clearly not a good idea. What you need is a pusher whose volume is much less than the volume of the object. A straightened paper clip or a pin will do (Figure 18).

Figure 18: *Finding the volume of something that floats*

Two Misconceptions

Early on, the children should come to grips with two important ideas concerning volume:

1. The volume of an object is independent of the material it is made of.
2. The volume of an object does not change when its shape changes.[2]

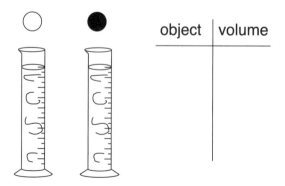

Figure 19: *Volume vs. material*

---

[2]Usually. See later discussion.

As to the first point, you can study spheres of the same volume but made of a wide variety of materials (steel, lucite, glass, even wood). The children should discover that their volumes are the same. As illustrated in Figure 19, students can fill two identical cylinders to the same level with water, carefully place both objects in, and see that the volume displaced is the same. Initially, many children will say that the heavier object has more volume and that the water will go up higher in its graduated cylinder. They are confusing mass and volume. If you take a clay cube and mash it into a thin disk, many children will say that the disk has less volume than the cube. Here they confuse one dimension, thinness, with volume: they mistakenly assume all thin objects have a small volume. Again, using the graduated cylinder the child can see that the volumes are the same. Figure 20. They can make all kinds of shapes out of a single piece of clay and determine that they all have the same volume. Indeed, the only way they can change its volume is to tear off a piece.

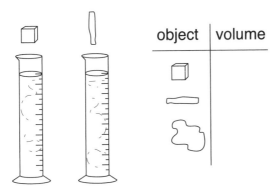

Figure 20: *Volume vs. shape*

The Concept of Mass

Defining Mass

Mass is one of the most difficult variables to understand. It is also one of the most important. Length, area, and volume have straightforward definitions. The volume of an object, for example, is defined as a measure of the space it occupies. Does mass have a similar straightforward definition? In a sense it does and in a sense it does not. Basically, **mass** is a measure of the quantity of matter in an object. That is its simple definition. Unfortunately, that begs the question. One can ask, what is matter, and we are back to where we started. So we have to look more closely at mass. And that is where things get difficult. Mass is defined through what it *does,* and this sets it apart from length, area, and volume. Moreover, mass does two things which means, in a sense, it has two definitions.

> Basically, **mass** is a measure of the quantity of matter in an object.

One of the things that mass does is absolutely crucial for the existence of our universe. Mass is the cause of the force of gravity. Without mass, there would be no gravity, and without gravity, matter would not have clumped into galaxies and stars and us. Since mass causes gravity, we can define mass through the pull of gravity—the greater the pull, the greater the mass an object has.

The other thing that mass does has to do with the motion of an object. All other variables being equal, the mass of an object determines how much the velocity of an object will *change* when subject to a given force. In layman's terms, the larger the mass of an object, the harder you have to push to change its speed. Since we are not ready to study motion, we will not discuss the details of this aspect of mass. Nevertheless, we might note that it was Einstein's contemplation of both properties of mass (gravity and motion) that led him to his general theory of relativity.

One way, then, to determine which of two objects has more mass is to determine which one is pulled on more strongly by the Earth's gravitational force. One possible way to do this is to drop two objects, as shown in Figure 1, and see which reaches the ground first. You might suppose, since the more mass an object has, the bigger the force of gravity, that the more massive object would fall faster and reach the ground first. If you do this exercise, however (as Galileo did), you will find that

Figure 1: *Dropping two objects*

both objects reach the ground at the same time! What went wrong? Well, we are breaking one of our cardinal rules, which is keeping variables fixed. When the objects fall, we not only have gravity pulling on them, but their velocity is changing as well. Therefore, both definitions of mass are involved and the overall effect is no longer obvious. It appears that in some way the effects cancel!

So we need a way of measuring the pull of gravity (i.e., using definition 1) without having the object move (i.e., eliminating definition 2). As we shall see in the next section, we can do this with a two-pan balance.

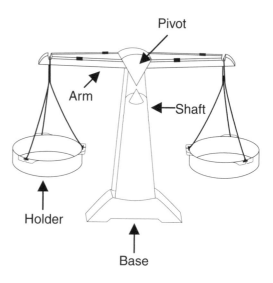

Figure 2: *A balance*

Equal Arm Balance

The equal arm, or two-pan, balance is the key to our operational definition of mass for children. If two objects balance, they have the same mass. If the arm tilts to one side, the object in the lower of the two pans has more mass than the object in the other pan.

Basically, the balance is a stick that is pivoted at its center and has two holders that are mounted on at points which are equidistant from the pivot (hence the name equal arm balance). Figure 2 pictures a balance that we often use in *Math Trailblazers*. It is quite sturdy and accurate enough for use in the elementary classroom. The tall shaft and long arms of the balance make it very useful in a variety of balancing experiments. If you would like to make your own, you can use a block of wood (Figure 3a) or a book to hold the pivot rod (Figure 3b). A ruler can act as the arm and the bottom of paper cups as pans. These latter pieces can be attached to the arm with string and paper clips.

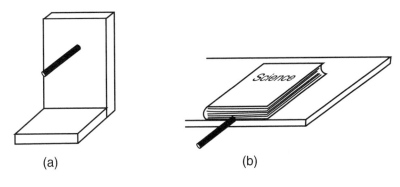

(a)   (b)

Figure 3: *Making a balance*

Once you have put your two-pan balance together, it must be zeroed. That is, the arm must be level before any masses are added. We suggest that you zero each balance and then have the children check to see that it is level before and during each experiment.

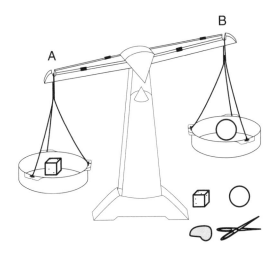

Figure 4: *Comparing masses*

A	B	More Mass
Cube	Ball	Cube
Scissors	Ball	Scissors

We are now ready to find out which of two objects, A or B, has greater mass. One is placed in each pan. Since the object with more mass will experience the bigger gravitational pull, the balance will tilt either one way or the other. If A has more mass it will tilt to the left, as shown in Figure 4, while if B has more mass it will tilt to the right. If the masses in the pans are equal, the pull of gravity on both is the same and the balance will remain level. One word of caution, though: If the masses are the same and the arm is tilted when the masses are placed on the balance, then the ruler will often remain tilted. Thus, to be sure, bring the arm back to level and see if it remains there.

One of the first exercises you can do with children in kindergarten through second grade is to have them compare, two at a time, the masses of a wide variety of objects. Then they should order the objects from the most massive to the least massive (see *Putting Masses in Order* in Grade 2 Unit 10). You can use a washer, connecting cube, small scissors, steel ball, and so on. Notice that the two-pan balance does away with the motion definition of mass since the balance is at rest when the measurement is made. Thus, the balance allows us to relate the object's mass directly to the pull of gravity.

Measuring Mass: The Mass Standard

The above is fine for comparing masses, but how do we measure *the* mass of an object? In other words, how do we assign a number to the mass of our object? Just as when we measure length, area, and volume, we need to decide on a unit. Say that we take as our standard masses a set of identical washers (paper clips would do as well). Let's call the mass of each washer 1 *ugh*. Then, if our object is balanced by 4 washers, its mass is 4 ughs, as shown in Figure 5. If the mass of the object is between 4 and 5 ughs, then the balance will not level out but tilt one way for 4 washers and the other way for 5. In this way, the child can assign unique masses to a wide range of objects. Clearly, the smaller the washer, the more accurately one can determine the mass of an object.

But washers are not a very satisfactory standard. The washers in your class may not have the same mass as those used in another school in your district, much less in another city or another country. What we need is a universal standard that is accepted by the entire scientific community. This problem was recognized by scientists a long time ago and was resolved when the Paris Academy of Sciences submitted a report to the French National Assembly in which 1 cc of

Object	Number of Washers	Mass in ughs
Ball	4	4
Cube	2	2

Figure 5: *Measuring masses*

water was defined to have a mass of 1 gm, the **gram** being the name chosen for the unit of mass. Then, using this definition, a platinum cylinder was made and declared to be the standard for 1000 grams. In 1875, an international treaty was signed by most "civilized" nations which established an International Bureau of Weights and Measures in Sevres, France, near Paris. The international prototype kilogram, made of platinum iridium alloy, is kept there. If you want your own kilogram, you have to go to Paris with an equal arm balance and some material and hack away at the material until it balances the platinum iridium standard. The National Bureau of Standards in Washington, DC, has an accurately constructed copy as do other governments throughout the world.

For small measurements, one needs a mass that is smaller than a kilogram, just as one needs a length that is smaller than a meter. The gram, like the centimeter, is perfect for this. Most objects you will deal with in the elementary school science program will have masses between 1 and 100 grams. Masses are commercially available, usually in 1-, 5-, 10-, 20-, 50-, 100-, 200-, 500-, and 1000-gram pieces. It might be a good idea to have one good set of very accurate standard masses for your school (locked in a closet marked "Paris," of course), but they are expensive. For general classroom use, there are less expensive sets of plastic masses available. However, since the plastic masses may not be as accurate, you may wish to compare them to a good set of standard masses or find their mass using a triple beam balance or other accurate scales.

The cheapest standard mass is a nickel. It has a mass very close to 5 grams! But alas, a dime does not have a mass of 10 grams. There are two ways to get around having to buy sets of expensive standard masses. To determine the mass of a small object, measure the mass of several of the objects and then divide the total mass by the number of objects. For example, if it turns out that 10 small objects balance a 5-gram piece, then each object will have a mass of 0.5 grams. (5 grams ÷ 10 objects = 0.5 grams per object.)

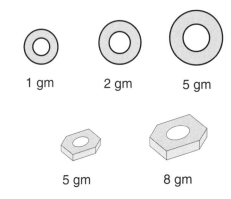

1 gm   2 gm   5 gm

5 gm   8 gm

Figure 6: *Using washers as standard masses*

If you go to a hardware store and make a pest of yourself— bring your two-pan balance—you can usually find washers that have "nice" masses, like 1, 2, 5, 8 grams, etc. Figure 6 shows such a collection that can be used as standard masses. Once you have the washers, give each child several of each and a lot of objects whose mass you want them to determine. A good data table is a big help since you want to keep track of the number of different washers it takes to balance the object.

Then, as shown in Figure 7, a little multiplication and addition is necessary to obtain the final mass in grams. In the example above, the total mass is:

$$m_{total} = 3 \times 1 \text{ gm} + 1 \times 2 \text{ gm} + 2 \times 5 \text{ gm} + 2 \times 8 \text{ gm} = 31 \text{ gm}.$$

Finding masses in grams is a great way to practice multiplication, addition, and mental math.

Object	Number of Standard Masses				Mass in gm
	1 gm	2 gm	5 gm	8 gm	
Plastic Cylinder	3	1	2	2	31

Figure 7: *Finding mass using washers*

A second way to get around using expensive standards is again to use washers but place them in packages of sets of 1, 5, 10, 20 grams, etc. The package can be composed of several washers wrapped in masking tape with enough tape or small washers to make an even 5 gm, 10 gm, and so on. Either way, the cost of a washer is small enough that children can have a set of masses for a few dollars.

Mass vs. Weight

In everyday language, we talk about the weight of an object rather than its mass. Are these two words for the same thing? Technically, weight and mass are distinct concepts. In scientific terms, the **mass** of an object is the amount of matter in the object. Mass is measured in kilograms and grams in the metric system and in pounds and ounces in the English system. The **weight** of an object is the measure of the pull of gravity on that object. Sir Isaac Newton first explained the importance of gravity for the motions of the planets and for the fall of an object more than 300 years ago.

Because of the awareness of space travel, most children know that the pull of gravity is different on different planets and that there is essentially no gravity in outer space. Many museums and planetariums have exhibits that show your weight on the moon and various planets. For example, since the moon's gravity is weaker than the Earth's, the pull on an individual object would be less. Thus, a human being would weigh less on the moon than on Earth.

How is the mass of an object affected by gravity? The mass of an object remains constant regardless of space travel since gravity does not influence mass. Since we use a two-pan balance to measure mass, both sides of the balance are equally affected by gravity. If an 11-gram pencil balances one 1-gram and two 5-gram standard masses on Earth, it will balance those same masses on the moon.

However, since most of us are likely to spend our lives on Earth, the distinction between mass and weight may be lost on many students.

We suggest two pedagogical alternatives with regard to the distinction between mass and weight:

1. Ignore it. This point is fairly subtle and eludes many adults.
2. Provide a simple explanation, but don't worry about it too much.

Building the *Math Trailblazers* Classroom

This section focuses on establishing a flexible and challenging learning environment for all students. Strategies include addressing classroom culture, effectively grouping students, managing manipulatives, and pacing instruction.

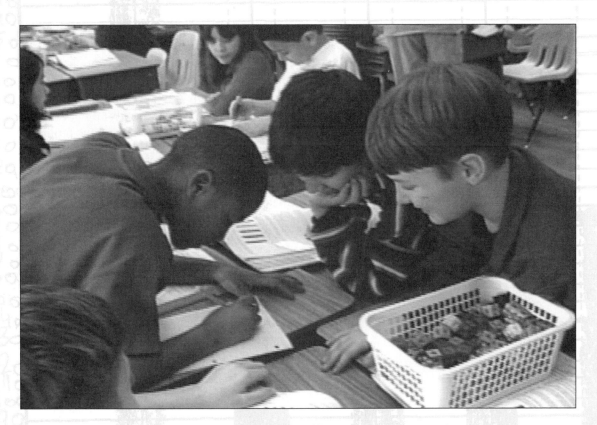

Students work effectively in groups assisted by easy access to math manipulatives.

Building the *Math Trailblazers* Classroom

Using strategies like those described here enables students to develop confidence and expertise in problem solving.

Two factors essential to student learning are the curriculum and a classroom environment that supports and challenges students (NCTM, 2000; Reys & Bay-Williams, 2003). Data on classroom implementation of the *Math Trailblazers* curriculum came from pilot test results, classroom observations, videos of lessons, and teacher feedback. From these sources, effective classroom management and teaching strategies emerged. These strategies enable students to develop confidence and expertise in problem solving. This section summarizes the following teaching and classroom management strategies: addressing classroom culture, student grouping, organization and management of manipulatives, and curriculum pacing.

Classroom Culture

Creating a classroom culture that promotes thinking and learning requires an explicit focus on high student expectations and cooperation. The following strategies result in high performance among students (Kersaint, 2007) and should become part of *Math Trailblazers* classrooms:

- *Allow time for students to reason mathematically.* While many teachers may think they have high expectations, their well-intentioned actions can lower the difficulty level of students' work (Smith, Stein, Henningson, & Silver, 2000). For example, a teacher may model a detailed solution path for a challenging problem. However, when students mimic the teacher's solution path, they lose the opportunity to think about the problem and attempt their own strategies. This reduces the challenge of the problem. Instead, develop a challenging classroom culture that encourages mathematical reasoning by allowing students to discuss their strategies and ideas with classmates prior to starting the problem.

- *Provide opportunities for students to freely discuss mathematical understandings.* One noticeable characteristic of an effective *Math Trailblazers* classroom is the nature of the discussion that takes place consistently. When discourse is part of the classroom culture of learning, students are confident in sharing their ideas and questioning other students' contributions. Good classroom discourse is vital to the implementation of *Math Trailblazers.* "Academically Productive Talk" (Chapin & O'Connor, 2007) is the vehicle through which students make sense of new concepts. The Language in the *Math Trailblazers* Classroom section explores the connection between classroom discourse and learning.

- *Have students explain how they solve problems.* Teachers can encourage students to persevere in the problem-solving process by having them try different approaches or seek help from their classmates. Support students' thinking and classroom discourse by asking them to reflect on earlier completed tasks. References to previously completed tasks helps students make connections in their learning and in their problem-solving processes. Once students have drawn parallels in their learning, have them communicate their understandings in writing or share their ideas in class discussions.

- *Let students be responsible for their own learning.* One indicator of a classroom culture that supports and challenges students is that students realize they alone are responsible for solving problems. The teacher only provides the tools that assist students in solving problems. Students further understand that the teacher is not the owner of answers. Students should solve problems and offer explanations, not the teacher. The following two anecdotes are examples of students taking responsibility for their learning:

Jeremy, a fifth grader, whispered to a math coach who came regularly to his classroom, "I think you've known the answers all year! But you want us to figure them out!"

Hannah, a second grader, raised her hand to answer a question the teacher had posed. She paused and before responding, asked, "Will I have to explain my answer?" When the teacher assured her she would have to explain, she said, "Then let me think about it a little longer."

Use of the above strategies results in students who value mathematics, increase their persistence in solving a problem, become confident in their ability to do mathematics, become mathematical problem solvers, and believe that mathematics makes sense.

Establishing Classroom Norms

Establishing a classroom culture that promotes high expectations and inquiry means establishing classroom norms for participation. When you enter a classroom that "works" it seems effortless. The students and teacher respect each other's ideas. There is a true sense of collaboration and exploration. To create such an environment requires intentional and ongoing effort on the part of the teacher. The following recommendations represent ideas from numerous effective *Math Trailblazers* teachers.

- *Set clear expectations and remind students of them daily.* Some teachers use a "Rights and Responsibilities" approach to classroom rules. These rights and responsibilities can be framed in a positive way and encourage student ownership. Some examples include:

1. I have the right to be heard when speaking.
2. I will speak clearly.
3. I will not interrupt others.
4. I will listen carefully when others speak.
5. I have the right to learn.
6. I will ask questions when I do not understand.
7. I will not distract others from learning.

> To create an environment of true collaboration and exploration requires intentional and ongoing effort on the part of the teacher.

Chapin and O'Connor (2007) use the concept of "obligations" when considering students' participation in classroom discourse. Regardless of the rules you select, or whether you negotiate those rules with students or set them yourself, it is essential that you teach and model those expectations for students. In the beginning of the year, dedicate time each day to teaching and practicing students' rights and responsibilities. Take easy tasks and use them to teach desired behaviors. Be explicit and let students know which outcomes are being practiced. Some teachers discuss the expectations and post them in the front of the room. The investment in the beginning of the year and daily reminders are powerful in creating a risk-taking learning environment. For video examples of how some teachers prepare for and begin the year with *Math Trailblazers* go to www.Trailblazers.com.

- *Teach children to be mathematicians.* Provide opportunities for students to work in groups, struggle to find a solution path, argue their mathematics solution, and settle differences. These opportunities mirror the work of mathematicians.

- *Create a flexible and dynamic classroom environment.* Allow opportunities for further exploration or extensions of a topic. Often as students explore new problems, they make connections to other mathematical teaching opportunities.

PART III

Grouping Students for Effective Instruction

Working with a partner or in small groups enhances students' opportunities to communicate about mathematics in a nonthreatening environment. Students learn from and help each other. However, selecting and managing effective groups requires important considerations. They include:

- Do I group heterogeneously?
- What size groups should I use?
- Do I just choose names randomly?
- Do I plan groups that mix students by ability, temperament, or both?
- Do I give students in a group "jobs" to ensure that everybody works?
- What individual accountability measures can I use?
- Will each student prepare a product, or will the group produce one shared product?

There are many ways to group students to ensure success. Some important considerations in grouping and facilitating group work follow.

Grouping needs to be flexible. Flexibility in grouping means that the number of people in the group changes based on the task. Also, sometimes pairing students with like abilities makes more sense then pairing a struggling learner with a very strong student. It may be effective to establish cooperative groups of three to four students that remain constant for a period of time, such as one month or one unit. Some days students may work in their cooperative group and other days they may be in a new partnership, based on your decision of what size group will best support student thinking and engagement.

The following are appropriate ways to group students for instruction:

- Small groups of two, three, or four students seem to be the most successful. In primary classrooms, pairs are the most effective groupings with the occasional exception of bringing two strong pairs together to form a group of four. Sometimes groups of three work best depending on the task. For example, in third grade, the *The Better Picker Upper* lab compares the absorbency of three types of paper towels. In this case it is best to assign each member of the group the responsibility of examining one type of paper towel. When it comes to grouping in your classroom, the important idea is to keep groupings flexible and to stress the importance of cooperation and respect no matter the group size.

Flexibility in grouping means that the number of people in the group changes based on the task.

- Teach pair-sharing where students turn quickly to a partner and discuss new concepts, strategies, or new vocabulary with a classmate. This breaks up teacher talk time and allows students to scaffold ideas for one another.
- Pick names randomly from a hat or jar when you want to increase the flexibility of students' working relationships.
- Have children choose partners.
- Place children in groups that match how they best work—the quiet ones all in one group and the boisterous all together.
- Assign groups by ability, heterogeneous or homogeneous when targeting specific skills with specific students.
- Keep the whole class together in one group.

While whole-class instruction and working individually are not often considered grouping strategies, both are appropriate and essential in learning mathematics. Whole-class instruction is especially useful when explaining the day's problem, introducing a new manipulative, correcting a common mistake, or summarizing the lesson. Whole-group instruction is most effective when it is brief, focused, and the information applies to all students. Clarity is enhanced when teachers provide a few minutes for pairs to discuss new ideas.

Working alone is powerful and effective as well. Giving students time to reflect and record their strategies before joining the group increases participation and helps students assess their own needs. When students do begin group time, they are able to focus on the lesson's goals and contribute thoughtfully to the discussion. In concluding the lessons, individual reflection in the form of journal writing can be a powerful assessment tool. Teachers can keep close tabs on student thinking as they develop from each day's lesson and also help catch any misinformation before big gaps in learning take place (DeBellis & Rosenstein, 2007).

Giving students time to reflect and record their strategies before joining the group increases participation and helps students assess their own needs.

Room Arrangement Matters. Seating students at tables or with desks pulled together does not necessarily guarantee that students will work well together, but sitting in rows and columns makes cooperation much more difficult. Have students sit around a group of desks that may be pulled together as a work surface to facilitate discussion and focus.

Build in Individual Accountability. Individual accountability is also important when students work in groups. To balance individual responsibility with cooperation, some teachers adopt a procedure that numbers students in each group 1, 2, 3, 4. The teacher prompts the class by saying, "3s may start the conversation at each table" or "odds talk to each other" or "1s and 3s talk and 2s and 4s listen." The important things to remember are that all students are held accountable and that the questions for groups are rich enough to push understanding.

Group members also need to be accountable to each other. They need to use one another as a resource before consulting the teacher. Be disciplined and not answer questions from group members unless they have carefully consulted each member. It is especially when working together on laboratory investigations that it is the group's responsibility to make sure all members have appropriate and accurate data tables and graphs. Students need to learn to rely on and trust one another for group work to be successful.

Here is a summary of how a *Math Trailblazers* classroom might use different student groupings:

- Students work independently giving each child a chance to think through a question and come up with a way to problem solve.

- Students turn to a partner to rehearse their answers or to make their answers more complete.

- Students work in groups to complete a task. They share ideas, responsibilities, and materials. These tasks would be difficult to complete independently. There are many ways to choose groups so that all students benefit from working with others.

- Students work as a whole class evaluating peer problem-solving strategies or receiving direction from the teacher.

Managing Math Manipulatives

Most *Math Trailblazers* lessons suggest or require the use of manipulatives. Manipulatives facilitate student learning, but effective manipulative use requires attention to their management. The following suggest ways to manage manipulatives within the classroom:

Manipulatives need to be prepared and organized ahead of time.

- When appropriate, the "Preparing for Upcoming Units" section of the Unit Planner identifies a manipulative to be used in the next unit. Gather manipulatives in advance and place them in a center for exploration.

- At the appropriate grade, have laminated copies of full-size or desk-size ten frames, *100 or 200 Charts,* and multiplication tables available for students.

- Store commonly used materials such as laminated flash cards and base-ten boards in accessible locations such as pocket charts. Make copies of these for students and allow them to take home their originals for practice.

- Allow students to explore manipulatives during indoor recess or center time. This casual experience helps them to be more focused when the lesson begins.

- Try all the manipulatives yourself before using them with students. Some grade levels use common planning time to try the lab activities together.

- Prepare and store copies of frequently-used items such as data tables and graphs. These can be copied in bulk before the school year saving both time and money.

Store manipulatives with easy access for students in mind.

- Have the most frequently used manipulatives, such as connecting cubes, links, coins, and base-ten pieces, available all year at student desks, on counters, or stored in nearby tubs for quick availability.

- If sharing a manipulative kit between teachers, develop a system to catalog manipulatives for easier accessibility.

- Store manipulatives in clear plastic bags, boxes, or cartons. Organize them so there are enough pieces in each bag or box for partners or whole tables. Have students who needs practice counting arrange links and connecting cubes in sets of ten by color.

- When working in groups with manipulatives, assign one person in each group the responsibility of collecting and returning items to their original location.

- Create a personal Daily Practice and Problem (DPP) manipulative kit for students to use when solving their DPPs each day. These kits include manipulatives frequently used to solve DPP problems. They may include things like links, coins, and connecting cubes at the primary grades, and base-ten pieces and pattern blocks at the middle grades.

- Label manipulative kits with quantities of materials to help prevent their loss. A label such as "This kit should contain 4 rulers, 4 calculators, and 4 sets of base-ten pieces" will help students (and teachers) track all materials before they are stored.

- Easy accessibility and visibility are key to efficient use of storage devices. Organizers, such as those with clear plastic shoe pockets designed to be hung on a door are a good resource for storing calculators or other manipulatives. By adding students' names to the outside of each pocket, you can tell quickly who has or has not returned their manipulatives.

Use manipulatives in instruction to promote understanding.

- Introduce each manipulative and discuss its use. For example, when students first use graduated cylinders, say, "What do you see when you look at a graduated cylinder?" Or for a balance ask, "What do you notice about this balance?" The conversations that groups have first and then share with the whole class are rich and exciting. Students often see interesting things that teachers may not.

- Include calculators as an option for students. As with most tools, the more they use them, the more commonplace they become. Be open about discussing when calculators are an appropriate choice.

- Post a list of the day's manipulatives to be used for each lesson. Make older students responsible for retrieving and returning their own supplies according to that list.

- Designate a "hands off" area on the desk or table for manipulatives to be kept while listening to a student or teacher.

Above all, remember that the more experience students have with manipulatives, the more equipped they will be for solving problems.

Ideas on the Pacing of *Math Trailblazers* Lessons

Teach math 60 minutes per day, every day. The National Council of Teachers of Mathematics established a standard of 60 minutes per day of mathematics instruction for children beginning in grade 1. *Math Trailblazers* is designed to be used for 60 minutes per day, every day. Sequence activities that follow the day's schedule and the children's ability to focus. For example, you can begin the day with a Daily Practice and Problem item, do a math activity that keeps the children working in groups at tables, and do an activity that has the children walking around to gather data later in the day. Not all 60 minutes of instruction need to be offered continuously.

Use manipulatives in instruction to promote understanding.

The National Council of Teachers of Mathematics established a standard of 60 minutes per day of mathematics instruction for children beginning in Grade 4.

Building the MTB Classroom

The early units in each grade contain many opportunities for teachers to get to know the children and to assess their math abilities from the first day. Encourage your colleagues to join you in reaching the goal of a full hour of math, every day.

Use the Pacing Suggestions in the *Unit Resource Guide*. Suggestions for pacing are given within each *Unit Resource Guide* at the beginning of the lessons and Unit Outlines. They are also in the Overview section of the *Teacher Implementation Guide*. Often the suggestions will recommend omitting or adding certain lessons if this is your first year with *Math Trailblazers*. For example, pacing suggestions for fifth grade will sometimes direct you to add a lesson from fourth grade or skip sections of the unit if your students are new to *Math Trailblazers*.

Use the multidisciplinary structure of *Math Trailblazers* to your advantage. Teach the lessons involving *Adventure Books* during literature blocks or read aloud times. Pull the science-heavy lessons or units into your science time. The lessons involving "Mr. Origin" can be completed during Social Studies lessons to address map skills. There are many creative ways to incorporate more mathematics into each day.

If this is your first year teaching *Math Trailblazers*, work towards teaching as much of the material as possible. This is especially true for teachers at grades 3–5. Teachers in the primary grades often complete all the lessons as outlined in the *Unit Resource Guide* with little trouble. To do this, teachers must start on the first day of school and dedicate an hour to math instruction each day through the last day of school. Completing all the lessons in the primary grades greatly impacts students at grades 3–5.

Teachers in the upper grades should strive to complete more and more of the curriculum each year. However, there is more content in grades 4–5 than can be taught in one school year. *Math Trailblazers* is aimed at a national audience. Because content expectations vary from state to state, some content included in grade 4 may be taught in grade 5 in your district. Thus, you and your colleagues need to carefully choose what content to teach at what time.

Upper-grade teachers in their first year with *Math Trailblazers* should teach the lessons as described and try not to stay too long on any one concept. Although this may be the first time your students see concepts presented in this way, they will have several opportunities to explore the ideas. Each lesson is not designed to be taught for mastery. The concepts will spiral back throughout the year in the Daily Practice and Problems and later units. Each time a concept is presented, the approach is slightly different. If students struggled the first time, they will have more opportunities as the year progresses to acquire the concept or skill.

Respecting differences in classrooms. Some schools or districts establish a pacing chart for each grade so classrooms stay together and all students will receive the same mathematics instruction. Asking teachers to move through a curriculum at exactly the same rate is very difficult to implement. Sometimes individual teachers find that students need more time with one concept and less time with another. We find that schools and districts with the best implementations recommend the lessons and units that need to be completed within a quarter and allow teachers some flexibility in the weekly pacing of the materials.

Rearranging lesson order. If changes must be made to the order of the lessons, make decisions as a grade level in a school or district. These decisions should be made with the advice of a math specialist or coordinator who understands the development of the mathematics content within and across grades. It is very important to the integrity of the curriculum that individual teachers not make pacing decisions on their own. Sometimes the timing of state tests determines when a particular unit should be covered. In these cases, teachers benefit from cross-grade level discussions.

Whole-group decisions can consider timing of the math facts program and Daily Practice and Problems. Teachers can use the *Facts Resource Guide* at grades 2–5 to keep on track with the math facts while making adjustments to other content. When making decisions as a school, teachers from one grade to the next can adjust for gaps in learning when items are missed or altered. It is very helpful to have at least one person with access to the entire curriculum to help guide these types of discussions for your school or district. If you do not have a qualified person in your district contact Kendall/Hunt for additional resources.

This section is just the beginning of what the *Math Trailblazers* classroom can be. The conversation continues with other sections of the *Teacher Implementation Guide.* Sections on classroom discourse, working with parents, and meeting the needs of individual students add to the information presented here. Also the online communities at Mathtrailblazers.com and the listserv give you direct access to teachers in the field. To join the *Math Trailblazers* Listserv, send a note to TIMS@uic.edu.

References

Chapin, Suzanne H., and Catherine O'Connor. "Academically Productive Talk: Supporting Students' Learning in Mathematics." *The Learning of Mathematics*. Portia C. Elliot, W. Gary Martin, and Marilyn E. Strutchens, eds., pp. 113–128. National Council of Teachers of Mathematics, Reston, VA, 2007.

Curriculum and Evaluation Standards for School Mathematics, National Council of Teachers of Mathematics, Reston, VA, 1989.

DeBellis, Valerie A., and Joseph G. Rosenstein. "Creating an Equitable Learning Environment for Teachers of Grades K–8 Mathematics." *The Learning of Mathematics*. Portia C. Elliot, W. Gary Martin, and Marilyn E. Strutchens, eds., pp. 271–288. National Council of Teachers of Mathematics, Reston, VA, 2007.

Kersaint, Gladis. "The Learning Environment: Its Influence on What is Learned." *The Learning of Mathematics*. Portia C. Elliot, W. Gary Martin, and Marilyn E. Strutchens, eds., pp. 83–96. National Council of Teachers of Mathematics, Reston, VA, 2007.

Principles and Standards for School Mathematics, National Council of Teachers of Mathematics, Reston, VA, 2000.

Reys, B.J., and J.M. Bay-Williams. "The Role of Curriculum Materials In Implementing the Curriculum and Learning Principles." *Mathematics Teaching in the Middle School.* 9(2), pp. 120–124, 2003.

Stein, M.K., M.S. Smith, M.A. Henningson, & E.A. Silver. *Implementing Standards-based Mathematics Instruction: A Casebook for Professional Development.* Teacher's College Press, New York, 2000.

Teaching the *Math Trailblazers* Student: Meeting Individual Needs

This section concentrates on meeting the needs of individual students, specifically focusing on the needs of English Language Learners, special education students, and talented or gifted students as they access the rigorous mathematics in *Math Trailblazers*.

Student and teacher working together to access the rigorous mathematics in Math Trailblazers.

Teaching the MTB Student

Teaching the *Math Trailblazers* Student: Meeting Individual Needs

Today's world is increasingly more diverse, and educators frequently need to attend to this diversity. New issues, ideologies, and calls for accountability surface almost daily, highlighting the need for teachers to address all forms of diversity within their classrooms. It may be surprising to some, but every classroom is diverse in some ways. Students vary in their prior knowledge, interests, and learning styles, among other things. Many classrooms have students from different cultures or ethnic groups. Within a student group, some may have special learning needs while others are gifted or talented in mathematics. All have the right to access the rigorous mathematics in *Math Trailblazers.*

The importance of making rigorous mathematics available to all students is articulated in the Equity Principle in the *Principles and Standards for School Mathematics* (NCTM, 2000). The Equity Principle states:

> Excellence in mathematics education requires equity—high expectations and strong support for all students. . . . All students, regardless of their personal characteristics, backgrounds, or physical challenges must have opportunities to study and support to learn mathematics. Equity does not mean that every student should receive identical instruction. . . . All students need access each year to a coherent, challenging mathematical curriculum taught by competent and well-supported mathematics teachers. (p. 12)

> *All students, regardless of their personal characteristics, backgrounds, or physical challenges must have opportunities to study and support to learn mathematics.*

From its inception, the *Math Trailblazers* writers intended to design a curriculum that would support all learners. According to Robert Marzano (2003), the school-level factor that has the most impact on student achievement for all students is a "guaranteed and viable curriculum." Marzano defines a guaranteed and viable curriculum as one in which students are provided with both the opportunity to learn and the time in which to learn. This means that the sequence and organization of the curriculum must support students as they learn.

Math Trailblazers materials (lessons, labs, games, and assessments) include a variety of strategies that address the needs of students of differing learning styles, cultural and linguistic differences, and mathematical abilities. To assist teachers in creating a flexible learning environment, these strategies as well as some of the opportunities for meeting the needs of a wide variety of learners are identified in the Unit Outline in grades 1–5.

While the design of *Math Trailblazers* makes great strides in supporting a wide range of learners, it is still important to consider the unique needs of learners and adapt lessons appropriately. English Language Learners, for example, benefit from the use of the language that is part of the *Math Trailblazers* design, but these learners will be more successful when teachers implement additional language support. Gifted learners certainly benefit from the challenging open-ended tasks that are found throughout the curriculum, but can learn more when these tasks include extensions or adaptations. Special education students are supported with the language, models, and strategies used throughout the curriculum, but additional scaffolding and reading and writing support can enhance their experience.

This section was created for teachers to understand how the curriculum design supports specific groups of learners *and* to provide ideas for additional strategies that can further support each learner. The populations addressed in this section are:

Part 1. English Language Learners

Part 2. Special Education Students

Part 3. Talented and Gifted Students

These sections are not a review of all research in the field nor are they intended to be exhaustive lists of appropriate strategies. Instead they are an overview of some math-specific issues that are likely to be true in many classrooms. They also include some tried and true strategies that *Math Trailblazers* teachers have found to support their efforts to provide a challenging and supportive learning environment for their students.

Resources

Marzano, Robert. *What Works in Schools: Translating Research into Action.* Association for Supervision and Curriculum Development, Alexandria, VA, 2003.

Principles and Standards for School Mathematics. National Council of Teachers of Mathematics, Reston, VA, 2000.

Using *Math Trailblazers* with English Language Learners

PART I

A. Introduction

Mathematics classrooms no longer operate within a universal environment of "just numbers." Students are now expected to reason, explore, justify, and record their strategies for solving complex problems. This shift in practice, while excellent in rigor, presents a different challenge for students who are learning English. Their needs are unique and, therefore, warrant special attention.

Whether your district has adopted a small group instruction model or a mainstream classroom model for English Language Learners (ELLs), they deserve access to the rich mathematics presented throughout *Math Trailblazers.* If you teach in a district that has adopted or is considering adopting *Math Trailblazers,* be prepared to instruct all students with this curriculum. You can be confident that students with special needs, whether linguistic or academic, will benefit immensely from the hands-on, concept-based instruction provided in *Math Trailblazers.*

Whether your district has adopted a small group instruction model or a mainstream classroom model for English Language Learners (ELLs), they deserve access to the rich mathematics presented throughout Math Trailblazers.

Teaching the MTB Student

With the move away from isolated computation as the primary focus of mathematics instruction, it is important to ask, "How can I help English Language Learners succeed in a language-rich math class?" Rather than seeing the amount of listening, reading, writing, and speaking in *Math Trailblazers* as an obstacle, consider it as an opportunity for ELLs to learn and use their new language in a meaningful way. In fact, the only way they will learn English and mathematics is if they have the opportunity to use language in their math class.

The section in the *Teacher Implementation Guide,* titled Language in the *Math Trailblazers* Classroom, provides many ideas for supporting language use in general. In this section, the focus is on the unique needs of ELLs. While certainly not exhaustive, the ideas presented in this section offer a starting point for further thought, discussion, and collaboration. The section begins with a brief overview of research and theory related to language learning. It identifies and discusses tools already in the structure of *Math Trailblazers* and shares additional strategies that will increase access to the content.

B. Second Language Learning: Theory in Review

Early theories of second language learning were rooted in behaviorist theories of education. Behaviorists believed that language was learned through exposure to controlled grammar and language structure with minimal thought to social or cultural impact. (Ricard-Amato and Snow, 2005) In a time when much of education was decontextualized and rote, language instruction was no different.

From research in the field of second language learning starting in the late 1970s, we now know that second languages are not "learned" through rules and structures. Rather, they are acquired through context-embedded interactions much as children learn their first language. The work of Stephen Krashen, James Cummins, and others greatly shape our current views of how children acquire a language (*Schooling and Language Minority Students: A Theoretical Framework* Pp. 3–79, 1991).

Krashen (ibid, 1991) proposes that children acquire a second language naturally as they are exposed to comprehensible input through a low affective filter. In other words, as students interact in a safe, concrete environment they are able to understand and take risks in language. Through high motivation and purposeful use of the new language over time, students move towards proficiency in that language.

Cummins (ibid, 1991) adds further insight into second language learning by documenting the amount of time it takes most students to become proficient in the target language as described above. According to his research, it takes approximately two years for a student to master face-to-face, context-embedded communicative fluency. This level of competency is necessary to succeed in day-to-day social conversations such as those on the playground for example.

Ease at simple exchanges by ELLs, however, is often mistaken for advanced fluency in the new language. Therefore, Cummins (1984) identified an important distinction between the ease of social language and the unique demands required to succeed in the classroom's academic environment. To become proficient in the cognitively demanding language of the classroom, students need five to seven years to reach the level of their native English-speaking peers. That means even though students seem proficient in everyday conversations, they have years of academic language to master. The distinction between the two language proficiencies is crucial in ensuring the success of English Language Learners in our schools. The distinction allows teachers and researchers to identify and address the unique demands of academic language instruction.

Donaldson (1978) predated Cummins in her identification of "embedded and disembedded thought and language." By expanding on Donaldson's ideas, Cummins developed a framework for defining language use in the classroom. Cummins (1984) cites her framework when explaining why students acquire conversational language more rapidly due to the embedded contextual clues and high motivation of face-to-face communication. In addition, the framework reiterates the difficulty experienced by students in completing the cognitive demands of abstract tasks within the classroom. Cummins articulates the major aim of schooling as developing students' abilities to manipulate and interpret abstract texts. Therefore, the more we can do as educators to relate the abstract, academic world to the concrete, familiar world of students, the more accessible that knowledge becomes.

C. Tools in *Math Trailblazers* to Support English Language Learners

By using *Math Trailblazers* you are already well on your way to providing ELLs access to rigorous mathematics. This curriculum has numerous effective tools for making the abstract come to life. As you plan your lessons using the *Unit Resource Guide* consider the following features:

- Abundance of visuals
- Extensive use of manipulatives
- Graphic organizers
- Labs
- Problem solving from everyday life
- Connections to literature
- Group and partner work
- Opportunities to write and read in English

Math Trailblazers uses many of these features daily. Simply implementing all aspects of the curriculum will increase the support of your English Language Learners.

> *By using* Math Trailblazers *you are already well on your way to providing English Language Learners access to rigorous mathematics.*

D. Language-rich Approach to Instruction

We now know that English Language Learners develop skills in listening, speaking, reading, and writing at the same time, although we once believed they progressed in a linear fashion (Richard-Amato and Snow, 2005). Therefore, every lesson should provide meaningful opportunities for English Language Learners to experience and use language. *Math Trailblazers* provides excellent opportunities for students to use and learn language in a safe environment. Language is two-way communication: receptive (listening and reading) and productive (speaking and writing). This section takes each of these four domains and explains what is built into *Math Trailblazers* along with a discussion of the related needs and strategies of English Language Learners.

Every math lesson should provide meaningful opportunities for English Language Learners to experience and use language.

Listening. *Math Trailblazers* provides problem solving in motivating scenarios. In these tasks, students listen to others in their groups as they work on solutions. For example, students sell lemonade and plan class parties in third grade. They track the weather and investigate healthy eating habits in first grade. They take trips to famous places to study mathematical concepts. They consider the height of the Sears Tower and the circumference of the large Ferris wheel at Navy Pier in Chicago. They even predict the number of pennies in a stack from Earth to the moon!

Students listen to original or adapted literature in the *Adventure Book* and trade books recommended in the curriculum. The *Unit Resource Guides* and the *Teacher Implementation Guides* list literature selections that are either suggested or essential to completing each unit. Research is overwhelming as to the benefits of daily read alouds for all students, especially English Language Learners (Krashen, 1993; Trelease, 2001). If you are unable to read each selection to the students, add math-related titles to your listening center, or for high motivation, your podcasting center.

For English Language Learners it is essential that you monitor their abilities to listen and comprehend what they hear, whether it is listening to you or their peers. Use strategies like "numbered heads together" where each group member is assigned a number for the teacher to use in monitoring participation or drawing names from a cup to ensure that all students share. Be careful, of course, to allow generous wait time for ELLs to form their thoughts, and even allow them to share in alternative ways like drawings or motions. Allow students to be the teacher as they share their strategies for solving problems. By limiting the sharing of duplicate strategies, you also encourage students to listen carefully and evaluate each other's ideas.

There are teacher actions that can improve the listening and comprehension skills of English Language Learners. These include:

- As you speak to your English Language Learners, use clear language with lots of expression and movement.
- Be your own dictionary, always explaining difficult words as you use them.

- Use Art Costa's 10/2 principle. Do not speak for more than 10 minutes without giving students at least 2 minutes to process and make connections with the new information (Brechtel, 1998).

- Familiarize students with the process of turning quickly to their neighbor and interacting with what they are hearing.

- Allow students time to draw a picture or do a quick write.

However you manage it, just give students time to connect the new learning to a familiar idea.

Reading. Math class is a great opportunity for students to apply all their reading skills in a different context. English Language Learners benefit from paired reading especially when paired with strong English readers. (Diaz-Rico and Weed, 2002) They also benefit when expository texts, such as the *Student Guide,* are reworded into summary statements. (Echevarria and Graves, 2003) These strategies encourage groups of students to rewrite each paragraph or section using one sentence. Summarizing helps English Language Learners focus on the important information and not get lost in the details.

Again, use all the reading resources in the curriculum:

- Use the literature in the Literature Connections and the *Adventure Book* in addition to the *Student Guide.*

- Transfer key sentences from the *Student Guide* to sentence strips for English syntax examination.

- Omit key words for vocabulary development or "cloze" activities where students use the context of the sentence to find the missing key term or terms.

- Consider using math-related words in your spelling or vocabulary program.

- Do NOT focus on teaching key words like "in all" or "how many left" as indicators of certain operations. These terms can mislead and distract students from thinking about the whole problem. Instead teach students to read the problem carefully by focusing on its action or by considering the picture it creates.

Speaking. Use cooperative groups to put English Language Learners into situations where they can use their language and hear other native speakers. The Lesson Guides suggest ways for students to work in groups. Keep the groups flexible while varying their size and purpose. Students may work in groups to complete labs or in pairs to share strategies for problem solving. Because students need constant guidance and encouragement when working with others, spend the time needed to create a classroom environment of constructive student-to-student relationships. Give children the language needed to help each other or clarify ideas. Be sensitive to cultural and dominance issues that hinder equity among students. Do not be discouraged if it takes longer than you expect for students to work well together. Suggestions include:

- Provide sentence frames and sentence starters for discussion.

- Teach new vocabulary. (For more information and teaching ideas refer to the end of this section.)

- In primary classes use a key term as the "word of the day." Each time you transition within the lesson use the new term as a signal to move or begin work. You may even want to associate a physical movement or sound with the term to further involve the children with the new concept. (Brechtel, 1998)

- Encourage students to share their thinking by refusing to be the only expert in the room.

- Foster a safe environment where students are not ridiculed for making mistakes in English (or in math). For more information on establishing classroom norms, see the Building the *Math Trailblazers* Classroom section.

- Try numbering the participants in each group to encourage each student to speak. Use numbers or other identifiers as triggers to begin conversations. For example, "Twos, begin the conversation on prime numbers." Or "Fours, be ready to report back to the class at the end of your discussion." Using numbers or other identifiers in this way provides gentle accountability for all students.

- Keep in mind that the less time you talk, the more time students will have to talk.

- Set time for students to 1) work alone, 2) work in small groups before coming together in a whole-group discussion. This gives students a chance to think about the problem and test their ideas with a few others, before sharing with the whole class.

Writing. Take advantage of the many opportunities for children to write that exist in *Math Trailblazers*. English Language Learners need to see good writing modeled for them everyday, especially in math class. Even native speaking English students struggle to express their thinking and strategies for problem solving. All students need the language of thought. They need words for what is happening in their head. Therefore, encourage the use of terms such as counting on, skip counting, and regrouping. Use this vocabulary in class, not as words to be tested, but rather as language that gives meaning to the solution paths that students present. In the beginning you do the drawing and the writing; students give the ideas. Little by little as students become more confident, encourage them to draw, and later write, about their solutions. Save student work and show problem-solving examples to your students. You can score those just as you would score formal writing pieces in other subjects.

In addition, consider the following suggestions for improving writing for English Language Learners:

- Use the journal prompts. Make the journal prompts interactive by responding to the students in writing whenever possible.

- Model mathematical language by using shared writing strategies in which you and your students write together (McCarrier, Pinnell, and Fountas, 2000).

- Use the writing required in *Math Trailblazers* to support good writing in general. For example, reinforce transition words in strategy explanations as you would in expository writing.

- Use sentence frames or sentence starters to help English Language Learners model correct structure.
- Develop a respectful safe environment for students to share their strategies, so that English Language Learners will have more opportunities to develop that inner sense of what "sounds right" in English.

E. Issues Frequently Raised in Discussions with Teachers of English Language Learners

Planning Lessons When Some or All of the Students are ELLs

Use the *Unit Resource Guide* in planning your lessons. This component remains the center of each daily activity. The *Unit Resource Guide* outlines the content goals for each lesson. For the English Language Learners in your room, it is extremely important that the grade-level content goals are as close to the goals of their peers as possible. Not only do they need access to the same rich mathematics, for English Language Learners each new lesson is another opportunity for language growth as well. Therefore every lesson now needs to accomplish two goals: learning rigorous mathematics content and improving English skills (Echevarria, Vogt, and Short, 2000).

The following lesson from Grade 2 Unit 3 is an example of one way you might adapt a *Math Trailblazers* lesson to accommodate English Language Learners. This level of detail is NOT necessary for each lesson, but might be useful in getting started. Once you become more familiar with these strategies, the lesson planning will become second nature. You will be more confident making the adaptations right from the *Unit Resource Guide.*

English Language Learners need access to the same rich mathematics as their classmates, and each new lesson is another opportunity for language growth as well.

Teacher:	Grade 2 Unit 3 Lesson 3	Date:

Envision Outcomes:

Content Goals:
- Sorting objects by size.
- Collecting and recording data in a table.
- Making and interpreting bar graphs.

Posted goal for students:

"Students will sort buttons into groups by size, record the numbers in each group in a data table, and study them in a graph"

Language Goals:
- "There are ___ (small, medium, large) buttons in our handful."
- _____ buttons are the most common in our handful.
- _____ buttons are the least common in our handful.
- See Journal Prompt.
- Student pairs discuss how to sort their piles of buttons.
- Students review their graph at the end of class focusing on trends in the data.

Vocabulary:

sort	size*
button	small
medium	large
data table	graph
label	handful
most/least	common
tally	

*Word of the day

Enlist Help:
Consult the TIMS Tutor: *The TIMS Laboratory Method.* Ask adult helpers, if available, to monitor partner discussions.

Equip the Learners:
- Ask partners to identify a small, medium, and large object in the room and share with their table. Report a few examples to the class.
- Break down the word "handful." Ask students to predict its meaning from its construction.
- Bring in a soup can to show an example of a label. Discuss the function of a label.
- Review the pictures from *The Button Box* by M. Reid read in Unit 3 Lesson 1.

Engage Motivation:
- Give student pairs a handful of buttons and ask them to sort them into three groups: small, medium, and large. Show the transparency and model with a small group of buttons.
- Remind students of the sentence starters listed in the "Language Goals" they can use for discussion.
- Walk around and observe students as they work together. Praise appropriate use of mathematical language and cooperative behavior.

Execute the Lesson:
- Using the data table as a visual, remind students how to fill out the bottom of page 57 in their *Student Guide.* Ask pairs how they can record "Number of Buttons."
- If no groups suggest it, remind them how to draw tallies to keep track of the buttons.
- On a transparency or chart paper, review the parts of a graph. Pay close attention to the "labels" on each axis. Remind them of the soup can.
- Ask students to graph their data.
- Refer to the sentence frames to help students discuss their graphs with the class. Encourage student pairs to share.

Evaluate the Progress:
- Use the addition and subtraction problems suggested on page 34 of the *Unit Resource Guide* to continue problem solving in pairs.
- Have groups compare and contrast their graphs using sentence starters like, "Our group had ___ more/less buttons than…" or "Our graph looks like a _____, while their graph looks like a _____."
- Place graphs in portfolios to use as a baseline for future activities.
- Interact with the students' entries in their math journals.
- Record observations as groups work together. (See the Assessment section.)

Teacher:	Grade __ Unit __ Lesson __ Date:	
Envision Outcomes:		
Content Goals:	**Language Goals:**	**Vocabulary:**

Enlist Help:

Equip the Learners:

Engage Motivation:

Execute the Lesson:

Evaluate the Progress:

Effective Lesson Planning for English Language Learners using the *Unit Resource Guide:*

ENVISION OUTCOMES:

Content Goals: These should be clear and posted for students at the beginning of the lesson. They may be in the form of a question that students will answer or a task they can complete. The Key Content section of the Lesson Guide is a good place to start formulating your goals. Regardless of their form, review them before the lesson begins and as you progress to help the students (and you) keep focus.

Language Goals: Here is the major adjustment needed for English Language Learners. As you review the lesson in the *Unit Resource Guide,* consider what language needs will arise for your students. Identify the English structure or vocabulary you must address as you proceed through the lesson. Be direct and explicit as you teach the language lessons. See below for more ideas on teaching new vocabulary.

ENLIST HELP:

Connect with other teachers in your building if you need help making your goals accessible to English Language Learners. If you have staff trained specifically in providing instruction to English Language Learners, ask them to team teach with you on occasion. If they work with some of your students in a small group either outside or inside the classroom, have them build background knowledge for your upcoming lessons. Be careful, however, to keep them from giving direct instruction before students have a chance to develop the concepts for themselves. Consult the *Teacher Implementation Guide* for any content-related questions involving the curriculum. You can also use the Background and Content Notes in the *Unit Resource Guides* to review the mathematics for yourself.

EQUIP THE LEARNERS:

Take a few minutes at the beginning of the lesson to awaken the background knowledge of your students. This is a great time to use picture or literature books recommended in the *Unit Resource Guide.* Also, as you review the *Unit Resource Guide* record any new vocabulary words that might pose a challenge to English Language Learners. This includes at least the Key Vocabulary section, but most likely additional terms as well. Remember to highlight new definitions of familiar terms or homophones relating to math. Take time to introduce new vocabulary before you begin the lesson as long as it does not take away from student exploration and discovery. (See the vocabulary section for more ideas.)

ENGAGE MOTIVATION:

Motivate students by providing manipulatives or engaging them in a real-life problem-solving scenario. Again the *Unit Resource Guide* is your best source for ideas regarding appropriate manipulatives for each lesson. Remind students of previous work they have done related to this topic. The *Student Guide* includes many opportunities for problem solving that relate to students.

EXECUTE THE LESSON:

Teach the lesson once the students are engaged. Use lots of visuals and graphic organizers to increase comprehension. For every ten minutes of instruction, give two minutes of process time. Remember to keep focused on the goals, language, and content that were introduced at the beginning of the lesson. Help the students remember the important, not just the interesting.

EVALUATE THE PROGRESS:

Finish the lesson by checking for understanding. Review the goals and check students' progress. Use response journals or pictures. Ask students to monitor their own learning as to how well they met the lesson's goals. Consult the lesson's Assessment section in the *Unit Resource Guide* for suggestions on assessment activities.

Strategies to Help English Language Learners Remember all the New Academic Language

The amount of new academic vocabulary can be overwhelming. As teachers we want to make every effort to familiarize the students with new vocabulary within the context of the lesson (Coggins, et al. 2007). This is not a directive for isolated vocabulary instruction.

- Help students to see new words all over the classroom.
- Include them in spelling lists and on word walls.
- Use a "word of the day" to signal transition times between activities.
- Create personal dictionaries that students update daily with pictures and descriptions of new terms.
- Remember that many terms specific to mathematics have multiple meanings from common words. For example, mean, average, foot, product, and difference are a few of the words that have new meanings related to math content. Other words are homophones like sum, whole, plane, or weight that have common definitions when spelled differently. It is important to acknowledge these nuances in meaning when it comes to content-specific vocabulary.

Help English Language Learners explore new words on a deeper level:

- Look for patterns between words and how words relate to each other.
- Uncover root words and prefixes to predict meanings.
- Map words according to their relationship to other words.
- Compare and contrast words.
- Consider non-examples as a way to define unfamiliar terms.
- Take words out of their original sentences or paragraphs to help students focus on context clues. This familiar technique is referred to as a "cloze" exercise, and it has been effective for years at helping students uncover meanings of new words from their surroundings.

Ultimately, students will leave your classroom and have to take responsibility for their own learning:

- Move students toward independence by teaching them to use available tools.

- Teach them to use the glossary or index section at the back of their *Student Guides.*

- Remind them that when they look up an unknown term in a standard dictionary, the definition relating to math may not be the first one mentioned.

- Help students assess their knowledge when they come across familiar or unfamiliar words. Teach them to ask themselves questions like, "Where have I heard that term before?" or "How is this familiar word being used in a new way?" Then, they can evaluate where they need to go for more information.

Strategies to Increase Use of Nonverbal Communication in the Classroom

Math Trailblazers includes many opportunities for students to discover knowledge and content through experience. Capitalize and extend those daily opportunities. For example, in the first-grade activity called *Sharing Cookies,* bring in a box of cookie-shaped cereal for the students to use instead of cubes. Use cardboard pizzas in third grade for the *Pizza Problems.* Have kids make a paper T-shirt to decorate for *T-shirt Factory Problems,* also in third grade. Collect actual coins for money problems. Whenever possible, use real or close to real objects in presenting lessons.

If the objects are too hard to gather, bring in pictures, videos, or online images to show new concepts. Save old magazines and laminate pictures to use for vocabulary development. Make your own Shape Book using digital photography during the first-grade *Shape Walk* activity. Enlist the help of older classes to make resources for the younger grades. Video and internet services like UnitedStreaming.com can also be useful for collecting visuals. Save your work in an organized file from year to year to make the task more manageable.

Help build background knowledge by setting up an exploratory center of the coming unit. Use the Preparing for Upcoming Lessons section of the *Unit Resource Guide* to give you ideas of what is coming. Have your English Language Learners explore some of the new vocabulary with a native speaking peer. Just try not to give direct instruction robbing the learner of the joy of future discovery.

In this growing field of education stay connected to current research through national organizations such as the National Council of Teachers of Mathematics, TODOS: Mathematics for All, and National Association of Bilingual Education.

> Math Trailblazers *includes many opportunities for students to discover knowledge and content through experience.*

References

Blachowicz, Camille, and Peter J. Fisher. *Teaching Vocabulary in All Classrooms.* Pearson Education, Upper Saddle River, NJ, 2002.

Brechtel, Marcia. *Bringing the Whole Together: An Integrated Whole Language Approach for the Multilingual Classroom.* Dominie Press, Carlsbad, CA, 1998.

Coggins, Debra, et al. *English Language Learners in the Mathematics Classroom.* Corwin Press, Thousand Oaks, CA, 2007.

Cummins, James. "Language Proficiency, Bilingualism, and Academic Achievement." *Academic Success for English Language Learners: Strategies for K–12 Mainstream Teachers.* Patricia A. Richard-Amato, and Marguerite Ann Snow, eds., pp. 76–86. Pearson Education, White Plains, NY, 2005.

Donaldson, Margaret. *Children's Minds.* Collins, Glasgow, 1978.

Diaz-Rico, L., and K. Weed. *The Crosscultural, Language, and Academic Development Handbook.* Allyn & Bacon, Needham Heights, MA, 2002.

Echevarria, Jana, and Anne Graves. *Sheltered Content Instruction: Teaching English-Language Learners with Diverse Abilities.* Allyn & Bacon, Boston, MA, 2003.

Echevarria, Jana, MaryEllen Vogt, and Deborah J. Short. *Making Content Comprehensible for English Language Learners: The SIOP Model.* Allyn and Bacon, Boston, MA, 2000.

Herrell, Adrienne, and Michael Jordan. *Fifty Strategies for English Language Learners.* Pearson Education, Upper Saddle River, NJ, 2004.

Hill, Jane D., and Kathleen M. Flynn. *Classroom Instruction That Works with English Language Learners.* Association for Supervision and Curriculum Development, Alexandria, VA, 2006.

Krashen, Stephen. "Bilingual Education and Second Language Acquisition Theory." *Schooling and Language Minority Students: A Theoretical Framework.* Charles F. Leyba, ed., pp. 51–79. Evaluation, Dissemination and Assessment Center, Los Angeles, CA, 1991.

Krashen, Stephen. *The Power of Reading.* Libraries Unlimited, Englewood, CO, 1993.

Leyba, Charles F, ed. *Schooling and Language Minority Students: A Theoretical Framework.* Evaluation, Dissemination and Assessment Center, Los Angeles, CA, 1991.

McCarrier, Andrea, Gay Su Pinnell, and Irene C. Fountas. *Interactive Writing: How Language and Literacy Come Together, K–2.* Heinemann, Portsmouth, NH, 2000.

Ortiz-Franco, Luis., et al., eds. *Changing the Faces of Mathematics: Perspectives on Latinos.* National Council of Teachers of Mathematics, Reston, VA, 1999.

Richard-Amato, Patricia A., and Marguerite Ann Snow, eds. *Academic Success For English Language Learners: Strategies for K–12 Mainstream Teachers.* Pearson Education, White Plains, NY, 2005.

Trelease, Jim. *The Read Aloud Handbook.* Penguin Books, New York, NY, 2001.

Using *Math Trailblazers* with Special Education Students

A. Introduction

Finding appropriate strategies for working effectively with students who receive special education services is a challenge in any classroom. Depending on a student's disability, he or she may struggle with some or many aspects of mathematics instruction. This section highlights strategies designed to help all students, including those who experience difficulties with mathematical concepts, access the mathematics concepts and skills as presented in the *Math Trailblazers* curriculum.

In particular, this section focuses on issues related to using *Math Trailblazers* with students who have mathematics learning disabilities. You may find the information useful for other students who do not have a diagnosed disability but are experiencing learning difficulties in mathematics.

The 2004 reauthorization of the *Individuals with Disabilities Education Act* (IDEA) and associated regulations on implementing the law outline the parameters that schools must follow in providing specially designed instruction for students with disabilities. This includes the provision that students with disabilities must receive education in the least restrictive environment possible, where they have access to the general education curriculum and role models of typically developing classmates. This often means that students with disabilities have opportunities to learn challenging curricula alongside their peers without disabilities.

As part of the *No Child Left Behind Act* (NCLB) of 2001, school districts are held accountable for ensuring that all students, including those with special needs, make adequate yearly progress in reading and mathematics. The combination of IDEA and NCLB regulations has created new challenges for teachers and schools. With special-needs students being assessed on the full mathematics curriculum and schools being held accountable for the progress in mathematics of most students with disabilities, schools and districts are exploring new ways to ensure that all students including those with disabilities have access to the district's general mathematics curriculum.

Math Trailblazers was developed with a strong commitment to providing high-quality mathematics instruction for all students, including those with special needs. As such, the authors of *Math Trailblazers* incorporated approaches and tools into the curriculum to address the diverse learning needs of a wide range of students and to assist teachers with the task of differentiating their instruction. The authors of *Math Trailblazers* have designed this section to provide greater detail about strategies to support teachers to effectively plan their *Math Trailblazers* lessons for use by students in need of additional support in mathematics.

> *This section highlights strategies designed to help all students, including those who experience difficulties with mathematical concepts, access the mathematics concepts and skills as presented in the Math Trailblazers curriculum.*

The following section (Part B) highlights how the approaches used in *Math Trailblazers* align with the best practice research on differentiating mathematics instruction for students with disabilities. Part C includes additional resources developed by the Addressing Accessibility in Mathematics Project at Education Development Center (EDC) that can help teachers develop appropriate accommodations for students who have special learning needs in mathematics. References are included at the end of Part II.

B. *Math Trailblazers* Instruction and Special Education Research

The study of mathematics learning disabilities is relatively new when compared with research into reading disabilities (Geary, 2005; Gersten et al., 2004). Much of the work with mathematics learning disabilities has focused on simple arithmetic competencies, with little research on more complex arithmetic and other mathematical domains (Geary, 2004). While more research is needed, there is a research base of modifications and accommodations that can support (or inhibit) a student with learning disabilities. Some of the most promising strategies are shared here.

There is no single method or approach you can adopt for all students with disabilities or even all those with a specific disability. By definition, appropriate services for students with disabilities must be individualized. An essential element of working effectively with a student struggling with mathematics is identifying the source(s) of the student's difficulties. Accurately diagnosing mathematics learning disabilities is tricky (Ginsburg, 1997; Geary, 2005; Gersten et al., 2005). Different cognitive competencies are required for counting, recalling basic facts quickly; developing effective arithmetic procedures with whole numbers, fractions, and decimals; and learning mathematics that requires visual or spatial understandings, such as geometry or data representation. Students may have disabilities in one domain but function well in another.

It is also true that a student with significant language-based disabilities may appear to have a mathematical-based disability. It is therefore important that the full range of available assessment data be utilized to determine appropriate accommodations for each child.

However, there are general research-based teaching practices that seem to enhance learning for children with some mathematics learning disabilities. This section discusses those practices in relation to *Math Trailblazers*.

Strategies used within *Math Trailblazers* for all students are consistent with approaches researchers recommend for students who either are struggling with mathematics or those receiving special education services. As a result, accommodations for many special needs students will not likely require the development of drastically different approaches or lessons. Rather, teachers will need to examine lessons in relation to the learning preferences and needs of individual students, and highlight the specific approaches and strategies from within *Math Trailblazers* that make good instructional sense for the individual child. Good instruction for children with special needs ultimately depends upon reflective, knowledgeable, and flexible teachers who plan lessons carefully (Kilpatrick et. al., 2001).

> *Good instruction for children with special needs ultimately depends upon reflective, knowledgeable, and flexible teachers who plan lessons carefully.*

Math Facts and Computation

Many students who are diagnosed with mathematics learning disabilities also have memory-related difficulties. Memory deficits can impact students' abilities to quickly recall math facts or routinely follow multiple steps in arithmetic procedures, but memory demands differ with the task. For example, the memory demands required for retrieval of math facts differ from those required for the recall of steps in a multistep procedure or to learn geometric shapes and properties.

Students with memory difficulties must use effective strategies to work around rote memorization of facts, procedures, or definitions. Following are examples that show how the design of the curriculum supports students with special needs.

> *Math Trailblazers interweaves conceptual understanding with development of procedural competency.*

1. Instruction on the math facts focuses on patterns and connections among and between facts. *Math Trailblazers* approach for teaching and learning math facts is an example of how a strategies-based approach can assist some students who are not able to memorize the math facts. For those children, explicitly teaching strategies for figuring out the answers to math facts can be helpful. Such instruction connects the learning of one fact with knowledge of another. Research has consistently affirmed that carefully constructed, explicit instruction on problem-solving strategies provides students with learning disabilities more opportunities to figure out the correct answer and can dramatically improve their computation skills (Bottge, 2001; Gersten and Chard, 2001). See the TIMS Tutor: *Math Facts* for more information on this strategies-based approach.

2. *Math Trailblazers* interweaves conceptual understanding with development of procedural competency. This aligns with best-practice recommendations for instructing students with learning disabilities (Bottge et al., 2001; Thorton & Jones, 1996; Rittle-Johnson et al., 2001; Ginsburg, 1997). The *Math Trailblazers* approach to teaching arithmetic operations draws attention to tools within the curriculum that can assist special-needs learners to develop the needed conceptual understanding of the operations in order to gain fluency with the procedures.

3. Students use a variety of strategies for doing computation. The introduction of more than one valid procedure for each arithmetic operation offers students alternative options that might align better with their learning strengths. The regular use of calculators may be of great assistance and is a common accommodation for students who can effectively set up problems but have difficulty developing facility with paper-and-pencil procedures.

4. Extensive and ongoing use of multiple representations of arithmetic operations, such as manipulatives (e.g., connecting cubes and base-ten pieces), pictures (e.g., tallies, base-ten shorthand), and other visual representations (e.g., mathhoppers, rulers and number lines, part-part-whole mats) support students with special needs by providing different "entry points" for understanding the operations.

Use of multiple representations or alternative procedures are not panaceas in and of themselves. Most learners, but especially those with learning disabilities, will require instruction that explicitly helps them connect the various models and visual representations with the symbolic (numerical) representations of the concept (Fuson, 1992; Ginsberg, 1997). Students with learning disabilities often have difficulty making choices when multiple options are presented, and they often need more practice than other students. Introducing too many representations or alternative procedures may make it difficult for some students to make effective use of the information (Gersten & Chard, 2001). A lesson adaptation may include more explicit guidance identifying which procedures and representations are best suited to individual students at different times.

5. Daily Practice and Problems (DPPs) provide additional opportunities to practice. Once an appropriate method is identified as best suited for an individual student, additional practice is important. Most times, the practice opportunities are within the DPP or simple extensions of problem-solving contexts in daily lessons. Occasionally, the teacher may need to seek other resources for the extra practice.

Facts about Practice

- Arithmetic worksheets with many practice problems may not be helpful to many students with learning disabilities.
- Shorter, carefully constructed problem sets may be more effective in helping students with special needs develop fluency with facts and procedures (Diezman et al., 2003).
- In their meta-analysis of research on learning disabilities, Swanson and Deshler (2003) stated, "Although intensive practice of newly learned information in the early stages of learning is necessary, the cognitive intervention literature suggests that distributed practice is better for retention. Several studies have also suggested that the long-term retention of all kinds of information and skills is greatly enhanced by distributed practice" (p. 129).

Problem Solving

A fundamental assumption in *Math Trailblazers* is that students learn mathematics more effectively if they are using mathematics in meaningful contexts to solve problems. Engagement in mathematical problem solving is particularly important for students with special needs. Rich problems add context that may help such students make sense of the mathematics, build upon their previous knowledge, and judge the reasonableness of results. The problems also provide a source for the extra practice that students may require. As such, researchers caution against holding off problem solving because some basic skills are not yet in place (Bottge et al., 2001; Ginsburg, 1997; Gersten & Chard, 2001). The games and puzzles included in every grade of *Math Trailblazers* provide another source of motivation and practice that can be used effectively with special needs students.

Engagement in mathematical problem solving is particularly important for students with special needs.

Problem-solving situations in *Math Trailblazers* require students to transfer their mathematical knowledge to new situations. While these situations may be challenging for some students with learning disabilities, researchers emphasize that these students not be excluded from this important part of the mathematics curriculum. The kinds of mathematics problems they will encounter in *Math Trailblazers* can be successfully solved by the great majority. Some recommendations for supporting students are offered here:

1. Explicitly teach strategies for solving different kinds of problems (Fuchs and Fuchs, 2002; Fuchs and Fuchs, 2003; Baker et al., 2002; Swanson and Deschler, 2003). Such instruction often offers a series of steps that help students navigate through a problem, find the relevant information, and connect the problem with previous learning.

2. Consistently use tools such as advance organizers, picture-based models, or other explicit learning strategies that help students successfully work through complicated problems (Swanson and Deschler, 2003).

3. Help students make connections between varied aspects of instruction. Students with learning disabilities may need extra assistance making the connection between problem-solving experiences, concrete representations, and formal procedures (Gersten and Baker, 1998; Gersten and Chard, 1999; Ginsburg, 1997). They also will likely require additional, specific assistance with decision making, information use, vocabulary, sequencing, and patterning (Bley and Thorton, 1995).

4. Explicitly connect current or upcoming lessons with previous learning in the form of advance organizers. This may also be helpful, particularly with older students (Swanson and Deshler, 2003; Gersten and Baker, 1998).

Communication about Mathematics

Regular communication of mathematical ideas using different representations is a hallmark of instruction with *Math Trailblazers*. Classrooms that encourage students to discuss their solution strategies and justify their answers enable students with learning disabilities to communicate their mathematical understandings in ways that align with their strengths—using actions, symbols, words, or manipulatives. Students with learning disabilities are more likely to understand and retain concepts when they:

* rephrase problems in their own words;

* describe solution approaches and results; and

* summarize what others have reported. (Diezman et al., 2003).

Multiple modes of classroom communication also provide teachers with richer data to assess student progress and offer regular feedback to students. Evidence suggests that students with learning disabilities tend to overestimate their academic performance and therefore depend even more than

> *Classrooms that encourage students to discuss their solution strategies and justify their answers enable students with learning disabilities to communicate their mathematical understandings in ways that align with their strengths—using actions, symbols, words, or manipulatives.*

Communication Strategies

Deizmann et al. (2003) suggest the following communication strategies, among others, to assist students with learning difficulties:

* Allow students to communicate their thinking and solution strategies in ways that align with their preferred learning styles and strengths, using actions, symbols, words, or manipulatives.
* Use a buddy system or other means to highlight the links between what is said, manipulated, and written during a task.
* Ask students to rephrase a task or problem in their own words because virtually all these students need to hear themselves so they can understand and retain ideas; ask them to repeat the solution strategies shared by other students in the class.
* Break tasks into smaller parts and require students to report in as each part is finished.
* Ask students to write on a slate or the board as opposed to paper.

other students on consistent feedback from teachers about their progress (Heath and Glenn, 2005; Bottge, 1999).

The balance in *Math Trailblazers* of whole class instruction, small group interactions, and individual work is well-suited to promoting the communication and learning needs of students with learning disabilities. Many special needs educators recommend varying group sizes to provide students with a range of opportunities for participation. Smaller groups also allow students with learning difficulties to experiment with ideas prior to sharing with a larger group.

Homework

Homework in *Math Trailblazers* presents special challenges because it often is atypical of parents' own experiences with mathematics homework. Parents may feel ill-equipped to assist with math homework and will likely need additional, explicit discussions about expectations for mathematics learning, homework policies, and ways to assist their children. Students with learning disabilities will benefit from strong, at-home homework support structures (parents, siblings, other relatives or adults, peers). The following suggestions may be helpful as teachers plan their homework assignments for students with learning disabilities. (ERIC/OSEP, 2001).

- Be sure the homework is meaningful and focuses on the essential mathematics that students must learn.

- The assignment should be clear and doable.

- Communicate clearly, taking extra time to explain assignments and use various means to remind students about the homework and due dates.

- Adjust the length of the assignment; assign the homework in small units.

- Adapt the assignment to address the individual needs and strengths of students; allow alternative methods for students to turn in their work, e.g., audio taping rather than writing assignments.

- Provide learning tools, such as calculators or manipulatives; don't assume those tools will be available at home.

- Identify a peer tutor or assign the student to a study group.

- Use various methods to communicate with parents about homework assignments; try to develop at-home homework support structures (e.g., parents, siblings, peers, other adults).

C. Lesson Planning Tools

The preceding section underscored two major points:

- The instructional approaches used regularly in *Math Trailblazers* align with the prevailing research on teaching students with learning disabilities.

- The curriculum already has many embedded tools and structures that can help students with mathematics learning disabilities succeed in mathematics.

Homework that prepares students for an upcoming lesson may be particularly useful for those with learning disabilities. Such homework may review previously taught concepts and skills needed in the upcoming lesson or preview some individual pieces of the upcoming lesson giving students some extra time prior to class to think about and process parts of problems they will see in class.

Careful lesson planning is the cornerstone of effective work with students who have mathematics learning disabilities. The Addressing Accessibility in Mathematics Project, based at the Education Development Center, has developed a lesson planning process and a set of tools that can assist teachers using *Math Trailblazers.* The project's goals are to make mathematics curricula and instruction more accessible to students with disabilities and to promote collaboration between mathematics teachers and special needs educators.

The Project's lesson planning process provides a framework for thinking proactively about the kinds of barriers that students may encounter in a lesson. Like many suggested planning routines for working with special needs students, the concept behind the Addressing Accessibility in Mathematics Project lesson planning process is that once barriers are identified, they can be addressed by providing the scaffolding and support that students need to reach the mathematics goals.

As part of the lesson planning, the Project suggests that teachers begin by considering instructional practices, such as pairing students or using large visuals, before deciding to alter the curriculum materials. They caution that some strategies can go too far and lose the integrity of the mathematics content and pedagogy or set expectations too low for students (Brodesky et al., 2004).

The steps in the Addressing Accessibility in Mathematics Project lesson planning process are summarized in the following table. Keep the guiding questions in mind as you plan. Making lessons accessible is a combination of proactive planning and on-the-spot decision-making. The expectation is not to make an individual lesson plan for each student; the goal is for teachers to create one lesson plan with accessibility strategies built in, recognizing that additional accommodations will be needed for some individuals. By examining the lesson through an accessibility lens, teachers can anticipate potential barriers for their students, plan strategies, and "keep them in their back pockets" to use as needed.

Addressing Accessibility in Mathematics Project Lesson Planning Process[1]	
Step	**Guiding Questions**
1. Focus on the mathematics of the lesson.	• What are the mathematics goals? What are the tasks? • What is most important for *all* students to learn?
2. Focus on the students.	• What are the student's strengths and weaknesses?
3. Identify potential barriers.	• What is the match or mismatch between the lesson's mathematics content and tasks and the student's strengths and weaknesses?
4. Consider accessibility strategies.	• What strategies might meet the student's needs and enable them to reach the mathematics goals?
5. Plan and implement the lesson.	• How do I integrate the accessibility strategies into my lesson plan? • How do I collect evidence to see if the strategies were effective?
6. Plan follow-up actions.	• Did the student achieve the mathematics goal for the lesson? Did the accessibility strategies help? How do you know? • How do the results of this lesson impact planning for future lessons?

[1] Adapted from Brodesky et al., 2004.

Tools for Planning Lessons

To assist *Math Trailblazers* teachers, we include several tools here that were developed by the Addressing Accessibility in Mathematics Project. These documents are reprinted here with permission from the Education Development Center for use by *Math Trailblazers* teachers. Teachers and school and district-based staff developers may make up to 10 copies. ***For all other uses, please contact Fred Gross (fgross@edc.org) for permission.*** These and other documents can also be accessed in electronic format from the Addressing Accessibility in Mathematics web site (http://edc.org/accessmath/).

• *Instructional Strategies to Increase Accessibility*
   This one-page document lists strategies to consider for planning and teaching accessible lessons. It is a good introduction to a more detailed resource developed by the Addressing Accessibility in Mathematics Project: the *Accessibility Strategies Toolkit for Mathematics,* which is available from the project web site (http://edc.org/accessmath/resources/strategies.asp).

The goal of the *Accessibility Strategies Toolkit for Mathematics* is to provide an organized list of strategies for making mathematics more accessible to students with disabilities. Students' strengths and needs in six areas—conceptual processing, language, visual-spatial processing, organization, memory, and attention—are examined. For each of these six areas, the authors identified common types of tasks in *Standards*-based mathematics curricula, student needs and challenges, and corresponding teaching strategies for promoting accessibility.

- *Accessibility Planners*
  The Accessibility Planners are templates that provide guiding questions for identifying mathematical goals, potential barriers, and strategies to enable students to reach the goals. The planners are typically used in professional development workshops and with groups where teachers work together to analyze lessons and brainstorm accessibility strategies. They can, however, be used by individual teachers. Two different Planners are included here. Additional Planners are available from the Addressing Accessibility in Mathematics web site (http://edc.org/accessmath/resources/planners.asp).

  - *Individual Focal Student Planner*
    This planner is designed for recording observations on the strengths and weaknesses of an individual student. There is a space for listing accessibility strategies that are helpful for the student.

  - *Lesson Planner*
    This template can be used to plan accessibility strategies for individual lessons.

Instructional Strategies to Increase Accessibility

Helping Students Understand Tasks
- Reword directions or questions
- Have students paraphrase directions and questions
- Provide visual *and* auditory directions
- Preview vocabulary
- Have students highlight key information
- Change context to make it more familiar or appealing to students
- Show examples of the finished product

Helping Students Access Math in Varied Ways
- Build on students' prior math knowledge
- Make connections across math topics
- Move from concrete to representational to abstract
- Use multiple representations
- Provide additional examples
- Offer manipulatives
- Use technology strategies
- Use visuals like charts or projected images
- Offer alternative ways for students to show what they know
- Provide kinesthetic learning opportunities

Building Student Independence
- Offer timers to help students with pacing
- Teach highlighting and color-coding
- Use "think alouds" and other metacognitive strategies
- Teach *and* model strategies for:
  - Organization
  - Self-questioning and self-monitoring
  - Problem-solving
  - Memory (such as mnemonics)
- Clarify expectations (use rubrics)

Providing Tools and Handouts
- Provide study guides with key information to reduce copying and note-taking
- Offer calculators and multiplication charts
- Provide resource sheets
- Provide templates for tables, graphs, writing, and other tasks
- Use graphic organizers
- Provide practice problems
- Provide a word bank with key vocabulary words and visuals

Promoting Understanding through Discourse
- Have students work in pairs or small groups
- Use cooperative learning
- Keep class discussions short and focused
- Provide timely and constructive feedback
- Check in frequently with students
- Use questions, prompts, and hints

Helping Students Manage Tasks and Organization
- Reformat handouts to provide more workspace
- Reduce amount of copying
- Provide a checklist
- Provide time management cues
- Set up a notebook organizational system
- Provide project organizers to help the students keep track of tasks
- Offer tools such as highlighters and post-its to help students focus

Adjusting Tasks to Student Needs
- Adjust level of difficulty
- Use friendlier numbers
- Break complex tasks into smaller parts
- Adjust amount of time for tasks
- Adjust amount of work
- Create multiple versions of a problem, in order to offer alternatives to a range of learners
- Adjust pacing to optimize attention

Creating a Supportive Environment
- Post and reinforce classroom expectations
- Post homework assignments in a consistent location
- Seat students strategically, based on needs like vision or hearing. Seat distractible students away from windows or doors.
- Use nonverbal signals to cue attention or behavior
- Use consistent and familiar routines
- Provide easy access to manipulatives, templates, and other tools in the classroom

Teaching the MTB Student

Observations and Strategies for Focal Student: _____

	Student's Strengths	Student's Difficulties
Conceptual		
Language		
Visual-Spatial		
Organization		
Memory		
Attention		
Other		

Helpful Strategies for this Student

Lesson Planner for _____

Math Goals: *What are the priorities?*		
Lesson Demands *What's involved for students? Consider tasks and content.*	**Potential Barriers & Student Difficulties** *What difficulties do you anticipate?*	**Accessibility Strategies** *What strategies would you use to meet students' needs?*

References

Baker, S., R. Gersten, and D. Lee. "A Synthesis of Empirical Research on Teaching Mathematics to Low-achieving Students." *The Elementary School Journal,* 103(1), pp. 51–74, 2002.

Bley, N.S., and C.A. Thornton. *Teaching Mathematics to Students with Learning Disabilities.* Pro-Ed, Austin, TX, 1995.

Bottge, B.A. Reconceptualizing Mathematics Problem Solving for Low-achieving Students. *Remedial and Special Education,* 22(2), pp. 102–112, 2001.

Bottge, B.A., M. Heinrichs, S.Y. Chan, and R.C. Serlin. "Anchoring Adolescents' Understanding of Math Concepts in Rich Problem-solving Environments." *Remedial and Special Education,* 22(5), pp. 299–326, 2001.

Brodesky, A.R., C. Parker, M. Murray, and L. Katzman. *Accessibility Strategies Toolkit for Mathematics.* Education Development Center, Newton, MA, 2002.

Brodesky, A.R., F.E. Gross, A.E. McTigue, and C.C. Tierney. "Planning Strategies for Students with Special Needs: A Professional Development Activity." *Teaching Children Mathematics,* 11(3), pp. 146–154, 2004.

Diezmann, C.M., C.A. Thornton, and J.J. Watters. "Addressing the Needs of Exceptional Students Through Problem Solving." F.K. Lester & R.I. Charles, eds. *Teaching Mathematics Through Problem Solving: Prekindergarten–Grade Six,* pp. 169–182. National Council of Teachers of Mathematics, Reston, VA, 2003.

ERIC/OSEP Special Project. "Homework Practices That Support Students with Disabilities." *Research Connections in Special Education No. 8.* (EC 308348), Spring 2001.

Fuchs, L.S., and D. Fuchs. "Enhancing the Mathematical Problem Solving of Students with Mathematics Disabilities." H.L. Swanson, K.R. Harris, and S.E. Graham, eds. *Handbook on Learning Disabilities,* pp. 306–322. Guilford, New York, 2003.

Fuchs, L.S, and D. Fuchs. "Mathematical Problem-solving Profiles of Students with Mathematics Disabilities with and without Comorbid Reading Disabilities." *Journal of Learning Disabilities,* 35(6), pp. 563–573, 2002.

Fuson, K.C. "Research on Learning and Teaching Addition and Subtraction of Whole Numbers." G. Lenihardt, R. Putnam, and R. Hattrup, eds. *Analysis of Arithmetic for Mathematics Teaching.* Lawrence Erlbaum Associates, Hillsdale, NJ, 1992.

Geary, D.C. "Mathematics and Learning Disabilities." *Journal of Learning Disabilities,* 37(1), pp. 4–15, 2004.

Geary, D.C. "Role of Cognitive Theory in the Study of Learning Disability in Mathematics." *Journal of Learning Disabilities,* 38(4), pp. 305–307, 2005.

Geary, D.C., M.K. Hoard, J. Byrd-Craven, and M.C. DeSoto. "Strategy Choices in Simple and Complex Addition: Contributions of Working Memory and Counting Knowledge for Children with Mathematical Disability." *Journal of Experimental Child Psychology,* 88, pp. 121–151, 2004.

Gersten, R., and D. Chard. "Number Sense: Rethinking Arithmetic Instruction for Students with Mathematical Disabilities." *The Journal of Special Education,* 33(1), pp. 18–28, 1999.

Gersten, R., N.C. Jordan, and J.R. Flojo. "Early Identification and Interventions for Students with Mathematics Difficulties." *Journal of Learning Disabilities,* 38(4), pp. 293–304, 2005.

Gersten, R., and S. Baker. "Real World Use of Scientific Concepts Integrating Situated Cognition with Explicit Instruction." *Exceptional Children,* 65(1), pp. 23–25, 1998.

Ginsburg, H.P. "Mathematics Learning Disabilities: A View from Developmental Psychology." *Journal of Learning Disabilities,* 30, pp. 20–33, 1997.

Heath, N., and T. Glen. "Positive Illusory Bias and the Self-protective Hypothesis in Children with Learning Disabilities." *Journal of Clinical Child and Adolescent Psychology.* 34 (2), pp. 272–281, 2005.

Kilpatrick, J., J. Swafford, and B. Findell, eds. *Adding It Up: Helping Children Learn Mathematics.* National Academy Press, Washington, DC, 2001.

Lovin, L., M. Kyger, and D. Allsopp. "Differentiation for Special Needs Learners." *Teaching Children Mathematics,* pp. 158–167, 2004.

Marolda, M.R., and P.S. Davidson, eds. "Assessing Mathematical Abilities and Learning Approaches" C.A. Thornton and N.S. Bley, eds. *Windows of Opportunity: Mathematics for Students with Special Needs,* pp. 41–60. National Council of Teachers of Mathematics, Reston, VA, 1994.

McGilly, K., ed. *Classroom Lessons.* Bradford, Cambridge, MA, 1994.

Rittle-Johnson, B., R.S. Siegler, and M.W. Alibali. "Developing Conceptual Understanding and Procedural Skill in Mathematics: An Iterative Process." *Journal of Educational Psychology,* 93(2), pp. 346–362, 2001.

Smith, D.D., ed. *Introduction to Special Education: Teaching in an Age of Opportunity* (5th ed.). Pearson Education, Inc., Boston, MA, 2004.

Swanson, H.L., and D. Deshler. "Instructing Adolescents with Learning Disabilities: Converting a Meta-analysis to Practice." *Journal of Learning Disabilities,* 36(2), pp. 124–35, 2003.

Thornton, C.A., and N.S. Bley, eds. *Windows of Opportunity: Mathematics for Students with Special Needs.* National Council of Teachers of Mathematics, Reston, VA, 1994.

Thornton, C.A., and G.A. Jones. "Adapting Instruction for Students with Special Learning Needs, K–8." *Journal of Education,* 178(2), pp. 59–69, 1996.

Womack, D. *Special Needs in Ordinary Schools: Developing Mathematical and Scientific Thinking in Young Children.* Cassell Educational Limited, London, 1988.

Teaching the MTB Student

Meeting the Needs of the Mathematically Gifted or Talented Student in the *Math Trailblazers* Classroom

A. Introduction

The design of Math Trailblazers is well aligned with the needs of talented or gifted students, and the curriculum provides many opportunities for extending and differentiating instruction.

Talented or gifted students are quite different from other students in the classroom. For example, they remember things easily, needing very little review. They like to be engaged in problem solving, can work with abstract concepts beyond the scope of their peers, and approach problems in novel ways (Wilkens, Wilkens, & Oliver, 2006). A teacher's challenge with talented or gifted students is unique; rather than finding ways to make the content comprehensible to students, the teacher must move beyond the curriculum to provide additional challenge. Given this fact and that high stakes assessments focus on bringing low achieving students up to proficient levels, attention has shifted away from the talented or gifted student. Fortunately, the design of *Math Trailblazers* is well aligned with the needs of talented or gifted students, and the curriculum provides many opportunities for extending and differentiating instruction.

According to Zaccaro (2006), mathematically gifted children need to be given material that truly and appropriately challenges them. Assouline and Lupkowski-Shoplik (2005) list key elements of a curriculum that supports mathematically talented or gifted students. These elements include a broad scope of content studied in depth and at a high level with problem solving at the core of the instruction. Students solve problems, communicate solution strategies, represent problem situations in a variety of ways, and reflect on the efficiency of their problem-solving methods. Students should discover mathematical content that connects to real life as well as to other subjects.

The *Math Trailblazers* curriculum was developed with a commitment to both equity and excellence for all students, including the talented or gifted student. The following are some *Math Trailblazers* features that align with the needs of talented or gifted students:

- Students construct new knowledge as well as practice mathematical concepts through rigorous and authentic problem-solving situations.
- Students are frequently asked to communicate their solution strategies orally and in writing.
- Students solve problems using multiple problem-solving processes and provide multiple representations for their solutions.
- Students are encouraged to reflect and evaluate the efficiency of both their problem-solving strategies and the strategies of others.

B. Talented or Gifted Students in Mathematics

The following topics explore issues related to teaching talented or gifted children. Information includes insights from research, work with teachers, and how the structure of *Math Trailblazers* addresses these issues.

Identifying Talented or Gifted Students

One prevailing myth about mathematically talented students is that only students identified for a gifted program can be mathematically talented. There are a range of ways to identify students as gifted, some based on IQ scores (above 130) or on standardized test scores (above 95%). These types of criteria, however, can eliminate a student who has a special talent in one area and average or above average abilities in other areas. As a result a mathematically talented student may not meet the criteria for his or her school's gifted program (Assouline and Lupkowski-Shoplik, 2005).

The National Association for Gifted Children (NAGC) calls for a more comprehensive definition of a gifted student. They describe a gifted person as:

. . . someone who shows, or has the potential for showing, an exceptional level of performance in one or more areas of expression.

Some of these abilities are very general and can affect a broad spectrum of the person's life, such as leadership skills or the ability to think creatively. Some are very specific talents and are only evident in particular circumstances, such as a special aptitude in mathematics, science, or music. The term giftedness provides a general reference to this spectrum of abilities without being specific or dependent on a single measure or index. It is generally recognized that approximately five percent of the student population, or three million children, in the United States are considered gifted.

A person's giftedness should not be confused with the means by which giftedness is observed or assessed. Parent, teacher, or student recommendations, a high mark on an examination, or a high IQ score are not giftedness; they may be a signal that giftedness exists. Some of these indices of giftedness are more sensitive than others to differences in the person's environment.

(http://www.nagc.org/index.aspx?id=574)

In this discussion, we consider the talented or gifted student as those formally identified as gifted in the area of mathematics through assessment procedures and those students not formally identified as talented, but whom a teacher determines, through assessments, observations, and classroom assessments to be talented in mathematics.

Content Note

Although students are referred to as being either talented or gifted, programs developed for such students use the title Talented and Gifted.

While every student is different, talented or gifted students in mathematics commonly exhibit particular traits in a mathematics classroom. They begin to grasp mathematical concepts at an early age. Many of these students enter school having established their own theories of number sense, computational strategies, problem solving, and patterns. Teachers describe these children as being able to see connections among topics and ideas without formal instruction. They are often able to discern answers with unusual speed and accuracy. Also, due to their intuitive understanding, they may skip steps and be unable to explain how they arrived at their answer (Rotigel & Fello, 2005). According to Sheffield (1999), students who demonstrate giftedness in mathematics may demonstrate uneven understanding of mathematical concepts. These students are frequently less interested in the computational "how to," preferring to engage in problem solving that is both challenging and interesting (Zaccaro, 2006).

Though these students are usually able to understand difficult mathematical concepts more readily than their same age peers, these same students may also appear to be disinterested or unmotivated in a one-size-fits-all classroom. Diezmann and Watters (2005) identify boredom as a major concern for gifted students, which results from a lack of challenging academic tasks and from a perception that the learning experience has limited value to them. This lack of challenge may be furthered when teachers try to address the needs of these students by: simply increasing the amount of work the students are to complete without addressing the complexity of the task; assigning these students to help others who are still working; or asking them to work on something else quietly while they wait for others to finish (Tomlinson, 1999; Diezmann and Watters, 2005). Both the *Principles and Standards* (NCTM, 2000) and Zaccaro (2006) caution educators that the practice of simply pushing students through the curriculum at a faster pace is not the answer.

The NCTM *Principles and Standards* states:

> One traditional way for students to learn additional mathematics in which they have a particular interest is differential pacing—allowing some students to move rapidly through the mathematical content expected of all so that they can go on to additional areas. However, some alternatives to differential pacing may prove advantageous. For example, curricula can be offered in which students can explore mathematics more deeply rather than more rapidly. This model allows them to develop deep insights into important concepts that prepare them well for later experiences instead of experiencing a more cursory treatment of a broader range of topics. (p. 369)

Zaccaro (2006) explains that expecting more work from students increases the likelihood that gifted students will develop a lack of interest. More work does not nurture the student's passion for mathematics. He compares this to "teaching all scales and no music." (p. 3)

This model (differential pacing) allows them [students] to develop deep insights into important concepts that prepare them well for later experiences instead of experiencing a more cursory treatment of a broader range of topics.

Teaching Talented or Gifted Students: Classroom Learning Community

Providing the best classroom support for talented or gifted students begins with a classroom learning community that focuses on deep understanding of important mathematics for all learners. Hiebert et al. (1997) explain that effective learning means providing rich environments for developing deep understanding of mathematics through collaboration, communication, and the creation of cognitive conflict. Having these foundations in place allows the teacher to facilitate the most effective work with talented or gifted students.

The literature suggests that there are some common foundations present in a healthy classroom learning community. They include:

- Ideas and methods expressed by all students deserve and are given respect.
- Students are encouraged to work out their own methods and communicate them with understanding to others.
- Teachers help students make their own sense of ideas and methods.
- Teachers provide high expectations and the necessary scaffolding to move each child to his or her next learning benchmark.
- Mistakes are seen as sites for learning. Challenge and frustration are a part of learning and life and should be viewed as part of the learning process.
- The authority for determining whether something is correct and sensible lies with the logic of the subject rather than with the status of the teacher. The teacher strives for student independence. (Hiebert, et al., 1997; Tomlinson, 1999; Zaccaro, 2006; Kilpatrick, Swafford, & Findell, 2001)

For additional information on establishing and maintaining effective classrooms, see the Building the *Math Trailblazers* Classroom section.

Teaching Talented or Gifted Students: Homogeneous and Heterogeneous Grouping

Appropriate grouping of students in math class is often a concern of both new and experienced teachers. In an attempt to meet the needs of all learners, educators have often separated students by achievement, grouping them with students who have similar achievement levels. Many educators believed that these homogeneous classrooms would allow students to learn at their own pace and would allow teachers to meet the needs of the students more consistently. According to the National Research Council, however, data from international comparisons (especially Asia) support the assumption that all students can achieve important mathematical learning goals within heterogeneously grouped classrooms. Tomlinson (1999) further argues that students learn best in a heterogeneous classroom only when teachers create "effective communities of learning in which all learners are specifically and systematically addressed." (p. 22) She further states that classroom learning communities grounded in best-practice and that are responsive to the diverse needs of the learners benefit all students through differentiation of instruction.

> *Providing the best classroom support for talented or gifted students begins with a classroom learning community that focuses on deep understanding of important mathematics for all learners.*

> *The tasks within* Math Trailblazers *lessons are challenging and involve problem solving and reasoning—curriculum qualities appropriate for the talented or gifted child.*

Math Trailblazers is designed for heterogeneous grouping and contains the strategies described above to support and challenge talented or gifted students. The tasks within lessons are challenging and involve problem solving and reasoning—curriculum qualities appropriate for the talented or gifted child. In addition, tasks are solved using a range of strategies, which allows those more advanced to implement more sophisticated strategies. *Math Trailblazers* lessons provide the support for discussion about math concepts. These supports help students learn to be effective communicators and to work collaboratively. Many of the lessons involve working in pairs or small groups. This sets the stage for providing the differentiation and individualization that may not occur in classrooms that are more teacher directed or designed exclusively for whole class instruction.

Tasks That Support the Learning of Mathematically Talented or Gifted Students

According to Doyle (1983, 1988) students learn from the kind of work they do. The tasks students are asked to complete determine the nature of that work. When designing mathematical tasks for talented or gifted students, Diezmann and Watters (2005) identify four defining characteristics, each of them at the heart of the *Math Trailblazers* curriculum.

Defining Characteristics of Curriculum that Challenges and Supports Talented or Gifted Students (Diezmann and Watters 2005)

1. The tasks are authentic. Students are able to emulate the practices of mathematicians at an appropriate level.

2. The tasks develop mathematical abstract reasoning. These allow the student who is gifted mathematically to explore patterns and relationships, produce holistic and lateral solutions, and work abstractly.

3. The tasks develop meta-cognitive skills. Hiebert et al. (1997) describes this as knowing how to use information as a result of understanding how it is connected or related to new knowledge or skills. Additionally, meta-cognition is being able to decide when to use a strategy by judging whether or not it is efficient.

4. The tasks increase motivation and passion for mathematics. Tasks that are challenging and meaningful allow mathematically talented students to construct meaning and develop autonomy as a learner.

One of the unique strengths of the *Math Trailblazers* curriculum is its integration with science and language arts. This interdisciplinary approach to problem solving allows students to emulate the real-world work of mathematicians and scientists. Throughout the curriculum, students are involved in scientific investigations of everyday phenomena that develop and apply mathematical skills and concepts to generate meaningful situations.

The laboratory experiments in *Math Trailblazers* are examples of authentic tasks, crucial to the success of talented or gifted students. In each experiment students identify variables, draw pictures of their methodology, collect and organize data in tables and graphs, and look for and use patterns to analyze their data. For example, in second grade, students compare the distance different vehicles can roll. Students are introduced to the concept of "multiple trials" in an investigation and to the use of the median as a way to average their data.

Students in fifth grade first explore the geometry of circles informally and then formally. Students use collected data to find an accurate approximation for the ratio of the circumference to diameter of a circle. Discussion ensues to cement the connection between this investigation and the constant pi (π). Students then use the constant to find a formula for the circumference of a circle. In each activity, the context of authentic tasks helps the talented or gifted students make connections between previous learning and new information. Students are able to apply what they have learned in a new or different context. According to the *Principles and Standards* (NCTM, 2000), students develop deeper and more lasting understanding when they can identify the rich connection among mathematical topics in contexts they can relate to other subjects, their own interests, and their experience. For a more in-depth discussion about *Math Trailblazers* integration with science and language arts, refer to the Foundations of *Math Trailblazers* section.

Communication is also an integral part of the *Math Trailblazers* curriculum. Students increase their understanding of mathematics by discussing the mathematics they are doing. Students are expected to share their strategies for problem solving during classroom discourse and through written explanations. Journal and discussion prompts are standard features in the lesson guide for many lessons. You can use these prompts to focus classroom discussions. Asking talented or gifted students to communicate the results of their thinking to others provides them an opportunity to clarify and deepen their understanding. Students become better able to justify their solution paths to others, especially when there are divergent solution paths. For a more in-depth discussion about communication in the *Math Trailblazers* classroom refer to the Language in the *Math Trailblazers* Classroom section.

The *Math Trailblazers* curriculum also emphasizes problems that have multiple solution paths. These problems give students opportunities to talk about their own thinking in both small group and whole-class discussions. As students share their problem-solving strategies with their classmates and teacher, and as they listen to the strategies of others, they become more reflective about mathematics. The consistent inclusion of opportunities for reflection helps the talented or gifted student think about his or her own learning and leads to more efficient strategies for problem solving.

Problems with multiple solutions give students opportunities to talk about their own thinking in both small group and whole-class discussions.

A Sample Task from *Math Trailblazers*

This sample task from *Math Trailblazers* includes the components discussed above, especially the importance of communication between student and teacher. Sharing such a task with parents, teachers of talented or gifted students, or administrators can illustrate the opportunities and challenge in this curriculum that make it appropriate for the talented or gifted student.

To develop an understanding of the base-ten number system, the students in first grade are asked to fill in numbers on an empty 50's chart, consisting of

5 rows of 10 squares per row, as shown in Figure 1. The students begin by choosing a number from a deck of digit cards. They then use a variety of strategies to determine where to record the selected number. Students continue this way until all the cards are used.

Figure 1: *A partially completed 50's chart*

Lessons are designed to encourage students to develop efficient strategies for problem solving as they build deep conceptual understandings of the mathematics.

This activity provides a launching point for developing important concepts in mathematics. The classroom described at left demonstrates that, when students are given the opportunity to construct meaning through open-ended problem solving and when they are provided the opportunity to reflect on and share their thinking with others, they are able to discover patterns and relationships, and deepen their understanding of mathematics.

C. Planning for Instruction

The *Math Trailblazers* curriculum was developed to provide high quality, rigorous mathematics for all students. Lessons are designed to encourage students to develop efficient strategies for problem solving as they build deep conceptual understandings of the mathematics. The teacher's role is integral to this process as he or she designs complex instruction with the needs of each learner in mind. Complex instruction is defined by Cohen (1994) as, "a rich strategy developed to deal with the sorts of academic ranges that frequently exist in classrooms that are academically, culturally, and linguistically heterogeneous." (p. 68)

Cohen's definition creates the underlying foundation for differentiated classrooms. In education, differentiation is defined as a teacher's responsive reaction to the needs of the learners in the classroom. In other words, differentiation is responding to individual or small group needs as opposed to teaching as if the class were a singular unit in which all students are alike.

50's Chart: From the Classroom

First graders were observed completing the task described above. They used a variety of problem-solving strategies to determine where to place the number represented on the selected card. Some students made a representation of that number using trains (or groups) of connecting cubes. The cubes were made into groups of tens and leftovers. The students placed the cubes directly onto the 50's chart to help them identify the correct box in which to record the number. Other students counted the squares, placing the number in the correct box. Still other students used the strategy of counting by tens and then by ones to identify where to place the number.

As the students continued to work, one child began to see a pattern emerging on the chart and was able to use this pattern to place the numbers. For example, he recognized that the number 47 would go in the same column as 17 only down 3 rows because 4 is 3 more than 1. This student may have been beginning to develop an abstract understanding of the value of 10 and using this to understand the relationship between the various numbers on his chart. He then asked the teacher, "Does this always work?" He was trying to make sense of the situation, make connections to what he knew, and devise a rule that explained how this system worked. The teacher continued to stretch this child's understanding by encouraging him to try to think about numbers greater than 50 asking, "Where would the number 93 fit on your chart?" He pointed to 43 and said, "Under this number, just more tens."

The goal of differentiation is maximum student growth and individual success (Tomlinson & Allen, 2000).

In the differentiated classroom, effective instruction begins with teacher planning. Tomlinson (1999) identifies the following three critical elements of the curriculum that must be linked for effective instruction:

- Content—The content is what we want students to know, understand, or do as a result of instruction. The content is the "input" for instruction.
- Process—The process includes the activities or tasks that allow a student to make sense of the content.
- Product—The product is the "output." The product represents the way in which a student demonstrates what he or she understands and can do as a result of learning.

The lessons in the *Math Trailblazers* curriculum are designed and organized to clearly focus on the content, the process, and the products so students develop understandings of the key concepts, guiding principles, essential skills, and necessary facts of mathematics. For the talented or gifted student, the teacher must consider if the content, processes, and products are appropriately challenging, and when necessary, to adapt the lesson.

There are many effective instructional strategies for working with talented or gifted students in a heterogeneous setting. Centers, stations, and using tiered lessons provide the greatest flexibility since the teacher can use these instructional strategies to differentiate instruction for all students in the classroom.

Instructional Strategies for Differentiation in the *Math Trailblazers* Classroom

In any lesson plan, a teacher needs to consider three important questions: What should be differentiated? For what purpose? And, how will this be accomplished? (Tomlinson, 1999)

When considering what to differentiate, a teacher needs to remember the three critical elements of the curriculum: content, process, and product. Additionally the teacher needs to consider the learning profile of each student, student interest, and student readiness. Another aspect that can be differentiated is the physical learning environment. Differentiating the physical learning environment might include the classroom configuration, use of specific grouping strategies, use of manipulatives both real and virtual, and student choice of product.

There are many effective instructional strategies for working with talented or gifted students in a heterogeneous setting. Centers, stations, and using tiered lessons provide the greatest flexibility since the teacher can use these instructional strategies to differentiate instruction for all students in the classroom.

Key Principles of a Differentiated Classroom

- The teacher is clear about the key concepts of the unit.
- The teacher is clear about which skills are fundamental to supporting conceptual learning.
- The teacher understands, appreciates, and builds upon student differences.
- Assessment and instruction are inseparable.
- The teacher adjusts content, process, and product in response to student readiness, interests, and learning profile.
- All students participate in respectful work.
- Students and teachers are collaborators in learning.
- Goals of a differentiated classroom are maximum growth and individual success.
- Flexibility is the hallmark of a differentiated classroom. (Tomlinson, 1999)

Centers. There are two types of centers that a teacher may use in a classroom to provide differentiation of instruction. The first, a learning center, is an area of the classroom that contains activities designed to teach, reinforce, or extend a skill or concept. Teachers can design classroom centers to focus on current instruction, review past instruction, or preview and explore an upcoming concept or skill set. The second type is the interest center. This center is designed to increase a student's motivation by providing opportunity to explore topics of interest to the student. In general a center provides students with materials and activities that address a wide range of instructional levels and learning styles. Center activities can vary from structured to open-ended, and promote individual learning toward a defined goal.

In the *Math Trailblazers* classroom, teachers can use centers effectively with talented or gifted students. A teacher may set up learning or interest centers with activities or materials that focus on practice or extension of a core concept or skill. Configuring a center for talented or gifted students is more than just giving them more work. The skillful use of centers permits the teacher to challenge talented or gifted students with content appropriate to their levels of understanding.

Stations. While similar to a center, stations provide a structure in which teachers can assign students to specific areas of the room to complete different tasks. The tasks can be varied according to the ability level of students assigned to that station. Stations invite flexibility in the classroom in that not all students need to go to every station. Stations may also be used sequentially to build desired skills or conceptual understandings.

Teachers in a *Math Trailblazers* classroom may develop stations in which all students are working on the same content but where each station represents a different entry point into the content. For example, at one station, students may work with manipulatives to construct concrete models for problem solving while at another station students might be asked to solve problems using more abstract representations for their solutions. The essential consideration in doing such lesson design is that each station is still focused on the goals of the lesson and of the unit. It is inappropriate to have stations that are limited to more trivial expectations—this interpretation of differentiated lessons has resulted in the propagation of inequities in the classroom.

In grades 3–5, the task and challenge items in the Daily Practice and Problems can be a rich resource for both centers and stations. The items identified as a task are designed to take about 15 minutes to complete, and often expand a concept or provide extra practice on a skill. Challenge items are designed to be more thought provoking and to stretch a student's problem-solving skills.

Tiered Lessons. Using tiered lessons is a differentiation strategy that allows teachers to develop multiple pathways for students to take as they address the same concept or skill. Although much of the content in *Math Trailblazers* is intentionally structured as tiered lessons, understanding how a tiered lesson is structured helps teachers more efficiently and effectively reach the talented or gifted student. Teachers can identify the challenge of each of the defined tiers in a lesson to determine which best meets the learning needs of the students in the classroom (Kingore, 2006; Pierce & Adams, 2005; Kettler & Curliss, 2005; Tomlinson, 1999).

Factors that Influence the Complexity of Tiered Learning Experiences

Degree of Assistance and Support
- Teacher directs instruction
- Teacher as facilitator
- Small group support
- Individual autonomy

Degree of Structure
- Clearly defined parameters
- Open ended

Complexity of Activity or Task
- Process and product are concrete
- Process and product involve abstract thinking

Complexity of Process
- Pacing
- Number and complexity of steps
- Simple to high levels of thinking
- Sophisticated research skills are required

Complexity of Product
- Simple, correct answers
- Varied and complex responses
- Integration of advanced skills and concepts is required

Adapted from Kingore (2006)

While there are several different models for developing a tiered lesson, some general characteristics span them all. The following list, which describes the tiered structure found in *Math Trailblazers* is adapted from Tomlinson (1999); Kingore (2006); and Pierce & Adams (2005).

1. Identify the key concepts, skills, or generalizations that are the focus of the lesson. Ask yourself the following: What do I want students to know and be able to do as a result of this lesson?

2. Think about the students in your classroom. Keep in mind that tiered lessons assume that all children are able to learn the same essential concepts, skills, or generalizations in different ways. The groups of students working at each tier should be flexible depending on the

content, process, and products assigned at each tier. As you define your groups consider the range of readiness in your classroom, as well as the interests, talents, and learning styles of each student.

3. Determine the complexity of the activity along a continuum from least complex to greatest complexity. In other words, will the task challenge your most talented or gifted students, your students working at grade level, or your less advanced students. Once you determine where this activity falls on the continuum you can determine if the task meets the needs of all in your classroom. One example of a lesson's tiered structure is that in the laboratory experiments, the questions are successively more difficult.

4. If you find that this activity does not meet the level of your most talented or gifted student, identify who needs another version of the learning experience.

5. Only when necessary, create a different version of the task to address the learners in your classroom. You will find that different *Math Trailblazers* lessons have different quantities of tiers depending on the concepts and skills.

6. Use appropriate assessment for the lesson. Assessments will vary depending on the tier.

Math Trailblazers was designed with many of its lessons structured according to the characteristics of tiered lessons. Lessons begin by clearly identifying the key content that is the focus for all students. Throughout the lesson students are presented with tasks and questions that allow for multiple solution paths that vary in complexity. The following is an example of a tiered lesson from *Math Trailblazers*.

In the fourth-grade lesson *Perimeter vs. Length,* students explore the relationship between the area and perimeter of a rectangle as the area is increased in a specified way. Students first create the rectangles with square inch tiles. They then record the rectangle on grid paper. This lesson is tiered because students are asked increasingly more complex questions about the area and perimeter of the rectangle. Students are provided multiple entry points to the problems presented. Some students will use the square-inch tiles to build concrete models to represent each figure and count the number of tiles to determine either the area or the perimeter. Other students will create representations of the figures using grid paper and rely on the figures they draw to solve the problem. Still others will begin to use mathematical formulas to find the area or perimeter of the figures as they build them.

Because this lesson is already "tiered," it allows children to access the mathematics in ways that make sense to them and to push their understanding as far as possible. The talented or gifted students engaged in this lesson are likely to apply mathematical formulas to find the area or perimeter of geometric figures. These learners are more likely to see that they can decompose more complex figures into simpler geometric shapes. For example they may decompose a trapezoid into a rectangle and two triangles. These students may also see the relationship between shapes, for example two triangles might make a square. These learners benefit from lessons such as this one that contain challenges that are an integral part of the curriculum.

D. Resources for Teachers

Meeting the needs of all learners in the classroom can be challenging but also very exciting. The *Math Trailblazers* curriculum provides many resources for teachers in the *Teacher Implementation Guide* (TIG). This resource includes information for teachers that explores mathematical concepts and ideas addressed in the curriculum.

To learn more about working with students identified as talented or gifted in the classroom the following websites may be helpful:

National Association for Gifted Children (NAGC) The NAGC has been in existence for more than 50 years. This organization is dedicated to serving professionals who work on behalf of gifted children. NAGC publishes a journal for professionals entitled, Gifted Child Quarterly.
http://www.nagc.org

The Association for the Gifted (TAG) TAG is a special interest group of the Council for Exceptional Children (CEC).
http://www.cec.sped.org

American Association for Gifted Children (AAGC) The AAGC is the oldest organization dedicated to advocacy for gifted children.
http://www.aagc.org

Hoagies Gifted Education Page An extensive listing of conferences, resources, articles, and support for teachers.
http://www.hoagiesgifted.com

References

Assouline, S., and A. Lupkowski-Shoplik. *Developing Mathematical Talent: A Guide for Challenging and Educating Gifted and Advanced Learners in Math.* Prufrock Press, Waco, TX, 2005.

Diezmann, C., and J. Watters. "Catering for Mathematically Gifted Elementary Students." *Math Education for Gifted Students.* S. Jensen and J. Kendrick, eds., pp. 33–46. Prufrock Press, Waco, TX, 2005.

Hiebert, J., T. Carpenter, E. Fennema, K. Fuson, D. Wearne, H. Murray, A. Olivier, and P. Human. *Making Sense Teaching and Learning Mathematics with Understanding.* Heinemann, Portsmouth, NH, 1997.

Kettler, T., and M. Curliss. "Mathematical Acceleration in a Mixed-Ability Classroom." *Math Education for Gifted Students.* S. Jensen and J. Kendrick eds., pp. 83–92. Prufrock Press, Waco, TX, 2005.

Kilpatrick, J, J. Swafford, and B. Findell, eds. *Adding it Up: Helping Children Learn Mathematics.* National Research Council (NRC), Washington, DC, 2001.

Kingore, B. "Tiered Instruction: Beginning the Process." *Teaching for High Potential.* NAGC, winter 2006.

Pierce, R., and C. Adams. "Tiered Lessons." *Math Education for Gifted Students.* S. Jensen and J. Kendrick, eds., pp. 49–60. Prufrock Press, Waco, TX, 2005.

Principles and Standards for School Mathematics. National Council of Teachers of Mathematics, Reston, VA, 2000.

Reed, C. "Mathematically Gifted in the Heterogeneously Grouped Mathematics Classroom." *Math Education for Gifted Students.* S. Jensen and J. Kendrick, eds., pp. 17–31. Prufrock Press, Waco, TX, 2005.

Rotigel, J., and S. Fello. "Mathematically Gifted Students How Can We Meet Their Needs?" *Math Education for Gifted Students.* S. Jensen & J. Kendrick, eds., pp. 3–16. Prufrock Press, Waco, TX, 2005.

Sheffield, L.J., ed. *Developing Mathematically Promising Students.* National Council of Teachers of Mathematics, Reston, VA, 1999.

Shore, B.M., and M.A.B. Delcourt. "Effective Curricular and Program Practices in Gifted Education and the Interface with General Education." *Journal for the Education of the Gifted* 20(2), pp. 138–154, 1996.

Tomlinson, C. *The Differentiated Classroom Responding to the Needs of all Learners.* Association for Supervision and Curriculum Development, Alexandra, VA, 1999.

Wilkins, M.M., J.L. Wilkins, and T. Oliver. "Differentiating the Curriculum for Elementary Gifted Mathematics Students." *Teaching Children Mathematics,* 13(1), pp. 6–13, 2006.

Zaccaro, E. "The Seven Components of Successful Programs for Mathematically Gifted Children." *Teaching for High Potential,* NAGC, winter 2006.

Language in the
Math Trailblazers Classroom

This section focuses on the use of language while students read, write, speak, and listen in the *Math Trailblazers* classroom. Students' language abilities increase while using a curriculum rich in opportunities to communicate mathematically.

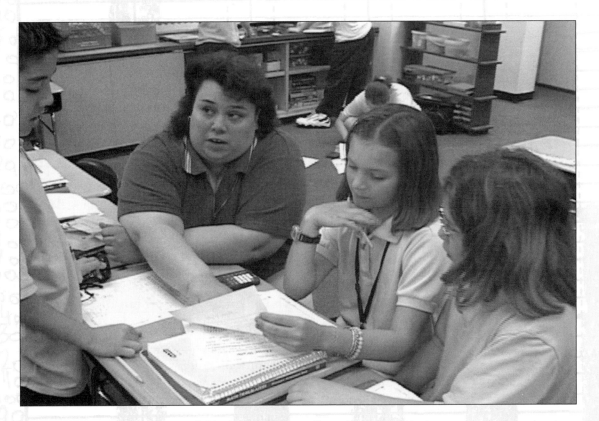

A teacher helps students solidify their understanding of mathematical concepts by listening to their explanations, helping them read the problems, and write their solutions.

Language in the
Math Trailblazers Classroom

The use of language—listening, reading, speaking, and writing—is emphasized throughout the *Math Trailblazers* curriculum. This enables students to consider and communicate ideas and solidify their understanding of mathematical concepts. In the past, many mathematics textbooks and lessons limited students' use of language. Parents, administrators, and other teachers may not understand the need for so much reading and writing in a mathematics class. Moreover, getting students to read, write, speak, and listen, while crucial to the learning process, is sometimes a challenge.

This section offers support for developing language use in your classroom. Part I provides a brief rationale of why language is important and how it is used in *Math Trailblazers*. This information is useful in working with colleagues and parents who may not understand the need for reading and writing in mathematics class. Part II provides additional background and support for incorporating language into your daily lessons. Specifically, support is provided on three overlapping areas of language use: reading, writing, and discourse strategies.

Incorporating Language into Mathematics Lessons

Using language to learn mathematics is grounded in learning theory and research. While there are many reasons to incorporate reading, writing, listening, and speaking into mathematics instruction, we discuss issues that may arise when discussing language with parents, administrators, and other teachers.

Reasons to Focus on Language in Mathematics Lessons

Language can help students understand mathematics. The value of studying mathematics is to learn both processes and skills necessary for solving real-life problems. In *Math Trailblazers,* students investigate and solve mathematical problems in real-world contexts. They design accurate and efficient strategies. Discussing possible approaches during the problem-solving process and presenting various solution strategies broadens and deepens students' understanding. It also solidifies their ideas as they learn to use mathematics language.

The context of many mathematics lessons are language-dependent. *Math Trailblazers* uses real-life contexts to develop mathematical concepts in a concrete, visual manner. The contexts actually help students understand math concepts and promote student interest in the math lessons. The contexts provide meaning and concrete examples for thinking about abstract concepts.

Listening, reading, speaking, and writing enable students to consider and communicate ideas and solidify their understanding of mathematical concepts.

Incorporating problem-solving contexts into the lessons, however, requires increased use of language in the text and in implementing of the lesson (through speaking, listening, and writing). For example, second-grade students use the context of a car moving through a neighborhood to develop initial concepts of geometry known as slides, flips, and turns. Without this context, which requires students to both read and listen as they solve the problems, the lesson would not be accessible to all learners. In later grades, these language-dependent contexts provide an opportunity for students to make sense of symbolic representations; e.g., 9×4 becomes 9 groups of 4 boxes, and so on. While tempting to remove the contexts to reduce the language demands, such adaptations interfere with a student's ability to make sense of what they are doing. The contexts also connect ideas within mathematics and between mathematics and their world.

Using language in mathematics results in improved literacy. Some teachers, parents, or principals may believe that the increased use of language interferes with the learning of mathematics. This is most often suggested for English-language learners and students with language-related learning disabilities. While such students may need additional support in interpreting the language in the problem, having a familiar context to ground thinking is more often a support to students, not a hurdle. In addition, English-language learners will only learn the language of mathematics if there is significant use of productive (speaking and writing) and receptive (listening and reading) forms of language. Language use in a mathematics classroom has the benefit of not just improving students' abilities to communicate mathematically, but to communicate in general. Everyday language is improved while using it within the context of math class.

Proficiency in mathematics language is essential for success in mathematics. There are three types of language involved in mathematical discourse. The first is conversational language used for giving instruction, explaining a process, and so on. The second is discrete language used for understanding symbols such as $+$, $-$, $\times$, $\div$, and the words and meaning attached to symbols. The third is mathematical language, which includes terms such as *range, product,* and *sample.* These have definitions specific to mathematics that are different from everyday usage. All three types of mathematical language are important to effectively communicate. Since mathematical language is not often a part of students' experiences outside the mathematics classroom, it is particularly important to make them a regular part of their mathematics learning.

Where Students Encounter Language in the *Math Trailblazers* Curriculum

In *Math Trailblazers,* students engage in all facets of language use including:

- reading introductory vignettes at the start of many lessons,
- explaining the process they used to solve a problem,
- listening to and comparing solution strategies,
- working collaboratively with classmates,
- writing responses to open-ended problems,
- reporting observations either orally or in writing, and
- reading and discussing the trade books and *Adventure Books.*

PART II | Assisting Students with Reading, Writing, and Discourse

Reading

Reading Comprehension: Background

George Polya (1973) outlined a 4-step problem-solving process. "Understand the problem" is the first step, followed by devising a plan, carrying out the plan, and looking back. Understanding first involves comprehending the text and then understanding what the mathematics is within the text. If students do not comprehend the text, they can't begin to understand the problem, therefore they cannot engage in doing mathematics. This is true even for reading symbolic expressions as simple as $8 \div 2 = 4$. At the beginning of the problem-solving process, it is important to realize the complexity of reading in mathematics. Mathematics text is different from other text; it is very dense, containing more ideas per sentence than any other type of text (Kenney, 2005). In addition, it can contain words as well as numeric and nonnumeric symbols. Students may have to comprehend illustrations that relate to the text, including tables, graphs, charts, pictures, and coordinate axes. Finally, the syntax of mathematics story problems is different from everyday language. Making these distinctions explicit supports reading comprehension for all students and is absolutely essential for those struggling with language or learning English.

> *Only if students comprehend the text can they begin to understand the problem and engage in doing mathematics.*

Reading Comprehension: Strategies

The following strategies can increase students' reading comprehension:

1. Help students understand the goal of the lesson. Understanding the lesson's goal helps them with reading comprehension.
2. Find out whether the context is familiar to students. Bring meaning to that context. For example, students may not know the meaning of sampling a population. Ask, "Can you share how you have heard the word 'sampling' used?" Students may report on sampling food, samples of wallpaper or paint, or other experiences. If not, share a personal experience such as when you participated in a survey.
3. Model the process of interpretation through "think aloud." This includes articulating what dilemmas or questions arise as you read and what words and phrases help you figure out what to do.
4. Ask students what difficulties they have understanding the problem. As students try to find words to describe what they don't understand, they often solve the problem themselves. Sometimes, other students offer helpful input.
5. Restate the problem in an interactive manner. Ask students to use the pair-share strategy: one partner tells what the problem is about (e.g., finding volunteers to work at the science fair) and the other partner tells the question they will need to answer (e.g., how many people will be needed).

6. Help students with phrases and their meanings. For example, consider the question: "Which group has twice as many small lids as large lids?" Ask students to think about what that phrase "twice as many . . . as" means and then describe how they know. Add these phrases to a journal or math word wall. Note that this helps students see how the meaning of words are influenced by other words around them. This is very different from a key-word approach, which can result in limited comprehension (see the section on using key words later in this document).

7. Allow students time to read aloud and time to listen to others read aloud. Follow with "What is this question asking you to do?" and "How did you know?" Asking "how" makes explicit the connection between words and mathematical concepts and procedures.

To support students as they read (or listen to) children's books connected to *Math Trailblazers* lessons, we recommend the following strategies:

- Preview or review vocabulary that may be problematic.
- Ask students to predict or summarize story contents.
- Ask questions related to the story, but beyond the discussion prompts.

Grades 1–5 in *Math Trailblazers* each has a series of *Adventure Books,* short stories written like graphic novels (comic book style) or illustrated, connected text. The stories are used to illustrate a math or science concept with children as the problem solvers.

You can share these stories in a variety of ways:

1. Read the story as students follow along.
2. Read the story, then have students read it with a partner.
3. Students read the story with a partner.
4. Assign the story for homework the night before for students to pre-read with family members.
5. Students read the story in a reader's theater format.
6. Record the story and place it in a listening center with accompanying questions for students to answer.

Reading Levels

In any classroom there is a range of reading abilities. While the curriculum is written to be accessible to all students, struggling readers or nonreaders may need additional support. One way is to read the text first as a whole class. Another is to group the nonreaders with the teacher at the start to be sure they understand the text. Heterogeneous grouping can support nonreaders or reluctant readers, especially if you insist that when you visit the group every student can explain the task. The following story demonstrates how one second-grade teacher organized her classroom with reluctant and nonreaders to provide access to all students.

A Classroom Example of Accommodating Different Reading Levels

(This second-grade lesson deals with making a map on the x- and y-axis with Mr. Origin (a referent object) at the origin of the coordinate plane.)

The room is full of second graders with varying degrees of reading abilities. I had planned the Mr. Origin lab for one class period, but didn't think we would get to the questions about the map. But these kids were wonderful and finished making their maps and measuring with ease. So, since they were in groups, I said to each group as they finished, "Go ahead and start answering the questions about your map."

There were groans, but each group began to read the questions and respond to them. One group put their heads together and answered all the questions. A second group got started but one child asked to be excused for a moment (a nonreader). A third group immediately split into two pairs and began answering questions (but didn't finish). When group 4 was stuck, I asked one boy to read the questions to the group. There was a nonreader in that group and he wouldn't listen to the questions being read. So, I asked him to read. He read the words but obviously couldn't read for meaning (yet). The first boy read it one more time and then the group answered the questions. Before they were finished they had read the question a total of 6 times and then answered the question.

Afterwards, I reflected on the lesson, in particular how the students were able to answer the questions. I thought that pairs might be better than larger groups for tasks involving reading.

I also thought about which child needed to be paired with which child during a reading part of a math lesson. One idea I had was to pull my nonreaders together and read to them before having them work in pairs on the questions.

When I looked at the papers, I found that only two children had not answered all or most of the questions successfully, both nonreaders. I made a mental note that I need to ask each nonreader to respond to me orally to check for understanding.

Working together, the students had helped each other understand the questions and respond to them successfully.

Caution: Key-Word Approach Can Limit Comprehension

Some reading strategies can inhibit learning. In mathematics, the most common is searching the story problem for key words that indicate a specific operation. Research shows that while teachers help identify what are sometimes called "key words" to support student thinking, students use these words to abandon reasoning about the problem (Kenney, Hancewicz, Heuer, Metsisto, Tuttle, 2005; Sowder, 1988). The reasons why a "key-word approach" can be detrimental to comprehension include:

1. Key words often have multiple meanings.
2. The list of key words continues to grow over the years making it difficult to remember.
3. The key words might indicate an operation, but the question may be asking for more than the response to a computation.
4. Key-word search doesn't help students understand the meaning of the problem.
5. For problems involving multiple steps, it doesn't work and students are then ill-prepared to read for understanding. Instead, students need opportunities to find meaning in the reading.
6. Phrases can shift the meaning of words in the phrase. For example "how," "many," and "how many" signify different things in mathematics.
7. Addition of (or removal of) a single letter changes meaning (e.g. "percent of" versus "percent off," "ten" versus "tens").

Appropriate Attention to Key Words

It is important to develop vocabulary that is specific to mathematics. Although, this point may seem to contradict the previous section, there is an important distinction. In the "keyword" approach, students memorize that a word (e.g., difference) means to "subtract" regardless of the content of the sentence; in a precision-of-vocabulary approach, students become familiar with the common phrases (e.g., more than) and relationships among words (e.g., if-then) and how they interact with the rest of the sentence. As a teacher, one way to support student-reading skills is to make explicit some of these vocabulary considerations specific to mathematics. Some common examples of the subtleties in mathematics language follow:

1. Here are two problems using the term *more than,* one requiring subtraction (or counting down) and one requiring addition (or counting up):
   - Jenny has 9 apples. She has 3 *more than* Linda. How many apples does Linda have?
   - Jenny has 9 apples. Linda has 3 *more than* Jenny. How many does Linda now have?
2. Here are two problems in which "by" indicates two different operations:
   - Linda had four cats in her stuffed animal collection. After her birthday, the number of cats *increased by* three. How many cats does Linda have?
   - Linda had four cats in her stuffed animal collection. After her birthday, the number of cats was *multiplied by* three. How many cats does Linda now have?

3. In this example, the operation is the same, but a different response is required for each:
   - The third grade went on a field trip. There are 50 students in the third grade. Twenty students fit on each bus. How many buses were needed?
   - The third grade went on a field trip. There are 50 students in the third grade. Twenty students fit on each bus. How many buses were full?
4. In these statements the key word *of* is used in different ways:
   - What is the area *of* a triangle? (indicating find the space inside)
   - What is one-half *of* 24? (indicating $\frac{1}{2} \times 24$ or $24 \div 2$)

     Find the perimeter *of* the rectangle. (indicating where the perimeter is).

Writing

Writing: Background

The value of having students write in math is quite simply that writing improves learning. Pugalee (2005) explains:

As students write, they manipulate, integrate, and restructure knowledge through using and reflecting on what they know and believe. This process facilitates the development of meaningful understanding: the more a student works with ideas and concepts, the more likely those ideas and concepts will be understood and remembered. (p. xii)

Writing can allow more flexibility in how much time a student has to describe a solution and provides the opportunity for reflection and correction. If students struggle with the words to explain, they can supplement or replace with illustrations. While writing has clear benefits, it is also very challenging. Students are learning to write as they are learning mathematics, so the thought processes are demanding, the precision required in communicating mathematically increases the difficulty of this task, and even students willing to share orally, may be reluctant to share their ideas in writing. Because writing does improve learning, but is difficult, it is essential that students have ample opportunity and support for writing.

Math Trailblazers offers many opportunities for students to write. Just as in a writing lesson, students benefit when they submit a written explanation, receive input from the teacher, and then revise the explanation based on feedback. In the early grades, writing might include a simple process of asking students to tell in words or sentences how many objects they found altogether. Teachers can help primary students learn to write by having them dictate their thinking to an adult or by drawing pictures. Teachers at all grade levels, including kindergarten, should expect students to submit written work, even if the thoughts are incomplete or inaccurate. Students become better writers by writing. As noted earlier, as students improve their writing in mathematics, they improve their writing skills in general. Math class is just one of many situations in which students need to learn effective written communication.

Writing: Strategies

Because writing may be the most difficult literacy skill, it is important to explicitly teach students to write (or illustrate) their work. Here are some ways teachers support student writing:

1. Use and display the *Math Trailblazers* Student Rubrics in grades 3–5. If students have the rubrics in front of them as they work, they will produce better products. If you use a sample, have students collectively respond to whether the sample meets the expectations in the *Telling* or other rubrics. Students will learn how to be more clear and thorough in their writing. For more information on rubrics, see the Assessment section.

TIMS Tip

Post enlargements of the rubrics in the classroom where they are easy to point to and read.

2. Prior to writing, ask students to verbally summarize the important concepts of the lesson. You can even list key points on the board so students can synthesize the information into complete sentences in their own way. Sharing key points can serve as a good review and an opportunity for speaking and reading that further solidifies the concept for students.

3. For students having trouble beginning, sentence starters are a good tool. Another related tool is a graphic organizer with sections where students are prompted to write the question, process, and solution. Some teachers use Polya's (1973) 4-step problem-solving process as a guide, asking students to (1) state the problem, (2) tell what approach they used, (3) explain what solution they got, and (4) tell how their solution answers the original problem.

4. Incorporate creative writing prompts that engage your students. For example, use a genre introduced in language arts, like poetry, fables, or persuasive narratives.

5. Ask students to draw pictures, diagrams or, for older students, concept maps of what they later explain in words. Using pictures can support writing and help you to see what they are trying to explain.

6. Have students keep a math journal of the written summaries of lessons or problems. In this way students can see their improvement in explaining mathematics and have a resource for looking up information they might have forgotten. See the TIMS Tutor: *Journals* for a range of prompts and tips on keeping a math journal.

7. Make a transparency of a well-written response to share with students. To preserve anonymity, use a sample from another class or save samples from year to year.

8. Ask students to fold a paper in half, solve the problem on the first half, and then open the paper and write the steps on the second half.

Regardless of the strategies you use, it is important to remember that the goal is to capture students' ideas and thinking. Creativity and novel solutions are important, and writing opportunities should not impose ways for students to begin or solve a problem.

Language in the Classroom

Discourse

Discourse: Background

Those who start teaching with a *Standards*-based curriculum like *Math Trailblazers* often see a change in their classroom discourse. Because *Math Trailblazers* engages students in problem solving and inquiry, there are opportunities for students to approach a problem differently and share different solution strategies. Students learn from hearing others' approaches, and such conversations allow teachers to help students focus on key mathematical ideas. This is different from asking questions to get students to a particular teacher-determined endpoint, a model of questioning often referred to as funneling, where the teacher uses questions to funnel students to a particular formula, approach, or term (Herbel-Eisenmann and Breyfogle, 2005).

Post-exploration discussions are essential to the learning process. As Chapin, O'Conner, and Anderson (2003) write, "When a teacher succeeds in setting up a classroom in which students feel obligated to listen to one another, to make their own contributions clear and comprehensible, and to provide evidence for their claims; that teacher has set in place a powerful context for student learning." (p. 9)

Discourse is not only a concluding activity in a lesson, however, but is important as student work is in progress. This can help stimulate new ideas across working groups. Whitin & Whitin (2000) call this "rough draft thinking" and argue that it allows classmates and the teacher to get a glimpse into other students' thought processes and to revise one's own thinking (p. 220).

Having classroom discourse means establishing norms for how students interact with each other. Hiebert, et al. (1996) describe four critical features of establishing a social culture for learning mathematics, shared in brief here:

Ideas are the currency of the classroom. Ideas, expressed by any participant, have the potential to contribute to everyone's learning and consequently warrant respect and response.

Students have autonomy with respect to the methods used to solve problems. Students must respect the need for everyone to understand their own methods and must recognize that there are often a variety of methods that will do the job.

The classroom culture exhibits an appreciation for mistakes as learning sites. Mistakes afford opportunities to examine errors in reasoning and thereby raise everyone's level of analysis. Do not cover up mistakes; use them constructively.

The authority for reasonability and correctness lies in the logic and structure of the subject, rather than in the social status of participants. The persuasiveness of an explanation or the correctness of a solution depends on the mathematical sense it makes, not on the popularity of the presenter. (pp. 9–10)

> *Because* Math Trailblazers *engages students in problem solving and inquiry, there are opportunities for students to approach a problem differently and share different solution strategies.*

Discourse: Strategies

Facilitating discourse improves with practice. As students become more accustomed to explaining their thinking, listening to others, and asking their own questions, knowing what questions you should ask and when to ask them is an important skill. Discourse that "focuses" rather than "funnels" is less predictable and requires skills on your part. Some strategies to support effective discourse include the following:

1. Allot time for students to share and compare strategies and solutions at the end of the lesson, even if it is not the end of the period. It takes time for students to articulate their ideas. If you are running out of time, build it into the next day. Reflecting about the lesson helps children develop an understanding of math concepts and helps you to understand what it is they learned.

2. Shift classroom procedures from general ones like "listen to one another" to specific ones, such as "We need to listen and understand what the speaker is saying. We all have an obligation to ask questions when we don't understand."

3. Focus on the important mathematical concepts in the lesson. If these objectives are written on the board it helps both you and students keep the dialogue focused.

4. Ask good questions. Interesting questions that have answers not already known support good classroom discussions. Use questions that prompt students to listen to each other. For example, "Can you repeat in your own words what you just heard?" "How is this strategy similar to or different from your strategy?" and "What can you add to what was just said?" "Do you agree or disagree with it? Why or why not?" In all cases, the response is neither punitive nor evaluative. If the student who is asked these questions cannot answer, he or she can always ask, "I didn't understand, could you please repeat what was said?" These questions communicate to students that you expect them to listen and learn from each other. Good questions for facilitating discourse are offered in *Professional Standards for Teaching Mathematics* (NCTM, 1991) or can be accessed through Public Broadcasting Service Teacherline.

5. Engage all students in discussion. Participation is not optional. If students are sharing with the whole group, stop at times and ask them to share their thoughts with a partner. Ask students to write an idea on paper or in their journals so they are ready to share.

6. Focus on student understanding. Kenney, et al. (2005) characterize three types of discourse. First, the traditional, in which the teacher and several students talk. Second is a "probing" discussion, where the teacher is still generating the questions, but the questions are more open-ended. Third, is "discourse-rich," where students are working together toward mathematical understanding. An important distinction in the third type is the student-to-student and student-to-class interactions.

7. Decide when to guide students and when to wait, when to ask a student for further elaboration and when to elicit input from others. Quiet pauses should not be uncomfortable dead time, but "think time" for all students to think about what was just said, process it, and then respond.

In addition to these strategies, Easley (1990) offers guidelines for establishing an environment that fosters discourse (see below).

Ten Suggestions for Practice in Communication

From *Dialogue and Conceptual Splatter in Mathematics Classes* by Jack Easley

1. Try to maintain an atmosphere of freedom in the classroom, that is, an atmosphere that encourages students* to feel free to express themselves.
2. When in doubt, remain silent! Give students a chance to work through their mathematical difficulties.
3. Don't paraphrase because paraphrasing is usually a technique for pushing the students too quickly towards the teacher's point of view. Let the students' words stand by themselves. Ask students to clarify the expression of their own thoughts rather than comply with your thoughts.
4. Encourage constructive arguments. For example, ask, "Do you believe that?" "Do you agree or disagree?" "How do you know?" or say, "Tell me what you mean."
5. Play dumb, but avoid condescension. Let the students teach you as well as each other.
6. Don't focus on "right" answers. Alternative answers can create a tension that leads to lively and fruitful interaction. In addition, many good problems have more than one right answer, or at least more than one possible solution technique.
7. Let students have time to work on a problem as individuals before you ask them to share their thoughts in a small or large group, thereby encouraging each student to get involved in the problem.
8. No best way exists to form small groups. For example, you can group students at random or on the basis of ability levels or of their conflicting opinions.
9. Dialogue groups, whether small or large, can be called "meetings." Take time to model expected etiquette for the meetings.
10. Save the written work of the students to evaluate and substantiate their learning. Record the classroom dialogues on videotapes, audiotapes, and in your own journal of the activities; share these recordings with the students. And finally, bring continuity to the dialogues by basing future sessions on your evaluation of the conceptual splatter that has been expressed. (p. 36)

*Students is used here to replace "pupils," which was used in the original publication.

For further information on developing a language-rich classroom for English Language Learners, see the Teaching the *Math Trailblazers* Student: Meeting Individual Needs section.

References

Assessment Standards for School Mathematics. National Council of Teachers of Mathematics, Reston, VA, 1995.

Burrill, G. "Changes in your Classrooms: From the Past to the Present to the Future." *Mathematics Teaching in the Middle School,* 4(3), pp. 184–190, 1998.

Chapin, S.H., C. O'Conner, and N.C. Anderson. *Classroom Discussions: Using Math Talk to Help Students Learn.* Math Solutions Publications, Sausalito, CA, 2003.

Cummins, J. "Supporting ESL Students in Learning the Language of Mathematics." *Research Says: Issues and Trends in Mathematics.* Pearson Education, New York, 2007.

Cuoco, A., E.P. Goldenberg, and J. Mark. "Habits of Mind: An Organizing Principle for Mathematics Curricula." *Journal of Mathematical Behavior,* 15, pp. 375–402, 1996.

Curriculum and Evaluation Standards for School Mathematics (1st ed.). National Council of Teachers of Mathematics, Reston, VA, 1989.

Easley, Jack. "Research into Practice. Dialogue and Conceptual Splatter in Mathematics Classes." *Arithmetic Teacher,* 37(7), pp. 34–37, 1990.

Galima, L., and T. Hirsch. "Making Mathematics Accessible to English Learners." Paper presented at the National Council of Teachers of Mathematics (NCTM) annual meeting, Atlanta, GA, March 2007.

Herbel-Eisenmann, B.A., and M.L. Breyfogle. "Questioning our Patterns of Questioning." *Mathematics Teaching in the Middle School,* 10(9), pp. 484–489, 2005.

Hiebert, J., et al. *Making Sense: Teaching and Learning Mathematics with Understanding.* Heinemann, Portsmouth, NH, 1997.

Kenney, J.M., E. Hancewicz, L. Heuer, D. Metsisto, and C.L. Tuttle. *Literacy Strategies for Improving Mathematics Instruction.* Association for Supervision and Curriculum Development, Alexandria, VA, 2005.

McIntosh, M.E. "500 Writing Formats." *Mathematics Teaching in the Middle School,* 2(5), pp. 354–358, 1997.

Polya, G. *How to Solve It: A New Aspect of Mathematical Method.* Princeton University Press, Princeton, NJ, 1973.

Principles and Standards for School Mathematics. National Council of Teachers of Mathematics, Reston, VA, 2000.

Professional Standards for Teaching Mathematics. National Council of Teachers of Mathematics, Reston, VA, 1991.

Pugalee, D.K. *Writing for Mathematical Understanding.* Christopher Gordon Publishers Norwood, MA, 2005.

Sowder, L. "Children's Solutions of Story Problems." *Journal of Mathematical Behavior* 7, pp. 227–238, 1988.

Van de Walle, J.A. *Elementary and Middle School Mathematics: Teaching Developmentally.* Pearson Education, New York, 2007.

Whitin, D.J., and P. Whitin. "Exploring Mathematics Through Talking and Writing." M.J. Burke, and F.R. Curcio, eds. *Learning Mathematics for a New Century: 2000 Yearbook,* pp. 213–222. NCTM, Reston, VA, 2000.

Wood, T. "Alternative Patterns of Communication in Mathematics Classes: Funneling or Focusing?" H. Steinbring, M.B. Bussi, and A. Sierpinska, eds. *Language and Communication in the Mathematics Classroom,* pp. 167–178. NCTM, Reston, VA, 1998.

Working with *Math Trailblazers* Parents and Families

The Parents and *Math Trailblazers* section provides suggestions and tips to help parents participate in their child's understanding of *Math Trailblazers* and to enhance its benefits for their children.

A teacher, student, and parent work together to solve a problem.

Working with *Math Trailblazers* Parents and Families

 PART I | ## *Math Trailblazers* Features

Parents' understanding and support of your mathematics curriculum plays an important role in its successful implementation and can be a key factor in children's success with mathematics. This section provides suggestions and tips to help parents understand the *Math Trailblazers* curriculum. It is arranged in three parts. The first part describes several built-in features to help you communicate with parents. The second part gives advice on preparing two types of special programs: math nights for families and parent presentations at school or district meetings. The third part provides blackline masters to copy and distribute to parents.

Parents want assurances that the content and approaches of the school's mathematics program will not only educate and interest their children now, but also benefit them later when test scores and school admissions become serious realities. Most adults experienced a mathematics curriculum that focused almost exclusively on teaching facts and standard procedures for computing. In contrast, *Math Trailblazers* maintains a careful balance between developing skills, underlying mathematical concepts, and problem solving. Parents need to understand this balance. Moreover, parents must understand the importance of teaching the other mathematics strands (algebra, geometry, measurement, and data analysis and probability). As you work with parents throughout the year, communicate the following:

> *Parents need to understand the careful balance that* Math Trailblazers *maintains between developing skills, underlying mathematical concepts, and problem solving.*

- Varied contexts for solving problems in *Math Trailblazers* help children learn to use mathematics in meaningful ways;

- The activities in *Math Trailblazers* are designed to provide children with the skills they will need in the workplace of the 21st century.

- Current research supports the approaches used in *Math Trailblazers* for teaching mathematics. In regard to computation and facts, the approaches in *Math Trailblazers* allow students to gain fluency with less drill and memorization than former methods and with better retention;

- Practice with skills and procedures is distributed between homework, Daily Practice and Problems, and within most problem-solving activities in the program;

- *Math Trailblazers* encourages students to develop varied ways to solve problems—not just the solutions that adults might select; and

- Mathematical ideas are represented with manipulatives, pictures, tables, graphs, and numbers—and how these representations allow children to access the mathematics in varied ways.

Communicating with Parents

Gaining parent support early will save effort in the long term. Anticipate potential parental concerns about a new math program and address them proactively through an ongoing parent education effort.

Math Trailblazers includes a parent brochure, letters home, homework notes, and parent information blackline masters to help you communicate about the curriculum.

Parent Brochure

The parent brochure provides an introduction to the curriculum. Blackline masters of this brochure (in English and Spanish) are at the end of this section. They are designed for you to send home at the beginning of the year or use as a handout at a fall parent meeting.

Letters Home

Parent letters are included at the beginning of each unit to give specific information about what children will study. These letters describe the concepts presented in each unit and how parents or family members can provide follow-up and encouragement at home. A sample Letter Home is shown in Figure 1.

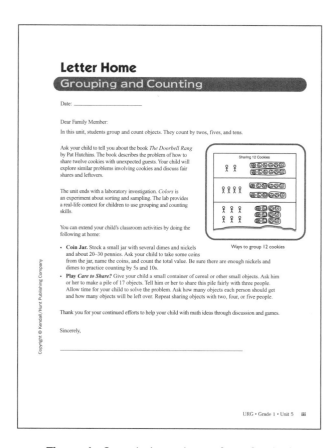

Figure 1: *Sample letter home from Grade 1*

Homework Notes

Many homework assignments, especially in grades K–3, include a separate explanation for family members, outlining the activity's purpose and providing hints for assisting with the assignment. An example of such a note is shown in Figure 2. These explanations are to help parents feel comfortable with the curriculum's content and goals. We encourage you to supplement the parent instructions with your own notes and to provide a way for parents to get their homework questions answered (e.g., via emails, phone, or after school).

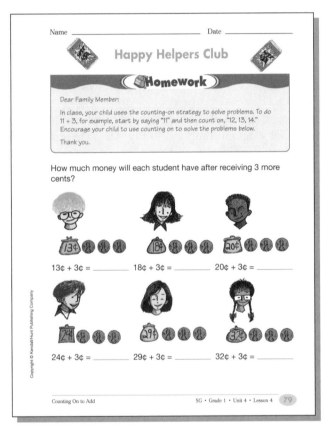

Figure 2: *Sample Grade 1 homework note for parents*

Parent Information Blackline Masters

Additional information on selected topics is available to be copied for parent at the end of this section. Topics include:

- Math Facts Philosophy
- Multiplication Methods in *Math Trailblazers*
- Long Division in *Math Trailblazers*
- Internet Resources for Families of *Math Trailblazers* Students

Roles for Parent Volunteers

Parent volunteers can support the implementation of *Math Trailblazers* in a variety of capacities.

Parent volunteers can be an important support to the implementation of Math Trailblazers in a variety of capacities.

Math Trailblazers incorporates many hands-on activities. In addition to the commercially purchased manipulatives such as base-ten pieces, many activities call for materials such as jars, container lids, paper towel cores, and so on. Parent volunteers can ease the job of gathering and managing these materials.

Parent volunteers also can assist with classroom activities. They can work on special projects or lesson extensions with small groups. Some teachers periodically invite several parents to assist with station activities, where student groups rotate from station to station. Often it is helpful to have an extra set of hands and eyes in the classroom to assist as needed.

Parents can assist students during a lesson. Assign parents to work with particular groups of students or with individual students who need extra assistance. With guidance on appropriate ways to support student thinking, this can be a great support for students, as well as educate parents in the instructional approaches used in *Math Trailblazers*.

You can obviously tailor the roles parents play in providing support to your needs and the interests and capabilities of individual parents. There is little doubt, however, that parent volunteers are a valuable asset as you work with *Math Trailblazers*.

Special Programs for Families and Parents

One way to help parents understand and support the goals and philosophy of *Math Trailblazers* is to organize special math-related programs for parents and families. One type of program is a math night, during which parents participate in math activities with their children. Another is a more formal presentation given by a teacher or other curriculum leader at a school parent night or special informational meeting. Many schools combine both types of programs by giving a short presentation as part of a math night. The following are suggestions to help you plan parent and family programs for your school.

Family Math Nights

A typical math night involves families coming to school to participate together in math activities. A variety of successful math night formats include:

- **Math Night Carnival**
  Families move from one math activity to another at their own pace. This format is typically held in a large space such as a gymnasium or lunchroom.

- **Teacher-Led Math Night**
  Families visit their child's math classroom and work together through grade-level specific activities and games.

- **Math Night Classroom Rotation**
  Families rotate through a series of classrooms. Each classroom presents a specific math activity or game. Families may encounter activities from a variety of grade levels.

> One way to help parents understand and support the goals and philosophy of Math Trailblazers *is to organize special math-related programs for parents and families.*

The best format of any math night differs from school to school and even from year to year within the same school. The following is what happened at one school.

The school invited parents and students to a math night designed as a carnival, held in the gym. Students and parents played a game at each booth and got a prize when they finished. As the evening progressed though, parents congregated in the middle of the gym while their children played the games alone. This event did not meet the goal of getting parents involved with and learning about Math Trailblazers.

The next year, the staff decided to reorganize the math night to keep parents involved in Math Trailblazers *activities with their children. In preparation for the math night, teachers chose primary and intermediate activities and planned them to be held in classrooms. They made a display about the activity that included information on how the activity aligned with the state and NCTM Standards. Teachers also hung estimation activities in the hallways to keep families busy as they moved through the school. As families worked their way from the primary to the middle grades, they saw how the mathematics develops across the grades. Parental involvement on this math night was a big improvement over previous years.*

Suggested Activities

When planning a math night, choose activities that illustrate key ideas from the *Math Trailblazers* curriculum and engage parents. For example, choose activities that focus on problem solving, address a range of mathematical content, or have connections to science.

Doing parts of one of the labs is an effective way for parents to experience how mathematics in the curriculum is embedded in meaningful contexts. Consider using labs you have already done in class. That way, students can lead their parents. Students won't mind repeating the lab, since in many cases, the data will be new to them.

Following is a list of activities that worked well in math night programs. We chose these activities because the concepts underlying them are easily understood, and require minimum preparation. They also show the impact of *Math Trailblazers* work with the scientific method and ways for children to practice computation in a context.

Kindergarten:
* sorting apples from *Data Collection* in the *Ongoing Content* section
* *A Garden's Area,* Month 7 Lesson 4

Grade 1:
* *Pockets* activities in Unit 3 (selected pieces)
* *More or Less Than 100,* Unit 9 Lesson 2

Grade 2:
* *High, Wide, and Handsome,* Unit 4 Lesson 1 (selected pieces)
* *Tile Designs,* Unit 2 Lesson 1
* *Marshmallows and Containers,* Unit 6, Lesson 5 (selected pieces)

Grade 3:
- *First Names,* Unit 1 Lesson 10
- *The Better "Picker Upper,"* Unit 5 Lesson 3
- *Floor Tiler,* Unit 11 Lesson 5

Grade 4:
- *Arm Span vs. Height,* Unit 1 Lesson 5 (selected pieces)
- *Investigating Area and Perimeter,* Unit 2 Lesson 1

Grade 5:
- *Three in a Row,* Unit 8 Lesson 2
- *Factor 40,* Unit 11 Lesson 1
- *Fraction Cover All,* Unit 5 Lesson 3

Tips for Math Nights

The following list of recommendations reflects the experiences of teachers in many different settings. The list is intended to help you make decisions for your own Math Night, but not all may be appropriate in your setting.

- Hold more than one math night, with different grade levels (e.g., K, 1–2, 3–5) grouped together. If you target multiple grades, families with children in different grades can participate together. On the other hand, if you offer grade-level classes, parents can learn more about their child's particular grade.

- Require that students come with an adult. Explain that this is not just a program for children, but a chance for families to enjoy mathematics together.

- If using the teacher-led classroom format, make sure there is enough room for everyone. Some schools divide participants into groups of eight to ten families, so there are about 25 people per class.

- Consider offering babysitting for younger siblings, so parents can devote their attention to their school-age children.

- Ask families to register in advance so you will know how many people to plan for. This also lets you know whether you need further recruitment efforts. However, some schools believe that asking families to register discourages some from attending.

- Involve as many people as you can. Include groups such as the parent-teacher organization. Ask high school students to help as volunteers—some schools offer credit for volunteer service.

- Involve parent volunteers in planning the event and leading the activities. This gives parents a first-hand look at the curriculum and makes the planning more manageable. Parents who are not comfortable leading activities can help with registration, shop for supplies, arrange for food, and babysit.

- Advertise. Send home fliers, have students make invitations for their parents, feature articles in school newsletters, put up posters.

- Offer rewards for coming, such as packages of manipulatives or math games that can be played at home. Offer a reward to the class that has the highest attendance.

- Provide food. Find local sponsors or ask the parent organization for donations of food or beverages.
- Have a raffle. Items can be donated by local businesses. Include information about the raffle in the flyer. Math trade books and gift certificates make great prizes.
- Be sure to try the activities yourself before leading them.
- Use manipulatives in the activities so parents can see how their children use them for meaningful math activities.
- Use one or more of the math facts games to illustrate one way to engage students in practicing math facts.
- Send home a packet of games so families can continue to play at home.
- Hand out an evaluation form to help plan for future programs.
- Have a math day, instead of math night. Parents can visit their children's math classes and stay for lunch. Or set up math stations around the school and have students as tour guides.

Content Note

Getting the most from your work with parents
Just as teachers ask students to reflect on their learning, be sure to ask parents what they learned from any *Math Trailblazers*-related parent activities. Invite parents to think about a question as the final activity. This can help provide insights into what parents have learned, but also provide feedback for the next parent session.

Here are some additional tips for programs that use a carnival or classroom rotation format:

- Hand out "passports." Ask families to get "stamped" at each station and enter their completed passports in a prize drawing.
- If you want participants to spend equal amounts of time at each station, then plan a second activity or open-ended task at short stations.
- Include stations that feature brief sessions on various aspects of *Math Trailblazers,* for example, how to use strategies to learn math facts, the TIMS Laboratory Method, and so on.

Other Resources for Planning Math Nights
- *Family Math* is an excellent resource for planning a math program for families. It describes stimulating math games and activities for a series of classes in which parents and children participate together. Included are an early childhood book and a K–8 book, and translations into Spanish. The goals of *Family Math* complement the goals of *Math Trailblazers* and as a result, parents who participate in *Family Math* are likely to have a good understanding of the approach used in *Math Trailblazers.* Whether you plan a one-night event to introduce *Math Trailblazers* or a longer series of classes, *Family Math* gives practical advice to help you plan. It also has useful handouts on topics such as math and careers that are interesting to families. For more information about the program, including training for Family Math workshop leaders, or to order a book, contact:

Family Math
Lawrence Hall of Science
University of California at Berkeley
Berkeley, CA 94720-5200
www.lhs.berkeley.edu/equals

- As part of their continued professional development and support for *Math Trailblazers* users, Kendall/Hunt Publishing Company offers assistance in planning math nights tailored to the needs of your school. You may contact them at 1-800-542-6657.

Presentations to Parents

Since the *Math Trailblazers* program is different from what is familiar to most parents and grandparents, curriculum presentations and the reasons your school selected it can help build support. These range from formal presentations at district-wide or school-wide meetings to less formal discussions at classroom parent nights. Some schools hold monthly meetings that focus on different grade levels or different topics. Others schedule one district-wide or school-wide presentation that gives an overview of the program. Suggestions of topics to include in a presentation are discussed below. Additional resources for preparing your presentation are at the end of this section.

> **Suggested Topics for a Parent Presentation**
> - Description of *Math Trailblazers*
> - Your District's Implementation
> - A Closer Look
> - Computation and Math Facts in *Math Trailblazers*

Description of *Math Trailblazers*

The following are ways to describe *Math Trailblazers*. For further elaboration, see the Foundations section.

- *Math Trailblazers* is a *Standards*-based curriculum. It follows the recommendations of the *Principles and Standards for School Mathematics,* developed by the National Council of Teachers of Mathematics (NCTM, 2000) to improve the teaching and learning of mathematics. These recommendations outline a vision for school mathematics that includes:
  - a mathematically challenging curriculum that covers a broad range of mathematical content;
  - a strong focus on engaging students in mathematical problem solving;
  - instruction that is conceptually oriented and stresses thinking, reasoning, and the application of appropriate uses of calculators and computers; and
  - a strong commitment to promoting success in mathematics among all students—not only those who traditionally do well.

- *Math Trailblazers* is a research-based curriculum. The first edition was the result of more than six years of work by the Teaching Integrated Math and Science Project (TIMS) at the University of Illinois at Chicago, including extensive pilot- and field-testing of the materials. In developing *Math Trailblazers,* the authors drew upon research findings from a wide variety of sources, as well as from the broad experiences of the authoring group, which included mathematicians, scientists, and former teachers. The National Science Foundation funded development of *Math Trailblazers* and has continued to support research on the impact of *Math Trailblazers* on student achievement and research-based development of revised editions.

- *Math Trailblazers* is a problem-solving curriculum. A fundamental principle is that mathematics is best learned through active involvement in solving real problems. Problem solving in *Math Trailblazers* is not a distinct topic, but one that permeates the entire program, providing a context for students to apply the mathematics they know and learn new

> *Since the* Math Trailblazers *program is different from what parents and grandparents are familiar with, presentations about the curriculum and the reasons your school selected it can help build support.*

mathematics. For example, in a third grade laboratory experiment, *The Better "Picker Upper,"* students investigate which paper towel is more absorbent. They explore the absorbency of various brands of paper towels by dropping water onto each and comparing the areas of the resulting spots. In the process, they learn about area, fractions, averaging, and computation. As students work on problems such as these, they develop skills, procedures, and concepts.

• *Math Trailblazers* is a full mathematics curriculum, with a focus on science and language arts. It uses science as a context for much of the problem solving built into the program. In Kindergarten students collect and analyze data at least once every week, and in each of grades 1–5, students engage in eight to ten laboratory investigations that serve as a rich source of real-world mathematics problems. In these investigations, students identify variables, draw pictures, take measurements, organize data in tables, graph data, and look for and use patterns—all important mathematics skills that are used by scientists. *Math Trailblazers* also focuses on language arts, with lessons that emphasize reading, writing, and oral communication. Collections of original math-related stories are found in the *Math Trailblazers Adventure Book*. Math trade books are recommended to accompany many lessons.

Your District's Implementation of *Math Trailblazers*

Include some of the following as you discuss your district's implementation:

• **Selection process.** Assure parents that a careful and thoughtful process was used to select the curriculum. Consider inviting a representative from the selection committee to describe the process.

• **Reasons for choosing *Math Trailblazers* over other curricula.** Describe the features of the program that appeal to the selection committee. How does *Math Trailblazers* help meet the goals of your school? If your district pilot-tested the curriculum before adoption, discuss feedback from teachers who have piloted the program. Invite one or more of those teachers to share their experiences.

• **Professional development.** Explain the program your district has in place to assure that teachers are trained to use the curriculum effectively. Describe the professional development opportunities teachers have had or will have to support their implementation.

• **Evidence of success.** If your district has used the program for a few years, describe teacher and student experiences with it. If you are new to the program, report on some of the experiences of other districts. Information on the success of *Math Trailblazers* around the country is available on the Kendall/Hunt web site, http://www.kendallhunt.com/mtb3.

• **Examples of what students are doing.** A good way to communicate to families that their children are learning more than just computational skills is to show examples of student work. Pick samples that illustrate how students solve complex multistep problems.

A Closer Look at *Math Trailblazers*

To help parents understand some of the strengths of *Math Trailblazers,* show them examples of specific lessons. If possible, ask them to solve a problem or play a game so they can experience firsthand the problem-solving approach to *Math Trailblazers.* Debrief from the activity in the way that you would with students. Ask parents to reflect on the lesson's content, how it compares to their experience, and what this means in terms of opportunities for students to learn. Consider using student work to show the kinds of problems *Math Trailblazers* students solve. Use work collected from your own students or samples available in the *Math Trailblazers* support material.

One source of student work examples is a component of *Math Trailblazers* called the Teacher Enhancement Resource Modules (TERMs). The TERMs were designed to help staff developers assemble workshops for teachers, but portions can also be presented to parents. They contain a guide for presenters with blackline masters, explanatory text, and discussion questions and answers. A set of TERMs is usually available in each district. Check with your principal or district office or call Kendall/Hunt at 1-800-KH-Books.

Most TERMs also include videos showing *Math Trailblazers* teachers and students engaged in activities from the curriculum. These streaming videos are available through the Kendall/Hunt website, mymathtrailblazers.com. Check with your principal or district office for information on how to access these resources.

Another source of appropriate sample student work, video, and explanatory text are from a grade 2 activity, *Measuring Volume.* This source contains a selection of relevant text, blackline masters, and the video you can use to develop a presentation for parents. These materials are available on the web, www.mymathtrailblazers.com.

The following are modules that can be adapted for use with parents (found in TERMS Set #1):

- **Why Reform?**

  This TERM presents information to introduce *Standards*-based mathematics. It includes a video *How Many in the Bag?* that shows students talking with their partners about their solutions to subtraction problems that arise from pulling handfuls of cubes from a bag. The interaction of the students talking about the problems shows how communication helps students clarify their thinking, correct mistakes, and hear different strategies from fellow students.

  A selection of text, blackline masters, and the video of one TERM, *Why Reform?* is available for download at www.mymathtrailblazers.com

- **Operations: Meaning, Invention, Efficiency, Power**

  Use this TERM to help guide the discussion of how the concept of division develops across grades K–5 and to describe the *Math Trailblazers* philosophy of computation. This TERM also shows how this philosophy applies to the development of other operations and to teaching the math facts.

- **Area: A Look Across the Grades**

  Use the *Area* TERM to help parents see how science is a rich context for applying and learning mathematics. This TERM includes representative area activities from each grade to show growth in mathematics and development of the concept of area through the grades.

- **Computation and Math Facts in *Math Trailblazers***

  Many parents think of computation when they think of mathematics, so it is natural for them to be curious about the way *Math Trailblazers* teaches computation. Explain that a balanced approach fosters the development of both mathematical concepts and skills. The following points might be useful in talking with parents about computation and basic math facts.

1. Computation. In today's world, students compute using paper-and-pencil algorithms, calculators, and mental arithmetic. They need to get exact answers to problems as well as make and recognize reasonable estimates. *Math Trailblazers* helps students develop efficient and accurate methods for computation with the four basic operations. The treatment of each operation proceeds in the following stages:

   - Developing meaning for the operation

   - Inventing procedures for solving problems

   - Becoming more efficient at carrying out procedures

   - Developing mathematical power

2. "Mathematical power" means that students understand when to apply the operation and how to use varied computational methods to solve problems. Students practice using the operations in activities, games, and laboratory investigations. More practice is provided in the Daily Practice and Problems in Grades 1–5 and in the Home Practice in Grades 3–5. Flexible thinking and mathematical power are our goals. The above computation stages are discussed more thoroughly in the Math Facts and Whole-Number Operations section.

3. The paper-and-pencil algorithms for multiplication and long division taught in *Math Trailblazers* are probably somewhat different from those that parents learned in school. We introduce the "all-partials method" for multiplication first since many children find it easier to learn. Then we introduce the more efficient "compact method," the algorithm traditionally taught. (See Figure 3.)

All-Partials Method	Compact Method
15	15
× 22	× 22
10 (2 × 5)	30 (2 × 15)
20 (2 × 10)	+ 300 (20 × 15)
100 (20 × 5)	330
+ 200 (20 × 10)	
330	

Figure 3: *Paper and pencil algorithms for multiplication*

For division, we teach the "forgiving method" because many students find it easier to learn than the traditional method. While this method involves making estimates about the quotient, as does the traditional method, the forgiving method encourages the use of "easy" numbers, such as division by 10 or 100 in the estimates. The forgiving method also allows underestimates so it doesn't involve as much erasing and re-calculating as done by some children when using the traditional method. In the case where the highest possible estimate is made, the two methods are essentially the same. (See Figure 4.) Parent information sheets that describe the multiplication and division algorithms used in *Math Trailblazers* are at the end of this section.

Forgiving Method		**Traditional Method**
$\begin{array}{r} 335 \\ 5\overline{)1675} \\ -1500 \\ \hline 175 \\ -150 \\ \hline 25 \\ -25 \\ \hline 0 \end{array}$	300 (estimate quotient 1675 ÷ 5) 30 (estimate quotient 175 ÷ 5) 5 (25 ÷ 5) $\overline{}$ 335	$\begin{array}{r} 335 \\ 5\overline{)1675} \\ -15 \\ \hline 17 \\ -15 \\ \hline 25 \\ -25 \\ \hline 0 \end{array}$

Figure 4: *Paper and pencil algorithms for division*

4. Math Facts. The goal of the *Math Trailblazers* math facts program is for students to learn the basic facts efficiently, gain fluency with their use, and retain that fluency over time. A large body of research supports an approach that is built on a foundation of work with strategies and concepts. This leads not only to more effective learning and better retention, but also to the development of mental math skills.

The *Math Trailblazers* math facts program is characterized by the elements below. These are summarized in the *Math Facts Philosophy* Blackline master at the end of this section.
- Early emphasis on problem solving
- Use of strategies to find facts and the de-emphasis of rote work
- Gradual and systematic introduction of the facts
- Ongoing practice
- Appropriate assessment
- Facts are not gatekeepers
- Multiyear approach

As you discuss the math facts program, give parents a few examples of math fact strategies such as the subtraction strategies of "counting up" and "using a ten." Other strategies are discussed in the *Math Facts* Tutor. This tutor is available to parents on the Kendall/Hunt website, as are several other TIMS Tutors.

Other Resources for Planning Your Presentation

The *Family* section of the Kendall/Hunt Website http://www.mymath trailblazers.com has several links to documents that can help you plan your presentation. Here are a few:

- *An Introduction for Families* includes answers to the following questions:
  What is in the *Math Trailblazers* curriculum?
  What is a *Math Trailblazers* classroom like?
  What connections does *Math Trailblazers* make with other school subjects?
  Why is my child using calculators with *Math Trailblazers?*
  How can parents talk with their children about math?

- *Frequently Asked Questions* includes answers to the following questions:
  How is *Math Trailblazers* different from other mathematics curricula?
  What is the opinion of the scientific community regarding the standards set by the National Council of Teachers of Mathematics?
  What science does *Math Trailblazers* include?
  How does *Math Trailblazers* integrate mathematics with other content areas?
  What kind of assessment does *Math Trailblazers* use?
  Does *Math Trailblazers* make use of collaborative learning?
  Can *Math Trailblazers* facilitate teaching children with learning styles and ability levels in a heterogeneous classroom?

Additional resources for working with parents include:

Stenmark, Jean Kerr, Virginia Thompson, and Ruth Cossey. *Family Math.* University of California, Lawrence Hall of Science, Berkeley, CA, 1986.

Funkhouser, J.E., and M.R. Gonzales. *Family Involvement in Children's Education: Successful Local Approaches: An Idea Book.* U.S. Department of Education, Washington, DC, 1997. http://www.ed.gov/pubs/FamInvolve/

Shartrand, A.M., H.B. Weiss, H.M. Kreider, and M. Lopez, *New Skills for New Schools: Preparing Teachers in Family Involvement.* Harvard Graduate School of Education, Harvard Family Research Project, Cambridge, 1997. (Available from the U. S. Department of Education http://www.ed.gov/pubs/NewSkills/index.html.)

Mira, A. *A Family's Guide: Fostering your Child's Success in School Mathematics.* National Council of Teachers of Mathematics, Reston, VA, 2005.

National Council of Teachers of Mathematics Families Web page, http://nctm.org/resources/families.aspx

Parent Information Blackline Masters

- Parent Brochure (English and Spanish versions)
- Math Facts Philosophy
- Multiplication Methods in *Math Trailblazers*
- Long Division in *Math Trailblazers*
- Internet Resources for Families of *Math Trailblazers* Students

Math Trailblazers™

A Mathematical Journey Using Science and Language Arts

An Introduction for Families

A TIMS® Curriculum from the University of Illinois at Chicago

Published by Kendall/Hunt Publishing Company

---

math!

Your child will have a lot to share with you about mathematics. Here are some conversation starters to help your child communicate what he or she is doing in mathematics:

☞ What problems did you solve in math today? How did you solve the problems? Are there other ways to solve that same problem?

☞ Did you use any special materials in math today? What were they? How did you use them?

☞ Did you measure anything in school today? What did you measure?

☞ Did you collect data in math today? How did you record the data?

☞ Did you hear a math story today? Please tell me the story.

> "One of the things I've noticed … is that when he [my child] brings home an activity and he brings a measuring tape or something kind of special, he's excited about doing it. The fact that we're involved in the games—he loves that—and he's proud of what he's doing."
>
> **Parent**

You can contact the developers of *Math Trailblazers* at the following address:

 UIC The University of Illinois at Chicago

TIMS Project
Institute for Mathematics and Science Education (M/C 250)
950 South Halsted Street, Room 2075 SEL
Chicago, IL 60607-7019
www.math.uic.edu/IMSE

 KENDALL/HUNT PUBLISHING COMPANY
4050 Westmark Drive   Dubuque, Iowa 52002
www.mathtrailblazers.com

Development of *Math Trailblazers* was supported in part by the National Science Foundation.

Math Trailblazers make with other school subjects?

> this carries over to different subject areas. It's not just isolated to math."
>
> **Teacher**

In *Math Trailblazers*, children learn mathematics, in part, by applying it in many different contexts. This makes mathematics meaningful for students and models the way mathematics is used outside of school.

Science investigations are used often in *Math Trailblazers* to provide a context for learning and applying mathematics. Children design experiments; collect, organize, and graph data; and analyze experimental results in much the same way scientists do. Measurement of length, area, volume, mass, and time is done repeatedly within the context of scientific experiments. This strong connection with science engages students in rich problem-solving activities and introduces students to the tools and methods scientists use.

Math Trailblazers also has many connections with language arts—communication of math ideas in writing and orally is an integral part of every lesson. Children write journal entries, record data, and share ideas. They also read children's books and *Math Trailblazers Adventure Books* that connect with many class lessons. As children communicate their methods for solving problems and justify their answers, they better understand important math concepts. Their writing and other communication skills also improve.

Why is my child using calculators with *Math Trailblazers*?

The calculator is a tool used in appropriate situations to help your child explore number ideas and relationships, solve more complex problems, and explore mathematics on his or her own. The use of calculators is supported by the National Council of Teachers of Mathematics.

The mathematics curriculum being taught in many schools today is very similar to the curriculum that was taught when the parents, grandparents, and even great-grandparents of today's school children attended school. Many of the math skills in that curriculum remain important today. But the world has changed considerably since the time of our grandparents. Advances in technology have created many other essential math skills that your children will need when they complete their formal schooling and enter tomorrow's work force. The National Council of Teachers of Mathematics recognized these needs when, in 1989 and 2000, it made a series of recommendations for updating math instruction in U.S. schools. *Math Trailblazers* was developed to reflect these national recommendations.

Math Trailblazers will prepare students to:

★ know and apply basic math skills;

★ solve problems using many different strategies;

★ be independent thinkers;

★ reason skillfully in diverse situations;

★ effectively communicate solutions to problems and methods for solving them;

★ work alone and in groups to solve problems.

Math Trailblazers was developed and tested over a seven-year period by a team from the Teaching Integrated Mathematics and Science (TIMS) Project at the University of Illinois at Chicago. Using the results of educational research and over 15 years of previous experience in curriculum development, the TIMS Project has written an innovative program that will prepare your children with math skills needed for the 21st century.

curriculum?

Math Trailblazers is a comprehensive curriculum that maintains a balance between the development of math concepts and basic skills. Students apply basic math skills while working on meaningful and challenging tasks. The math content of the traditional math curriculum is studied; but other topics—estimation, geometry, measurement, patterns and relationships, algebra concepts, and statistics and probability—are investigated at an appropriate level in each grade.

The curriculum includes different types of lessons:

Activities—explorations of math concepts and skills that use a variety of tools and methods.

Labs—extended investigations that use a simplified version of the method scientists use.

Daily Practice and Problems—items that provide practice in math skills and concepts.

Games—math games that build familiarity with math skills and concepts.

Adventure Books—illustrated stories that deal with math and science ideas.

Assessments—activities that allow the teacher and student to assess progress.

classroom like?

When you walk into your child's *Math Trailblazers* class, you will probably notice that it does not look like the mathematics classroom you experienced when you were your child's age. Children might be working in groups, rolling cars down ramps, dropping water onto paper towels, or pulling jellybean samples from bags. As they work, children discuss different ways to solve problems. The room is filled with a feeling of excitement and discovery.

In a *Math Trailblazers* classroom, children are:

☆ learning mathematics by using it to solve many different kinds of problems;

☆ drawing on their own experiences and working with real-world problems;

☆ using concrete objects to understand abstract mathematical concepts;

☆ communicating mathematical ideas to their peers and teacher;

☆ gaining confidence in mathematics and developing an "I can do it" feeling.

Math Trailblazers™*

Una Aventura en Matemáticas usando Ciencias y el Arte de Lenguaje

Una Introducción para Familias

Desarrollando por el Proyecto de TIMS—Teaching Integrated Mathematics and Science— (Integrando la Enseñanza de las Matemáticas y de las Ciencias) de la Universidad de Illinois en Chicago

Publicado por Kendall/Hunt Publishing Company

* Abriendo un camino de matemáticas

---

con otras materias escolares ?

En *Math Trailblazers*, los estudiantes aprenden matemáticas, en parte, aplicandolo a diversas situaciones. De esta manera las matemáticas se hacen interesantes y adquieren sentido.

Investigaciones científicas en *Math Trailblazers* proveen la oportunidad frecuente de la aplicación de las matemáticas. Los estudiantes diseñan experimentos; acumulan y organizan datos; hacen gráficas de datos; y analizan los resultados de los experimentos en una manera semejante a lo que hacen los científicos. Se hacen mediciónes de longitud, area, volumen, masa, y tiempo como parte de experimentos científicos. Esta fuerte conexión con la ciencia hace que los estudiantes resuelvan problemas como "científicos," usando métodos y herramientas de la ciencias.

Math Trailblazers también tiene muchas conexiones con el arte de lenguaje. La comunicación de ideas en matemáticas—a través de escribir, hablar, y dibujar—es una parte integral de cada lección. Los estudiantes escriben en sus diarios, registran datos, y comparten ideas. Ellos también leen libros infantiles y "libros de aventuras" que se conectan con muchas lecciónes. Los estudiantes mejoran en su entendimiento de conceptos matemáticos al comunicar sus métodos de resolver problemas y explicar sus respuestas. Sus habilidades en escribir y comunicar también mejoran.

¿Por qué mi hijo/a está usando calculadoras en *Math Trailblazers*?

Las calculadoras son instrumentos usados para ayudar a su hijo/a a investigar ideas con números y sus relaciones, resolver problemas complejos, y explorar la matemática. El uso de estas herramientas es recomendado por el Concejo Nacional de Maestros de Matemáticas.

---

hacer ?

Su hijo/a tendrá mucho que compartir con usted acerca de matemáticas. Aquí hay algunos temas para iniciar conversaciones que ayudarán a su hijo/a a que él o ella comunique lo que esté haciendo en matemáticas.

☞ ¿Qué problema resolviste el día de hoy en tu clase de matemáticas? ¿Cómo lo resolviste? ¿Hay alguna otra forma de resolver ese mismo problema?

☞ ¿Utilizaste algúnos materiales especiales en tu clase de matemáticas? ¿Qué eran? ¿Cómo los usaste?

☞ ¿Mediste hoy algo en la escuela? ¿Qué fue lo que mediste?

☞ ¿Acumulaste algunos datos en matemáticas? ¿Cómo registraste esos datos?

☞ ¿Escuchaste alguna historia en matemáticas? Por favor cuéntame la historia.

> "Una de las cosas que he notado… es que cuando él [mi hijo] trae una actividad a la casa y trae una cinta métrica o algo especial, está emocionado para hacerlo. El hecho que nosotros estamos enredados en los juegos—le encanta—y está orgulloso de lo que está haciendo."
>
> **Un padre de familia**

Se puede comunicar con los diseñadores de *Math Trailblazers* a la siguiente dirección:

The University of Illinois at Chicago

TIMS Project
Institute for Mathematics and Science Education (M/C 250)
950 South Halsted Street, Room 2075 SEL
Chicago, IL 60607-7019
www.math.uic.edu/IMSE

KENDALL/HUNT PUBLISHING COMPANY
4050 Westmark Drive   Dubuque,   Iowa   52002
www.mathtrailblazers.com

El desarrollo de *Math Trailblazers* fue ayudado en parte por la National Science Foundation.

Los programas de matemáticas que se encuentran hoy día en muchas escuelas son muy semejantes a las classes que tenían los padres, abuelos, y aún bisabuelos de los estudiantes de hoy. Mucha del material de esos programas todavía se necesita hoy. Pero el mundo ha cambiado desde el tiempo de nuestros abuelos. Avances en tecnología han creado la necesidad de desarrollar otras técnicas especiales que sus hijos necesitarán en el mundo de trabajo del futuro. El Concejo Nacional de Maestros de Matemáticas reconoció estas necesidades cuando hizo una serie de recomendaciones para mejorar la enseñanza de matemáticas en las escuelas de los Estados Unidos. Hemos desarrollado el programa *Math Trailblazers* para incorporar esas recomendaciones nacionales.

Math Trailblazers preparará estudiantes para:

★ aprender y usar técnicas básicas en matemáticas;

★ resolver problemas usando varias estrategias diferentes;

★ pensar independientemente;

★ razonar con habilidad en diversas situaciones;

★ comunicar efectivamente tanto las soluciones como los métodos;

★ resolver problemas trabajando solos y en grupos.

El programa *Math Trailblazers* fue desarrollado y ensayado por un equipo del Proyecto de TIMS—Teaching Integrated Mathematics and Science—(Integrando la Enseñanza de las Matemáticas y de las Ciencias) de la Universidad de Illinois en Chicago. Han creado un programa innovativo que proveerá a sus hijos con los bases matemáticos necesarios para poder competir en el campo del trabajo en el Siglo XXI.

El programa *Math Trailblazers* es un programa integral que mantiene un balance entre el desarrollo de los conceptos y las técnicas básicas de matemáticas. Los estudiantes usan las técnicas básicas mientras están trabajando con problemas interesantes y estimulantes. Se estudian los tópicos matemáticos de un programa tradicional; pero también se investigan otras materias—estimación, geometría, medición, patrones y relaciones, conceptos de álgebra, estadística y probabilidad—en un nivel apropiado para los niños.

El programa contiene varios tipos de lecciones:

Actividades—exploraciones de conceptos matemáticos y técnicas usando diferentes herramientas y métodos.

Laboratorios—investigaciones que usan una versión simplificada del método que los científicos usan.

Prácticas y Problemas Diarios—problemas breves que proveen práctica con técnicas y conceptos matemáticos.

Juegos—juegos matemáticos que estimulan familiaridad con técnicas y conceptos matemáticos.

Libros de Aventuras—historietas ilustradas que tratan con conceptos de las ciencias y matemáticas.

Evaluaciones—actividades que permiten al maestro y a los estudiantes evaluar el progreso.

> **"Cuando mi hija mayor comenzó, no tenía confianza con las matemáticas. Y ahora que ha tenido *Math Trailblazers*, dice que es buena en las matemáticas. Eso me hace sentir bien."**
>
> **Un padre de familia**

Trailblazers!

Si usted entra a un salón de clases *Math Trailblazers*, probablemente notará que no se parece al que usted asistía cuando tenía esa edad. En ese salón, los niños pueden estar trabajando en grupos, poniendo gotas de agua a toallas de papel, o analizando muestras de confites. Mientras los estudiantes trabajan, ellos discuten diferentes formas para resolver los problemas matemáticos. Se percibe en clases *Math Trailblazers* los sentimientos y la emoción de descubrimiento matemático.

En un salón de estas clases los alumnos están:

☆ aprendiendo matemáticas en la resolución de problemas;

☆ usando experiencias propias y trabajando con problemas verdaderas;

☆ usando objetos concretos para entender conceptos matemáticos abstractos;

☆ comunicando sus ideas de matemáticas a sus compañeros y maestros;

☆ adquiriendo confianza en las matemáticas y desarrollando un sentimiento de, "Yo sí lo puedo hacer."

> **"Me encanta llegar a una clase donde los estudiantes están recolectando datos. Algunos están en el piso midiendo esto o trabajando con papel o haciendo preguntas. Es tan emocionante ver los niños enredados en este tipo de descubrimiento de matemáticas."**
>
> **Director de escuela primaria**

Math Facts Philosophy

The goal of the math facts strand in *Math Trailblazers* is for students to learn basic facts efficiently, gain fluency with their use, and retain that fluency over time. A large body of research supports an approach in which students develop strategies for figuring out the facts rather than relying solely on rote memorization. This not only leads to more effective learning and better retention, but also to the development of mental math skills. Therefore, the teaching of the basic facts in *Math Trailblazers* is characterized by the following elements:

Use of Strategies. Students first approach the basic facts as problems to solve rather than as facts to memorize. We encourage the use of strategies to find facts, so students become confident that they can find answers to fact problems they do not immediately recall. In this way, students learn that math is more than memorizing facts and rules that "you either get or you don't." (For information on common math fact strategies, see the *Math Facts* Tutor on the *Just for Math Trailblazers Families* page of the Kendall Hunt website http://kendallhunt.com. Click on "K–12," then "Just For Families," then "Math Trailblazers Families." Then scroll down to the list of TIMS Tutors.)

Distributed Facts Practice. Students study small groups of facts they found using similar strategies. They review the facts as they use them to solve problems in labs, activities, and games. In Grades 2–5, students are given flash cards to study each group of facts at home.

Appropriate Assessment. Teachers assess students' knowledge of the facts through observations as they work on activities, labs, and games as well as through the appropriate use of written tests and quizzes. Quizzes follow the study of small groups of facts organized around specific strategies. In Grades 2–5, students take inventory tests of facts at the end of each semester. In grades 3–5, each student records his or her progress on *Facts I Know* charts and determines which facts he or she needs to study.

A Multiyear Approach. In Grades 1 and 2, the curriculum emphasizes strategies that enable students to develop fluency with the addition and subtraction facts. In Grade 3, students gain fluency with the multiplication facts while reviewing the addition and subtraction facts. In Grade 4, the addition and subtraction facts are checked, the multiplication facts are reviewed, and students develop fluency with the division facts. In Grade 5, the multiplication and division facts are systematically reviewed and assessed.

Facts Will Not Act as Gatekeepers. Use of strategies and calculators allows students to continue to work on interesting problems and experiments while learning the facts. Thus students are not prevented from learning more complex mathematics because they do not have quick recall of the facts.

Multiplication Methods in *Math Trailblazers*

As your child learns paper-and-pencil multiplication in *Math Trailblazers,* he or she is introduced to more than one method. The **all-partials method** is introduced first since many children find it easier to learn. Then the more efficient **compact method**—the method traditionally taught in schools in the United States—is introduced. After children work with both methods, they choose which is most comfortable for them. We present both methods below so you will be familiar with them.

Both methods are based on the same idea, but the recording is different. In the all-partials method, every step is written down. In the compact method, some steps are not recorded.

Example 1. Compute 6×73.

In both methods, we break 73 into two parts: $73 = 3 + 70$. Then we multiply each part by 6 and add:

$$6 \times 73 = 6 \times 3 + 6 \times 70.$$

All-Partials Method	Compact Method
In this method, every step is written down on separate lines. $\begin{array}{r} 73 \\ \times\,6 \\ \hline 18 \\ 420 \\ \hline 438 \end{array}$ (This is 6×3) (This is 6×70) The partial products are recorded in the lines under the multiplication sign, then the lines are added.	In this method, some steps are combined and the answer is recorded on one line. $\begin{array}{r} {}^{1} \\ 73 \\ \times\,6 \\ \hline 438 \end{array}$ (This is $6 \times 3 + 6 \times 70$) The partial products are added as they are recorded: First compute $6 \times 3 = 18$; then write the 8 in the ones' column and carry the 1 into the tens' column (some people write down the carry, others just remember it). Next, compute 6×7 tens $= 42$ tens. Add the 1 that was carried to get 43 tens. Write the 3 in the tens' column and the 4 in the hundreds' column.

Multiplication Methods in *Math Trailblazers (continued)*

Example 2: Compute 73×46.

Again, both methods involve breaking the numbers into two parts and multiplying. Since $46 = 6 + 40$, the product is

$$73 \times 46 = 73 \times (6 + 40)$$
$$= 73 \times 6 + 73 \times 40$$
$$= (6 \times 3 + 6 \times 70) + (40 \times 3 + 40 \times 70)$$

All-Partials Method	**Compact Method**
In this method, every step is written down on separate lines.	In this method, some steps are combined and recorded on one line.
| ```
   73
 × 46
─────
   18   (6 × 3)
  420   (6 × 70)
  120   (40 × 3)
 2800   (40 × 70)
─────
 3358
``` | ```
   73
 × 46
─────
  438   (This is 6 × 73)
 2920   (This is 40 × 73 or 4 tens × 73)
─────
 3358
``` |
The partial products are recorded in the rows under the multiplication sign, then the rows are added.	For the first line, compute $6 \times 73 = 438$ as in Example 1.
	For the second line, compute $40 \times 73 = 2920$. (Some people omit the 0 in the ones' column because 2920 is 292 tens and no ones. In this case, be sure nothing is written in the ones' column.)
	Here are the details for the second line:
	$40 \times 73 = 40 \times 3 + 40 \times 70$. First compute $40 \times 3 = 120$; record the 20 tens by writing 2 in the tens' column and 0 in the ones' column, then carry the 1 into the hundreds' column (you can write the carry or just remember it). Next, compute $40 \times 70 = 2800$. That is 28 hundreds. Add the one 1 hundred that was carried to get 29 hundreds. Write the 9 in the hundreds' column and the 2 in the thousands' column.
	Finally, add both lines.

Long Division in *Math Trailblazers*

In *Math Trailblazers,* your child will learn a long division method that may be different from the method you learned. We teach the **forgiving method** because many students find it easier to learn than the traditional method. Both methods make estimates about the quotient (the answer to the division problem), but the forgiving method allows underestimates, so it doesn't involve as much erasing and recalculating as the traditional method sometimes does.

As an example, let's divide 95 by 3. Think of dividing 95 objects such as marbles into groups of 3. How many groups will there be? (Or, think of putting the objects into 3 groups. How many will be in each group?)

First, estimate the answer. A good estimate would be 30, but lower numbers would work too. Suppose we choose 20. Then, since $3 \times 20 = 60$, we have taken care of 60 marbles. Subtract 60 from 95 and record the estimate to the right of the problem.

$$
\begin{array}{r}
3\overline{)95} \\
-\ 60 \quad\ \ \ \ 20 \\
\hline
35
\end{array}
$$

Now divide the remaining 35 marbles by 3. Let's estimate that $35 \div 3$ is about 10. Since $3 \times 10 = 30$, write

$$
\begin{array}{r}
3\overline{)95} \\
-\ 60 \quad\ \ \ \ 20 \\
\hline
35 \\
-\ 30 \quad\ \ \ \ 10 \\
\hline
5
\end{array}
$$

Since 3 "goes into" 5 one time, write

$$
\begin{array}{r}
3\overline{)95} \\
-\ 60 \quad\ \ \ \ 20 \\
\hline
35 \\
-\ 30 \quad\ \ \ \ 10 \\
\hline
5 \\
-\ 3 \quad\ \ \ \ 1 \\
\hline
2
\end{array}
$$

Since 3 does not divide 2, there are 2 marbles left over. This is the remainder. Add up the number of 3s we took away: $20 + 10 + 1 = 31$. Thus, 95 divided by 3 is 31 with remainder 2. We write this on top of the problem, as in the traditional division method.

$$
\begin{array}{r}
31\,R2 \\
3\overline{)95} \\
-\ 60 \quad\ \ \ \ 20 \\
\hline
35 \\
-\ 30 \quad\ \ \ \ 10 \\
\hline
5 \\
-\ 3 \quad\ \ \ \ 1 \\
\hline
2 \quad\ \ \ \ 31
\end{array}
$$

As students become familiar with the forgiving method, they make better estimates to keep the number of steps at a minimum. Below is another way to do this problem using the forgiving method. Note that this time, making the highest possible estimates (without overestimating) results in the same number of steps as the traditional method. If the highest estimate is made each time, the two methods are essentially the same.

$$
\begin{array}{r}
31\,R2 \\
3\overline{)95} \\
-\ 90 \quad\ \ \ \ 30 \\
\hline
5 \\
-\ 3 \quad\ \ \ \ 1 \\
\hline
2 \quad\ \ \ \ 31
\end{array}
$$

The forgiving method allows students to underestimate as they develop their estimation skills. But, although this method forgives underestimates, overestimates are not forgiven. When students overestimate, they have to erase, just as with the traditional method.

This method can be extended to solve problems with multidigit divisors. However, *Math Traiblazers* students usually use calculators for such problems.

Internet Resources for Families of *Math Trailblazers* Students

Here are several websites that can help families support their children's learning of Mathematics:

Mymathtrailblazers.com Family section

The publisher of *Math Trailblazers,* Kendall/Hunt, maintains a website at http://www.mymathtrailblazers.com to help the families of children using *Math Trailblazers* understand the curriculum. It contains an introduction to the program and a discussion of its research basis, answers to frequently asked questions, glossaries, TIMS Tutors (which provide an in-depth exploration of the mathematical concepts and ideas behind *Math Trailblazers*), homework help, and recommended software and literature lists. Contact Kendall/Hunt regarding granting families access to this site.

NCTM Families Web page

http://nctm.org/resources/families.aspx

The National Council of Teachers of Mathematics (NCTM) Families Web page includes lessons and activities, resources, links to other family sites, as well as brochures that answer questions such as

Why does my child's math look different from the math I remember?

What can I do to make sure my child succeeds in math?

Math homework is due tomorrow—how can I help?

NCTM Illuminations

http://illuminations.nctm.org

This site contains a library of online math activities and interactive tools for students to use to explore, learn, and apply mathematics in the classroom and at home. It also has links to hundreds of online resources that an editorial panel has reviewed and rated as exemplary.

The Math Forum

http://mathforum.org

The Math Forum is a very broad-based website maintained by Drexel University. It has such features as Ask Dr. Math, where students can ask mathematical questions, and an extensive mathematics resource library for students in elementary school through graduate school. Other features include discussion groups, a collection of good problems, teacher resources, and information on issues in mathematics education.

National Library of Virtual Manipulatives for Interactive Mathematics

http://nlvm.usu.edu

Utah State University developed and maintains this web site. It includes an extensive collection of virtual manipulatives and accompanying activities. Students can work interactively with geoboards, pattern blocks, tangrams, base-ten pieces, balance scales, and other materials. This provides the opportunity to work with materials that are perhaps not otherwise available.

Helping Your Child Learn Mathematics http://www.ed.gov/parents/academic/help/math/index.html

This is a downloadable booklet available at the website of the Department of Education that contains "fun activities that parents can use with their children from preschool age through grade 5 to strengthen their math skills and build strong positive attitudes toward math."

Figure This!

http://www.figurethis.org

The Family Corner of the Figure This! website provides math challenges for families. It has downloadable brochures on topics such as Families and School, Families and Math, Families and Homework, and Math and Literature, as well as recommended books. The focus is on families of middle-school students, but much of the advice is appropriate for families of elementary-school students as well.

Manipulatives List

The Manipulatives List outlines all manufactured manipulatives and other materials needed to implement *Math Trailblazers* successfully.

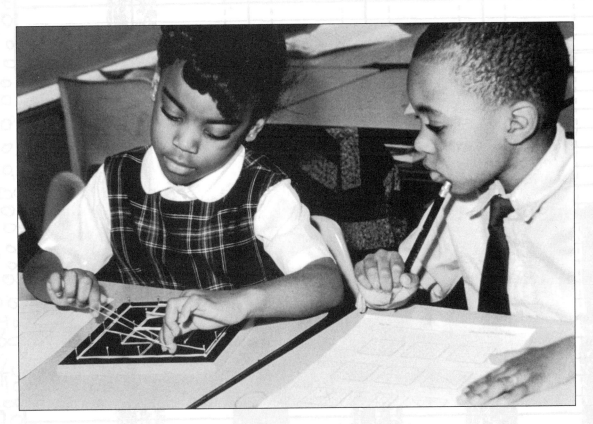

Students explore shapes using geoboards.

Manipulatives List

Following are the manipulatives for fourth grade. There are several categories of manipulatives listed here:

Manufactured Manipulatives: a list of each of the manipulatives needed to implement fully the *Math Trailblazers* curriculum. Many of these manipulatives may be available already in your classroom or school.

Manufactured manipulatives can be purchased:

- in grade-level complete kits from Kendall/Hunt Publishing Company;
- as a customized kit from Kendall/Hunt;
- or individually for your specific needs.

Please contact Kendall/Hunt directly for additional information.

Other materials are needed for the successful implementation of the *Math Trailblazers* curriculum for the entire year. These materials are listed in three categories to aid in planning for the year:

- **Consumables** (one-use items such as beans, paper towels, etc.)
- **Collectibles** (throwaway items such as magazines, egg cartons, jars, etc.)
- **School Supplies** (items usually available in classrooms such as tape, glue, markers, etc.)

Manipulatives for *Math Trailblazers* Grade 4

Manufactured Manipulative, Classroom	Number per Group	TOTAL per Classroom of 30 Students
balls, Super	1 per group of 3	10
balls, tennis	1 per group of 3	10
base-ten pieces, set consists of: 2 packs (10 cm × 10 cm × 10 cm), 14 flats (10 cm × 10 cm × 1 cm), 30 skinnies (10 cm × 1 cm × 1 cm), 50 bits (1 cm × 1 cm × 1 cm)	1 set per student pair	15 sets
*calculator	1 per student	30
connecting cubes, (Hex-a-Link™, Multilink®, or equivalent)	40 per student	1200
connecting cubes, centimeter	75 per group of 3	750
eyedropper, plastic	1 per student pair	15
geometric wooden solids	1 set per classroom	1
graduated cylinder, 100-cc	1 per student pair	15
graduated cylinder, 250-cc	1 per student pair	15
gram masses, consists of: 10 5-gram masses 5 10-gram masses 2 20-gram masses 10 1-gram masses	1 set per student pair	15 sets

*Students need a calculator with addition, subtraction, multiplication, and division with a constant operation function and Algebraic Operating System (AOS). We recommend using a calculator that has the following keys: parentheses, change sign ($+/-$), and square root.

Manipulatives for *Math Trailblazers* Grade 4 (*Continued*)

Manufactured Manipulative, Classroom	Number per Group	TOTAL per Classroom of 30 Students
marbles, standard size	25 per student pair	375
marbles, large (approx. $\frac{3}{4}$ inch)	12 per student pair	180
number cubes	1 per group of 3	10
overhead base-ten pieces	1 set	1 set
overhead square-inch tiles, colored	1 set	1 set
pattern blocks, fraction (1 cm or $\frac{1}{2}$ cm to match size of standard pattern blocks used)	6 brown trapezoids per student pair	90 brown trapezoids
pattern blocks, standard	10 green triangles per student pair	150 green triangles
	10 blue rhombuses per student pair	150 blue rhombuses
	2–3 yellow hexagons per student pair	30–45 yellow hexagons
	and 6 red trapezoids per student pair	90 red trapezoids
protractors	1 per student	30
ruler, cm/inch, transparent	1 per student	30
spinners, clear plastic	1 per student pair	15
square-inch tiles, colored	60 per group of 3	600
standard masses (See gram masses.)		
two-pan balance	1 per student pair	15
wood or metal incline (at least 50 cm long)	1 per group of 3	10
yardsticks/metersticks	1 per student	30
*wall chart, laminated: data tables & graph	1 set per classroom	1

*The wall chart is available through Kendall/Hunt Publishing Company 1-800-228-0810.

Additional Materials or Equipment Needed
for *Math Trailblazers* Grade 4

Collectible Materials	Number Required
bags, paper lunch	1 per student
bags, resealable	1 per student
boxes, small cardboard and cereal	1 per student
containers to hold water, marbles, etc.	1 per student
jars, clear; large and small	1 small and 1 large
milk cartons or small containers for planting	1 per student
newspapers or magazines	1 per student
roller skates or toy cars	1 per student group
small objects to measure mass	2–3 per student group
string or twine	1 ball
wire	1 24-inch piece per student group

Consumable Materials	Number Required
adding machine tape	8 rolls
beans: red, navy, or pinto	1 handful per student
paper towels	2 rolls
potting soil	1 cup per student
seeds, lima or sunflower	2 per student

School Supplies	Number Required
construction paper	25 sheets
easel paper	16 sheets
envelopes	15–20 per student
file rack	1 per classroom
index cards, 3 inch by 5 inch	1 per student
manila folders	2 per student

The following supplies are used throughout the year:

colored pencils, crayons, or markers

glue

hole puncher

masking tape

overhead markers

paper clips

scissors

Scotch tape

self-adhesive notes

transparencies

Literature List

The Literature List provides suggested titles and recommended reading of commercially available trade books which are used in many *Math Trailblazers* lessons.

Students connect math and literature by reading a trade book.

Literature List

Literature List

Many lesson guides in *Math Trailblazers* suggest the use of commercially available trade books. A listing of these trade books is provided here. These books can be used to extend or enhance a particular lesson.

Unit 1—Data About Us

- Bishop, Claire Huchet, and Kurt Wiese. *The Five Chinese Brothers.* Coward-McCann, Inc., New York, 1999. (Lesson 4)
- Glass, Dr. Julie. *Fly on the Ceiling.* Random House Books for Young Readers, New York, 1998.
- "How Six Men Traveled Through the Wide World" and "The Six Servants" from *The Complete Grimm's Fairy Tales.* Introduction by Padraic Colum and commentary by Joseph Campbell. Pantheon Books, Inc., New York, 1976. (Lesson 4)
- "How Six Men Traveled Through the Wide World" in Andrew Lang (Ed.) *The Yellow Fairy Book.* Dover Publications Inc., New York, 1979. (Lesson 4)
- Mahy, Margaret, and Jean and Mon-Sien Tsaug. *The Seven Chinese Brothers.* Scholastic Inc., New York, 1992. (Lesson 4)
- Nagda, Ann Whitehead, and Cindy Bickel. *Tiger Math: Learning to Graph from a Baby Tiger.* Henry Holt and Company, New York, 2000.

Unit 2—Geometric Investigations: A Baseline Assessment Unit

- Burns, Marilyn. *Spaghetti and Meatballs for All!* Illustrated by Debbie Tilley. Scholastic Inc., New York, 1997.
- Neuschwander, Cindy. *Sir Cumference and the Great Knight of Angleland.* Illustrated by Wayne Geehan. Charlesbridge Publishing, Watertown, MA, 2001.
- Neuschwander, Cindy. *Sir Cumference and the Isle of Immeter.* Charlesbridge Publishing, Watertown, MA, 2006.

Unit 3—Numbers and Number Operations

- Burns, Marilyn. *The I Hate Mathematics! Book.* Little, Brown, and Company, Boston, MA, 1976. (Lesson 2)
- Calvert, Pam. *Multiplying Menace: The Revenge of Rumpelstiltskin (A Math Adventure).* Charlesbridge Publishing, Watertown, MA, 2006.
- Haskins, Jim. *Count Your Way through the Arab World.* Illustrated by Dana Gustafson. Scott Foresman, Glenview, IL, 1988. (Lesson 2)
- Ifrah, Georges. *The Universal History of Numbers: From Prehistory to the Invention of the Computer.* John Wiley & Sons, Hoboken, NJ, 2000. (Lesson 2)
- Owen, Claire. *All Roads Lead to Rome.* ETA/Cuisenaire, Vernon Hills, IL, 2005.
- St. John, Glory. *How to Count Like a Martian.* Hill & Wang Publishing, New York, 1975. (Lesson 2)
- Schmandt-Besserat, Denise. *The History of Counting.* Morrow Junior, New York, 1999. (Lesson 2)
- Thompson, Lauren. *One Riddle, One Answer.* Scholastic Press, Inc., New York, 2001.

Unit 4—Products and Factors

- Demi. *One Grain of Rice.* Scholastic Press, Inc., New York, 1997.
- Hulme, Joy N. *Sea Squares.* Illustrated by Carol Schwartz. Hyperion Books for Children, New York, 1993. (Lesson 1)
- Neuschwander, Cindy. *Amanda Bean's Amazing Dream.* Scholastic Press, Inc., New York, 1998.
- Tang, Greg. *The Best of Times: Math Strategies that Multiply.* Scholastic Press, Inc., New York, 2002.
- Tang, Greg. *The Grapes of Math: Mind Stretching Math Riddles.* Scholastic Press, Inc., New York, 2003.

Unit 5—Using Data to Predict

- Peterson, Ivars and Nancy Henderson. *Math Trek: Adventures in the Math Zone.* Jossey-Bass, San Francisco, 2000.
- Tang, Greg. *The Grapes of Math: Mind-Stretching Math Riddles.* Scholastic Press, Inc., New York, 2003.

Unit 6—Place Value Patterns

- Birch, David. *The King's Chessboard.* Penguin Putnam Books, New York, 1993. (Lesson 2)
- Demi. *One Grain of Rice.* Scholastic Press, Inc., New York, 1997.
- Handford, Martin. *Where's Waldo?* Candlewick Press, Cambridge, MA, 1997. (Lesson 5)
- McKissack, Patricia. *A Million Fish . . . More or Less.* Random House, New York, 1996. (Lesson 6)
- Pittman, Helena Clare. *A Grain of Rice.* Bantam Doubleday Dell, New York, 1996. (Lesson 2)
- Schwartz, David. *How Much Is a Million?* William Morrow and Company, New York, 1993. (Lesson 6)

Unit 7—Patterns in Multiplication

- Anno, Masaichiro and Mitsumasa. *Anno's Mysterious Multiplying Jar.* Penguin Putnam Books for Young Readers, New York, 1983.
- Clemson, Wendy. *Math Magic—Multiplying and Dividing.* Two-Can Publishing, London, UK, 2002.
- Leedy, Loreen. *2 × 2 = Boo! A Set of Spooky Multiplication Stories.* Holiday House, New York, 1995.

Unit 8—Measuring Up: An Assessment Unit

- Adler, David A. *How Tall, How Short, How Far Away?* Holiday House, New York, 2000.
- *Aesop's Fables.* Compiled and illustrated by Jerry Pinkney. SeaStar Books, New York, 2000. (Lesson 1)
- Allen, Pamela. *Mr. Archimedes' Bath.* HarperCollins Publishers, New York, 1998.
- Jenkins, Steve. *Hottest, Coldest, Highest, Deepest.* Houghton Mifflin, New York, 2004.

Literature List

- Jenkins, Steve. *The Top of the World: Climbing Mount Everest.* Houghton Mifflin, New York, 1999.
- Myller, Rolf. *How Big Is a Foot?* Yearling, New York, 1991.
- Owen, Claire. *A Simple System.* ETA/Cuisenaire, Vernon Hills, IL, 2005.
- Schwartz, David A. *Millions to Measure.* Harper Trophy, New York, 2006.

Unit 9—Shapes and Solids

- Birmingham, Duncan. *M Is for Mirror.* Tarquin, St. Albans, UK, 1988.
- Burns, Marilyn. *The Greedy Triangle.* Scholastic Press, New York, 1995.
- Coerr, Eleanor. *Sadako and the Thousand Paper Cranes.* Puffin, London, UK, 2005.
- Coffland, Jack and David. *Football Math: Touchdown Activities and Projects for Grades 4–8.* Good Year Books, Tucson, AZ, 1995.
- Murphy, Stuart J. *Captain Invincible and the Space Shapes.* Harper Trophy New York, 2001.
- Murphy, Stuart J. *Let's Fly a Kite.* Harper Trophy, New York, 2000.
- Neuschwander, Cindy. *Mummy Math—An Adventure in Geometry.* Henry Holt and Company, Inc., New York, 2005.
- Neuschwander, Cindy. *Sir Cumference and the Knights of Angleland.* Charlesbridge Publishing, Watertown, MA, 2001.
- Neuschwander, Cindy. *Sir Cumference and the Sword and the Cone.* Charlesbridge Publishing, Watertown, MA, 2001.
- Owen, Claire. *Building Blocks.* ETA/Cuisenaire, Vernon Hills, IL, 2005.
- Owen, Claire. *Perfect Patterns.* ETA/Cuisenaire, Vernon Hills, IL, 2005.
- Owen, Claire. *Precise Patterns.* ETA/Cuisenaire, Vernon Hills, IL, 2005.
- Owen, Claire. *Rainforest Math.* ETA/Cuisenaire, Vernon Hills, IL, 2005.

Unit 10—Using Decimals

- Allen, Pamela. *Mr. Archimedes' Bath.* HarperCollins Publishers, New York, 1998.
- Carroll, Lewis. *The Annotated Alice: The Definitive Edition. Alice's Adventures in Wonderland;* and *Through the Looking-Glass and What Alice Found There.* Introduction by Martin Gardner. Illustrated by John Tenniel. W.W. Norton, New York, 1999. (Lesson 6)
- Coffland, Jack and David. *Football Math: Touchdown Activities and Projects for Grades 4–8.* Good Year Books, Tucson, AZ, 1995.
- Gifford, Scott, and Shmuel Thaler. *Piece = Part = Portion.* Tricycle Press, Berkeley, CA, 2003.
- Leedy, Loreen. *Fraction Action.* Holiday House, New York, 1996.
- Lo Presti, Angeline Sparagna. *A Place for Zero.* Charlesbridge Publishing, Watertown, MA, 2003.
- Myller, Rolf. *How Big Is a Foot?* Yearling, New York, 1991.
- Owen, Claire. *A Simple System.* ETA/Cuisenaire, Vernon Hills, IL, 2005.
- Schwartz, David M. *Millions to Measure.* Harper Trophy, New York, 2006.

Unit 11—Multiplication

* Birch, David, and Devis Grebu. *The King's Chessboard.* Puffin, London, UK, 2003.
* Burns, Marilyn. *The I Hate Mathematics! Book.* Little, Brown and Company, New York, 1975. (Lesson 6)
* Calvert, Pam. *Multiplying Menace: The Revenge of Rumpelstiltskin (A Math Adventure).* Charlesbridge Publishing, Watertown, MA, 2006.
* Haskins, Jim. *Count Your Way Through the Arab World*, illustrated by Dana Gustafson. Carolrhoda Books, Minneapolis, 1987. (Lesson 6)
* Ifrah, Georges. *The Universal History of Numbers: From Prehistory to the Invention of the Computer.* John Wiley & Sons, New York, 2000. (Lesson 6)
* Lumpkin, Beatrice. *Senefer.* Africa World Press, Trenton, NJ, 1997.
* Owen, Claire. *Picture Numbers.* ETA/Cuisenaire, Vernon Hills, IL, 2005.
* St. John, Glory. *How to Count Like a Martian.* Henry Z. Walch, New York, 1975. (Lesson 6)
* Schmandt-Besserat, Denise. *The History of Counting,* illustrated by Michael Hays. Morrow Junior Books, New York, 1999. (Lesson 6)
* Sitomer, M., and H. Sitomer. *How Did Numbers Begin?,* illustrated by Richard Cuffari. Thomas J. Crowell, New York, 1976. (Lesson 6)

Unit 12—Exploring Fractions

* Adler, David A. *Fraction Fun.* Holiday House, New York, 1997.
* Pallotta, Jerry. *Hershey's Fraction Book.* Cartwheel Press, New York, 1999.
* Stamper, Judith Bauer. *Go Fractions.* Grosset and Dunlap, New York, 2003.

Unit 13—Division

* Bruce, Sheila. *Everybody Wins!* Kane Press, New York, 2003.
* Burnie, David. *Eyewitness Books: Plants.* D.K. Publishing, New York, 2000.
* Calvert, Pam. *Multiplying Menace: The Revenge of Rumpelstiltskin (A Math Adventure).* Charlesbridge Publishing, Watertown, MA, 2006.
* Murphy, Stuart. *Divide and Ride.* Harper Trophy, New York, 1997.

Unit 14—Chancy Predictions: An Introduction to Probability

* Cushman, Jean. *Do You Wanna Bet?* Your Chance to Find Out about Probability. Clarion Books, New York, 1991.
* Murphy, Stuart. *Probably Pistachio.* Harper Trophy, New York, 2001.

Unit 15—Using Patterns

- Baptista, Lynne Hardie. *Discover Rain Forests.* Publications International, Ltd., Lincolnwood, IL, 1993. (Lesson 2)
- Cherry, Lynne. *The Great Kapok Tree: A Tale of the Amazon Rain Forest.* Voyager Books, New York, 2000. (Lesson 2)
- Glass, Dr. Julie. *The Fly on the Ceiling.* Random House for Young Readers, New York, 1998.
- Jordan, Martin and Janis. *Journey of the Red-Eyed Tree Frog.* Simon & Schuster, New York, 1992. (Lesson 2)
- Perez, Ed. *A Look Around Rain Forests.* Willowisp Press, Inc., St. Petersburg, FL, 1993. (Lesson 2)

Unit 16—Assessing Our Learning

None

Games List

The Games List includes descriptions of games used in *Math Trailblazers*.

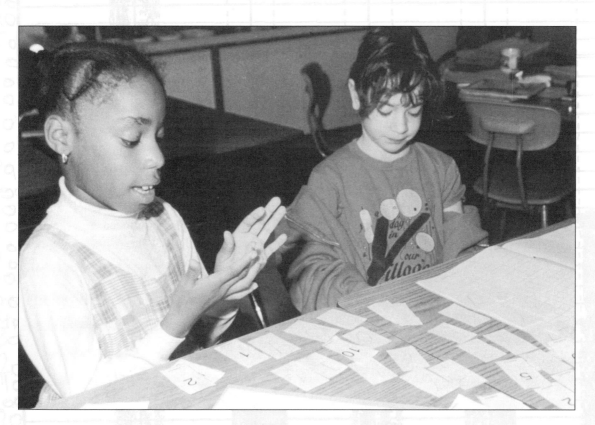

A student uses counting strategies while playing a math game.

Games List

Games are often used in *Math Trailblazers* to engage students in practicing basic arithmetic and other math concepts. A complete listing of the games fo your grade and a description of the games are provided below.

Once introduced, these games can be used throughout the year for ongoing practice. We suggest that after the games have been introduced and played in class, they be added to a "Games Menu," with necessary materials placed in math center somewhere in the classroom. Students can then replay the game: during indoor recess, when they have completed other assignments, and at other times during the day. TIMS Tips in the lesson guides will remind you t add each game to the Games Menu.

Unit 1—Data About Us
None

Unit 2—Geometric Investigations: A Baseline Assessment Unit
Digits Game in *Unit Resource Guide* Unit 2 Page 23 DPP item N

Students draw boxes on their papers as shown.

$$\begin{array}{r} \square\ \square \\ +\ \square\ \square \\ \hline \end{array}$$

The teacher chooses a digit at random from a set of digit cards (0–9). Students place the digit drawn in a box in such a way as to get the largest sum. Once a digit is placed, it cannot be moved. The teacher chooses a second digit without replacing the first. Play continues until the teacher has read enough digits. The player with the largest sum wins.

Digits Game in *Unit Resource Guide* Unit 2 Page 24 DPP item P

Students draw boxes on their papers as shown.

$$\begin{array}{r} \square\ \square \\ -\ \square\ \square \\ \hline \end{array}$$

The teacher chooses a digit at random from a set of digit cards (0–9). Students place the digit drawn in a box in such a way as to get the largest difference. Once a digit is placed, it cannot be moved. The teacher chooses a second digit without replacing the first. Play continues until the teacher has read enough digits. The player with the largest difference wins.

Unit 3—Numbers and Number Operations
None

Unit 4—Products and Factors

Digits Game in *Unit Resource Guide* Unit 4 Page 22 DPP item O

Students draw boxes on their papers as shown.

The teacher chooses a digit at random from a set of digit cards (0–9). Students place the digit drawn in a box in such a way as to get the largest sum. Once a digit is placed, it cannot be moved. The teacher chooses a second digit without replacing the first. Play continues until the teacher has read enough digits. The player with the largest sum wins. Play again; however, change the addition sign to a subtraction sign. This time, students try to find the largest difference.

Floor Tiler in *Unit Resource Guide* Unit 4 Lesson 3 Pages 60–66, *Discovery Assignment Book* Page 47, and *Student Guide* Pages 107–108

After spinning two numbers, players use the products of the numbers to form a rectangle and to color in the shape on their grid paper. Players take turns spinning and filling in their grids.

Product Bingo in *Unit Resource Guide* Unit 4 Lesson 5 Pages 83–90, *Discovery Assignment Book* Page 49, and *Student Guide* Pages 116–117

Students use two spinners to generate multiplication problems. They find the products and place markers showing the products on a bingo card. Players find that one card of four cards is most likely to win because more of its numbers can be obtained as products in several ways.

Unit 5—Using Data to Predict
None

Unit 6—Place Value Patterns

Draw, Place, and Read in *Unit Resource Guide* Unit 6 Lesson 3 Pages 52–65, *Discovery Assignment Book* Page 75, and *Student Guide* Page 159

A caller draws seven numbers. As each number is called, players record the number on their place value charts, trying to create the highest number. The player who makes and reads the highest number wins.

9 to 5 War in *Unit Resource Guide* Unit 6 Lesson 7 Pages 110–115, *Discovery Assignment Book* Pages 79–82, and *Student Guide* Pages 175–177

Students each use two decks of cards: one deck with nines and fives and one deck with the numbers one through ten to play a variation of war. Players draw one card from each of their decks and multiply the two numbers on the cards drawn. The highest product wins the cards.

Unit 7—Patterns in Multiplication

Draw, Place, and Read in *Unit Resource Guide* Unit 7 Page 16 DPP item D

Record 7 blanks on a sheet of paper as shown below.

$$\underline{\quad\quad}\;,\;\underline{\quad\quad}\;\;\underline{\quad\quad}\;\;\underline{\quad\quad}\;,\;\underline{\quad\quad}\;\;\underline{\quad\quad}\;\;\underline{\quad\quad}$$

1. A caller draws 7 numbers.
2. After each draw, players record the digit drawn in any of the seven places. Once a digit is recorded, it cannot be moved.
3. After all seven draws, the person who makes and reads the highest number earns a point.

Operation Target in *Unit Resource Guide* Unit 7 Lesson 1 Pages 30–44, *Student Guide* Page 183, and *Unit Resource Guide* Page 14 DPP item H

Students use four digits and the four arithmetic operations ($+$, $-$, $\div$, $\times$) to generate as many different whole numbers as possible.

Unit 8—Measuring Up: An Assessment Unit

Fill It First in *Unit Resource Guide* Unit 8 Lesson 2 Pages 53–59, *Discovery Assignment Book* Page 107, and *Student Guide* Pages 221–222

Teams predict the rise in water level as marbles are added to a graduated cylinder. Fill a graduated cylinder to the 50-cc mark. Make a score sheet as shown.

Predicted Volume in cc	Actual Volume in cc	Points

Spin the spinner to find out whether to add one, two, three, or four marbles to the graduated cylinder. The first team predicts the volume of the marbles before adding them to the cylinder. If the prediction is correct, the team scores a point for each marble added. Then, team 2 takes a turn. The first team to have a total of 20 cc of marbles in their cylinder scores an extra 3 points. That team then waits for the other team to have a total of 20 cc of marbles. The team with the highest score wins.

Operation Target in *Unit Resource Guide* Unit 8 Lesson 2 Pages 53–59 and *Student Guide* Pages 223–224

Students make all the numbers 0 to 9 using the digits 1, 4, 6, and 8 and the four operations ($+$, $-$, $\times$, and $\div$).

Unit 9—Shapes and Solids

None

Unit 10—Using Decimals

Decimal Hex in *Unit Resource Guide* Unit 10 Lesson 5 Pages 104–107 and *Discovery Assignment Book* Pages 179–181

Players place game markers on a game board and spin to see if they can move to adjacent game spaces with decimals greater than, less than, or equivalent to their current game space. The winner of the game is the first player to move his or her game piece across the board to a position opposite the starting position.

Unit 11—Multiplication

None

Unit 12—Exploring Fractions

Frabble Game in *Unit Resource Guide* Unit 12 Lesson 4 Pages 64–70, *Discovery Assignment Book* Pages 203–209, and *Student Guide* Pages 339–342

Students use a deck of fraction cards to order fractions according to size by strategically placing cards on a table. The winner of the game is the player who has the highest number of points for cards played.

Unit 13—Division

None

Unit 14—Chancy Predictions: An Introduction to Probability

Bean Counter's Game in *Unit Resource Guide* Unit 14 Lesson 2 Pages 39–45 and *Student Guide* Page 387

Players draw a line and make six tick marks on it. They then draw one of each of the six faces of a number cube below the marks. Players distribute 12 beans in any manner above the six faces drawn. Players roll a number cube and remove a bean from the face rolled. The first player to remove all the beans from his or her playing line is the winner.

Unit 15—Using Patterns

Guess My Rule in *Unit Resource Guide* Unit 15 Lesson 4 Pages 73–86 and *Student Guide* Page 414

One player is the function machine who thinks of a rule such as "Add 1 then Double" and secretly writes it down on a piece of paper. Other players then take turns giving input and output numbers until one player is able to guess the rule.

Unit 16—Assessing Our Learning

None

Games List

Software List

The Software List outlines recommended computer software used to enhance *Math Trailblazers* lessons.

Students use software to practice math facts and solve problems.

Software List

Software Titles by Topic

Applying Mathematics to Other Disciplines
A Field Trip to the Rainforest Deluxe

Data Collection/Reading and Interpreting Graphs
A Field Trip to the Rainforest Deluxe
Graph Master
Ice Cream Truck
Tabletop Jr.
TinkerPlots

Fractions/Decimals/Percents
Fraction Attraction
Math Arena
Math Munchers Deluxe
Math Mysteries: Fractions
Mighty Math Number Heroes
Tenth Planet: Fraction Operations
Tenth Planet: Representing Fractions

Geometry
Building Perspective Deluxe
The Factory Deluxe
Math Arena
Math Munchers Deluxe
Math Workshop Deluxe
MicroWorlds Ex
Mighty Math Calculating Crew
Mighty Math Number Heroes
Shape Up!
Tessellation Exploration

Integers
Mighty Math Calculating Crew
Number Sense and Problem Solving:
   How the West Was One + Three × Four

Logical Thinking/Problem Solving/Patterns
Building Perspective Deluxe
Carmen Sandiego's Math Detective
The Factory Deluxe
Ice Cream Truck
Math Mysteries: Advanced Whole Numbers
Math Mysteries: Fractions
Math Mysteries: Measurement
Math Mysteries: Whole Numbers
Number Sense and Problem Solving:
   Divide and Conquer, How the West Was
   One + Three × Four, Puzzle Tanks
Tabletop Jr.
Ten Tricky Tiles
Zoombinis Logical Journey

Measurement
The Factory Deluxe
Math Mysteries: Measurement
Mighty Math Carnival Countdown
Shape Up!

Number Theory (Factors and Primes)
Math Munchers Deluxe
Mighty Math Calculating Crew

Practice with Basic Operations
Carmen Sandiego's Math Detective
Math Arena
Math Munchers Deluxe
Math Mysteries: Advanced Whole Numbers
Math Mysteries: Whole Numbers
Math Workshop Deluxe
Number Facts Fire Zapper
Number Sense and Problem Solving:
   How the West Was One + Three × Four
Ten Tricky Tiles

Probability
Mighty Math Number Heroes

Programs for Illustrating
Kid Pix

Understanding of Basic Operations
Fraction Attraction
Number Sense and Problem Solving:
   Divide and Conquer
Mighty Math Calculating Crew
Ten Tricky Tiles
Tenth Planet: Fraction Operations

Websites
The Math Forum: www.mathforum.org
National Library of Virtual Manipulatives for
   Interactive Mathematics: www.matti.usu.edu
One resource for additional mathematics links and
   sites: http://illuminations.nctm.org/swr/index.asp

Recommended Software for Fourth-Grade Units

Unit 1—Data About Us

Carmen Sandiego's Math Detective provides practice with math facts, estimation, ordering numbers, and word problems.

Graph Master allows students to organize data and create graphs.

Ice Cream Truck develops problem solving, money skills, and arithmetic operations.

Kid Pix allows students to create their own illustrations.

Math Mysteries: Measurement develops multistep problem solving with distance, weight, and capacity.

Math Mysteries: Whole Numbers is a series of structured word problems dealing with whole numbers.

Number Facts Fire Zapper provides practice with math facts in an arcade-like game.

Number Sense and Problem Solving: Puzzle Tanks develops logical thinking while practicing math facts.

Ten Tricky Tiles provides practice with math facts through engaging puzzles.

TinkerPlots allows students to record, compare, and analyze data in tables and graphs.

Unit 2—Geometric Investigations: A Baseline Assessment Unit

Carmen Sandiego's Math Detective provides practice with math facts, estimation, ordering numbers, and word problems.

The Factory Deluxe promotes spatial reasoning and practice finding area.

Graph Master allows students to collect data and create their own graphs.

Ice Cream Truck develops problem solving, money skills, and arithmetic operations.

Kid Pix allows students to create their own illustrations.

Math Arena is a collection of math activities that reinforces many math concepts.

Math Mysteries: Whole Numbers is a series of structured word problems dealing with whole numbers.

MicroWorlds Ex is a drawing program that helps students develop spatial reasoning and an understanding of coordinates while making shapes.

Mighty Math Number Heroes poses short answer questions about fractions, number operations, polygons, and probability.

Number Facts Fire Zapper provides practice in number facts in an arcade-like game.

Number Sense and Problem Solving: Puzzle Tanks develops logical thinking while practicing math facts.

Shape Up! is a geometry program that contains five sets of shapes that students can manipulate and explore.

Ten Tricky Tiles provides practice with number facts through engaging puzzles.

TinkerPlots allows students to record, compare, and analyze data in tables and graphs.

Unit 3—Numbers and Number Operations

Ice Cream Truck develops problem solving, money skills, and arithmetic operations.

Math Arena is a collection of math activities that reinforces many math concepts.

Math Workshop Deluxe develops math facts proficiency.

Mighty Math Calculating Crew poses short answer questions about number operations and money skills.

National Library of Virtual Manipulatives website (http://matti.usu.edu) allows students to work with manipulatives including base-ten pieces.

Unit 4—Products and Factors

Math Arena is a collection of math activities that reinforces many math concepts.

Math Munchers Deluxe provides practice with basic facts, factors, and multiples in an arcade-like game.

Math Mysteries: Advanced Whole Numbers is a series of structured multistep word problems dealing with whole numbers.

Mighty Math Calculating Crew poses short answer questions about number operations and money skills.

Mighty Math Number Heroes poses short answer questions about fractions, number operations, polygons, and probability.

National Library of Virtual Manipulatives website (http://matti.usu.edu) allows students to work with manipulatives including rectangle multiplication.

Number Sense and Problem Solving: Puzzle Tanks develops logical thinking while students practice math facts.

Unit 5—Using Data to Predict

Graph Master provides practice with collecting data and creating graphs. (Lessons 1, 3, and 4)

Kid Pix helps students create their own illustrations.

Math Mysteries: Measurement provides practice with multistep problem solving involving distance, weight, and capacity.

TinkerPlots allows students to record, compare, and analyze data in tables and graphs.

Unit 6—Place Value Patterns

Carmen Sandiego's Math Detective provides practice with math facts, estimation, ordering numbers, and word problems.

Math Arena is a collection of math activities that reinforces many math concepts

Math Munchers Deluxe provides practice in basic facts and finding equivalent fractions, decimals, and percents in an arcade-like game.

Mighty Math Calculating Crew poses short answer questions about number operations and money skills.

Mighty Math Number Heroes poses short answer questions about number operations.

National Library of Virtual Manipulatives website (http://matti.usu.edu) allows students to work with manipulatives including base-ten pieces, the abacus, and many others.

Unit 7—Patterns in Multiplication

Ice Cream Truck provides practice with problem solving, money skills, and arithmetic operations.

Math Arena is a collection of math activities that reinforces many math concepts.

Math Munchers Deluxe provides practice with basic facts and identifying factors and multiples in an arcade-like game.

Math Workshop Deluxe develops math facts proficiency.

Mighty Math Calculating Crew provides practice with number operations and money skills.

Number Sense and Problem Solving: How the West Was One + Three × Four provides practice with the order of operations.

Unit 8—Measuring Up: An Assessment Unit

Graph Master allows students to organize data and create graphs.

Kid Pix allows students to create their own illustrations.

Math Mysteries: Measurement develops multistep problem solving with distance, weight, and capacity.

TinkerPlots allows students to record, compare, and analyze data in tables and graphs. (Lesson 3)

Unit 9—Shapes and Solids

Building Perspective Deluxe develops spatial reasoning and visual thinking in three dimensions.

Carmen Sandiego's Math Detective provides practice with math facts, estimation, ordering numbers, and word problems.

The Factory Deluxe promotes spatial reasoning and practices finding area.

Math Arena is a collection of math activities that reinforces many math concepts.

Math Workshop Deluxe develops spatial sense and math facts proficiency.

MicroWorlds Ex is a drawing program that helps students develop spatial reasoning and an understanding of coordinates while making shapes.

Mighty Math Calculating Crew poses short answer questions about three-dimensional shapes.

Mighty Math Number Heroes poses short answer questions about polygons.

National Library of Virtual Manipulatives website (http://matti.usu.edu) allows students to work with manipulatives including geoboards and tangrams.

Shape Up! is a geometry program that contains five sets of shapes that students can manipulate and explore.

Tessellation Exploration develops understanding of the geometry of tessellations and allows students to create their own.

Unit 10—Using Decimals

Fraction Attraction develops understanding of fractions using fraction bars, pie charts, hundreds blocks, and other materials.

Graph Master allows students to collect data and create their own graphs.

Ice Cream Truck develops problem solving, money skills, and arithmetic operations.

Kid Pix allows students to create their own illustrations.

Math Arena is a collection of math activities that reinforces many math concepts.

Math Munchers Deluxe provides practice in basic facts and finding equivalent fractions, decimals, and percents in an arcade-like game.

Math Mysteries: Fractions develops problem solving with fractions.

Math Mysteries: Measurement develops multistep problem solving with distance, weight, and capacity.

Math Workshop Deluxe allows students to explore fractions and decimals.

Mighty Math Number Heroes poses short answer questions about fractions and number operations.

Tenth Planet: Fraction Operations develops conceptual understanding of fraction operations.

TinkerPlots allows students to record, compare, and analyze data in tables and graphs.

Unit 11—Multiplication

Ice Cream Truck develops problem-solving and computation skills.

Math Arena is a collection of math activities that reinforces many math concepts.

Math Mysteries: Advanced Whole Numbers is a series of structured multistep word problems.

Math Mysteries: Whole Numbers is a series of structured word problems.

Mighty Math Calculating Crew poses short answer questions about number operations and money.

Mighty Math Number Heroes poses short answer questions about operations and other math concepts.

Number Facts Fire Zapper provides practice with number facts in an arcade-like game.

Unit 12—Exploring Fractions

Fraction Attraction develops understanding of fractions using fraction bars, pie charts, hundreds blocks, and other materials.

Math Arena is a collection of math activities that reinforces many math concepts.

Math Munchers Deluxe provides practice with equivalent fractions and other skills in an arcade-like game.

Math Mysteries: Fractions develops multistep problem solving with fractions.

Math Workshop Deluxe allows students to explore fractions and decimals.

Mighty Math Number Heroes poses short answer questions about fractions and other number operations.

National Library of Virtual Manipulatives website (http://matti.usu.edu) allows students to work with fractions using pattern blocks and other manipulatives on the computer.

Tenth Planet: Fraction Operation develops conceptual understanding of fraction operations.

Tenth Planet: Representing Fractions provides a conceptual introduction to fractions.

Unit 13—Division

Graph Master allows students to collect data and create their own graphs.

Kid Pix allows students to create their own illustrations.

Math Munchers Deluxe provides practice with basic facts in an arcade-like game.

Math Mysteries: Advanced Whole Numbers is a series of structured multistep word problems dealing with whole numbers.

Math Workshop Deluxe develops math fact proficiency.

Mighty Math Calculating Crew poses short answer questions about number operations and money.

Mighty Math Number Heroes poses short answer questions about number operations.

Number Sense and Problem Solving: Divide and Conquer develops conceptual understanding of the division process.

TinkerPlots allows students to record, compare, and analyze data in tables and graphs.

Unit 14—Chancy Predictions: An Introduction to Probability

Math Arena provides practice with many math concepts.

Mighty Math Number Heroes provides practice with fractions, number operations, polygons, and probability.

National Library of Virtual Manipulatives website (http://matti.usu.edu) allows students to work with manipulatives including geoboards, base-ten pieces, the abacus, and many others.

Unit 15—Using Patterns

Building Perspective Deluxe develops spatial reasoning and visual thinking in three dimensions.

The Factory Deluxe promotes spatial reasoning and provides practice with finding area.

A Field Trip to the Rainforest Deluxe integrates mathematics with science.

Math Arena is a collection of math activities that reinforces many math concepts.

Math Workshop Deluxe provides practice with fractions and decimals and develops spatial sense and math facts proficiency.

National Library of Virtual Manipulatives website (http://matti.usu.edu) allows students to work with number patterns and number puzzles.

Number Sense and Problem Solving: Puzzle Tanks develops logical thinking while practicing math facts.

Shape Up! provides activities with five different sets of shapes.

TinkerPlots allows students to record, compare, and analyze data in tables and graphs.

Zoombinis Logical Journey provides practice with finding patterns to solve puzzles.

Unit 16—Assessing Our Learning

Graph Master allows students to collect data and create their own graphs.

Kid Pix allows students to create their own illustrations.

TinkerPlots allows students to record, compare, and analyze data in tables and graphs.

Recommended Software List–
Brief Descriptions of the Programs

Building Perspective Deluxe by Sunburst
This program develops students' problem-solving skills, spatial perception, and visual thinking skills. Students are presented with ground-level views of an array of buildings. The task is to predict how the buildings will look when viewed from above. This program is recommended for Grades 4–adult.

Carmen Sandiego's Math Detective by Riverdeep—The Learning Company
In this program students work as detectives to foil the evil Carmen Sandiego's plot to crystallize famous world landmarks. In order to do so they must collect clues from five different math activities. The activities can be accessed in a practice mode. The activity Atom Smasher works on developing accuracy and speed with math facts. Teachers can customize the problems in this part of the program. Crime Wave Sensor develops estimation. Students are presented with math equation with a missing number. Students then click on a number chart to begin guessing the missing number. The program calculates the equation with the student's guess so that the student can refine the guess. This provides a powerful tool to develop mental imagery of numbers and their proximity to one another. Light Spectrometer requires students to place numbers in one pile from smallest to largest, much like the Tower of Hanoi puzzle. Microchip Decoder asks students to draw shapes and asks multiple-choice questions focusing on vocabulary. In Molecular Scope students write equations from word problems. The teacher's manual is well organized and there are many support materials provided as well. The program is recommended for Grades 3 to 7.

The Factory Deluxe by Sunburst
Students are asked to produce or duplicate products in a simulated assembly line. Students direct the machines to punch, rotate, and stripe a variety of geometric shapes. Students explore sequences, patterns, and spatial relationships. There are also two games in the program. Ship It! is a game that develops logical thinking. Several shapes with a variety of attributes are presented. The student must place the shapes in the best containers. The containers are labeled with various attributes. At the advanced levels, it is possible that more than one shape fits an attribute, i.e., goes into a container. In the second game, Deliver It!, students control trucks that compete on a racecourse. The trucks move as correct answers to area problems are given. This game develops estimation of area using a grid as well as measuring and using formulas. The program is recommended for Grades 4 to 8.

A Field Trip to the Rainforest Deluxe by Sunburst
This program integrates mathematics with science. Children explore plants and animals indigenous to a rain forest. In the activities, children use data tables to gather information and explore various aspects of the rain forest. The program allows children to create their own tables. It is recommended for Grades 2 and up.

Fraction Attraction by Sunburst
Fraction Attraction provides conceptual development of fractions in four games. Students develop understanding of equivalent fractions by turning a Ferris wheel. Other games address ordering fractions and positioning fractions on the number line. The concept of fraction as a distance is included also. In every game students can get an explanation of the mathematics, not just correct answers, in the diagnostic help section. The explanations use fraction bars, pie charts, and hundreds blocks to show alternate representations. There are different levels of difficulty and students can choose to work with decimal and percent equivalents as well. The teachers' guide offers other off-computer activities and teaching suggestions to build understanding. The program is recommended for Grades 3 to 8.

Graph Master by Tom Snyder Productions
Graph Master allows students to collect data into the program or import data from outside. There are 9 different types of graphs available, depending on the type of data: bar graph, pictograph, circle graph, line graph, scatterplot, frequency chart, histogram, line plot, and box plots. The user decides on graph type, scale, variables, and labels. The program allows two graphs to be open side by side so that students can compare the same data in different formats or compare different data. Students can also sort and tally data, get statistics (mean, median, mode, and range) and filter data. The program provides help in interpreting the types of graphs and there are ten sample data sets available. The program is recommended for Grades 4 to 8.

Ice Cream Truck by Sunburst
Ice Cream Truck simulates a real-life business. Students own an ice cream truck and their goal is to make as big a profit as possible. Students buy ice cream from a warehouse. They decide how much to buy, what to charge, and where to sell. The program provides information about the temperature outside and the time of day they will be selling. The program then simulates the customers and determines how much ice cream was sold that day. Students must make informed decisions. They have a spreadsheet available and must keep track of their profits and expenses, including gas. This program promotes multistep problem solving and decision making. The program is recommended for Grades 3 to 6.

Kid Pix by Riverdeep—The Learning Company
This program allows students to create their own illustrations for many different applications throughout the curriculum. In mathematics, students can use this program to illustrate problems they have been given to solve or they can create and illustrate their own patterns and problems. The program is recommended for Grades K–4.

Math Arena by Sunburst
Math Arena is a collection of 20 well thought-out problem solving and skill reinforcing games. Each activity begins with a short tutorial, which can be

skipped. The games include practice in estimating angles, using symmetry to finish a quilt, finding a person lost in a coordinate grid, using transformations to form triangular designs, and forming arrays consisting of a given number of squares. Students practice making change and estimating if the total bill at a store is over an allotted amount of money, as well as finding the sale price of an item, given the discount percent. Other games provide practice with arithmetic skills. Students must recognize equivalent amounts and catch arithmetic errors. In other activities students must find equivalent fractions and find the next number in a pattern. In another game students practice forming Venn diagrams. The level of play can be changed and there are teacher options. The manual comes with worksheets to complement the computer work. This program is recommended for Grades 4 to 7.

The Math Forum (www.mathforum.org)
The Math Forum is a very broad-based website maintained by Drexel University. The site has such features as Ask Dr. Math, where students can ask mathematical questions. There is an extensive mathematics resource library for students in elementary school through graduate school. Other features include discussion groups, an extensive collection of good problems, teacher resources, and issues in mathematics education.

Math Munchers Deluxe by Riverdeep—The Learning Company
Math Munchers Deluxe allows students to practice operations and identify primes, multiples, and factors. The student moves a Muncher, which devours expressions that fit a given criterion, around the screen. For example, one task is to devour all expressions that are equivalent to .5. The Muncher tries to avoid being eaten by Troggles, but this feature can be turned off, allowing the student to focus on the mathematics. The program allows the user to choose a grade level, and to choose between whole numbers, fractions, decimals, and geometry. Within the topics students can choose evaluating expressions, finding equivalent expressions, and comparing expressions. The program is recommended for students in Grades 3–6.

Math Mysteries: Advanced Whole Numbers by Tom Snyder Productions
Math Mysteries: Advanced Whole Numbers has the same type of problems as *Math Mysteries: Whole Numbers.* They differ in the amount of extraneous information, the number of steps, and how the questions are embedded in the stories. The program is recommended for students in Grades 4–7.

Math Mysteries: Fractions by Tom Snyder Productions
Math Mysteries: Fractions focuses on problem solving using fraction problems. The program is designed for group work. Students watch a short cartoon where they gather data and gain an understanding of the problem. They solve the problem and check their work using provided guides. The problems involve creating fractions, adding, subtracting, multiplying, and dividing fractions. There are a total of 24 problems with reproducible pages to help structure problem solving and answers for the teacher. The program is recommended for students in Grades 4–7.

Math Mysteries: Measurement by Tom Snyder Productions
Math Mysteries: Measurement focuses on problem solving using measurement problems. The program is designed for group work. Students

watch a short cartoon where they gather data and gain an understanding of the problem. They solve the problem and check their work using provided guides. The problems involve metric and customary length, weight, volume, and rates. There are a total of 24 problems with reproducible pages to help structure problem solving and answers for the teacher. The program is recommended for students in Grades 4–7.

Math Mysteries: Whole Numbers by Tom Snyder Productions
Math Mysteries: Whole Numbers focuses on problem solving using whole numbers and time problems. The program is designed for group work. Students watch a short cartoon where they gather data and gain an understanding of the problem. They solve the problem and check their work using provided guides. The problems involve adding, subtracting, multiplying, and dividing with whole numbers, working with time, working with rates, and interpreting remainders. There are a total of 24 problems with reproducible pages to help structure problem solving and answers for the teacher. The program is recommended for students in Grades 4–7.

Math Workshop Deluxe by Riverdeep—The Learning Company
This program is a collection of math activities. There are several activities that foster the development of spatial sense. Students have three different puzzle activities to choose from and they can create their own patterns in Pattern Windows. Bowling for Numbers is a fact practice activity. The teacher can set the parameters for the facts to be practiced. In the Rhythm Shop students get an introduction to fraction concepts. The fractions created are then tied to music rhythms. The Rockets activity is a computerized version of the ancient game of Nim. The program comes with many teacher support materials and is recommended for Grades K to 7.

MicroWorlds Ex by LCSI
MicroWorlds Ex is an interactive program that allows users to create geometric shapes by issuing commands. As students construct figures, they learn about the geometric properties of shapes. There are several commercially available programs. Recent versions include MicroWorlds JR and MicroWorlds Ex by LCSI. In these versions, students can add text, animation, and sound. It also includes web-integration. This program is recommended for Grades 2 to adult.

Mighty Math Calculating Crew by Riverdeep—The Learning Company
This very versatile skills program has four sections with about 20 specific goals in each section. The Nautical Number Line presents lost treasures under a number line. Students must move a ship to the correct number to achieve a treasure. The skills here focus on locating numbers on the line, rounding, adding and subtracting whole numbers, fractions, and decimals, and working with negative numbers. The Superhero Superstore focuses on money skills and operations involving numbers with ending zeros. Dr. Gee's 3D Lab acquaints students with nets of solids. Students must match nets with solids and identify attributes of the nets and solids. Nick Knack, Supertrader, develops conceptual understanding of multiplication as repeated addition and division as partitioning equally. There are long division practice problems too. The program is recommended for Grades 3 to 6.

Mighty Math Carnival Countdown by Riverdeep—The Learning Company
The program provides students with logic activities, basic operations, tasks, and work with two-dimensional objects and place value. Each of the 5 activities is further divided into 13 to 26 different types of problems. Carnival Cars focuses on sets and sorting by attributes, using > and < symbols and distinguishing even and odd numbers. Snap Clowns practices the basic operations and helps students gain conceptual understanding of the operations that they are performing. Bubble Band focuses students' attention on place value. The beginning activities focus on the ones place but later students work in the hundreds and see how groups of 10 are traded. Giggle Factory focuses on number sense and the concept of equivalence. Students can work up to 1000 in these activities. Pattern Block Round Up uses the manipulative to pose questions about symmetry, area, perimeter, and basic fraction ideas. The program is recommended for Grades K–2.

Mighty Math Number Heroes by Riverdeep—The Learning Company
This very versatile skills program has four sections with about 20 specific goals in each section. Fraction Fireworks asks students questions about fractions and decimals. The questions range from identifying fractions to comparing, adding, and subtracting fractions with like and unlike denominators. It also includes multiplying fractions and questions about decimals. The GeoComputer section uses the geoboard to practice identifying different types of angles and polygons. Students answer questions about symmetry, different transformations, perimeter, area, and tessellations. In the Quizzo section students compete in a game show in various categories. Questions include multiplication and division facts, adding and subtracting 2-digit and 3-digit numbers, identifying patterns, and operations with decimals. In the probability section students answer questions with spinners, coins, and graphs. The questions range from exploring possible/impossible events to finding probabilities, comparing probabilities, and identifying independent events. The program is recommended for Grades 3 to 6.

National Library of Virtual Manipulatives for Interactive Mathematics (www.matti.usu.edu)
This website was developed and is maintained at Utah State University. It includes an extensive collection of virtual manipulatives and accompanying activities. Students can work with geoboards, pattern blocks, tangrams, base-ten pieces, balance scales, and other materials interactively. This provides the opportunity to work with materials that are perhaps otherwise not available. For students who have access to the concrete materials, using the interactive manipulatives provides opportunity to move from concrete to pictorial representations.

Number Facts Fire Zapper by Gamco
Number Facts Fire Zapper's goal is to develop proficiency and speed at basic math facts in a fun arcade-type game. Students must move firefighters around a screen and spray math facts with the correct answer in order to extinguish the flames. Students choose which operation they want to practice. The length of the game and the speed at which the number facts appear can be changed. The program allows the teacher to keep track of individual student progress. The teacher can also see an analysis of how a student did on particular fact groups. For example the program shows the percent correct o

all problems involving the multiples of seven. The program is recommended for Grades 1 to 8.

Number Sense and Problem Solving by Sunburst
  Divide and Conquer
  The program helps develop conceptual understanding of dividends, divisors, quotients, and remainders. Ten letters are used to represent the 10 digits in code. The goal is to break the code by figuring out what digit is represented by what letter. The program presents a dividend and the student chooses divisors. The program then computes the quotient and remainder. Depending on the level, some of the information provided is in code as well. By using addition, subtraction, multiplication, and division, students must analyze the equations they generate to match the letters with the numbers. The program also allows the user to switch to Greek letters commonly used in mathematics. The program is an excellent tool for developing logical thinking and hypothesis testing and is recommended for Grades 4 to 8.

  How the West Was One + Three × Four
  Students learn about order of operations as they race their stagecoach or locomotive along the number line trail. The computer generates three numbers. The players make combinations of these numbers using the four basic operations and parentheses to be the first to reach Red Gulch. Teachers can customize the program. The program is recommended for Grades 4–8.

  Puzzle Tanks
  This program develops logical thinking. Students must fill a truck with exactly a given amount of liquid. Two tanks are used to fill the truck. The tanks hold a certain amount of liquid, which changes with each game. The tanks can be refilled indefinitely, but the entire tank is emptied at once. Students must use the basic operations to get the right amount into the tank. Besides basic operations and number sense, the concept of equality and algebra skills are also reinforced. The program is recommended for Grades 4 to 8.

Shape Up! by Sunburst
Shape Up! is a very versatile geometry program consisting of five sets of shapes. The user can choose to work with pattern blocks or tangrams designed to correspond to the manipulatives. Another set of shapes involves regular triangles, pentagons, hexagons, octagons, squares, and circles. These shapes can be dissected and put back together in any desired fashion. In addition, the user can choose from two sets of three-dimensional shapes. One set is the platonic solids and the other a variety of shapes. Students can explore area, symmetry, tessellations, similarity, and congruence. The program allows users to view inside 3-dimensional shapes using the Transparent function. Any of the shapes can be moved and rotated. The teacher's guide includes an extensive implementation guide to use the program to its fullest capacity and an in-depth reference section. This program develops student van Hiele levels with opportunities to explore shapes more easily than working with concrete materials. The program is recommended for Grades K–8.

Tabletop Jr. by Sunburst
This program focuses on developing logical thinking and working with data as an age-appropriate introduction to statistics. Students make objects from thirteen different possible kits. The objects have a variety of attributes. Students can then use these objects as data to manipulate. The data can be arranged, for example, on axes, as pictographs, and Venn diagrams. Students sharpen their discrimination skills as they look for like and unlike objects and patterns in the data. There are many excellent classroom activities in the teacher's manual. The program is recommended for Grades K to 5.

Ten Tricky Tiles by Sunburst
Ten Tricky Tiles develops understanding of number relations and logical thinking, and provides addition and subtraction fact practice. Students must fit number tiles 0–9 into the correct places to make number sentences true. The number tiles must be arranged so that all the sentences are correct in order to get points. The program also reinforces the concept of equality with operations on both sides of the equals sign. There are three activities with increasing difficulty to choose from. The most challenging activity is a number crossword puzzle where the number sentences are all interrelated. The ten number tiles must be placed so horizontal and vertical number sentences are true. There are accompanying worksheets and suggestions for helping students develop efficient strategies. The program is recommended for Grades 2 to 6.

Tenth Planet: Fraction Operations by Sunburst
Tenth Planet: Fraction Operations develops conceptual understanding of fraction operations. The program has short video clips of fraction operations in real life and multistep fraction problem situations. The program has interactive fraction bars to help students understand common denominators. Students keep dividing a bar until they can make the given bars (fractions) with the same size parts. Several different activities allow practice in adding and subtracting fractions. The teachers' guide provides supporting blackline masters. The program is recommended for Grades 4 to 7.

Tenth Planet: Representing Fractions by Sunburst
The program contains video clips and activities that promote conceptual understanding of what a fraction is. The focus is on fractions: naming equal parts of a whole and different ways to cut a whole into equal pieces. Through real-life examples students see that a fraction of one object may be very different in size from the same fractional part of another object. The notion that as the denominator gets bigger, the fractional piece that it represents gets smaller is also addressed. There are several activities where students cut fractions, identify fractions, and construct the whole. Fractions are used in linear, area, and volume models. The program is recommended for Grades 2 to 4.

Tessellation Exploration by Tom Snyder Productions
Tessellation Exploration allows students to create, animate, and print their own tessellations. The program reinforces the mathematics of slide, rotation and reflection transformations as students explore and draw connections between art and mathematics. After creating a shape, students can add artwork. Students explore the rules that govern tessellations. There are

suggested class activities and worksheets in the teachers' guide. A tessellation tutorial and many examples of tessellations are included. The program is recommended for Grades 4 and above.

TinkerPlots by Key Curriculum Press
This program allows students to record, explore, compare, and analyze data in tables and graphs they design themselves. The data can be entered or imported into the program. Students can edit data in tables, then display the data in a bar graph, point graph, or circle graph. Tables and graphs can be compared side-by-side to examine relationships in data. This program is recommended for Grades 4–8.

Zoombinis Logical Journey by Riverdeep—The Learning Company
This program builds thinking skills. The student must guide the Zoombinis to a new land by solving logic puzzles. The Zoombinis are little creatures that have different attributes (feet, hair, noses, etc.). In many of the challenges, students must discover how the attributes are grouped in order to proceed. Patterning, collecting evidence, graphing, sorting, and hypothesis testing are developed as the game progresses. There are twelve different puzzles with four levels of difficulty that change each time the program is played. The program is recommended for Grades 3 to 8.

Software Companies Addresses and Telephone Numbers

Gamco
The Siboney Learning Group
325 N. Kirkwood Road, Suite 200
Saint Louis, MO 63122
1-888-726-8100
www.gamco.com
www.siboneylearninggroup.com

Key Curriculum Press
1150 65th Street
Emeryville, CA 94608
1-888-881-8885
www.keypress.com

LCSI
P.O. Box 162
Highgate Springs, VT 05460
1-800-321-5646
www.microworlds.com

Riverdeep—The Learning Company
100 Pine Street, Suite 1900
San Francisco, CA 94111
1-888-242-6747
www.riverdeep.net

Sunburst Technology
1550 Executive Drive
Elgin, IL 60123
1-888-492-8817
www.sunburst.com

Tom Snyder Productions
80 Coolidge Hill Road
Watertown, MA 02472
1-800-342-0236
www.tomsnyder.com

Glossary

This glossary provides definitions of key vocabulary terms in the Grade 4 lessons. Locations of key vocabulary terms in the curriculum are included with each definition. Components Key: URG = *Unit Resource Guide,* SG = *Student Guide,* DAB = *Discovery Assignment Book,* and TIG = *Teacher Implementation Guide.*

A

Acre (URG Unit 6 p. 32; SG p. 153)
A measure of land area equal to 43,560 square feet.

Acute Angle (URG Unit 2 p. 104 & Unit 9 p. 45; SG p. 50)
An angle that measures less than 90°.

All-Partials Algorithm
(URG Unit 7 pp. 10, 99; SG p. 197;
TIG p. 230)
A paper-and-pencil method for solving
multiplication problems. Each partial
product is recorded on a separate line.
(*See also* partial product.)

$$\begin{array}{r} 186 \\ \times\ 3 \\ \hline 18 \\ 240 \\ 300 \\ \hline 558 \end{array}$$

Angle (URG Unit 2 p. 101; SG p. 42)
The amount of turning or the amount of opening between two rays that have the same endpoint.

Angle of Turning (URG Unit 9 pp. 10, 65)
The smallest angle through which a figure can be turned about the center of turning so that the figure coincides with itself.

Area (SG p. 29; TIG p. 329)
The area of a shape is the amount of space it covers, measured in square units.

Array (URG Unit 4 p. 8)
An array is an arrangement of elements into a rectangular pattern of (horizontal) rows and (vertical) columns.

Average (URG Unit 1 p. 67 & Unit 5 p. 8; SG pp. 13, 125; TIG p. 241)
A number that can be used to represent a typical value in a set of data. (*See also* mean and median.)

B

Base (of an exponent) (SG p. 113)
When exponents are used, the number being multiplied. In $3^4 = 3 \times 3 \times 3 \times 3 = 81$, the 3 is the base and the 4 is the exponent. The 3 is multiplied by itself 4 times.

Base-Ten Board (URG Unit 3 p. 51; SG p. 68)
A tool to help children organize base-ten pieces when they are representing numbers.

Base-Ten Pieces (URG Unit 3 p. 8; SG p. 68)
A set of manipulatives used to model our number system as shown in the figure below. Note that a skinny is made of 10 bits, a flat is made of 100 bits, and a pack is made of 1000 bits.

Nickname	Picture	Shorthand
bit		•
skinny		/
flat		
pack		

Glossary

Base-Ten Shorthand (URG Unit 3 pp. 9, 65; SG p. 71)
A pictorial representation of the base-ten pieces as shown on page 365.

Benchmarks (URG Unit 6 pp. 69, 95; SG p. 169)
Numbers convenient for comparing and ordering numbers, e.g., 0, $\frac{1}{2}$, 1 are convenient benchmarks for comparing and ordering fractions.

Best-Fit Line (URG Unit 5 pp. 8, 27, 28; SG p. 123)
The line that comes closest to the points on a point graph.

Binning Data (URG Unit 13 p. 39)
Placing data from a data set with a large number of values or large range into intervals in order to more easily see patterns in the data.

Bit (URG Unit 3 pp. 8, 51, 62, 63 & Unit 6 p. 56; SG p. 68)
A cube that measures 1 cm on each edge. It is the smallest of the base-ten pieces and is often used to represent 1. (*See also* base-ten pieces.)

C

Categorical Variable (URG Unit 1 pp. 9, 51; SG p. 7; TIG p. 309)
Variables with values that are not numbers. (*See also* variable and value.)

Center of Turning (URG Unit 9 p. 65; SG p. 251)
A point on a plane figure around which it is turned. In particular, the point about which an object with turn symmetry is rotated.

Centimeter (SG p. 272)
A unit of length in the metric system. A centimeter is $\frac{1}{100}$ of a meter.

Certain Event (URG Unit 14 pp. 8, 29, 30; SG p. 385)
An event that has a probability of 1 (100%).

Common Fraction (URG Unit 10 p. 50)
Any fraction that is written with a numerator and denominator that are whole numbers. For example, $\frac{3}{4}$ and $\frac{9}{4}$ are both common fractions. (*See also* decimal fraction.)

Commutative Property of Multiplication (URG Unit 3 p. 31 & Unit 4 p. 30)
This is also known as the Order Property of Multiplication. Changing the order of the factors does not change the product. For example, $3 \times 5 = 5 \times 3 = 15$. Using variables, $n \times m = m \times n$.

Composite Number (URG Unit 4 pp. 9, 34)
A number that has more than two distinct factors. For example, 9 has three factors (1, 3, 9) so it is a composite number.

Convenient Number (URG Unit 1 p. 117 & Unit 7 p. 109; SG pp. 202, 203)
A number used in computation that is close enough to give a good estimate, but is also easy to compute with mentally, e.g., 25 and 30 are convenient numbers for 27.

Cubic Centimeter (URG Unit 8 p. 37; SG p. 216; TIG p. 335)
The volume of a cube that is one centimeter long on each edge.

D

Decimal (URG Unit 3 p. 84)
1. A number written using the base-ten place value system.
2. A number containing a decimal point. (*See also* decimal fraction.)

Decimal Fraction (URG Unit 10 p. 50)
A fraction written as a decimal. For example, 0.75 and 0.4 are decimal fractions and $\frac{75}{100}$ and $\frac{4}{10}$ are called common fractions.

Decimeter (URG Unit 10 p. 34; SG p. 271)
A unit of length in the metric system. A decimeter is $\frac{1}{10}$ of a meter.

Degree (URG Unit 2 p. 103; SG p. 47)
A degree (°) is a unit of measure for angles. There are 360 degrees in a circle.

Denominator (URG Unit 10 p. 65 & Unit 12 pp. 32, 34; SG pp. 276, 326)
The number below the line in a fraction. The denominator indicates the number of equal parts in which the unit whole is divided. For example, the 5 is the denominator in the fraction $\frac{2}{5}$. In this case the unit whole is divided into five equal parts.

Dividend (URG Unit 3 p. 28; SG p. 58)
The number that is divided in a division problem, e.g., 12 is the dividend in $12 \div 3 = 4$.

Divisible (URG Unit 7 p. 49; SG p. 184)
A number a is divisible by a number b, if there is no remainder when a is divided by b. For example, 12 is divisible by 4 ($12 \div 4 = 3$), but **not** by 5 ($12 \div 5 = 2$ R2).

Division Sentence (SG p. 58)
A number sentence involving division.

Divisor (URG Unit 3 p. 28 & Unit 8 p. 131; SG pp. 58, 235, 236)
In a division problem, the number by which another number is divided. In the problem $12 \div 4 = 3$, the 4 is the divisor, the 12 is the dividend, and the 3 is the quotient.

E

Edge (URG Unit 9 p. 87; SG p. 256)
A line segment where two faces of a three-dimensional figure meet.

Equilateral Triangle (URG Unit 2 p. 119 & Unit 9 p. 78; SG p. 241)
A triangle with all sides and all angles equal.

Equivalent Fractions (URG Unit 12 pp. 36, 37, 73, 75; SG p. 343)
Fractions that have the same value, e.g., $\frac{2}{4} = \frac{1}{2}$.

Estimate (URG Unit 3 p. 112 & Unit 7 p. 109; SG p. 202; TIG p. 249)
1. (verb) To find *about* how many.
2. (noun) An approximate number.

Even Number (SG p. 98)
Numbers that are multiples of 2 (2, 4, 6, 8, etc.) are called even numbers.

Exponent (URG Unit 4 p. 72; SG pp. 98, 113)
The number of times the base is multiplied by itself. In $= 3 \times 3 \times 3 \times 3 = 81$, the 3 is the base and the 4 is the exponent. The 3 is multiplied by itself 4 times.

Extrapolation (URG Unit 5 p. 28; SG p. 124; TIG p. 321)
Using patterns in data to make predictions or to estimate values that lie beyond the range of values in the set of data.

F

Face (URG Unit 9 p. 87; SG p. 256)
A plane figure that is one side of a three-dimensional figure.

Fact Family (URG Unit 3 pp. 28, 29 & URG Unit 8 p. 130; SG pp. 59, 234; TIG p. X)
Related math facts, e.g., $3 \times 4 = 12$, $4 \times 3 = 12$, $2 \div 3 = 4$, $12 \div 4 = 3$.

Factor (URG Unit 3 p. 30 & Unit 4 p. 49; SG pp. 61, 103, 184)
In a multiplication problem, the numbers that are multiplied together. In the problem $3 \times 4 = 12$, 3 and 4 are the factors.
Whole numbers that can be multiplied together to get a number. That is, numbers that divide a number evenly, e.g., 1, 2, 3, 4, 6, and 12 are all the factors of 12.

Factor Tree (URG Unit 4 p. 70; SG p. 111)
A diagram that shows the prime factorization of a number.

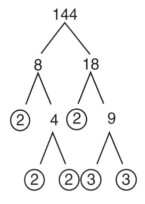

Fair Game or Fair Number Cube (URG Unit 14 p. 52)
A game in which it is equally likely that any player will win. A number cube is fair if all the faces are equally likely to appear.

Fewest Pieces Rule
(URG Unit 3 pp. 53, 62, 64 & Unit 10 p. 53; SG p. 74)
Using the least number of base-ten pieces to represent a number. (*See also* base-ten pieces.)

Fixed Variables (URG Unit 1 p. 96, Unit 2 p. 57, & Unit 5 pp. 77, 79; SG p. 141; TIG p. 310)
Variables in an experiment that are held constant or not changed.

Flat (URG Unit 3 pp. 9, 63 & Unit 6 p. 56; SG p. 68)
A block that measures 1 cm × 10 cm × 10 cm. It is one of the base-ten pieces and is often used to represent 100. (*See also* base-ten pieces.)

Forgiving Method of Division
(URG Unit 13 p. 59; SG p. 366)
A paper-and-pencil method for division in which successive partial quotients are chosen and partial products are subtracted from the dividend, until the remainder is less than the divisor. The sum of the partial quotients is the quotient. For example, $644 \div 7$ can be solved as shown at the right. This method of division is called the forgiving method because it "forgives" estimates of the partial quotients that are too low.

$$\begin{array}{r} 92 \\ 7\overline{\smash{\big)}644} \\ \underline{140} \quad 20 \\ 504 \\ \underline{350} \quad 50 \\ 154 \\ \underline{140} \quad 20 \\ 14 \\ \underline{14} \quad 2 \\ 0 \quad 92 \end{array}$$

Front-End Estimation (URG Unit 3 pp. 10, 85)
Estimation by looking at the left-most digit.

Function (URG Unit 15 pp. 9, 76; TIG pp. 265, 269)
A rule that assigns to any input number exactly one output number. More generally, a rule that assigns to the elements of one set (the domain) exactly one element of another set (the target).

Glossary

G

H

Hexagon (URG Unit 2 p. 124)
A six-sided polygon.

Hieroglyphics (URG Unit 11 p. 97)
An ancient Egyptian form of writing.

I

Identity Property of Multiplication (URG Unit 3 p. 31)
This is also known as the Property of One for
Multiplication. One times any number is that number.
Using variables, $n \times 1 = n$.

Impossible Event (URG Unit 14 pp. 8, 29; SG p. 384)
An event that has a probability of 0 or 0%.

Infinite (URG Unit 9 p. 82)
Cannot be counted in a finite amount of time. More than
any number.

Interpolation (URG Unit 5 p. 28; SG p. 124; TIG p. 321)
Making predictions or estimating values that lie between
data points in a set of data.

Intersect (SG p. 238)
To meet or cross.

J

K

L

Likely Event (URG Unit 14 pp. 8, 30; SG p. 385)
An event that has a high probability of occurring.

Line (URG Unit 9 pp. 10, 34; SG p. 239)
A set of points that form a straight path extending infinitely
in two directions.

Line Segment (URG Unit 9 p. 34; SG p. 239)
A part of a line between and including two points called
the endpoints.

Line of Symmetry (URG Unit 9 pp. 11, 63; SG p. 251)
A line is a line of symmetry for a plane figure if, when the
figure is folded along this line, the two parts match exactly.

Line Symmetry (URG Unit 9 pp. 11, 63; SG p. 251)
A figure has line symmetry if it has at least one line
of symmetry.

Liter (SG p. 219)
Metric unit used to measure volume. A liter is a little more
than a quart.

M

Manipulated Variable (URG Unit 5 pp. 77, 78, 79 &
Unit 10 p. 87; SG p. 140; TIG p. 309)
In an experiment, the variable with values known at the
beginning of the experiment. The experimenter often
chooses these values before data is collected. The manipu
lated variable is often called the independent variable.

Mass (URG Unit 8 p. 36 & Unit 15 pp. 92, 94; SG pp. 41
418; TIG p. 349)
The amount of matter in an object.

Mean (URG Unit 1 p. 67 & Unit 5 pp. 49, 50;
SG pp. 125, 135; TIG p. 241)
An average of a set of numbers that is found by adding the
values of the data and dividing by the number of values.

Measurement Division (URG Unit 4 p. 9; TIG p. 303)
Division as equal grouping. The total number of objects
and the number of objects in each group are known. The
number of groups is the unknown. For example, tulip bulb
come in packages of 8. If 216 bulbs are sold, how many
packages are sold?

Measurement Error (TIG p. 256)
The unavoidable error that occurs due to the limitations
inherent to any measurement instrument.

Median (URG Unit 1 p. 67 & Unit 5 pp. 49, 50;
SG pp. 13, 125; TIG p. 244)
For a set with an odd number of data arranged in order, it
the middle number. For an even number of data arranged i
order, it is the number halfway between the two middle
numbers.

Megabit (URG Unit 6 p. 57)
A base-ten model that is a cube with an edge of length
100 cm. It represents 1,000,000 since it has a volume of
1,000,000 cubic cm.

Meniscus (URG Unit 8 p. 35; SG p. 221; DAB p. 101;
TIG p. 342)
The curved surface formed when a liquid creeps up the si
of a container (for example, a graduated cylinder).

Meter (SG p. 270; TIG p. 326)
A unit of length in the metric system. A meter is a bit mor
that 39 inches.

Milliliter (ml) (URG Unit 8 p. 37; SG p. 219; TIG p. 342
A measure of capacity in the metric system that is the
volume of a cube that is one centimeter long on each side.

Millimeter (SG p. 273; TIG p. 326)
A unit of length in the metric system. A millimeter is one-
thousandth of a meter, i.e., one-tenth of a centimeter.

Millions Period (URG Unit 6 p. 30; SG pp. 151, 158, 159)
The sequence of digits (if any) in the millions place, the ten-millions place, and the hundred millions place. In the number 12,**456**,789,987 the millions period is in bold type.

Multiple (URG Unit 4 p. 34 & Unit 7 p. 83; SG pp. 98, 185)
A number is a multiple of another number if it is evenly divisible by that number. For example, 12 is a multiple of 2 since 2 divides 12 evenly.

Multiplicand (URG Unit 11 pp. 8, 35)
Either of the numbers being multiplied in a multiplication problem.

N

Negative Number (URG Unit 3 p. 102; SG p. 87)
A number less than zero; a number to the left of zero on a horizontal number line.

Net (URG Unit 9 pp. 11, 91; SG p. 258)
A way of representing the surface of a three-dimensional solid in two-dimensions. A net can be obtained by cutting the surface along edges until it can be laid flat on a plane.

Number Sentence
An equation or inequality with numbers. For example, $3 \times 2 + 5 = 10 + 1$ and $2 < 3 + 1$

Numeral (URG Unit 3 p. 42)
A symbol used to represent a number.

Numerator (URG Unit 10 p. 65 & Unit 12 pp. 32, 34; SG pp. 276, 326)
The number written above the line in a fraction. For example, the 2 is the numerator in the fraction $\frac{2}{5}$. (*See also* denominator.)

Numerical Variable (URG Unit 1 pp. 9, 51; SG p. 7; TIG p. 309)
Variables with values that are numbers. (*See also* variable and value.)

O

Obtuse angle (URG Unit 2 p. 105 & Unit 9 p. 45; SG p. 51)
An angle that measures more than 90°.

Odd Number (SG p. 98)
Numbers that are not multiples of 2 (1, 3, 5 ,7, etc.) are called odd numbers.

Ones Period (URG Unit 6 p. 31; SG pp. 151, 158)
The sequence of digits (if any) in the ones place, the tens place, and the hundreds place. In the number 12,456,789,**987** the ones period is in bold type.

Operation (SG p. 180)
A process that takes two numbers and results in a third. This, more precisely, is called a binary operation. For example, addition, subtraction, multiplication, and division are operations.

Order of Operations (URG Unit 7 p. 33; SG p. 180)
A convention that determines how to find the value of an expression that has more than one operation.

P

Pack (URG Unit 3 pp. 9, 64; SG p. 68)
A cube that measures 10 cm on each edge. It is one of the base-ten pieces and is often used to represent 1000. (*See also* base-ten pieces.)

Papyrus (URG Unit 11 p. 99)
A type of writing paper used by the ancient Egyptians.

Parallel Lines (URG Unit 9 pp. 33, 34, 36; SG p. 238)
Lines that are in the same direction. In the plane, parallel lines are lines that do not intersect.

Parallelogram (URG Unit 9 p. 35; SG p. 241)
A quadrilateral with two pairs of parallel sides.

Partitive Division (URG Unit 4 p. 9; TIG p. 303)
Division as equal sharing. The total number of objects and the number of groups are known. The number of objects in each group is the unknown. For example, Frank has 144 marbles that he divides equally into 6 groups. How many marbles are in each group?

Perimeter (URG Unit 2 p. 39; SG pp. 29, 33)
The distance around a two-dimensional shape.

Period (URG Unit 6 p. 31; SG p. 151)
A group of three places in a large number, starting on the right, often separated by commas as shown at the right.

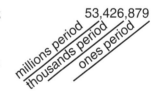

Perpendicular (URG Unit 9 p. 33; SG p. 238)
Perpendicular lines are lines that meet at right angles.

Perspective (URG Unit 9 p. 90)
The art of drawing solid objects on a flat surface so that it produces the same impression as do the actual objects when viewed from a particular point.

Glossary

Point (URG Unit 9 p. 44)
An exact position in the plane or in space.

Polygon (URG Unit 9 p. 49; SG p. 247)
A two-dimensional connected figure made of line segments in which each endpoint of every side meets with an endpoint of exactly one other side.

Polyhedron (URG Unit 9 p. 94)
A connected geometric solid whose surface is made of polygons.

Portfolio (URG Unit 2 p. 93; TIG p. 289)
A collection of student work that shows how a student's skills, attitudes, and knowledge change over time.

Positive Number (URG Unit 3 p. 102; SG p. 88)
A number greater than zero; a number to the right of zero on a horizontal number line.

Powers of Two (URG Unit 6 p. 40; SG p. 155)
2 multiplied by itself a certain number of times. $2^1 = 2$, $2^2 = 2 \times 2 = 4$, $2^3 = 2 \times 2 \times 2 = 8$, etc.

Prime Factor (URG Unit 4 p. 70; SG p. 110)
A factor of a number that is itself prime.

Prime Number (URG Unit 4 pp. 9, 34, 52; SG pp. 98, 104)
A number that has exactly two factors, itself and 1. For example, 7 has exactly two distinct factors, 1 and 7.

Prism (URG Unit 9 pp. 12, 94; SG p. 259)
A polyhedron that has two congruent faces, called bases, that are parallel to each other, and all other faces are parallelograms. If the other faces are rectangles the prism is called a right prism.

Prisms   Not a prism

Probability (URG Unit 14 pp. 8, 30, 52; SG pp. 385, 390)
A number from 0 to 1 (0% to 100%) that describes how likely an event is to happen. The closer that the probability of an event is to one, the more likely the event will happen.

Product (URG Unit 3 p. 30; SG pp. 61, 107)
The answer to a multiplication problem. In the problem $3 \times 4 = 12$, 12 is the product.

Q

Quadrilateral (URG Unit 9 pp. 35, 49; SG pp. 56, 248)
A polygon with four sides. (*See also* polygon.)

Quick Paper-and-Pencil Method for Addition
(URG Unit 3 p. 83; SG p. 79)
A traditional method for adding multidigit numbers. See example at right:

$$\begin{array}{r} 1\overset{1}{3}\overset{1}{2}6 \\ +575 \\ \hline 1901 \end{array}$$

Quick Paper-and-Pencil Method for Subtraction
(SG p. 82)
A traditional method for subtraction. For example:

$$\begin{array}{r} \overset{0}{\cancel{1}}\overset{1}{\cancel{2}}\overset{12}{\cancel{3}}\overset{1}{7} \\ -459 \\ \hline 778 \end{array}$$

Quotient (URG Unit 3 p. 28 & Unit 13 p. 59; SG pp. 58, 235, 236)
The answer to a division problem. In the problem $12 \div 3 = 4$, the 4 is the quotient.

R

Ray (URG Unit 9 pp. 34, 44; SG p. 240)
A part of a line that has one endpoint and extends indefinitely in one direction.

Recording Sheet (URG Unit 3 p. 51; SG pp. 68, 79)
A place value chart used for addition and subtraction problems.

Rectangle (URG Unit 2 p. 84 & Unit 9 p. 80)
A quadrilateral with four right angles.

Reflex Angle (URG Unit 2 p. 105)
An angle larger than 180° but less than 360°.

Regular (URG Unit 9 p. 79)
A polygon is regular if all sides are of equal length and all angles are equal.

Remainder (URG Unit 13 p. 58)
Something that remains or is left after a whole number division problem. The portion of the dividend that is not evenly divisible by the divisor, e.g., $16 \div 5 = 3$ with 1 as a remainder.

Responding Variable (URG Unit 5 pp. 77, 79 & Unit 10 p. 87; SG p. 140; TIG p. 309)
The variable whose values result from the experiment. Experimenters find the values of the responding variable by doing the experiment. The responding variable is often called the dependent variable.

Rhombus (URG Unit 2 p. 124)
A quadrilateral with four sides of equal length.

Right Angle (URG Unit 2 p. 104 & Unit 9 p. 45; SG p. 48)
An angle that measures 90°.

Roman Numeral (URG Unit 3 pp. 42, 43; SG p. 64)
A system of representing numbers used by the Romans. The symbol I represents 1, V represents five, X represents ten, etc.

Rounded Number (URG Unit 6 pp. 95, 96 & Unit 7 p. 119)
See rounding.

Rounding (URG Unit 6 p. 71; TIG p. 253)
Replacing a number with the nearest convenient number.
Numbers are often rounded to the nearest whole number,
ten, hundred, fifty, etc.

S

Skinny (URG Unit 3 pp. 9, 51, 62, 63 & Unit 6 p. 56;
SG p. 68)
A block that measures 1 cm × 1 cm
× 10 cm. It is one of the base-ten
pieces that is often used to represent 10.
(*See also* base-ten pieces.)

Solid (URG Unit 9 pp. 11, 87, 94; SG p. 256)
A three-dimensional figure that has volume greater than 0.

Square (URG Unit 2 pp. 84, 119, 124)
A polygon with four equal sides and four right angles.

Square Inch (SG p. 29)
The area of a square with a side length of one inch.

Square Number (URG Unit 4 p. 34; SG p. 98)
A number that is the result of multiplying a whole number by
itself. For example, 36 is a square number since $36 = 6 \times 6$.

Square Root (URG Unit 15 p. 59)
The square root of a number N is the number whose square is
N. The symbol for square root is $\sqrt{\ }$. For example, the
square root of 25 is 5, since $5 \times 5 = 25$. In symbols we write
$\sqrt{25} = 5$. The square root of 26 is not a whole number.

Subtractive Principle (URG Unit 3 p. 43; SG p. 66)
A method of interpreting certain Roman numerals.
For example, IX represents 9 while XI represents 11.

Super Bit (URG Unit 6 pp. 55, 56)
A base-ten model that is a cube with an edge of length
10 cm. It represents 1,000 since it has a volume of 1,000
cubic centimeters. It is usually called a pack.

Super Flat (URG Unit 6 p. 56)
A base-ten model that is a rectangular solid that measures
10 cm × 100 cm × 100 cm. It represents 100,000 since it
has a volume of 100,000 cubic cm.

Super Skinny (URG Unit 6 p. 56)
A base-ten model that is a rectangular solid that measures
10 cm × 10 cm × 100 cm. It represents 10,000 since it has
a volume of 10,000 cubic cm.

Survey (SG p. 358)
An investigation conducted by collecting data from a
sample of a population and then analyzing it. Usually
surveys are used to make predictions about the entire
population.

T

Tally
A way of recording a count by making marks. Usually
tallies are grouped in fives. ⊪⊪ |||

Ten Percent (10%) (URG Unit 6 p. 82 & Unit 7 p. 109)
10 out of every hundred or $\frac{1}{10}$.

Thousands Period (URG Unit 6 p. 30; SG pp. 151,
158, 159)
The sequence of digits (if any) in the thousands place,
the ten-thousands place, and the hundred-thousands place.
In the number 12,456,**789,**987 the thousands period is in
bold type.

TIMS Laboratory Method (URG Unit 1 p. 9;
SG pp. 17–20; TIG p. 307)
A method that students use to organize experiments and
investigations. It involves four phases: draw, collect, graph,
and explore. It is a way to help students learn about the scientific method.

Translational Symmetry (URG Unit 9 p. 11)
A pattern has translational symmetry if there is a transla-
tion that moves the pattern so it coincides with itself.

Trapezoid (URG Unit 2 p. 124)
A quadrilateral with exactly one pair of parallel sides.

Triangle (URG Unit 2 p. 124)
A polygon with three sides.

Turn-Around Facts (URG Unit 3 p. 29; SG p. 61)
Multiplication facts that have the same factors but in a
different order, e.g., $3 \times 4 = 12$ and $4 \times 3 = 12$.
(*See also* commutative property of multiplication.)

Turn-Around Rule (URG Unit 4 p. 30)
A term used to describe the commutative property of
multiplication. (*See also* commutative property of
multiplication.)

Turn Symmetry (URG Unit 9 pp. 10, 65; SG p. 251)
A figure has turn symmetry if it can be rotated around a
point (called the center of turning) through an angle less
than 360° and so that the turned figure matches the original.

Type of Turn Symmetry (URG Unit 9 p. 65)
The number of times a figure coincides with itself when
it is rotated about its center of turning. For example, a
square has 4-fold turn symmetry. This is also called $\frac{1}{4}$ turn
symmetry.

Glossary

U

Undefined (Division by Zero) (URG Unit 13 p. 87; SG p. 376)
We say division by 0 is undefined because there is no number that satisfies the definition of division when 0 is the divisor. For example, if there were a number $N = 3 \div 0$, it would be the unique number N that makes $N \times 0 = 3$ a true statement. There is no such N.

Unlikely Event (URG Unit 14 p. 29; SG p. 384)
An event that has small probability.

V

Value (URG Unit 1 pp. 35, 51; SG pp. 3, 7; TIG p. 309)
The possible outcomes of a variable. For example, red, green, and blue are possible values for the variable *color*. Two meters and 1.65 meters are possible values for the variable *length*.

Variable (URG Unit 1 pp. 9, 35; SG p. 3; TIG p. 309)
1. An attribute or quantity that changes or varies. (*See also* categorical variable and numerical variable.)
2. A symbol that can stand for a variable.

Vertex (URG Unit 2 p. 103 & Unit 9 pp. 44, 87; SG pp. 46, 243, 256)
The common endpoint of two rays or line segments.

Volume (URG Unit 8 p. 36 & Unit 9 p. 109; SG p. 216; TIG p. 335)
The measure of the amount of space occupied by an object.

Volume by Displacement (SG p. 217; DAB p. 101; TIG p. 344)
A way of measuring volume by measuring the amount of water (or some other fluid) it displaces.

W

Weight (URG Unit 15 p. 92; SG p. 417)
A measure of the pull of gravity on an object. One unit for measuring weight is the pound.

X

Y

Z

Zero Property of Multiplication (URG Unit 3 p. 31)
Any number times zero is zero. Using variables, $n \times 0 = 0$.

SECTION 19

Grade 4 Index

This index provides the unit number in parentheses followed by the page number for the multivolume URG (*Unit Resource Guide*). It provides page references for the SG (*Student Guide*), the DAB (*Discovery Assignment Book*), the AB (*Adventure Book*), and the TIG (*Teacher Implementation Guide*). Definitions or explanations of key terms can be found on the pages listed in bold type.

A

Abacus, AB 69
Abstract reasoning, TIG 400
Academic language, TIG 378
Accountability, measures of, TIG 361–362
Accuracy, TIG 77, 243, 261, 299, 327, 345–346, URG (6) 82. *See also* Approximation, Closeness, Estimation, Ten percent benchmark
   TIMS Tutor on, TIG 249–264
Acre(s), URG (6) 25, **32**
Acute angles, DAB 13, 126–129, SG **50**–51, 54–55, URG (2) iii, 30, **104** 120–121, URG (3) 17, URG (5) 16, 133, URG (8) 110, URG (9) 17, 21–22, **45**, URG (11) 16
Addends, URG (3) 84
Adding It Up: Helping Children Learn Mathematics **(National Research Council),** URG (13) 10
Addition, DAB 3, 6, 86, 124, 157, 186, SG 78–85, TIG 66, URG (1) 15–16, 22, URG (3) 79–92, URG (4) 20, 23, URG (5) 13, URG (7) 25, URG (9) 27, URG (10) 21, URG (14) 22, URG (16) 12, 18
  with base-ten pieces, SG 78–80, 84–85, URG (3) 83–85
  estimation, DAB 68, TIG 251–252
  of fractions, TIG 104, URG (12) 48–52
  Math Facts, TIG 169, 277–278, URG (1) 29–30
  multidigit, SG 174, TIG 277
  number sentences, URG (12) 99–100
  paper-and-pencil, SG **79**–80, 84, 174, URG (3) **83**
  problem types, TIG 300–302
  quick paper-and-pencil method for addition, URG (3) 83
  quiz on, URG (1) 29–30, URG (3) 92
  repeated, URG (3) 28
  word problems, URG (3) 109–115
Additive property of mass, URG (15) 91
Addressing Accessibility in Mathematics Project, Education Development Center (EDC), TIG 383, 388–393
Advance organizers, TIG 386

Adventure Book (AB), TIG 12, 24, 39, 49, 54, 58, 75, 92, 98, 101, 117
Alberto in TenthsLand, AB 45–56, TIG 98, URG (10) 108–115
Algebra, TIG 11, 132, 134, 136, 138, 140, 142, 144, 146, 148, 150, 152, 154, 156, 158, 160, 162, URG (15) 8, 76. *See also* Function machines, Functions, Number sentences, Patterns, Variables
Algebra Standards for Grades 3–5 **(National Council of Teachers of Mathematics),** URG (15) 8–10
Algorithms, TIG 15, 230, 434
  all-partials, SG 197, TIG 230, 434, 479, URG (7) 10
  compact (traditional), URG (11) 9, 61–68
  quick paper-and-pencil method for addition, URG (3) 83
  quick paper-and-pencil method for subtraction, SG 82
All-Partials method of multiplication, TIG 100–102, 442, URG (7) iii, 10, 99, URG (11) iii, 8–9, 53, 64, 79, 87
American Association for Gifted Children (AAGC), TIG 409
Analyzing data, in TIMS Laboratory Method, TIG 321–322
Angle of turning, URG (9) 10, 64–**65**, 70, 126, 129
Angles, SG 41–56, **42**, 243–250, TIG 60, 63, 90–91, URG (2) 9, 97–108, **101**, URG (9) iii, 10, 17, 21–22, 41–52, URG (15) 16, 23
  acute, SG **50**–51, 54–55, URG (2) iii, 30, **104**, 120–121
  circles for, URG (2) 108
  comparing, SG 43–44, 53
  descriptions of, URG (9) 44–46
  drawing, DAB 126, SG 47, 54, URG (5) 16
  estimating sizes of, URG (3) 17
  of hexagons, DAB 145
  measurement of, DAB 13, 127–129, SG 243–250, URG (9) 46–48, URG (10) 23
  obtuse, SG **51**, 54–55, URG (2) iii, 30, **105,** 120–121
  in pattern blocks, DAB 17–19, SG 55–56, URG (2) 116–124
  in pentagons, URG (11) 16
  reflex, URG (2) **105**

Divisors, SG **58, 235–236,** URG (3) **28,** URG (8) **131,** URG (10) 17

Dodgson, Charles, URG (10) 86

Doubling, SG 154, 156–158, TIG 78, 278–280, URG (1) 20, 29, URG (2) 14, 26, 34, URG (6) 23, 37–49, URG (7) 16, 20, URG (11) iii, URG (15) 8–9
  in ancient Egypt (duplation), AB 62, 67–68, URG (11) iii, 106
  function machines for, URG (15) 76–77

Downhill Racer Lab, DAB 250, SG 288–295, TIG 95–97, URG (10) 80–98, URG (16) 27, 31

Draw, Place, and Read Game, DAB 75, SG 159, TIG 459–460, URG (7) 16, URG (11) 19

Drop heights, AB 17–28, DAB 56, URG (12) 72–90, 95–101, URG (12) 84

Duplation, AB 62, 67–68, URG (11) iii, 106

E

Edges
  of polygons, URG (9) 79
  of prisms, URG (9) **87**
  of shapes, SG **256–259**

Education Development Center (EDC), TIG 383, 388–393

Egypt, ancient, URG (11) 104–107. *See also* Phil and Howard's Excellent Egyptian Adventure

Einstein, Albert, TIG 349

Endpoints, URG (9) 49

English language learners, TIG 3, 369–381
  improving skills of, TIG 411
  introduction to, TIG 369–370
  language-rich approach to, TIG 372–373
  lesson plan examples for, TIG 376–377
  nonverbal communication and, TIG 380
  outcomes, TIG 376
  strategies for, TIG 379–380
  support, TIG 371
  teacher issues with, TIG 375
  theory on, TIG 370–371
  tools supporting, TIG 371

Equal-Arm balance, TIG 272, 350–352. *See also* Two-Pan balance

Equal grouping model of division, URG (13) 8

Equal sharing model of division, URG (4) 9, URG (13) 8

Equator, AB 93

Equilateral triangles, SG **241,** URG (2) **119,** URG (9) 36, 63, 66, **78,** 121, 126

Equity Principle, TIG 9, 368

Equivalent fractions, SG **343**–345, TIG 105, URG (12) 11, 35–37, 71–77, **73, 74**

Equivalent sets, TIG 302–303

Error. *See* Experimental error

Estimation, DAB 94–95, TIG 17, 79–80, 83, 88, 249–264, 299, 345, URG (1) 81, 99, 104, 117, URG (2) 27, URG (3) 20, 112–113, URG (4) 13–14, URG (6) 24, 91–103, URG (7) iii, 9–10, 106–112, URG (13) 14. *See also* Accuracy
  of angle size, URG (9) 45–46
  of area, URG (7) 29
  benchmarks for, SG 169
  of calculations, TIG 251–257
  closeness and, TIG 259–260, URG (6) 77–87
  with convenient numbers, DAB 87, SG 202–206
  definition of, TIG **249**–250
  front-end, URG (3) 9, **85**
  of growth patterns, URG (15) 57, 59
  of large numbers, URG (6) 95–96, URG (7) 26, URG (8) 23
  of length, SG 35, URG (1) 28, URG (7) 20
  of measurements, TIG 260–262
  of mileage, URG (7) 110–111
  of money, URG (6) 97–98
  with multiplication, TIG 252–253, URG (7) 109–110
  number sense and, URG (6) 9
  of numbers of objects, TIG 262–264, URG (6) 80–84
  place value and, DAB 68
  of probability, URG (14) 8
  in problem solving, TIG 299
  of products, SG **202**–206, 306–307, 311, 315, URG (8) 19
  of quantities by comparing, SG 162–167
  of quotients, URG (13) 8, 74–75
  reasonable, URG (6) 84–85
  of steps walked per hour, URG (8) 85–99
  of sums and differences, SG 171–174, URG (6) 96–97
  teaching, TIG 250
  ten percent benchmark for. *See* Ten percent benchmark
  TIMS Tutor on, TIG 249–264
  of volume, URG (8) 20–21, 36–37, URG (9) 111–112
  word problems in, TIG 56, URG (5) 119–123, URG (7) 128–133

Estimation and Number Sense **(Threadgill-Sowder),** TIG 250

Euclid, URG (4) 9

Evaluation of Learning in Arithmetic, The **(Brownell),** URG (8) 90

Evening out, URG (5) 62, URG (14) 51

Even numbers, SG **98,** URG (7) 48–49, URG (12) 25

Events
  certain, SG **385,** URG (14) 29
  chance of, URG (14) 26–37
  impossible, SG **384,** URG (14) 8
  likely, AB 78, SG **385,** URG (14) 29
  unlikely, SG **384,** URG (14) 29

Expectations, TIG 17, 359

special education students, TIG 382–395
  introduction to, TIG 382–383
  lesson planning for, TIG 387–393
  research on, TIG 383–387
Individualized Education, TIG 383. *See also* Special
  education students
Individuals with Disabilities Education Act of 2004,
  TIG 382
Infinite numbers, AB 40, URG (9) **82**
Information for parents
  English, URG (3) 11
  Spanish, URG (3) 12
Input, in functions, URG (15) 76, 78
Interest centers, in classrooms, TIG 404
International Bureau of Weights and Measures,
  TIG 353
International Wildlife Association, AB 92
Internet resources for parents, TIG 445–446
Interpolation, SG **124,** TIG **321,** 345, URG (5) **28,** 98,
  134, URG (8) 112, 121, URG (10) 89, URG (12)
  125, URG (16) 28
  in Bouncing Ball Lab, URG (5) 82
Intersecting lines, SG **238,** URG (1) 94
Intervals, in bar graphs, URG (13) 41
Intuitive understanding, of gifted or talented children,
  TIG 398
Inventory tests, URG (3) 16, URG (16) 8
  division, URG (16) 21–22
  multiplication, URG (8) 130
Inverse relationship (multiplication and division), URG
  (12) 10, URG (13) 87
Investigation, TIG 311–312
IQ scores, TIG 397

Join **problem types,** TIG 300
Journals, math, TIG 174, 184, 190, 197, 204, 271–274
Journey to Flatopia, AB 29–44, TIG 92, URG (9) 76–83
Juice boxes, volume of, URG (9) 111–112
Jupiter (planet), AB 77

K

Karplus, Robert, TIG 15
Key words, reading and, TIG 415–416
Kilograms (kg), URG (15) 100
Knowing **rubric,** SG 441, TIG 200–201, URG (6) 91–92,
  97–99, URG (7) 61–73, URG (8) 85–97, URG
  (10) 67–69, URG (16) 71–75

L

Labeling axes, TIG 317–318, URG (1) 38
Labs
  Area *vs.* Length, SG 435–438, TIG 120, URG (16)
    46–60
  Arm Span *vs.* Height, SG 17–23, TIG 58–59, URG (1)
    89–106
  assessment, TIG 185, 204
  Bouncing Ball, AB 15–28, SG 139–145, TIG 75, URG
    (5) iii, 8, 18, 72–90
  Downhill Racer, DAB 250, SG 288–295, TIG 97, URG
    (10) 80–98, URG (16) 27, 31
  Fill 'er Up!, URG (5) 19
  Perimeter *vs.* Length, SG 31–36, URG (2) 50–65
  Plant Growth, SG 379–381, 402–405, TIG 111, 117,
    URG (13) 97–106, URG (14) 15, URG (15) 8,
    24–25
  review of, DAB 113–114, 251–252, SG 232–238, 430,
    TIG 88, 120–121, 198–199, URG (8) 116–123,
    URG (16) 23–38
  Rolling a Number Cube, SG 388–391, URG (14) 39–44
  Stencilrama, URG (1) 80
  Taste of TIMS, SG 419–423, TIG 118, URG (15)
    87–101
  Volume *vs.* Number, SG 225–229, TIG 88, URG (8)
    60–73
Language arts connections, TIG 10, 12, URG (1) 86,
  URG (14) 101
Large numbers, TIG 66, 77, URG (6) 25–34, URG (7) 24,
  URG (14) 10–11, 51
  estimation of, URG (6) 95–96, URG (7) 26, URG (8) 23
  in news, URG (6) 30–31
  place value chart for, URG (6) 31–32
Latitude, URG (9) 82
Law of large numbers, URG (14) 10–11, 51
Learning centers, in classrooms, TIG 399, 404
Length. *See* Measurement of length
Length × width **formula,** TIG 331
Lesson planning
  for English language learners, TIG 377–379
  for gifted or talented students, TIG 402–407
  for special education students, TIG 387–393
Lessons, assessment, TIG 185–186
Less than or equal to **(<),** DAB 179–181, URG (12) 58
Letter Home
  English, URG (1) iii, URG (2) iii, URG (3) iii, URG (4)
    iii, URG (5) iii, URG (6) iii, URG (7) iii, URG (8)
    iii, URG (9) iii, URG (10) iii, URG (11) iii, URG
    (12) iii, URG (13) iii, URG (14) iii, URG (15) iii,
    URG (16) iii
  Spanish, URG (1) iv, URG (2) iv, URG (3) iv, URG (4)
    iv, URG (5) iv, URG (6) iv, URG (7) iv, URG (8)

M

URG (11) iv, URG (12) iv, URG (13) iv, URG (14) iv, URG (15) iv, URG (16) iv

Math Facts information for, TIG 426, 441–444

Math Facts philosophy for, TIG 426, 441, URG (3) 10

programs for, TIG 427–431

Spanish language materials for, TIG 439–440

TV survey activity and, URG (13) 44

Multidigit numbers, URG (7) 53

Multiples, SG **98,** 185, URG (4) iii, **34**–35, 93, URG (5) 13–14, URG (7) 48–53, **83,** URG (13) 89, URG (14) 16

of one hundred, URG (13) 19

of ten, URG (7) 26, URG (9) 25, URG (11) 22, 53–54, URG (13) 19

Multiple representations of procedures, TIG 385

Multiple trials, SG 141, TIG 257, 314, 401, URG (10) 88–89, URG (15) 48, URG (16) 27–28

Multiplicands, URG (11) **8, 35,** 87

Multiplication, AB 58–59, DAB 6, 37–49, 83–89, 157, 183–189, 193, 214, 228, 240, SG 96–101, 298, TIG 81–84, 99–102, URG (2) 28, URG (4) 17–18, 20, URG (7) 27–28, 94–103, URG (8) 27, 29, 107–108, URG (9) 19, URG (10) 21, URG (11) 8–9, 15, 26–43, 49–57, 79, URG (12) 18, 20, 122, URG (13) 14, 16, 91, URG (15) 16, 21, URG (16) 18, 90

all-partials method of, SG **197**–201, 305–307, 313–316, URG (7) iii, URG (11) iii

array model of, SG 96–108, 234, URG (4) iii, 8

on Base-Ten Board, URG (11) 33–35

with base-ten pieces, URG (11) 20

break-apart products of, SG 190–192, 298–303, URG (11) 30–33

compact method of, SG 308–312, 317–321, URG (7) iii, URG (11) 61–68, 85–90

divisibility rules and, DAB 188

division and, DAB 216, URG (13) 84–92

estimation in, TIG 252–253, URG (7) 109–110

fact families for, URG (7) 15

Facts I Know, chart for, DAB 33, SG **62,** URG (3) 15, URG (5) 12

Facts Inventory Test on, TIG 89

by five, TIG 65, URG (3) 24–36

grouping in, DAB 88

inventory test on, URG (8) 130

Last Six Facts in, DAB 89

Math Facts on, SG 58–63, 234–236, TIG 169, 280–282, URG (3) 3–4, 8, 22, URG (4) 14, URG (5) 8, 11, URG (8) 13–14, 17, 21, 25, 28, 126–137, URG (9) 18, 22, 24, 27, URG (10) 18, 26, URG (11) 18, URG (12) 21–22, URG (14) 20, URG (15) 18, URG (16) 17

with money, URG (5) 15

by multiples of ten, URG (11) 53–54

by nine, URG (6) 16, 19–22, 24

9-to-5 War Game and, URG (6) 110–114

number sentences for, SG 100, 303, URG (8) 130, URG (12) 99–100

by one, SG 61, URG (3) 30

by one hundred, DAB 186–187

order of operations in, DAB 85, SG **180**–183, **223,** TIG 82, URG (7) 9, 18, 30–38, **33,** URG (8) 18, 107, URG (15) 20

patterns in, TIG 81–82, URG (7) 9–10

problem types in, TIG 302–303

Product Bingo Game Boards for, DAB 49

properties of, URG (3) 31

rectangles and, DAB 45, TIG 69, URG (4) 26–40

of round numbers, SG 207–210, URG (7) 116–123

spinners and, DAB 47

square numbers and, DAB 189

table completion exercise in, DAB 67, 105–106, 239, 247

table on, URG (8) 15

by ten, DAB 87, 186–187, SG 193–195, TIG 65, 83, URG (3) 24–36, URG (7) 21, 79–90, URG (9) 25

by three, DAB 39, 43, URG (4) 24

of three factors, URG (4) 70–71

turn-around facts in, SG **61,** URG (3) **29,** URG (7) 82

by two, DAB 39, 41, URG (4) 16, 24, URG (7) 23

volume calculation by, TIG 339–341

word problems in, DAB 40, 241, 249, TIG 71, 302–303, URG (4) 90–94, URG (11) 105–107, URG (13) 84–92

by zero, SG 61, URG (3) 30

Multiplication sentences, SG 100, URG (4) 49

Multiplication tables, URG (4) 63, 93

Multi-step logic, TIG 11

Multi-step word problems, URG (3) 112–113, URG (12) 96–101

Mymathtrailblazers.com, TIG 445

N

National Assessment of Educational Progress, URG (12) 10

National Association for Gifted Children (NAGC), TIG 397, 407

National Association of Bilingual Education, TIG 380

National Bureau of Standards, TIG 353

National Council of Teachers of Mathematics (NCTM), TIG 2–3, 8–10, 15–16, 123–128, 178–179, 219–220, 276, URG (1) 116, URG (8) 90, URG (15) 8–10

National Research Council (NRC), TIG 308, URG (13) 8

***National Science Education Standards* (National Research Council),** TIG 308

National Science Foundation (NSF), TIG 15

NCTM Families Web page, TIG 445

NCTM Illuminations Web page, TIG 445

Negative numbers, SG 86–91, **87,** TIG 66, URG (3) iii, 99–106, **102,** URG (7) 35, URG (15) 77

Nets, DAB 141–143, 151, SG **258**–262, URG (9) **11**–12, 91–92, 98–99, 121, 129

Newton, Sir Isaac, TIG 354

Nine
divisibility by, URG (7) 51–53
division by, URG (6) 16, 19–22, 24
multiplication by, URG (6) 16, 17–22, 24
Triangle Flash Cards for, DAB 67, 71, 193, 197, 239, URG (6) 14, URG (12) 17, URG (15) 38, URG (16) 35

9-to-5 War Game, DAB 79–81, SG 175–176, TIG 80, 459, URG (6) 110–114

No Child Left Behind Act of 2001, TIG 382

Non-canonical number sentences, TIG 297

Nonsquare rectangles, AB 36

Nonstandard units, TIG 325

Norms, classroom, TIG 359–360

Number and operations, TIG 132, 134, 136, 138, 140, 142, 144, 146, 148, 150, 152, 154, 156, 158, 160, 162

Number cubes, AB 77, 86, SG 392, TIG 113, URG (14) 24, **52,** 100. *See also* Rolling a Number Cube Lab, Fairness
fair *versus* loaded, URG (14) 10–11
spinners from, DAB 231–236, URG (14) 47–59, 63–70

Number facts, TIG 223–224

Number lines, DAB 35, 70, SG 169–171, 173, TIG 79, URG (3) 99–106, URG (6) 66–74, URG (14) 52
decimals on, URG (10) 21
fractions on, URG (10) 10, URG (12) 10

Number puzzles, URG (5) 18, URG (9) 29

Numbers, TIG 64–67
composite, URG (4) **9, 34**
convenient, DAB 70, 87, 95, 155, SG **202, 203,** TIG 253, URG (1) **117,** URG (3) 9, 96, URG (6) 96, URG (7) iii, 120, URG (8) 19, URG (11) 22, URG (13) 58
Egyptian, URG (11) 97
even, SG **98,** URG (7) 48
infinite, AB 40, URG (9) **82**
large, DAB 155, 185, TIG 77–78, URG (6) 25–34, 37, 95–96, URG (7) 24–25, URG (14) 10–11, 51
negative, SG 86–91, **87,** TIG 66, URG (3) iii, 3, 99–106, **102,** URG (7) 35, URG (15) 77
in news, DAB 69
odd, SG **98,** URG (7) 48
positive, SG 88–91
prime, DAB 39, 54, 93, SG **98, 104,** URG (4) iii, 8–**9,** 31–35, **34,** 51–52, 75, URG (5) 132

round, SG 207–210, TIG 84, URG (7) 116–123
square, DAB 39, 53, 57, 185, 189, 227, SG **98,** URG (4) iii, 8, 34–35, URG (5) iii, 8, 11–12, 14, 17, 21, URG (6) 22, URG (11) 14, 17, URG (14) 37, URG (16) 37
volume *versus,* URG (8) 60–73
whole, TIG 3, 17, 165–169, 224–231, URG (5) 50, URG (7) 35, 49, URG (12) 11
writing, DAB 69, 186, URG (12) 24

Number sense, TIG 17, URG (2) 14, URG (6) 9, URG (7) 9

Number sentences, DAB 54, 95, 155, 157, SG 199, TIG 297, URG (1) 24, URG (3) 19, 22, URG (4) 17, 35, 49–50, URG (5) 17, URG (6) 102, URG (7) 9, URG (10) 20
addition, URG (12) 99–100
division, SG 58–60, 104, URG (15) 21
fraction, URG (12) 50–51, 85
multiplication, SG 100, 303, URG (8) 25, URG (12) 99–100, URG (15) 21
on time, URG (13) 17

Numerals, URG (3) **42–43**

Numeration, TIG 220–222

Numerator, SG **276, 326,** URG (10) 50, **65,** URG (12) 10, **32, 34,** 50, 58, 73, 99

Numerical variables, DAB 3, 11, 55–56, SG **7,** 20, TIG **309,** 315, URG (1) **9,** 19, **51**–52, 67, URG (2) 54, URG (5) 20, URG (10) 90

O

Observational assessment, TIG 30, 181–183, 188–189, 197, 204. *See also* all URGs

Obtuse angles, DAB 13, 126–129, SG **51,** 54–55, URG (2) iii, 30, **105,** 120–121, URG (3) 17, URG (5) 16, URG (9) 17, 21–22, **45,** URG (11) 16

Octahedrons, DAB 151, TIG 93, URG (9) 12, 120–122

Odd numbers, SG **98,** URG (7) 48

Olympics, DAB 55, URG (5) 26, 32, 34, 128

One
multiplication by, URG (3) 30
ones' period, SG **151,** 158, URG (6) **31**
"whole" as, URG (12) 88–89

One-fourth (1/4), URG (10) 19

100 Chart, TIG 127, 221, URG (7) 48–49, 56

180° angle, URG (5) 16

Open-Response assessment, URG (7) 66–74

Open-Response problems, TIG 185–186, 191–197

Operation, SG **180**

Operation cards, URG (7) 41

Operation Target Game, DAB 85, SG 183, 224, TIG 82, 460, URG (7) 18, 35, URG (8) 18

of convenient numbers, DAB 70

of decimals, SG 276–287

estimation and, DAB 68

Fewest Pieces Rule of, SG **74**–75, 281, URG (3) **53, 62–64,** URG (10) 18, 36, **53,** URG (11) 20

number sense and, URG (6) 5

of numbers in news, DAB 69

ordering numbers by, SG 160–161

periods in, SG 150–155, **151,** 158–159, URG (6) **31**

reading and writing numerals in, SG 150, 152–155, 157–159

ten percent chart for, DAB 77

Plane, URG (9) 94

Plant Growth Lab, DAB 243, SG 379–381, 402–405, TIG 111, 117, URG (13) 97–106, URG (14) 15, URG (15) 7, 24–39

Point graphs, AB 9, DAB 59–64, URG (1) 9, 97–100, 106, URG (6) 42, URG (8) 121, URG (15) 93–94, URG (16) 28. *See also* Best-Fit lines

bar graphs *versus,* DAB 56, TIG 314–316, URG (2) **57**–59

making, SG 157

plotting, DAB 7–8

of powers of two, SG 155

predictions from, SG 120–124, 146–148, URG (5) 22–36

Points, URG (9) 34, **44,** URG (15) 28

Point system, TIG 198–199

Polya, George, TIG 299

Polygons, AB 36, DAB 145, SG **247,** URG (9) 48–**49**

regular, AB 38, URG (9) **79,** 93

Polyhedron, URG (9) 94

Pooling data, URG (14) 51, 56, 67, 70, 76, 84

Portfolios, SG 39–40, 233, 439, TIG 62, 89, 121, 187, 190–191, 197, 205, 289–294, URG (2) iii, 9, 54, 91–95, **93,** URG (5) 8, URG (8) 116–123, URG (16) 8, 49, 56, 95–99

Positive numbers, SG **88**–91, URG (3) 102

Powers of ten, DAB 229, TIG 254, URG (6) 58

Powers of two, SG **155**–156, URG (6) **40**

Precision, TIG 261

Prediction, DAB 51–64, SG 143–145, TIG 112–115, 267, 320–324, URG (5) iii, 8, 134, URG (8) 112, URG (10) 86, 89. *See also* Probability, Labs

of averages, URG (5) 52

from best-fit lines, DAB 59–64

data for, TIG 72–75

of doubling, URG (6) 41

of drop and bounce heights, AB 19–20, 26

from graphs, DAB 55–56, 109–111, 250, SG 120–124, URG (1) 84, URG (5) 22–36, 95–101, URG (15) 6, 27

of height, URG (1) 95, 99

from labs, URG (8) 121, URG (15) 94–95, URG (16) 27–28

of mass, URG (15) 101

from patterns, URG (15) iii

of random events, URG (14) 11

before surveys, URG (13) 34, 36

of volume measurement, URG (8) 56, URG (9) 26

word problems in, URG (5) 119–123

Primary growth, URG (13) 104

Prime factors, SG **110**–115, TIG 69–71, URG (4) 67–76, **70,** URG (5) 13–14, URG (8) 110, URG (12) 20

Prime numbers, DAB 39, 54, 93, SG **98, 104,** URG (4) iii, 8–9, **34**–35, 51–52, 75

Principles and Standards for School Mathematics (National Council of Teachers of Mathematics), TIG 2–3, 8–10, 123–128, 178–179, 219–220, 276, URG (1) 116, URG (15) 8

Prisms, SG 256–267, **259,** TIG 92–94, 339–341, URG (9) **11,** 84–99, **87, 93–94**

constructing, URG (9) 123–129

description of, URG (9) 87–90

drawing, SG 257, URG (9) 88–90

hexagonal, DAB 145–147

nets of, DAB 147–149, URG (9) **91**–92

right triangular, DAB 149

types of, URG (9) 93–94

volume of, SG 263–267, TIG 92–93, URG (9) 105–116

Probability, DAB 225–236, SG 385–399, **390,** TIG 112–115, 132, 134, 136, 138, 140, 142, 144, 146, 148, 150, 152, 154, 156, 158, 160, 162, URG (12) 10, URG (13) 101, 105, URG (14) iii, **8–11,** 24–25, 26–33, **30,** 52–54, 57, 83, 96–101. *See also* Bean Counter's Game, Probe Quest, Rolling a Number Cube Lab

as fraction, SG 390–391

probability lines and, AB 80–81, DAB 229, SG 385–386

spinners and, DAB 231–236, SG 392–399, URG (14) 78–81, 88–93

Probe Quest, AB 71–90, URG (14) 96–101

Problems, open-response, TIG 185–186, 191–197

Problem solving, TIG 10, 16. *See also* Word problems

as process standard, TIG 124–125

in scope and sequence, TIG 133, 135, 137, 139, 141, 143, 145, 147, 149, 151, 153, 155, 157, 159, 161, 163

Process standards, TIG 125–127

Product Bingo Game, DAB 49, SG 116–117, TIG 70–71, 459, URG (4) 83–89

Products, DAB 37–49, SG **61, 107**–108, TIG 68–71, URG (3) **30,** URG (7) 60, 87, URG (7) 66, URG (10) 22, URG (11) 22

break-apart, TIG 280, URG (11) 9

Cartesian, TIG 303

estimation of, DAB 87

even, URG (12) 25

partial, URG (11) 71–79

of prime numbers, DAB 54

T

graphing data (phase 3) in, TIG 314–321
science view of, TIG 307–308
TIMS Tutor on, TIG 307–324
variables and values in, TIG 309–311
TIMS Multidimensional Rubric, TIG 191–192, 198, 200,
URG (2) 73–80, URG (16) 51–54, 71–75
TIMS philosophy, TIG 230–231
TIMS Tutors, TIG 3, 217–355
Area, TIG 329–333
Arithmetic, TIG 219–239
Averages, TIG 241–248
Estimation, Accuracy, and Error, TIG 249–264,
URG (5) 80
Functions, TIG 265–270
Journals, TIG 271–274
Length, TIG 325–328
Mass, TIG 349–355
Math Facts, TIG 275–287
Portfolios, TIG 289–294
TIMS Laboratory Method, TIG 307–324
Volume, TIG 335–347
Word Problems, TIG 295–306
TODOS: Mathematics for all, TIG 380
Trading rules, decimals, URG (10) 70
Traditional method of division, URG (13) 8–9, 61
Translational symmetry, URG (9) 10–**11**
Translations, TIG 297–298
Trapezoids, DAB 17–19, URG (2) 119–121, 124, URG (9)
63, 66, URG (12) 83–84, 88–89, 112–113
Trends, TIG 267
Trials, DAB 56, 113–114, 251–252, SG 141, URG (5)
80–81, URG (8) 120–121, URG (10) 88, URG
(15) 48, URG (16) 27–28
Triangle Flash Cards, DAB 93
activities with, SG 61–62
division, DAB 247, URG (14) 17, URG (15) 15, URG
(16) 13
for five, DAB 23, 29, 115, 123, 227, URG (3) 35, URG
(8) 131–132, 136, URG (14) 35, URG (16) 34
for last six facts, DAB 85, 213, 217, 239, URG (7) 14,
URG (13) 15, URG (15) 39, URG (16) 38
master, DAB 97–99
for nine, DAB 67, 71, 193, 197, 239, URG (6) 14, URG
(12) 17, URG (15) 38, URG (16) 35
sorting, URG (3) 15
for square numbers, DAB 53, 57, 185, 189, 227,
URG (5) 11–12, URG (11) 14, URG (14) 37,
URG (16) 37
for ten, DAB 23, 31, 117, 123, 227, URG (3) 36, URG
(8) 131–132, 137, URG (14) 36, URG (16) 36
for three, DAB 43, 155, 161, 239, URG (4) 15, URG
(10) 17, URG (15) 37, URG (16) 33
for two, DAB 41, 155, 159, 227, URG (4) 15, URG (10)
17, URG (14) 34, URG (16) 32

Triangles, AB 79, DAB 17–19, URG (1) 15–17, URG (2)
103, 120–121, 124, URG (4) 16, URG (9) 26,
URG (10) 23, URG (12) 83–84, 88–89, 113
equilateral, SG **241,** URG (2) **119,** URG (9) 36, 63, 66,
78, 121, 126
patterns of, URG (15) 64–68
right, AB 37, 42, URG (9) 10, 17, 21–22, 45, 63, 81
Triangular prisms, URG (9) 93, 110
Turn-Around facts, SG **61,** URG (3) **29,** URG (7) 82
Turn-Around rule, URG (4) **30**
Turning, URG (2) 101, 104
angles as, URG (9) 64–68
center of, SG **251–254**
Turn symmetry, DAB 135, 139, 248, SG **251–254,** TIG
91–92, URG (9) iii, **10,** 64–68, **65,** 126, 129, URG
(12) 124
Twelfths, URG (12) 35–37, 43
Twenty, skip counting by, DAB 53
Twin primes, URG (4) 8
Two
divisibility by, URG (7) 48–51
doubling, URG (1) 20, 29
Math Facts on, URG (10) 29
multiplication by, DAB 39, URG (4) 16, 24, URG (7) 23
power of, SG **155–158**
powers of, URG (6) **40**
Triangle Flash Cards for, DAB 41, 155, 159, 227,
URG (4) 15, URG (10) 17, URG (14) 34, URG
(16) 32
Two Heads Are Better Than One, AB 15–28, TIG 75,
URG (5) 95–101
Two-Column data tables, URG (1) 51–52, URG (2) 39,
45, URG (5) 68, URG (8) 65, 72, URG (15) 36,
76–77, URG (16) 81
Two-Pan balance, URG (15) 90–91, 99. *See also* Equal-
Arm balance
Type of turn symmetry, URG (9) 64–68, **65,** URG
(12) 124

Undefined (division by zero), SG 376, URG (13) 25,
87–88
Unique solution, URG (13) **87**
Unit planner, URG (1) 4–6, URG (2) 4–6, URG (3) 4–6,
URG (4) 4–6, URG (5) 4–6, URG (6) 4–6, URG
(7) 4–6, URG (8) 4–6, URG (9) 4–7, URG (10)
4–6, URG (11) 4–6, URG (12) 4–7, URG (13)
4–6, URG (14) 4–6, URG (15) 4–5, URG (16) 4–5
Unit Resource Guides (URG), TIG 24–40
Adventure Book lesson guide, TIG 39
answer keys, TIG 41

V

W

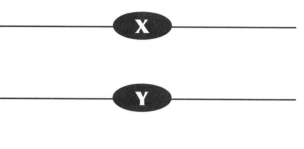